# Online Research and Reference Aids

Whether you want to investigate the ideas behind a thought-provoking topic or conduct in-depth research for a paper, our Online Research and Reference Aids can help you refine your research skills, find the information you need on the Web, and use that information effectively. You can access these resources through the companion Web site for *America: A Concise History*, Third Edition, at **bedfordstmartins.com/henrettaconcise** or by using the URLs given below.

## DocLinks

**bedfordstmartins.com/doclinks**

Annotated links to primary documents online. Search by topic, date, or textbook chapter.

## HistoryLinks

**bedfordstmartins.com/historylinks**

Annotated links to selected U.S. history Web sites, including those containing image galleries, maps, and audio and video clips for supplementing research. Search by date, subject, medium, keyword, or textbook chapter.

## A Student's Online Guide to History Reference Sources

**bedfordstmartins.com/benjamin**

A collection of links to history-related electronic reference sources such as databases, indexes, and journals, plus contact information for state, provincial, local, and professional history organizations. Based on the appendix to Jules Benjamin's *A Student's Guide to History*, Ninth Edition.

## Research and Documentation Online

**bedfordstmartins.com/resdoc**

Clear advice on how to conduct research, integrate primary and secondary sources into research papers, and cite sources correctly.

## The St. Martin's Tutorial on Avoiding Plagiarism

**bedfordstmartins.com/plagiarismtutorial**

An online tutorial that explains what plagiarism is and how to avoid it by keeping good notes, staying organized, knowing what to ask, and integrating sources appropriately. Includes exercises on integrating sources and recognizing acceptable summaries.

*Third Edition*

# America
## A CONCISE HISTORY

**Volume 1: To 1877**

*Third Edition*

# America

## A CONCISE HISTORY

**Volume 1: To 1877**

James A. Henretta
University of Maryland

David Brody
University of California, Davis

Lynn Dumenil
Occidental College

**BEDFORD / ST. MARTIN'S**
Boston   •   New York

*For Bedford / St. Martin's*

*Executive Editor for History:* Mary Dougherty
*Director of Development for History:* Jane Knetzger
*Development Editor:* William J. Lombardo
*Senior Production Editor:* Lori Chong Roncka
*Production Supervisor:* Jennifer L. Wetzel
*Senior Marketing Manager:* Jenna Bookin Barry
*Editorial Assistant:* Elizabeth Wallace
*Production Assistants:* Kristen Merrill and Amy Derjue
*Art Director:* Donna Lee Dennison
*Text Design:* Wanda Kossak
*Copy Editor:* Mary Lou Wilshaw-Watts
*Indexer:* EdIndex
*Photo Research:* Pembroke Herbert and Sandi Rygiel/Picture Research Consultants & Archives
*Cartography:* Mapping Specialists, Ltd.
*Cover Design:* Billy Boardman
*Cover Art: Giant Steamboats at New Orleans,* by Hippolyte Sebron, 1853, oil on canvas, 48 × 72 in.
    Newcomb Art Gallery, Tulane University, New Orleans. Gift of D. H. Holmes Company,
    New Orleans. Photo by Owen Murphy.
*Composition:* TechBooks
*Printing and Binding:* R.R. Donnelley & Sons Company

*President:* Joan E. Feinberg
*Editorial Director:* Denise B. Wydra
*Director of Marketing:* Karen Melton Soeltz
*Director of Editing, Design, and Production:* Marcia Cohen
*Managing Editor:* Elizabeth M. Schaaf

Library of Congress Catalog Card Number: 2004110495

Manufactured in the United States of America.

0   9   8   7   6   5
f   e   d   c   b   a

*For information, write:* Bedford / St. Martin's, 75 Arlington Street, Boston,
MA 02116 (617-399-4000)

ISBN: 0–312–41364–5 (Combined Volume)     EAN: 978–0–312–41364–4
ISBN: 0–312–41563–X (Volume 1: To 1877)     EAN: 978–0–312–41563–1
ISBN: 0–312–41641–5 (Volume 2: Since 1865)   EAN: 978–0–312–41641–6

### Credits

*Credits and copyrights are printed at the back of the book on pages C-1–C-3, which constitute an extension of the copyright page.*

*For Emily and Rebecca;*
*Siena, Cameron, Alex, Lea, and Eleanor;*
*and Norman*

# PREFACE

$\mathbf{N}$ow, as never before, Americans realize the importance of History. When the administration of George W. Bush invaded Iraq in the spring of 2003, it hoped in a single dramatic act to transform the Middle East and, indeed, to change the course of history. But History—the cumulative weight of the past—is not so easily overthrown. As the sobering events that followed the toppling of Saddam Hussein's dictatorial regime have shown, the hope of swiftly creating an American-style democracy in Iraq has come up against the historical identity and institutions of its people, as well as their ethnic and religious diversity. In the pages that follow, we will tell that story and many similar stories of the collision in American history between the grand hopes of ambitious individuals and governments and the stubborn persistence of past customs and institutions.

The interaction between past and present is one of the motifs of this third edition of the concise version of our comprehensive text, *America's History*. As we develop this perspective, we remain committed to the historical vision that has informed this textbook project from its very inception. We are bent on writing a democratic history, one that captures the experiences of ordinary people even as it records the achievements of the great and powerful. Throughout the book, we focus not only on the marvelous diversity of peoples who became American but also on the institutions—political, economic, social and cultural—that forged a common national identity. We want to show how people of all classes and groups make their own history while simultaneously being influenced and constrained by circumstances, by the customs and institutions inherited from the past, and by the hierarchy of power in the present. And we believe that the best way to convey the agency of historical actors is through a narrative, but a narrative that is harnessed to historical argument and explanation—not simply a retelling of "this happened, then that happened." The story, we hope, tells not only what happened, but *how* and *why*.

## Organization and Structure

Good narrative history is, of course, primarily a product of good sentences and good paragraphs. So our labors have been mostly in the trenches, so to speak, in a line-by-line striving toward the vividness and human presence that are the hallmarks of narrative history. But there are also larger strategies that can be called into play. Within chapters we have been especially attentive to chronology, which sometimes involved a significant reordering of the material. For example, we now begin Chapter 13 with a section on "The Mature Cotton Economy," whose existence encouraged westward expansion, the annexation of Texas, and the fateful war with Mexico. For reasons of continuity we have also reordered Chapters 18 and 19 so that "Politics in the Age of Enterprise" now follows "The Rise of the City." This new organization provides students with a seamless transition to our discussion of the political reforms of the Progressive Era (Chapter 20). Chapter 31 likewise received considerable revision and now provides a compact and coherent overview of the period from the early 1980s to the present. By being forced to think hard about how to organize materials, we have come up with a stronger periodization and clearer thematic development.

To assist students in grasping the meaning and complexity of the past, we have grounded *America: A Concise History* in a clear chronology and strong conceptual framework. Each of the two volumes is divided into three parts, with each part corresponding to a distinct phase of development. Every part begins at a crucial turning point, such as the American Revolution or the Cold War, and emphasizes the dynamic forces at work. Part openers contain **thematic timelines** that highlight key developments and **part essays** that set out clearly and concisely the main themes of our story and, through a combination of quotations from historical actors and careful analysis, explore the crucial engines of historical change that create new conditions of life. This structure will help students understand the major themes in each period of American history, to discover how the bits and pieces of historical data acquire significance as part of a larger pattern of development.

Moreover, to capture the reader's attention, each chapter opens with an anecdote or scene that establishes the chapter's main ideas and topics. Our chapter endings eschew the usual textbook summary in favor of apt statements bringing the discussion to a satisfying close and opening the way for what follows.

# New Perspectives

The revising process is also an opportunity to incorporate new scholarship. Our treatment of Native Americans in the colonial era incorporates recent anthropologically influenced work showing how Indian peoples maintained elements of their traditional culture in the face of European domination. We draw on new work dealing with the role of women and gender in eighteenth-century religion and antebellum politics and recent scholarship on the crisis over slavery after Independence. We offer an expanded treatment of the role of state policy during the antebellum Market Revolution, and we make full use of recent Reconstruction scholarship that sees the transition from slavery to freedom as largely a battle over labor systems. We continue to incorporate more about the Far West into the nation's historical narrative, relying on the new western history for insight into the interactions among environment, peoples, and economic development.

Advances in gender history enable us to offer a new discussion of bachelorhood and masculinity in the late nineteenth century and to temper our treatment of progressive welfare policy as we become aware of its patriarchal underpinnings. New scholarship on ethnic minorities similarly enables us to amplify our discussion of Native Americans during World War I and the New Deal, Asian Americans during the Great Depression, and black women during the 1920s and the later civil rights struggles. Recent scholarship based on hitherto closed Soviet and U.S. archives continues to inform our treatment of the Cold War, and an analysis of the turbulent years following the attack by Muslim extremists on September 11, 2001, brings the book to a thoughtful close. In these ways, and others, we strive to maintain the reputation of *America: A Concise History* as a fresh and timely text.

## Features in This Edition

In the first edition of *America: A Concise History*, our main goal was to shorten the original text by 40 percent—in effect, to make six words do the work of ten—without compromising its balanced coverage and explanatory power. In the second edition, we undertook the equally ambitious objective of writing a more compelling *narrative* text. Our goal was to produce a book that students would actually enjoy reading, not merely a set of assignments to be gotten through. The number of instructors who now use our text on a regular basis suggests the success of that endeavor.

In this third edition we have turned our attention to some nuts-and-bolts issues of teaching history. Keenly aware that today's students lack geographic literacy, we have beefed up the **map program**. We have added over thirty new maps, redrawn every existing map to reflect recent advances in cartography, and, to assist students to become better map readers, have added "call-outs" to particular maps. As a further aid to readers, we have included a **glossary** that provides a historically appropriate definition of challenging or unfamiliar terms and concepts. Recognizing also that students increasingly live in a mental world shaped by the World Wide Web, we have combed through hundreds of **Web sites** to find those that best supplement the material in the text and integrated them with the "**For Further Exploration**" bibliographical essays found at the end of each chapter. To assist instructors and advanced students, a **full bibliography** is available on the Web at bedfordstmartins.com/henrettaconcise. Our goal is ultimately to write a history that moves seamlessly between the written text and the bountiful images and sources available at the click of a mouse.

To strengthen our commitment to putting a human face on historical experience, each chapter contains two boxed **voices**, first-person excerpts from letters, diaries, autobiographies, and public testimony that paint a vivid picture of the social or political life of the time. Some are **American Voices**; others, new to this edition, are **Voices from Abroad**. These voices deepen the international dimension to our analysis of American life. To enliven students' understanding of history, we have peppered the text with more than 150 paintings, illustrations, and photographs, most of them in full color and many new to this edition. We have also provided detailed captions that set the illustrations in context and extend the discussion in the text.

Taken together, these documents and illustrations provide instructors with a trove of teaching materials, and students with a chance to enter the life of the past and see it from within.

# Supplements

Readers of *America: A Concise History* often cite its ancillary package as a key to the book's success in the classroom. Most of the ancillaries are customized for the concise edition, providing a flexible yet targeted collection of resources for instructors and a helpful set of study tools for students.

## *For Students*

**Online Study Guide at bedfordstmartins.com/henrettaconcise.** The popular Online Study Guide for *America: A Concise History* is a free and uniquely personalized learning tool to help students master themes and information in the textbook and improve their historical skills. Assessment quizzes help students evaluate their textbook comprehension and provide customized plans for further study through a variety of activities. Instructors can monitor student progress through the online Quiz Gradebook or receive e-mail updates.

**Documents to Accompany AMERICA'S HISTORY, Fifth Edition.** Edited by Melvin Yazawa (University of New Mexico) and Kevin J. Fernlund (University of Missouri, St. Louis), this collection of over 350 primary source documents with editorial apparatus is constructed to facilitate students' comprehension and analysis of the readings, and is easily assigned with the concise edition.

NEW **Maps in Context: A Workbook for American History.** Written by historical cartography expert Gerald A. Danzer (University of Illinois at Chicago), this skill-building workbook helps students comprehend the essential connections between geographic literacy and historical understanding. Organized to correspond to the typical U.S. survey course, *Maps in Context* presents a wealth of map-centered projects and convenient pop-quizzes that give students hands-on experience working with maps.

NEW **History Matters: A Student Guide to U.S. History Online.** This new resource, edited by Alan Gevinson, Kelly Schrum, and Roy Rosenzweig (all of George Mason University), provides an illustrated and annotated guide to 250 of the most useful Web sites for student research in U.S. history, as well as advice on evaluating and using Internet sources. This essential guide is based on the acclaimed "History Matters" Web site developed by the American History Social Project and the Center for History and New Media.

**Bedford Series in History and Culture.**   Over 70 titles in this highly praised series combine first-rate scholarship, historical narrative, and important primary documents for undergraduate courses. Each book is brief, inexpensive, and focused on a specific topic or period. Package discounts are available.

*Historians at Work* **Series.**   Brief enough for a single assignment yet meaty enough to provoke thoughtful discussion, each volume in this series examines a single historical question by combining unabridged selections by distinguished historians, each with a differing perspective on the issue, with helpful learning aids. Package discounts are available.

*NEW*  **PlaceLinks at bedfordstmartins.com/henrettaconcise.**   PlaceLinks provides access to resources on the Web for over 100 historical sites in all fifty states, such as specific monuments, parks, and museums that connect students to the places where history happened. This new online feature makes history tangible and local.

**DocLinks at bedfordstmartins.com/doclinks.**   This Web site provides over 750 annotated Web links to online primary documents, including links to speeches, legislation, treaties, social commentary, Supreme Court decisions, essays, travelers' accounts, personal narratives and testimony, newspaper articles, visual artifacts, songs, and poems. Students and teachers alike can search documents by topic, date, or specific chapter of *America: A Concise History*. Links can be selected and stored for later use or published to a unique Web address.

**HistoryLinks at bedfordstmartins.com/historylinks.**   Recently updated, HistoryLinks directs instructors and students to over 500 carefully selected and annotated links to history-related Web sites, including those containing image galleries, maps, and audio and video clips for supplementing lectures or assignments. Users can browse these Internet starting points by date, subject, medium, keyword, or specific chapter in *America: A Concise History*. Instructors can assign these links as the basis for homework assignments or research projects, or students can use them in their own history research. Links can be selected and stored for later use or published to a unique Web address.

**A Student's Online Guide to History Reference Sources at bedfordstmartins .com/benjamin.**   This Web site provides links to history-related electronic reference sources such as databases, indexes, and journals, plus contact information for state, provincial, local, and professional history organizations.

**Research and Documentation Online at bedfordstmartins.com/resdoc.**   This Web site provides clear advice on how to integrate primary and secondary sources into research papers, how to cite sources correctly, and how to format in MLA, APA, Chicago, or CBE style.

**The St. Martin's Tutorial on Avoiding Plagiarism at bedfordstmartins.com/ plagiarismtutorial.**    This online tutorial reviews the consequences of plagiarism and explains what sources to acknowledge, how to keep good notes, how to organize research, and how to appropriately integrate sources. The tutorial includes exercises to help students practice integrating sources and recognizing acceptable summaries.

**Critical Thinking Modules at bedfordstmartins.com/historymodules.**    This Web site offers over two dozen online modules for interpreting maps, audio, visual, and textual sources, centered on events covered in the U.S. history survey. An online guide correlates modules to textbook chapters and books in the Bedford Series in History and Culture.

## *For Instructors*

**Instructor's Resource Manual.**    This popular manual by Bradley T. Gericke (U.S. Army Command and General Staff College) offers both experienced and first-time instructors a wealth of tools—annotated chapter outlines and summaries, lecture strategies, discussion starters, and suggested research assignments—for presenting textbook material in exciting and engaging ways.

**Computerized Test Bank.**    This test bank by Thomas L. Altherr (Metropolitan State College of Denver) and Adolph Grundman (Metropolitan State College of Denver) provides easy-to-use software to create tests. Over 80 exercises are provided per chapter, including multiple-choice, fill-in-the-blank, map analysis, short essay, and full-length essay questions. Instructors can customize quizzes, add or edit both questions and answers, as well as export them to a variety of formats, including WebCT and Blackboard. The disc includes correct answers and essay outlines.

**Transparencies.**    This set of over 250 full-color acetate transparencies includes all maps and many images from *America: A Concise History* and the parent text, *America's History*, Fifth Edition. A guide correlating all the maps and art to the concise edition is available on the Book Companion Site.

**Instructor's Resource CD-ROM.**    This disc provides instructors with ready-made and customizable PowerPoint multimedia presentations built around chapter outlines, maps, figures, and selected images from the textbook. The disc also includes images in JPEG format, an electronic version of the *Instructor's Resource Manual*, outline maps in PDF format for quizzing or handouts, and quick-start guides to the Online Study Guide.

**Book Companion Site at bedfordstmartins.com/henrettaconcise.**    The companion Web site gathers all the electronic resources for the text, including the Online Study Guide and related Quiz Gradebook, at a single Web address, providing convenient links to such helpful lecture, assignment, and research materials as PowerPoint chapter outlines, a transparency correlation guide, DocLinks, HistoryLinks, and Map Central.

**Map Central at bedfordstmartins.com/mapcentral.**   Map Central is a searchable database of over 750 maps from Bedford/St. Martin's history texts for classroom presentation and over 50 basic political and physical outline maps for quizzing or handouts.

**Using the Bedford Series in History and Culture in the U.S. History Survey at bedfordstmartins.com/usingseries.**   This online guide helps instructors integrate volumes from the highly regarded Bedford Series in History and Culture into their U.S. history survey course. The guide not only correlates themes from each series book with the survey course but also provides ideas for classroom discussions.

**Blackboard Course Cartridge and WebCT e-Pack.**   Blackboard and WebCT content are available for this book.

**Videos and Multimedia.**   A wide assortment of videos and multimedia CD-ROMs on various topics in American history is available to qualified adopters.

# Acknowledgments

The scholars and teachers who reviewed *America: A Concise History* made suggestions that we gratefully incorporated into the new edition. Most of our reviewers have used concise texts in their courses, and their classroom experience has helped us to craft a book that meets the needs of today's diverse students. Thanks are due to: Ginette Aley, Virginia Tech; Rosemary Brogan, Cabrillo Community College; Nichole Etcheson, University of Texas at El Paso; Paul Faler, University of Massachusetts–Boston; David Farber, University of New Mexico; Linda Gies, Eastern New Mexico University; Craig Hendricks, Long Beach City College; Johanna Hume, Alvin Community College; Susan Johnson, Ohio State University; Kathleen Kennedy, Western Washington University; Andrew Kersten, University of Wisconsin, Green Bay; Michael Mangus, Ohio State University, Newark; Jimmie McGee, South Plains College; Carol O'Connor, Arkansas State University; Eric Rauchway, University of California, Davis; Paul Rosier, Villanova University; Bradford Sample, Indiana University; Rhonda Smith, Eastern Kentucky University; Sean Taylor, Minnesota State University, Moorehead; Michael Topp, University of Texas at El Paso; Robert Zeidel, University of Wisconsin, Stout.

As the authors of *America: A Concise History*, we know better than anyone else how much this book is the work of other hands and minds. We are grateful to Mary Dougherty, Jane Knetzger, and Patricia Rossi who oversaw the project, and William

Lombardo, who used his extensive knowledge and critical skills as a well-trained historian to edit our text and suggest a multitude of improvements. Elizabeth M. Welch offered invaluable insight and guidance along the way. As usual, Joan E. Feinberg has been generous in providing the resources we needed to produce the third edition. Lori Chong Roncka did more than we had a right to expect in producing an outstanding volume. Karen Melton Soeltz and Jenna Bookin Barry in the marketing department have been instrumental in helping this book reach the classroom. We also thank the rest of our editorial and production team for their dedicated efforts: Elizabeth Wallace, Kristen Merrill, Amy Derjue, and Anne True; Pembroke Herbert and Sandi Rygiel at Picture Research Consultants and Archives; Jennifer Wetzel and Sandy Schechter. Finally, we want to express our appreciation for the invaluable assistance of Patricia Deveneau, Jonathan White, David Axeen, James Halstead, and Norman S. Cohen, whose work contributed in many ways to the intellectual vitality of this new edition of *America: A Concise History.*

James A. Henretta
David Brody
Lynn Dumenil

# BRIEF CONTENTS

*Part One*

THE CREATION OF AMERICAN SOCIETY, 1450–1775  **2**

1   WORLDS COLLIDE: EUROPE, AFRICA, AND AMERICA, 1450–1620  6

2   THE INVASION AND SETTLEMENT OF NORTH AMERICA, 1550–1700  37

3   THE BRITISH EMPIRE IN AMERICA, 1660–1750  68

4   GROWTH AND CRISIS IN COLONIAL SOCIETY, 1720–1765  99

5   TOWARD INDEPENDENCE: YEARS OF DECISION, 1763–1775  131

*Part Two*

THE NEW REPUBLIC, 1775–1820  **162**

6   WAR AND REVOLUTION, 1775–1783  166

7   THE NEW POLITICAL ORDER, 1776–1800  196

8   THE DYNAMICS OF WESTERN SETTLEMENT AND EASTERN CAPITALISM, 1790–1820  227

9   THE QUEST FOR A REPUBLICAN SOCIETY, 1790–1820  257

*Part Three*

ECONOMIC REVOLUTION AND SECTIONAL STRIFE, 1820–1877  **288**

10   THE ECONOMIC REVOLUTION, 1820–1860  292

11   A DEMOCRATIC REVOLUTION, 1820–1844  322

12   RELIGION AND REFORM, 1820–1860   352

13   THE CRISIS OF THE UNION, 1844–1860   382

14   TWO SOCIETIES AT WAR, 1861–1865   412

15   RECONSTRUCTION, 1865–1877   442

# CONTENTS

Preface   vii

List of Maps   xxvi

About the Authors   xxviii

*Part One*

THE CREATION OF AMERICAN SOCIETY, 1450–1775   **2**

*Chapter 1*
**WORLDS COLLIDE: EUROPE, AFRICA, AND AMERICA, 1450–1620**   6

**Native American Worlds**   7

The First Americans   7   •   The Mayas and the Aztecs   9   •   The Indians of the North   10

**Traditional European Society in 1450**   14

The Peasantry   14   •   Hierarchy and Authority   16   •   The Power of Religion   17

**Europe Encounters Africa and the Americas, 1450–1550**   18

The Renaissance   18   •   West African Society and Slavery   20   •   Europe Reaches the Americas   23   •   The Spanish Conquest   25

**The Protestant Reformation and the Rise of England**   29

The Protestant Movement   29   •   The Dutch and the English Challenge Spain   31 •   The Social Causes of English Colonization   33

VOICES FROM ABROAD
FATHER LE PETITE: The Customs of the Natchez, 1730   13

AMERICAN VOICES
FRIAR BERNARDINO DE SAHAGÚN: Aztec Elders Describe the Spanish Conquest   26

VASION AND SETTLEMENT OF NORTH AMERICA,
–1700   37

**Imperial Conflicts and Rival Colonial Models**   38

New Spain: Colonization and Conversion   38   •   New France: Furs and Souls   41
•   New Netherland: Commerce   43   •   English Virginia: Settlers and
a Staple Crop   44

**The Chesapeake Experience**   47

Settling the Tobacco Colonies   47   •   Masters, Servants, and Slaves   50   •   The
Seeds of Social Revolt   51   •   Bacon's Rebellion   52

**Puritan New England**   53

The Puritan Migration   53   •   Puritanism and Witchcraft   57   •   A Yeoman
Society, 1630–1700   58

**The Eastern Indians' New World**   59

Puritans and Pequots   59   •   Metacom's (King Philip's) Rebellion   61   •   The Fur
Trade and the Inland Peoples   63

> VOICES FROM ABROAD
> SAMUEL DE CHAMPLAIN: Going to War with the Hurons   42

> AMERICAN VOICES
> MARY ROWLANDSON: A Captivity Narrative   64

*Chapter 3*
**THE BRITISH EMPIRE IN AMERICA, 1660–1750**   68

**The Politics of Empire, 1660–1713**   69

The Great Aristocratic Land Grab   69   •   From Mercantilism to Imperial Dominion
70   •   The Glorious Revolution in England and America   72   •   Imperial Wars
and Native Peoples   74

**The Imperial Slave Economy**   76

The South Atlantic System   77   •   Slavery in the Chesapeake and
South Carolina   80   •   The Emergence of an African American Community   84
•   Resistance and Accommodation   85   •   The Southern Gentry   87   •
The Northern Maritime Economy   88

**The New Politics of Empire, 1713–1750**   91

The Rise of Colonial Assemblies   91   •   Salutary Neglect   92   •   Protecting the
Mercantile System   94   •   The American Economic Challenge   95

VOICES FROM ABROAD
OLAUDAH EQUIANO: The Brutal "Middle Passage"    81

AMERICAN VOICES
GOVERNOR JOSEPH DUDLEY AND JOHN WINCHESTER: A "Leveling" Spirit in the Colonies    93

*Chapter 4*
GROWTH AND CRISIS IN COLONIAL SOCIETY, 1720–1765    99

Freehold Society in New England    100

Farm Families: Women's Place    100    •    Farm Property: Inheritance    102    •
The Crisis of Freehold Society    103

The Middle Atlantic: Toward a New Society, 1720–1765    104

Economic Growth and Social Inequality    104    •    Cultural Diversity    106
•    Religious Identity and Political Conflict    111

The Enlightenment and the Great Awakening, 1740–1765    112

The Enlightenment in America    112    •    American Pietism and the Great
Awakening    114    •    Religious Upheaval in the North    116    •    Social and
Religious Conflict in the South    117

The Midcentury Challenge: War, Trade, and Social Conflict, 1750–1765    119

The French and Indian War Becomes a War for Empire    119    •    British Economic
Growth and the Consumer Revolution    122    •    The Struggle for Land in
the East    124    •    Western Uprisings and Regulator Movements    125

AMERICAN VOICES
Runaway Servants and Slaves    107

AMERICAN VOICES
CHARLES WOODMASON: Social Chaos on the Carolina Frontier    127

*Chapter 5*
TOWARD INDEPENDENCE: YEARS OF DECISION, 1763–1775    131

The Imperial Reformers, 1763–1765    132

The Legacy of War    132    •    The Sugar Act and Colonial Rights    134    •    An Open
Challenge: The Stamp Act    137

The Dynamics of Rebellion, 1765–1766    138

Politicians Protest and the Crowd Rebels    138    •    Ideological Roots
of Resistance    142    •    Parliament Compromises, 1766    143

The Growing Confrontation, 1767–1770    145

The Townshend Initiatives    145    •    America Again Debates and Resists    147
•    Lord North Compromises, 1770    149

**The Road to War, 1771–1775**    151

The Compromise Ignored    151    •    The Continental Congress Responds    153
•    The Rising of the Countryside    155    •    The Failure of Compromise    158

> AMERICAN VOICES
> SAMUEL ADAMS: An American View of the Stamp Act    144

> VOICES FROM ABROAD
> LIEUTENANT COLONEL FRANCIS SMITH: A British View of Lexington and
> Concord    159

*Part Two*

## THE NEW REPUBLIC, 1775–1820    **162**

*Chapter 6*
### WAR AND REVOLUTION, 1775–1783    166

**Toward Independence, 1775–1776**    167

The Second Continental Congress and Civil War    167    •    Common Sense    168
•    Independence Declared    171

**The Trials of War, 1776–1778**    172

War in the North    172    •    Armies and Strategies    174    •    Victory at Saratoga    175
•    Social and Financial Perils    176

**The Path to Victory, 1778–1783**    178

The French Alliance    179    •    War in the South    180    •    The Patriot
Advantage    183    •    Diplomatic Triumph    183

**Republicanism Defined and Challenged**    184

Republican Ideals under Wartime Pressures    184    •    The Loyalist Exodus    187
•    The Problem of Slavery    188    •    A Republican Religious Order    190

> AMERICAN VOICES
> MARY HOOKS SLOCUMB: The Meaning of War    169

> VOICES FROM ABROAD
> ALEXANDER COVENTRY: The Character of Northern Slavery    191

*Chapter 7*
### THE NEW POLITICAL ORDER, 1776–1800    196

**Creating Republican Institutions, 1776–1787**    197

The State Constitutions: How Much Democracy?    197    •    The Articles
of Confederation    202    •    Shays's Rebellion    206

The Constitution of 1787    207

The Rise of a Nationalist Faction    207    •    The Philadelphia Convention    208    •
The People Debate Ratification    211    •    The Federalists Implement the
Constitution    214

The Political Crisis of the 1790s    215

Hamilton's Financial Program    216    •    Jefferson's Agrarian Vision    218    •
The French Revolution Divides Americans    219    •    The Rise of Political
Parties    221    •    Constitutional Crisis, 1798–1800    222

AMERICAN VOICES
ABIGAIL AND JOHN ADAMS: The Status of Women    200

VOICES FROM ABROAD
WILLIAM COBBETT: Peter Porcupine Attacks Pro-French Americans    223

## Chapter 8
## THE DYNAMICS OF WESTERN SETTLEMENT AND
## EASTERN CAPITALISM, 1790–1820    227

Westward Expansion    228

Native American Resistance    228    •    Migration and the Changing Farm Economy
232    •    The Transportation Bottleneck    235

The Republicans' Political Revolution    237

The Jeffersonian Presidency    237    •    Jefferson and the West    239    •    Conflict with
Britain and France    240    •    The War of 1812    242

The Capitalist Commonwealth    246

Banks, Manufacturing, and Markets    246    •    Public Policy: The Commonwealth
System    249    •    Federalist Law: John Marshall and the Supreme Court    250

AMERICAN VOICES
RED JACKET: A Seneca Chief's Understanding of Religion    232

VOICES FROM ABROAD
ALEXIS DE TOCQUEVILLE: Law and Lawyers in the United States    254

## Chapter 9
## THE QUEST FOR A REPUBLICAN SOCIETY, 1790–1820    257

Democratic Republicanism    258

Social and Political Equality for White Men    258    •    Toward a Republican Marriage
System    260    •    Republican Motherhood    261    •    Raising and Educating
Republican Children    263

**Aristocratic Republicanism and Slavery**    266

The North and South Grow Apart    266    •    Toward a New Southern Social
Order    268    •    Slave Society and Culture    271    •    The Free Black Population    272
•    The Missouri Crisis    275

**Protestant Christianity as a Social Force**    277

The Second Great Awakening    277    •    Women's New Religious Roles    284

> AMERICAN VOICES
> JACOB STROYER: A Child Learns the Meaning of Slavery    273

> VOICES FROM ABROAD
> FRANCES TROLLOPE: A Camp Meeting in Indiana    279

## *Part Three*

## ECONOMIC REVOLUTION AND SECTIONAL STRIFE, 1820–1877    **288**

*Chapter 10*
### THE ECONOMIC REVOLUTION, 1820–1860    292

**The Coming of Industry: Northeastern Manufacturing**    293

Division of Labor and the Factory    293    •    The Textile Industry and British
Competition    294    •    American Mechanics and Technological Innovation    297
•    Wage Workers and the Labor Movement    299

**The Market Revolution**    301

Migration to the Southwest and the Midwest    301    •    The Transportation
Revolution Forges Regional Ties    302    •    The Growth of Cities and Towns    308

**Changes in the Social Structure**    309

The Business Elite    310    •    The Middle Class    311    •    Urban Workers and the
Poor    313    •    The Benevolent Empire    314    •    Revivalism and Reform    315    •
Immigration and Cultural Conflict    317

> AMERICAN VOICES
> LUCY LARCOM: Early Days at Lowell    298

> AMERICAN VOICES
> JOHN GOUGH: The Vice of Intemperance    318

*Chapter 11*
### A DEMOCRATIC REVOLUTION, 1820–1844    322

**The Rise of Popular Politics, 1820–1829**    323

The Decline of the Notables and the Rise of Parties    323    •    The Election
of 1824    325    •    The Last Notable President: John Quincy Adams    327    •
"The Democracy" and the Election of 1828    328

The Jacksonian Presidency, 1829–1837    330

Jackson's Agenda: Patronage and Policy    332    •    The Tariff and Nullification    333    •    The Bank War    334    •    Indian Removal    336    •    The Jacksonian Impact    340

Class, Culture, and the Second Party System    342

The Whig Worldview    342    •    Labor Politics and the Depression of 1837–1843    345    •    "Tippecanoe and Tyler Too!"    347

AMERICAN VOICES
MARGARET BAYARD SMITH: Republican Majesty and Mobs    331

AMERICAN VOICES
BLACK HAWK: A Sacred Reverence for Our Lands    338

Chapter 12
RELIGION AND REFORM, 1820–1860    352

Individualism    353

Emerson and Transcendentalism    353    •    Emerson's Literary Influence    355    •    Brook Farm    357

Communalism    358

The Shakers    358    •    The Fourierist Phalanxes    361    •    John Humphrey Noyes and the Oneida Community    361    •    The Mormon Experience    362

Abolitionism    367

Uplift, Race-Equality, and Rebellion    367    •    Garrison and Evangelical Abolitionism    368    •    Opposition and Internal Conflict    371

The Women's Rights Movement    374

Origins of the Women's Movement    374    •    Abolitionism and Women    376    •    The Program of Seneca Falls and Beyond    378

AMERICAN VOICES
An Illinois "Jeffersonian" Attacks the Mormons    365

AMERICAN VOICES
KEZIAH KENDALL: A Farm Woman Defends the Grimké Sisters    377

Chapter 13
THE CRISIS OF THE UNION, 1844–1860    382

Manifest Destiny    383

The Mature Cotton Economy, 1820–1860    383    •    The Independence of Texas    386    •    The Push to the Pacific: Oregon and California    387    •    The Fateful Election of 1844    390

**War, Expansion, and Slavery, 1846–1850**   392

The War with Mexico, 1846–1848   **392**   •   A Divisive Victory   **393**   •   1850: Crisis and Compromise   **396**

**The End of the Second Party System, 1850–1858**   398

Resistance to the Fugitive Slave Act   **399**   •   The Political System in Decline   **400** • The Kansas-Nebraska Act and the Rise of New Parties   **401**   •   The Election of 1856 and Dred Scott   **403**

**Abraham Lincoln and the Republican Triumph, 1858–1860**   406

Lincoln's Political Career   **407**   •   The Party System Fragments   **409**

> AMERICAN VOICES
> MARY BOYKIN CHESNUT: A Slaveholding Woman's Diary   **385**

> AMERICAN VOICES
> AXALLA JOHN HOOLE: "Bleeding Kansas": A Southern View   **404**

*Chapter 14*
**TWO SOCIETIES AT WAR, 1861–1865**   412

**Secession and Military Stalemate, 1861–1862**   413

Choosing Sides   **413**   •   Setting War Aims and Devising Strategies   **418**

**Toward Total War**   423

Mobilizing Armies and Civilians   **423**   •   Mobilizing Resources   **426**

**The Turning Point: 1863**   428

Emancipation   **428**   •   Vicksburg and Gettysburg   **430**

**The Union Victorious, 1864–1865**   432

Soldiers and Strategy   **432**   •   The Election of 1864 and Sherman's March to the Sea   **436**

> VOICES FROM ABROAD
> ERNEST DUVEYIER DE HAURANNE: German Immigrants and the Civil War within Missouri   **417**

> AMERICAN VOICES
> DOLLY SUMNER LUNT: Sherman's March through Georgia   **439**

*Chapter 15*
**RECONSTRUCTION, 1865–1877**   442

**Presidential Reconstruction**   443

Lincoln's Approach   **443**   •   Johnson Seizes the Initiative   **444**   •   Acting on Freedom   **446**   •   Congress versus President   **450**

**Radical Reconstruction**    452

Congress Takes Command    **453**    •    Woman Suffrage Denied    **456**    •    Republican Rule in the South    **457**    •    The Quest for Land    **460**

**The Undoing of Reconstruction**    464

Counterrevolution    **465**    •    The Acquiescent North    **468**    •    The Political Crisis of 1877    **469**

AMERICAN VOICES
JOURDON ANDERSON: Relishing Freedom    **447**

AMERICAN VOICES
HARRIET HERNANDES: The Intimidation of Black Voters    **466**

**DOCUMENTS**    D-1
The Declaration of Independence    D-1
The Articles of Confederation and Perpetual Union    D-4
The Constitution of the United States    D-9
Amendments to the Constitution    D-18

**APPENDIX**    A-1
Territorial Expansion    A-1
The Labor Force    A-2
Changing Labor Patterns    A-3
American Population    A-4
Presidential Elections    A-5

**GLOSSARY**    G-1

**CREDITS**    C-1

**INDEX**    I-1

# LIST OF MAPS

1.1 The Ice Age and the Settling of the Americas    8
1.2 West Africa and the Mediterranean in the Fifteenth Century    21
1.3 The Spanish Conquest of the Great Indian Civilizations    28

2.1 New Spain Looks North, 1513–1610    39
2.2 River Plantations in Virginia, c. 1640    49
2.3 Settlement Patterns within New England Towns, 1630–1700    60

3.1 Britain's American Empire, 1713    76
3.2 Africa and the Atlantic Slave Trade, 1700–1810    78
3.3 The Rise of the American Merchant, 1750    89

4.1 The Hudson River Manors    105
4.2 Religious Diversity in 1750    108
4.3 European Spheres of Influence, 1754    120
4.4 Westward Expansion and Land Conflicts, 1750–1775    126

5.1 Britain's American Empire in 1763    133
5.2 British Troop Deployments, 1763 and 1775    149
5.3 British Western Policy, 1763–1774    154

6.1 The War in the North, 1776–1777    174
6.2 The War in the South, 1778–1781    181
6.3 The Status of Slavery, 1800    192

7.1 The Confederation and Western Land Claims    203
7.2 Land Division in the Northwest Territory    205
7.3 Ratifying the Constitution of 1787    214

8.1 Indian Cessions and State Formation, to 1840    231
8.2 The War of 1812    243
8.3 Defining the National Boundaries, 1800–1820    245

9.1  The Expansion of Voting Rights for White Men, 1800–1830    259
9.2  Distribution of the Slave Population in 1790 and 1830    269
9.3  The Missouri Compromise, 1820–1821    276
9.4  The Second Great Awakening, 1790–1860    283

10.1  Western Land Sales, 1830–1839 and 1850–1862    303
10.2  The Transportation Revolution: Roads and Canals, 1820–1850    306
10.3  Railroads of the North and South, 1850–1860    307

11.1  Presidential Election of 1824    326
11.2  The Removal of Native Americans, 1820–1843    340

12.1  Major Communal Experiments before 1860    359
12.2  The Mormon Trek, 1830–1848    364
12.3  Women and Antislavery, 1837–1838    373

13.1  American Settlements in Texas, 1821–1836    387
13.2  Routes to the West, 1835–1860    389
13.3  The Mexican War, 1846–1848    394
13.4  The Compromise of 1850 and the Kansas-Nebraska Act of 1854    399
13.5  Political Realignment, 1848–1860    405

14.1  The Process of Secession, 1860–1861    414
14.2  The Eastern Campaigns of 1862    419
14.3  The Western Campaigns, 1861–1862    422
14.4  Lee Invades the North, 1863    431
14.5  The Closing Virginia Campaign, 1864–1865    435
14.6  Sherman's March through the Confederacy, 1864–1865    438

15.1  Reconstruction    453
15.2  The Barrow Plantation, 1860 and 1881    463

The United States (physical)    at the back of the book
Major World Trading Blocs    at the back of the book

# ABOUT THE AUTHORS

**James A. Henretta** is Priscilla Alden Burke Professor of American History at the University of Maryland, College Park. He received his undergraduate education at Swarthmore College and his Ph.D. from Harvard University. He has taught at the University of Sussex, England; Princeton University; UCLA; Boston University; as a Fulbright lecturer in Australia at the University of New England; and at Oxford University as the Harmsworth Professor of American History. His publications include *The Evolution of American Society, 1700–1815: An Interdisciplinary Analysis; "Salutary Neglect": Colonial Administration under the Duke of Newcastle; Evolution and Revolution: American Society, 1600–1820;* and *The Origins of American Capitalism.* Recently he coedited and contributed to a collection of original essays, *Republicanism and Liberalism in America and the German States, 1750–1850,* as part of his larger research project on "The Liberal State in America: New York, 1820–1975." In 2002–2003, he held the John Hope Franklin Fellowship at the National Humanities Center in North Carolina.

**David Brody** is Professor Emeritus of History at the University of California, Davis. He received his B.A., M.A., and Ph.D. from Harvard University. He has taught at the University of Warwick in England, at Moscow State University in the former Soviet Union, and at Sydney University in Australia. He is the author of *Steelworkers in America; Workers in Industrial America: Essays on the Twentieth-Century Struggle;* and *In Labor's Cause: Main Themes on the History of the American Worker.* He has been awarded fellowships from the Social Science Research Council, the Guggenheim Foundation, and the National Endowment for the Humanities. He is past president (1991–1992) of the Pacific Coast branch of the American Historical Association. His current research is on labor law and workplace regimes during the Great Depression.

**Lynn Dumenil** is Robert Glass Cleland Professor of American History at Occidental College in Los Angeles. She is a graduate of the University of Southern California and received her Ph.D. from the University of California, Berkeley. She has written *The Modern Temper: American Culture and Society in the 1920s* and *Freemasonry and American Culture: 1880–1930.* Her articles and reviews have appeared in the *Journal of American History;* the *Journal of American Ethnic History; Reviews in American History;* and the *American Historical Review.* She has been a historical consultant to several documentary film projects and is on the Pelzer Prize Committee of the Organization of American Historians. Her current work, for which she received a National Endowment for the Humanities Fellowship, is on World War I, citizenship, and the state. In 2001–2002 she was the Bicentennial Fulbright Chair in American Studies at the University of Helsinki.

*Third Edition*

# America

## A CONCISE HISTORY

**Volume 1: To 1877**

# Part One

# THE CREATION OF AMERICAN SOCIETY

## 1450–1775

| ECONOMY | SOCIETY | GOVERNMENT |
|---|---|---|
| From Staple Crops to Internal Growth | Ethnic, Racial, and Class Divisions | From Monarchy to Republic |
| **1450** ▸ Native American subsistence economy<br><br>Europeans fish off North American coast | ▸ Sporadic warfare among Indian peoples<br><br>Spanish conquest of Mexico (1519–1521) | ▸ Rise of monarchical nation-states in Europe |
| **1600** ▸ First staple export crops: furs and tobacco | ▸ English-Indian warfare<br><br>African servitude begins in Virginia (1619) | ▸ James I claims divine right to rule England<br><br>Virginia House of Burgesses (1619) |
| **1640** ▸ New England trade with sugar islands<br><br>Mercantilist regulations: first Navigation Act (1651) | ▸ White indentured servitude in Chesapeake<br><br>Indians retreat inland | ▸ Puritan Revolution<br><br>Stuart restoration (1660)<br><br>Bacon's Rebellion in Virginia (1675) |
| **1680** ▸ Tobacco trade stagnates<br><br>Rice cultivation expands | ▸ Indian slavery in the Carolinas<br><br>Ethnic rebellion in New York (1689) | ▸ Dominion of New England (1686–1689)<br><br>Glorious Revolution ousts James II (1688–1689) |
| **1720** ▸ Mature yeoman farm economy in North<br><br>Imports from Britain increase | ▸ Scots-Irish and German migration<br><br>Growing rural inequality | ▸ Rise of the colonial representative assemblies<br><br>Challenge to "deferential" politics |
| **1760** ▸ Trade boycotts encourage domestic manufacturing | ▸ Uprisings by tenants and backcountry farmers<br><br>Artisan protests | ▸ Ideas of popular sovereignty<br><br>Battles of Lexington and Concord (1775) |

| RELIGION | CULTURE |
|---|---|
| **From Hierarchy to Pluralism** | **The Creation of American Identity** |
| ▶ Protestant Reformation begins (1517) | ▶ Diverse Native American cultures in eastern woodlands |
| ▶ Persecuted English Puritans and Catholics migrate to America | ▶ Puritans implant Calvinism, education, and freehold ideal |
| ▶ Religious liberty in Rhode Island | ▶ Aristocratic aspirations in the Chesapeake |
| ▶ Rise of toleration | ▶ Emergence of African American language and culture |
| ▶ German and Scots-Irish Pietists in Middle Atlantic region<br><br>Great Awakening | ▶ Expansion of colleges, newspapers, and magazines<br><br>Franklin and the American Enlightenment |
| ▶ Evangelical Baptists in Virginia<br><br>Quebec Act allows Catholicism (1774) | ▶ First signs of an American identity<br><br>Republican innovations in political theory |

Societies are made, not born. They are the creation of decades, even centuries, of human endeavor and experience. The first American societies were formed by hunting and gathering peoples who migrated to the Western Hemisphere from Asia many centuries ago. Over numerous generations these migrants— the Native Americans—came to live in a wide variety of environments and cultures. In much of North America they developed kinship-based societies that relied on farming and hunting. But in the lower Mississippi Valley, Native Americans developed a hierarchical

3

social order similar to that of the great civilizations of the Aztecs, Mayas, and Incas of Mesoamerica. The coming of Europeans and their diseases tore the fabric of most Native American cultures into shreds. Nearly everywhere, men and women of European origins—the Spanish in Mesoamerica, the French in Canada, the English along the Atlantic coast—gradually achieved domination over the native Indian peoples.

The Europeans who settled in the English mainland colonies initially sought to transplant their traditional society to the New World—their farming practices, their social hierarchies, their culture and heritage, and their religious ideas. But in learning to live in the new land, the English, Germans, and Scots-Irish who came to England's North American colonies eventually created societies that were distinctly different from those of their homelands in their economies, social character, political systems, religion, and culture.

**ECONOMY** Many European settlements were very successful in economic terms. Traditional Europe was made up of poor, overcrowded, and unequal societies that periodically suffered devastating famines. But with few people and a bountiful natural environment, the settlers in North America created a bustling economy and, in the northern mainland colonies, prosperous communities of independent farm families. Indeed, this region became known to migrants from the British Isles and Germany as "the best poor man's country."

**SOCIETY** Some of the European settlements, however, became places of oppressive captivity for Africans. Aided by African traders and political leaders, Europeans bought hundreds of thousands of enslaved workers, from many African regions. They transported these slaves to the West Indies and the southern mainland colonies and forced them to labor on sugar, tobacco, and rice plantations. Slowly and with great effort, the slaves and their descendants created an African American culture within a social order dominated by Europeans.

**GOVERNMENT** In the meantime, whites in the emerging American societies created an increasingly free and competitive political system. The
first English settlers transplanted authoritarian institutions to America,
and the English government continued to manage their lives. However,
after 1689 traditional controls gradually gave way to governments based
in part on representative assemblies. Eventually, the growth of self-rule
would lead to demands for political independence from England.

**RELIGION** The American experience profoundly changed religious
institutions and values. Many migrants left Europe because of the
conflicts among rival Christian churches in the wake of the Protestant
Reformation and came to America seeking to practice their religion
without interference. The societies they created became increasingly
religious, especially after the evangelical revivals of the 1740s. By this
time, many Americans had rejected the harshest tenets of Calvinism
(a strict Protestant faith), and others had embraced the rationalist
view of the European Enlightenment. As a result, American Protestant
Christianity became increasingly tolerant, democratic, and optimistic.

**CULTURE** The new American society witnessed the appearance of new
forms of family and community life. The first English settlers lived in
patriarchal families ruled by dominant fathers and in communities
controlled by men of high status. By 1750, however, many American
fathers no longer strictly managed their children's lives. As these communities became more diverse and open, many men and some women
began to enjoy greater personal independence. This new American society was increasingly pluralistic, composed of migrants from many
European ethnic groups—English, Scots, Scots-Irish, Dutch, and
Germans—as well as enslaved West Africans and many different
Native American peoples. Distinct regional cultures developed in New
England, the Middle Atlantic colonies, and the Chesapeake and
Carolina areas. Consequently, an overarching American identity based
on the English language, English legal and political institutions, and
shared experiences emerged very slowly.

The story of the English colonial experience is thus both tragic and
exciting. The European settlers warred with Native Americans and
condemned most African Americans to bondage while themselves enjoying rich opportunities for economic security, political freedom, and
spiritual fulfillment.

# Chapter 1

## WORLDS COLLIDE: EUROPE, AFRICA, AND AMERICA
### 1450–1620

Soon there will come from the rising sun a different kind of man from
any you have yet seen . . . [after that,] the world will fall to pieces.

A Spokane Indian Prophet

"Before the French came among us," an elder of the Natchez people
of Mississippi exclaimed, "we were men . . . and we walked with boldness every
road, but now we walk like slaves, which we shall soon be, since the French already
treat us . . . as they do their black slaves." Before the 1490s the native peoples of the
Western Hemisphere knew absolutely nothing about the light-skinned inhabitants
of Europe and the dark-complexioned peoples of Africa. However, Portuguese
merchants hungry for the riches of Asia were already sailing along the west coast
of Africa and were trading for African slaves. When Christopher Columbus, another European searching for a sea route to Asia, encountered the peoples of the
Western Hemisphere, the destinies of four continents quickly became intertwined.
On his second voyage, Columbus carried a cargo of enslaved Africans, beginning
the centuries-long trade that created a multitude of triracial societies in the
Americas.

As the Natchez elder knew well, the resulting mixture of peoples was based not
on equality but on exploitation. By the time he urged his people to resist, the
European invaders were too numerous and strong to be dislodged. Aided by Indian
allies, the French killed hundreds of the Natchez rebels and sold the survivors into
slavery on the sugar plantations of the West Indies. The fate of the Natchez was
hardly unique. In the three centuries following Columbus's voyage, many Native
American peoples came under the domination of the Spanish, Portuguese, French,
English, and Dutch who colonized the Western Hemisphere and used enslaved
Africans to work agricultural plantations.

How did this happen? How did Europeans become leaders in world trade and
extend their influence across the Atlantic? What made Native American peoples

vulnerable to conquest by European adventurers? And what led to the transatlantic trade in African slaves? In the answers to these questions lie the origins of the United States and the dominant position of people of European descent in the modern world.

# Native American Worlds

When the Europeans arrived, most Native Americans—about 45 million—lived in Mesoamerica (present-day Mexico and Guatemala) and along the western coast of South America (present-day Peru); another 15 million resided in lands to the north (present-day United States and Canada). Some lived in simple hunter-gatherer or agricultural communities governed by kin ties, but the majority resided in societies ruled by warrior-kings and priests. In Mesoamerica and Peru, Indian peoples created civilizations whose art, religion, society, and economy were as complex as those of Europe and the Mediterranean.

## *The First Americans*

According to the elders of the Navajo people, history began when their ancestors emerged from under the earth; for the Iroquois, the story of their Five Nations began when people fell from the sky. However, most twenty-first-century anthropologists and historians believe that the first inhabitants of the Western Hemisphere were migrants from Asia. Some migrants came by water, but most probably came by land. Strong archaeological and genetic evidence suggests that late in the last Ice Age, which took place from 20,000 B.C. until 9000 B.C., small bands of Asian tribal hunters followed herds of game across a hundred-mile-wide land bridge between Siberia and Alaska. An oral history of the Tuscarora Indians, who lived in present-day North Carolina, tells of a famine in the old world and a journey over ice toward where "the sun rises," a trek that brought their ancestors to a lush forest with abundant food and game.

Most anthropologists believe that the main migratory stream from Asia lasted from about 13,000 B.C. to 9000 B.C., when the glaciers melted and the rising ocean waters submerged the land bridge and created the Bering Strait. A second movement of peoples around 6000 B.C., now traveling by water across the narrow strait, brought the ancestors of the Navajos and the Apaches to North America, while a third migration around 3000 B.C. introduced the forebears of the Aleut and Inuit peoples—the "Eskimos." Subsequently, the people of the Western Hemisphere, who were now settled as far south as the tip of South America and as far east as the Atlantic coast of North America, were largely cut off from the rest of the world for three hundred generations (Map 1.1).

For many centuries the first Americans lived as hunter-gatherers, subsisting on the abundant vegetation and wildlife. Gradually, the larger species of animals—mammoths, giant beaver, and horses—died out because of overhunting and

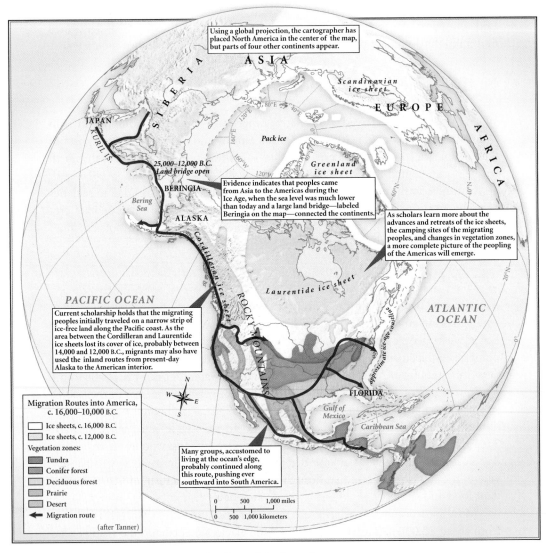

Using a global projection, the cartographer has placed North America in the center of the map, but parts of four other continents appear.

Evidence indicates that peoples came from Asia to the Americas during the Ice Age, when the sea level was much lower than today and a large land bridge—labeled Beringia on the map—connected the continents.

As scholars learn more about the advances and retreats of the ice sheets, the camping sites of the migrating peoples, and changes in vegetation zones, a more complete picture of the peopling of the Americas will emerge.

Current scholarship holds that the migrating peoples initially traveled on a narrow strip of ice-free land along the Pacific coast. As the area between the Cordilleran and Laurentide ice sheets lost its cover of ice, probably between 14,000 and 12,000 B.C., migrants may also have used the inland routes from present-day Alaska to the American interior.

Many groups, accustomed to living at the ocean's edge, probably continued along this route, pushing ever southward into South America.

**Migration Routes into America, c. 16,000–10,000 B.C.**

- ☐ Ice sheets, c. 16,000 B.C.
- ☐ Ice sheets, c. 12,000 B.C.

**Vegetation zones:**

- ◼ Tundra
- ◼ Conifer forest
- ☐ Deciduous forest
- ◼ Prairie
- ☐ Desert
- ◀ Migration route

(after Tanner)

### MAP 1.1 The Ice Age and the Settling of the Americas

Some sixteen thousand years ago, a sheet of ice covered much of Europe and North America. Taking advantage of a broad bridge of land connecting Siberia and Alaska, hunting peoples from Asia migrated into North America, searching for large game animals, such as woolly mammoths, and ice-free habitats. By 10,000 B.C. the descendants of the migrant peoples had moved as far south as present-day Florida and central Mexico.

climatic change, and hunters became adept at killing more elusive and faster rabbits, deer, and elk. About 3000 B.C. some Native American peoples began to develop farming, most notably in the region near present-day Mexico. These inventive horticulturists planted beans, squash, and maize (corn), as well as tomatoes, potatoes, and manioc—crops that would eventually enrich the food supply of the entire world. Indeed, the Indian peoples gradually bred maize into an extremely nutritious plant that had a higher yield per acre than wheat, barley, and rye, the staple cereals of Europe. They also learned to plant beans and squash together with corn, creating a mix of crops that provided a nutritious diet and preserved soil fertility. The resulting agricultural surplus laid the economic foundation for populous and wealthy societies in Mexico, Peru, and the Mississippi River Valley.

## The Mayas and the Aztecs

The flowering of civilization in Mesoamerica began among the Olmec people, who lived along the Gulf of Mexico around 700 B.C. Subsequently, the Mayan peoples of the Yucatán Peninsula of Mexico and the neighboring rain forests of Guatemala built large urban religious centers with elaborate systems of water storage and irrigation. By A.D. 300 the Mayan city of Tikal [*t-CALL*] contained at least 20,000 inhabitants, mostly farmers whose labor built huge stone temples. An elite class claiming descent from the gods ruled Mayan society and lived in splendor on goods and taxes extracted from peasant families. Drawing on religious and artistic traditions that stretched back to the Olmecs, skilled Mayan artisans decorated temples and palaces with art depicting warrior-gods and complex religious rituals. Mayan astronomers created a calendar that recorded historical events and accurately predicted eclipses of the sun and the moon. Mayas drawn from the elite class also developed hieroglyphic writing to record royal lineages, wars, and other noteworthy events. These skills in calculation and writing enhanced the authority of the priestly class and provided the Mayan peoples with a sense of their history and identity. By facilitating the movement of goods and ideas, they also increased the prosperity of Mayan society and the complexity of its culture.

Beginning around A.D. 800, Mayan civilization went into decline. Evidence suggests that a two-century-long dry period caused an economic crisis and prompted overtaxed peasants to desert the temple cities and retreat to the countryside. By A.D. 900 many religious centers had been abandoned, but some Mayan city-states lasted until the Spanish invasion in the 1520s.

A second major Mesoamerican civilization developed in the central highlands of Mexico around the city of Teotihuacán [*tea-o-ti-hue-CON*], with its magnificent Pyramid of the Sun. At its zenith about A.D. 500, Teotihuacán had more than one hundred temples, about four thousand apartment buildings, and a population of at least 100,000. By A.D. 800 Teotihuacán had also declined, probably because of a long-term drought and recurrent invasions by seminomadic warrior peoples. Eventually one of these peoples, the Aztecs, established an even more extensive empire.

The Aztecs entered the highlands of Mexico from the north and settled on an island in Lake Texcoco. There, in A.D. 1325, they began to build a new city, Tenochtitlán [*ten-och-tit-LAWN*] (present-day Mexico City). The Aztecs learned the settled ways of the resident peoples, mastered their complex irrigation systems and written language, and established an elaborate culture with a hierarchical social order. Priests and warrior-nobles ruled over twenty clans of free Aztec commoners who farmed communally owned land. The nobles also used huge numbers of non-Aztec slaves and serfs to labor on their private estates. Skilled artisans worked in stone, pottery, cloth, leather, and especially obsidian (hard volcanic glass that made sharp-edged weapons and tools).

The Aztecs remained an aggressive tribe and soon subjugated most of central Mexico. Their rulers demanded both economic and human tribute from scores of subject tribes, gruesomely sacrificing untold thousands of men and women to ensure agricultural fertility and the daily return of the sun. Aztec merchants created trading routes that crisscrossed the empire and imported furs, gold, textiles, food, and obsidian from as far north as the Rio Grande and as far south as present-day Panama. By A.D. 1500, Tenochtitlán had grown into a great metropolis with magnificent palaces and temples and over 200,000 inhabitants. Its splendor dazzled subject peoples as well as Spanish soldiers. "These great towns and pyramids and buildings arising from the water, all made of stone, seemed like an enchanted vision," marveled one Spaniard. The Aztecs' wealth, strong institutions, and military power posed a formidable challenge to any adversary, at home or from afar.

### The Indians of the North

The Indians who resided north of the Rio Grande lived in societies that were less complex and less coercive because, unlike those to the south, they lacked a diversity of occupations and a social hierarchy. Most of the northern peoples lived in self-governing tribes composed of **clans**—groups of related families with a common identity and a real or legendary common ancestor. Clan elders and local chiefs conducted ceremonies, resolved personal feuds, and disciplined individuals who violated customs. They also decided war policy and banned marriage between members of the same clan, a rule that helped prevent inbreeding. However, the elders and chiefs did not form a distinct ruling class—like that of the Mayan and Aztec nobles—and, because their kinship system of government was locally based and worked by consensus, they had only limited powers. Moreover, the culture of these lineage-based societies did not encourage the accumulation of material goods. Indeed, the individual ownership of land was virtually unknown; as a French missionary among the Iroquois noted, they "possess hardly anything except in common." The elders urged individuals to share food and other scarce goods, encouraging an ethic of reciprocity rather than one of accumulation. "You are covetous, and neither generous nor kind," the Micmac Indians of Nova Scotia told acquisitive-minded French fur traders around 1600. "As for us, if we have a morsel of bread, we share it with our neighbor."

Over the centuries some Indian peoples did develop a materialistic outlook and engaged in trade or conquest. The earliest expansive Indian cultures appeared in the areas of present-day Ohio. By A.D. 100 the vigorous Hopewell people had increased the food supply by domesticating plants, organized themselves in large villages, and set up a trading network that stretched from Louisiana to Wisconsin and beyond. They imported obsidian from the Yellowstone region of the Rocky Mountains, copper from the Great Lakes, and pottery and marine shells from the Gulf of Mexico. The Hopewell built large burial mounds and surrounded them with extensive circular, rectangular, or octagonal earthworks that in some cases still survive. Skilled craftsmen fashioned striking ornaments that they buried with the dead: copper beaten into intricate artistic designs, mica cut into the shapes of serpents and human hands, and stone pipes carved to represent frogs, hawks, bears, and other animals—figurines evidently representing spiritually powerful beings. For unknown reasons, the elaborate trading network of the Hopewell gradually collapsed around A.D. 400.

A second complex culture developed among the Pueblo peoples of the Southwest—the Hohokams, Mogollons, and Anasazis. By A.D. 600 Hohokam [ho-HO-kam] peoples in the high country along the border of present-day Arizona and New Mexico were using irrigation to grow two crops a year, fashioning fine pottery with red-on-buff designs, and worshiping their gods on Mesoamerican-like platform mounds; by A.D. 1000, they were living in elaborate multiroom stone structures (or pueblos). To the east, in the Mimbres Valley of New Mexico, the Mogollon [mo-gee-YON] peoples developed a distinctive black-on-white pottery. In the north of present-day New Mexico, the Anasazi (now known as the people of the Ancestral Pueblo) culture emerged around A.D. 900. The Anasazis were master architects, building residential-ceremonial villages in steep cliffs, a pueblo in Chaco Canyon that housed 1,000 people, and four hundred miles of straight roads. However, the culture of the Anasazis, Mogollons, and Hohokams gradually collapsed after A.D. 1150 as long periods of drought and soil exhaustion disrupted maize production and prompted the abandonment of Chaco Canyon and other long-established communities. The descendants of these Pueblo peoples—including the Zunis and the Hopis—later built strong but smaller and more dispersed village societies.

The last large-scale culture to emerge north of the Rio Grande was the Mississippian civilization. Beginning about A.D. 800, the advanced farming technology of Mesoamerica spread into the Mississippi River Valley, perhaps carried by Mayan emigrants from the Yucatán Peninsula. By planting new strains of maize and beans, the Mississippian peoples produced an agricultural surplus and a robust culture based on small, fortified temple cities. By A.D. 1150 the largest city, Cahokia [ca-HO-key-ah] (near present-day St. Louis), boasted a population of 15,000 to 20,000 and more than one hundred temple mounds, one of them as large as the great Egyptian pyramids. As in Mesoamerica, the tribute paid by peasant cultivators supported a privileged class of nobles and priests who waged war against neighboring chiefdoms, patronized skilled artisans, and may have been worshiped as quasi-sacred beings related to the sun god.

By A.D. 1350, this six-hundred-year-old Mississippian civilization was in rapid decline, undermined by overpopulation, warfare, and urban diseases such as

**Chaco Canyon**

Chaco Canyon was a major center of ancestral Pueblo culture between A.D. 850 and 1250. In this high desert landscape, with its long winters, short growing seasons, and marginal rainfall, the Chacoan peoples constructed massive stone buildings. Well-built roads connected these "great houses," which were used for ceremonial and administrative purposes, to more than 150 other great houses scattered throughout the region. NPS Photo / D. Six.

tuberculosis. Nonetheless, its values and institutions endured for centuries. When the Spanish adventurer Hernán de Soto invaded the region in the 1540s, he found the Apalachee [*ap-a-LA-chee*] and Timucua [*tee-MOO-cwa*] Indians living in permanent settlements and fiercely resistant to his commands. "If you desire to see me, come where I am," a chief told de Soto, "neither for you, nor for any man, will I set back one foot." A century and a half later, French traders and priests who encountered the Natchez people (and who would soon help to conquer them) found a society rigidly divided among hereditary chiefs, two groups of nobles and honored people, and a bottom class of peasants. "Their chiefs possess all authority," a Frenchman noted. "They distribute their favors and presents at will." Undoubtedly influenced by Mayan or Aztec rituals, the Natchez marked the death of a chief by sacrificing his wives and burying their remains in a ceremonial mound (see Voices from Abroad, "The Customs of the Natchez, 1730," p. 13).

Other peoples in the region, such as the Creeks, Chickasaws, Cherokees, and Seminoles, resided in small and dispersed agricultural communities. In these societies—and among the Algonquian peoples who lived farther to the east— farming was the work of women. While men hunted and fished, Indian women

**VOICES FROM ABROAD**

# The Customs of the Natchez, 1730

### FATHER LE PETITE

*B*eliefs and institutions from the earlier Mississippian culture (A.D. 1000–1450) lasted for
centuries among the Natchez, who lived in present-day Mississippi. Father le Petite was
one of the hundreds of Jesuits who lived among—and wrote detailed accounts of—the Indians
in the French colonies of Louisiana and Canada. Here, he accurately describes many Natchez
customs but fails to understand that the rules governing the succession of the chief simply follow the normal practice of descent in a matrilineal society.

My Reverend Father, This Nation of Savages inhabits one of the most beautiful and fertile
countries in the World, and is the only one on this continent which appears to have any
regular worship. Their Religion in certain points is very similar to that of the ancient
Romans. They have a Temple filled with Idols, which are different figures of men and of
animals, and for which they have the most profound veneration. Their Temple in shape
resembles an earthen oven, a hundred feet in circumference. They enter it by a little door
about four feet high, and not more than three in breadth. Above on the outside are three
figures of eagles made of wood, and painted red, yellow, and white. Before the door is a
kind of shed with folding-doors, where the Guardian of the Temple is lodged; all around it
runs a circle of palisades, on which are seen exposed the skulls of all the heads which their
Warriors had brought back from the battles in which they had been engaged with the enemies of their Nation. . . .

The Sun is the principal object of veneration to these people; as they cannot conceive of
anything which can be above this heavenly body, nothing else appears to them more wor-
thy of their homage. It is for the same reason that the great Chief of this Nation, who knows
nothing on the earth more dignified than himself, takes the title of brother of the Sun, and
the credulity of the people maintains him in the despotic authority which he claims.

The old men prescribe the Laws for the rest of the people, and one of their principles
is . . . the immortality of the soul, and when they leave this world they go, they say, to live
in another, there to be recompensed or punished.

In former times the Nation of the Natchez was very large. It counted sixty Villages and
eight hundred Suns or Princes; now it is reduced to six little Villages and eleven Suns. [Its]
Government is hereditary; it is not, however, the son of the reigning Chief who succeeds
his father, but the son of his sister, or the first Princess of the blood. This policy is founded
on the knowledge they have of the licentiousness of their women. They are not sure, they
say, that the children of the chief's wife may be of the blood Royal, whereas the son of the
sister of the great Chief must be, at least on the side of the mother.

SOURCE: *The Jesuit Relations and Allied Documents*, ed. Reuben Gold Thwaites (Cleveland: Murrow
Brothers, 1900), 68:121–35.

became adept horticulturists, using flint hoes to plant corn, squash, and beans. Because of the importance of farming, a **matrilineal** inheritance system developed among many eastern Indian peoples, including the Five Nations of the Iroquois (the Mohawks, Oneidas, Onondagas, Cayugas and Senecas who lived in present-day New York State). Women cultivated the fields around semi-permanent settlements and passed the right to use them to their daughters. In these matrilineal societies, fathers stood outside the main lines of kinship; the principal responsibility for childraising fell upon the mother and her brothers, who often lived with her (rather than with their wives). The ritual and religious lives of these farming peoples focused on the agricultural cycle, such as the Iroquois green corn and strawberry festivals. Because of women's labor, the eastern Indian peoples of A.D. 1500 ate better than their ancestors had, but they enjoyed few material comforts and their populations grew slowly.

When Europeans intruded into their lives after 1500, most Indians north of the Rio Grande had resided on the same lands for generations. However, the strong city-states that had once flourished in the Southwest and in the Mississippi valley had vanished. Consequently, there were no great Indian empires or religious centers that could lead a sustained campaign of military and spiritual resistance. "When you command, all the French obey and go to war," the Chippewa chief Chigabe [*chig-AH-be*] remarked to a general, but "I shall not be heeded and obeyed by my nation." Because household and lineage were the basis of his society, Chigabe explained, "I cannot answer except for myself and for those immediately allied to me."

# Traditional European Society in 1450

In A.D. 1450 few observers would have predicted that the European peoples would become the overlords of the Western Hemisphere. A thousand years after the fall of the great Roman empire, Europe was divided into many small kingdoms. Indeed, around 1350 a vicious epidemic from the subcontinent of India—the Black Death—had killed one-third of Europe's peoples. Other areas of the world, such as China, were much more economically advanced and were dispatching commercial fleets to far-flung lands, including the eastern coast of Africa.

## *The Peasantry*

There were only a few large cities in Western Europe—in A.D. 1450 only Paris, London, and Naples had 100,000 residents and thus equaled the size of Teotihuacán at its zenith. More than 90 percent of the European population consisted of **peasants** living in small rural communities. Peasant families usually owned or leased a small dwelling in the village center and had the right to farm the surrounding fields. The fields were "open"—not divided by fences or hedges—making cooperative farming a necessity. The village community decided which crops would be grown,

**Artisan Family**

Work was slow and output was limited in the preindustrial world, and survival required the efforts of all family members. Here a fifteenth-century French woodworker planes a panel of wood while his wife twists flax fibers into linen yarn for the family's clothes and their son fashions a basket out of reeds.

Giraudon / Art Resource, NY.

and every family followed its dictates. Because there were few merchants or good roads, most families exchanged surplus grain and meat with their neighbors or bartered their farm products for the services of local millers, weavers, and blacksmiths. Most peasants yearned to be **yeomen**—members of a household that owned enough land to support its members in comfort—but relatively few achieved that goal.

As among the Native Americans, the rhythms of European peasant life followed the seasons. The agricultural year began in March or April, when the ground thawed and dried and the villagers began the exhausting work of spring plowing and the planting of wheat, rye, and oats. During these busy months men sheared the thick winter wool of their sheep, which the women washed and spun into yarn. Peasants cut the first crop of hay in June and stored it as winter fodder for their livestock. In the summer, life became more relaxed, and families repaired their houses and barns. Fall brought the strenuous harvest time, followed by solemn feasts of thanksgiving and riotous bouts of merrymaking. As winter approached, peasants slaughtered excess livestock and salted or smoked the meat. During the cold months peasants completed the tasks of threshing grain and weaving textiles, visited friends and relatives, and held celebrations to mark the pagan winter solstice or birth of Christ. Just before the farming cycle began again in March, rural residents held carnivals to celebrate with drink and dance the end of the long winter night.

Even births and deaths followed the seasons. Many rural people died in January and February, victims of viral diseases, and again in August and September, casualties of epidemics of fly-borne dysentery. More mysteriously, in European villages (and later in rural British America), the greatest numbers of babies were born in February and March, with a smaller peak in September and October. The precise causes of this pattern are unknown; most likely, seasonal fluctuations in female work patterns or the food supply altered a woman's ability to carry a child to full term. One thing is certain. This pattern of births does not exist in modern urban societies, so it must have reflected the rigors of the traditional agriculture cycle.

For most peasants survival required unremitting labor. Horses and oxen strained to break the soil with primitive wooden plows, while workers harvested hay and grain with small hand sickles. Because of the lack of high-quality seeds, chemical fertilizers, and pesticides, output was pitifully small—less than one-tenth of present-day yields. The margin of existence was thin and corroded family relations. Malnourished mothers fed their babies sparingly, calling them "greedy and gluttonous," and many newborn girls were "helped to die" so that their older brothers would have enough to eat. Disease killed about half of all peasant children before the age of twenty-one. Violence—assault, murder, rape—was part of the fabric of daily life, and hunger was a constant companion. "I have seen the latest epoch of misery," a French doctor reported as famine and plague struck. "The inhabitants . . . lie down in a meadow to eat grass, and share the food of wild beasts."

Often destitute, usually exploited and dominated by landlords and aristocrats, many peasants simply accepted their condition. Others hoped for a better life for themselves and their children. In Spain, Germany, and Britain, the deprived rural classes would supply the majority of white migrants to the Western Hemisphere.

## Hierarchy and Authority

In the traditional European social order, as among the Aztec and Mayan peoples, authority came from above. Kings and princes owned vast tracts of land, conscripted men for military service, and lived in splendor off the labor of the peasantry. Yet monarchs were far from supreme because of the power of local nobles, each of whom also owned large estates and controlled hundreds of peasant families. Collectively, these noblemen challenged royal authority. They had their own legislative institutions, such as the French *parlements* and the English House of Lords, and enjoyed special privileges. However, after 1450 kings expanded their powers by fashioning new royal courts of law and forming alliances with wealthy merchants. These initiatives gradually undermined the power of the nobility and created more centralized and better financed states, thereby laying the administrative basis for overseas expansion.

Just as kings and nobles ruled society, so men governed families. Among rich and poor, the man was the head of the house, his power justified by the teachings of the Christian Church. As one English clergyman put it, "The woman is a weak creature not embued with like strength and constancy of mind"; law and custom consequently "subjected her to the power of man." Upon marriage, an English woman assumed her husband's surname and had to submit (under threat of legally sanctioned physical "correction") to his orders. Moreover, she surrendered to her husband the legal right to all her property; upon his death she received a **dower**, usually the use during her lifetime of one-third of the family's land and goods.

A father controlled the lives of his children with equal authority, demanding that they work for him until their middle or late twenties. Then landowning peasants would provide land to sons and dowries to daughters and choose marriage partners of appropriate wealth and status. In many regions fathers bestowed most of the land on the eldest son, an inheritance practice known as **primogeniture**, which forced many younger children to join the ranks of the roaming poor. In such a society few men—and even fewer women—had much personal freedom or individual identity.

Hierarchy and authority prevailed in traditional European society both because of the power of established institutions, such as the family, church, and village community, and because, in a violent and unpredictable world, they offered ordinary people a measure of security. These values of order and security, which migrants carried with them to America, would shape the character of family life and the social order there well into the eighteenth century.

### The Power of Religion

For centuries, the Roman Catholic Church was the only Christian Church in Western Europe and served as one of the great unifying social institutions. By A.D. 1000, Catholic priests had converted most of pagan Europe. The pope, as head of the Catholic Church, directed a vast religious hierarchy of cardinals, bishops, and priests. Catholic books and theologians preserved Latin, the great language of classical scholarship, and Christian dogma provided a common understanding of God, the world, and human history. Equally important, the Church provided a bulwark of authority and discipline. Every village had a church, and the holy shrines that dotted the byways of Europe were constant reminders of the Church's power and teachings.

Christian doctrine penetrated deeply into the everyday lives of peasants. Originally, most Europeans were pagans; like many of the Indians of North America, they were animists who believed that the entire natural world contained unpredictable spiritual forces that had to be paid ritual honor. Then, Christian priests taught them that spiritual power came from outside of nature, from a great God who had sent his divine son, Jesus Christ, into the world to save humanity from its sins. The Church also devised a religious calendar that transformed pagan agricultural festivals into Christian holy days. Thus, the winter solstice, which for pagans marked the return of the sun, became the feast of Christmas, to mark the coming of the Savior. To avert famine and plague, Christianized peasants did not make ritual offerings to nature but offered prayers to Christ and the saints.

The Church also taught that Satan, a lesser and evil supernatural being, constantly challenged God by tempting people to sin. If a devout Christian fell mysteriously ill, the sickness might be the result of an evil spell cast by a witch in league with Satan. If prophets spread unusual doctrines, or **heresies**, they were surely the tools of Satan. Suppressing false doctrines among Christians became an obligation of rulers, while combating Islam was a principal task of new orders of Christian knights. Following the death in A.D. 632 of the prophet Muhammad, the founder of Islam, the newly converted Arab peoples of the Mediterranean used force and persuasion to spread the Islamic faith and Arab civilization into sub-Saharan Africa, India, and Indonesia and deep into Spain and the Balkan region of eastern Europe. Between A.D. 1096 and 1291 Christian armies undertook a series of Crusades to halt this advance.

The Crusaders had some military successes against their Muslim Arab foes, but their most profound impact was on European society. Religious warfare intensified Europe's Christian identity and prompted the persecution of Jews and their expulsion from many European countries. The Crusades also broadened the intellectual and economic horizons of the privileged classes of Western Europe, who absorbed the advanced scholarship of the Arab world and set out to capture the Arab-dominated trade routes that stretched from Mongolia to Constantinople and from the East Indies to the Mediterranean.

# Europe Encounters Africa and the Americas, 1450–1550

Around A.D. 1400 Europeans experienced a major revival of learning—the **Renaissance** (from the French word for "rebirth"). Drawing inspiration from classical Greek and Roman (rather than Christian) sources and from Europe's rapid recovery from the devastating Black Death of the 1340s, Renaissance intellectuals were optimists. They saw themselves not as victims of the forces of nature but as many-sided individuals with the capacity to change the world. Inspired by new knowledge, the rulers of Portugal and Spain commissioned Italian mariners to find trade routes to India and China. These maritime adventurers soon brought Europeans into direct contact with the peoples of Africa, Asia, and the Americas, beginning a new era in world history.

## The Renaissance

Stimulated by exposure to the Arab world, first Italy and then the countries of northern Europe experienced a rebirth of learning and cultural life. Arab traders had access to the silks and spices of the East, and Arab societies had acquired

**Astronomers at Istanbul, 1581**

Arab and Turkish scholars transmitted ancient texts and learning to Europeans during the Middle Ages and provided much of the geographical and astronomical knowledge used by European explorers during the sixteenth century, the great Age of Discovery.

Ergun Cagutay, Istanbul.

magnetic compasses, water-powered mills, and mechanical clocks. Moreover, Arab scholars carried on the legacy of Byzantine civilization, which, in the centuries following the collapse of the Roman empire in Western Europe, had preserved the great achievements of the Greeks and Romans in medicine, philosophy, mathematics, astronomy, and geography. As the Crusades of the twelfth and thirteenth centuries exposed Europeans to Byzantine and Arab learning, they reacquainted themselves with their own classical heritage.

The Renaissance had the most profound impact on the upper classes. Merchants from the Italian city-states of Venice, Genoa, and Pisa dispatched ships to Alexandria, Beirut, and other eastern Mediterranean ports, where they purchased goods from China, India, Persia, and Arabia and sold them throughout Europe. The enormous profits from this commerce created powerful merchants, bankers, and textile manufacturers who conducted trade, lent vast sums of money, and spurred technological innovation in silk and wool production. This moneyed elite ruled the republican city-states of Italy and created the concept of **civic humanism**, an **ideology** that celebrated public virtue and service to the state and would profoundly influence European and American conceptions of government.

Perhaps no other age in European history has produced such a flowering of artistic genius. Michelangelo, Andrea Palladio, and Filippo Brunelleschi [*bru-nel-LESS-key*] designed and built great architectural masterpieces, while Leonardo da Vinci, Jacopo Bellini, and Raphael produced magnificent religious paintings, creating styles and setting standards that have endured into the modern era.

This creative energy inspired Renaissance rulers. In *The Prince* (1513), Niccolò Machiavelli provided unsentimental advice on how monarchs could increase their political power. The kings of Western Europe followed his advice, creating royal law courts and bureaucracies to reduce the power of the landed classes and forging alliances with merchants and urban artisans. Monarchs allowed merchants to trade throughout their realms and granted privileges to artisan guilds, thereby encouraging domestic manufacturing and foreign trade. In return, kings and princes extracted taxes from towns and loans from merchants to support their armies and officials. This alliance of monarchs, merchants, and royal bureaucrats (which eventually became known as **mercantilism**) propelled Europe into its first age of overseas expansion.

Under the direction of Prince Henry (1394–1460), Portugal led a great surge of maritime commercial expansion. Henry was at once a Christian warrior and a Renaissance humanist. As a general of the Crusading Order of Christ, he had fought the Muslims in North Africa. As a humanist, Henry patronized Renaissance thinkers. And, as an explorer, he retained the services of Arab and Italian geographers. Imbued with the spirit of the Renaissance, he tried to fulfill the mission assigned to him by an astrologer: "to engage in great and noble conquests and to attempt the discovery of things hidden from other men."

Because Arab and Italian merchants dominated trade in the Mediterranean, Henry sought an alternative route to Asia. In the 1420s he established a center for exploration near Lisbon and sent newly designed and strongly constructed three-masted ships (caravels, with a lateen—or triangular—sail) to navigate the African coast. His seamen soon discovered and settled three sets of islands—the Madeiras, the Canaries, and the Azores. By 1435 Portuguese sea captains were roaming the coast of West Africa, seeking ivory and gold in exchange for salt, wine, and fish. By the 1440s they were trading in humans as well, the first Europeans to engage in the long-established trade in African slaves.

## West African Society and Slavery

Vast and diverse, West Africa stretches along the coast from present-day Senegal to Angola. In the 1400s tropical rain forest covered much of the coast, but a series of great rivers—the Senegal, Gambia, Volta, Niger, and Congo—provided relatively easy access to the woodlands, plains, and savanna of the interior (Map 1.2).

Most West Africans farmed modest plots and lived in extended families in small villages. Normally, men cleared the land and women planted and harvested the

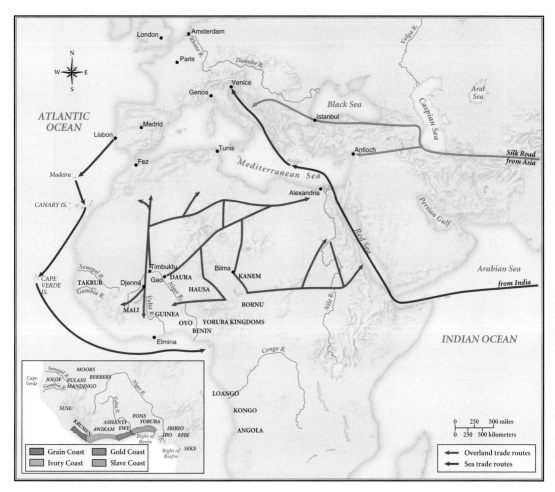

**MAP 1.2 West Africa and the Mediterranean in the Fifteenth Century**

Trade routes across the Sahara Desert had long connected West Africa with the Mediterranean region. Gold, ivory, and slaves moved northward; fine textiles, spices, and the Muslim faith traveled to the south. Beginning in the 1430s, the Portuguese opened up a maritime trade with the coastal regions of West Africa, which were home to many peoples and dozens of large and small states.

crops. On the plains of the savanna, millet, cotton, and livestock were the primary products, while the forest peoples grew yams and harvested oil-rich palm nuts. Forest dwellers exchanged palm oil and kola nuts, a mild stimulant, for the textiles and leather goods produced by savanna dwellers. Similarly, salt produced along the seacoast was traded for iron or gold mined in the hills of the interior.

West Africans spoke many different languages and lived in hundreds of distinct cultural and political groups. A majority of the people resided in hierarchical, socially stratified societies ruled by princes. Other West Africans dwelled in stateless societies organized by household and lineage (much like those of the woodland

**Fulani Village in West Africa**

Around 1550 the Fulani people conquered the lands to the south of the Senegal River. To protect themselves from subject peoples and neighboring tribes, the Fulani constructed fortified villages, such as the one depicted here. Previously the Fulani had been nomadic herders and, as the enclosed pasture shows, continued to keep livestock. Note the cylindrical houses of mud brick, surmounted by thatched roofs. Frederic Shoberl, ed., *The World in Miniature*, 1821.

FOR MORE HELP ANALYZING THIS IMAGE, see the Online Study Guide at **bedfordstmartins.com/henrettaconcise**.

Indians of eastern North America). Most peoples had secret societies, such as the Poro for men and the Sande for women, that united people from different lineages and clans. These societies provided education in sexual practices, conducted adult initiation ceremonies, and, by shaming individuals and officials, enforced codes of public conduct and private morality.

Spiritual beliefs varied greatly. Although some West Africans had been converted to Islam by Arab missionaries and believed in a single god, most recognized a variety of deities—ranging from a remote creator-god who seldom interfered in human affairs to numerous animistic spirits that lived in the earth, animals, and plants. Africans viewed their ancestors with great respect, believing that they inhabited a nearby spiritual world from which they could intercede on behalf of their descendants.

At first European traders had a positive impact on life in West Africa by introducing new plants and animals. Portuguese merchants carried coconuts from East Africa, oranges and lemons from the Mediterranean, pigs from Western Europe, and (after 1500) maize, manioc, and tomatoes from the Americas. Portuguese merchants also expanded existing African trade networks. From small, fortified trading posts on the coast, they shipped metal products and manufactures to inland areas and took gold, ivory, and pepper in return. Africans handled this trade; yellow fever, malaria, and dysentery quickly struck down Europeans who ventured inland, and their death rate often reached 50 percent a year.

Europeans soon joined Arab merchants and Africans in the slave trade. Unfree labor was the norm in most premodern societies, and in West Africa it took the form of slavery. Some people were held in bondage as security for debts; others were sold into servitude by their kin, often in exchange for food in times of famine; still others were war captives. Although treated as property and exploited as agricultural laborers, slaves were usually considered members of the society that had enslaved them. Most retained the right to marry, and their children were often free. A small proportion of unfree West Africans were **trade slaves**, mostly war captives and criminals sold from one kingdom to another or carried overland in caravans by Arab traders to the Mediterranean region. Thus, the first Portuguese in Senegambia found that a Wolof [WOE-*lof*] king

> supports himself by raids which result in many slaves. . . . He employs these slaves in cultivating the land allotted to him; but he also sells many to the Azanaghi [Arab] merchants in return for horses and other goods.

Subsequently, Portuguese traders established "forts" at small port cities—Gorée, Elmina, Mpinda, and Loango—where they bought slaves from African princes and warlords. Initially they carried a few thousand African slaves each year to sugar plantations in Madeira and the Canary Islands and to Lisbon, which soon had a black population of 9,000. After 1550 the maritime slave trade expanded enormously as Europeans set up sugar plantations in Brazil and the West Indies. By 1700, slave traders were carrying hundreds of thousands of enslaved Africans to toil and die on American plantations.

### Europe Reaches the Americas

As they traded with Africans, Portuguese adventurers continued their quest for an ocean route to Asia. In 1488, Bartolomeu Dias rounded the Cape of Good Hope, the southern tip of Africa, and ten years later Vasco da Gama reached India. Although the Arab, Indian, and Jewish merchants who controlled the trade along India's Malabar Coast tried to exclude him, da Gama acquired a highly profitable cargo of cinnamon and pepper—spices used to flavor and preserve meat. To capture the trade in spices and Indian textiles, da Gama returned to India in 1502 with twenty-one fighting vessels, which outmaneuvered and outgunned the Arab fleets. Soon the Portuguese government set up fortified trading posts for its merchants at key points around the Indian Ocean, in Indonesia, and along the coast of Asia to China and

Japan. In a transition that helped to lay the foundations for the momentous growth of European wealth and power, the Portuguese replaced Arabs as the leaders in world commerce.

Spain quickly followed Portugal's example. As Renaissance rulers, King Ferdinand of Aragon and Queen Isabel of Castile saw national unity and commerce as the keys to power and prosperity. Married in their teens in an arranged match, the young rulers (r. 1474–1516) combined their kingdoms and completed the centuries-long *reconquista* by ousting the Muslims from their realm. In 1492 their armies captured Granada, the last outpost of Islam in Western Europe. Using Catholicism to build a sense of "Spanishness," Ferdinand and Isabel launched a brutal Inquisition against suspected Christian heretics and expelled or forcibly converted thousands of Jews and Arabs. Simultaneously they sought trade and empire and enlisted the services of Christopher Columbus, a mariner from Genoa. Misinterpreting the findings of Italian geographers, Columbus believed that the Atlantic Ocean, long feared by Arab sailors as a ten-thousand-mile-wide "green sea of darkness," was little more than a narrow channel of water separating Europe from Asia. Although dubious about Columbus's theory, Ferdinand and Isabel arranged financial backing from Spanish merchants and charged Columbus to find a new trade route to Asia and carry Christianity to its peoples.

Columbus set sail in three small ships in August 1492. Six weeks later, after a perilous voyage of three thousand miles, he found land, disembarking on October 12 on an island in the present-day Bahamas. Believing he had reached Asia— "the Indies," in fifteenth-century parlance—Columbus called the native inhabitants Indians and the islands the West Indies. Surprised by the rude living conditions of the native people, Columbus expected them to "easily be made Christians, for it appeared to me that they had no religion." With ceremony and solemnity, he bestowed the names of the Spanish royal family and Catholic holy days on the islands, thereby intending to claim them for Spain and for Christendom. Columbus then explored the neighboring Caribbean islands and demanded tribute from the local Taino [*TIE-no*], Arawak [*AR-a-wak*], and Carib peoples. Buoyed by the natives' stories of rivers of gold lying "to the west," Columbus left forty men on the island of Hispaniola (present-day Haiti and the Dominican Republic) and returned triumphantly to Spain.

Although Columbus brought back no gold, the Spanish monarchs supported three more voyages over the next twelve years. During those expeditions Columbus began the colonization of the West Indies, transporting more than a thousand Spanish settlers—all men—and hundreds of domestic animals. He also began the transatlantic trade in slaves by carrying hundreds of Indians to bondage in Europe and importing black slaves from Africa to work as artisans and farmers in the new Spanish settlements. Because Columbus failed to find either golden treasures or great kingdoms, his death in 1506 went virtually unnoticed.

Other explorers continued the quest, and a German geographer named the continents after a Genoese mariner, Amerigo Vespucci, who had traveled to South

America around 1500 and called it a *nuevo mundo*, a new world. For its part, the Spanish crown continued to call the new lands *Las Indias* (the Indies) and determined to make them part of a new Spanish world.

## The Spanish Conquest

Columbus and other Spanish adventurers ruled the peoples of the Caribbean islands with an iron hand. After subduing the Arawaks and Tainos on Hispaniola, the Spanish probed coastal settlements on the mainland in search of gold and slaves. In 1513 Juan Ponce de León explored the coast of Florida and gave the peninsula its name. That same year Vasco Núñez de Balboa crossed the Isthmus of Darien (Panama), becoming the first European to see the Pacific Ocean. Rumors of rich Indian kingdoms in the interior encouraged other Spaniards, including many hardened veterans of the wars against the Muslims, to launch an invasion. To encourage these adventurers to expand its American empire, the Spanish crown offered successful conquistadors (conquerors) titles of nobility, the ownership of vast estates, and Indian laborers to farm them.

The first great success of the conquistadors came in present-day Mexico. In 1519 the ambitious and charismatic adventurer Hernán Cortés landed on the Mexican coast with 600 men and marched toward the Aztec capital of Tenochtitlán. Fortunately for the Spaniards, Cortés arrived in the very year that Aztec mythology had predicted for the return of the god Quetzalcoatl. Fearful that Cortés might be the returning god, Moctezuma [*mock-ta-zoo-ma*], the Aztec ruler, acted indecisively. After an Aztec ambush failed, Moctezuma allowed Cortés to proceed without challenge to Tenochtitlán and received him with great ceremony, only to become Cortés's captive.

When Moctezuma's forces finally attempted to expel the invaders, they faced superior European military technology. The sight of the Spaniards in full armor, with guns that shook the heavens and inflicted devastating wounds, made a deep impression on the Aztecs, who knew how to purify gold but not how to produce iron tools or weapons. Moreover, the Aztecs had no wheeled carts or cavalry, and their warriors, fighting on foot with flint- or obsidian-tipped spears and arrows, were no match for mounted Spanish conquistadors wielding steel swords and aided by vicious attack dogs. Although heavily outnumbered and suffering great losses, Cortés and his men were able to fight their way out of the Aztec capital (see American Voices, "Aztec Elders Describe the Spanish Conquest," p. 26).

Still, the Indian peoples of Mexico could easily have crushed the European invaders if they had remained united. But Cortés deftly exploited the widespread resentment against the Aztecs. With the assistance of Malinche, his Indian interpreter and mistress, he formed military alliances and raised thousands of troops from subject peoples who had seen their wealth expropriated by Aztec nobles and their people sacrificed to the Aztec sun god. The Aztec empire collapsed, the victim not of superior Spanish military technology but of a vast internal rebellion of Indian peoples.

**AMERICAN VOICES**

## Aztec Elders Describe the Spanish Conquest

### FRIAR BERNARDINO DE SAHAGÚN

*During the 1550s Friar Bernardino de Sahagún published the* Florentine Codex: General History of New Spain. *According to Sahagún, the authors of the codex were Aztec elders who lived through the conquest. Here the elders describe their reaction to the invading Europeans and the devastating impact of smallpox.*

Moctezuma enjoyed no sleep, no food, no one spoke to him. Whatsoever he did, it was as if he were in torment. Ofttimes it was as if he sighed, became weak, felt weak. . . . Wherefore he said, "What will now befall us? Who indeed stands [in charge]? Alas, until now, I. In great torment is my heart; as if it were washed in chili water it indeed burns." . . .

And when he had so heard what the messengers reported, he was terrified, he was astounded. . . . Especially did it cause him to faint away when he heard how the gun, at [the Spaniards'] command, discharged: how it resounded as if it thundered when it went off. It indeed bereft one of strength; it shut off one's ears. And when it discharged, something like a round pebble came forth from within. Fire went showering forth; sparks went blazing forth. And its smoke smelled very foul; it had a fetid odor which verily wounded the head. And when [the shot] struck a mountain, it was as if it were destroyed, dissolved . . . as if someone blew it away.

All iron was their war array. In iron they clothed themselves. With iron they covered their heads. Iron were their swords. Iron were their crossbows. Iron were their shields. Iron were their lances. And those which bore them upon their backs, their deer [horses], were as tall as roof terraces.

And their bodies were everywhere covered; only their faces appeared. They were very white; they had chalky faces; they had yellow hair, though the hair of some was black. . . . And when Moctezuma so heard, he was much terrified. It was as if he fainted away. His heart saddened; his heart failed him. . . .

[Soon] there came to be prevalent a great sickness, a plague. It was in Tepeilhuitl that it originated, that there spread over the people a great destruction of men. Some it indeed covered [with pustules]; they were spread everywhere, on one's face, on one's head, on one's breast. There was indeed perishing; many indeed died of it. No longer could they walk; they only lay in their abodes, in their beds. No longer could they move. . . . And when they bestirred themselves, much did they cry out. There was much perishing. Like a covering, covering-like, were the pustules. Indeed, many people died of them, and many just died of hunger. There was death from hunger; there was no one to take care of another; there was no one to attend to another.

SOURCE: Friar Bernardino de Sahagún, *Florentine Codex: General History of New Spain*, trans. Arthur J. O. Anderson and Charles E. Dibble (Santa Fe and Salt Lake City: School of American Research and University of Utah Press, 1975), 12:17–20, 26, 83.

The Spanish also had a silent ally—disease. Separated from Eurasia for thousands of years, the inhabitants of the Western Hemisphere had no immunities to common European diseases. A massive smallpox epidemic lasting seventy days ravaged Tenochtitlán following the Spanish exodus, "striking everywhere in the city," according to an Aztec source, killing Moctezuma's brother and many others. "They could not move, they could not stir. . . . Covered, mantled with pustules, very many people died of them." Subsequent outbreaks of smallpox, influenza, and measles killed hundreds of thousands of Aztecs and their subject peoples and sapped the morale of the survivors. Exploiting this demographic weakness, Cortés quickly extended Spanish rule over the entire Aztec empire. His lieutenants then moved against the Mayan city-states in the Yucatán Peninsula, eventually conquering them as well.

In 1532 the Spanish conquest entered a new phase. Francisco Pizarro led a military expedition to Peru, home of the rich and powerful Inca empire that stretched 2,000 miles along the Pacific coast of South America. To govern this far-flung empire, the Inca rulers had built 24,000 miles of roads and dozens of carefully placed administrative centers, which were constructed of finely crafted stone. A semidivine Inca king ruled the empire, assisted by a hierarchical bureaucracy staffed by noblemen, many of whom were his relatives. By the time Pizarro and his small force of 168 men and 67 horses reached Peru, half of the Inca population had died from European diseases, which had been spread by Indian traders. Weakened militarily and fighting over succession to the throne, the Inca nobility was easy prey for Pizarro's army. In little more than a decade Spain had become the master of the wealthiest and most populous regions of the Western Hemisphere (Map 1.3).

The Spanish invasion and European diseases changed life forever throughout the Americas. Disease and warfare wiped out virtually all the Indians of Hispaniola—at least 300,000 people. In Peru the population plummeted from nine million in 1530 to fewer than half a million a century later. Likewise, diseases carried by Spanish adventurers into the area of the present-day United States inflicted catastrophic losses on the Pueblo peoples of the Southwest and the Mississippian chiefdoms of the Southeast. Mesoamerica suffered the greatest decline. In 1500, it boasted a population of 40 million; by 1650, its Native American population had fallen to a mere 3 million people—one of the greatest demographic disasters in world history.

Once the conquistadors had triumphed, the Spanish government quickly created an elaborate bureaucratic empire. From its headquarters in Madrid, the Council of the Indies issued laws and decrees to viceroys and other Spanish officials in America. Nonetheless, the conquistadors remained powerful because they held royal grants (*encomiendas*) giving them legal control of the native population. They ruthlessly exploited the surviving Native Americans, forcing them to raise crops and cattle for local consumption and export to Europe. The Spaniards also permanently altered the natural environment by introducing grains and grasses that supplanted the native flora. Horses, once native to the Western Hemisphere but now extinct, were

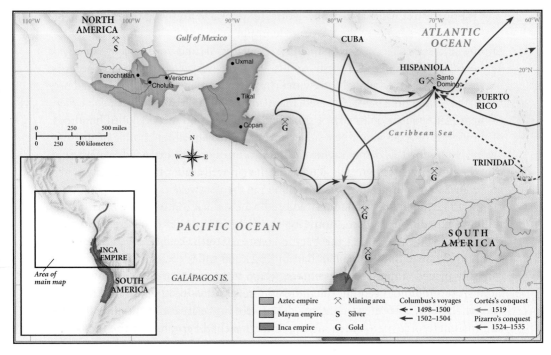

**MAP 1.3 The Spanish Conquest of the Great Indian Civilizations**

The Spanish first invaded the islands of the Caribbean. Rumors of a magnificent golden civilization led to Cortés's invasion of the Aztec empire in 1519. By 1535 other Spanish conquistadors had conquered the Mayan temple cities and the Inca empire in Peru, completing one of the great conquests in world history.

FOR MORE HELP ANALYZING THIS MAP, see the Online Study Guide at **bedfordstmartins.com/henrettaconcise**.

reintroduced by Cortés and dramatically changed the way of life of many Indian peoples, especially on the Great Plains.

The Spanish invasion of the Americas had a significant ecological impact on Europe and Africa as well. In a process of transfer known to historians as the **Columbian Exchange**, the food products of the Western Hemisphere—especially maize, potatoes, and cassava (manioc)—became available to the peoples of other continents, significantly increasing agricultural yields and stimulating the growth of population. Similarly, the livestock and crops—and weeds and human diseases—of African and Eurasian lands became part of the lives of residents of the Americas. Nor was that all. The gold and silver that had formerly honored Aztec gods now gilded the Catholic churches of Europe and flowed into the countinghouses of Spain, making that nation the richest and most powerful in Europe.

By 1550 the once magnificent civilizations of Mexico and Peru lay in ruins. "Of all these wonders"—the great city of Tenochtitlán, the rich orchards, the overflowing markets—"all is overthrown and lost, nothing left standing," recalled the Spanish chronicler Bernal Díaz, who had been a young soldier in Cortés's army. Moreover, the surviving Indian peoples had lost vital parts of their cultural identity, as Spanish priests suppressed their worship of traditional gods and converted them to Catholicism. As early as 1531 an Indian convert reported a vision of a dark-skinned Virgin Mary, later known as the Virgin of Guadalupe, a Christian version of the "corn mother" who traditionally protected the maize crop.

A new society took shape on the recently emptied land. Between 1500 and 1650, no fewer than 350,000 Spanish migrants settled in areas previously occupied by the native peoples of Mesoamerica and South America. Because over 75 percent of the Spanish settlers were men who took Indian women as wives or mistresses, the result was a substantial **mestizo** (mixed-race) population and an elaborate race-based **caste system**. Around 1800, at the end of the colonial era, Spanish America was a vast empire that stretched from the tip of South America to present-day Oregon and contained about 17 million people: a dominant caste of 3.2 million Europeans; 5.5 million people of mixed race and cultural heritage; 7.5 million Indians, most of whom were poor; and 1 million enslaved Africans. For the original Native American peoples, the consequences of the European invasion in 1492 were tragic and irreversible.

# The Protestant Reformation and the Rise of England

Religion formed a central aspect of European life and played a crucial role in the settlement of America. Even as Catholic fervor in Spain prompted the forced conversion of Muslims, Jews, and Native Americans, Christianity ceased to be a unifying force in European society. New religious doctrines preached by Martin Luther and other reformers divided Europe between Catholic and Protestant states and plunged the continent into religious wars. These struggles resulted in the emergence of Holland and England as Protestant nations determined to challenge Spain's dominant position in the Western Hemisphere.

## The Protestant Movement

Over the centuries, the Catholic Church had become a large and wealthy institution. Renaissance popes and cardinals used the Church's wealth to patronize the arts and some clerics used their power for personal gain. Pope Leo X (r. 1513–1521) received half a million ducats a year from the sale of religious offices. Corruption at the top encouraged ordinary priests and monks to use status to obtain economic or sexual favors. One English reformer denounced the clergy as a "gang of scoundrels" who should be "rid of their vices or stripped of their authority," but he was ignored. Other reformers, such as Jan Hus of Bohemia, were tried and executed as heretics.

In 1517 Martin Luther, a German monk and professor at the university in Wittenberg, took up the cause of reform. His Ninety-five Theses condemned many Catholic practices, including the use of **indulgences**—church certificates that allegedly pardoned a sinner from punishments in the afterlife. Outraged by Luther's charges, the pope dismissed him from the Church and the Holy Roman Emperor, King Charles I of Spain (r. 1516–1556), threatened Luther with punishment. However, the princes of northern Germany, who were resisting the emperor's authority for political reasons, protected Luther from arrest, thus allowing the Protestant movement to survive.

Luther broadened his attack and took issue with Roman Catholic doctrine in three major respects. First, he rejected the doctrine that Christians could secure salvation through good deeds or the purchase of indulgences; instead, Luther argued that people could be saved only by grace, which came as a free gift from God. Second, the German reformer downplayed the role of the clergy and the pope as mediators between God and the people, proclaiming, "Our baptism consecrates us all without exception and makes us all priests." Third, Luther said that believers must look to the Bible (not Church officials or doctrine) as the ultimate authority in matters of faith. So that every literate German-speaking believer could read the Bible, he translated it from Latin into German.

Peasants as well as princes heeded Luther's attack on authority and, to his dismay, mounted social protests of their own. In 1524 some German peasants rebelled against their manorial lords. Fearing social revolution, Luther urged obedience to established political institutions and condemned the teachings of new groups of religious dissidents, such as the Anabaptists (so called because they rejected infant baptism). Reassured of Luther's social conservatism, most princes in northern Germany embraced his teachings and broke from Rome, thereby gaining the power to appoint bishops and control the Church's property within their domains. To restore Catholic doctrine and his political authority, the emperor dispatched armies to Germany, unleashing a generation of warfare. Eventually, the Peace of Augsburg (1555) restored order by dividing Germany into Lutheran states in the north and Catholic principalities in the south.

John Calvin, a French theologian, established the most rigorous Protestant regime in Geneva, Switzerland. Even more than Luther, Calvin stressed the weakness of men and women and the omnipotence of God. His *Institutes of the Christian Religion* (1536) depicted God as an awesome and absolute sovereign who governed the "wills of men so as to move precisely to that end directed by him." Calvin preached the doctrine of **predestination**—the idea that God had chosen certain people for salvation even before they were born and condemned the rest to eternal damnation. In Geneva he set up a model Christian community, eliminating bishops and placing spiritual power in the hands of ministers chosen by the members of each congregation. Ministers and pious laymen ruled the city, prohibiting frivolity and luxury and imposing religious discipline on the entire society. "We know," wrote Calvin, "that man is of so perverse and crooked a nature, that everyone would scratch out his neighbor's eyes if there were no bridle to hold them in." Calvin's doctrines won converts all over Europe, becoming the theology of the Huguenots in France, the Reformed churches in Belgium and Holland, and the Presbyterians and Puritans in Scotland and England.

In England, King Henry VIII (r. 1509–1547) initially opposed Protestantism. However, in 1534, when the pope refused to annul his marriage to Catherine of Aragon, Henry broke with Rome and placed himself at the head of a national Church of England (which promptly approved the annulment). Although Henry made few changes in Church doctrine, organization, and ritual, he allowed the spread of Protestant beliefs and teachings. Faced with popular pressure for religious reform, Henry's daughter and successor, Queen Elizabeth I (r. 1558–1603) approved a Protestant confession of faith that incorporated both the Lutheran doctrine of salvation by grace and the Calvinist belief in predestination. To mollify traditionalists, Elizabeth retained the Catholic ritual of Holy Communion—now conducted in English rather than in Latin—as well as the hierarchy of bishops and archbishops.

Elizabeth's compromises angered radical Protestants, who condemned the power of bishops as "anti-Christian and devilish and contrary to the Scriptures." Many of these reformers took inspiration from the Presbyterian system pioneered in Calvin's Geneva and developed by John Knox for the Church of Scotland; in Scotland local congregations elected lay elders (presbyters), who assisted ministers in running the Church, and sent delegates to synods (councils) that decided Church doctrine. By 1600, at least five hundred ministers in the Church of England wanted to eliminate bishops and install a Presbyterian form of church government.

Other radical English Protestants called themselves "unspotted lambs of the Lord" or "Puritans." These extraordinarily intense and devout Calvinist Protestants wanted to "purify" the Church of Catholic teachings and magical or idolatrous practices. Thus, Puritan services avoided appeals to dead saints or the burning of incense; instead, they focused on a carefully argued sermon on ethics or dogma. Puritans also placed special emphasis on the "conversion experience," the felt infusion of God's grace, and the "calling," the duty to serve God in one's ordinary life and work. To ensure that all men and women had access to God's commands, they encouraged everyone to read the Bible, thus promoting widespread literacy. Finally, most Puritans wanted authority over spiritual and financial matters to rest primarily with local congregations or Presbyterian synods (elected church councils). Eventually, thousands of Puritan migrants would establish churches in North America based on these radical Protestant doctrines.

### The Dutch and the English Challenge Spain

Luther's challenge to Catholicism in 1517 came just two years before Cortés conquered the Aztec empire, and the two events remained linked. Gold and silver from Mexico and Peru made Spain the wealthiest nation in Europe and King Philip II

**Elizabeth I (r. 1558–1603)**

Attired in richly decorated clothes that symbolize her power, Queen Elizabeth I relishes the destruction of the Spanish Armada (pictured in background) and proclaims her nation's imperial ambitions. The queen's hand rests on a globe, asserting England's claims in the Western Hemisphere.

(r. 1556–1598), the successor to Charles I, its most powerful ruler. In addition to Spain, Philip presided over wealthy city-states in Italy, the commercial and manufacturing provinces of the Spanish Netherlands (present-day Holland and Belgium), and, after 1580, Portugal and all its possessions in America, Africa, and the East Indies. "If the Romans were able to rule the world simply by ruling the Mediterranean," a Spanish priest boasted, "what of the man who rules the Atlantic and Pacific oceans, since they surround the world?"

Philip, an ardent Catholic, tried to root out Protestantism in the Netherlands, which had become wealthy from trade with the vast Portuguese empire and from the weaving of wool and linen. To protect their Calvinist faith and political liberties, the Dutch and Flemish provinces revolted in 1566, and in 1581, the seven northern provinces declared their independence, becoming the Dutch Republic (or Holland). When Elizabeth I of England dispatched 6,000 troops to assist the Dutch cause,

Philip found a new enemy. In 1588, he sent the Spanish Armada—130 ships and 30,000 men—against England. Philip planned to reimpose Catholicism in England and then wipe out Calvinism in Holland. However, the Armada failed utterly, as English ships and a fierce storm destroyed the Spanish fleet. Philip continued to spend his American gold on religious wars, undermining the Spanish economy and prompting the migration of hundreds of thousands of Spaniards to America. By the time of his death in 1598, Spain was in serious decline.

As Spain faltered, Holland prospered—the economic miracle of the seventeenth century. Amsterdam emerged as the financial capital of northern Europe, and the Dutch Republic became the leading commercial power by replacing Portugal as the dominant trader in Indonesia and West Africa. The Dutch merchants also looked across the Atlantic and created the West India Company, which invested in sugar plantations in Brazil and established the fur-trading colony of New Netherland in North America.

England also emerged as an important European state, its economy stimulated by a rise in population from 3 million in 1500 to 5 million in 1630. Equally important, the royal government supported the expansion of commerce and manufacturing. English merchants had long supplied European weavers with high-quality wool, and around 1500, they created their own textile industry. In this **outwork** (or putting-out) system merchants bought wool from the owners of great estates and provided it to landless peasants, who spun and wove the wool into cloth. The government helped these textile manufacturers by setting low rates for wages and by opening up foreign markets. To encourage merchant enterprise, Queen Elizabeth granted special monopoly privileges to the Levant Company (Turkey) in 1581, the Guinea Company (Africa) in 1588, and the East India Company (India) in 1600.

This system of state-assisted manufacturing and trade became known as mercantilism. Elizabeth encouraged domestic manufacturing in order to reduce imports and increase exports—and give England a favorable balance of trade. The queen and her advisors wanted gold and silver to flow into the country in payment for English goods, stimulating further economic expansion and enriching the merchant community. Increased trade also meant higher revenues from import duties, which swelled the royal treasury and enhanced the power of the national government. By 1600 these merchant-oriented policies had laid the foundations for overseas colonization. The English (as well as the Dutch) now had the merchant fleets and economic wealth needed to challenge Spain's monopoly in the Western Hemisphere.

### The Social Causes of English Colonization

The growth of the English population combined with unsettling economic changes to provide a large body of settlers willing to go to America. The massive expenditure of American gold and silver by Philip II had doubled the money supply of Europe and sparked a major inflation between 1530 and 1600—known today as the **Price Revolution**.

In England the nobility was the first casualty of the Price Revolution. Aristocrats had customarily rented out their estates on long leases for fixed rents, giving them a secure income and plenty of leisure. As one English nobleman put it, "We eat and drink and rise up to play and this is to live like a gentleman." Then inflation struck. In less than two generations the price of goods more than tripled while the nobility's rent income barely increased. As the wealth of the aristocracy declined, that of the **gentry** and the yeomen rose. The gentry (nonnoble landholders with substantial estates) kept pace with inflation by renting land on short leases at higher rates. Yeomen, described by a European traveler as "middle people of a condition between gentlemen and peasants," owned small farms that they worked with family help. As wheat prices tripled, yeomen used the profits to build larger houses and provide their children with land.

Economics influenced politics. As aristocrats lost wealth, their branch of Parliament, the House of Lords, declined in influence. At the same time, members of the rising gentry entered the House of Commons, the political voice of the propertied classes. Supported by the yeomen, the gentry demanded new rights and powers for the Commons, such as control of taxation. Thus the Price Revolution encouraged the rise of representative institutions in which rich commoners and small property owners had a voice, a development with profound consequences for English—and American—political history.

The Price Revolution likewise transformed the lives of peasants and landless farm laborers, who made up three-fourths of the population. The rise of the textile industry increased the demand for wool and led profit-minded landlords and wool merchants to persuade Parliament to pass **enclosure acts**. These acts allowed owners to fence in the open fields that surrounded many peasant villages and put sheep to graze on them. Now dispossessed of land, peasant families lived on the brink of poverty, spinning and weaving wool or working as wage laborers on large estates. Wealthy men had "taken farms into their hands," an observer noted in 1600, "whereby the peasantry of England is decayed and become servants to gentlemen."

A series of crop failures caused by cold weather precipitated the migration across the Atlantic. Between 1590 and 1640, land prices rose and the danger of starvation increased, prompting thousands of yeomen families to look to America for land for their children. Dispossessed peasants and weavers, their livelihoods threatened by a recession in the cloth trade, were likewise on the move. "Thieves and rogues do swarm the highways," warned one justice of the peace, "and bastards be multiplied in parishes." Seeking food and security, tens of thousands of young propertyless laborers contracted to go to America in the lowly condition of indentured servants. This massive migration of English yeomen families and impoverished laborers would bring about a new collision between the European and Native American worlds.

## TIMELINE

| | | | |
|---|---|---|---|
| 13,000–3000 B.C. | Main settlement of North America | 1492 | Christopher Columbus's first voyage to America |
| 3000–2000 B.C. | Cultivation of crops begins in Mesoamerica | 1513 | Juan Ponce de León explores Florida |
| | | 1517 | Martin Luther sparks Protestant Reformation |
| 100 B.C.–A.D. 400 | Flourishing of Hopewell culture | 1519–1521 | Hernán Cortés conquers Aztec empire |
| 300 | Rise of Mayan civilization | 1531–1538 | Francisco Pizarro vanquishes Incas in Peru |
| 500 | Zenith of Teotihuacán civilization | 1534 | Henry VIII establishes Church of England |
| 600 | Emergence of Pueblo cultures | 1536 | John Calvin, *Institutes of the Christian Religion* |
| 700–1100 | Spread of Arab Muslim civilization | | |
| 800–1350 | Development of Mississippian culture | 1550–1630 | Price Revolution / English mercantilism / Enclosure acts |
| 1096–1291 | Crusades link Europe with Arab learning | 1556–1598 | Philip I, king of Spain |
| 1325 | Aztecs establish capital at Tenochtitlán | 1558–1603 | Elizabeth I, queen of England |
| 1400–1550 | Italian Renaissance | 1560s | English Puritan movement begins |
| 1440s | Portugal enters trade in African slaves | | |

# For Further Exploration

Kenneth Pomeranz, *The Great Divergence: Europe, China, and the Making of the Modern World Economy* (2000), sets the settlement of America in the perspective of world history. Alvin M. Josephy Jr., ed., *America in 1492: The World of the Indian Peoples before the Arrival of Columbus* (1991), offers a panorama of early Indian societies. Recent scholarship on the prehistoric Indians of the United States is brought to life by Brian M. Fagan, *The Great Journey: The People of Ancient America* (1987). For the European background of colonization, begin with George Huppert, *After the Black Death* (2nd ed., 1998), a highly readable introduction to Western Europe's recovery from the devastating epidemic of the mid-fourteenth century. William D. Phillips with Carla Rahn Phillips continue the story of European expansion in *The Worlds of Christopher Columbus* (1992), an engaging biography that describes the enormous consequences of Columbus's voyages.

Peter Laslett, *The World We Have Lost* (3rd ed., 1984), offers a vivid portrait of society in seventeenth-century England, while Susan Doran and Christopher Durston, *Princes, Pastors, and People: The Church and Religion in England, 1529–1689* (1991), discuss the impact of the Protestant Reformation on theology, the role of the clergy, and church services.

Two interesting Public Broadcasting Service (PBS) videos examine the ancient civilizations of Mesoamerica: *Odyssey: Maya Lords of the Jungle* (1 hour) and *Odyssey: The Incas* (1 hour). For additional information log on to "1492: An Ongoing Voyage" at <http://lcweb.loc.gov/exhibits/1492/intro.html>, which provides a survey of the native cultures of the Western Hemisphere, the impact of discovery, and full-color images of artifacts and art. Material on an early Indian civilization in the southwestern United States is available at "Sipapu: The Anasazi Emergence into the Cyber World," <http://sipapu.gsu.edu/>.

---

For definitions of key terms boldfaced in this chapter, see the glossary at the end of the book.

To assess your mastery of the material covered in this chapter, see the Online Study Guide at **bedfordstmartins.com/henrettaconcise**.

For map resources and primary documents, see **bedfordstmartins.com/henrettaconcise**.

---

# Chapter 2

# THE INVASION AND SETTLEMENT OF NORTH AMERICA
## 1550–1700

Human life is reduced to real suffering, to hell, only when . . .
cultures and religions overlap.

ALBRECHT VON HALLER

E stablishing colonies in the distant land of North America was not for the faint of heart. First came a long voyage in small ships over stormy, dangerous waters. Then the migrants, weakened by weeks of travel, spoiled food, and shipboard diseases, faced potentially hostile Indian peoples. "We neither fear them or trust them," declared Puritan settler Francis Higginson, but rely on "our musketeers." Although the risks were great and the rewards uncertain, Europeans by the tens of thousands crossed the Atlantic during the seventeenth century. They were either driven by poverty and religious persecution at home or drawn by the lures of the New World: land, gold, and—as another Puritan migrant put it—the hope of "propagating the Gospel to these poor barbarous people."

For Native Americans, the European invasion was nothing short of catastrophic. Whether they came as settlers or missionaries or fur traders, the white-skinned people spread havoc, bringing new diseases and religions and threatening Indians with the loss of their cultures, lands, and lives. "Our fathers had plenty of deer and skins, . . . and our coves were full of fish and fowl," the Narragansett chief Miantonomi reminded the neighboring Montauk people in 1642, "but these English having gotten our land . . . their cows and horses eat the grass, and their hogs spoil our clam banks, and we shall all be starved." The Narragansetts called for united resistance. "We [are] all Indians," Miantonomi continued, and must "say brother to one another, . . . otherwise we shall all be gone shortly." But Indian unity was fragmentary and brittle, and foretold the course of North American history: the advance of the European invaders and the dispossession of the Indian peoples.

# Imperial Conflicts and Rival Colonial Models

In Mesoamerica the Spanish converted the Indians to Catholicism and made them dig gold and farm large estates. In the more sparsely populated region of eastern North America, the French and the Dutch created fur-trading empires and the native peoples retained their lands and political autonomy. However, in the English colonies, settlers sought to expel Indians from their lands. Whatever the goals of the invaders, nearly everywhere Indian peoples eventually rose in revolt.

## *New Spain: Colonization and Conversion*

In their ceaseless quest for gold, Spanish adventurers penetrated deeply into the southern and western United States. In the 1540s Francisco Vásquez de Coronado searched in vain for the fabled seven golden cities of Cíbola, but his men discovered the Grand Canyon in Arizona, the Pueblo peoples of New Mexico, and the grasslands of central Kansas. Simultaneously, Hernán de Soto and a force of 600 adventurers cut a bloody swath across the Southeast, doing battle with the Apalachees of northern Florida and the Coosas of northern Alabama but finding no gold and few other riches (Map 2.1).

By the 1560s Spanish officials gave up the search for rich Indian peoples and focused on the defense of the existing empire. Roving English "sea dogs" were plundering Spanish treasure ships and Caribbean seaports, and French Protestants began to settle in Florida, long claimed by Spain. Following King Philip II's order to cast out the trespassing Frenchmen "by the best means," Spanish troops massacred 300 members of the "evil Lutheran sect." To safeguard Florida, in 1565 Spain established a fort at St. Augustine, which became the first permanent European settlement in the future United States. However, Indian raids wiped out a dozen other Spanish military outposts and religious missions, one as far north as Chesapeake Bay.

These military setbacks prompted the Spanish crown to adopt a new policy toward the Indian peoples. The Comprehensive Orders for New Discoveries, issued in 1573, placed the "pacification" of new lands primarily in the hands of missionaries, not conquistadors. Franciscan friars promptly set up missions among the settled agricultural Pueblo peoples visited by Coronado two generations before and named the area *Nuevo México*. Although the friars often learned Indian languages, they systematically attacked the natives' culture. Protected by Spanish soldiers, missionaries whipped sexual sinners and smashed the Indians' religious idols. To win the allegiance of Native Americans to the Christian God, they tried to impress them with rich vestments, gold crosses, and silver chalices.

For the Franciscans, religious conversion and cultural assimilation went hand in hand. They introduced the European practice of having men instead of women grow most of the crops and encouraged the Indians to talk, cook, dress, and walk like Spaniards. Moreover, they generally ignored Spanish laws intended to protect

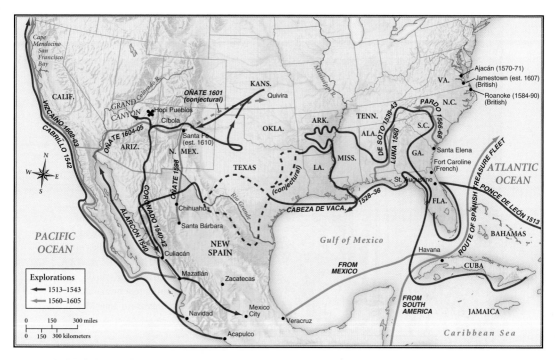

**MAP 2.1 New Spain Looks North, 1513–1610**

The quest for gold drew Spanish adventurers first to Florida and then deep into the present-day United States. When the wide-ranging expeditions of Hernán de Soto and Francisco Vásquez de Coronado failed to find gold or flourishing Indian civilizations, authorities in New Spain confined northern settlements to St. Augustine in Florida (to protect the treasure fleet) and Santa Fe in the upper Rio Grande Valley.

FOR MORE HELP ANALYZING THIS MAP, see the Online Study Guide at **bedfordstmartins.com/henrettaconcise**.

the native peoples from coerced labor. This neglect allowed privileged Spanish landowners (***encomenderos***) to collect tribute from the native population, both in goods and in forced labor. The missions also depended on Indian workers, who grew the crops and carried them to market, often on their backs.

Native Americans initially tolerated the Franciscan rule out of fear of military reprisals or in hopes of learning their spiritual secrets. But when Christian prayers failed to protect their communities from European diseases, droughts, and raids by the nomadic Apaches, many Pueblo people returned to their ancestral religions and blamed Spanish rule for their ills. Thus, the people of Hawikuh refused to become "wet-heads" (as the Indians called baptized Christians) "because with the water of baptism they would have to die."

In 1598 the tense relations between Indians and Spaniards in New Mexico exploded into open warfare. An expedition of 500 Spanish soldiers and settlers led

### Conversion in New Mexico

Franciscan friars, assisted by nuns of various religious orders, introduced Catholicism to the Indian peoples north of the Rio Grande. This 1631 engraving shows one of those nuns, María de Jesús de Agreda, preaching to a nomadic people (*los chichimecos*) in New Mexico. Nettie Lee Benson Latin American Collection, University of Texas at Austin.

by Juan de Oñate seized corn and clothing from the Pueblo peoples and murdered or raped those who resisted. When Indians of the Acoma pueblo killed 11 soldiers, the Spanish troops destroyed the pueblo, killing 500 men and 300 women and children. Now faced by bitterly hostile Indian peoples, most of the settlers withdrew from New Mexico.

However, in 1610 the Spanish returned, founded the town of Santa Fe, and reestablished the system of missions and forced labor. Over the next two generations, European diseases, forced tribute, and raids by nomadic Navajos and Apaches threatened many Pueblo peoples with extinction. By 1680 their population, which had once numbered 60,000, had declined to a mere 17,000. In desperation the Indian shaman (priest) Popé led the peoples of two dozen pueblos in a carefully coordinated rebellion that killed over 400 Spaniards. As the uprising continued, the Indians forced the remaining 2,000 Spanish colonists to flee three hundred miles to El Paso. Repudiating Christianity, the Pueblo peoples desecrated churches and tortured and killed 21 missionaries.

Reconquered a decade later, the Indians rebelled again in 1696, only to be subdued. Exhausted by a generation of warfare, the Pueblo peoples agreed to a compromise that allowed them to practice their own religion and avoid forced labor. In return, they accepted a dependent position in New Mexico and joined with the Spanish to defend their settlements and farms against attacks by nomadic Indians.

Spain had maintained its northern empire but had largely failed to achieve its goals of religious conversion and cultural assimilation. Taken aback by the military costs of expansion, Spanish officials delayed settlement of the distant region of California until the 1760s. For the time being, Florida and New Mexico stood as the defensive outposts of Spain's North American empire.

### New France: Furs and Souls

Far to the northeast the French likewise tried to convert the native peoples to Catholicism. In the 1530s Jacques Cartier had claimed the lands bordered by the Gulf of St. Lawrence for France, but the first permanent French settlement came only in 1608, when Samuel de Champlain founded Quebec. Despite a series of brutal famines in northwestern France and the offer of leaseholds in the fertile St. Lawrence Valley, few peasants migrated to America. France's Catholic monarchs discouraged migration to preserve an ample supply of military recruits at home. They also barred Huguenots (French Protestants) from Quebec, fearing they would not be loyal to the crown. Moreover, French peasants held strong legal rights to their village lands and feared the long, bitter winters in Quebec. Many regarded Canada "as a country at the end of the world" and living there a virtual sentence of "civil death." Of the 27,000 men and women who migrated to Quebec, nearly two-thirds eventually returned to France. In 1698 the European population of New France was only 15,200, compared with 100,000 settlers in the English colonies.

Rather than developing as a settler colony, New France instead became a vast enterprise for acquiring furs, which were in great demand in Europe. To secure plush beaver pelts from the Huron Indians (who lived to the north of the Great Lakes), Champlain provided them with guns to fight the expansionist-minded Five Nations of the Iroquois (see Voices from Abroad, "Going to War with the Hurons," p. 42). Searching for furs and a water route to Asia, the French explorer Jacques Marquette reached the Mississippi River in present-day Wisconsin in 1673 and traveled as far south as Arkansas. In 1681 Robert de La Salle traveled down the Mississippi to the Gulf of Mexico, completing exploration of the majestic river and claiming new lands for France, while also enriching himself. As a French priest noted with disgust, La Salle's expedition hoped "to buy all the Furs and Skins of the remotest Savages, who, as they thought, did not know their Value; and so enrich themselves in one single voyage." To honor King Louis XIV (r. 1643–1714), La Salle named the region he explored Louisiana; soon it included the thriving port of New Orleans on the Gulf of Mexico.

Despite their small numbers, French traders had a disastrous impact on Native Americans of the Great Lakes region. By unwittingly introducing European diseases, they triggered epidemics that killed 25 to 90 percent of the residents of many Indian villages, including those of their Huron allies. Moreover, by buying furs for export to Europe, the French sparked a devastating series of wars among Indian peoples. In the 1640s, the New York Iroquois defeated the Hurons, forced them to migrate to the north and west, and took control of their rich fur-bearing territory.

# Going to War with the Hurons

## SAMUEL DE CHAMPLAIN

*B*est known as the founder of Quebec, Samuel de Champlain was primarily a soldier and an adventurer. Champlain joined the Company of New France and in 1603 traveled to North America, determined to create a French empire there. To ensure French access to western fur trade, in 1609 Champlain joined the Hurons in a raid against the Iroquois, which he described in a book of his American adventures.

Pursuing our route, I met some two or three hundred savages. . . . We made a reconnaissance, and found that they were tribes of savages called Ochasteguins [Hurons] and Algonquins, on their way to Quebec to assist us in exploring the territory of the Iroquois, with whom they are in deadly hostility. . . .

In all their encampments, they have their Pilotois, or Ostemoy, a class of persons who play the part of soothsayers, in whom these people have faith. One of these builds a cabin, surrounds it with small pieces of wood and covers it with his robe: after it is built, he places himself inside, so as not to be seen at all, when he seizes and shakes one of the posts of his cabin, muttering some words between his teeth, by which he says he invokes the devil, who appears to him in the form of a stone, and tells them whether they will meet their enemies and kill many of them. . . .

Now, as we began to approach within two or three days' journey of the abode of our enemies, we advanced only at night. . . . By day, they withdraw into the interior of the woods, where they rest, without straying off, neither making any noise, even for the sake of cooking, so as not to be noticed in case their enemies should by accident pass by.

In order to ascertain what was to be the result of their undertaking, they often asked me if I had had a dream, and seen their enemies, to which I replied in the negative. . . . [Then one night] while sleeping, I dreamed that I saw our enemies, the Iroquois, drowning near a mountain, within sight. When I expressed a wish to help them, our allies, the savages, told me we must let them all die. . . . This, upon being related [to our allies], gave them so much confidence that they did not doubt any longer that good was to happen to them. . . .

[After our victory over the Iroquois] they took one of the prisoners, to whom they made a harangue, enumerating the cruelties which he and his men had already practiced toward them without any mercy, and that, in like manner, he ought to make up his mind to receive as much.

Meanwhile, our men kindled a fire; and, when it was well burning, they brand, and burned this poor creature gradually, so as to make him suffer greater torment. Sometimes they stopped, and threw water on his back. Then they tore out his nails, and applied fire to the extremities of his fingers and private member. Afterwards, they flayed the top of his head, and had a kind of gum poured all hot upon it. . . .

SOURCE: Samuel de Champlain, *Voyages of Samuel de Champlain, 1604–1618*, ed. W. L. Grant (New York: Charles Scribner's Sons, 1907), 79–86.

French priests sought converts among both the defeated Hurons and the belligerent Iroquois. Most were Jesuits, members of the Society of Jesus—a religious order originally founded to combat the Reformation. Between 1625 and 1763, hundreds of Jesuits lived among the Indian peoples and, to a greater extent than the Spanish Franciscans, came to understand their values. Thus, one Jesuit noted the Huron belief that "our souls have desires which are inborn and concealed, yet are made known by means of dreams." As among the Pueblo peoples, many eastern Indians initially welcomed the French "Black Robes" as powerful spiritual beings with magical secrets, such as the ability to forge iron. But when prayers to the Christian God did not protect them from disease and attack, they grew skeptical. A Peoria chief charged that the priest's "fables are good only in his own country; we have our own [religious beliefs], which do not make us die as his do." When epidemics came, some Indians vented their anger by killing French missionaries and fur traders.

Whatever their shortcomings, the French Jesuits did not exploit the labor of the Indian peoples. Moreover, they tried to keep alcoholic beverages, which wreaked havoc among the natives, from becoming a bargaining item in the French fur trade. Finally, the French Jesuits won converts by adapting Christian beliefs to address Indian needs. Thus, in the 1690s they introduced the cult of the Virgin Mary to the young women of the Illinois people, who used its emphasis on chastity to assert the Algonquian belief that unmarried women were "masters of their own body."

Still, the French fur-trading system brought war and cultural devastation to the Indian peoples. According to an oral history of the Iroquois, "Everywhere there was peril and everywhere mourning. Feuds with outer nations, feuds with brother nations, feuds of . . . sister towns and feuds of families and of clans made every warrior a stealthy man who liked to kill."

## New Netherland: Commerce

By 1600 the Dutch Republic was the trading hub of northern Europe, and its agents in North America had little interest in religious conversion. Their eyes were fastened on commerce. In 1609 Henry Hudson, an Englishman employed by the Dutch East India Company, encountered and named the Hudson River in present-day New York. Soon Dutch merchants established fur-trading posts on Manhattan Island and at Fort Orange (present-day Albany). In 1621 the Dutch government chartered the West India Company, giving it a monopoly of trade in West Africa and in the Americas. Three years later the company founded the town of New Amsterdam on Manhattan Island and made it the capital of New Netherland.

Few Dutch settlers moved to these fur-trading posts, making them vulnerable to a takeover by rival European nations. To encourage migration, the West India Company granted huge estates along the Hudson River to wealthy Dutchmen and stipulated that each proprietor settle fifty tenants within four years or lose his grant; by 1646 only one proprietor, Kiliaen van Rensselaer, had succeeded. The population in Dutch North America remained small, reaching only 1,500 in 1664.

Although New Netherland failed to attract settlers, it flourished briefly as a fur-trading enterprise. In 1633 Dutch traders at Fort Orange exported thirty thousand beaver and otter pelts. Subsequently, the Dutch seized prime farming land from the Algonquian-speaking peoples and took over their trading network, in which corn and wampum from Long Island were exchanged for furs from Maine. The Algonquians responded with force. A bloody two-year war killed more than 200 Dutch residents and 1,000 Indians, many in brutal massacres of women, children, and elderly men. After the war the Dutch provided guns and entered into an alliance with the Mohawks, one of the Iroquois Nations of New York and a long-time foe of the Algonquians. However, the West India Company now largely ignored its crippled North American settlement and concentrated on the profitable importation of African slaves to its sugar plantations in Brazil.

In New Amsterdam, Dutch officials ruled shortsightedly. Governor Peter Stuyvesant rejected the demands of English Puritan settlers on Long Island for a representative system of government and alienated the colony's increasingly diverse population of Dutch, English, and Swedish migrants. Consequently, in 1664, during an Anglo-Dutch war, the residents of New Amsterdam offered little resistance to an English invasion and subsequently accepted English rule. For the rest of the century, the renamed towns of New York and Albany remained small fur-trading centers, Dutch-English outposts in a region still dominated by Native Americans. In Albany, Mohawk remained the language of business until the 1720s.

## English Virginia: Settlers and a Staple Crop

The first English ventures in North America, undertaken by minor nobility in the 1580s, were abject failures. Sir Humphrey Gilbert's settlement in Newfoundland collapsed for lack of financing, and Sir Ferdinando Gorges's colony along the coast of Maine floundered because of the harsh climate. Sir Walter Raleigh's three expeditions to North Carolina likewise ended in disaster when the colony at Roanoke vanished without a trace (and today is known as the "lost" colony). Following these failures, merchants replaced landed gentry as the leaders of English expansion; initially, their goal was trade rather than settlement. To provide adequate funding, the merchants formed **joint-stock companies** that sold shares to many investors and sought royal support. In 1606, King James I (r. 1603–1625) granted a group of ambitious London merchants a trading monopoly in the lands stretching from present-day North Carolina to southern New York. To honor the memory of Elizabeth I, the "Virgin Queen," the company's directors named the region Virginia. To prevent the spread of Spanish Catholicism among the natives, they promised to "propagate the [true] Christian religion" among the "infidels and Savages."

However, trade remained the main goal of the Virginia Company. The first expedition in 1607 included only adventurers—no farmers, ministers, or women. The company retained ownership of the land and appointed a governor and a small

**Carolina Indians Fishing, 1585**

The artist John White was one of the English settlers in Sir Walter Raleigh's ill-fated colony on Roanoke Island, and his watercolors provide a rich visual record of Native American life. Here the Indians who resided near present-day Albemarle Sound in North Carolina are harvesting a protein-rich diet of fish from its shallow waters. Trustees of the British Museum.

council to direct the adventurers, who were its employees or "servants." The directors expected them to procure their own food and ship gold, exotic crops, and Indian merchandise to England. Some adventurers were young gentlemen with personal ties to the shareholders of the company: a bunch of "unruly Sparks, packed off by their Friends to escape worse Destinies at home." The rest were cynical men bent on turning a quick profit by trading for gold or finding it. All they wanted, as one of them said, was to "dig gold, refine gold, load gold."

Unfortunately, such traders were unprepared for the challenges of the new environment. Arriving in Virginia after a hazardous four-month voyage, the newcomers settled on a swampy and unhealthful peninsula. They named both their new home (Jamestown) and the waterway (James River) after the king. Because the adventurers lacked access to fresh water and refused to plant crops, their fate was sealed. Of the 120 Englishmen who embarked on the expedition, only 38 were alive nine months later, and death continued to take a high toll. By 1611 the Virginia Company had sent 1,200 settlers to Jamestown, but fewer than half had survived. "Our men were destroyed with cruell diseases, as Swellings, Fluxes, Burning Fevers, and by warres," reported one of the leaders, "but for the most part they died of meere famine."

Native American hostility gradually developed into a major threat. The Pamunkey [pa-MUN-key] chief Powhatan, leader of the Algonquian-speaking tribes of the region, initially treated the traders as a source of valuable goods. A "grave majestical man," according to the adventurer John Smith, Powhatan allowed his followers—some 14,000 people in all—to exchange their corn for English cloth and iron hatchets. As conflicts over food and land increased, Powhatan accused the English of coming "not to trade but to invade my people and possess my country" and threatened war. In 1614 the Indian leader tried to integrate the newcomers into his chiefdom through a family alliance, by marrying his daughter Pocahontas to the adventurer John Rolfe. This tactic also failed, partly because Rolfe imported tobacco seed from the West Indies and cultivated the crop, which fetched a high price in England. Eager to become rich by planting tobacco, English settlers embarked for Virginia by the thousands, threatening to overrun Powhatan's kingdom.

To attract migrants to its increasingly valuable colony, the Virginia Company instituted a new set of policies. In 1617 it allowed individual settlers to own land, granting one hundred acres to every freeman and allowing masters to claim an additional fifty acres for every servant. Next, the company issued a "greate Charter" that swept away the military-style regime of Governor Sir Thomas Dale and created a system of representative government. The House of Burgesses, which first convened in Jamestown in 1619, could make laws and levy taxes, although the governor and the company council in England could veto its legislative acts. By 1622 these incentives of land ownership, self-government, and a judicial system based on "the lawes of the realme of England" had attracted about 4,500 new recruits. Virginia was on the verge of becoming a settler-colony.

However, the influx of English migrants sparked all-out war with the Indians. Land-hungry tobacco planters demanded access to Native American farming lands, alarming Opechancanough, Powhatan's brother and successor. Mobilizing the peoples of many Chesapeake tribes, in 1622 Opechancanough launched a surprise attack that killed nearly a third of the white population. The English fought back by seizing the Indians' cornfields and harvesting the food for themselves. By depriving the native peoples of sustenance, they gradually secured the safety of the colony.

The cost of the war was high for both sides. The Indian revolt killed many settlers and destroyed much property but failed to halt English expansion. The victorious invaders sold captured warriors into slavery, "destroy[ing] them who sought to destroy us," and took control of "their cultivated places . . . possessing the fruits of others' labour." By 1630 the colonists in Virginia had created a flourishing tobacco economy and a stable English-style local polity, controlled by landed gentlemen sitting as justices of the peace.

# The Chesapeake Experience

The English colonies in the Chesapeake brought wealth to some people but poverty and moral degradation to many more. Settlers forcefully dispossessed Indians of their lands, and prominent families ruthlessly pursued their dreams of wealth by exploiting the labor of English indentured servants and enslaved African laborers.

## Settling the Tobacco Colonies

Shocked by the Indian uprising, James I accused the Virginia Company of misman-agement and, in 1624, made Virginia a royal colony. Under the terms of the colony's charter, the king and his ministers appointed the governor and a small advisory council. The king allowed the House of Burgesses to continue but stipulated that his Privy Council ratify all legislation. James also decreed the legal establishment of the Church of England, which meant that all property owners had to pay taxes to sup-port its clergy. These institutions—a royal governor, an elected assembly, and an established Anglican Church—became the model for royal colonies throughout English America.

A second tobacco-growing settler-colony, which developed in neighboring Maryland, had a different set of institutions. In 1632 King Charles I (r. 1625–1649), the successor to James I, conveyed the territory bordering the vast Chesapeake Bay to Cecilius Calvert, an aristocrat who carried the title Lord Baltimore. As the pro-prietor of Maryland (named in honor of Queen Henrietta Maria, Charles's wife), Baltimore could sell, lease, or give this land away as he pleased. He also had the authority to appoint public officials and to found churches and appoint ministers.

Baltimore wanted Maryland to become a refuge from persecution for his fellow English Catholics. He therefore devised a policy of religious restraint to minimize confrontations between Catholics and Protestants, instructing the governor (his brother, Leonard Calvert) to allow "no scandall nor offence to be given to any of the Protestants" and to "cause All Acts of Romane Catholicque Religion to be done as privately as may be." In 1634, twenty gentlemen (mostly Catholics) and two hundred artisans and laborers (mostly Protestants) established St. Mary's City, which over-looked the mouth of the Potomac River. Maryland's population grew quickly, for the Calverts carefully supervised its development by hiring skilled artisans and offering ample grants of land to wealthy migrants. However, political conflict constantly

### The Tobacco Economy

Most farmers—poor or rich—raised tobacco because it grew just as well in small fields as on vast plantations. Large-scale operations, such as the one pictured here, used indentured servants and slaves to grow and process the crop. The workers cured the tobacco stalks by hanging them for several months in a well-ventilated shed; then they stripped the leaves and packed them tightly into large plantation-made barrels, or "hogsheads," for shipment to Europe.
Library of Congress.

FOR MORE HELP ANALYZING THIS IMAGE, see the Online Study Guide at **bedfordstmartins.com/henrettaconcise**.

threatened Maryland's stability. When Governor Leonard Calvert violated the terms of the charter by governing without the "Advice, Assent, and Approbation" of the freemen, they elected a representative assembly and insisted on the right to initiate legislation, which Lord Baltimore grudgingly granted. Uprisings by Protestant settlers also endangered Maryland's religious mission. To protect his Catholic coreligionists, who remained a minority, Lord Baltimore persuaded the assembly to enact a Toleration Act (1649) granting religious freedom to all Christians.

In Maryland, as in Virginia, tobacco was the basis of the economy. Indians had long used tobacco as a medicine and a stimulant. By the 1620s English men and women had come to crave tobacco and the nicotine it contained, smoking, chewing, and snorting it with abandon. Initially James I condemned tobacco as a "vile Weed" whose "black stinking fumes" were "baleful to the nose, harmful to the brain, and dangerous to the lungs." But the king's attitude changed as revenues from an import tax on tobacco filled the royal treasury.

European demand for tobacco set off a forty-year economic boom in the Chesapeake. "All our riches for the present do consist in tobacco," a planter

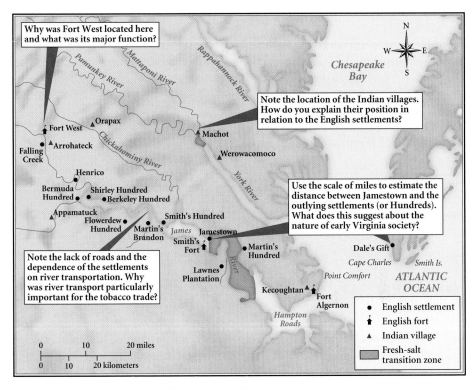

**MAP 2.2 River Plantations in Virginia, c. 1640**

The first migrants settled in widely dispersed plantations—and different disease environments—along the James River. The growth of the tobacco economy continued this pattern as wealthy planter-merchants traded with English ship captains from their riverfront plantations. Consequently, few substantial towns or trading centers developed in the Chesapeake region.

remarked in 1630. Exports rose from about 3 million pounds in 1640 to 10 million pounds in 1660. Newly arrived planters moved up the river valleys, establishing large farms (plantations) that were distant from one another but easily reached by water (Map 2.2).

Despite the economic boom, life in the Chesapeake colonies remained harsh, brutish, and short. The scarcity of towns deprived settlers of mutual assistance and the benefits of community life. Families were equally scarce because there were few women settlers, and marriages were often disrupted by early death. Pregnant women were especially vulnerable to malaria, which was spread by the mosquitoes that flourished in the mild Chesapeake climate. Many mothers died after bearing a first or second child, so that orphaned children (along with unmarried young men) formed a large fraction of the society. In Middlesex County, Virginia, more than 60 percent of children had lost one or both of their parents by the time they were thirteen. Although 15,000 settlers arrived in Virginia between 1622 and 1640, the number of English colonists rose only from 2,000 to 8,000.

## Masters, Servants, and Slaves

Nonetheless, the prospect of owning land continued to lure migrants to the Chesapeake region. By 1700 more than 80,000 English settlers had moved to Virginia, and another 20,000 had arrived in Maryland, the great majority not as free men and women but as indentured servants. English shipping registers provide insight into their backgrounds. Three-quarters of the 5,000 indentured servants who embarked from the port of Bristol were young men; many had traveled hundreds of miles searching for work. Once in Bristol, these penniless wanderers were persuaded by merchants and sea captains to sign labor contracts called **indentures** and embark for the Chesapeake. The indentures bound servants to work for a master for four or five years, after which they would be free men and women, able to marry and work for themselves.

For merchants, servants represented valuable cargo because their contracts fetched high prices from Chesapeake planters. For the plantation owners, they were an incredible bargain. During the tobacco boom a male servant could produce five times his purchase price in a single year. To ensure maximum production, most masters ruled their servants strictly, beating them for bad behavior and withholding permission to marry. If servants ran away or became pregnant, masters went to court to increase the term of service. Female servants were especially vulnerable to abuse. As a Virginia law of 1692 stated, "dissolute masters have gotten their maids with child; and yet claim the benefit of their service." Planters got rid of uncooperative servants by selling their contracts to new masters. As an Englishman remarked in disgust, in Virginia "servants were sold up and down like horses."

Despite this ordeal, most indentured servants did not escape from poverty. Half the men died before receiving their freedom, and another quarter remained poor. Only a quarter acquired the property and respectability they had sought. If they survived, female servants generally fared better because men in the Chesapeake had grown "very sensible of the Misfortune of Wanting Wives." Many female servants married their masters or other well-established men. By migrating to the Chesapeake, these few—and very fortunate—men and women escaped a life of landless poverty in England.

The first African workers fared worse. In 1619 John Rolfe noted that "a Dutch man of warre . . . sold us twenty Negars," but for a generation the numbers of Africans remained small. About 400 Africans lived in the Chesapeake colonies in 1649, making up 2 percent of the population, and by 1670 the proportion of blacks had reached only 5 percent. Although many Africans served their English masters for life, they were not legally enslaved. English common law acknowledged indentured servitude but not **chattel slavery**—the ownership as property of one human being by another. Moreover, some of these Africans had labored as slaves in African seaports and had some knowledge of European traders and Atlantic commerce. By cunning calculation, hard work, or conversion to Christianity many of them escaped bondage. Some ambitious African Christian freemen even purchased slaves, bought the labor contracts of white servants, or married English women, suggesting that at that time religion and personal initiative were as important as race in determining social status. By becoming a Christian and a planter, an enterprising African could aspire to near equality.

This mobility for Africans came to end in the 1660s because legislatures in the Chesapeake colonies enacted laws that lowered their status. One cause was the growing consciousness of race among the English-born elite. Even more important, the end of the tobacco boom prompted planters to turn to slave labor. The "low price of Tobacco requires it should bee made as cheap as possible," declared Colonel Nicholas Spencer, and "blacks can make it cheaper than whites." By 1671 the Virginia House of Burgesses had forbidden Africans to own guns or join the militia. It had also barred them — "tho baptized and enjoying their own Freedom" — from buying the labor contracts of white servants and from winning their freedom by converting to Christianity. Being black was a mark of inferior legal status, and slavery was becoming a permanent and hereditary condition. As an English clergyman observed around 1680, "These two words, Negro and Slave, had by custom grown Homogeneous and convertible."

## The Seeds of Social Revolt

By the 1660s the growing size of the tobacco crop triggered a collapse of the market. Tobacco had once sold for 24 pence a pound; now it fetched one-tenth as much. As the economic boom turned into a "bust," long-standing social conflicts flared up in political turmoil.

Political decisions in England were one reason for the decline of tobacco prices. In 1651, Parliament passed an Act of Trade and Navigation designed to exclude Dutch ships from England's colonies. As revised in 1660 and 1663, the Navigation Acts permitted only English or colonial-owned ships to enter American ports, thereby excluding Dutch merchants, who paid the highest prices for tobacco. The acts also required the colonists to ship tobacco and other "enumerated articles" only to England, where monarchs continually raised the import duty on tobacco, thereby stifling growth of the market. By the 1670s planters were getting only one penny a pound for their crop.

Nonetheless, the number of Chesapeake planters continued to grow and tobacco exports doubled between the 1670s and the 1690s. Profit margins grew thin, and yeomen families earned just enough to scrape by. Even worse off were newly freed indentured servants, who could not pay the fees to claim the 50 acres of land to which they were entitled or to buy the necessary tools and seed. Many former servants had to sell their labor again, by signing new indentures or becoming wageworkers or tenant farmers.

Gradually the Chesapeake colonies came to be dominated by an elite of planter-merchants whose power rivaled that of the English gentry. Owners of large estates prospered by leasing small plots to the growing army of former servants. They also lent money at high interest rates to hard-pressed yeomen families. Some well-to-do planters became commercial middlemen, setting up retail stores or charging a commission for selling the tobacco of their poorer neighbors to English merchants.

In Virginia this elite accumulated nearly half the land by securing grants from royal governors. In Maryland well-connected Catholic planters were equally powerful; by 1720 Charles Carroll owned 47,000 acres of land, which was farmed by scores of tenants, indentured servants, and slaves.

As these aggressive planter-entrepreneurs confronted a multitude of young, landless laborers, social conflicts intensified. In Virginia, they reached a breaking point during the corrupt regime of Governor William Berkeley. Berkeley first served as governor between 1642 and 1652; appointed governor again in 1660, he made large land grants to members of his council, who promptly exempted their lands from taxation and appointed friends as local justices of the peace and county judges. To suppress dissent in the House of Burgesses, Berkeley bought off legislators with land grants and appointments to lucrative positions as sheriffs, tax collectors, and estate appraisers. Unrest increased when the corrupt Burgesses changed the voting system to exclude landless freemen, who constituted half of all adult white men. Property-holding yeomen retained the vote but—distressed by tobacco prices, rising taxes, and political corruption—they were no longer willing to support the rule of Berkeley and the power-hungry landed gentry.

### Bacon's Rebellion

An Indian conflict lit the flame of social rebellion. By 1675 the number of Native Americans in Virginia had dwindled from 30,000 in 1607 to a mere 3,500, as compared to 38,000 Europeans and about 2,500 Africans. Although most Indians lived on treaty-guaranteed lands along the frontier, their presence remained controversial. Hundreds of impoverished English **freeholders** and aspiring tenants wanted cheap land and insisted that the natives be expelled or exterminated. Wealthy seacoast planters, who wanted a ready supply of white labor, opposed expansion into Indian territory, as did Berkeley and the planter-merchants who traded with the Native Americans for furs.

Fighting broke out late in 1675 when a band of Virginia militia murdered 30 Indians. Defying orders from Governor Berkeley, a larger force of 1,000 militiamen then surrounded a fortified Susquehannock village and killed five chiefs who came out to negotiate. The militarily strong Susquehannocks, recent migrants from present-day northern Pennsylvania, retaliated by raiding outlying plantations and killing 300 whites. To avoid war, Berkeley proposed a defensive military policy. However, settlers dismissed his strategy of building frontier forts as useless militarily and simply a plot by planters and merchants to impose high taxes and take "all our tobacco into their own hands."

Nathaniel Bacon emerged as the leader of the protesters. An English migrant, Bacon had settled on a frontier estate and commanded the respect of his neighbors because of his youthful vigor and his English connections, which had secured him an appointment to the governor's council. When Berkeley refused to grant Bacon a military commission, the headstrong planter marched his frontiersmen against the Indians anyway and slaughtered some of the peaceful Doeg [DO-g] people. Condemning the frontiersmen as "rebels and mutineers," Berkeley expelled Bacon from the council and arrested him. But Bacon's men quickly won his release and forced the governor to hold legislative elections. The newly elected House of Burgesses enacted far-reaching political reforms that curbed the powers of the governor and the council and restored voting rights to landless freemen.

These much-needed reforms came too late. Bacon was bitter about Berkeley's arbitrary actions, and the poor farmers and indentured servants in his army resented years of exploitation by wealthy men and arrogant justices of the peace. As one yeoman rebel put it, "A poor man who has only his labour to maintain himself and his family pays as much [in taxes] as a man who has 20,000 acres." Backed by 400 armed men, Bacon seized control of the colony and issued a "Manifesto and Declaration of the People," that demanded the death or removal of all Indians and an end to the rule of wealthy "parasites." "All the power and sway is got into the hands of the rich," Bacon proclaimed, as his army burned Jamestown to the ground and plundered the plantations of Berkeley's allies. When Bacon died suddenly from dysentery in October 1676, the governor took his revenge, dispersing the rebel army, seizing the estates of well-to-do rebels, and hanging 23 men.

Bacon's Rebellion was a pivotal event in Virginia's history and, indeed, in American history. Thereafter, landed planters remained dominant in Virginia by curbing corruption and finding public positions for politically ambitious yeomen. They also appeased the lower social orders by cutting their taxes and supporting the expansion onto Indian lands. Finally, the uprising confirmed the planters' growing commitment to African slavery. To forestall another rebellion by poor whites, Chesapeake planters turned away from indentured servitude, explicitly legalized slavery in 1705, and imported thousands of African laborers. Those decisions committed subsequent generations of Americans to a social system based on racial exploitation.

# Puritan New England

The Puritan exodus from England between 1620 and 1640 was both a worldly quest for land and a spiritual effort to preserve the "pure" Christian faith. By creating a "holy commonwealth" in America, pious migrants hoped to reform the established Church of England. By distributing land broadly, they tried to build a society of independent property-owning farm families. And by defining their mission in spiritual terms, the Puritans gave a moral dimension to American history.

## The Puritan Migration

From the beginning New England differed from other European colonies. Unruly male adventurers began New Spain and Jamestown, and commercial-minded fur traders dominated life in New France and New Netherland. By contrast, women and children as well as men settled Plymouth, the first permanent community in New England, and its leaders were pious Protestants—the Pilgrims.

The Pilgrims were Puritans who had left the Church of England, thus earning the name "Separatists." When King James I threatened to harry Puritans "out of the land, or else do worse," the Pilgrims left England and settled among Dutch Calvinists in Holland. Subsequently, 35 of these exiles resolved to migrate to America to maintain their English identity. Led by William Bradford and joined by 67 other migrants from England, they sailed to America aboard the *Mayflower* in 1620. Arriving in America without a royal charter, they created their own covenant of government, the Mayflower Compact, to "combine ourselves together into a civill body politick." This document was the first "constitution" adopted in North America and used the Puritan model of a self-governing religious congregation as the blueprint for political society.

The first winter in America tested the Pilgrims. As in Virginia, hunger and disease took a heavy toll; of the 102 migrants who arrived in November, only half survived until the spring. Thereafter the Plymouth colony—unlike Virginia—became a healthy and thriving community. The cold climate inhibited the spread of mosquito-borne diseases, and the Pilgrims' religious discipline established a strong work ethic. Moreover, because a severe smallpox epidemic in 1618 had killed most of the local Wampanoag people, the migrants faced few external threats. The Pilgrims built solid houses, planted ample crops, and their numbers grew rapidly to 3,000 by 1640. To ensure political stability, they issued a written legal code that provided for a colony-wide system of representative self-government, broad political rights, and a prohibition of government interference in spiritual matters.

Meanwhile, England was plunging deeper into religious turmoil. King Charles I repudiated some Protestant doctrines, such as the role of grace in salvation. English Puritans, who had gained many seats in Parliament, accused the king of "popery"—holding Catholic beliefs. In 1629 Charles dissolved Parliament, claimed the power to rule by "divine right," and raised money through royal edicts and the sale of monopolies. When Archbishop William Laud, whom Charles chose to head the Church of England, dismissed hundreds of Puritan ministers, thousands of Puritans fled to America.

The exodus began in 1630, when 900 Puritans sailed across the Atlantic under the leadership of John Winthrop, a well-educated country squire. Calling England morally corrupt and "overburdened with people," Winthrop sought land and opportunity for his children and a place in Christian history for his people. "We must consider that we shall be as a City upon a Hill," Winthrop told his fellow passengers. "The eyes of all people are upon us." Like the Pilgrims, the Puritans envisioned a reformed Christian society, a genuinely "New" England that would preserve the true faith and inspire religious change in England.

Winthrop and his associates established the Massachusetts Bay colony in the area around present-day Boston and transformed their joint-stock business corporation, the General Court of shareholders, into a colonial legislature. Over the next decade about 10,000 Puritans migrated to the colony, along with 10,000 others fleeing hard times in England. The Puritans created representative political institutions, with an elected governor, council, and assembly. However, to ensure rule by the godly, the Puritans limited the right to vote and hold office to men who were church members. Eschewing the policy of religious toleration in Plymouth colony, they established Puritan congregationalism as the state-supported religion, barred other faiths from conducting services, and used the Bible as a legal was well as a spiritual guide. "Where there is no Law," the colony's government advised local magistrates, they should rule "as near the law of God as they can."

In establishing churches, New England Puritans tried to re-create the simplicity of the first Christians. They eliminated bishops and placed power in the hands of the laity, or the ordinary members of the congregation—hence their name, Congregationalists. Influenced by John Calvin, Puritans embraced **predestination**, the doctrine that God had decided, or "predestined," the fates of all people before they were born and had chosen only a few "elect" men and women (the Saints) for salvation. Many church members lived in great anxiety, for they could never be sure whether God had selected them for salvation or damnation.

Puritans dealt with the uncertainties of divine election in three ways. Some congregations stressed the conversion experience—the intense spiritual sensation of being "born again" upon receiving God's grace. Other Puritans stressed ministerial "preparation," the confidence in salvation that came from years of spiritual guidance. Still others believed that God considered the Puritans as his "chosen people," who would be saved as long as they obeyed his laws.

To maintain God's favor, the Puritan magistrates of Massachusetts Bay purged their society of religious dissidents. One target was Roger Williams, who in 1634 had become the minister of the Puritan church in Salem, a new coastal town just north of Boston. Williams endorsed the Pilgrims' separation of church and state in Plymouth colony and condemned the legal establishment of Congregationalism in Massachusetts Bay. He taught that political magistrates should have authority over only the "bodies, goods, and outward estates of men," not their spiritual lives. Moreover, he questioned the Puritans' seizure (rather than purchase) of Indian lands. In response, the Puritan magistrates banished him from Massachusetts Bay.

In 1636 Williams and his followers resettled in Rhode Island, founding the town of Providence on land purchased from the Narragansett Indians. Other religious dissidents founded Portsmouth and Newport. In 1644 these towns obtained a corporate charter from the English Parliament that granted them full authority "to rule themselves." In Rhode Island as in Plymouth, there was no legally established church; every congregation was autonomous, and individual men and women could worship God as they pleased.

Puritan magistrates in Massachusetts Bay also felt threatened by Anne Hutchinson, the wife of a merchant and a mother of seven who worked as a midwife. Hutchinson held weekly prayer meetings for women in her house and accused certain Boston clergymen of placing undue emphasis on good behavior. In words that recalled Martin Luther's rejection of indulgences, Hutchinson argued that salvation could not be earned through good deeds; there was no "covenant of works." Rather, God bestowed salvation through the "covenant of grace" and "revealed" divine truth directly to the individual believer. The doctrine of revelation diminished the role of ministers, and Puritan magistrates denounced it as heretical.

The magistrates also resented Hutchinson because of her sex. Like other Christians, Puritans believed that both men and women could be saved. When it came to the governance of church and state, however, women were seen as distinctly inferior to men. As the Pilgrim minister John Robinson put it, women "are debarred by their sex from ordinary prophesying, and from any other dealing in the church wherein they take authority over the man." Puritan women could never be ministers, lay preachers, or even voting members of the congregation.

In 1637 the magistrates put Hutchinson on trial for the heresy of teaching that inward grace freed an individual from the rules of the church. Hutchinson defended her views with great skill, and even Winthrop admitted that she was "a woman of fierce and haughty courage." But the judges scolded her for not attending to "her household affairs, and such things as belong to women" and found her guilty. Banished, she followed Roger Williams into exile in Rhode Island.

These coercive policies, along with the desire for better land, prompted other Puritans to leave Massachusetts Bay. In 1636 pastor Thomas Hooker led his congregation to the Connecticut River Valley, where they established the town of Hartford; other migrants settled along the river at Wethersfield and Windsor. In 1639 the Connecticut Puritans adopted the Fundamental Orders, a plan of government that included an established church, a popularly elected governor and assembly, and voting rights for most property-owning men—not just church members.

As Puritans established themselves in America, England fell into a religious war. When Archbishop Laud imposed a Church of England prayer book on Presbyterian Scotland in 1642, a Scottish army invaded England. Thousands of English Puritans (and hundreds of American Puritans) joined the invaders, demanding greater authority for Parliament and reform of the established church. After four years of civil war, the Parliamentary forces led by Oliver Cromwell were victorious. In 1649 Parliament executed Charles I, proclaimed a republican Commonwealth, and banished bishops and elaborate rituals from the Church of England.

The Puritan triumph was short-lived. Popular support for the Commonwealth ebbed, especially after 1653 when Cromwell took dictatorial control. Following Cromwell's death, moderate Protestants and a resurgent aristocracy summoned the son of Charles I from Europe and restored the monarchy and the power of bishops in the Church of England. For many Puritans, Charles II's accession in 1660 represented the victory of the Antichrist—the false prophet described in the final book of the New Testament.

For the Puritans in America, the restoration of the monarchy began a new phase of their "errand into the wilderness." They had come to New England to preserve the "pure" Christian Church, expecting to return to Europe in triumph. When that sacred mission was dashed by the failure of the English Revolution, Puritan ministers exhorted their congregations to create a new society in America based on their faith and ideals.

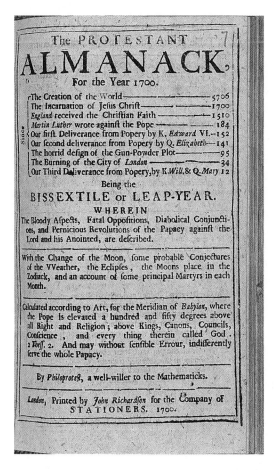

**The Protestant Almanack, 1700**

The conflict between Protestants and Catholics took many forms. To reinforce the religious identity of English Protestants, the Company of Stationers (or printers) published a yearly almanac that charted not only the passage of the seasons but also the "Pernicious Revolutions of the Papacy against the Lord and his Anointed."

By permission of the Syndics of Cambridge University Library.

## Puritanism and Witchcraft

Like the Native Americans they encountered in New England, Puritans thought that the physical world was full of supernatural forces. This belief in "spirits" stemmed in part from Christian teachings, such as the Catholic belief in miracles and the Protestant faith in the powers of "grace." Devout Christians saw signs of God's (or Satan's) power in blazing stars, birth defects, and other unusual events. Noting that many ministers' houses "had been smitten with Lightning," Cotton Mather, a prominent theologian, wondered "what the meaning of God should be in it."

The Puritans' respect for spiritual forces also reflected widespread pagan assumptions. When Samuel Sewall, a well-educated Puritan merchant and judge, moved into a new house, he fended off evil spirits by driving a metal pin into the floor. Thousands of ordinary Puritan farmers followed the pagan astrological charts printed in almanacs to determine the best times to plant crops, marry, and make other important decisions.

Zealous ministers attacked many of these beliefs and practices as "superstition" and condemned "cunning" individuals who claimed to have special powers as healers or prophets. Indeed, many Christians looked on such conjurers as "wizards" or "witches" who acted at Satan's command. The people of Andover, Massachusetts, "were much addicted to sorcery," claimed one observer, and "there were forty men in it that could raise the Devil as well as any astrologer." Between 1647 and 1662 civil authorities in New England hanged 14 people for witchcraft, mostly older women who, their accusers claimed, were "double-tongued" or "had an unruly spirit."

The most dramatic episode of witch-hunting took place in Salem, Massachusetts, in 1692. Initially, a few young girls experienced strange seizures and accused various neighbors of bewitching them. When judges allowed the introduction of "spectral" evidence—visions seen only by the young accusers—the number of accusations spun out of control. Eventually, Massachusetts authorities arrested 175 people and executed 20 of them. The causes of this mass hysteria were complex and are still hard to fathom. Some historians point to group rivalries: many of the accusers were the daughters and young servants of poor farmers in a rural area of Salem, whereas many of the accused witches were wealthier church members or their friends. Because 14 women were executed, other historians view the witchcraft trials as part of a broader attempt to keep women in a subordinate position. Still other scholars focus on the fears raised by recent Indian attacks in nearby Maine, which killed the parents of some of the young accusers who sparked the Salem prosecutions.

Whatever the cause, the Salem episode marked a turning point. Popular revulsion against the executions brought an end in New England to legal prosecutions for witchcraft and heresy. The European Enlightenment, a major intellectual movement that began around 1675, also discouraged witchcraft accusations by promoting a more rational view of the world. Increasingly, educated people explained accidents and sudden deaths through theories that drew upon the "laws of nature," not through religion, astrology, and witchcraft. In contrast to Cotton Mather (d. 1728), who believed that lightning might be a supernatural sign, well-read men of the next generation—such as Benjamin Franklin—would conceive of lightning as a natural phenomenon.

## A Yeoman Society, 1630–1700

In building communities in New England, Puritans consciously shunned the worst features of traditional Europe. They did not wish to live in towns dominated by a few wealthy landowners or controlled by a distant government that levied oppressive taxes. Consequently, the migrants created self-governing towns and encouraged broad property ownership. Instead of granting thousands of acres to wealthy planters (as occurred in the Chesapeake colonies), the General Courts of Massachusetts Bay and Connecticut bestowed the title to a township on a group of settlers, or **proprietors**, who distributed the land among themselves.

Widespread ownership of land did not mean equality of wealth or status. "God had Ordained different degrees and orders of men," proclaimed the Boston merchant

John Saffin, "some to be Masters and Commanders, others to be Subjects, and to be commanded." Town proprietors normally gave the largest plots to men of high social status, who often became selectmen and justices of the peace. However, all male heads of families received some land, creating a freehold society of independent households. Even as the sons of smallholders were forced, at least temporarily, into the ranks of tenants and laborers, the vast majority of men remained landowners with a vote in the **town meeting**, the main institution of local government (Map 2.3).

Consequently, ordinary farmers in New England communities had much more political power than did most European peasants and most yeomen in the planter-dominated Chesapeake colonies. Each year the town meeting chose selectmen to manage its affairs. The meeting also levied taxes; enacted ordinances regarding fencing and road building; and regulated the use of common fields for grazing livestock. Finally, towns elected representatives to the General Court, which gradually displaced the governor as the center of political authority.

Because of these Puritan-inspired policies, nearly all New England households had an opportunity to acquire freehold property, participate in the political life of the community, and enjoy some economic security. When he died in the 1690s, Nathaniel Fish was one of the poorest men in Barnstable, Massachusetts, yet he owned a two-room cottage, eight acres of land, an ox, and a cow. For him and thousands of other settlers, New England had proved to be the promised land, a new world of opportunity.

# The Eastern Indians' New World

Native Americans throughout the eastern woodland region were also living in a new world, but for them it was a bleak, dangerous, and conflict-ridden place. Some Indian peoples, like the Pequots in New England, the Susquehannocks in Virginia, and the Iroquois in the trans-Appalachian region, resisted the invaders by force. Others retreated into the mountains or moved farther west to preserve their traditional culture or to band together in new tribes.

## *Puritans and Pequots*

Even before the Puritans came to New England, they pondered the morality of intruding on Native American lands. "By what right or warrant can we enter into the land of the Savages?" they asked themselves. John Winthrop answered this query by detecting God's hand in a disastrous smallpox epidemic that reduced the Indian population from 13,000 to 3,000. "If God were not pleased with our inheriting these parts," he asked, "why doth he still make roome for us by diminishing them as we increase?" Citing the book of Genesis, the magistrates of Massachusetts Bay declared that the Indians had not "subdued" their land and therefore had no "just right" to it.

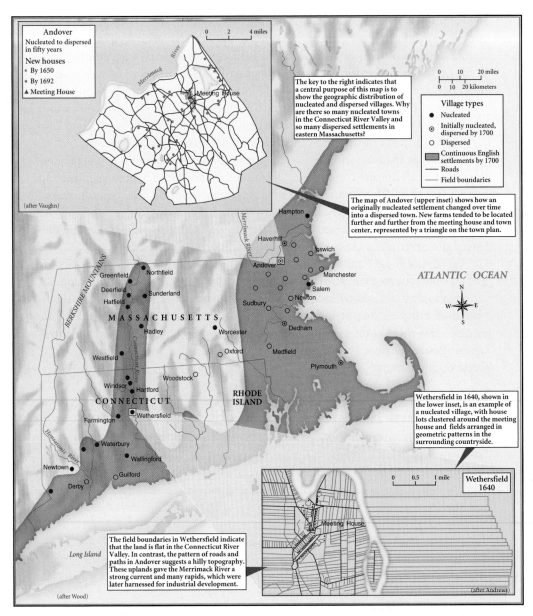

**Andover**
Nucleated to dispersed
in fifty years
New houses
• By 1650
• By 1692
▲ Meeting House

(after Vaughn)

The key to the right indicates that
a central purpose of this map is to
show the geographic distribution of
nucleated and dispersed villages. Why
are there so many nucleated towns
in the Connecticut River Valley and
so many dispersed settlements in
eastern Massachusetts?

Village types
• Nucleated
◉ Initially nucleated,
  dispersed by 1700
○ Dispersed
▨ Continuous English
  settlements by 1700
— Roads
— Field boundaries

The map of Andover (upper inset) shows how an
originally nucleated settlement changed over time
into a dispersed town. New farms tended to be located
further and further from the meeting house and town
center, represented by a triangle on the town plan.

Hampton

Haverhill

Ipswich

Andover

Manchester

ATLANTIC OCEAN

Greenfield    Northfield

Deerfield    Sunderland

Hatfield

M A S S A C H U S E T T S

Salem

Newton

Sudbury

Hadley    Worcester

Dedham

Westfield    ○ Oxford    Medfield

Woodstock ○

Windsor    Hartford

CONNECTICUT    RHODE
ISLAND

Farmington    ◉ Wethersfield

Waterbury

Wallingford

Newtown ●

Derby ○    ○ Guilford

BERKSHIRE MOUNTAINS

Merrimack River

Plymouth

Wethersfield in 1640, shown in
the lower inset, is an example of
a nucleated village, with house
lots clustered around the meeting
house and fields arranged in
geometric patterns in the
surrounding countryside.

The field boundaries in Wethersfield indicate
that the land is flat in the Connecticut River
Valley. In contrast, the pattern of roads and
paths in Andover suggests a hilly topography.
These uplands gave the Merrimack River a
strong current and many rapids, which were
later harnessed for industrial development.

Long Island

Meeting House

Wethersfield
1640

(after Wood)

(after Andrews)

## MAP 2.3 Settlement Patterns within New England Towns, 1630–1700

Initially, most Puritan towns were compact. Regardless of the local topography (hills or plains),
families lived close to one another in the nucleated village center and traveled daily to work in the
surrounding fields. This pattern is clearly apparent in the 1640 map of Wethersfield, Connecticut,
which is situated on the broad plains of the Connecticut River Valley. The first settlers of Andover,
Massachusetts, also chose to live in the village center. However, the rugged topography of eastern
Massachusetts encouraged a dispersed form of settlement, and by 1692 many residents of Andover
lived on their own farms.

Because of their moral righteousness, the Puritans often treated Native Americans with a brutality equal to that of the Spanish conquistadors and Nathaniel Bacon's frontiersmen in Virginia. When Pequot warriors attacked English farmers who had intruded into the Connecticut River Valley in 1636, Puritan militia and their Indian allies led a surprise attack on a Pequot village and massacred about 500 men, women, and children. "God laughed at the Enemies of his People," one soldier boasted, "filling the Place with Dead Bodies."

Like most Europeans, English Puritans viewed the Indians as "savages," culturally inferior people who did not deserve civilized treatment. But the Puritans were not racist as the term is understood today. To them, Native Americans were not genetically inferior—they were white people with sun-darkened skins—and "sin" or Satan, rather than race, accounted for their degenerate condition. "Probably the devil" delivered these "miserable savages" to America, the Puritan minister Cotton Mather suggested, "in hopes that the gospel of the Lord Jesus Christ would never come here to destroy or disturb his absolute empire over them."

This interpretation of the Indians' history inspired the Puritan minister John Eliot to convert them to Christianity. Eliot translated the Bible into Algonquian and undertook numerous missions to Indian villages in eastern Massachusetts. Because Puritans demanded that Indians understand the complexities of Protestant theology, only a few Native Americans became full members of Puritan congregations. However, the Puritans created "**praying towns**" that, like the Spanish Franciscans' missions in New Mexico, supervised the Indian population; by 1670, more than 1,000 Indians lived in fourteen special mission towns. At the close of the seventeenth century, the combination of Christianization, European diseases, and military force had destroyed the autonomy and culture of many of the Algonquian-speaking peoples in coastal New England.

## Metacom's (King Philip's) Rebellion

By the 1670s there were three times as many whites as Indians in New England. The English population now totaled some 55,000, while the number of Indians had plummeted: from an estimated 120,000 in 1570, to 70,000 in 1620, to barely 16,000. To Metacom, leader of the Wampanoags, the future looked grim. When his people copied English ways by raising hogs and selling pork in Boston, Puritan officials accused them of selling at "an under rate" and placed restrictions on their trade. When they killed wandering livestock that damaged their cornfields, authorities denounced them for violating English property rights. Like Opechancanough [op-e-CHAN-canoe] and the Susquehannocks [sus-kwa-HAN-oks] in Virginia and Popé in New Mexico, Metacom finally concluded that only military resistance could save Indian lands and culture. So in 1675 Metacom (whom the English called King Philip) forged a military alliance with the Narragansetts and Nipmucks and attacked white settlements throughout New England. Bitter fighting continued into 1676, ending only

**Metacom (King Philip), Chief of the Wampanoag**

The Indian uprising of 1675 left an indelible mark on the historical memory of New England. This painting from the 1850s, done on semitransparent cloth and lit from behind for dramatic effect, was used by traveling performers to tell the story of King Philip's War. Note that Metacom is not depicted as a savage but as a dignified man; freed from fear of Indian attack, nineteenth-century New England whites could adopt a romanticized version of their region's often brutal history.
Shelburne Museum.

when Indian warriors ran short of guns and powder, and Mohegans and Mohawks in alliance with the Massachusetts Bay government ambushed and killed Metacom.

The rebellion was a deadly affair. The Indians had fought long and hard, a party of Narragansetts told Roger Williams, because the English "had forced them to it." Indeed, the Indians destroyed 20 percent of the English towns in Massachusetts and Rhode Island and killed 1,000 whites, about 5 percent of the adult population. Almost every day, recalled settler William Harris, he had heard new reports of the Indians' "burneing houses, takeing cattell, killing men & women & Children: & carrying others captive." But the Indians' own losses—from famine and disease as well as battle—were much larger: as many as 4,500, or 25 percent of an already diminished population. Many of the surviving Algonquian peoples migrated farther into the New England backcountry, where they intermarried with other Algonquian tribes tied to the French. Over the next century, these displaced Indian peoples would take their revenge, allying with the French to attack their Puritan enemies (see American Voices, "A Captivity Narrative," p. 64).

## The Fur Trade and the Inland Peoples

As English settlers slowly advanced up the river valleys from the Atlantic coast, the Indians who lived near the Appalachian Mountains and in the great forested areas beyond remained independent. Yet these distant Indian peoples felt the European presence because they entered the fur trade to obtain woolen blankets, iron cookware, knives, and guns, which they used to kill deer and their enemies. Thanks in part to their strategic geographic location in present-day central New York, which enabled them to bargain for goods from different European officials and merchants, the militarily aggressive and diplomatically astute Iroquois peoples were the most successful. Iroquois warriors moved quickly to the east and south along the Mohawk, Hudson, Delaware, and Susquehanna Rivers to exchange goods with (or threaten) the English and Dutch colonies. They traveled north via Lake Champlain and the Richelieu River to deal with French traders in Quebec. And they journeyed west by means of the Great Lakes and the Allegheny-Ohio river system to exploit the rich fur-bearing lands of the Mississippi Valley.

The rise of the Iroquois was breathtakingly rapid, just as their subsequent decline was tragically sobering. In 1600 the Iroquois in New York numbered about 30,000 and lived in large towns of 500 to 2,000 inhabitants. Two decades later they had organized themselves in a great "longhouse" confederation of the Five Nations: the Senecas, Cayugas, Onondagas, Oneidas, and Mohawks. Although a virulent smallpox epidemic in 1633 cut their numbers by a third, the Iroquois waged a successful series of wars against the Iroquoian-speaking Hurons (1649), Neutrals (1651), Eries (1657), and Susquehannocks (1669). The victorious warriors carried hundreds of captives to New York, where Iroquois kin tortured and killed many of the captives to atone for those lost in battle.

These triumphs gave the Iroquois control of the fur trade with the French in Quebec and the Dutch in New York. Equally important, it replenished the populations of villages hard hit by epidemics and wartime losses. To assimilate war captives that were spared, Iroquois families conducted "requickening" ceremonies that transferred to the captives the names of their dead relatives, along with their social roles and duties. By 1667 half of the population of many Mohawk towns consisted of adopted prisoners. Cultural diversity within Iroquoia increased because the Five Nations now

AMERICAN VOICES

# A Captivity Narrative

## MARY ROWLANDSON

*Mary Rowlandson, a minister's wife in Lancaster, Massachusetts, was one of many settlers taken captive by the Indians during Metacom's war. Mrs. Rowlandson spent twelve weeks in captivity, traveling constantly, until her family ransomed her for the considerable sum of £20. Her account of this ordeal,* The Sovereignty and Goodness of God, *published in 1682, became one of the most popular prose works of its time.*

On the tenth of February 1675, came the Indians with great numbers upon Lancaster: their first coming was about sunrising; hearing the noise of some guns, we looked out; several houses were burning, and the smoke ascending to heaven. . . . [T]he Indians laid hold of us, pulling me one way, and the children another, and said, "Come go along with us"; I told them they would kill me: they answered, if I were willing to go along with them, they would not hurt me. . . .

The first week of my being among them I hardly ate any thing; the second week I found my stomach grow very faint for want of something; and yet it was very hard to get down their filthy trash; but the third week . . . they were sweet and savory to my taste. I was at this time knitting a pair of white cotton stockings for my [Indian] mistress; and had not yet wrought upon a sabbath day. When the sabbath came they bade me go to work. I told them it was the sabbath-day, and desired them to let me rest, and told them I would do as much more tomorrow; to which they answered me they would break my face. . . .

During my abode in this place, Philip [Metacom] spake to me to make a shirt for his boy, which I did, for which he gave me a shilling. I offered the money to my master, but he bade me keep it; and with it I bought a piece of horse flesh. Afterwards he asked me to make a cap for his boy, for which he invited me to dinner. I went, and he gave me a pancake, about as big as two fingers. It was made of parched wheat, beaten, and fried in bear's grease, but I thought I never tasted pleasanter meat in my life. . . .

My master had three squaws, living sometimes with one, and sometimes with another one. . . . [It] was Weetamoo with whom I had lived and served all this while. A severe and proud dame she was, bestowing every day in dressing herself near as much time as any of the gentry of the land: powdering her hair, and painting her face, going with necklaces, with jewels in her ears, and bracelets upon her hands. When she had dressed herself, her work was to make girdles of wampom and beads. . . .

On Tuesday morning they called their general court (as they call it) to consult and determine, whether I should go home or no. And they all as one man did seemingly consent to it, that I should go home. . . .

SOURCE: C. H. Lincoln, ed., *Original Narratives of Early American History: Narratives of Indian Wars, 1675–1699* (New York: Barnes and Noble, 1952), 14: 139–41.

made peace with their traditional French foes and allowed Jesuit missionaries to live among them. Soon about 20 percent of the Iroquois were Catholics, some living under French protection in separate mission-towns.

In 1680 the Iroquois repudiated their ties to the French and traded with the English and Dutch merchants in New York. Seeking furs, they embarked on a new series of western wars. Warriors of the Five Nations pushed a dozen Algonquian-speaking peoples allied with the French—the Ottawas, Foxes, Sauks, Kickapoos, Miamis, and Illinois—out of their traditional lands north of the Ohio River and into a newly formed multitribal region (present-day Wisconsin) west of Lake Michigan. The cost of these victories was high. After losing about 2,200 warriors, in 1701 the Iroquois again made treaties with the French, bringing peace to the inland region for two generations.

However, the character of Indian society throughout the eastern woodland region had been permanently altered. Most tribes had diminished in size as warfare, European diseases, and the rum and corn liquor sold by fur traders took their toll. "Strong spirits . . . Causes our men to get very sick," a Catawba leader in Carolina protested, "and many of our people has Lately Died by the Effects of that Strong Drink." Many Indian peoples also lost their economic independence. As they exchanged furs for European-made iron utensils and woolen blankets, Indians neglected traditional artisan skills—making fewer flint hoes, clay pots, and skin garments. As a Cherokee chief complained in the 1750s, "Every necessity of life we must have from the white people." Religious autonomy vanished as well. When French missionaries won converts among the Hurons and Iroquois, they divided Indian communities into hostile religious factions.

Equally striking, constant warfare altered the dynamics of tribal politics by shifting power from cautious elders, the sachems, to headstrong young warriors. The sachems, one group of Seneca warriors said with scorn, "were a parcell of Old People who say much but who Mean or Act very little." The position and status of women changed in complex and contradictory ways. Traditionally, eastern woodland women had asserted authority as the chief providers of food and handcrafted goods. As a French Jesuit noted of the Iroquois, "The women are always the first to deliberate . . . on private or community matters. They hold their councils apart and . . . advise the chiefs . . . , so that the latter may deliberate on them in their turn." The influx of European goods and the disruption of farming by warfare threatened the economic basis of women's power. At the same time, the influence of women in victorious tribes increased because they assumed responsibility for the cultural assimilation of hundreds of captives.

Finally, the sheer extent of the fur industry—the trapping and killing of hundreds of thousands of beaver, deer, otter, and other animals—profoundly altered the natural environment. Streams ran faster and forest underbrush grew denser because there were fewer beavers to build dams and fewer deer to trim the vegetation. Native animals as well as the native peoples now lived in a new American world.

| | TIMELINE | | |
|---|---|---|---|
| 1539–1543 | Coronado and de Soto seek gold and explore parts of present-day United States | 1625–1649 | Charles I, king of England |
| 1565 | Spain establishes St. Augustine, Florida | 1630 | Puritans found Massachusetts Bay colony |
| 1598 | Acoma rebellion in New Mexico | 1634 | Maryland settled |
| 1603–1625 | James I, king of England | 1636–1637 | Pequot war |
| | | | Roger Williams and Anne Hutchinson banished |
| 1607 | English adventurers settle Jamestown, Virginia | 1640s | Puritan revolution in England |
| 1608 | Samuel de Champlain founds Quebec | | Iroquois go to war over fur trade |
| 1613 | Dutch set up fur-trading post on Manhattan Island | 1651 | First Navigation Act |
| | | 1660 | Restoration of English monarchy |
| 1619 | First Africans arrive in the Chesapeake region | | Tobacco prices fall and remain low |
| | Virginia House of Burgesses convened | 1664 | English conquer New Netherland |
| 1620 | Pilgrims found Plymouth colony | 1675–1676 | Bacon's Rebellion |
| | | | Metacom's uprising |
| 1620–1660 | Tobacco boom in Chesapeake colonies | | Expansion of African slavery in the Chesapeake region |
| 1621 | Dutch West India Company chartered | 1680 | Popé's Rebellion in New Mexico |
| 1622 | Opechancanough's uprising | 1692 | Salem witchcraft trials |
| 1624 | Virginia becomes a royal colony | | |

# For Further Exploration

For a comprehensive and insightful narrative of the Spanish exploration and settlement of the lands to the north of the Rio Grande, consult David Weber, *The Spanish Frontier in North America* (1992). Bernard Bailyn, *The Peopling of British North America: An Introduction* (1986), presents a brief, vivid history of English migration and settlement. In *American Slavery, American Freedom* (1975) Edmund Morgan offers a compelling portrayal of white servitude and black slavery in early Virginia, while John Demos, *The Unredeemed Captive: A Family Story from Early America* (1994), relates the gripping tale of Eunice Williams, a captured Puritan girl who lived her life among the Mohawks. Two other fine studies of Native American life are James Merrell, *The Indians' New World: Catawbas and Their Neighbors from European Contact through the Era of Removal* (1989), and Colin Calloway, *New Worlds for All: Indians, Europeans, and the Remaking of Early America* (1997). William Cronon, *Changes in the Land: Indians, Colonists, and the Ecology of New England* (1983), is a succinct analysis of the impact of the Indians and the English on the ecology of New England. Arthur Quinn, *A New World: An Epic of Colonial America from the Founding of Jamestown to the Fall of Quebec* (1994), is a lively narrative filled with portraits of important political figures, macabre events, and high hopes that end disastrously.

A PBS video, *Surviving Columbus* (2 hours), traces the experiences of the Pueblo Indians over 450 years. "First Nations Histories," at <http://www.tolatsga.org/Compacts.html>, presents short histories of many North American Indian peoples and information on their politics, language, culture, and demography. Two fine Web sites explore the history of the Pilgrims at Plymouth: "Caleb Johnson's Mayflower History," at <http://www.mayflowerhistory.com/>, and "The Plymouth Colony Archive Project," at <http://etext.lib.virginia.edu/users/deetz/>. "Colonial Williamsburg," at <http://www.colonialwilliamsburg.org/history/>, offers an extensive collection of documents, illustrations, and secondary texts about colonial life, as well as information about the archeological excavations at Williamsburg. Extensive materials on the Salem witchcraft episode can be viewed at <http://etext.lib.virginia.edu/salem/witchcraft/>.

---

For definitions of key terms boldfaced in this chapter, see the glossary at the end of the book.

To assess your mastery of the material covered in this chapter, see the Online Study Guide at **bedfordstmartins.com/henrettaconcise**.

For map resources and primary documents, see **bedfordstmartins.com/henrettaconcise**.

---

## Chapter 3

# THE BRITISH EMPIRE IN AMERICA
## 1660–1750

These two words, Negro and Slave, [have become] Homogeneous and convertible; even as Negro and Christian, Englishman and Heathen, are [now] . . . made opposites.

REVEREND MORGAN GODWYN, 1680

When Charles II came to the throne in 1660 England was a second-class trading country, picking up the crumbs left by Dutch merchants. "What we want is more of the trade the Dutch now have," declared the duke of Albemarle. To secure this trade, the English government passed the Acts of Trade and Navigation, which excluded Dutch merchants from its growing colonies, and then went to war to enforce the new legislation. By the 1720s the newly unified kingdom of Great Britain (comprising England and Scotland) controlled the North Atlantic trade. "Our trade is our chief support," Lord Carteret told the House of Lords in 1739. As the ardent imperialist Malachy Postlethwayt put it a few years later, the British empire "was a magnificent superstructure of American commerce and naval power on an African foundation."

As Postlethwayt noted, the wealth of the British empire rested on the predatory trade in African slaves and the sugar those slaves produced on the plantations of the West Indies. To protect these valuable sugar colonies from European rivals—the Dutch in New Netherland, the Spanish in Florida, and especially the Catholic French in Quebec and the West Indies—British officials repeatedly went to war. Boasted one English pamphleteer, "We are, of any nation, the best situated for trade, . . . capable of giving maritime laws to the world."

As the Navigation Acts regulated colonial commerce, British officials tried to subject colonial political institutions to imperial direction. Although this initiative met with less success, by 1713 Britain had become a significant power in Europe and the Western Hemisphere. The cost was high. While most white colonists on the North American mainland enjoyed modest prosperity, thousands of enslaved Africans endured brutal work and early death.

**Power and Race in the Chesapeake**

Lord Baltimore holds a map of his proprietary colony, Maryland, in this 1670 painting by Gerard Soest. The colony will soon belong to his grandson Cecil Calvert, who points to his magnificent inheritance. The presence of a young African servant foreshadows the importance of slave labor in the post-1700 Chesapeake economy.

Enoch Pratt Free Library of Baltimore.

FOR MORE HELP ANALYZING THIS IMAGE, see the Online Study Guide at **bedfordstmartins. com/henrettaconcise**.

stipulated that colonial sugar, tobacco, and indigo could be shipped only to England. To provide even more business for English merchants, the acts required that European exports to America pass through England. To pay the customs officials that enforced these mercantilist laws, the Revenue Act of 1673 imposed a "plantation duty" on sugar and tobacco exports.

The English government backed its mercantilist policy with the force of arms. In three commercial wars between 1652 and 1674, the English navy drove the Dutch from New Netherland and ended Dutch supremacy in the West African slave trade. Meanwhile, English merchants expanded their fleets and seized control of North Atlantic commerce.

Many Americans resisted these mercantilist laws as burdensome and intrusive. Edward Randolph, an English customs official in Massachusetts, reported that the Puritan-dominated government took "no notice of the laws of trade," welcomed Dutch merchants, imported goods from the French sugar islands, and claimed that its royal charter exempted it from the new regulations. Outraged, Randolph called for English troops to "reduce Massachusetts to obedience." Instead, the Lords of

Trade—the administrative body charged with colonial affairs—pursued a puni-tive legal strategy. In 1679 the lords denied the claim of Massachusetts Bay to the adjoining province of New Hampshire and created a separate colony there with a royal governor. Then, in 1684, the lords persuaded the English Court of Chancery to annul the charter of Massachusetts Bay on the grounds that the Puritan govern-ment had violated the Navigation Acts and virtually outlawed the Church of England.

That was just the beginning. The accession to the throne of James II (r. 1685–1688) prompted new imperial initiatives. James had grown up in France during the reign of Oliver Cromwell and was an admirer of France's authoritarian king, Louis XIV. Believing that monarchs had a "divine-right" to rule, James in-structed the Lords of Trade to subject the American colonies to royal control. In 1686 the Lords revoked the corporate charters of Connecticut and Rhode Island and merged them with the Massachusetts Bay and Plymouth colonies to form a new royal province, the Dominion of New England. Two years later the home govern-ment added New York and New Jersey to the Dominion, creating a vast colony that stretched from the Delaware River to Maine.

This administrative innovation went far beyond mercantilism, which regulated trade while respecting the political autonomy of the American colonies. Rather, it extended to America the authoritarian model of colonial rule imposed on Catholic Ireland. When James II took control of New York in 1674, he refused to allow an elective assembly and ruled by decree. Now he imposed absolutist rule on the entire Dominion by appointing Sir Edmund Andros, a former military officer, as governor and empowering him to abolish the existing legislative assemblies. In Massachusetts, Andros immediately banned town meetings, angering villagers who prized local self-rule. He also advocated public worship in the Church of England, offending Puritan Congregationalists. Even worse from the colonists' perspective, the governor chal-lenged all land titles granted under the original Massachusetts charter. Andros of-fered to provide new deeds but only if the colonists would agree to pay an annual fee (or quit-rent).

## The Glorious Revolution in England and America

Fortunately for the colonists, James II angered English political leaders as much as Andros alienated the Americans. The king revoked the charters of many English towns, rejected the advice of Parliament, and aroused popular opposi-tion by openly practicing Roman Catholicism. When James's Spanish Catholic wife gave birth to a son in 1688, it raised the prospect of a Catholic heir to the throne. To forestall such an event, English parliamentary leaders led a quick and bloodless coup known as the Glorious Revolution. Backed by popular sentiment and military leaders, they forced James into exile and enthroned Mary, his Protestant daughter by his first wife, and her Dutch Protestant husband, William of Orange. Queen Mary II and King William III agreed to rule as constitutional monarchs loyal to "the Protestant reformed religion." They accepted a bill of rights limiting royal prerogatives and increasing personal liberties and parliamentary powers.

To justify their coup, parliamentary leaders relied on the political philosopher John Locke. In his *Two Treatises on Government* (1690), Locke rejected divine-right theories of monarchical rule; he argued that the legitimacy of government rests on the consent of the governed and that individuals have inalienable natural rights to life, liberty, and property. Locke's celebration of individual rights and representative government had a lasting influence in America, where many political leaders wanted to expand the powers of the colonial assemblies.

More immediately, the Glorious Revolution sparked rebellions by colonists in Massachusetts, Maryland, and New York. When the news of the coup reached Boston in April 1689, Puritan leaders seized Governor Andros and shipped him back to England. Responding to American protests, the new monarchs broke up the Dominion of New England. However, they refused to restore the old Puritan-dominated government; instead, in 1692 they created a new royal colony of Massachusetts (which included Plymouth and Maine). The colony's charter empowered the king to appoint the governor (and customs officials) and stipulated that the Massachusetts assembly be elected by all male property owners (not just Puritan church members). It further undermined Puritan rule by prohibiting restrictions on members of the Church of England.

In Maryland the uprising of 1689 had economic as well as religious causes. Since 1660 falling tobacco prices had threatened the livelihoods of smallholders, tenant farmers, and former indentured servants. These economically vulnerable people were mostly Protestant, and they resented the rising taxes and the high fees imposed by wealthy proprietary officials, who were primarily Catholic. When Parliament ousted James II, a Protestant association in Maryland quickly removed the Catholic officials. The Lords of Trade supported this Protestant initiative; they suspended Baltimore's proprietorship, imposed royal government, and legally established the Church of England. This arrangement lasted until 1715, when Benedict Calvert, the fourth Lord Baltimore, converted to the Anglican faith, and the king restored the proprietorship to the Calvert family.

In New York the rebellion against the Dominion of New England began a decade of violent political conflict. New England settlers on Long Island, angered by James's prohibition of representative institutions, began the uprising and quickly won the support of Dutch Protestant artisans in New York City, who welcomed the succession of Queen Mary and her Dutch husband. The Dutch militia ousted Lieutenant Governor Nicholson, an Andros appointee and an alleged Catholic sympathizer. They rallied behind a new government led by Jacob Leisler, a militant German Protestant merchant who had married into a prominent New York Dutch family. Leisler hoped to win the support of all classes and ethnic groups, but his denunciations of political rivals as "popish dogs" and "Roages, Rascalls, and Devills" alienated many New Yorkers. When Leisler imprisoned his opponents, imposed new taxes, and championed the artisans' cause, the wealthy merchants who had traditionally controlled the city's government condemned his rule. In 1691 the merchants won the support of the new English governor, who had Leisler indicted for treason. Convicted by an English jury, Leisler was hanged and then decapitated, an act of vengeance that corrupted New York politics for a generation.

In both America and England the Glorious Revolution of 1688 and 1689 began a new historical era. The uprisings in Boston and New York toppled the authoritarian Dominion of New England and, because King William wanted colonial support for a war against Catholic France, won the restoration of internal self-government. In England, William and Mary ruled as constitutional monarchs and promoted an empire based on commerce. Although Parliament created a new Board of Trade (1696) to supervise the American settlements, it had little success. Settlers and proprietors resisted the board's attempt to install royal governments in every colony, as did many English political leaders, who feared an increase in monarchical power. The result was a period of lax administration. The home government imposed only a few laws and taxes on the colonies and allowed enterprising merchants and financiers to develop them as a source of trade.

### Imperial Wars and Native Peoples

In a world of competing mercantilist nations, the expansion of British trade depended on the growth of its military power. Between 1689 and 1815 Britain fought a series of increasingly intense wars with France for dominance in western Europe. To win this struggle, British political leaders created a powerful central state that spent three-quarters of its revenue on military expenses. As these wars spread to the Western Hemisphere, they involved growing numbers of colonists and Native American warriors, who were now armed with European guns. Indeed, many Indian peoples were now familiar enough with European goals and diplomacy to turn the fighting to their own advantage.

The first significant battles in North America occurred during the War of the Spanish Succession (1702–1713), which pitted Britain against France and Spain and prompted English settlers in the Carolinas to attack Spanish Florida. The Carolinians armed the Creeks, whose 15,000 members lived in matrilineal clans and farmed the fertile lands along the present-day Georgia-Alabama border. A joint English-Creek expedition burned the Spanish town of St. Augustine but failed to capture the nearby fort. Fearing that future Carolinian-backed Indian raids would endanger its colony of Florida and pose a threat to Havana in nearby Cuba, the Spanish reinforced St. Augustine and unsuccessfully attacked Charleston, South Carolina.

The Creeks had their own quarrels to settle with the pro-French Choctaws to the west and the Spanish-allied Apalachees to the south and used this opportunity to become the dominant tribe in the region. Beginning in 1704 a force of Creek and Yamasee warriors destroyed the remaining Franciscan missions in northern Florida, attacked the Spanish settlement at Pensacola, and captured 1,000 Apalachees, whom they sold to South Carolinian slave traders for sale in the West Indies. Simultaneously, a Carolina-supplied Creek expedition attacked the Iroquois-speaking Tuscarora people of North Carolina, killing hundreds, executing 160 male captives, and sending 400 women and children into slavery. The surviving Tuscaroras migrated to the north and joined the New York Iroquois (who then became the Six Nations). Having ruled by the guns of their Indian allies, the Carolinians now died by them. When traders demanded the payment of debts in 1715, the Yamasee and Creek revolted and killed 400 colonists before being overwhelmed by the Carolinians and their new Cherokee allies.

Native Americans also played a central role in the fighting in the Northeast, where French Catholics from Canada confronted English Protestants from New England. Aided by the French, Abenaki and Mohawk warriors took revenge on their Puritan enemies. They destroyed English settlements in Maine and in 1704 attacked the western Massachusetts town of Deerfield, where they killed 48 residents and carried 112 into captivity. In response, New England militia attacked French settlements and, in 1710, joined British naval forces and troops to seize Port Royal in French Acadia (Nova Scotia). However, a major British-American expedition against the French stronghold at Quebec failed miserably.

The New York frontier remained quiet because France and England did not want to disrupt the lucrative fur trade and because most of the Iroquois Nations had tired of war and adopted a policy of "aggressive neutrality." In 1701 the Iroquois concluded a peace treaty with France and its Indian allies. Simultaneously, they renewed their "covenant chain" of military alliances with the English governors of New York and the Algonquian tribes of New England. For the next half-century the Iroquois exploited their geographic location by trading with both the English and the French but refusing to fight for either one. The Delaware leader Teedyuscung urged an alliance with the Iroquois by showing his people a pictorial message: "You see a Square in the Middle, meaning the Lands of the Indians; and at one End, the Figure of a Man, indicating the English; and at the other End, another, meaning the French. Let us join together to defend our land against both."

Despite the military stalemate in the colonies, Britain won major territorial and commercial concessions through its victories in Europe. In the Treaty of Utrecht (1713), Britain obtained Newfoundland, Acadia, and the Hudson Bay region of northern Canada from France, as well as access to the western Indian trade (Map 3.1). From Spain, Britain acquired the strategic fortress of Gibraltar at the entrance to the Mediterranean and a thirty-year contract to supply slaves to Spanish America. These

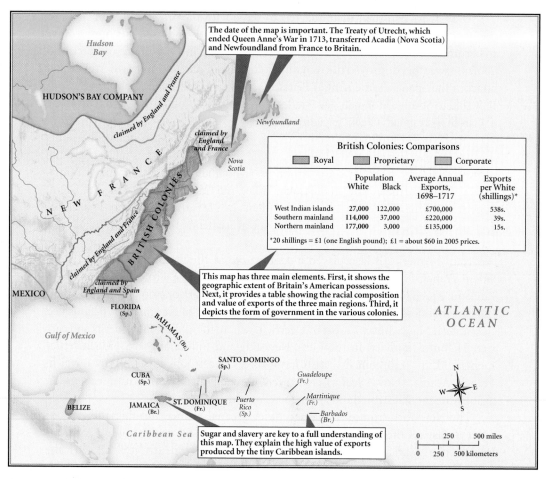

The date of the map is important. The Treaty of Utrecht, which ended Queen Anne's War in 1713, transferred Acadia (Nova Scotia) and Newfoundland from France to Britain.

| British Colonies: Comparisons | | | |
|---|---|---|---|
| Royal | Proprietary | Corporate | |

| | Population White | Black | Average Annual Exports, 1698–1717 | Exports per White (shillings)* |
|---|---|---|---|---|
| West Indian islands | 27,000 | 122,000 | £700,000 | 538s. |
| Southern mainland | 114,000 | 37,000 | £220,000 | 39s. |
| Northern mainland | 177,000 | 3,000 | £135,000 | 15s. |

*20 shillings = £1 (one English pound); £1 = about $60 in 2005 prices.

This map has three main elements. First, it shows the geographic extent of Britain's American possessions. Next, it provides a table showing the racial composition and value of exports of the three main regions. Third, it depicts the form of government in the various colonies.

Sugar and slavery are key to a full understanding of this map. They explain the high value of exports produced by the tiny Caribbean islands.

**MAP 3.1 Britain's American Empire, 1713**

Britain's possessions in the West Indies consisted of tiny islands—mere dots on the Caribbean Sea. However, in 1713 they were by far the most valuable parts of the empire. Their sugar crops brought wealth to English merchants, trade to the northern colonies, and a brutal life (and early death) to African workers.

gains solidified Britain's commercial supremacy, preserved the Protestant monarchy instituted in 1689, and brought peace to eastern North America for a generation.

# The Imperial Slave Economy

Britain's increasing interest in American affairs reflected the growth of a new agricultural and commercial order—the South Atlantic system—which produced sugar, tobacco, rice, and other subtropical products. At the center of this economic regime stood plantations worked by enslaved labor from Africa.

## The South Atlantic System

The South Atlantic system had its center in Brazil and the West Indies and had sugar as its main product. Before 1500 people in most lands had few sweeteners—mostly honey and the juices of fruits, such as apples and oranges. Then Portuguese planters developed sugar plantations in the Madeira Islands and, after 1550, in Brazil. As the production of sugarcane spread, first Europeans and then other peoples developed a craving for the potent new sweetener.

European merchants, investors, and planters ran the system. They provided the organizational skill, ships, and money needed to grow and process sugarcane, carry the refined sugar to market, and supply the plantations with European tools and equipment. To provide labor for the sugar plantations, the merchants imported slaves from Africa. Between 1550 and 1700, Portuguese and Dutch traders annually transported about 10,000 Africans across the Atlantic. Subsequently, British and French merchants took over this commerce. They developed African-run slave-catching systems that extended far into the interior of Africa and funneled captives to the slave ports of Elmina, Whydah, Loango, and Cabinda. Between 1700 and 1810 European ships carried about 7 million Africans—800,000 in the 1780s alone—to toil in the Americas (Map 3.2).

Beginning in the 1620s, Dutch merchants introduced sugar cultivation to English and French settlements in the West Indies, and a "sugar revolution" quickly transformed their economies. In the 1650s most residents of the island of Barbados were English planters and their white indentured servants, who exported tobacco and livestock hides. Fifty years later, the majority of Barbadians were enslaved Africans, and hundreds of English settlers were departing for the Carolinas. By 1700 English sugar planters were investing heavily in the Leeward Islands and Jamaica, which soon had populations that were 85 to 90 percent African. In 1750 Jamaica—the largest island in the British West Indies—had seven hundred large sugar plantations worked by more than 105,000 slaves.

Sugar was a rich man's crop because it required many laborers to plant and cut the cane and expensive equipment to process it into raw sugar and molasses. Consequently, an affluent planter-merchant elite financed the sugar industry and grew even wealthier from its produce, drawing annual profits of more than 10 percent on their investment. As the Scottish economist Adam Smith noted in his famous treatise *The Wealth of Nations* (1776), sugar was the most profitable crop in Europe and America.

In fact, the South Atlantic system brought wealth to the entire European economy. To take England as an example, the owners of most British West Indian plantations lived as absentees in England and spent their profits there. Moreover, the Navigation Acts required that sugar produced in the British West Indies be sold to British consumers or exported by British merchants to continental markets. By 1750 British reshipments of sugar and tobacco from America accounted for half of all British exports. Substantial profits also flowed into Britain from the

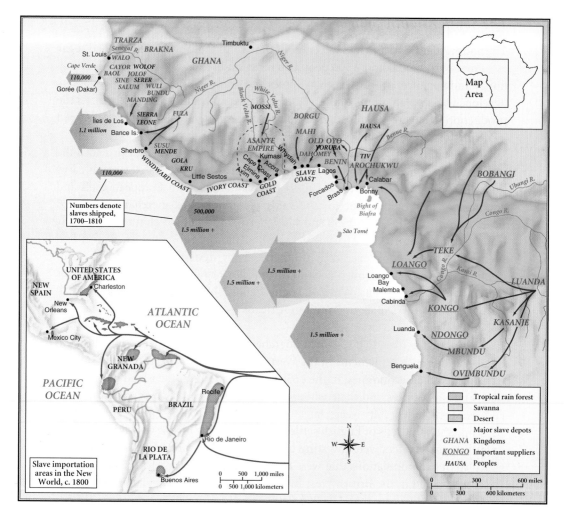

**MAP 3.2 Africa and the Atlantic Slave Trade, 1700–1810**

The tropical rain forest region of West Africa was home to scores of peoples and dozens of kingdoms. Some kingdoms, such as Dahomey, became aggressive slavers, taking tens of thousands of war captives and funneling them to the seacoast, where they were sold to European traders. About 15 percent of the Africans died during the grueling Middle Passage, the transatlantic voyage between Africa and the Americas. Most of the survivors labored on sugar plantations in Brazil and the British and French West Indies.

FOR MORE HELP ANALYZING THIS MAP, see the Online Study Guide at **bedfordstmartins.com/henrettaconcise**.

slave trade because the Royal African Company and other English traders sold male slaves in the West Indies for three to five times what they paid for them in Africa. In addition, the trade in American sugar and tobacco stimulated British manufacturing. To transport slaves (and machinery and settlers) to America, English shipyards built hundreds of vessels. Thousands of English and Scottish

**Shipping Sugar from Antigua**

Sugar was a valuable commodity and also a heavy one. Few sugar plantations had wharves that could accommodate large vessels. Consequently, slaves had to maneuver the heavy barrels of sugar onto small boats and row them to the oceangoing ships, which used winches and pulleys to lift them on board. National Maritime Museum, London.

men and women worked in trade-related industries: building port facilities and warehouses, refining sugar and tobacco, distilling rum from molasses (a by-product of sugar), and manufacturing textiles and iron products for the growing markets in Africa and America. Finally, commercial expansion provided Britain with a supply of experienced sailors and thus helped the Royal Navy become the most powerful fleet in Europe.

As the South Atlantic system enhanced prosperity in Europe, it brought economic decline, political change, and human tragedy to West Africa. Between 1550 and 1870 the Atlantic slave trade uprooted about 15 million Africans, diminishing the population and wealth of much of the continent. Moreover, the value of the guns, iron, rum, cloth, and other European products that entered the African economy in exchange for slaves amounted only to about one-tenth (in the 1680s) to one-third (by the 1780s) the value of the goods those slaves subsequently produced in America.

Equally important, the slave trade changed the nature of West African society by promoting centralized states and military conquest. In 1739 an observer noted that "whenever the King of Barsally wants Goods or Brandy . . . the King goes and ransacks some of his enemies' towns, seizing the people and selling them." War and slaving became a way of life in Dahomey, where the royal house made the sale of slaves a state monopoly and used the resulting access to European guns to create a military despotism. Dahomey's army, which included a contingent of 5,000 women, systematically raided the interior for captives and exported thousands of slaves each year. The Asante kings also used the firearms and wealth acquired through the Atlantic trade to create a bureaucratic empire of 3 million to 5 million people. Yet slaving remained a choice for Africans, not a necessity. The old and still powerful kingdom of Benin, famous for its cast bronzes and carved ivory, prohibited the export of slaves for over a century.

The trade in humans produced untold misery—bringing early death to hundreds of thousands of Africans and lifelong slavery to millions more. In many African societies class divisions hardened as people of noble birth enslaved and sold those of lesser status. Gender relations shifted as well. Men constituted two-thirds of the slaves sent across the Atlantic both because European planters paid more for "men and stout men boys," "none to exceed the years of 25 or under 10," and because African traders directed women captives into local slave markets for sale as agricultural workers and house servants. The resulting imbalance between the sexes in Africa allowed some men to take several wives, changing the nature of marriage. Moreover, the Atlantic trade prompted harsher forms of slavery in Africa and eroded the dignity of human life there as well as in the Western Hemisphere.

Those Africans sold into the heart of the South Atlantic system had the bleakest fate. Torn from their village homes, captives were marched in chains to coastal ports such as Elmina on the Gold Coast. From there they made the perilous **Middle Passage** to the New World in hideously overcrowded ships. The captives had little to eat and drink, and the stench of excrement was nearly unbearable. Some slaves jumped overboard, choosing to drown rather than endure more suffering (see Voices from Abroad, "The Brutal 'Middle Passage,'" p. 81). Nearly a million Africans (15 percent of the 8 million who crossed the Atlantic between 1700 and 1810) died on the journey, mostly from dysentery, smallpox, or scurvy.

For the survivors of the Middle Passage, things only got worse. Life on the sugar plantations of northwest Brazil and the West Indies was a lesson in relentless exploitation and systematic violence. Enslaved Africans labored for ten hours a day under a hot semitropical sun, slept in flimsy huts, lived on a starchy diet of corn, yams, and dried fish, and were subject to brutal discipline. With sugar prices high and the cost of slaves low, many planters worked slaves to death and then imported more. Between 1708 and 1735, British planters imported about 85,000 Africans into Barbados, but the island's black population increased by only 4,000 (from 42,000 to 46,000) during those three decades.

### Slavery in the Chesapeake and South Carolina

In the aftermath of Bacon's Rebellion, planters in Virginia and Maryland took advantage of the increased British trade in slaves to import thousands of Africans (see Chapter 2). In a "tobacco revolution," they created a new plantation regime based

# The Brutal "Middle Passage"

## OLAUDAH EQUIANO

*Olaudah Equiano, known also as Gustavus Vassa, claimed to have been born in the an-
cient kingdom of Benin (in present-day southern Nigeria). However, two scholars, writing independently, have recently argued that Equiano was actually born into slavery in
America and drew upon conversations with African-born slaves to create a fictitious history of
an idyllic childhood, kidnapping and enslavement at the age of eleven, and a traumatic Middle
Passage across the Atlantic. Whatever the validity of their arguments, Equiano apparently endured plantation slavery in Barbados and Virginia, where he was purchased by an English sea
captain. Buying his freedom in 1766, Equiano settled in London, became an antislavery activist, and, in 1789, published the memoir containing this selection.*

My father, besides many slaves, had a numerous family of which seven lived to grow up,
including myself and a sister who was the only daughter. . . . I was trained up from my earliest years in the art of war, my daily exercise was shooting and throwing javelins, and my
mother adorned me with emblems after the manner of our greatest warriors. One day,
when all our people were gone out to their works as usual and only I and my dear sister
were left to mind the house, two men and a woman got over our walls, and in a moment
seized us both, and without giving us time to cry out or make resistance they stopped our
mouths and ran off with us into the nearest wood. . . .

At length, after many days' travelling, during which I had often changed masters, I got
into the hands of a chieftain in a very pleasant country. This man had two wives and some
children, and they all used me extremely well and did all they could to comfort me, particularly the first wife, who was something like my mother. . . . I was again sold and carried
through a number of places till . . . at the end of six or seven months after I had been kid-
napped I arrived at the sea coast.

The first object which saluted my eyes when I arrived on the coast was the sea, and a slave
ship which was then riding at anchor and waiting for its cargo. I now saw myself deprived
of all chance of returning to my native country . . . ; and I even wished for my former slavery in preference to my present situation, which was filled with horrors of every kind. . . . I
was soon put down under the decks, and there I received such a salutation in my nostrils as
I had never experienced in my life; so that with the loathsomeness of the stench and crying
together, I became so sick and low that I was not able to eat, nor had I the least desire to taste
any thing. I now wished for the last friend, death, to relieve me; but soon, to my grief, two
of the white men offered me eatables, and on my refusing to eat, one of them held me fast
by the hands and laid me across I think the windlass, and tied my feet while the other flogged
me severely. . . . One day, when we had a smooth sea and moderate wind, two of my wearied
countrymen who were chained together (I was near them at the time), preferring death to
such a life of misery, somehow made it through the nettings and jumped into the sea.

At last we came in sight of the island of Barbados; the white people got some old slaves
from the land to pacify us. They told us we were not to be eaten but to work, and were soon
to go on land where we should see many of our country people. This report eased us much;
and sure enough soon after we were landed there came to us Africans of all languages.

SOURCE: *The Interesting Narrative of the Life of Olaudah Equiano, or Gustavus Vassa, the African, Written
by Himself* (London, 1789), 15, 22–23, 28–29.

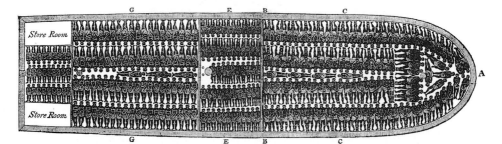

**Two Views of the Middle Passage**

As the slave trade boomed during the eighteenth century, ship designers packed in more and more human cargo, treating enslaved Africans with no more respect than hogsheads of sugar or tobacco. By contrast, a watercolor of 1846, painted by a ship's officer on a voyage to Brazil, captures the humanity and dignity of the enslaved Africans.

Peabody & Essex Museum / Royal Albert Memorial Museum, Exeter, England / Bridgeman Art Library.

on African slavery rather than English indentured servitude. By 1720 Africans numbered 20 percent of the Chesapeake population, and slavery had become a defining principle of the social order, not just one of several forms of bound labor. Equally important, slavery was now defined in racial terms. A Virginia law of 1692 prohibited sexual intercourse between the English and Africans, and in 1705 another statute defined virtually all resident Africans as slaves: "All servants imported or brought into this country by sea or land who were not Christians in their native country shall be accounted and be slaves."

Living conditions for enslaved Africans in Maryland and Virginia were much less severe than in the West Indies, and they lived relatively long lives. In terms of labor, tobacco was not as physically demanding a crop as sugar. Slaves planted the young tobacco seedlings in the spring, hoed and weeded the crop throughout the summer, and in the fall picked and hung up the leaves to cure over the winter. Moreover, epidemic diseases did not spread easily in the Chesapeake because the plantation quarters were small and dispersed. Also, because tobacco profits were low, planters could not afford to buy new slaves and therefore treated those they had less harshly than West Indian planters did.

Indeed, some tobacco planters increased their workforce through reproduction by purchasing female slaves and encouraging large families. In 1720 women made up about a third of the African population of Maryland, and the black population had begun to increase naturally. One absentee owner instructed his plantation agent "to be kind and indulgent to the breeding wenches, and not to force them when with child upon any service or hardship that will be injurious to them." And, he added, "the children are to be well looked after." By midcentury slaves constituted over 30 percent of the Chesapeake population, and over three-quarters of them were American born.

Slaves in South Carolina labored under much more oppressive conditions. The colony grew slowly until 1700, when Africans from rice-growing societies, who knew how to plant and process that nutritious grain, turned it into a profitable export. To expand production, white planters imported tens of thousands of slaves—and a "rice revolution" changed the face of the colony. By 1720 a majority of South Carolinians were of African birth or descent, and slaves constituted 80 percent of the population in rice-growing areas. Growing rice in inland swamp areas was dirty and dangerous work. Slaves planted, weeded, and harvested the crop in ankle-deep mud, amidst pools of putrid water. Mosquitoes were legion and transmitted epidemic diseases to densely populated plantations, where they took hundreds of African lives. Other slaves died from exhaustion as they moved tons of dirt to build irrigation works. "The labour required for [growing rice] is only fit for slaves," a Scottish traveler remarked, "and I think the hardest work I have seen them engaged in." As in the West Indies, there were many deaths and few births, and the importation of new slaves constantly "re-Africanized" South Carolina's black population.

**"Virginian Luxuries"**

This painting by an unknown artist (c. 1810) depicts the exploitation inherent in a slave society. On the right, an owner chastises a male slave by beating him with a cane; on the left, ignoring the cultural and legal rules prohibiting such affairs, a white master prepares to engage in sex with his black mistress. Abby Aldrich Rockefeller Folk Art Collection, Colonial Williamsburg Foundation.

## The Emergence of an African American Community

Slaves came from many regions of West Africa. South Carolina slave owners preferred laborers from the Gold Coast and Gambia, who had a reputation as hardworking farmers. However, as African sources of slaves shifted southward after 1730, more than 30 percent of the colony's workforce came from the Congo and Angola. Some white planters welcomed such ethnic diversity as a deterrent to slave revolts. "The safety of the Plantations," declared a widely read English pamphlet, "depends upon having Negroes from all parts of Guiny, who do not understand each other's languages and Customs and cannot agree to Rebel."

In fact, slaves initially did not think of themselves as "Africans" or "blacks" but as members of a specific family, clan, or people — Mende, Hausa, Ibo, Yoruba — and they associated mostly with those who shared their language. Gradually, however, enslaved peoples transcended these cultural barriers. In the West Indies and the Carolina lowlands, the largely African-born population created new languages, such as the Gullah dialect, that combined English and African words in an African grammatical structure. "They have a language peculiar to themselves," a missionary reported, "a wild confused medley of Negro and corrupt English, which makes them very unintelligible except to those who have conversed with them for many years." In the Chesapeake, where there were more American-born slaves, most people of African descent gradually gave up their native tongues. In the 1760s a European visitor to Virginia reported with surprise that "all the blacks spoke very good English."

A common language, whether Gullah or English, was a prerequisite for the creation of an African American community. A more equal sex ratio, which encouraged marriage and stable families, was another. In South Carolina a high death rate undermined ties of family and kinship, but after 1725 Chesapeake-area blacks created strong nuclear families and extended kin relationships. For example, all but 30 of the 128 slaves on one of Charles Carroll's estates in Maryland were members of two extended families. These "African Americans" had gradually developed a culture of their own, passing on family names, traditions, and knowledge to the next generation. As one observer suggested, blacks had created a separate society, "a Nation within a Nation."

As enslaved blacks forged a new identity, they integrated some African practices into their new American existence. Many Africans arrived in the colonies with ritual scars that white planters called "country markings" but these signs of tribal identity fell into disuse because slaves no longer lived in ethnic-based communities. However, their African heritage took tangible form in wood carvings inspired by traditional motifs, the large wooden mortars and pestles that slaves used to hull rice, and the design of dwellings, which often had rooms arranged from front to back in a distinctive "I" pattern (not side by side, as was common in English houses). African values also persisted, as some slaves retained Muslim religious beliefs and many more relied on the spiritual powers of conjurers, who knew the ways of African gods. As an English missionary reported from Georgia in the 1750s, many slaves clung to "the old Superstition of a false Religion." Other slaves adopted Protestant Christianity but reshaped its doctrines, ethics, and rituals to fit their needs.

### Resistance and Accommodation

There were drastic limits on African American creativity because slaves were denied education, accumulated few material goods, and had little leisure time. A well-traveled European who visited a slave hut in Virginia in the late eighteenth century found it "more miserable than the most miserable of the cottages of our peasants. The husband and wife sleep on a mean pallet, the children on the ground; a very bad fireplace, some utensils for cooking. . . . They work all week, not having a single day for themselves except for holidays."

Slaves resisted this rigorous work routine at their peril. To punish slaves who refused to work or ran away, planters resorted to the lash and the amputation of fingers, toes, and ears. Declaring the chronic runaway Ballazore an "incorrigeble rogue," a Virginia planter ordered all his toes cut off: "nothing less than dismembering will reclaim him." Thomas Jefferson, who witnessed such cruelty on his father's Virginia plantation, noted that each generation of whites was "nursed, educated, and daily exercised in tyranny," for the relationship "between master and slave is a perpetual exercise of the most unremitting despotism on the one part, and degrading submission on the other."

The extent of white violence depended on the size and density of the slave population. Because their numbers were small, blacks in rural areas of the northern colonies endured low status but little violence. Conversely, assertive slaves on the predominantly African sugar plantations in the West Indies routinely suffered branding with hot irons. In the South Carolina rice districts, where Africans outnumbered Europeans eight to one, planters prohibited slaves from leaving the plantation without special passes and forced their poor white neighbors to patrol the countryside.

Slaves dealt with their plight in a variety of ways. Some newly arrived Africans fled to the frontier, where they tried to reestablish traditional villages or married into Indian tribes. Blacks who were fluent in English fled to towns, where they tried to pass as free. But most African Americans worked out their destinies as enslaved agricultural laborers and bargained continually with their masters over the terms of their bondage. Some blacks undertook extra work to obtain better food and clothes; others seized a small privilege and dared the master to revoke it. Thus, Sundays gradually became a day free of labor—a right rather than a privilege. When bargaining failed, slaves protested silently by working slowly or stealing. Other blacks, provoked beyond endurance, attacked their owners or overseers, although such assaults were punishable by mutilation or death. A few blacks even plotted rebellion, despite white superiority in guns and, usually, in numbers as well.

Predictably, South Carolina witnessed the largest slave uprising—the Stono Rebellion of 1739. The governor of the neighboring Spanish (and Catholic) colony of Florida instigated the revolt by promising freedom to slaves who ran away from their English owners. By February 1739 at least sixty-nine slaves had escaped to St. Augustine, and rumors circulated "that a Conspiracy was formed by Negroes in Carolina to rise and make their way out of the province." When war between England and Spain broke out in September, seventy-five Africans—some of them Portuguese-speaking Catholics from the African kingdom of Kongo—rose in revolt and killed a number of whites near the Stono River. Displaying their skills as former soldiers in the war-torn Kongo, the rebels took up arms and marched south toward Catholic Florida "with Colours displayed and two Drums beating." Unrest swept the countryside, but the white militia killed many of the Stono rebels and prevented a general uprising. Frightened whites imported fewer new slaves and tightened plantation discipline.

## The Southern Gentry

As the southern colonies became full-fledged slave societies, the character of life changed for whites as well as for blacks. After 1675 most colonists in the Chesapeake region no longer lived in the disease-ridden swampy lowlands and consequently lived longer and formed stable families. Similarly, white rice planters in South Carolina maintained their health by moving to Charleston during the hot, mosquito-ridden summer months. As longevity increased, men reassumed their customary control of family property. When death rates had been high and took the lives of kin, husbands gave their widows large inheritances and named them as the executors of their estates and the legal guardians of their children. After 1700 most wealthy planters had living male kin and named them as executors and guardians. They also favored their male children by limiting the widow's portion of the estate to the traditional one-third share during her lifetime.

The reappearance of **patriarchy** within the family mirrored broader social developments. A planter and merchant elite used its financial power to control yeomen families and white tenant farmers and resorted to brute power to exploit the labor of enslaved blacks, the American equivalent of the oppressed peasants and serfs of Europe. Wealthy planters used Africans to grow food as well as tobacco; build houses, wagons, and tobacco casks; and make shoes and clothes. By making their plantations self-sufficient, the Chesapeake elite survived the depressed tobacco market between 1660 and 1720. Small-scale planters who used family labor to grow tobacco fared less well and fell into debt.

To prevent another rebellion like Bacon's uprising, the Chesapeake gentry addressed the concerns of middling and poor whites. With some success, they urged smallholders to seek wealth by investing in slaves; by 1770, 60 percent of the English families in the Chesapeake owned at least one slave. In addition, the gentry gradually reduced the taxes paid by poorer whites; in Virginia the annual poll tax fell from 45 pounds of tobacco in 1675 to 5 pounds in 1750. The political elite also allowed poor yeomen and some tenants to vote. The strategy of the leading families—the Carters, Lees, Randolphs, Robinsons—was to curry favor with these voters by bribing them with rum, money, and the promise of minor offices in county governments. In return, they expected yeomen and tenants to elect them to office and defer to their authority. This "horse trading" solidified the social position of the planter elite, which used its control of the House of Burgesses to undermine the power of the royal governor to dispense patronage and land grants. Hundreds of yeomen farmers benefited as well, tasting political power and garnering substantial fees and salaries as deputy sheriffs, road surveyors, estate appraisers, and grand jurymen.

Even as wealthy Chesapeake gentlemen created alliances with yeomen farmers, they consciously set themselves apart from their less affluent neighbors. Until the 1720s the ranks of the gentry were filled with boisterous, aggressive men who enjoyed the amusements of common folk—from hunting, hard drinking, and gambling on horse races to sharing tales of their manly prowess in seducing female servants and slaves. As time passed, however, affluent Chesapeake landholders took on the trappings of wealth and modeled themselves on the English aristocracy. Beginning in the 1720s they replaced their modest wooden houses with mansions of brick and mortar. The plantation house of Robert "King" Carter was over seventy-five feet long, forty-four feet wide, and forty feet high. Genteel planters entertained their neighbors in lavish style and sent their sons to London to be educated as lawyers and gentlemen. Most of the young men returned to America, married well-to-do heiresses, and followed in their fathers' footsteps, managing plantations, socializing with fellow gentry, and running the political system.

Wealthy Chesapeake and South Carolina women likewise emulated the refined ways of the English elite. They read English newspapers and fashionable magazines, wore English clothes, and dined in the English fashion, with an elaborate afternoon tea. To improve their daughters' marriage prospects, they hired English tutors to teach them etiquette. Once married, affluent gentry women deferred to their husbands' authority, reared pious children, and maintained elaborate social networks—gradually creating the new ideal of the southern genteel woman. Using the profits of the South Atlantic system, the planter elite formed an increasingly well-educated, refined, and stable ruling class.

### The Northern Maritime Economy

The South Atlantic system had a broad geographic reach. As early as the 1640s, New England farmers provided the sugar islands with bread, lumber, fish, and meat. As a West Indian explained, planters in the islands "had rather buy food at very dear rates than produce it by labour, so infinite is the profit of sugar works." By 1700 the economies of the West Indies and New England were tightly interwoven. Soon farmers and merchants in New York, New Jersey, and Pennsylvania were also shipping wheat, corn, and bread to the sugar islands.

The South Atlantic system tied together the entire British empire. In return for the sugar they sent to England, West Indian planters received bills of exchange (credit slips) from London merchants. The planters used those bills to buy slaves from Africa and to reimburse North American farmers and merchants for their provisions and shipping services. The American farmers and merchants then exchanged the bills for British manufactures, primarily textiles and iron goods (Map 3.3).

The West Indian trade created the first American merchant fortunes and the first urban industries. Merchants in Boston, Newport, Providence, Philadelphia, and New York invested their profits in new ships and in factories that refined raw sugar into finished loaves (which previously had been imported from England). They also distilled West Indian molasses into rum; by the 1740s Boston distillers were exporting half a million gallons of rum annually. In addition, merchants in smaller ports, such as Salem and Marblehead, built a major fishing industry by selling salted mackerel and cod to the sugar islands and to southern Europe.

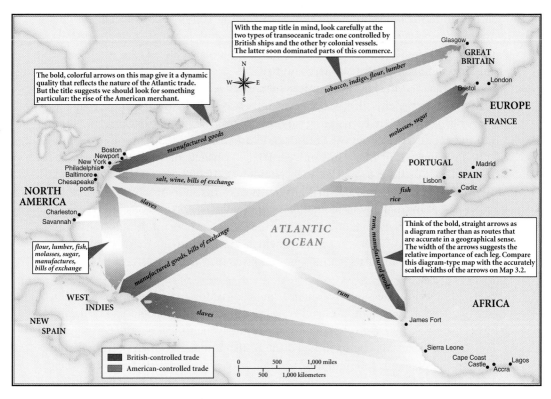

**MAP 3.3 The Rise of the American Merchant, 1750**

In accordance with mercantilist doctrine, British merchant houses controlled most of the transatlantic trade in manufactures, sugar, tobacco, and slaves. However, merchants in Boston, New York, and Philadelphia dominated trade between the mainland and the West Indies. In addition, Newport traders played a small role in the slave trade from Africa, while Boston and Charleston merchants grew rich by carrying fish and rice to southern Europe.

Southern merchants transformed Baltimore into a major port by developing a bustling trade in wheat, while Charleston traders exported deerskins, indigo, and rice to European markets.

The expansion of Atlantic commerce fueled the rapid growth of American port cities and coastal towns. Seeking jobs and excitement, British and German migrants and young people from the countryside—servant girls, male laborers and apprentice artisans—flocked to urban areas. By 1750 Newport, Rhode Island, and Charleston had nearly 10,000 residents apiece, Boston had 15,000, and New York had almost 18,000. The largest port was Philadelphia, whose population by 1776 reached 30,000, the size of a large European provincial city. Smaller coastal towns emerged as centers of the shipbuilding and lumber industries. Seventy sawmills dotted the Piscataqua River in New Hampshire, providing low-cost wood for homes, warehouses, and especially shipbuilding. Taking advantage of the Navigation Acts, which allowed colonists to build and own trading vessels, scores of shipwrights turned out oceangoing vessels, while hundreds of other artisans made ropes, sails, and metal fittings for the new fleet. By the 1770s colonial-built ships made up about one-third of the entire British merchant fleet.

The impact of the South Atlantic system extended far into the interior. A small fleet of trading vessels sailed back and forth between Philadelphia and the villages along the Delaware Bay, exchanging cargoes of European goods for barrels of flour and wheat for export to the West Indies and Europe. By the 1750s hundreds of professional teamsters in Maryland moved 370,000 bushels of wheat and corn and 16,000 barrels of flour to market each year—over 10,000 wagon trips. To service this traffic, entrepreneurs and artisans set up taverns, horse stables, and barrel-making shops in small towns along the wagon roads. The prosperous interior town of Lancaster, Pennsylvania, boasted more than 200 German and English artisans. The South Atlantic system not only provided markets for northern farmers but also opportunities for artisans in country towns and merchants and laborers in seaport cities.

Wealthy landowners and prosperous merchants dominated seaport society. In 1750 about forty merchants controlled over 50 percent of Philadelphia's trade and had taxable assets averaging £10,000, a huge sum at the time. Like the Chesapeake gentry, these urban merchants imitated the British upper classes, importing design books from England and building Georgian-style mansions to showcase their wealth. Their wives created a genteel culture by decorating their houses with fine furniture and entertaining guests at elegant dinners.

Artisan and shopkeeper families formed the middle ranks of seaport society and numbered nearly half the population. Innkeepers, butchers, seamstresses, shoemakers, weavers, bakers, carpenters, masons, and dozens of other specialists formed mutual self-help societies and worked to gain a competency—an income sufficient to maintain their families in modest comfort and dignity. Wives and husbands often worked as a team, teaching the "mysteries of the craft" to their children. Some artisans aspired to wealth and status, an entrepreneurial ethic that prompted them to hire apprentices and expand production. However, most craft workers were not well-to-do, and many of them were quite poor. In his entire lifetime a tailor was lucky to accumulate £30 worth of property—far less than the £2,000 owned at death by an ordinary merchant or the £300 listed in the **probate inventory** of a successful blacksmith.

Laboring men and women formed the lowest ranks of urban society. Merchants needed hundreds of dockworkers to unload manufactured goods and molasses from inbound ships and reload them with barrels of wheat, fish, and rice. Sometimes they filled these demanding jobs with black slaves, who numbered 10 percent of the workforce in Philadelphia and New York City; otherwise, they hired unskilled men who worked for wages. Poor women—whether single, married, or widowed—eked out a living by washing clothes, spinning wool, or working as servants or prostitutes. To make ends meet, most laboring families sent their children out to work at an early age. Indispensable to the economy yet without property, urban laborers rented rooms in crowded tenements in back alleys. In good times, their jobs bought security for their families or as much cheap New England rum as they could drink.

Periods of stagnant commerce threatened merchants with bankruptcy and artisans with irregular work. For laborers and seamen, whose household budgets left no margin for sickness or unemployment, depressed trade meant hunger, dependence on charity from the overseers of the poor, and—for the most desperate—a life of petty thievery. Involvement in the sugar- and slave-based South Atlantic system between 1660 and 1750 brought economic uncertainty as well as jobs and opportunities to farmers and workers in the northern colonies.

# The New Politics of Empire, 1713–1750

The success of the South Atlantic system of production and trade changed the politics of empire. British ministers, pleased with the prosperous commerce in staple crops, ruled the colonies with a gentle hand. The colonists took this opportunity to strengthen their political institutions and, eventually, to challenge the rules of the mercantilist system.

## The Rise of Colonial Assemblies

Before 1689 the authority of the representative assemblies in most colonies was weak. Political power rested in the hands of proprietors, royal governors, and authoritarian elites and reflected the traditional view that "Authority should Descend from Kings and Fathers to Sons and Servants," as a royal-minded political philosopher put it. In the Glorious Revolution of 1688 the political faction known as the Whigs challenged that hierarchical outlook in England and secured a constitutional monarchy that limited the authority of the crown. English Whigs did not advocate democracy but wanted substantial property owners in the House of Commons to have political power, especially over the levying of taxes. When Whig politicians forced King William and Queen Mary to accept a Declaration of Rights in 1689, they strengthened the powers of the Commons at the expense of the crown.

American representative assemblies also wished to limit the powers of crown officials. In Massachusetts during the 1720s the assembly repeatedly rebuffed the king's instructions to provide the royal governor with a permanent salary. Legislatures in North Carolina, New Jersey, and Pennsylvania likewise declined for several years to pay a salary to their governors. Through such tactics, the colonial legislatures gradually won control over taxation and local appointments, which angered imperial bureaucrats and absentee proprietors. "The people in power in America," complained the proprietor William Penn during a struggle with the Pennsylvania assembly, "think nothing taller than themselves but the Trees."

The rising power of the colonial assemblies created an elitist rather than a democratic political system. Although most property-owning white men had the right to vote after 1700, only men of considerable wealth and status stood for election. In Virginia in the 1750s seven members of the influential slave-owning Lee family sat in the House of Burgesses and, along with other powerful families, dominated its major committees. In New England descendants of the original Puritans intermarried and formed a core of political leaders. "Go into every village in New England," John Adams noted in 1765, "and you will find that the office of justice of the peace, and even the place of representative, have generally descended from generation to generation, in three or four families at most."

However, neither elitist assemblies nor wealthy property owners could impose unpopular edicts on the people. The crowd actions that overthrew the Dominion of New England in 1689 were a regular part of political and social life in America. In New York mobs closed houses of prostitution, while in Salem, Massachusetts, they ran people with infectious diseases out of town. In Boston in 1710 angry crowds prevented merchants from exporting scarce grain, and in New Jersey in the 1730s and 1740s they battled with proprietors who were forcing tenants from disputed lands. When Boston officials restricted the sale of farm produce to a single public market, a crowd destroyed the building and defied the authorities to arrest them. "If you touch One you shall touch All," an anonymous letter warned the sheriff, "and we will show you a Hundred Men where you can show one" (see American Voices, "A 'Leveling' Spirit in the Colonies," p. 93). Such expressions of popular power, combined with the growing authority of the assemblies, undermined the old hierarchical system. By the 1750s colonial political institutions were broadly responsive to popular pressure and increasingly immune from British control.

## Salutary Neglect

British colonial policy during the reigns of George I (r. 1714–1727) and George II (r. 1727–1760) contributed significantly to the rise of American self-government. Royal bureaucrats relaxed their supervision of internal colonial affairs, focusing instead on defense and trade. Two generations later the British political philosopher Edmund Burke would praise this strategy as "**salutary** [healthy] **neglect**."

Salutary neglect was a by-product of the political system developed by Sir Robert Walpole, the leader of the British Whigs in the House of Commons between 1720 and 1742. By strategically dispensing appointments and pensions in the name of the king, Walpole won parliamentary support for his policies. However, Walpole's use of patronage weakened the imperial system because it filled the Board of Trade and the royal governorships with men of little talent. When Governor Gabriel Johnson arrived in North Carolina in the 1730s, he vowed to curb the powers of the assembly and "make a mighty change in the face of affairs." Quickly discouraged by the lack of support from the Board of Trade, Johnson renounced

**AMERICAN VOICES**

~

# A "Leveling" Spirit in the Colonies

### GOVERNOR JOSEPH DUDLEY AND JOHN WINCHESTER

*I*n *1705 legal authorities in Massachusetts prosecuted two woodcutters, John Winchester and Thomas Trowbridge, for insubordination because they defied orders from the royal governor, Joseph Dudley. The following extracts from the testimony during their trial illustrates both the disdain of the upper classes for ordinary folk and popular resistance to the arbitrary exercise of authority.*

Account of Governor Joseph Dudley:
The Charet [coach] wherein the Governour was had three sitters and their Servants . . . drawn by four horses, one very unruly, & was attended only at that instant by Mr. William Dudley, the Governour's son.

When the Governour saw the two carts approaching he directed his son to bid them to give him the way . . . Who accordingly did Ride up & told them the Govr was there, & they must give way. Immediately upon it the second Carter came up to ye first . . . & one of them says aloud he would not go out the way for the Governour whereupon the Govr came out of the Charet and told Winchester he must give way to the Charet. Winchester answered boldly . . . I am as good flesh & blood as you. I will not give way. You may go out the way, & came towards the Governour. Whereupon the Governour drew his sword to secure himself & command the Road & went forward . . . and again commanded them to give way. Winchester answered that he was a Christian & would not give way & as the Governour came toward him he advanced & at length laid hold of the Govr & broke the sword in his hands. . . . And this is averred upon the honour of the Governour. . . .

Then came up John Winchester . . . who gives the following account.
. . . I left my cart and . . . asked Mr. William Dudley why he was so rash. He replied this dog [Trowbridge] won't turn out the way for the Governour. . . . I then told his excellency, if he would have patience a minute or two I would clear that way for him. . . . The Governour followed me with his drawn sword and said run the dogs through and with his naked sword stabbed me in the back. I facing about, he struck me on the head . . . giving me there a bloody wound. . . . I caught hold of his sword and broke it.

SOURCE: David Brion Davis and Steven Mintz, *The Boisterous Sea of Liberty: A Documentary History of America from Discovery through the Civil War* (New York: Oxford University Press, 1998), 105–6.

reform and decided "to do nothing which can be reasonably blamed, and leave the rest to time, and a new set of inhabitants."

Walpole's tactics also weakened the empire by undermining the integrity of the political system. **Radical Whigs** protested that Walpole had betrayed the Glorious Revolution by using patronage and bribery to create a strong Court Party. A Country

**Sir Robert Walpole, the King's Minister**

All eyes are on Walpole (left) as he offers advice to the Speaker of the House of Commons. A brilliant politician, Walpole used patronage to command a majority in the Commons and to win the support of George I and George II—the German-speaking monarchs from the duchy of Hanover. Walpole's personal motto, "Let sleeping dogs lie," helps to explain his colonial policy of salutary neglect.

© National Trust Photographic Library / John Hammond.

Party of landed gentlemen likewise warned that Walpole's policies of high taxes and a bloated royal bureaucracy threatened British liberties. Politically minded colonists adopted these arguments and complained that royal governors likewise abused their patronage powers. To preserve American liberty, they set about enhancing the powers of the representative assemblies, unintentionally laying the foundation for the American independence movement.

## Protecting the Mercantile System

Apart from patronage, Walpole's American policy had as its prime goal the protection of British commercial interests from military threats from the Spanish and French colonies. Initially, Walpole pursued a cautious foreign policy to allow Britain to recover from the generation of war (1689–1713) against Louis XIV of France. However, in 1732 he provided a parliamentary subsidy for the new colony of Georgia, which had been founded by its reform-minded trustees as a refuge for Britain's poor. Envisioning a society of independent family farmers, the trustees limited most land grants to 500 acres and initially outlawed slavery.

Walpole had little interest in social reform and subsidized Georgia to protect the valuable rice colony of South Carolina. Britain's expansion into Georgia, where

Spanish Franciscans had Indian missions, outraged Spanish officials. They were also angry because British merchants were taking over the trade in slaves and manufactured goods to Spain's American colonies. To resist Britain's commercial and geographic expansion, in 1739 Spanish naval forces stepped up their seizure of illegal traders—and mutilated the English sea captain, Robert Jenkins.

Yielding to Parliamentary pressure, Walpole launched the so-called "War of Jenkins' Ear," a predatory, but largely unsuccessful, attack against Spain's American empire. In 1740 British regulars failed to capture St. Augustine because South Carolina whites—still shaken by the Stono revolt—refused to commit militia units to the expedition. A year later a major British and American assault on the prosperous Spanish seaport of Cartagena (in present-day Colombia) likewise failed. Instead of enriching themselves with Spanish booty, hundreds of troops from the mainland colonies died of tropical diseases.

The War of Jenkins' Ear quickly became part of a general European conflict, the War of the Austrian Succession (1740–1749). Massive French armies battled British-subsidized German forces in Europe, and French naval forces roamed the West Indies, vainly trying to conquer a British sugar island. There was little fighting in North America until 1745, when 3,000 New England militiamen, supported by a British naval squadron, captured the powerful French naval fortress of Louisbourg at the entrance to the St. Lawrence River. To the dismay of New England Puritans, who feared invasion from Catholic Quebec, the Treaty of Aix-la-Chapelle (1748) returned Louisbourg to France. The treaty ensured British control over Georgia and reaffirmed its military superiority over Spain, but the New England colonists now understood that England would act in its own interests, not theirs.

### The American Economic Challenge

During these years the Walpole ministry confronted an unexpected American threat to Britain's economic expansion. According to the mercantilist Navigation Acts, the colonies were to produce staple crops and to consume British manufactured goods. To enforce the manufacturing monopoly enjoyed by British firms, Parliament passed a series of acts prohibiting Americans from selling colonial-made textiles (1699), hats (1732), and iron products such as plows, axes, and skillets (1750). As staple exports from the mainland settlements grew by 400 percent between 1700 and 1750, Americans purchased increasing amounts of British textiles and iron goods.

However, the Navigation Acts had a major loophole because they allowed Americans to own ships and transport goods. Colonial merchants exploited those provisions to control 95 percent of the commerce between the mainland and the West Indies and 75 percent of the transatlantic trade in manufactures. Quite unintentionally, the mercantilist system had created a dynamic community of colonial merchants.

Moreover, by the 1720s the British sugar islands could not absorb all the flour, fish, and meat produced by the rapidly growing mainland settlements. Ignoring Britain's intense rivalry with France, colonial merchants sold this produce in the French West Indies. These supplies helped French planters produce low-cost sugar and outsell Britain in the European sugar market. When American rum distillers began to buy cheap molasses from the French islands, British planters petitioned Parliament for help. The resulting Molasses Act of 1733 permitted the mainland colonies to export fish and farm products to the French islands but—to give a price advantage to British molasses—placed a high tariff on imports of French molasses. American merchants and public officials protested that the act would cut farm exports, cripple the distilling industry, and make it more difficult for colonists to purchase British goods. When Parliament ignored their petitions, American merchants smuggled in French molasses by bribing customs officials. Luckily for the Americans, sugar prices rose sharply in the late 1730s and enriched planters in the British West Indies; so the act was not rigorously enforced.

The lack of adequate currency in the colonies led to another confrontation. American merchants sent most of the gold and silver coins and **bills of exchange** they earned in the West Indian trade to Britain to pay for manufactured goods and thereby drained the domestic supply of money. To remedy this problem, ten colonial assemblies established land banks that lent paper money to farmers, who used their land as collateral for the loans. Farmers used the paper money to buy tools or livestock or to pay their creditors, thereby stimulating trade. However, some assemblies, such as that of Rhode Island, issued large amounts of currency (which consequently fell in value) and required merchants to accept it as legal tender. English merchants and other creditors rightly complained that they were being forced to accept worthless money. So in 1751 Parliament passed the Currency Act, which barred the New England colonies from establishing new land banks and prohibited the use of public currency to pay private debts.

These economic conflicts and the assertiveness of the American assemblies angered a new generation of British political leaders, who believed that the colonies already had too much autonomy. In 1749 Charles Townshend of the Board of Trade charged that American legislatures had assumed many of the "ancient and established prerogatives wisely preserved in the Crown"; he vowed to replace salutary neglect with more rigorous imperial control.

The wheel of empire had come full circle. In the 1650s England had set out to build a colonial empire and, over the course of a century, achieved the economic part of that goal. Mercantilist legislation, commercial warfare against European rivals, and the forced labor of a million African slaves brought economic prosperity to Britain. However, because of the Glorious Revolution and the era of salutary neglect, the empire unexpectedly dissolved into a group of politically self-governing colonies. So in the late 1740s British officials vowed once again to create a politically centralized colonial system.

## TIMELINE

| | | | |
|---|---|---|---|
| 1651 | First Navigation Act | 1720–1742 | Sir Robert Walpole serves as chief minister |
| 1660s | Virginia moves toward slave system | | |
| 1663 | Charles II grants Carolina proprietorship | 1720–1750 | African American community forms<br>Rice exports from Carolina soar |
| 1664 | English capture New Netherland, rename it New York | | Planter aristocracy emerges<br>Seaport cities expand |
| 1681 | William Penn founds Pennsylvania | 1732 | Parliament charters Georgia, challenging Spain |
| 1686–1689 | Dominion of New England | | Hat Act |
| 1688–1689 | Glorious Revolution in England; William and Mary ascend throne | 1733 | Molasses Act |
| | | 1739 | Stono Rebellion in South Carolina |
| | Revolts in Massachusetts, Maryland, and New York | | War with Spain in the Caribbean |
| 1689–1713 | England, France, and Spain at war | 1740 | Veto of Massachusetts land bank |
| | | 1750 | Iron Act restricts colonial iron manufactures |
| 1696 | Parliament creates Board of Trade | | |
| 1705 | Virginia enacts slavery legislation | 1751 | Currency Act prohibits land banks and use of paper money as legal tender |
| 1714–1750 | British follow policy of "salutary neglect" | | |
| | American assemblies gain power | | |

# For Further Exploration

The best concise overview of England's empire is Michael Kammen, *Empire and Interest: The American Colonies and the Politics of Mercantilism* (1970), while Linda Colley, *Britons: Forging the Nation, 1707–1837* (1992), explores the impact of empire on Britain. A clearly written study of multicultural tensions in early New York is Joyce Goodfriend, *Before the Melting Pot: Society and Culture in Colonial New York City, 1664–1730*. Two fine portrayals of imperial military and political affairs in the eighteenth century are Fred Anderson, *A People's Army: Massachusetts Soldiers and Society in the Seven Years' War* (1984), a compelling picture of army life, and Richard Bushman, *King and People in Provincial Massachusetts* (1985), a nicely crafted story of the decline of British authority in New England.

Betty Wood, *Origins of American Slavery* (1998), offers a survey of this important topic. For a lucid discussion of the diversity and evolving character of African bondage, see Ira Berlin, *Many Thousands Gone: The First Two Centuries of Slavery in North America* (1999), and Philip D. Morgan, *Slave Counterpoint: Black Culture in the Eighteenth-Century Chesapeake and Low Country* (1998). Olaudah Equiano, *The Interesting Narrative of the Life of Olaudah*

*Equiano* (originally published 1789; Bedford/St. Martin's, 1995), provides a powerful first-person account of a child's life in Africa, his kidnapping and sale into slavery in America, and his odyssey toward freedom and fame. On Africa, consult Paul Bohannan and Philip Curtin, *Africa and the Africans* (3rd ed., 1988).

The PBS video *Africans in America*, "Part 1: Terrible Transformation, 1450–1750" (1.5 hours) covers the African American experience in the colonial period; the Web site at <http://www.pbs.org/wgbh/aia/part1/title.html> contains a wide variety of pictures, historical documents, and scholarly commentary. Excerpts from Slave Narratives, at <http://vi.uh.edu/pages/mintz/primary.htm>, present materials selected by Steven Mintz from forty-six accounts, arranged in eleven chronological and thematic categories. Jerome S. Handler and Michael L. Tuite Jr. present a comprehensive Visual Record of the Atlantic Slave Trade and Slave Life in the Americas at <http://hitchcock.itc.virginia.edu/Slavery/>.

For definitions of key terms boldfaced in this chapter, see the glossary at the end of the book.

To assess your mastery of the material covered in this chapter, see the Online Study Guide at **bedfordstmartins.com/henrettaconcise**.

For map resources and primary documents, see **bedfordstmartins.com/henrettaconcise**.

# Chapter 4

## GROWTH AND CRISIS IN COLONIAL SOCIETY
### 1720–1765

The thirst after Indian lands, is become almost universal.

SIR WILLIAM JOHNSON TO THE EARL OF SHELBURNE, 1766

In 1736 Alexander MacAllister left the Highlands of Scotland for the backcountry of North Carolina, where his wife and three sisters soon joined him. Over the years MacAllister prospered as a landowner and mill proprietor and had only praise for his new home. Carolina was "the best poor man's country I have heard in this age," he wrote to his brother Hector, urging him to "advise all poor people . . . to take courage and come." In North Carolina there were no landlords to keep "the face of the poor . . . to the grinding stone," and so many Highlanders were arriving that "it will soon be a new Scotland." Here, on the far margins of the British empire, people could "breathe the air of liberty, and not want the necessarys of life." Tens of thousands of European migrants—Highland Scots, English, Scots-Irish, Germans—heeded such advice and helped to increase the population of Britain's North American settlements from 400,000 in 1720 to almost 2 million by 1765.

The rapid increase in the number of settlers—and slaves—transformed the character of life in every region of British America. Long-settled towns in New England became densely settled and then overcrowded. Antagonistic ethnic and religious communities jostled uneasily with one another in the Middle Atlantic region, and the influx of the MacAllisters and thousands of others into the backcountry of the South altered the dynamics of politics and social conflict there as well. Moreover, in every colony European intellectual and spiritual movements—the Enlightenment and Pietism—changed the tone of secular thought and religious life. Finally, and perhaps most important, as the immigrants and the landless children of long-settled families moved inland, they sparked warfare with the native peoples and with France and Spain, the other European powers contesting for North America. A generation of growth produced a decade of warfare.

# Freehold Society in New England

In the 1630s the Puritans left a country where a handful of nobles and gentry owned 75 percent of the arable land and farmed it by using servants, leaseholding tenants, and wage laborers. In America the Puritans consciously created a yeoman society consisting primarily of independent farm families. However, by 1750 New England's rapidly growing population occupied most of the best farmland, challenging the future prospects of the freehold ideal.

## *Farm Families: Women's Place*

The Puritans' commitment to family independence did not extend to gender relations. Puritan ideology celebrated the husband as head of the household and accorded him nearly complete control over his dependents. As the Reverend Benjamin Wadsworth of Boston advised women in *The Well-Ordered Family* (1712), being richer, more intelligent, or of higher social status than their husbands mattered little: "Since he is thy Husband, God has made him the head and set him above thee." Therefore, Wadsworth concluded, it was a woman's duty "to love and reverence him."

Throughout their lives women saw firsthand that their role was a subordinate one. Small girls watched their mothers defer to their fathers. As young women they saw the courts prosecute many women and very few men for the crime of fornication (having sexual union outside of marriage). And they learned that their marriage portions would be inferior in kind and size to those of their brothers; daughters usually received not highly prized land but rather livestock or household goods. Thus, Ebenezer Chittendon of Guilford, Connecticut, left all his land to his sons, decreeing that "Each Daughter have half so much as Each Son, one half in money and the other half in Cattle." Because English law had eliminated many customary restrictions over the disposition of wealth, fathers had nearly complete freedom to devise their property as they pleased.

In rural New England—indeed, throughout the colonies—women were raised to be dutiful helpmeets (helpmates) to their husbands. Farmwives spun thread and yarn from flax or wool and wove it into cloth for shirts and gowns. They knitted sweaters and stockings, made candles and soap, churned milk into butter and pressed curds into cheese, fermented malt for beer, preserved meats, and mastered dozens of other household tasks. The most exemplary or "notable" practitioners of these domestic arts won praise from the community because their physical labor was crucial to the rural household economy.

Bearing and rearing children were equally important tasks. Most women married in their early twenties and by their early forties had given birth to six or seven children, usually delivered with the assistance of midwives. These large families sapped the physical and emotional strength of most wives, and focused their attention on domestic activities for about twenty of their most active years.

**The Character of Family Life: The Cheneys**

Life in a large colonial-era family was very different from that in a small modern one.
Mrs. Cheney's face shows the rigors of having borne many children, a task that has occupied
her entire adult life (and may continue still, if the child she holds is her own). Her eldest daughter
has married the man standing at the rear and holds two of her own children, who are not much
younger than the last of her mother's brood. In such families, the lines between the generations
were blurred. National Gallery of Art, Washington, DC; gift of Edgar William and Bernice Chrysler Garbisch.

A Massachusetts mother explained that she had little room for religious activities
because "the care of my Babes takes up so large a portion of my time and attention."
Yet more women than men became full members of the Puritan congregations of
New England. As the revivalist Jonathan Edwards explained, many women joined
the church so "that their children may be baptized" and because they feared the dangers of childbirth.

As the size of farms shrank in long-settled communities, many couples chose to
have fewer children. After 1750, women in the typical farm village of Andover,
Massachusetts, bore an average of only four children and thus could pursue other
tasks. Farm women now made extra yarn, cloth, or cheese to exchange with neighbors or sell to shopkeepers and thereby enhanced their families' standard of living.
Or like Susan Huntington of Boston (the wife of a prosperous merchant), women
spent more time in "the care & culture of children, and the perusal of necessary
books, including the scriptures."

Yet women's lives remained tightly bound by a web of legal and cultural restrictions. While ministers often praised the women's piety, they excluded them from
an equal role in the church. When Hannah Heaton grew dissatisfied with her
Congregationalist minister, thinking him unconverted and a "blind guide," she

sought out Quaker and Baptist churches that welcomed questioning women and allowed them to become spiritual leaders. However, by the 1760s even evangelical Baptist congregations were stressing traditional male privileges. "The government of Church and State must be . . . family government" controlled by its "king," declared the Danbury (Connecticut) Baptist Association. Willingly or not, most New England women abided by the custom that, as the essayist Timothy Dwight put it, they should be "employed only in and about the house and in the proper business of the sex."

### Farm Property: Inheritance

By contrast, European men who migrated to the colonies escaped many traditional constraints, including the curse of landlessness. "The hope of having land of their own & becoming independent of Landlords is what chiefly induces people into America," an official noted in the 1730s. For men who had been peasants in Europe, owning property was a key element of their social identity.

Indeed, property ownership and family authority were closely related. Most migrating Europeans wanted large farms that would provide sustenance for themselves and ample land for their children. Parents with small farms could not provide their offspring with farms and had to adopt different strategies. Many placed their sons and daughters as indentured servants in more prosperous households, where they would have enough to eat. When the indentures ended at age eighteen or twenty-one, their propertyless sons faced the daunting challenge of a ten-to-twenty-year climb up the agricultural ladder, from laborer to tenant and finally to freeholder.

Luckier sons and daughters in successful farm families received a marriage portion when they reached the age of twenty-three to twenty-five. The marriage portion—land, livestock, or farm equipment—repaid children for their past labor and allowed parents to choose their children's partners, which they did not hesitate to do. The parents' security during old age depended on a wise choice of a wife or husband. Normally, children could refuse an unacceptable match, but they did not have the luxury of "falling in love" with whomever they pleased.

Marriage under English common law was hardly a contract between equals. A bride relinquished to her husband the legal ownership of her land and personal property. After his death, she received her dower—the right to use (but not to sell) a third of the family's estate. The widow's death or remarriage canceled this use-right, and her portion was divided among the children. The widow's property rights were subordinate to those of the family "line," which stretched, through the children, across the generations.

Indeed, it was the father's cultural duty to provide inheritances for his children, and men who failed to do so lost status in the community. Some fathers willed the family farm to a single son and provided their other children with money, apprenticeship contracts, or uncleared frontier tracts (or they required the inheriting son to do so). Alternatively, yeomen moved their families to an unsettled region, where life was hard but land for the children was cheap and abundant. "The Squire's House stands on the Bank of the Susquehannah," the traveler Philip Fithian reported from the Pennsylvania backcountry in the early 1760s. "He tells me that he will be able to settle all his sons and his fair Daughter Betsy on the Fat of the Earth."

These farmers' historic accomplishment was the creation of whole communities composed of independent property owners. A French visitor noted the sense of personal dignity in this rural world, which contrasted sharply with European peasant life. Throughout the northern colonies, he found "men and women whose features are not marked by poverty, by lifelong deprivation of the necessities of life, or by a feeling that they are insignificant subjects and subservient members of society."

## The Crisis of Freehold Society

How long would this happy circumstance last? Because of high rates of natural increase, New England's population doubled with each generation. The Puritan colonies had about 100,000 people in 1700, nearly 200,000 in 1725, and almost 400,000 in 1750. In long-settled areas many farms had been divided and then subdivided; now they consisted of fifty acres or less and many parents were unable to provide an adequate inheritance. In the 1740s the Reverend Samuel Chandler of Andover, Massachusetts, was "much distressed for land for his children," seven of whom were male. A decade later in the neighboring town of Concord, about 60 percent of the farmers owned less land than their fathers had.

Because parents had less to give their sons and daughters, they had less control over their children's lives. The system of arranged marriages broke down as young people engaged in premarital sex and used the urgency of pregnancy to win their fathers' permission to marry. Throughout New England the number of premarital conceptions rose spectacularly, from about 10 percent of firstborn children in the 1710s to 30 percent or more in the 1740s. Given another chance, young people "would do the same again," an Anglican minister observed, "because otherwise they could not obtain their parents' consent to marry."

New England families met the threat to the freeholder ideal through a variety of strategies. Many parents chose to have smaller families by using primitive methods of birth control. Others petitioned the provincial government for frontier land grants and hacked new farms out of the forests of central Massachusetts and western Connecticut—and eventually New Hampshire and the future Vermont. Still other farmers used their small plots more productively by replacing the traditional English crops of wheat and barley with high-yielding potatoes and Indian corn. Corn offered a hearty food for humans, and its leaves furnished feed for cattle and pigs, which in turn provided milk and meat. Gradually New England changed from a grain to a livestock economy and became the major supplier of salted and pickled meat to the slave plantations of the West Indies.

Finally, New England farmers survived on their smaller farms by exchanging goods and labor, developing the full potential of their household-based productive system. In this system, women and children joined other families in spinning yarn, sewing quilts, and shucking corn. Men lent each other tools, draft animals, and grazing land. Farmers plowed fields owned by artisans and shopkeepers, who repaid them with shoes, furniture, or store credit. Typically, no money changed hands; instead farmers, artisans, and shopkeepers recorded their debts and credits in personal account books and every few years "balanced" the books by transferring small amounts of cash to one another. The system of community exchange allowed households—and the entire economy—to achieve maximum output, thereby preserving the freehold ideal.

# The Middle Atlantic: Toward a New Society, 1720–1765

The Middle Atlantic colonies of New York, New Jersey, and Pennsylvania became home to peoples of differing origins, languages, and religions. These settlers—Scots-Irish Presbyterians, English and Welsh Quakers, German Lutherans, Dutch Reformed Protestants, and others—created ethnic and religious communities that coexisted uneasily with one another.

## *Economic Growth and Social Inequality*

Ample fertile land and a long growing season attracted migrants to the Middle Atlantic colonies, and profits from grain exports financed their rapid settlement. Between 1720 and 1770 a population explosion in western Europe increased the demand for wheat and doubled its price. By increasing their exports of wheat, corn, flour, and bread, Middle Atlantic farmers brought prosperity to the region and helped its population to surge from 120,000 in 1720 to 450,000 in 1765.

Even as the population rose, many migrants refused to settle in New York's fertile Hudson River Valley. There, the Van Rensselaers and other Dutch landlords presided over manors created by the Dutch West India Company in the 1620s and wealthy British families, such as the Clarkes and the Livingstons, dominated vast tracts granted by English governors between 1700 and 1714 (Map 4.1). Like the slave-owning Chesapeake planters, these landlords aspired to live like European gentry, but few migrants wanted to labor as poor and dependent peasants. Eventually the manorial lords were able to attract tenants but only by granting them long leases and the right to sell their improvements—their houses and barns—to the next tenant. The number of tenants on the vast Van Rensselaer estate rose slowly from 82 to 345 between 1714 and 1752 but then jumped to 700 by 1765.

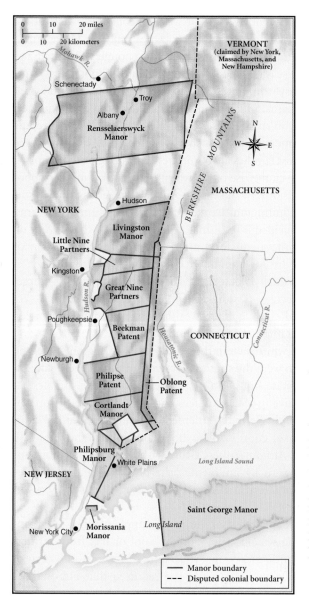

**MAP 4.1 The Hudson River Manors**

Dutch and English manorial lords dominated the fertile eastern shores of the Hudson River Valley, where they leased farms, on perpetual contracts, to German tenants and refused to sell land to freehold-seeking migrants from overcrowded New England. This powerful landed elite produced Patriot leaders, such as Gouverneur Morris and Robert Livingston, and leading American families, such as the Roosevelts.

Most tenant families hoped that with hard work and luck they could sell enough wheat to buy freehold farmsteads. However, preindustrial technology limited their output, especially during the crucial harvest season. As the wheat ripened, it had to be harvested quickly; any ripe uncut grain promptly sprouted and became useless. Yet a worker with a hand sickle could reap only half an acre a day, which limited the number of acres a family could harvest. The cradle scythe, an agricultural tool introduced during the 1750s, doubled or tripled the amount of grain a worker could cut. Even so, during the harvest season a family with two adult workers could reap only about twelve acres of grain—perhaps 150 to 180 bushels of wheat and rye. After family needs were met, the remaining grain might be worth £15—enough to buy salt and sugar, tools, and cloth but little else. The road to landownership was not an easy one.

Unlike New York, rural Pennsylvania and New Jersey were initially marked by relative economic equality. The original Quaker migrants arrived with approximately equal resources and lived simply in small houses with one or two rooms, a sleeping loft, a few benches or stools, some wooden trenchers (platters), and a few wooden noggins (cups). Only the wealthiest families ate off pewter or ceramic plates imported from England or Holland. However, the rise of the wheat trade and an influx of poor settlers created marked social divisions. By the 1760s some eastern Pennsylvania farmers used the labor of slaves and immigrant workers to grow wheat on large farms. Others bought up land and subdivided it into small tenancies, which they let out on profitable leases. Still others became successful commercial entrepreneurs by providing newly arrived settlers with farming equipment, sugar and rum from the West Indies, and financial services. Gradually a new class of agricultural capitalists—large-scale farmers, rural landlords, speculators, storekeepers, and gristmill operators—accumulated substantial estates and exhibited their wealth by buying mahogany tables, four-poster beds, table linen, and imported Dutch dinnerware.

By the 1760s, one-half of all white men in the Middle Atlantic region owned no property. Some propertyless men were the sons of farmers and would eventually inherit at least part of the family estate, but just as many were Scots-Irish "inmates"— single men or families "such as live in small cottages and have no taxable property, except a cow." In the predominantly German settlement of Lancaster, Pennsylvania, a merchant noted an "abundance of Poor people" who "maintain their Families with great difficulty by day Labour." Although these Scots-Irish and German migrants hoped to become tenants and eventually landowners, sharply rising land prices prevented many from realizing their dreams (see American Voices, "Runaway Servants and Slaves," p. 107).

Merchants and artisans took advantage of the ample supply of labor by organizing an outwork manufacturing system. They bought wool or flax from farmers and paid propertyless workers and land-poor farm families to spin it into yarn or weave it into cloth. In the 1760s an English traveler reported that hundreds of Pennsylvanians had turned "to manufacture, and live upon a small farm, as in many parts of England." Indeed, many eastern areas had become as crowded and socially divided as rural England, and farmers feared a return to the lowly status of the European peasant.

## Cultural Diversity

The middle colonies were not a melting pot in which European cultures quickly blended into a homogeneous "American" society; rather, they consisted of a patchwork of ethnically and religiously diverse communities. In 1748 a traveler found no

## AMERICAN VOICES

# Runaway Servants and Slaves

*B*etween 1720 and 1775 tens of thousands of poor Europeans and English convicts came to the mainland colonies as indentured servants and redemptioners and were sold to the highest bidder. "They sell the servants here as they do their horses, and advertise them as they do their beef and oatmeal," wrote an astonished British officer. Many of these servants labored side by side with enslaved Africans, and as shown by these newspaper advertisements from the Pennsylvania Gazette, the two groups found that they shared a passion for freedom.

October 12, 1752

Run away from doctor Thomas Graeme's plantation, in Horsham township, Philadelphia county, a Molatto slave, named Will, about 29 years of age, approaching very near the Negroe complexion, being of a Negroe father, and Indian mother, about five feet eight inches high, of an open bold countenance, somewhat pitted with the small-pox, speaks both English and Dutch, and is a very cunning sensible fellow. There went with him, a labouring man, that work'd by the day or month, called Thomas Stillwell, a tall smooth fac'd fair complexion'd fellow, with pale strait hair. . . . The said Stillwell is supposed to countenance the escape of the Molatto, by assuming the character of his master, or some such false pretence.

May 21, 1761

FIVE POUNDS Reward

Run away from the Subscribers, living at Little-Elk, Caecil County, Maryland, a Servant Woman named Margaret Sliter (but probably will change her Name) about 28 Years old, fresh colour, darkish brown Hair, born in England; had on when she ran away, two Bed-Gowns, one blue and white, the other dark Brown, both Callicoe. . . . Also a Negroe Man, named Charles, a lusty able Fellow, about 29 Years of Age, pitted with the Small-Pox, speaks good English, talks fast, is apt to get drunk, and pretends to be married to the aforesaid Margaret Sliter; had on when he ran away, a Pair of Thickset Breeches . . . a light coloured Jacket, an old brown Body-coat. . . .

Virginia, Lancaster County, Sept. 22, 1752

RUN away from the subscriber . . . on the 4th of May, A convict servant woman, named Sarah Knox (alias Howard, alias Wilson) of a middle size, brown complexion, short notes, talks broad, and said she was born in Yorkshire . . . and is a very deceitful, bold, insinuating woman, and a great liar. . . . I find [in the *Gazette*] an extract of a letter from Chester, in Pennsylvania, mentioning a quack Doctor, by the name of Charles Hamilton . . . who turns out to be a woman in mens cloaths, and now assumes the name of Charlotte Hamilton. . . . If she talks broad, I have reason to believe that she is the very servant who belongs to me.

SOURCE: Billy G. Smith and Richard Wojtowicz, *Blacks Who Stole Themselves: Advertisements for Runaways in the* Pennsylvania Gazette, *1728–1790* (Philadelphia: University of Pennsylvania Press, 1989), pp. 35, 50, 164.

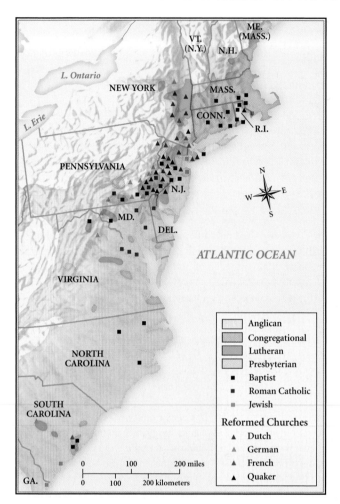

**MAP 4.2 Religious Diversity in 1750**

By 1750 religious diversity among European colonists was on the rise and not only in the ethnically disparate Middle Atlantic colonies. Baptists had increased their numbers in New England, long the stronghold of Congregationalism, and would soon be an important sect in Virginia. Already there were good-sized pockets of Presbyterians, Lutherans, and German Reformed in the South, where the Church of England (Anglicanism) was the established religion.

FOR MORE HELP ANALYZING THIS MAP, see the Online Study Guide at **bedfordstmartins.com/henrettaconcise**.

fewer than twelve religious denominations in Philadelphia, including Anglicans, Quakers, Swedish and German Lutherans, Scots-Irish Presbyterians, and even Roman Catholics (Map 4.2).

Migrants usually tried to preserve their cultural identities by marrying within their own ethnic groups or maintaining the customs of their native lands. The major exception was the Huguenots—Protestant Calvinists who were expelled from

Catholic France. They settled in New York and various seacoast cities and lost their French ethnic identity by intermarrying with other Protestants. More typical were the Welsh Quakers. Seventy percent of the children of the original Welsh migrants to Chester County, Pennsylvania, married other Welsh Quakers, as did 60 percent of the third generation.

Throughout Pennsylvania, Quakers became the dominant social group, at first because of their numbers and later because of their wealth and influence. Quakers controlled Pennsylvania's representative assembly until the 1750s and exercised considerable power in New Jersey as well. Because Quakers were pacifists, they dealt with Native Americans by negotiating treaties and buying land rather than seizing it. These conciliatory policies enabled Pennsylvania to avoid a major war with the Indian peoples until the 1750s. Some Quakers extended their religious values of equality and justice to African Americans. After 1750 many Quaker meetings condemned the institution of slavery, and some expelled members who continued to keep slaves.

The Quaker vision of a "peaceable kingdom" attracted German settlers who were fleeing their homelands because of war, religious persecution, and poverty. First to arrive, in 1683, was a group of religious dissenters—the Mennonites—attracted by the promise of religious freedom. In the 1720s religious upheaval and population growth in southwestern Germany and Switzerland brought a larger wave of migrants. "Wages were far better" in Pennsylvania, Heinrich Schneebeli reported to his friends in Zurich, and "one also enjoyed there a free unhindered exercise of religion." A third wave of Germans and Swiss—nearly 40,000 strong—landed in Philadelphia between 1749 and 1756. Some of these newcomers were redemptioners—a type of indentured servant—but many more were propertied farmers and artisans in search of ample land for their children.

Germans soon dominated many districts of eastern Pennsylvania, and thousands more moved down the Shenandoah Valley into the western parts of Maryland, Virginia, and the Carolinas. The migrants carefully guarded their language and cultural heritage. A minister in North Carolina admonished the young people in his congregation "not to contract any marriages with the English or Irish," explaining that "we owe it to our native country to do our part that German blood and the German language be preserved in America." Well beyond 1800 these settlers spoke German, read German-language newspapers, conducted church services in German, and preserved German farming practices, which sent women into the fields to plow and reap. English travelers remarked that German women were "always in the fields, meadows, stables, etc. and do not dislike any work whatsoever." Most German migrants were Protestants and lived easily as subjects of Britain's German-born and German-speaking monarchs, George I and George II. They engaged in politics only to protect their churches and cultural practices—insisting, for example, that as in Germany, married women should have the right to hold property and write wills.

**German Farm in Western Maryland**

Beginning in the 1730s, wheat became a major export crop in Maryland and Virginia. This engraving probably depicts a German farm because the harvesters are using oxen, not horses, and women are working in the field alongside men. Using "a new method of reaping" that is possibly of German origin, the harvesters cut only the grain-bearing tip and leave the wheat stalks in the fields, to be eaten by livestock. Library of Congress.

FOR MORE HELP ANALYZING THIS IMAGE, see the Online Study Guide at **bedfordstmartins.com/henrettaconcise**.

Migrants from Ireland formed the largest group of incoming Europeans, about 150,000 in number. Most were the descendants of the Presbyterian Scots who had been sent to Ireland by the English government during the seventeenth century to solidify its rule over Ireland's Catholic population. Once in Ireland, the Scots faced religious and economic discrimination from the English ruling classes. The Irish Test Act of 1704 excluded Presbyterians as well as Catholics from holding public office in Ireland; English mercantilist regulations placed heavy import duties on the woolens made by Scots-Irish weavers; and Scots-Irish farmers faced heavy taxes. "Read this letter, Rev. Baptist Boyd," a migrant to New York wrote back to his minister, "and tell all the poor folk of ye place that God has opened a door for their deliverance . . . all that a man works for is his own; there are no revenue hounds [tax collectors] to take it from us here." Lured by such reports, thousands of Scots-Irish sailed for Philadelphia beginning in the 1720s and then moved to central Pennsylvania and southward down the Shenandoah Valley into the backcountry of Maryland and Virginia. Like the Germans, the Scots-Irish retained their culture, holding firm to the Presbyterian faith.

## Religious Identity and Political Conflict

In Western Europe the leaders of church and state condemned religious diversity, and some German ministers carried these sentiments to Pennsylvania. "The preachers do not have the power to punish anyone, or to force anyone to go to church," complained the minister Gottlieb Mittelberger. As a result, "Sunday is very badly kept. Many people plough, reap, thresh, hew or split wood and the like." Thus, Mittelberger concluded, "Liberty in Pennsylvania does more harm than good to many people, both in soul and body."

As Mittelberger noted, ministers in Pennsylvania could not invoke government authority to uphold religious values. However, the result was not social anarchy because religious sects in the colonies enforced moral behavior through communal self-discipline. Quaker families attended a weekly worship meeting and a monthly discipline meeting. Every three months, a committee from the monthly meeting reminded each family to provide their children with proper religious instruction and fathers acted accordingly. "If thou refuse to be obedient to God's teachings," Walter Faucit of Chester admonished his son, "thou will be a fool and a vagabond." The committee also supervised adult behavior; a Chester County meeting disciplined one of its members "to reclaim him from drinking to excess and keeping vain company." Significantly, Quaker meetings regulated marriages and granted permission only to couples with land and livestock sufficient to support a family. As a result, the children of well-to-do Friends usually married within the sect, while poor Quakers remained unmarried, wed at later ages, or married without permission—in which case they were often barred from Quaker meetings. These sanctions effectively sustained a self-contained and prosperous Quaker community.

In the 1750s Quaker dominance in Pennsylvania came under attack. Scots-Irish Presbyterians along the frontier challenged the pacifism of the Quaker-dominated assembly by demanding an aggressive Indian policy. New German migrants also opposed the Quakers because they were denied fair representation in the provincial assembly and laws that respected their inheritance customs. As a European visitor noted, Scots-Irish Presbyterians, German Baptists, and German Lutherans were trying to form "a general confederacy" against the Quakers; however, they could not unite because of "a mutual jealousy, for religious zeal is secretly burning."

These ethnic and religious passions embittered Middle Atlantic politics. In Pennsylvania Benjamin Franklin disparaged the "boorish" character and "swarthy complexion" of German migrants, while in New York a Dutchman declared that he "Valued English Law no more than a Turd." The region's experiment in cultural and religious diversity prefigured the passionate ethnic and social conflicts that would characterize much of American society in the centuries to come.

# The Enlightenment and the Great Awakening, 1740–1765

Two great European cultural movements reached America between the 1720s and the 1760s: the Enlightenment and Pietism. The Enlightenment, which emphasized the power of human reason to understand and shape the world, appealed especially to well-educated men and women from merchant or planter families and to urban artisans. Pietism, an emotional, evangelical religious movement that stressed a Christian's personal relation to God, attracted even more adherents, primarily farmers and urban laborers. The two movements promoted independent thinking in different ways; together they transformed American intellectual and cultural life.

## *The Enlightenment in America*

Many early Americans turned to folk wisdom to explain the workings of the natural world. Thus, Swedish settlers in Pennsylvania attributed medicinal powers to the great white mullein, a common wildflower, and treated fevers by tying its leaves around their feet and arms. Others relied on religion. Most Christians believed the earth stood at the center of the universe and that God (and Satan, by witchcraft and other means) intervened directly and continuously in human affairs. When a measles epidemic struck Boston in the 1710s, the Puritan minister Cotton Mather thought that only God could end it.

Colonists held to these beliefs despite the scientific revolution of the sixteenth and seventeenth centuries, which challenged both traditional Christian and folk worldviews. In the 1530s the astronomer Copernicus observed that the earth traveled around the sun rather than vice versa, implying a more modest place for humans in the universe than had previously been assumed. Eventually the English scientist Isaac Newton, in his *Principia Mathematica* (1687), used mathematics to explain the movement of the planets around the sun. Newton's laws of motion and concept of gravity described how the universe could operate without the constant intervention of a supernatural being, undermining traditional Christian explanations of the cosmos.

In the century between *Principia Mathematica* and the outbreak of the French Revolution in 1789, the philosophers of the European Enlightenment used empirical (experience- or fact-based) research and scientific reasoning to study all aspects of life, including social institutions and human behavior. Enlightenment thinkers advanced four fundamental principles: the lawlike order of the natural world, the power of human reason, the natural rights of individuals (including the right to self-government), and the progressive improvement of society.

In his *Essay Concerning Human Understanding* (1690), the English philosopher John Locke emphasized the impact of environment, experience, and reason on human behavior. He argued that the character of individuals and societies was not fixed but could be changed through education and purposeful action. Locke's *Two Treatises on Government* (1690) advanced the revolutionary theory that political authority was not given by God to monarchs (as kings such as James II had insisted). Rather, it derived from social compacts that people made to preserve their "natural rights" to life, liberty, and property. In Locke's view, a people should have the right to change government policies—or even the form of government—through the decision of a majority.

The ideas of Locke and other Enlightenment thinkers came to America through books, travelers, and educated migrants. As early as the 1710s the Reverend John Wise of Ipswich, Massachusetts, used Locke's political principles to defend the Puritans' practice of vesting power in ordinary church members. Wise argued that just as the social compact formed the basis of political society, the religious covenant made the congregation—not the bishops of the Church of England or even the ministers—the proper interpreter of religious truth. The Enlightenment influenced Cotton Mather as well. When a smallpox epidemic threatened Boston in the 1720s, Mather turned to a scientific rather than a religious remedy by joining with physician Nicholas Boyleston to publicize the new technique of inoculation.

Benjamin Franklin was the exemplar of the American Enlightenment. Born in Boston in 1706 to a devout Calvinist family and apprenticed to a printer as a youth, Franklin was a self-taught man. While working as a printer and journalist in Philadelphia, he formed "a club of mutual improvement" that met weekly to discuss "Morals, Politics, or Natural Philosophy." These discussions and Enlightenment literature, rather than the Bible, shaped Franklin's imagination. As Franklin explained in his *Autobiography*, written in 1771, "from the different books I read, I began to doubt of Revelation [God-revealed truth] itself."

Like many urban artisans, wealthy Virginia planters, and affluent seaport merchants, Franklin became a **deist**. Influenced by Enlightenment science, deists believed that God had created the world but allowed it to operate in accordance with the laws of nature. The deists' God was a divine "watchmaker" who did not intervene directly in history or in people's lives. Rejecting the authority of the Bible, deists relied on people's "natural reason" (their innate moral sense) to define right and wrong. A sometime slave owner himself, Franklin used his reason to question the moral legitimacy of racial bondage and repudiated it once he became a defender of American freedom from British political "slavery."

Franklin popularized the practical-minded outlook of the Enlightenment in *Poor Richard's Almanack* (1732–1757), an annual publication read by thousands. In 1743 he helped found the American Philosophical Society, an institution devoted to "the promotion of useful knowledge." Taking this message to heart, Franklin himself invented bifocal lenses for eyeglasses, the Franklin stove, and the lightning rod. His book on electricity, published in England in 1751, won praise as the greatest contribution to science since Newton. Inspired by Franklin's example, ambitious printers in the American seaport cities published newspapers and gentleman's magazines, the first significant nonreligious publications to appear in the colonies. Thus, the

European Enlightenment added a secular dimension to colonial intellectual life, preparing the way for the great American contributions to republican political theory by John Adams, James Madison, and other Patriots during the Revolutionary era.

## American Pietism and the Great Awakening

As many educated Americans turned to deism, many other colonists embraced European Pietism, a Christian evangelical outlook. Pietists emphasized devout, or "pious," behavior, emotional church services, and a striving for a mystical union with God; they appealed to the heart, rather than the mind. In the 1720s German migrants carried this outlook to America, where they quickly sparked a religious revival. In Pennsylvania and New Jersey the Dutch minister Theodore Jacob Frelinghuysen moved from church to church, preaching rousing, emotional sermons to German settlers. In private prayer meetings he encouraged church members to spread the message of spiritual urgency. A decade later William Tennent and his son Gilbert copied Frelinghuysen's approach and led revivals among Scots-Irish Presbyterians throughout the Middle Atlantic region.

Simultaneously, an American-born Pietistic movement appeared in Puritan New England. The original Puritan settlers were emotionally intense, but over the decades since the 1630s, many congregations had lost their religious zeal. In the 1730s the minister Jonathan Edwards restored spiritual enthusiasm to the Congregational churches in the Connecticut River Valley. An accomplished philosopher as well as an effective preacher, Edwards urged his hearers—especially young men and women—to commit themselves to a life of piety and prayer.

George Whitefield, a young English evangelist, transformed these local revivals into a "Great Awakening" that spanned British North America. Whitefield had experienced conversion after reading German Pietistic tracts and became a follower of John Wesley, the founder of English Methodism. In 1739 Whitefield carried Wesley's fervent preaching style to America and over the next two years attracted huge crowds of "enthusiasts" from Georgia to Massachusetts. "Religion is become the Subject of most Conversations," the *Pennsylvania Gazette* reported. "No books are in Request but those of Piety and Devotion." The usually skeptical Benjamin Franklin was so impressed by Whitefield's oratory that when the preacher asked for contributions, Franklin emptied the coins in his pockets "wholly into the collector's dish, gold and all." When the evangelist reached Boston, the Reverend Benjamin Colman reported, the people were "ready to receive him as an angel of God."

Whitefield owed his appeal partly to his compelling personal presence. "He looked almost angelical; a young, slim, slender youth . . . cloathed with authority from the Great God," wrote a Connecticut farmer. Like most evangelical preachers, Whitefield did not read his sermons but spoke from memory. He preached as if inspired: gesturing eloquently, raising his voice for dramatic effect, using striking biblical metaphors, and even at times assuming a female persona—as a woman in labor struggling to deliver the word of God. When the young preacher told his

**George Whitefield, c. 1742**

No painting captured Whitefield's magical appeal, although this image conveys his open demeanor and religious intensity. When Whitefield spoke to a crowd near Philadelphia, an observer noted, his words were "sharper than a two-edged sword. . . . Some of the people were pale as death; others were wringing their hands . . . and most lifting their eyes to heaven and crying to God for mercy."

listeners they had all sinned and must seek salvation, hundreds of men and women suddenly felt the "new light" of God's grace within them. As "the power of god come down," Hannah Heaton recalled, "my knees smote together . . . it seemed to me I was a sinking down into hell . . . but then I resigned my distress and was perfectly easy quiet and calm . . . it seemed as if I had a new soul & body both." Strengthened and self-confident, these "New Lights" were eager to spread Whitefield's message throughout their communities.

## Religious Upheaval in the North

Like all cultural explosions, the Great Awakening was controversial. Conservative (or "Old Light") ministers such as Charles Chauncy of Boston condemned the "cryings out, faintings and convulsions" produced by emotional preachers. Chauncy likewise attacked the New Lights' practice of allowing women to speak in public as "a plain breach of that commandment of the LORD, where it is said, Let your WOMEN keep silence in the churches." In Connecticut, the Old Lights persuaded the legislative assembly to prohibit evangelists from speaking to established congregations without the ministers' permission. When Whitefield returned to Connecticut in 1744, he found many pulpits closed to him. But the New Lights resisted attempts to silence them. Dozens of farmers, women, and artisans roamed the countryside, condemning the Old Lights as "unconverted" sinners and willingly accepting imprisonment: "I shall bring glory to God in my bonds," a dissident preacher wrote from jail.

As the Awakening proceeded, it undermined support for established churches and challenged their tax-supported status. In New England many New Lights left the legally established Congregational Church. By 1754 they had founded 125 "separatist" churches which supported their ministers through voluntary contributions. Other religious dissidents joined Baptist congregations, which also favored the separation of church and state. "God never allowed any civil state upon earth to impose religious taxes," declared the Baptist preacher Isaac Backus. In New York and New Jersey the Dutch Reformed Church split in two because New Lights resisted conservative church authorities in the Netherlands.

The Awakening challenged the authority of ministers, whose education and biblical knowledge had traditionally commanded respect. In an influential pamphlet, *The Dangers of an Unconverted Ministry* (1740), Gilbert Tennent asserted that the minister's authority came not from theological training but from the conversion experience. Reaffirming Martin Luther's belief in the priesthood of all Christians, Tennent suggested that anyone who had experienced the saving grace of God could speak with ministerial authority. Isaac Backus likewise celebrated this spiritual democracy, noting that "the common people now claim as good a right to judge and act in matters of religion as civil rulers or the learned clergy."

In many rural villages, revivalism reinforced the communal values of farm families by questioning the competitive and mercenary values of the marketplace. Suspicious of merchants and land speculators, Jonathan Edwards spoke for many rural colonists when he charged that a "private niggardly [miserly] spirit" was more suitable "for wolves and other beasts of prey, than for human beings." As Gilbert Tennent put it, "In any truly Christian society mutual love is the Band and Cement."

As religious enthusiasm spread, churches founded new colleges to educate their youth and train ministers. New Light Presbyterians established the College of New Jersey (Princeton) in 1746, and New York Anglicans founded King's College (Columbia) in 1754. Baptists set up the College of Rhode Island (Brown) while the

Dutch Reformed Church subsidized Queen's College (Rutgers) in New Jersey. The true intellectual legacy of the Awakening, however, was not education for the few but a new sense of authority among the many. As a European visitor to Philadelphia remarked in surprise, "the poorest day-laborer . . . holds it his right to advance his opinion, in religious as well as political matters, with as much freedom as the gentleman."

## Social and Religious Conflict in the South

In the southern colonies religious enthusiasm also sparked social conflict. In Virginia the Church of England was legally established and supported by public taxes. However, Anglican ministers generally ignored the spiritual needs of African Americans (about 40 percent of the population), and landless whites (another 20 percent) attended irregularly. Middling white freeholders (35 percent of the residents) formed the core of most Anglican congregations. Prominent planters and their families (a mere 5 percent) held real power in the Church and used their control of parish finances to discipline Anglican ministers. One clergyman complained that dismissal awaited any minister who "had the courage to preach against any Vices taken into favor by the leading Men of his Parish."

The Great Awakening challenged both the dominance of the Church of England and the planter elite. In 1743 the bricklayer Samuel Morris, inspired by reading George Whitefield's sermons, led a group of Virginia Anglicans out of the Church. Seeking a more vital religious experience, Morris and his followers invited New Light Presbyterian ministers to lead their prayer meetings. Soon these Presbyterian revivals spread among Scots-Irish in the backcountry and English settlers in the Tidewater region, threatening the social authority of the Virginia gentry. Traditionally, planters and their well-dressed families arrived at Anglican services in elaborate carriages drawn by well-bred horses, and the men flaunted their power by marching in a body to their reserved front pews. Such potent reminders of the gentry's social superiority would vanish if freeholders attended New Light Presbyterian rather than Church of England services. Moreover, religious pluralism would threaten the tax-supported status of the Anglican Church.

To halt the spread of New Light doctrines, Virginia's governor denounced them as "false teachings," and Anglican justices of the peace closed down Presbyterian meetinghouses. This harassment kept most white yeomen families and poor tenants within the Church of England, as did the fact that most Presbyterian ministers were highly educated and sought converts mainly among skilled workers and propertied farmers.

Baptists succeeded where Presbyterians failed. The Baptists were a radical and widely persecuted Reformation sect that grew rapidly in number during and after the Great Awakening. The Baptists' central ritual was adult baptism, often involving complete immersion in water. Once men and women had experienced the infusion of grace—had been "born again"—they were baptized in an emotional public ceremony. The enthusiasm and democratic ways of the Baptist preachers who came to Virginia in the 1760s drew thousands of yeomen and tenant farm families into their congregations by offering them solace and emotional release in a troubled world.

Even slaves were welcome at Baptist revivals. In 1740 George Whitefield had condemned the brutality of slaveholders and urged that blacks be brought into the Christian fold. In South Carolina and Georgia a few New Light planters took up Whitefield's challenge, but white hostility and the commitment of Africans to their ancestral religions kept the number of converts low. The first significant conversion of slaves to Christianity came in Virginia in the 1760s, as second- and third-generation English-speaking African Americans responded positively to the Baptist message that all people were equal in God's eyes.

The ruling planters reacted violently to the Baptists, viewing them as a threat to hierarchical authority and their way of life. The Baptists emphasized spiritual equality by calling one another "brother" and "sister," and their preachers condemned the customary pleasures of Chesapeake planters—gambling, drinking, whoring, and cockfighting. Hearing Baptist Dutton Lane condemn "the vileness and danger" of drunkenness, planter John Giles took the charge personally: "I know who you mean! and by God I'll demolish you." In Caroline County, Virginia, an Anglican posse attacked a prayer meeting led by Brother John Waller; Waller, a fellow Baptist reported, "was violently jerked off the stage; they caught him by the back part of his neck, beat his head against the ground, and a gentleman gave him twenty lashes with his horsewhip."

Despite such attacks, Baptist congregations continued to multiply. By 1775 about 20 percent of Virginia's whites and hundreds of enslaved blacks had joined Baptist churches. To signify their state of grace, some Baptist men "cut off their hair, like Cromwell's round-headed chaplains." Many others refused to attend "a horse race or other unnecessary, unprofitable, sinful assemblies." Still others forged a new ethic of evangelical masculinity, "crying, weeping, lifting up the eyes, groaning" when touched by the Holy Spirit but defending themselves with vigor. "Not able to bear the insults" of heckler Robert Ashby, a group of Baptists "took Ashby by the neck and heels and threw him out of doors," sparking a bloody brawl.

However, the revival in the Chesapeake did not bring radical changes to the social order. Rejecting the requests of evangelical women, Baptist men kept church authority in the hands of "free born male members." Anglican slaveholders likewise retained power within the polity. Nonetheless, the Baptist insurgency gave spiritual meaning to the lives of the poor and empowered yeomen and tenants to defend their economic interests. Moreover, as Baptist ministers spread Christianity among slaves, the cultural gulf between blacks and whites shrank, undermining one justification for slavery and giving blacks a new religious identity. Within a generation African Americans would develop their own versions of Protestant Christianity.

# The Midcentury Challenge: War, Trade, and Social Conflict, 1750–1765

Between 1750 and 1765 a series of events transformed colonial life. First, Britain embarked on the French and Indian War in America, which became a worldwide conflict—the Great War for Empire. Second, a surge in trade boosted colonial consumption but put Americans deeply in debt to British creditors. Third, a great westward migration sparked new battles with Indian peoples, armed conflicts between settlers and landowners, and frontier rebellions against eastern-controlled governments (Map 4.3).

## The French and Indian War Becomes a War for Empire

In 1750 Indian peoples controlled the interior of eastern North America—the great valleys of the Ohio and Mississippi Rivers. Only a few Anglo-Americans had ventured across the Appalachian Mountains because there were few natural transportation routes and because of Indian resistance. The Iroquois in particular had firmly opposed white settlement and used their control of the fur trade to bargain for guns and subsidies from British and French officials.

However, the Iroquois strategy of playing off the French against the British was breaking down. The Europeans resented the rising cost of "gifts" of arms and money; equally important, Indian alliances began to crumble in the face of escalating Anglo-American demands for land. In the late 1740s the Mohawks rebuffed attempts by Sir William Johnson, a British Indian agent and land speculator, to settle Scottish migrants west of Albany. To the south, the Iroquois were infuriated when Governor Dinwiddie of Virginia and a group of prominent planters proposed "the Extension of His Majesties Dominions" into the upper Ohio River Valley, an area that the Iroquois controlled through alliances with the Delawares and the Shawnees. Supported by influential London merchants, the Virginia speculators formed the Ohio Company in 1749 and obtained a royal grant of 200,000 acres. "We don't know what you Christians, English and French intend," the outraged Iroquois complained, "we are so hemmed in by both, that we have hardly a hunting place left."

To maintain influence with the Iroquois Nations, the British Board of Trade called a great intercolonial meeting with the Indians at Albany, New York, in June 1754. At Albany the American delegates declared they had no designs on the lands of the Iroquois and sought their assistance against the French. To protect the British colonies from the French, Benjamin Franklin proposed a Plan of Union with a continental assembly that would manage all western affairs: trade, Indian policy, and defense. But neither Franklin's Albany Plan nor a proposal by the Board of Trade for a political "union between ye Royal, Proprietary, & Charter Governments" was in the cards. Both the provincial assemblies and British ministers feared that a consolidated American government would undermine their authority.

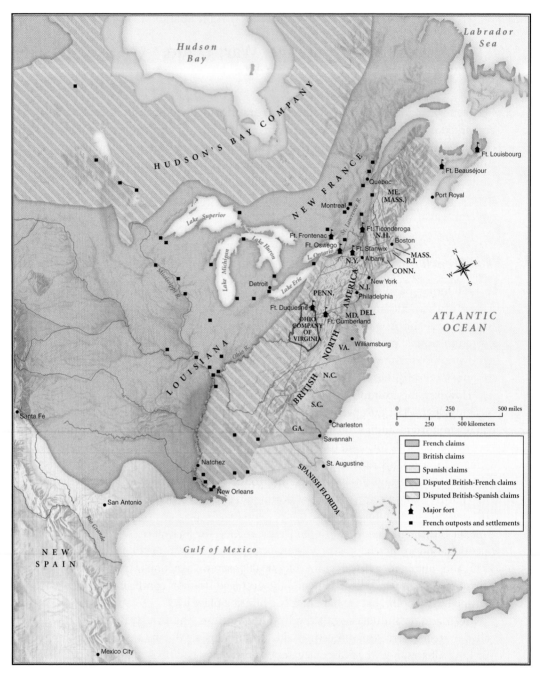

## MAP 4.3 European Spheres of Influence, 1754

France and Spain laid claim to vast areas of North America and used their Indian allies to combat the numerical superiority of British settlers. For their part, Native Americans played off one European power against another. As a British official observed, "To preserve the Ballance between us and the French is the great ruling Principle of Modern Indian Politics." By expelling the French from North America, the Great War for Empire disrupted this balance and left the Indian peoples on their own to resist encroaching Anglo-American settlers.

The Ohio Company's land grant alarmed French authorities as well as the Iroquois. To counter it, they constructed a series of forts, including Fort Duquesne at the point where the Monongahela and Allegheny Rivers join to form the Ohio (present-day Pittsburgh). The confrontation escalated when Dinwiddie dispatched an expedition led by Colonel George Washington, a young Virginia planter and Ohio Company stockholder. In July 1754 French troops seized Washington and his men and expelled them from the Ohio Valley, prompting expansionists in Virginia and Britain to demand war. Henry Pelham, the British prime minister, urged calm: "There is such a load of debt, and such heavy taxes already laid upon the people, that nothing but an absolute necessity can justifie our engaging in a new War."

Pelham could not control the march of events. In Parliament William Pitt, a rising British statesman, and Lord Halifax, the new head of the Board of Trade, strongly advocated a policy of colonial expansion. They persuaded Pelham to dispatch military forces to America, where they joined with colonial militia in attacking French forts. In June 1755 British and New England troops captured Fort Beauséjour in Nova Scotia (Acadia). Subsequently, troops from Puritan Massachusetts seized nearly 10,000 French Catholic Acadians, permanently deported them to France, Louisiana, and the West Indies, and settled English and Scottish Protestants on their farms.

These Anglo-American successes were quickly offset by a stunning defeat. As 1,400 British regulars and Virginia militiamen advanced on Fort Duquesne in July 1755, they came under attack by a small force of French and a larger group of Delawares and Shawnees, who had allied with the French. In the ensuing battle the British commander, General Edward Braddock, lost his life and nearly two-thirds of his troops. "We have been beaten, most shamefully beaten, by a handfull of Men," Washington complained bitterly as he led the militiamen back to Virginia.

By 1756 the fighting in America had spread to Europe, where it arrayed France, Spain, and Austria against Britain and Prussia. When Britain mounted major offensives in India and West Africa as well as in North America, the conflict became a Great War for Empire (known as the Seven Years' War in Europe and the French and Indian War in the colonies). Since 1700 Britain had reaped unprecedented profits from its overseas trading empire and was determined to crush France, the main obstacle to its expansion.

William Pitt, the new secretary of state, was the grandson of the East Indies merchant "Diamond" Pitt, a committed expansionist, and an arrogant leader. "I know that I can save this country and that I alone can," he declared. Indeed, Pitt was a master of strategy, both commercial and military, and planned to cripple France by attacking its colonies. In designing the critical campaign against New France, Pitt exploited a demographic advantage: on the North American mainland, King George II's two million subjects outnumbered the French by 14 to 1. To mobilize the colonists, Pitt paid half the cost of their troops and supplied them with arms and equipment, an expenditure in America of nearly £1 million a year. Moreover, he committed a major British fleet and 30,000 British regulars to the American conflict.

Beginning in 1758 the powerful Anglo-American forces moved from one triumph to the next. They forced the French to abandon Fort Duquesne (which they renamed Fort Pitt) and then captured the major fortress of Louisbourg at the mouth of the St. Lawrence. In 1759 a force led by General James Wolfe sailed up the St. Lawrence and captured Quebec, the heart of France's American empire. Quebec's fall was the turning point of the war. The Royal Navy prevented French reinforcements from crossing the Atlantic, and in 1760 British forces captured Montreal and completed the conquest of Canada.

Elsewhere the British also went from success to success. Fulfilling Pitt's dream, the East India Company ousted French traders from India. British forces seized French Senegal in West Africa, the French sugar islands of Martinique and Guadeloupe, and the Spanish colonies of Cuba and the Philippine Islands. The Treaty of Paris of 1763 confirmed this triumph. It granted Britain sovereignty over half the continent of North America, including French Canada, all French territory east of the Mississippi River, and Spanish Florida. The French empire in North America was reduced to a handful of sugar islands in the West Indies and two rocky islands off the coast of Newfoundland.

Britain's victory alarmed Indian peoples from New York to Michigan, who feared an influx of Anglo-American settlers. Hoping that the French would return as a counterweight to British power, the Ottawa chief Pontiac declared, "I am French, and I want to die French." Neolin, a Delaware prophet, went further; he taught that the suffering of the Indian peoples stemmed from their dependence on the Europeans' goods, guns, and rum and called for the expulsion of all Europeans. Inspired by Neolin's vision and his own anti-British sentiments, in 1763 Pontiac led a group of loosely confederated tribes in a major uprising known as "Pontiac's rebellion." The Indian force seized nearly every British garrison west of Fort Niagara, besieged the fort at Detroit, and killed or captured over 2,000 frontier settlers. But the Indian alliance gradually weakened, and British military expeditions defeated the Delawares near Fort Pitt and broke the siege of Detroit. In the peace settlement, Pontiac and his allies accepted the British as their new political "fathers." In return, the British established the Proclamation Line of 1763 that closed the trans-Appalachian west to Anglo-American settlement.

## British Economic Growth and the Consumer Revolution

Britain owed its military and diplomatic success to its unprecedented economic resources. Since 1700, when it had wrested control of many oceanic trade routes from the Dutch, Britain had been the dominant commercial power in the Atlantic and Indian Oceans. By 1750 it had also become the first country to use new manufacturing technology and work discipline. This combination of commerce and industry would soon make Britain the most powerful nation in the world.

**Pipe of Peace**

In 1760 the Ottawa chief Pontiac welcomed British troops to his territory, offering a pipe of peace to their commander, Major Robert Rogers. Three years later, Pontiac led a coordinated uprising against British troops, traders, and settlers, accusing them of cheating Native American peoples of their furs and lands. Library of Congress.

Mechanical power was a key ingredient of Britain's Industrial Revolution. British artisans designed and built mills and engines that efficiently used water and steam to power a wide array of other machines: lathes for shaping wood, jennies and looms for spinning and weaving textiles, and hammers for forging iron. The new power-driven machinery produced woolen and linen textiles, iron tools, furniture, and chinaware in greater quantities than traditional manufacturing methods—and at lower cost. Moreover, the entrepreneurs who ran the new workshops drove their employees hard, forcing them to keep pace with the machines and work long hours. To market the abundant products of these factories, English and Scottish merchants extended a full year's credit to colonial shopkeepers instead of the traditional six months. Americans were soon purchasing 20 percent of all British exports.

To pay for these goods, the colonists increased their exports of tobacco, rice, indigo, and wheat. In Virginia, farmers moved into the Piedmont, a region of plains and rolling hills just inland from the Tidewater counties. Using credit advanced by Scottish merchants, planters bought land, slaves, and equipment. The merchants took the planters' tobacco in payment and exported it to expanding markets in France and central Europe. In South Carolina planters supported their luxurious lifestyle by using British government subsidies to develop indigo plantations. By the 1760s they were exporting large quantities of the deep blue dye to English textile factories as well as selling 65 million pounds of rice a year to Holland and southern Europe. Simultaneously, New York, Pennsylvania, Maryland, and Virginia became the breadbasket of the Atlantic world by supplying Europe's exploding population with wheat at ever-increasing prices. In Philadelphia wheat prices jumped almost 50 percent between 1740 and 1765.

Americans used the profits of this trade to buy English manufactures in a "consumer revolution" that raised their standard of living. However, this first American spending binge, like most subsequent splurges, landed many consumers in debt. Even during the boom years of the 1750s, exports paid for only 80 percent of the imported British goods. The remaining 20 percent—millions of pounds—was financed from Britain by the extension of mercantile credit and by Pitt's military expenditures. When the end of military subsidies prompted an economic recession, colonial merchants looked anxiously at their overstocked warehouses and feared bankruptcy. "I think we have a gloomy prospect before us," a Philadelphia trader noted in 1765, "as there are of late some Persons failed, who were in no way suspected." The increase in transatlantic trade had raised living standards but also made Americans more dependent on overseas credit and international economic conditions.

## The Struggle for Land in the East

In good times and bad, the colonial population continued to grow, intensifying the demand for arable land. The families who founded the town of Kent, Connecticut, in 1738 were descendants of the first settlers; like earlier generations, they had moved westward to establish new farms. Now they lived at the western boundary of the colony. To provide for the next generation, many Kent families joined to form the Susquehanna Company, a land-speculating venture created in 1749. Hoping to settle the Wyoming Valley in present-day northeastern Pennsylvania, the company asked the Connecticut legislature to assert its jurisdiction over that region on the basis of Connecticut's "sea-to-sea" royal charter of 1662. However, King Charles II had also granted the Wyoming Valley to William Penn, and the Penn family had issued its own land grants in the region. By the late 1750s settlers from the two colonies were asserting their claims by burning down their rivals' houses and barns.

Simultaneously, three distinct but related land disputes broke out in the Hudson River Valley. Wappinger Indians, Massachusetts migrants, and Dutch tenant farmers asserted ownership rights on lands long claimed by the Van Rensselaer, Livingston, and other manorial families. When the manorial lords turned to the legal system to uphold their claims, Dutch and English farmers in Westchester, Dutchess, and Albany Counties used mob violence to close the courts. At the behest of the royal governor, General Thomas Gage and two British regiments joined local sheriffs and manorial bailiffs to suppress the Dutch tenants, intimidate the Wappinger Indians, and evict the Massachusetts squatters.

Other land disputes erupted in New Jersey and the southern colonies, where resident landowners and English aristocrats successfully asserted legal claims based on long-dormant seventeenth-century charters. One court decision upheld the right of Lord Granville, an heir of one of the Carolina proprietors of 1660, to collect an annual tax on land in North Carolina; another decision awarded ownership of the entire northern neck of Virginia (along the Potomac River) to Lord Fairfax.

This revival of proprietary power stemmed from an expanding demand for land (and its increasing value) that prompted the landed gentry to reassert long-dormant claims. It also reflected the maturity of the colonial courts, which now had the authority to uphold many of these claims. These developments underscored the increasing resemblance between rural society in Europe and America. High-quality land on the Atlantic coastal plain was getting more expensive, and English aristocrats, manorial landlords, and wealthy speculators had control of much of it. Tenants and even yeomen farmers feared they soon might be reduced to the status of European peasants and looked westward for cheap freehold land near the Appalachian Mountains.

## Western Uprisings and Regulator Movements

As farmers moved westward, they sparked new disputes over Indian policy, political representation, and debts. During the war with France, Delaware and Shawnee warriors had attacked frontier farms throughout central and western Pennsylvania, destroying property and killing and capturing hundreds of residents. Subsequently, Scots-Irish settlers demanded military action to expel all Indians, but Quaker leaders refused. In 1763 the Scots-Irish Paxton Boys took matters into their own hands and massacred twenty members of the peaceful Conestoga tribe. When Governor John Penn tried to bring the murderers to justice, about 250 armed Scots-Irish advanced on Philadelphia. Benjamin Franklin intercepted the angry mob at Lancaster and arranged a truce, narrowly averting a pitched battle with the militia. Prosecution of the Paxton Boys failed for lack of witnesses and the Scots-Irish dropped their demands, but the episode left a legacy of racial hatred and political resentment (Map 4.4).

Violence also broke out in the backcountry of South Carolina, where land-hungry Scottish and Anglo-American settlers clashed repeatedly with Cherokees during the war with France. When the war ended in 1763, a group of landowning vigilantes, the Regulators, tried to suppress outlaw bands of whites that were stealing cattle and other

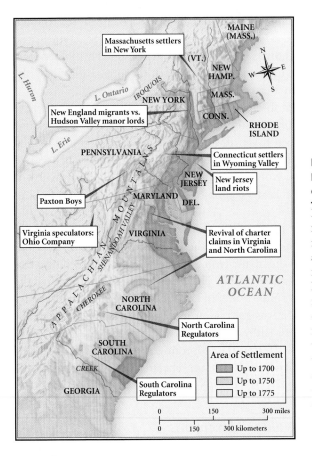

**MAP 4.4 Westward Expansion and Land Conflicts, 1750–1775**

Between 1750 and 1775 the mainland population doubled— from 1.2 million to 2.5 million— and spurred both westward migration and legal battles over land, which had become increasingly valuable. Violence broke out in eastern areas, as tenant farmers and smallholders contested landlord titles, and also in the backcountry, where migrating settlers fought with Indians, rival claimants, and the officials of eastern-dominated governments.

property (see American Voices, "Social Chaos on the Carolina Frontier," p. 127). The Regulators also wanted greater political rights and demanded that the eastern-controlled government provide their region with more courts, fairer taxes, and greater representation in the provincial assembly. Fearing slave revolts, the lowland rice planters who ran the South Carolina government chose to compromise with the Regulators rather than to fight them. In 1767 the assembly created locally controlled courts in the western counties and reduced the fees for legal documents. However, it refused to reapportion the assembly or lower western taxes. Like the Paxton Boys in Pennsylvania, the South Carolina Regulators attracted attention to western needs but ultimately failed to wrest power from the eastern elite.

In 1766 a more radical Regulator movement arose in the backcountry of North Carolina. The recession of the early 1760s caused a sharp fall in tobacco prices, and many farmers could not pay their debts. When creditors filed lawsuits, judges directed sheriffs to seize the indebted farmers' property and sell it to pay creditors and court costs. Backcountry farmers—including many German migrants—denounced the merchants' lawsuits, both because they generated high fees for lawyers and court

**AMERICAN VOICES**

~

## Social Chaos on the Carolina Frontier

### CHARLES WOODMASON

*T*o Charles Woodmason, a minister of the Church of England (the Anglican or Episcopal Church), the Carolina backcountry was a disorderly place. His journal contains vivid portraits of poor farming villages filled with immoral and violence-prone people—a chaotic mixture of ethnic and religious groups who had little respect for established authority. But a careful reading of his entries reveals a great deal of social and political cohesion, thanks to the influence of dissenting Protestant congregations led by affluent planters and politically astute lawyers.

[February 1767] I had appointed a [Church of England] Congregation to meet me at the Head of Hanging Rock Creek—Where I arriv'd on Tuesday Evening—Found the Houses filled with debauch'd licentious fellows, and Scot Presbyterians who had hir'd these lawless Ruffians to insult me, which they did with Impunity—Telling me, they wanted no D——d Black Gown Sons of Bitches among them—and threatening to lay me behind the Fire, which they assuredly would have done had not some travellers alighted very opportunely, and taken me under Protection—These Men sat up with, and guarded me all the Night. . . .

[June 1768] You must understand that all (or greatest Part) of this Part of the Province where I am, has been settled within these 5 years by Irish Presbyterians from Belfast, or Pennsylvania and they imagin'd that they could secure this large Tract of fine country to themselves and their Sect. Hereon, they built Meeting Houses, and got Pastors from Ireland, and Scotland. But with these there has also a Great Number of New Lights and Independants come here from New England, and many Baptists. . . .

To preserve their People from falling off to the Church established [Woodmason's Episcopal Church], . . . the [Presbyterian] Synods of Pensylvania and New England send out a Sett of Rambling fellows Yearly—who do no Good to the People, no Service to Religion—but turning of their Brains and picking up their Pockets of ev'ry Pistreen the Poor Wretches have. . . .

These Sects are eternally jarring among themselves—The Presbyterians hate the Baptists far more than they do the Episcopalians, and so of the Rest—but (as in England) they will unite altogether in a body to distress or injure the Church established. . . . Hence it is, that when any Bills have been presented to the Legislature to promote the Interests of Religion, these Sectaries have found Means to have them overruled, for the leading men of the House being all Lawyers, those People know how to grease Wheels as make them turn.

If Numbers were to be counted here, the Church People would have the Majority—but in Point of Interest, I judge that the Dissenters possess most Money—and thereby they can give a Bias to things at Pleasure.

SOURCE: Charles Woodmason, *The Carolina Backcountry on the Eve of the Revolution*, edited by Richard Hooker (Chapel Hill: University of North Carolina Press, 1953), 16–18, 41–46.

OF TWELVE REGULATORS CONDEMNED AT
HILLSBORO, THE FOLLOWING SIX WERE EXECUTED
BY THE BRITISH GOVERNOR: JAMES PUGH, ROBERT
MATEAR, BENJAMIN MERRILL, CAPTAIN MESSER,
AND TWO OTHERS, WHOSE NAMES ARE NOW
UNKNOWN. "OUR BLOOD WILL BE AS GOOD SEED IN
GOOD GROUND, THAT WILL SOON PRODUCE ONE
HUNDRED FOLD — JAMES PUGH, UNDER THE GALLOWS
AT HILLSBORO, N.C., JUNE 19th, 1771.

### History and Memory

This visually striking highway marker, erected by a government agency in North Carolina, offers an official—and only partially correct—view of the past. Rather than assail the Regulators as extralegal vigilantes or outright lawbreakers (as many observers did at the time), the marker shrouds them in patriotism, as innocent victims of a vengeful British governor.

Alamance Battlefield, photo by Mike Mayse.

officials and because they violated rural customs, which allowed loans to remain unpaid for years.

To save their farms from grasping creditors and tax-hungry officials, North Carolina debtors joined together in a Regulator movement. Disciplined mobs of farmers intimidated judges, closed courts, and freed their comrades from jail. However, the Regulators also proposed a coherent set of reforms. They demanded legislation to lower legal fees and allow payment of taxes in the "produce of the country" rather than in cash. They also insisted on greater legislative representation and a fairer tax system, proposing that each person be taxed "in proportion to the profits arising from his estate." But it was all to no avail. In May 1771 royal governor William Tryon decided to suppress the Regulators. Mobilizing British troops and the eastern militia, Tryon defeated a large Regulator force at the Alamance River. When the fighting ended, thirty men lay dead and Tryon summarily executed seven insurgent leaders. Not since Leisler's regime in New York in 1689 (see Chapter 3) had a domestic political conflict caused so much bloodshed.

In 1771 as in 1689, colonial conflicts became intertwined with imperial politics. In Connecticut, the Reverend Ezra Stiles defended the North Carolina Regulators. "What shall an injured & oppressed people do," he asked, when faced with "Oppression and tyranny (under the name of Government)?" Stiles's remarks reflected growing resistance to British imperial control. America was still a dependent society closely tied to Britain by trade, culture, and politics, but it was also an increasingly complex society with the potential for an independent existence. British policies would determine the direction the maturing colonies would take.

## TIMELINE

| | | | |
|---|---|---|---|
| 1700–1714 | New Hudson River manors created | 1743 | Benjamin Franklin founds the American Philosophical Society |
| 1710s–1730s | Enlightenment ideas spread from Europe to America<br>Deists rely on "natural reason" to define a moral code | 1749 | Virginia speculators create the Ohio Company<br>Connecticut farmers form the Susquehanna Company |
| 1720s | Germans and Scots-Irish settle in the Middle Atlantic colonies<br>Theodore Jacob Frelinghuysen preaches Pietism to German migrants | 1750s | Industrial Revolution begins in England<br>Consumer revolution increases American imports and debt |
| | | 1754 | French and Indian War begins<br>Meeting of Iroquois and Americans at Albany; Plan of Union |
| 1730s | William and Gilbert Tennent lead Presbyterian revivals among Scots-Irish<br>Jonathan Edwards preaches in New England | 1756 | Britain begins the Great War for Empire |
| 1739 | George Whitefield sparks the Great Awakening | 1759 | Britain captures Quebec |
| 1740s–1760s | Growing shortage of farmland in New England<br>Religious and ethnic pluralism in the Middle Atlantic colonies<br>Rising grain and tobacco prices<br>Increasing social inequality in rural areas | 1760s | Land conflict along the border between New York and New England<br>Regulator movements in the Carolinas suppress outlaw bands and seek power<br>Baptist revivals in Virginia |
| 1740s | Great Awakening sparks conflict between Old Lights and New Lights<br>Colleges established by religious denominations | 1763 | Pontiac's uprising leads to the Proclamation of 1763<br>Treaty of Paris ends the Great War for Empire<br>Scots-Irish Paxton Boys massacre Indians in Pennsylvania |

# For Further Exploration

The social history of eighteenth-century America comes alive in studies of individual lives. In *Good Wives: Image and Reality in the Lives of Women in Northern New England, 1650–1750* (1982), Laurel Thatcher Ulrich paints a vivid picture of the everyday lives of women as they assumed a variety of roles. Benjamin Franklin's *Autobiography* (available in many editions) provides an entertaining look at the bustling city of Philadelphia and demonstrates Franklin's Enlightenment sensibility and his pursuit of wealth and influence. A less successful quest for self-betterment is the subject of another autobiography, *The Infortunate: The Voyage and Adventures of William Moraley, an Indentured Servant*, edited by Susan E. Klepp and Billy G. Smith (1992). Harry S. Stout's *The Divine Dramatist: George Whitefield and the Rise of Modern Evangelicalism* (1991) shows how the charismatic preacher's flair for theatrics and self-promotion enabled him to preach effectively and fulfill his sense of duty to God.

Other well-written social histories are Rhys Isaac, *The Transformation of Virginia, 1740–1790* (1982); Patricia U. Bonomi, *A Factious People: Politics and Society in Colonial New York* (1971); and Fred Anderson, *A People's Army: Massachusetts Soldiers and Society in the Seven Years' War* (1984).

For insight into the day-to-day lives of women, see the PBS video *A Midwife's Tale* (1.5 hours), which tells the story of Martha Ballard, who lived at the end of the eighteenth century; additional materials on Ballard's experiences are available at <http://www.pbs.org/amex/midwife> and <http://www.DoHistory.org>. On day-to-day economic life, see the Colonial Currency and Colonial Coin site at <http://www.coins.nd.edu/ColCurrency/index.html>, which contains detailed essays as well as pictures of colonial money. Franklin's life and times are presented at The Electric Franklin, <http://www.ushistory.org/franklin/index.htm>. Jonathan Edwards On-Line, at <http://www.JonathanEdwards.com/>, provides access to the writings of the great philosopher and preacher, but note that this site uses Edwards's arguments to advance one side of a present-day theological debate. For a rich collection of documents and visual materials on the lives of migrant German sectarians, see the Bethlehem Digital History Project at <http://bdhp.moravian.edu/>.

---

For definitions of key terms boldfaced in this chapter, see the glossary at the end of the book.

To assess your mastery of the material covered in this chapter, see the Online Study Guide at **bedfordstmartins.com/henrettaconcise**.

For map resources and primary documents, see **bedfordstmartins.com/henrettaconcise**.

# Chapter 5

# TOWARD INDEPENDENCE:
# YEARS OF DECISION
## 1763–1775

The said [Stamp] act is contrary to the rights of mankind, and
subversive of the English Constitution.

TOWN MEETING OF LEICESTER, MASSACHUSETTS, 1765

As the Great War for Empire ended in 1763, Seth Metcalf joined many other American colonists celebrating the triumph of British arms. A Massachusetts soldier during the war, Metcalf thanked "the Great Goodness of God" for the "General Peace" that was so "perculary Advantageous to the English Nation." A mere two years later, Metcalf saw God's dialogue with his chosen Puritan people very differently. "God is angry with us of this land," the pious Puritan wrote in his journal, "and is now Smiting [us] with his Rod Especially by the hands of our [British] Rulers."

The rapid disintegration of the bonds uniting Britain and America—an event that Metcalf could explain only in terms of Divine Providence—mystified many Americans. How had it happened, the president of King's College in New York asked in 1775, that such a "happily situated" people had armed themselves and were ready to "hazard their Fortunes, their Lives, and their Souls, in a Rebellion"? Unlike other colonial peoples of the time, white Americans lived in a prosperous society with a strong tradition of self-government. They had little to gain and much to lose by rebelling.

Or so it seemed in 1765, before the British government attempted to reform the imperial system. These long overdue administrative reforms prompted a violent response, which began a downward spiral of ideological debate and political conflict. "This year Came an act from England Called the Stamp Act . . . ," Metcalf reflected, "which is thought will be very oppressive to the Inhabitants of North America." "But," he added, "Mobbs keep it back." The course of events that ended finally in civil war was far from inevitable. Careful statecraft and political compromise could have saved the empire. Instead, inflexible responses by British ministers and passionate agitation by Patriot leaders brought about its demise.

131

# The Imperial Reformers, 1763–1765

The Great War for Empire left a mixed legacy. Britain had driven the French out of Canada and now dominated eastern North America. But the cost was high: a mountain of debt that prompted the British ministry to impose new taxes on its American possessions. More fundamentally, the war spurred Parliament to redefine the character of the empire. The policy of salutary neglect, with its emphasis on trade and self-government, gave way to an emphasis on imperial power and direct Parliamentary rule.

## The Legacy of War

The war changed the dimensions of the colonial relationship. During the fighting, colonial leaders and British generals disagreed sharply on military strategy. Moreover, the presence of 25,000 British troops revealed sharp cultural differences. The arrogance of British officers and their demands for deference shocked many Americans, including a Massachusetts militiaman who declared that British soldiers "are but little better than slaves to their officers." The disdain was mutual. British general James Wolfe complained that colonial troops were drawn from the dregs of society and that "there was no depending on them in action."

The war also exposed the weak authority of British royal governors. In theory, governors had extensive political powers, including command of the provincial militia; in reality, they had to share power with the colonial assemblies, which outraged British officials. In Massachusetts, complained the Board of Trade, "almost every act of executive and legislative power is ordered and directed by votes and resolves of the General Court." To enhance royal authority, British officials ordered a strict enforcement of the Navigation Acts. Before the war colonial merchants routinely bribed customs officials to avoid the duties imposed by the Molasses Act of 1733. To curb such corruption, in 1762 Parliament passed the Revenue Act, which tightened up the customs service. In addition, the ministry instructed the Royal Navy to seize vessels that were carrying goods between the mainland colonies and the French islands. It was absurd, declared an outraged British politician, that French armies which were attempting "to Destroy one English province, are actually supported by Bread raised in another."

Britain's victory over France provoked a fundamental shift in imperial military policy. In 1763 the ministry decided to deploy a peacetime army of ten thousand men in North America. The decision had many causes. King George III (r. 1760–1820) wanted patronage positions for his military friends, so he needed a large army, someplace to station it, and somebody to pay for it. His ministers worried about newly acquired colonies; they feared a rebellion by the 60,000 French residents of Canada or a Spanish invasion of Florida. Moreover, Pontiac's rebellion had nearly overwhelmed Britain's frontier forts and underscored the need for military garrisons to restrain the Indian peoples and to deter land-hungry whites from settling west of the Proclamation Line of 1763. Finally, some British politicians worried about the loyalty of the American settlers now that they no longer needed

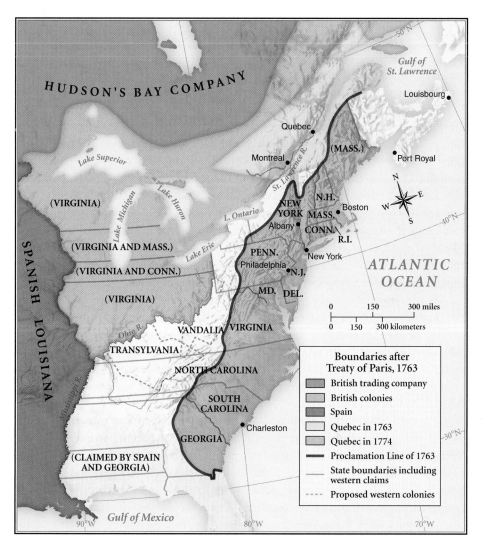

**MAP 5.1 Britain's American Empire in 1763**

Following the Great War for Empire and the Treaty of Paris of 1763, Britain held a dominant position in the West Indies and controlled all of eastern North America. British ministers dispatched troops to the conquered colonies of Florida and Quebec and, with the Proclamation Line of 1763, tried to prevent Anglo-American settlement west of the Appalachian Mountains.

protection from the French in Canada. As William Knox, a treasury official who had once served the crown in Georgia, put it: "The main purpose of Stationing a large Body of Troops in America is to secure the Dependence of the Colonys on Great Britain." By stationing an army in America, the British ministry was indicating its willingness to use force—whether against rebellious Indians, conquered Frenchmen, or dissident American colonists (Map 5.1).

Another significant result of the war was the growth of Britain's national debt, which soared from £75 million in 1754 to £133 million in 1763. The interest charges on the war debt now consumed 60 percent of the national budget and forced cutbacks in other government expenditures. To restore fiscal stability, Lord Bute, who became prime minister in 1760, needed to raise taxes. However, the Treasury Department opposed any increase in the British land tax, which was already at an all-time high and was paid by members of the propertied classes, who had great influence in Parliament. Therefore, Bute taxed the underrepresented poor and middling classes by imposing higher import duties on tobacco and sugar, which manufacturers passed on to consumers in the form of higher prices. The ministry also increased excise levies—essentially sales taxes—on goods such as salt, beer, and distilled spirits, once again passing on the costs of the war to the king's ordinary subjects. Left unresolved was the question of taxing the American colonists, who, like the British poor, had little influence in Parliament. However, ministers knew that free Americans contributed only about five shillings a year to the imperial budget, while British taxpayers paid nearly five times as much.

To collect existing taxes and duties, the British government doubled the size of the tax bureaucracy and increased its powers. Customs agents and informers patrolled the coasts of southern Britain, arresting smugglers and seizing tons of French wines and Flemish textiles. Convicted smugglers faced heavy penalties, including death or "transportation" to America as indentured servants. Despite protests by colonial assemblies, nearly fifty thousand English criminals had already been banished to America.

The price of empire had turned out to be debt and a more intrusive government, which confirmed the worst fears of the British opposition parties, the Radical Whigs and Country Party landlords. Both groups argued that the huge war debt had placed the treasury at the mercy of the "monied interest," the banks and financiers who were reaping millions of pounds in interest from government bonds. Moreover, the expansion of the tax bureaucracy had created thousands of patronage positions filled with "worthless pensioners and placemen." To reverse the growth of government power—and the consequent threats to personal liberty and property rights—reformers in Britain demanded that Parliament be made more representative of the property-owning classes. The Radical Whig John Wilkes called for an end to **rotten boroughs**—tiny districts whose voters were controlled by wealthy aristocrats and merchants. In domestic affairs as in colonial policy, the war had transformed British political life.

### The Sugar Act and Colonial Rights

The active exercise of government power was particularly apparent in American affairs, thanks to the reforms implemented by a new generation of British officials. George Grenville, who became prime minister in 1763, launched the first initiatives. First Grenville won Parliamentary approval of the Currency Act of 1764, which

**George Grenville, Architect of the Stamp Act**

As prime minister from 1764 to 1766, Grenville assumed leadership of the movement for imperial reform and taxation. This portrait of 1763 suggests Grenville's energy and ambition. As events were to show, the new minister was determined to reform the imperial system and ensure that the colonists shared the cost of the empire. The Earl of Halifax, Garrowby, Yorkshire.

protected British merchants by banning the colonies from using paper money (which was often worth less than its face value) as legal tender. Now American merchants, planters, and ordinary farmers would have to pay their debts in gold or silver coin, which was always in short supply.

Then Grenville proposed a new Navigation Act, the Sugar Act of 1764, to replace the widely evaded Molasses Act of 1733. The new legislation was well designed. Treasury officials, who understood the pattern of colonial trade, convinced Grenville that the mainland settlers had to sell some of their wheat, fish, and lumber in the French islands. Without the molasses, sugar, and bills of exchange derived from those sales, the colonists would lack the funds to buy British manufactured goods. Grenville consequently resisted demands from British sugar planters for a duty of 6 pence per gallon, which would completely cut off colonial imports of

French molasses. Instead, he settled on a smaller duty of 3 pence per gallon, which would allow molasses from the British islands to compete with the cheaper French product.

This carefully crafted policy garnered little support in America because it threatened American merchants and distillers. Many New England merchants, such as John Hancock of Boston, had made their fortunes by smuggling French molasses and their profits would be cut severely if the new regulations were enforced. These merchants and New England distillers, who feared a rise in the price of molasses, claimed publicly that the Sugar Act would wipe out trade with the French islands. Privately, they vowed to evade the duty by smuggling or by bribing officials.

More important, the political allies of the merchants raised constitutional objections to the new legislation. The speaker of the Massachusetts House of Representatives argued that the duties constituted a tax, making the Sugar Act "contrary to a fundamental Principall of our Constitution: That all Taxes ought to originate with the people." The Sugar Act raised other constitutional issues as well. Merchants prosecuted under the act would be tried by **vice-admiralty courts**— maritime tribunals composed only of a British-appointed judge—and not by a friendly, local common-law jury. American legislatures had long opposed vice-admiralty courts and had found ways to curtail their legal powers so that merchants accused of violating the Navigation Acts were tried in common-law courts. The Sugar Act closed this legal loophole by extending the jurisdiction of vice-admiralty courts to all customs offenses.

The new powers given to the vice-admiralty courts revived old American fears. The influential Virginia planter Richard Bland reminded his fellow settlers that the colonies had long been subject to the Navigation Acts, which restricted their manufactures and commerce. But, he protested, the colonists "were not sent out to be the Slaves but to be the Equals of those that remained behind." John Adams, a young Massachusetts lawyer who was defending merchant John Hancock on a charge of smuggling, similarly condemned the new vice-admiralty courts, saying that they "degrade every American . . . below the rank of an Englishman."

While the logic of these arguments for equal treatment was compelling, some of the facts were wrong. The Navigation Acts certainly discriminated against the colonists in order to assist British-based merchants and manufacturers. However, the new vice-admiralty legislation was not discriminatory; similar rules had long been in force in Britain. The real issue was the new spirit of imperial reform and the growing administrative power of the British state. Having lived for decades under a policy of salutary neglect, Americans knew immediately that the new British policies challenged existing constitutional practices and understandings. As a committee of the Massachusetts House of Representatives put it, the Sugar Act and other British edicts "have a tendency to deprive the colonies of some of their most essential Rights as British subjects."

For their part, British officials insisted on the supremacy of Parliamentary laws and denied that the colonists enjoyed special privileges or even the traditional legal rights of Englishmen. When royal governor Francis Bernard heard that the Massachusetts House had objected to the Sugar Act, claiming no taxation without representation, he asserted that Americans did not have that constitutional right. "The rule that a British subject shall not be bound by laws or liable to taxes, but what he has consented to by his representatives," Bernard argued, "must be confined to the inhabitants of Great Britain only." In the eyes of most imperial officials and British reformers, the Americans were second-class subjects of the king, their rights limited by the Navigation Acts and the interests of the British state, as determined by Parliament.

### *An Open Challenge: The Stamp Act*

Taxation sparked the first great imperial crisis. Grenville's plan was to follow the Sugar Act of 1764 with a stamp act in 1765. This new levy would cover part of the cost of keeping British troops in America—some £200,000 per year (about $50 million today). The tax would require stamps (or printed markings) on all court documents, land titles, contracts, playing cards, newspapers, and other printed items. A similar stamp tax in England was yielding £290,000 a year; Grenville hoped the American levy would raise at least £60,000. The prime minister knew that some Americans would object to the tax on constitutional grounds, so in 1764 he asked explicitly whether any member of the House of Commons doubted "the power and sovereignty of Parliament over every part of the British dominions, for the purpose of raising or collecting any tax." No one rose to object.

Confident of Parliament's support, Grenville vowed to impose a stamp tax unless the colonists would lay taxes for their own defense. The London merchants who served as agents and lobbyists for the colonial legislatures immediately protested that the Americans lacked a continent-wide body that could decide matters of taxation and defense. Representatives from the various colonies had met together officially only once, at the Albany Congress of 1754, and not a single assembly had accepted that body's proposals. Benjamin Franklin, who was in Britain as the agent of the Pennsylvania assembly, proposed another solution to Grenville's challenge: American representation in Parliament. "If you chuse to tax us," he suggested, "give us Members in your Legislature, and let us be one People."

With the exception of William Pitt, British politicians rejected Franklin's idea as too radical. They argued that the colonists were already **"virtually" represented** in Parliament by the members who were transatlantic merchants and West Indian sugar planters. Colonial leaders were equally skeptical. Americans were "situate at a great Distance from their Mother Country," the Connecticut assembly declared, and therefore "cannot participate in the general Legislature of the Nation." Influential Philadelphia merchants, perceiving that a handful of mainland delegates would be powerless in Parliament, warned Franklin "to beware of any measure that might extend to us seats in the Commons."

The way was clear for Grenville to introduce the Stamp Act. His goal was not only to raise revenue but also to assert a constitutional principle: "the Right of Parliament to lay an internal Tax upon the Colonies," as his chief assistant declared. The ministry's plan worked smoothly. The House of Commons ignored the American petitions opposing the act and passed the new legislation by an over-whelming vote of 205 to 49. At the request of General Thomas Gage, the British mil-itary commander in America, Parliament also passed the Quartering Act of 1765 directing colonial governments to provide barracks and food for the British troops. Finally, Parliament approved Grenville's proposal that violations of the Stamp Act be tried in vice-admiralty courts.

The design was complete. Using the doctrine of Parliamentary supremacy, Grenville had begun to fashion a genuinely imperial administrative system in America. As in Ireland, it would be run by British officials with little regard for the local assemblies. He thus provoked a constitutional confrontation not only on the specific issues of taxation, jury trials, and quartering of the military but also on the fundamental question of representative self-government.

# The Dynamics of Rebellion, 1765–1766

Grenville had thrown down the gauntlet to the Americans. Although the colonists had often been forced to deal with unpopular laws and arrogant governors, they had faced an all-out attack on their institutions only once—in 1686 when James II had arbitrarily imposed the Dominion of New England. Now the danger was even greater, because the new reforms were backed not only by the king but also by the Parliament. However, the Patriots—as the defenders of American rights came to be called—met Grenville's challenge by organizing protests, encouraging riots, and ar-ticulating an ideology of resistance.

## Politicians Protest and the Crowd Rebels

Addressing the Virginia House of Burgesses in May 1765, Patrick Henry attacked King George III for supporting Grenville's new legislation. Indeed, by comparing George III to the tyrannical Charles I, who had sparked the Puritan Revolution of the 1640s, Henry seemed to call for a new republican revolution. Although Henry's remarks bordered on treason and dismayed most Burgesses, they condemned the Stamp Act as "a manifest Tendency to Destroy American freedom." In Mas-sachusetts, James Otis, another republican-minded firebrand, persuaded the House of Representatives to call a meeting of all the colonies "to implore Relief" from the act.

Nine colonial assemblies sent delegates to the Stamp Act Congress, which met in New York City in October 1765. The Congress issued a set of Resolves challeng-ing the constitutionality of the Stamp and Sugar Acts and declaring that only the

### The Intensity of Patrick Henry

This portrait, painted in 1795 when Henry was in his sixties, captures his lifelong seriousness and intensity. As an orator, Henry drew on evangelical Protestantism to create a new mode of political oratory. "His figures of speech . . . were often borrowed from the Scriptures," a contemporary noted, and the content of his speeches mirrored "the earnestness depicted in his own features." Mead Art Museum, Amherst College.

colonists' elected representatives could tax them. The Resolves also protested against the loss of American "rights and liberties," especially trial by jury. However, most delegates were moderate men who sought compromise, not confrontation. They concluded the Resolves by assuring Parliament that Americans "glory in being subjects of the best of Kings" and humbly petitioning for repeal of the Stamp Act. Other influential Americans advocated nonviolent resistance through a boycott of British goods.

Popular resentment was not so easily contained. When the law went into effect on November 1, disciplined mobs acted immediately. Led by men who called themselves the **Sons of Liberty**, the mobs demanded the resignation of stamp tax collectors, most of whom were native-born colonists. In Boston, the Sons of Liberty made an effigy of the collector Andrew Oliver, which they beheaded and burned; then they destroyed Oliver's new brick warehouse. Two weeks later Bostonians attacked the house of Lieutenant Governor Thomas Hutchinson, a defender of social privilege and imperial authority, breaking the furniture, looting the wine cellar, and burning the library.

The men who led the mobs on the streets were usually middling artisans and minor merchants. Behind them stood major merchants, such as John Hancock, and Patriot lawyers, such as Patrick Henry. "Spent the evening with the Sons of Liberty," lawyer John Adams wrote in his diary, "John Smith, the brazier [metalworker], Thomas Crafts, the painter, Edes, the printer, Stephen Cleverly, the brazier; Chase,

The BOSTONIAN'S Paying the EXCISE-MAN, or TARRING & FEATHERING

Plate I.

## A British View of American Mobs

This satiric view of the Sons of Liberty attacks their brutal treatment of John Malcolm, the commissioner of customs in Boston, who was threatened with death (note the noose hanging from the tree) and then tarred and feathered and forced to drink huge quantities of tea. Note the men in the background, disregarding property rights by pouring tea into Boston Harbor. The presence of a "Liberty Tree" implicitly poses the question: Does liberty mean anarchy?

Courtesy, John Carter Brown Library at Brown University.

the distiller; [and] Joseph Field, Master of a vessel." These men knew each other through their work or as drinking buddies at the many taverns that dotted the streets of the major port cities and soon became centers of Patriot agitation.

However, resistance to the Stamp Act spread far beyond the port cities. In nearly every colony, crowds of angry people—the "rabble," as their detractors called them—intimidated royal officials. Near Wethersfield, Connecticut, five hundred farmers and artisans held tax collector Jared Ingersoll captive until he resigned his office. This was "the Cause of the People," shouted one rioter. In New York nearly three thousand shopkeepers, artisans, laborers, and seamen marched through the streets, breaking street lamps and windows and crying "Liberty!"

Such plebeian crowd actions were a fact of life in both Britain and America. Governments tolerated the mobs because, short of calling out the militia, they had no means to stop them and because they usually did little damage. Every November 5, Protestant mobs on both sides of the Atlantic burned effigies of the pope to celebrate Guy Fawkes Day, which commemorated the failure in 1605 of a plot by Fawkes and other English Catholics to blow up the Houses of Parliament. Likewise, colonial mobs regularly destroyed houses used as brothels and rioted to protest the impressment of merchant seamen by the Royal Navy.

If rioting was traditional, its political goals were new. In New York City the leaders of the Sons of Liberty were Radical Whigs who feared that reform of the imperial system would undermine political liberty. These men, minor merchants such as Isaac Sears and Alexander McDougall, tried to focus the raw energy of the crowd on the new taxes. However, mob members had their own agendas and goals. Some well-established artisans and their journeymen joined the crowds because imports of low-priced British shoes and other manufactured goods threatened their livelihoods, and they feared the additional burden of a stamp tax. Unlike "the Common people of England," a well-traveled colonist observed, "the people of America . . . never would submitt to be taxed that a few may be loaded with palaces and Pensions . . . , while they themselves cannot support themselves and their needy offspring with Bread."

The religious passions of the Great Awakening motivated other members of the crowd. As evangelical Protestants who led disciplined, hardworking lives, they resented the arrogance of British military officers and the corruption of royal bureaucrats. In New England, where many people lived into their 60s and memories lived even longer, some protesters looked back to the Puritan Revolution and revived the antimonarchical sentiments of their great-grandparents. A letter to a Boston newspaper carrying the name of "Oliver Cromwell," the English republican revolutionary of the 1640s, promised to save "all the Freeborn Sons of America." Finally, the mobs in all areas included apprentices, journeymen, day laborers, and unemployed sailors—young men seeking excitement who, when fortified by drink, were ready to resort to violence.

Throughout the colonies popular resistance nullified the Stamp Act. Fearing a massive assault on Fort George on Guy Fawkes Day (November 5, 1765), New York lieutenant governor Cadwallader Colden called on General Gage to use his small military force to protect the stamps. Gage refused. "Fire from the Fort might disperse the Mob, but it would not quell them," he told Colden, and the result would be "an Insurrection, the Commencement of Civil War." Frightened collectors gave up their stamps, and angry Americans coerced officials into accepting legal documents without them. This popular insurrection gave a democratic cast to the emerging American Patriot movement and extended it far beyond the ranks of elected officials who called the Stamp Act Congress and even those merchants and lawyers, like Adams, who had helped to organize the Sons of Liberty. "Nothing is wanting but your own Resolution," declared a New York rioter, "for great is the Authority and Power of the People."

Slow communication across the Atlantic meant that the ministry's response to the Stamp Act Congress and the Liberty mobs would not be known until the spring of 1766. But royal officials in America knew already that they had lost the popular support that had ensured the empire's stability for three generations. As the collector of the customs in Philadelphia lamented, "What can a Governor do without the assistance of the Governed?"

### *Ideological Roots of Resistance*

The American resistance movement emerged first in the seaport cities because British policies directly affected urban residents. The Stamp Act taxed the newspapers sold by printers and the contracts and court documents used by merchants and lawyers; the Sugar Act raised the cost of molasses to distillers; and the flood of British manufactures threatened the livelihood of urban artisans. Consequently, the first protests focused narrowly on these economic and political grievances. An official in Rhode Island reported that most colonists deemed the interests of Britain and the colonies "almost altogether incompatible in a Commercial View." A pamphleteer focused on taxes and complained that the colonists were being compelled to give the British "our money, as oft and in what quantity they please to demand it." Other writers alleged that the British had violated specific "liberties and privileges" embodied in colonial charters.

Initially the resistance movement had no acknowledged leaders, no organization, and no clear goals. However, men trained as lawyers gradually took the lead, partly because merchants hired them to protect their goods from seizure by customs officials. The lawyers' professional values provided another motive; as practitioners of the **common law** they opposed extension of vice-admiralty courts and favored trial by juries. Composing pamphlets of remarkable political sophistication, Patriot lawyers and publicists provided the resistance movement with an intellectual rationale, a political agenda, and a visible cadre of leaders.

Patriot publicists drew on three intellectual traditions. The first was English common law—the centuries-old body of legal rules and procedures that protected the lives and property of the king's subjects. In 1761 the Boston lawyer James Otis invoked English legal precedent in the famous Writs of Assistance case; in that instance Otis disputed the legitimacy of a general search warrant permitting customs officials to inspect any person's property and possessions. Similarly, in demanding a jury trial for John Hancock, John Adams appealed to the jury-trial provision in the "29th Chap. of Magna Charta," an ancient English document that "has for many Centuries been esteemed by Englishmen, as one of the . . . firmest Bulwarks of their Liberties." Other lawyers protested when the ministry changed the terms of appointment for colonial judges from "during good behavior" to "at the pleasure" of the royal governor because this change undermined the independence of the judiciary.

A second major intellectual resource for educated Americans was the rationalist thought of the Enlightenment. Unlike American common-law attorneys, who invoked legal precedents to criticize British measures, the Virginia planter Thomas Jefferson invoked Enlightenment philosophers, such as David Hume and Francis Hutcheson, who questioned past practices and relied on reason to correct social ills. Jefferson and other Patriot authors also drew on the Enlightenment political philosopher John Locke, who argued that all individuals possessed certain "natural rights," such as life, liberty, and property, which government must protect. And they celebrated the French theorist Montesquieu, who praised institutional arrangements, such as the separation of powers among government departments, which prevented arbitrary rule.

The republican and Whig strands of the English political tradition provided a third ideological source for American Patriots. Puritan New England had long venerated the Commonwealth era—the brief period between 1649 and 1660 when England was a republic. After the Glorious Revolution of 1688, colonists in all regions praised the constitutional restrictions placed on the monarchy by English Whigs, such as the ban on royally imposed taxes. Later, educated Americans such as Samuel Adams of Boston applauded when Radical Whigs denounced political corruption. This republican and Radical Whig outlook made many Americans suspicious of royal officials. Joseph Warren, a physician and Patriot, reported that many Bostonians believed the Stamp Act was intended "to force the colonies into rebellion," after which the ministry would use "military power to reduce them to servitude" (see American Voices, "An American View of the Stamp Act," p. 144).

This suspicion-minded Radical Whig outlook—swiftly disseminated in newspapers and pamphlets—convinced many Americans of the evil intentions of the British ministry and helped to turn a series of impromptu riots and tax protests into a coherent political movement.

## *Parliament Compromises, 1766*

In Britain, Parliament was in turmoil. Although George III had dismissed Grenville as prime minister, his supporters continued to demand reform. When Benjamin Franklin declared that Americans would "never" pay a stamp tax "unless compelled by force of arms," Grenville's hard-line supporters demanded the dispatch of British soldiers to uphold the constitutional supremacy of Parliament and maintain its status as one of the few powerful representative bodies in eighteenth-century Europe. "The British legislature," declared Chief Justice Sir James Mansfield, "has authority to bind every part and every subject, whether such subjects have a right to vote or not."

## AMERICAN VOICES

# An American View of the Stamp Act

### SAMUEL ADAMS

*T*hanks *to his education at Harvard College, distiller Samuel Adams had impressive intellectual and literary skills. In this private letter to an English friend, Adams undertakes, in reasoned prose, to refute the arguments used by British ministers to defend the new measures of imperial taxation and control.*

To John Smith

December 19, 1765

Your acquaintance with this country . . . makes you an able advocate on her behalf, at a time when her friends have everything to fear for her. . . . The [British] nation, it seems, groaning under the pressure of a very heavy debt, has thought it reasonable & just that the colonies should bear a part; and over & above the tribute which they have been continually pouring into her lap, in the course of their trade, she now demands an internal tax. The colonists complain that this is both burdensome & unconstitutional. They allege, that while the nation has been contracting this debt solely for her own interest, they have [been] subduing & settling an uncultivated wilderness, & thereby increasing her power & wealth at their own expense. . . .

But it is said that this tax is to discharge the colonies' proportion of expense in carrying on the [recent] war in America, which was for their defense. To this it is said, that it does by no means appear that the war in America was carried on solely for the defense of the colonies; . . . there was evidently a view of making conquests, [thereby] . . . advancing her dominion & glory. . . .

There are other things which perhaps were not considered when the nation determined this to be a proportionate tax upon the colonies. . . . The [British] nation constantly regulates their trade, & lays it under what restrictions she pleases. The duties upon the goods imported from her & consumed here . . . amount to a very great sum. . . .

There is another consideration which makes the Stamp Act obnoxious to the people here, & that is, that it totally annihilates, as they apprehend, their essential rights as Englishmen. The first settlers . . . solemnly recognized their allegiance to their sovereign in England, & the Crown graciously acknowledged them, granted them charter privileges, & declared them & their heirs forever entitled to all the liberties & immunities of free & natural born subjects of the realm. . . .

The question then is, what the rights of free subjects of Britain are? . . . It is sufficient for the present purpose to say, that the main pillars of the British Constitution are the right of representation & trial by juries, both of which the Colonists lose by this act. Their property may be tried . . . in a court of Admiralty, where there is no jury. [As for representation], if the colonists are free subjects of Britain, which no one denies, it should seem that the Parliament cannot tax them consistent with the Constitution, because they are not represented. . . .

SOURCE: Harry Alonzo Cushing, ed., *The Writings of Samuel Adams* (New York: G. P. Putnam, 1904), 78–79.

However, three other parliamentary factions advocated repeal of the Stamp Act. The Old Whigs, now led by Lord Rockingham, the new prime minister, favored repeal because they believed that America was more important for its "flourishing and increasing trade" than for its tax revenues. A second faction, composed of the supporters of British merchants and manufacturers, pointed out an American boycott of British goods cut deeply into their sales. A committee of "London Merchants trading to America" mobilized support for repeal, and in January 1766 the commercial centers of Liverpool, Bristol, and Glasgow deluged Parliament with petitions. "The Avenues of Trade are all shut up," complained a Bristol merchant. "We have no Remittances and are at our Witts End for want of Money to fulfill our Engagements with our Tradesmen." Finally, former prime minister William Pitt and his friends demanded that "the Stamp Act be repealed absolutely, totally, and immediately" as a failed policy. Pitt tried to draw a subtle distinction between taxation and legislation; he argued both that Parliament could not tax the colonies and that British authority over America was "sovereign and supreme, in every circumstance of government and legislation whatsoever." As Pitt's ambiguous—and perhaps contradictory—position indicated, the controversy had raised difficult constitutional questions to which there were few clear answers.

Rockingham played for time by arranging a compromise. To mollify colonial opinion and assist British merchants, he repealed the Stamp Act and modified the Sugar Act by reducing the duty on French molasses from 3 pence to 1 penny a gallon. Then Rockingham pacified imperial reformers and hard-liners with the Declaratory Act of 1766, which explicitly reaffirmed the British Parliament's "full power and authority to make laws and statutes . . . to bind the colonies and people of America . . . in all cases whatsoever."

Because the Stamp Act crisis ended swiftly, it might have been forgotten just as quickly. As of 1766 political positions had not yet hardened. Through compromise, leaders of goodwill could still hope to work out an imperial relationship acceptable both to British officials and American settlers.

# The Growing Confrontation, 1767–1770

The compromise of 1766 was short lived. Within a year political rivalries in Britain sparked a more prolonged struggle with the American colonies and revived the passions of 1765. Increasing ideological rigidity among key British ministers and American Patriots dashed prospects for a quick political resolution.

## The Townshend Initiatives

Often the course of history is changed by a small event—a leader's illness, a personal grudge, a chance remark. So it was in 1767, when Rockingham's ministry collapsed because of its domestic policies and George III named William Pitt to head the new government. Pitt, the master strategist of the Great War for Empire, was chronically ill with gout and frequently missed Parliamentary debates, leaving Chancellor of the Exchequer Charles Townshend in command. Pitt was sympathetic toward America; Townshend was not. As a member of the Board of Trade in the 1750s, Townshend strongly favored restrictions on the colonial assemblies, a view reinforced by his service on a parliamentary law-reform committee. So in 1767, when Grenville attacked the military budget and demanded that the colonists pay for the British troops in America, Townshend made an unplanned, fateful policy decision. Convinced of the necessity of imperial reform and eager to reduce the English land tax, he promised to find a new source of revenue in America.

The new tax legislation, the Townshend Act of 1767, had a political as well as a financial goal. The statute imposed duties on colonial imports of paper, paint, glass, and tea and would raise about £40,000 a year. To pacify Grenville, part of this sum would defray American military expenses. However, most of the revenue would create a colonial civil list—a fund to pay the salaries of royal governors, judges, and other imperial officials. Once freed from financial dependence on the American legislatures, royal officials would be able to enforce Parliamentary laws and the king's instructions. To increase royal power still further, Townshend devised the Revenue Act of 1767. This act created a Board of American Customs Commissioners in Boston and vice-admiralty courts in Halifax, Boston, Philadelphia, and Charleston. By using Parliamentary-imposed tax revenues to finance administrative and judicial innovations, Townshend directly threatened the autonomy and authority of American political institutions.

The full implications of Townshend's policies became clear in New York, where the assembly refused to comply with the Quartering Act of 1765. Fearing an unlimited drain on its treasury, the New York legislature first denied General Gage's requests for barracks and supplies for British troops and then limited its assistance. In response, the ministry demanded full compliance; if the assembly refused, some members of Parliament threatened to impose a special duty on New York's imports and exports. The earl of Shelburne, the new secretary of state, went even further. He proposed the appointment of a military governor with authority to seize funds from New York's treasury and "to act with Force or Gentleness as circumstances might make necessary." Townshend decided on a less provocative but equally coercive measure, the Restraining Act of 1767, which suspended the New York assembly until it submitted to the Quartering Act. Faced with the loss of self-government, New Yorkers reluctantly appropriated the required funds.

The Restraining Act raised the stakes of the contest. The British Privy Council had traditionally supervised the assemblies by invalidating unacceptable colonial laws (and, over the decades, voided about 5 percent of all colonial statutes, such as those establishing land banks). Townshend's Restraining Act went much further by declaring that New York's assembly (and, indeed, every American representative body) was completely dependent on the will of Parliament.

## America Again Debates and Resists

The Townshend duties revived the constitutional debate over taxation. During the Stamp Act crisis some Americans, including Benjamin Franklin, had made a distinction between "external" and "internal" taxes. They suggested that "external" duties on trade, which Britain had long regulated through the Navigation Acts, were acceptable to Americans but that direct or "internal" taxes, which had not previously been levied, were not. Townshend thought this distinction between internal and external taxes "perfect nonsense," but he indulged the American argument and laid duties only on trade.

However, most colonial leaders refused to accept the legitimacy of Townshend's measures. They agreed with John Dickinson, author of *Letters from a Farmer in Pennsylvania* (1768), that the real issue was not whether the tax was internal or external but the intention of the legislation. These Americans argued that the Townshend duties were designed to raise revenue and therefore were taxes imposed without consent.

Townshend's measures turned American resistance into an organized movement. In February 1768 the Massachusetts House of Representatives sent a letter

WILLIAM JACKSON,

an IMPORTER; at the

BRAZEN HEAD,

North Side of the TOWN-HOUSE,

and Opposite the Town-Pump, i

Corn-hill, BOSTON.

It is desired that the Sons and Daughters of LIBERTY, would not buy any one thing of him, for in so doing they will bring Disgrace upon *themselves*, and their Posterity, for ever and ever, AMEN.

**A Nonimportation Broadside**

To punish merchants who defied the boycott against the Townshend duties, Patriots in Boston and other seaports posted simply worded broadsides urging residents not to patronize their businesses. Some Sons and Daughters of Liberty resorted to more violent tactics, harassing the merchants' customers and vandalizing their buildings.
Massachusetts Historical Society.

condemning the Townshend Act to the other assemblies, and in the spring Boston and New York merchants began a new boycott of British goods. Philadelphia merchants, sailors, and dockworkers refused to join the boycott because they were heavily involved in direct trade with Britain and believed they had too much to lose. Nonetheless, public support for nonimportation quickly emerged in the smaller port cities of Salem, Newport, and Baltimore. Throughout Puritan New England, ministers and public officials discouraged the purchase of "foreign superfluities" and promoted the domestic manufacture of cloth and other necessities.

American women, ordinarily excluded from public affairs, became crucial to the nonimportation through their production of **homespun** textiles. During the Stamp Act boycott of English goods, the wives and daughters of Patriot leaders had increased their output of yarn and cloth. Resistance to the Townshend duties mobilized many more women, including pious farmwives who spun yarn at the homes of their ministers. Some gatherings were openly patriotic, such as one in Berwick, Maine, where "true Daughters of Liberty" celebrated American products by "drinking rye coffee and dining on bear venison." Other women's groups combined support for nonimportation with charitable work by spinning flax and wool to donate to the needy. Just as men followed tradition in joining crowd actions to attack imperial policy, so women's customary attention to the well-being of their communities guided their protest efforts.

Newspapers celebrated these "Daughters of Liberty." One Massachusetts town proudly claimed an annual output of thirty thousand yards of cloth; East Hartford, Connecticut, reported seventeen thousand yards. Although this surge in domestic production did not compensate for the loss of British imports, which had averaged about ten million yards of cloth each year, it inspired support for nonimportation by thousands of women in many communities.

Indeed, the boycott mobilized Americans, especially in the seaport cities, into an organized political action. The Sons of Liberty published the names of merchants who imported British goods, broke their store windows, and harassed their employees. By March 1769 most Philadelphia merchants finally responded to public pressure and joined the nonimportation movement. Two months later the members of the Virginia House of Burgesses vowed not to buy dutied articles, luxury goods, or slaves imported by British merchants. "The whole continent from New England to Georgia seems firmly fixed," the *Massachusetts Gazette* proudly announced. "Like a strong, well-constructed arch, the more weight there is laid upon it, the firmer it stands; and thus with America, the more we are loaded, the more we are united." Reflecting colonial self-confidence, Benjamin Franklin called for a return to the pre-1763 mercantilist system and proposed a "plan of conciliation" that was really a demand for British capitulation: "repeal the laws, renounce the right, recall the troops, refund the money, and return to the old method of requisition."

American resistance only increased British determination. When the Massachusetts House's letter opposing the Townshend duties reached London, Lord

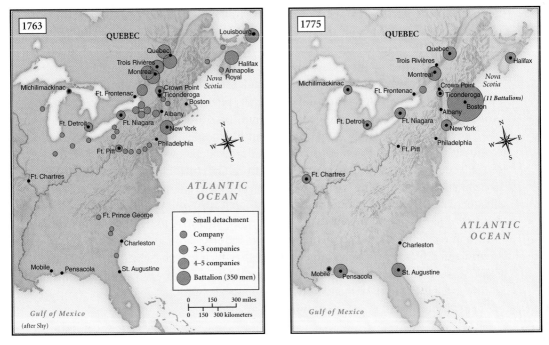

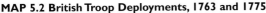

**MAP 5.2 British Troop Deployments, 1763 and 1775**

As the imperial crisis deepened, British military priorities changed. In 1763 most British battalions were stationed in Canada to deter Indian uprisings and French-Canadian revolts. After the Stamp Act riots of 1765, the British established large garrisons in New York and Philadelphia. By 1775 eleven battalions of British regulars occupied Boston, the center of the American Patriot movement.

Hillsborough, the secretary of state for American affairs, branded it as "unjustifiable opposition to the constitutional authority of Parliament." To strengthen the "Hand of Government" in Massachusetts and assist the customs commissioners there, Hillsborough dispatched four thousand British regular troops to Boston (Map 5.2). By the end of 1768, military coercion was a very real prospect. General Gage accused Massachusetts leaders of "Treasonable and desperate Resolves" and advised the ministry to "Quash this Spirit at a Blow." Parliament threatened to appoint a special commission to hear evidence of treason, and Hillsborough proposed to isolate Massachusetts from the other colonies and then use the army to bring the rebellious New Englanders to their knees. In 1765 American resistance to taxation had provoked a Parliamentary debate. In 1768 it produced a plan for military coercion.

## Lord North Compromises, 1770

At this critical moment the British ministry's resolve faltered. A series of harsh winters and drought-ridden summers cut grain output and raised prices. In Scotland and northern England, thousands of tenants deserted their farms and boarded ships bound for America. Food riots spread across the English countryside and, in the highly publicized Massacre of Saint George Fields, troops killed seven protesters. The Radical Whig John Wilkes, supported by associations of merchants, tradesmen, and artisans, stepped up his attacks on government corruption and won election to Parliament. Overjoyed, American Patriots drank toasts to Wilkes and bought thousands of teapots and mugs emblazoned with his picture. Riots in Ireland over the growing military budget there added to the ministry's difficulties.

The American trade boycott also began to have a major impact on the British economy. Normally the colonies had an annual trade deficit with the home country of £500,000, but in 1768 they imported less from Great Britain, cutting the deficit to £230,000. By continuing to provide staple goods and shipping services to overseas markets while cutting imports of British goods, in 1769 Americans amassed a balance of payments surplus of £816,000. To revive their flagging sales to America, British merchants and manufacturers petitioned Parliament for repeal of the Townshend duties. British government revenues, which were heavily dependent on excise taxes and duties on imported goods, had also suffered. By late 1769 some ministers felt that the Townshend duties were a mistake, and the king no longer supported Hillsborough's plan to use military force against Massachusetts.

Early in 1770 Lord North became prime minister and arranged a new compromise. Arguing that it was foolish to tax British exports to America (thereby raising their price and decreasing consumption), North persuaded Parliament to repeal most of the Townshend duties. However, he retained the tax on tea as a symbol of Parliament's supremacy. Gratified by North's initiative, colonial merchants called off the boycott.

Even the outbreak of violence did not rupture the compromise. During the boycott New York artisans and workers had taunted British troops, mostly with words but occasionally with stones and fists. In retaliation the soldiers tore down a Liberty Pole (a Patriot flagpole), setting off a week of street fighting. In Boston friction between the residents and British soldiers over constitutional principles and everyday issues, such as competition for part-time jobs, sparked a violent conflict. In March 1770, a group of soldiers fired into a rowdy crowd of demonstrators, killing five men, including one of the leaders, Crispus Attucks, an escaped slave who was working as a seaman. Reviving fears of a ministerial conspiracy against liberty, Radical Whigs labeled the incident a "massacre" and filled the popular press with accusations that the British had deliberately planned it.

Although most Americans ignored such charges and remained loyal to the empire, five years of conflict over taxes and constitutional principles had taken their toll. In 1765 American leaders had accepted Parliament's authority; the Stamp Act Resolves had opposed only certain "unconstitutional" legislation. By 1770 the most outspoken Patriots—Benjamin Franklin in Pennsylvania, Patrick Henry in Virginia, and Samuel Adams in Massachusetts—had repudiated Parliamentary supremacy and claimed equality for the American assemblies within the empire. Perhaps thinking of various European "composite monarchies" (in which kings ruled far-distant provinces acquired by inheritance or conquest), Franklin suggested that the colonies were now "distinct and separate states" with the "the same Head, or Sovereign, the King."

Franklin's suggestion outraged Thomas Hutchinson, the American-born royal governor of Massachusetts. Hutchinson emphatically rejected the idea of "two independent legislatures in one and the same state"; in his mind, the British empire was a single whole, its sovereignty indivisible. "I know of no line," he told the Massachusetts assembly, "that can be drawn between the supreme authority of Parliament and the total independence of the colonies."

There the matter rested. The British had twice tried to impose taxes on the colonies, and American Patriots had twice forced a retreat. If Parliament insisted on exercising Britain's claim to sovereign power, at least some Americans were prepared to resist by force. Nor did they flinch when reminded that George III condemned their agitation. As the Massachusetts House told Hutchinson, "There is more reason to dread the consequences of absolute uncontrolled supreme power, whether of a nation or a monarch, than those of total independence." Fearful of civil war, the ministry hesitated to take the final, fateful step.

# The Road to War, 1771–1775

The repeal of the Townshend duties in 1770 restored harmony to the British empire. Yet below the surface lay strong fears and passions and mutual distrust. Suddenly, in 1773 those undercurrents erupted, overwhelming any hope for compromise. In less than two years the Americans and the British stood on the brink of war.

## The Compromise Ignored

Once roused, political passions are not easily quelled. In Boston, radical Patriots continued to warn Americans of the dangers of imperial domination. In November 1772 Samuel Adams persuaded the Boston town meeting to establish a Committee of Correspondence to urge Patriots in other towns "to state the Rights of the Colonists of this Province." Within a few months eighty Massachusetts towns had similar committees, all in communication with one another. Then smugglers burned the *Gaspée*, a customs vessel, in Rhode Island, and the British government set up a royal commission to investigate the incident. The commission's broad powers, particularly its authority to send Americans to Britain for trial, aroused the Virginia House of Burgesses to set up its own Committee of Correspondence "to communicate with the other colonies" about the situation in Rhode Island. By mid-1773 similar committees appeared in Connecticut, New Hampshire, and South Carolina.

These committees sprang into action when Parliament passed the Tea Act in May 1773. The act provided financial relief for the British East India Company, which was deeply in debt because of military expeditions that extended British trade and political influence in India. The Tea Act provided the company with a government loan and, more important, relieved the company of paying tariffs on the tea it imported into Britain or sent to the colonies. However, Lord North failed to realize how unpopular the Tea Act would be in America. Since 1768, when the Townshend Act had placed a duty of 3 pence a pound on tea, many Americans had bought smuggled tea provided by Dutch traders. By relieving the East India Company of English tariffs, the Tea Act gave its tea a competitive price advantage over that sold by Dutch merchants. Thus, the act encouraged Americans to drink East India tea—and in the process pay the Townshend duty that Lord North had continued.

Radical Patriots smelled a plot and accused the ministry of bribing Americans to give up their principled opposition to British taxation. As an anonymous woman wrote in the *Massachusetts Spy*, "the use of [British] tea is considered not as a private but as a public evil . . . a handle to introduce a variety of . . . oppressions amongst us." American merchants joined the protest because the East India Company planned to distribute its tea directly to shopkeepers, thereby excluding most colonial merchants from the profits of the trade. "The fear of an Introduction of a Monopoly in this Country," General Haldimand reported from New York, "has induced the mercantile part of the Inhabitants to be very industrious in opposing this Step and added Strength to a Spirit of Independence already too prevalent."

The newly formed Committees of Correspondence took the lead in organizing resistance to the Tea Act. They held public bonfires at which they persuaded their fellow citizens (sometimes gently, sometimes not) to consign British tea to the flames. The Sons of Liberty patrolled the wharves and prevented East India Company ships from landing new supplies. By forcing the company's captains to return the tea to Britain or store it in public warehouses, the Patriots effectively nullified the legislation.

However, Governor Thomas Hutchinson of Massachusetts hatched a scheme to land the tea and collect the tax. When a shipment of tea arrived on the *Dartmouth*, Hutchinson immediately passed the ship through customs so that it could dock in the harbor. If the Sons of Liberty blocked the tea from coming ashore, Hutchinson was prepared to order the British troops to unload the tea and supervise its sale by auction. Patriots foiled the governor's plan by raiding the *Dartmouth*: a group of artisans and laborers disguised as Indians boarded the ship, broke open the 342 chests of tea (valued at about £10,000, or roughly $800,000 today), and threw them into the harbor. "This destruction of the Tea is so bold and it must have so important Consequences," John Adams wrote in his diary, "that I cannot but consider it as an Epoch in History."

The British Privy Council was outraged, as was the king. "Concessions have made matters worse," George III declared. "The time has come for compulsion." Early in 1774 Parliament decisively rejected a proposal to repeal the duty on

American tea; instead, it enacted four Coercive Acts to force Massachusetts into submission. The Port Bill closed Boston Harbor until the East India Company was paid for its tea. The Government Act annulled the Massachusetts charter and prohibited most local town meetings. The new Quartering Act required the colony to build barracks or accommodate soldiers in private houses. Finally, to protect royal officials from Patriot-dominated juries in Massachusetts, the Justice Act allowed trials for capital crimes to be transferred to other colonies or to Britain.

Patriot leaders throughout the mainland branded these measures as "Intolerable" and rallied support for Massachusetts. In far-off Georgia, a Patriot warned the "Freemen of the Province" that "every privilege you at present claim as a birthright, may be wrested from you by the same authority that blockades the town of Boston." "The cause of Boston," George Washington declared from Virginia, "now is and ever will be considered as the cause of America." The activities of the Committees of Correspondence had created a firm sense of unity among Patriots.

In 1774 Parliament passed the Quebec Act, which heightened the sense of common danger among Americans of European Protestant descent. The law extended the boundaries of Quebec into the Ohio River Valley, thus restricting the western boundaries of Virginia and other coastal colonies and angering influential land speculators and politicians. The act also gave legal recognition in Quebec to Roman Catholicism. This humane concession to Quebec's predominantly Catholic population reignited religious passions in New England, where Puritans associated Catholicism with arbitrary royal government and popish superstition. Although the ministry had not intended the Quebec Act as a coercive measure, many colonial leaders saw it as another demonstration of Parliament's power to intervene in American domestic affairs (Map 5.3).

## The Continental Congress Responds

Patriot leaders called a meeting of a new all-colony assembly, the Continental Congress. The newer mainland colonies—Florida, Quebec, Nova Scotia, and Newfoundland—did not attend, nor did Georgia, where the royal governor controlled the legislature. And the assemblies of the West Indian sugar islands, such as Barbados and Jamaica, fearful of revolts by their predominately African populations, reaffirmed their allegiance to the crown. However, delegates chosen by twelve mainland assemblies met in Philadelphia in September 1774 and addressed a set of controversial and divisive issues. Southern leaders, fearing a British plot "to overturn the constitution and introduce a system of arbitrary government," favored a new economic boycott. Bellicose representatives from New England advocated a political union and defensive military preparations. However, many delegates from the Middle Atlantic colonies wanted to seek a political compromise.

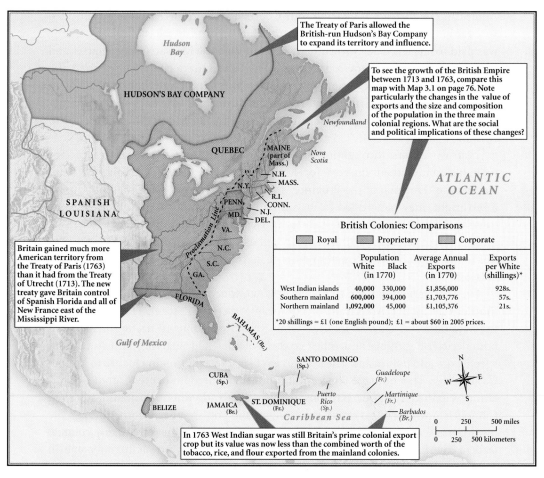

The Treaty of Paris allowed the British-run Hudson's Bay Company to expand its territory and influence.

To see the growth of the British Empire between 1713 and 1763, compare this map with Map 3.1 on page 76. Note particularly the changes in the value of exports and the size and composition of the population in the three main colonial regions. What are the social and political implications of these changes?

Britain gained much more American territory from the Treaty of Paris (1763) than it had from the Treaty of Utrecht (1713). The new treaty gave Britain control of Spanish Florida and all of New France east of the Mississippi River.

### British Colonies: Comparisons

| | Royal | | Proprietary | | Corporate |
|---|---|---|---|---|---|

| | Population White   Black (in 1770) | Average Annual Exports (in 1770) | Exports per White (shillings)* |
|---|---|---|---|
| West Indian islands | 40,000   330,000 | £1,856,000 | 928s. |
| Southern mainland | 600,000   394,000 | £1,703,776 | 57s. |
| Northern mainland | 1,092,000   45,000 | £1,105,376 | 21s. |

*20 shillings = £1 (one English pound); £1 = about $60 in 2005 prices.

In 1763 West Indian sugar was still Britain's prime colonial export crop but its value was now less than the combined worth of the tobacco, rice, and flour exported from the mainland colonies.

**MAP 5.3 British Western Policy, 1763–1774**

Challenging the Proclamation Line of 1763, which restricted white settlement west of the Appalachian Mountains, Anglo-American settlers and land speculators proposed the new western colonies of Vandalia and Transylvania. However, the Quebec Act of 1774 designated most western lands as Indian reserves and, by vastly enlarging the boundaries of Quebec, eliminated the sea-to-sea land claims of many colonies along the Atlantic Coast. The Quebec Act also angered New England Protestants, who condemned its provisions allowing French residents to practice Catholicism, and colonial political leaders, who condemned its failure to provide a representative assembly.

FOR MORE HELP ANALYZING THIS MAP, see the Online Study Guide at **bedfordstmartins.com/henrettaconcise**.

Led by Joseph Galloway of Pennsylvania, these men of "loyal principles" out-lined a new imperial system that resembled the Albany Plan of Union of 1754. Under Galloway's proposal, the king would appoint a president-general and the colonial assemblies would select a legislative council, which would have veto power over Parliamentary legislation that affected America. Despite this feature, delegates refused to endorse Galloway's plan. With British troops occupying Boston, the majority thought it was too conciliatory.

Instead, the First Continental Congress passed a Declaration of Rights and Grievances that condemned the Coercive Acts and demanded their repeal. It also repudiated the Declaratory Act of 1766, which had proclaimed Parliament's supremacy, and demanded that Britain restrict its control of American affairs to matters of external trade. Finally, the Congress approved a program of economic retaliation that would begin in December 1774 with a new nonimportation agreement. If Parliament did not repeal the Intolerable Acts by September 1775, the Congress vowed to cut off virtually all colonial exports to Britain, Ireland, and the British West Indies. Ten years of constitutional conflict had culminated in a threat of all-out commercial warfare.

Even at this late date a few British leaders hoped for compromise. In January 1775 William Pitt, now sitting in the House of Lords as the earl of Chatham, asked Parliament to renounce its power to tax the colonies and recognize the Continental Congress as a lawful body. In return for these concessions, he suggested, the Congress should acknowledge Parliamentary supremacy and grant a continuing revenue to help defray the British national debt.

The British ministry rejected Chatham's plan. Twice it had backed down in the face of colonial resistance; a third retreat was impossible. The honor of the nation was at stake. Branding the Continental Congress an illegal assembly, the ministry also ruled out Lord Dartmouth's proposal to send commissioners to America to negotiate a settlement. Instead, Lord North set stringent terms: Americans must pay for their own defense and administration and acknowledge Parliament's authority to tax them. To put teeth in these demands, North imposed a naval blockade on American trade with foreign nations and ordered General Gage to suppress dissent in Massachusetts. "Now the case seemed desperate," the prime minister told former Massachusetts governor Thomas Hutchinson, who had been forced into exile in London by Patriot agitators. "Parliament would not—could not—concede. For aught he could see it must come to violence."

## The Rising of the Countryside

Ultimately, the success of the urban-led Patriot movement would depend on the large rural population. Traditionally, most farmers had little interest in imperial affairs. Their lives were deeply rooted in the soil, and their prime allegiance was to family and community. But imperial policy increasingly intruded into their isolated domestic worlds by taking their sons for military duty and raising their taxes. Before the outbreak of the French and Indian War in 1754, farmers in Newtown, Long Island, had paid an average of 10 shillings a year in taxes; by 1756 their taxes had jumped to 30 shillings. Peace brought only slight relief, because in 1771 the British-imposed Quartering Act kept taxes at the high rate of 20 shillings. Such levies angered rural Americans, though in fact they paid much lower taxes than did most Britons.

A SOCIETY of PATRIOTIC LADIES,
AT
EDENTON in NORTH CAROLINA.

Plate V.

**Political Propaganda: The Empire Strikes Back**

A British cartoon satirizes the women of Edenton, North Carolina, for supporting the boycott of British trade by hinting at their sexual lasciviousness and— by showing an enslaved black woman holding an inkstand for these supposed advocates of liberty—their moral hypocrisy. Library of Congress.

FOR MORE HELP ANALYZING THIS IMAGE, see the Online Study Guide at **bedfordstmartins.com/ henrettaconcise**.

The urban-led boycotts of 1765 and 1769 also raised the political consciousness of rural Americans. When the Continental Congress placed a new ban on British goods in 1774, it easily established a network of local Committees of Safety and Inspection to support it. Appealing to rural thriftiness, the Congress discouraged the wearing of expensive imported clothes to funerals, approving only "a black crape or ribbon on the arm or hat for gentlemen, and a black ribbon and necklace for ladies." In Concord, Massachusetts, 80 percent of the male heads of families and a number of single women signed a Solemn League and Covenant supporting nonimportation. In other towns men blacked their faces, disguised themselves in blankets "like Indians," and threatened violence against "those that trade in rum, molasses, & Sugar, &c." in violation of the boycott.

Patriots also appealed to the yeoman tradition of freehold ownership, which was everywhere under attack. In long-settled communities, arable land was now scarce and expensive, and in new communities merchants were seizing farmsteads for delinquent debts. Money was always in short supply among rural households, and the town meeting of Petersham, Massachusetts, complained that the new tax demands of the British government would further drain "this People of the Fruits of their Toil." "The duty on tea," warned a Patriot pamphlet, "was only a prelude to a window-tax, hearth-tax, land-tax, and poll-tax, and these were only paving the way for reducing the country to lordships." By the 1770s many northern yeomen felt personally threatened by British imperial policy.

Despite their higher standard of living, southern slave owners had similar fears. Many Virginia Patriots—including Patrick Henry, George Washington, and Thomas Jefferson—speculated in western lands and reacted angrily when first the Proclamation Line of 1763 and then the Quebec Act of 1774 invalidated their claims. Moreover, many Chesapeake planters were deeply in debt to British merchants; a debt of £1,000 had once been considered excessive, a planter observed in 1766, but "ten times that sum is now spoke of with indifference and thought no great burthen on Some Estates." Although extravagant spending threatened many planters with financial disaster, George Washington noted, they were determined to live "genteely and hospitably" and were "ashamed" to adopt frugal ways. Accustomed to being absolute masters on their slave-labor plantations, they resented their financial dependence on British merchants and dreaded the prospect of political subservience. Once Parliament used the Coercive Acts to subdue Massachusetts, the planters feared, it might seize control of the House of Burgesses and Virginia's county courts and assist British merchants to seize their debt-burdened property. Consequently, the Patriot gentry supported demands by yeomen planters to close the law courts so they could bargain with Scottish merchants over debts and tobacco prices without the threat of legal action. "The spark of liberty is not yet extinct among our people," one planter declared, "and if properly fanned by the Gentlemen of influence will, I make no doubt, burst out again into a flame."

While many wealthy planters and affluent merchants supported the Patriot cause, other prominent Americans worried that resistance to Britain would destroy respect for all political institutions and end in mob rule. Their fears increased when the Sons of Liberty used force to uphold nonimportation. As a well-to-do New Yorker complained, "No man can be in a more abject state of bondage than he whose Reputation, Property and Life are exposed to the discretionary violence . . . of the community." As the crisis continued, these men rallied to the support of the royal governors.

Other social groups likewise refused to support the Patriot movement. In Pennsylvania and New Jersey, many Quakers and Germans tried to remain neutral because of pacifist religious principles and fear of political change. In regions where many wealthy landowners became Patriots, such as the Hudson Valley of New York, tenant farmers supported the king because they hated their landlords. Similar social divisions prompted some Regulators in the North Carolina backcountry and many farmers on the eastern shore of Chesapeake Bay in Maryland to oppose the Patriots there. Enslaved blacks had even less reason to support the cause of their Patriot masters. In November 1774, James Madison reported that one group of Virginia slaves planned to flee from their Patriot owners "when the English troops should arrive."

To mobilize support for the king, prominent Americans of "loyal principles" denounced the Patriot leaders and accused them of seeking independence. These Loyalists—mostly royal officials, merchants with military contracts, clergy of the Church of England, and well-established lawyers—formed an articulate pro-British party, but one that remained small and ineffective. A Tory Association started by Governor Wentworth of New Hampshire enrolled just fifty-nine members, fourteen of whom were the governor's relatives. At this crucial juncture Americans who favored resistance to British rule commanded the allegiance—or at least the acquiescence—of the majority of white Americans.

## The Failure of Compromise

When the Continental Congress met in September 1774, New England was already openly defying British authority. In August, the 150 delegates at an extra-legal Middlesex County Congress advised Patriots to close the royal courts of justice and transfer their political allegiance to the popularly elected House of Representatives. Following the congress, armed crowds harassed Loyalists and ensured Patriot rule in most of New England.

General Thomas Gage, the military governor of Massachusetts, tried desperately to maintain imperial power. In September 1774 he ordered British troops in Boston to seize Patriot armories and storehouses at Charlestown and Cambridge. In response, twenty thousand colonial militiamen mobilized to safeguard other military supply depots. The Concord town meeting voted to raise a defensive force, the famous **Minutemen**, to "Stand at a minutes warning in Case of alarm." Increasingly, Gage's authority was limited to Boston, where it rested primarily on the bayonets of his thirty-five hundred troops. Meanwhile, the Massachusetts House met on its own authority, collected taxes, bolstered the militia, and assumed the responsibilities of government.

In London, the colonial secretary, Lord Dartmouth, proclaimed Massachusetts to be in "open rebellion." Declaring that "force should be repelled by force," he ordered Gage to march quickly against the "rude rabble." On the night of April 18, 1775, Gage dispatched seven hundred soldiers to capture colonial leaders and supplies at Concord. But Paul Revere and two other Bostonians warned the Patriots, and at dawn local militiamen met the British troops first at Lexington and then at Concord. The skirmishes took a dozen lives. As the British retreated to Boston, militiamen from neighboring towns repeatedly ambushed them. By the end of the day, 73 British soldiers were dead, 174 wounded, and 26 missing. British fire had killed 49 American militiamen and wounded 39 (see Voices from Abroad, "A British View of Lexington and Concord," p. 159). Too much blood had now been spilled to allow another compromise. Twelve years of economic conflict and constitutional debate had ended in civil war.

**VOICES FROM ABROAD**

# A British View of Lexington and Concord

## LIEUTENANT COLONEL FRANCIS SMITH

*T*he past vanishes as soon as it occurs, and must be reconstructed by historians from documentary evidence. On April 26, 1775, a week after British troops marched on Lexington and Concord, the Patriot-controlled Massachusetts Provincial Congress issued what it called a "true, and authentic account" of the hostilities. The Congress alleged that at Lexington "the regulars rushed on with great violence and first began the hostilities" and that in the retreat of the British troops from Concord "houses on the road were plundered, . . . women in child-bed were driven by soldiery naked in the streets,[and] old men peaceably in their houses were shot dead." Four days earlier, in his official report to General Gage, British lieutenant colonel Francis Smith offered an account that presented British actions in a much more favorable light. Which version should the historian find more "true, and authentic"?

Sir,—In obedience to your Excellency's commands, I marched on the evening of the 18th inst. with the corps of grenadiers and light infantry for Concord, . . . to destroy all ammunition, artillery, tents &c. . . . Notwithstanding we marched with the utmost expedition and secrecy, we found the country had intelligence or strong suspicion of our coming. . . .

At Lexington . . . [we] found on a green close to the road a body of the country people drawn up in military order, with arms and accoutrements, and, as appeared afterward, loaded. . . . Our troops advanced towards them, without any intention of injuring them . . . ; but they in confusion went off, principally to the left, only one of them fired before he went off, and three or four more jumped over a wall and fired from behind it among the soldiers; on which the troops returned it, and killed several of them. They likewise fired on the soldiers from the Meeting[house] and dwelling-houses. . . .

While at Concord we saw vast numbers assembling in many parts; at one of the bridges they marched down, with a very considerable body, on the light infantry posted there. On their coming pretty near, one of our men fired on them, which they returned; on which an action ensued and some few were killed and wounded. In this affair, it appears that, after the bridge was quitted, they scalped and otherwise ill treated one or two of [our] men who were either killed or severely wounded. . . .

On our leaving Concord to return to Boston they began to fire on us from behind walls, ditches, trees, &c., which, as we marched, increased to a very great degree, and continued . . . for, I believe, upwards of eighteen miles; so that I can't think but it must have been a preconcerted scheme in them, to attack the King's troops the first favorable opportunity that offered; otherwise, I think they could not, in such a short a time from our marching out, have raised such a numerous body. . . .

SOURCE: Massachusetts Historical Society, *Proceedings, 1876* (Boston, 1876), 350ff.

## TIMELINE

| | | | |
|---|---|---|---|
| **1754–1763** | Great War for Empire<br>British national debt doubles | **1766** | First compromise: Stamp Act repealed and Declaratory Act passed |
| **1760** | George III becomes king | **1767** | Townshend duties on certain colonial imports<br>Restraining Act in New York temporarily suspends colonial assembly there<br>Daughters of Liberty make "homespun" cloth |
| **1762** | Revenue Act reforms customs service<br>Royal Navy arrests smugglers | | |
| **1763** | Treaty of Paris ends war<br>Proclamation Line restricts settlement west of Appalachians<br>George Grenville becomes British prime minister<br>John Wilkes demands political reform in England | **1768** | Second nonimportation movement<br>British army occupies Boston |
| | | **1770** | Second compromise: Townshend duties repealed<br>Boston Massacre |
| **1764** | Currency Act protects British merchants<br>Sugar Act places duty on imported French molasses<br>Colonists oppose vice-admiralty courts | **1772** | Committees of Correspondence formed |
| | | **1773** | Tea Act assists British East India Company<br>Boston Tea Party |
| **1765** | Stamp Act imposes direct tax on colonists<br>Quartering Act provides barracks for British troops<br>Riots by Sons of Liberty<br>Stamp Act Congress<br>First nonimportation movement | **1774** | Coercive Acts punish Massachusetts<br>Quebec Act offends Patriots<br>First Continental Congress<br>Third nonimportation movement<br>Loyalists organize |
| | | **1775** | General Thomas Gage marches to Lexington and Concord |

# For Further Exploration

Jack P. Greene and J. R. Pole, eds., *The Blackwell Encyclopedia of the American Revolution* (1991), illuminates both obscure and well-known aspects of the Revolutionary era, as do the personal testimonies in Barbara DeWolfe, *Discoveries of America: Personal Accounts of British Emigrants to North American during the Revolutionary Era* (1997). Edward Countryman, *The American Revolution* (1985), is a well-written scholarly overview, which tells the story through the lives of ordinary people. For a more journalistic account that focuses on leading men, see A. J. Langguth's *Patriots: The Men Who Started the American Revolution* (1988), a suspenseful story of such famous figures as George Washington, John Adams, Samuel Adams, and Patrick Henry. Edmund Morgan and Helen Morgan also use a biographical approach to tell the story of *The Stamp Act Crisis* (1953). Philip Lawson's *George Grenville* (1984) offers a sympathetic portrait of a reform-minded prime minister. The coming of the revolution is covered in three lucidly written and broadly conceived studies. Hiller B. Zobel's *The Boston Massacre* (1970) captures the social unrest and latent violence of these years, while Benjamin Labaree's *The Boston Tea Party* suggests how one "small" event altered the course of history and David Hackett Fischer explains the rise of the Radical Patriots and the outbreak of fighting in Massachusetts in *Paul Revere's Ride* (1994). For events in Virginia, see the probing study by Woody Holton, *Forced Founders: Indians, Debtors, Slaves, and the Making of the American Revolution in Virginia* (1999).

*Liberty! The American Revolution* (6 hours), a six-part video available through PBS, provides a coherent narrative of the movement for independence and has a fine companion Web site at <http://www.pbs.org/ktca/liberty/>. Two good collections of pamphlets, other political materials, and visual images pertaining to the Revolutionary era are available at Web sites at the University of Groningen in the Netherlands, <http://odur.let.rug.nl/~usa/D/index.htm> and at the University of Maryland, Baltimore County, <http://www.research.umbc.edu/~bouton/Revolution.links.htm>. The Web site of the National Gallery of Art, <http://www.nga.gov>, has an interesting section devoted to American paintings of the colonial and Revolutionary periods, including a detailed analysis of a work by Jonathan Copley. See its Index of American Design for a collection of eighteenth-century German American folk art.

---

For definitions of key terms boldfaced in this chapter, see the glossary at the end of the book.

To assess your mastery of the material covered in this chapter, see the Online Study Guide at **bedfordstmartins.com/henrettaconcise**.

For map resources and primary documents, see **bedfordstmartins.com/henrettaconcise**.

# Part Two

# THE NEW REPUBLIC
## 1775–1820

| GOVERNMENT | DIPLOMACY | ECONOMY |
|---|---|---|
| **Creating Republican Institutions** | **European Entanglements** | **Expanding Commerce and Manufacturing** |
| **1775** ▶ State constitutions devised and implemented <br><br> Monarchy-friendly Loyalists depart | ▶ Independence declared (1776) <br><br> French alliance (1778) | ▶ Wartime expansion of manufacturing <br><br> Severe inflation threatens economy |
| **1780** ▶ Articles of Confederation ratified (1781) <br><br> Legislatures assert supremacy in states <br><br> Philadelphia convention drafts U.S. Constitution (1787) | ▶ Treaty of Paris (1783) <br><br> Britain restricts U.S. trade with West Indies <br><br> U.S. government signs treaties with Indian peoples | ▶ Bank of North America founded (1781) <br><br> Commercial recession (1783–1789) <br><br> Western land speculation |
| **1790** ▶ Conflict over Hamilton's economic policies <br><br> First national parties: Federalists and Republicans | ▶ Wars of the French Revolution <br><br> Jay's and Pinckney's Treaties (1795) <br><br> Undeclared war with France (1798) | ▶ First Bank of the United States (1792–1812) <br><br> States charter business corporations <br><br> Outwork system grows |
| **1800** ▶ Revolution of 1800 reduces activism of national government <br><br> Chief Justice Marshall asserts judicial power | ▶ Napoleonic Wars (1802–1815) <br><br> Louisiana Purchase (1803) <br><br> Embargo of 1807 | ▶ Cotton expands into Old Southwest <br><br> Farm productivity improves <br><br> Embargo encourages U.S. manufacturing |
| **1810** ▶ Triumph of Republican Party and demise of Federalist Party <br><br> State constitutions democratized | ▶ War of 1812 <br><br> Treaty of Ghent (1816) ends war <br><br> Monroe Doctrine (1823) | ▶ Second Bank of the United States (1816–1836) <br><br> Supreme Court aids business <br><br> Emergence of a national economy |

| SOCIETY | CULTURE |
|---|---|
| **Defining Liberty and Equality** | **Pluralism and National Identity** |
| ▶ Emancipation of slaves in the North<br><br>Judith Sargent Murray, *On the Equality of the Sexes* (1779) | ▶ Thomas Paine's *Common Sense* calls for a republic |
| ▶ Virginia Statute of Religious Freedom (1786)<br><br>Idea of republican motherhood<br><br>French Revolution sparks ideological debate | ▶ State cessions and land ordinances create national domain in the West<br><br>German settlers keep own language<br><br>Noah Webster defines American English |
| ▶ Bill of Rights ratified (1791)<br><br>Sedition Act limits freedom of the press (1798) | ▶ Indians form Western Confederacy<br><br>Sectional divisions emerge between South and North |
| ▶ Youth choose own marriage partners<br><br>New Jersey decrees male-only suffrage (1807)<br><br>Atlantic slave trade legally ended (1808) | ▶ African Americans absorb Protestant Christianity<br><br>Tenskwatawa and Tecumseh revive Indian identity |
| ▶ Expansion of suffrage for white men<br><br>New England abolishes established churches (1820s) | ▶ War of 1812 tests national unity<br><br>Second Great Awakening shapes American culture |

"The American war is over," the Philadelphia Patriot Benjamin Rush declared in 1787, "but this is far from being the case with the American Revolution. On the contrary, nothing but the first act of the great drama is closed. It remains yet to establish and perfect our new forms of government." The job was even greater than Rush imagined, because the republican revolution of 1776 challenged nearly all the values and institutions of the colonial social order and forced changes not only in politics but also in economic, religious, and cultural life. By 1820 the new republic boasted activist state governments and vibrant movements for social reform and religious revival.

**GOVERNMENT** The first and most fundamental task was to create a republican system of government. But what precisely did that mean? In 1775, no one knew how the states should go about setting up republican institutions. Nor did American leaders know if there should be a permanent central authority along the lines of the Continental Congress. It would take time and experience to find out. It would take even longer to assimilate a new institution—the political party—into the workings of government. However, by 1820 difficult years of political compromise and constitutional revision had created state and national republican governments that commanded the allegiance of their citizens.

**DIPLOMACY** To create and preserve their new republic, Americans of European descent had to fight two wars against Great Britain, an undeclared war against France, and many battles with Indian peoples and confederations. The wars against Britain divided the country into bitter factions—Patriots against Loyalists in 1776, and prowar Republicans against antiwar Federalists in 1812—and expended much blood and treasure. Tragically, the extension of American sovereignty and settlement into the trans-Appalachian West brought cultural disaster to many Indian peoples, as their lives were cut short by European diseases and alcohol and their lands were seized by white settlers. Despite these external wars and internal conflicts, by 1820 the United States emerged as a strong independent state. Freed from a half century of entanglement in the wars and diplomacy of Europe, its people began to exploit the riches of the continent.

**ECONOMY** Already the expansion of markets and commerce had established the foundations for a strong national economy. Beginning in the 1780s northern merchants financed a banking system and organized a rural-based system of manufacturing, while state governments used charters and legal incentives to assist business entrepreneurs and provide improved roads, bridges, and waterways. Simultaneously, southern planters carried slavery westward to Alabama and

Mississippi and grew rich by exporting a new staple crop—cotton—to markets in Europe and the North. Some yeomen farm families migrated to the West to grow grain; those in the East turned to the production of raw materials such as leather and wool for the burgeoning manufacturing enterprises and worked part-time as handicraft workers. As a result of these activities, by 1820 the young American republic was on the verge of achieving economic as well as political independence.

**SOCIETY** As Americans undertook to create a republican society, they divided along lines of gender, race, religion, and class and disagreed over fundamental issues: legal equality for women, the status of slavery, the meaning of free speech and religious liberty, and the extent of public responsibility for social inequality. They resolved some disputes. Legislatures abolished slavery in the North, broadened religious liberty by allowing freedom of conscience, and (except in New England) ended the system of established churches. However, Americans continued to argue over social equality, in part because their republican creed placed authority in the family and society in the hands of men of property. This arrangement denied power not only to slaves but also to free blacks, women, and poor white men.

**CULTURE** The diversity of peoples and regions complicated efforts to define a distinct American culture and identity. Native Americans still lived in their own clans and nations, while black Americans, one-fifth of the enumerated population, were developing a new African American culture. The white inhabitants created vigorous regional cultures and preserved parts of their ancestral heritage—English, Scottish, Scots-Irish, German, and Dutch. Nevertheless, political institutions began to unite Americans, as did their increasing participation in the market economy and in evangelical Protestant churches. By 1820, to be an American meant, for many members of the dominant white population, to be a republican, a Protestant, and an enterprising individual in a capitalist-run market system.

# Chapter 6

# WAR AND REVOLUTION
## 1775–1783

A government of our own is our natural right. . . . 'TIS TIME
TO PART.

THOMAS PAINE, 1776

**W**hen the Patriots of Frederick County, Maryland, demanded allegiance to the American cause in 1776, Robert Gassaway would have none of it. "It was better for the poor people to lay down their arms and pay the duties and taxes laid upon them by King and Parliament," he told the local Council of Safety, "than to be brought into slavery and commanded and ordered about [by you]." The story was much the same in Farmington, Connecticut, where Patriot officials imprisoned Nathaniel Jones and seventeen other men for "remaining neutral" and not opposing a British raid. Everywhere, the logic of events was forcing families to choose sides between the Loyalists and the Patriots.

In this battle for the hearts and minds of ordinary men and women, the Patriots had an edge. Using their control of local governments, Patriot officials organized their neighbors into militia units and recruited volunteers for the Continental army. Gradually the American rebels forged an army that, despite its ragged appearance, held its own on the battlefield. "I admire the American troops tremendously!" exclaimed a French officer toward the end of the war. "It is incredible that soldiers composed of every age, even children of fifteen, of whites and blacks, almost naked, unpaid, and rather poorly fed, can march so well and withstand fire so steadfastly."

Military mobilization created political commitment. To encourage ordinary Americans to support the war—as soldiers, taxpayers, and hardworking citizens—the Patriot leadership prompted them to take an active role in the new republican governments. As the common people became the rulers rather than the ruled, the character of politics changed. "From subjects to citizens the difference is immense," remarked the South Carolina Patriot David Ramsay. "Each citizen of a free state contains . . . as much of the common sovereignty as another." By raising a democratic army and repudiating aristocratic and monarchical rule, the Patriots launched the age of republican revolutions first in Europe and then in Spain's American empire.

166

# Toward Independence, 1775–1776

The Battle of Concord set the Patriots on the road to independence. During the following months Patriot legislators in the thirteen colonies stretching from New Hampshire to Georgia threw out their royal governors and created the two essentials for independence: a provisional government and a credible army.

## *The Second Continental Congress and Civil War*

In May 1775 Patriot leaders gathered in Philadelphia for a Second Continental Congress. Soon after the Congress opened, more than 3,000 British troops attacked American fortifications on Breed's Hill and Bunker Hill overlooking Boston. After three assaults and 1,000 casualties, they finally dislodged the Patriot militia. Inspired by his countrymen's valor, John Adams exhorted the Congress to rise to the "defense of American liberty" by creating a Continental army and nominated George Washington of Virginia to lead it. After bitter debate Congress approved the proposals—but, Adams lamented, only "by bare majorities."

Despite the blood that had been shed, a majority in Congress still hoped for reconciliation with Britain. Led by John Dickinson of Pennsylvania, these moderates won approval of a petition that expressed loyalty to George III and requested repeal of oppressive Parliamentary legislation. But zealous Patriots such as Samuel Adams of Massachusetts and Patrick Henry of Virginia drummed up support for a Declaration of the Causes and Necessities of Taking Up Arms. Americans dreaded the "calamities of civil war," the declaration asserted, but were "resolved to die Freemen rather than to live [as] slaves." George III chose not to exploit these divisions among the Patriots; instead, in August 1775 he issued a Proclamation for Suppressing Rebellion and Sedition.

Even before the king's proclamation reached America, the radicals in Congress had won support for an invasion of Canada. Their goal was to unleash a popular French uprising and add a fourteenth colony to the rebellion. Patriot forces easily took Montreal, but in December 1775 they failed to capture Quebec City. Meanwhile, American merchants waged financial warfare by carrying out the promise of the First Continental Congress to cut off all exports to Britain and its West Indian sugar islands. With the tobacco and sugar trades in disarray, Parliament retaliated with the Prohibitory Act, which outlawed all trade with the rebellious colonies.

Skirmishes between Patriot and Loyalist forces broke out in many colonies. In Virginia the Patriot-dominated House of Burgesses forced the royal governor, Lord Dunmore, to take refuge on a British warship in Chesapeake Bay. Branding the Patriots as "traitors," the governor organized two military forces—one white, the Queen's Own Loyal Virginians, and one black, the Ethiopian Regiment, which enlisted about 1,000 slaves who had fled from their Patriot owners and were eager to fight for their liberty. In November 1775 Dunmore issued a controversial proclamation

**George III, 1771**

Like George Washington (b. 1732), King George III (b. 1738) was a young man when the American troubles began in 1765. In 1771, when Johann Zoffany painted this portrait of the king, George III was a headstrong monarch who was determined to impose his will on Parliament. Although he strongly supported Parliament's attempts to tax the colonies, his active involvement in the affairs of state sparked political confusion and contributed to the inept policy-making that led to the American rebellion.

The Royal Collection. © Her Majesty Queen Elizabeth II.

promising freedom to slaves and indentured servants who joined the Loyalist cause. White planters denounced this "Diabolical scheme" as "pointing a dagger to their Throats." Faced with black unrest and pressed by yeoman and tenant farmers demanding independence, Patriot planters called for a final break with Britain.

In North Carolina, military clashes likewise prompted demands for independence. Early in 1776 Josiah Martin, North Carolina's royal governor, raised a Loyalist force of 1,500 Scottish Highlanders in the Carolina backcountry. In response, Patriots mobilized the low-country militia and in February defeated Martin's army at the Battle of Moore's Creek Bridge, capturing more than 800 Highlanders (see American Voices, "The Meaning of War," p. 169). Following this victory, radical Patriots turned the North Carolina assembly into an independent Provincial Congress, which instructed its representatives in Philadelphia "to concur with the Delegates of other Colonies in declaring Independence, and forming foreign alliances." In May, Virginia Patriots followed suit; led by James Madison, Edmund Pendleton, and Patrick Henry, they met in convention and resolved unanimously to support independence.

## Common Sense

As the Patriots moved toward independence, many colonists retained a deep loyalty to the crown. Joyous crowds had toasted the health of George III when he ascended the throne in 1760 and when his ministers repealed the Stamp Act. Even as

**AMERICAN VOICES**

# The Meaning of War

MARY HOOKS SLOCUMB

*For sixteen-year-old Mary Hooks Slocumb, the outbreak of fighting in 1776 had a personal meaning. Already married and the mother of a young child, Slocumb so feared for the safety of her husband, a member of the North Carolina Light Horse Rangers, that, as she noted in a memoir written many years later, she threw caution to the wind, rushed to his side, and found herself in the role of a battlefield nurse.*

The men all left on Sunday morning. More than eighty went from this house with my husband. . . . I kept thinking where they had got to—how far; where and how many of the regulars and tories they would meet. . . . [That night] I had a dream. . . . I saw distinctly a body wrapped in my husband's guard cloak—bloody—dead; and others dead and wounded on the ground around him. . . . If ever I felt fear it was at that moment. . . . I went to the stable, saddled my mare—as fleet and easy a nag as ever travelled; and in one minute we were tearing down the road at full speed. . . .

When day broke I was some thirty miles from home. . . . The blind path I had been following brought me into the Wilmington road leading to Moore's Creek Bridge. . . . [A] few yards from the road, under a cluster of trees were lying perhaps twenty men. . . . In an instant my whole soul was centered in one spot; for there, wrapped in his bloody guard-Cloak, was my husband's body! . . . I remember uncovering his head and seeing a face clothed with gore from a dreadful wound across the temple. I put my hand on the bloody face; 'twas warm; and an *unknown voice* begged for water. . . . I brought it; poured some in his mouth; washed his face; and behold—it was Frank Cogdell. He soon revived and could speak. I was washing the wound in his head. Said he, "It is not that; it is that hole in my leg that is killing me." A puddle of blood was standing on the ground around his feet. I took his knife, cut away his trousers and stocking, found the blood came from a shot-hole through and through the fleshy part of his leg. I looked about and could see nothing that looked as if it would do for dressing wounds but some heart-leaves. I gathered a handful and bound them tight to the holes; and the bleeding stopped. . . . I dressed the wounds of many a brave fellow who did good fighting long after that day! . . . . Just then I looked up, and my husband, as bloody as a butcher, and as muddy as a ditcher, stood before me.

"Why Mary," he exclaimed, "What are you doing there?" . . . I would not tell my husband what brought me there. . . . In the middle of the night I again mounted my mare and started for home. . . . What a happy ride I had back! and with what joy did I embrace my child as he ran to meet me!

SOURCE: Elizabeth F. Ellet, *The Women of the American Revolution* (1850; New York: Haskell House, 1969), I, 316–21.

the imperial crisis worsened, Benjamin Franklin proposed that the king rule over autonomous American assemblies. This loyalty to the king stemmed in part from the character of social authority and family values. Every father was "a king, and governor in his family," according to the Stonington (Connecticut) Baptist Association. Just as the settlers submitted to male elders in their town meetings, churches, and families, so they should obey the king, their imperial "father." Denial of the king's legitimacy might threaten all paternal authority and disrupt the hierarchical social order.

Nonetheless, by 1775 many Americans had turned against the monarch. As the military conflict escalated, they accused George III of supporting oppressive legislation and ordering armed retaliation against them. Surprisingly, agitation became especially intense in Philadelphia, the largest—but hardly the most radical— seaport city. Many Philadelphia merchants harbored Loyalist sympathies and had been slow to join the boycott against the Townshend duties. However, artisans, who numbered about half the city's workers, had become a powerful force in the Patriot movement. Worried that British imports threatened their small-scale manufacturing enterprises, they organized a Mechanics Association to protect America's "just Rights and Privileges." By February 1776, forty artisans sat with forty-seven merchants on the Philadelphia Committee of Resistance, the extralegal body that enforced the latest trade boycott.

Many Scots-Irish artisans and laborers in Philadelphia became Patriots for cultural and religious reasons. They came from Presbyterian families who had fled from British-controlled Ireland to escape religious discrimination; moreover, many of them had embraced the egalitarian message preached by Gilbert Tennent and other New Light ministers. As pastor of Philadelphia's Second Presbyterian Church, Tennent had told his congregation that all men and women were equal before God. Applying that idea to politics, New Light Presbyterians shouted in street demonstrations that they had "no king but King Jesus." Republican ideas derived from the European Enlightenment also circulated freely in Pennsylvania. Well-educated scientists and political leaders such as Benjamin Franklin and Benjamin Rush questioned not only the wisdom of George III but also the idea of monarchy itself.

With popular sentiment in flux, a single pamphlet tipped the balance toward the Patriot side. In January 1776 Thomas Paine published *Common Sense*, a call for independence and a republican (nonmonarchical) form of government. Paine had served as a minor bureaucrat in the Customs Service in England and was fired for protesting low wages. He found his way to London, where he wangled a meeting with Benjamin Franklin. In 1774 Paine migrated to Philadelphia, where he met Benjamin Rush and other Patriots who shared his republican sentiments. In *Common Sense* Paine launched a direct assault on the traditional political order in rousing language that stirred popular emotions.

"Monarchy and hereditary succession have laid the world in blood and ashes," Paine proclaimed, leveling a personal attack against George III, "the hard hearted sullen Pharaoh of England." Mixing insults with biblical quotations, Paine blasted the British system of "mixed government" among the three estates of king, lords, and commoners. "That it was noble for the dark and slavish times in which it was created," Paine granted, but now this system of governance yielded only "monarchical tyranny in the person of the king" and "aristocratical tyranny in the persons of the peers."

Paine also made a compelling case for American independence. Turning the traditional metaphor of patriarchal authority on its head, he asked, "Is it the interest of a man to be a boy all his life?" Within six months *Common Sense* went through twenty-five editions and reached hundreds of thousands of people throughout the colonies. "There is great talk of independence," a worried New York Loyalist noted, "and the unthinking multitude are mad for it. . . . A pamphlet called Common Sense has carried off . . . thousands." Paine called on Americans to reject the king and Parliament and create independent republican states. "A government of our own is our natural right. . . . 'TIS TIME TO PART."

### Independence Declared

Inspired by Paine's arguments and beset by armed Loyalists, Patriot conventions called urgently for a break from Britain. In June 1776 Richard Henry Lee presented the Virginia Convention's resolution to the Continental Congress: "That these United Colonies are, and of right ought to be, free and independent states . . . absolved from all allegiance to the British Crown." Faced with certain defeat, staunch Loyalists and anti-independence moderates withdrew from the Congress, and left committed Patriots to take the fateful step. On July 4, 1776, the Congress approved the Declaration of Independence (see Documents, p. D-1).

The main author of the Declaration was Thomas Jefferson, a young Virginia planter. As a member of the Virginia legislature, Jefferson had mobilized resistance to the Coercive Acts with the pamphlet *A Summary View of the Rights of British America*. To persuade Americans and foreign observers to support independence, Jefferson vilified George III: "He has plundered our seas, ravaged our coasts, burned our towns, and destroyed the lives of our people. . . . A prince, whose character is thus marked by every act which may define a tyrant," Jefferson concluded, conveniently ignoring his own actions as a slave owner, "is unfit to be the ruler of a free people."

Employing the ideas of the European Enlightenment (see Chapter 4), Jefferson justified **republicanism** by proclaiming a series of "self-evident" truths: "that all men are created equal"; that they possess the "unalienable rights" of "Life, Liberty, and the pursuit of Happiness"; that government derives its "just powers from the consent of the governed" and can rightly be overthrown if it "becomes destructive of these ends." By linking these doctrines of individual liberty, popular sovereignty, and a republican form of government with independence, Jefferson established them as defining values of the new nation.

For Jefferson, as for Paine, the pen proved mightier than the sword. In rural hamlets and seaport cities, crowds celebrated the Declaration by burning George III in effigy and toppling statues of the king. These acts of destruction broke the Patriots' psychological ties to the father-monarch and established the legitimacy of republican state governments. On July 8, 1776, in Easton, Pennsylvania, a "great number of spectators" heard a reading of the Declaration, "gave their hearty assent with three loud huzzahs, and cried out, 'May God long preserve and unite the Free and Independent States of America.'"

# The Trials of War, 1776–1778

The Declaration of Independence coincided with a full-scale British military assault against the Patriots. For two years British forces won nearly every battle against the Continental army commanded by George Washington. A few inspiring American victories kept the rebellion alive, but during the winters of 1776 and 1777 the Patriot cause hung in the balance.

## War in the North

When the British resorted to military force, few European observers gave the rebels a chance. Great Britain had 11 million people, compared with the colonies' 2.5 million, nearly 20 percent of whom were enslaved Africans. Economically, the British had an even greater advantage thanks to the immense wealth generated by the South Atlantic system and the emerging Industrial Revolution. Its financial resources paid for the most powerful navy in the world, a standing army of 48,000 men, and thousands of hired German soldiers. British military officers had experience in America during the Seven Years' War, and their soldiers were well armed. Finally, the imperial government had the support of thousands of American Loyalists and many Indian tribes. The Cherokees in the Carolinas were firmly committed to the British side, as were four of the six Iroquois Nations of New York—the Mohawks, Senecas, Cayugas, and Onondagas—who were led by the pro-British Mohawk chief Joseph Brant.

By contrast, the rebellious Americans were militarily weak. General Washington's army consisted of about 18,000 poorly trained, short-term recruits hastily assembled by state governments in Virginia and New England. The Patriots could field thousands more militiamen but only near their own farms. Although many American officers had fought during the French and Indian War, they had never commanded a large force or faced a disciplined European army.

To exploit this military advantage, Britain's prime minister, Lord North, assembled a large invasion force and selected General William Howe to lead it. North ordered Howe to capture New York City and seize control of the Hudson River, thereby isolating the radical Patriots in New England from the other colonies. As the Continental Congress was declaring independence in Philadelphia in July 1776, Howe landed 32,000 troops—British regulars and German mercenaries—outside New York City.

**Joseph Brant**

The Mohawk chief Thayendanegea, known to the whites as Joseph Brant, was a devout member of the Church of England who had helped to translate the Bible into the Iroquois language. An influential leader, Brant secured the support of four of the six Iroquois Nations for the British. In 1778 and 1779, he led Iroquois warriors and Tory Rangers in devastating attacks on American settlements in the Wyoming Valley of Pennsylvania and the Cherry Valley in New York. This portrait by Charles Willson Peale was painted in 1797. Independence National Historic Park.

FOR MORE HELP ANALYZING THIS IMAGE, see the Online Study Guide at **bedfordstmartins.com/henrettaconcise**.

British superiority was immediately apparent. In August 1776 Howe attacked the Americans in the Battle of Long Island and forced their retreat to Manhattan Island. There Howe outflanked Washington's troops and nearly trapped them. Outgunned and outmaneuvered, the Continental army again retreated, first to Harlem Heights, then to White Plains, and finally across the Hudson River to New Jersey. By December, the British army had pushed the rebels out of New Jersey and across the Delaware River into Pennsylvania (Map 6.1).

From the Patriots' perspective winter came just in time. Following eighteenth-century military custom, the British halted their campaign for the cold months and allowed the Americans to catch them off guard. On Christmas night in 1776 Washington led his troops across the Delaware River and staged a surprise attack on Trenton, New Jersey, where he forced the surrender of 1,000 German soldiers. In early January 1777 the Continental army won another small victory at nearby Princeton. Bright stars in a dark night, these minor triumphs could not mask British military superiority. These are the times, wrote Tom Paine, that "try men's souls."

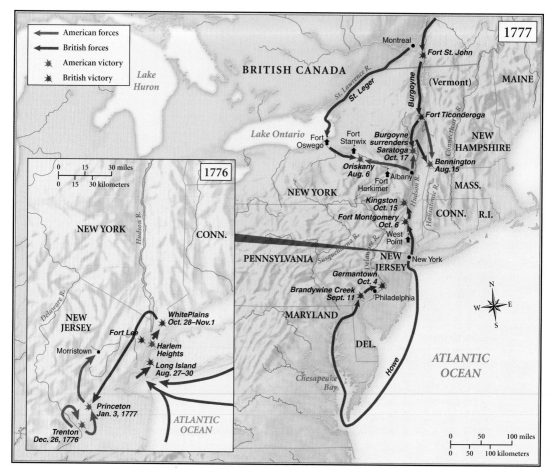

**MAP 6.1 The War in the North, 1776–1777**

In 1776 the British army drove Washington's forces across New Jersey into Pennsylvania. The Americans counterattacked successfully at Trenton and Princeton and then set up winter headquarters at Morristown. In 1777 British forces stayed on the offensive. General Howe attacked the Patriot capital of Philadelphia from the south, capturing it in early October. Meanwhile, General Burgoyne and Colonel St. Leger launched simultaneous invasions from Canada. Aided by thousands of New England militia, American troops commanded by General Horatio Gates defeated Burgoyne at Bennington, Vermont, and, in October 1777, at Saratoga, New York, the military turning point of the war.

FOR MORE HELP ANALYZING THIS MAP, see the Online Study Guide at **bedfordstmartins.com/henrettaconcise**.

## Armies and Strategies

British superiority did not break the will of the Continental army and, thanks partly to General Howe's tactical decisions and mistakes, the rebellion continued. Howe had opposed the Coercive Acts of 1774, and he still hoped for a political compromise. Indeed, he had authority from Lord North to allow the rebels to surrender on honorable terms. Consequently, instead of ruthlessly pursuing the retreating American army, Howe was content to show his superior power and convince the Continental Congress that resistance was futile. Howe's tactics also reflected eighteenth-century military practices, which focused on winning the surrender of opposing forces rather than destroying them. Moreover, the British general knew that he could not afford a major defeat because he was 3,000 miles and many months away from reinforcements. Although Howe's prudent tactics were understandable, they cost the British the opportunity to nip the rebellion in the bud.

Howe's failure to win a decisive victory was paralleled by Washington's success in avoiding a major defeat. He too was cautious; as Washington advised Congress, "On our Side the War should be defensive." His strategy was to draw the British away from the seacoast, extend their lines of supply, and sap their morale while keeping the Continental army intact as a symbol and instrument of American resistance.

Congress had promised Washington a regular force of 75,000 men, but the Continental army never reached a third of that number. Yeomen farmers preferred to serve in the local militia so that they could continue to work their farms; consequently, many recruits in the regular army were propertyless farmers and laborers. The Continental soldiers recruited by the state of Maryland and commanded by General William Smallwood were either poor American-born youths or older foreign-born men—often British ex-convicts and former indentured servants. Such men enlisted not out of patriotism but for a bonus of $20 in cash (about $1,000 today) and the promise of 100 acres of land. Molding such recruits into a fighting force took time. Many men panicked in the face of a British artillery bombardment or flank attack; hundreds deserted, unwilling to submit to the discipline of military life. The soldiers who stayed resented the contemptuous way their officers treated the "camp followers," the women who fed and cared for the troops.

Such personal support was crucial, for the Continental army was poorly supplied and faintly praised. Radical Whig Patriots viewed a standing army as a threat to liberty and even in wartime preferred the militia to a professional force. General Philip Schuyler of New York complained that his troops were "weak in numbers, dispirited, naked, destitute of provisions, without camp equipage, with little ammunition, and not a single piece of cannon." Given these handicaps, Washington was fortunate to have escaped an overwhelming defeat.

## Victory at Saratoga

Howe's failure to achieve a quick victory dismayed Lord North and his colonial secretary, Lord George Germain. Accepting the challenge of a long-term military commitment, the British leaders increased the land tax to finance the war and prepared to mount a major campaign in 1777.

The isolation of New England remained the primary British goal. To achieve it, Germain planned a three-pronged attack converging on Albany, New York. General John Burgoyne would lead a large contingent of British regulars from Quebec to Albany.

Colonel Barry St. Leger and a force of Iroquois warriors would attack from the west, and General Howe would dispatch a force northward from New York City (see Map 6.1).

Howe had a different scheme and it led to a disastrous result. Howe wanted to attack Philadelphia, the home of the Continental Congress, and end the rebellion with a single victory over Washington's army. With Germain's apparent approval, he set his plan in motion—but very slowly. Rather than march quickly through New Jersey, British troops sailed south from New York, then up the Chesapeake Bay to attack Philadelphia from the south. This strategy worked brilliantly, as Howe's troops easily outflanked the American positions along Brandywine Creek in Delaware and forced Washington to withdraw. On September 26 the British marched triumphantly into Philadelphia, expecting the capture of the rebels' capital would end the uprising. But the Continental Congress fled into the interior, determined to continue the struggle.

Moreover, Howe's slow attack against Philadelphia contributed directly to the defeat of Burgoyne's army. Initially Burgoyne's troops advanced quickly from Canada, crossing Lake Champlain, overwhelming the American defenses at Fort Ticonderoga and driving toward the upper reaches of the Hudson River. Then they stalled, for Burgoyne—"Gentleman Johnny," as he was called—fought with style and was slowed down by the extra weight of comfortable tents and ample stocks of food and wine. The American troops led by General Horatio Gates further impeded Burgoyne's progress by felling huge trees to delay his wagons and by raiding his long supply lines to Canada.

By the summer's end, Burgoyne's army of 6,000 British and German troops and 600 Loyalists and Indians was bogged down near Saratoga, New York. Desperate for food and horses, the British force staged a raid on nearby Bennington, Vermont, where 2,000 American militiamen repulsed them. Patriot forces in the Mohawk Valley likewise forced St. Leger and the Iroquois to retreat. To make matters worse, the British commander in New York City recalled the 4,000 troops he had sent toward Albany and dispatched them instead to bolster Howe's force in Philadelphia. While Burgoyne waited in vain for help, thousands of Patriot militiamen from Massachusetts, New Hampshire, and New York joined Gates's forces. They "swarmed around the army like birds of prey," reported an alarmed English sergeant, and in October 1777 forced Burgoyne to surrender.

The battle at Saratoga proved to be the turning point of the war. The Patriots captured more than 5,000 British troops and their equipment. Equally important, the victory ensured the success of American diplomats in Paris, who were seeking a military alliance with France.

## Social and Financial Perils

As Patriots on the home front celebrated the triumph at Saratoga, their joy was muted by wartime difficulties. The fighting exposed tens of thousands of civilians to deprivation, displacement, and death. "An army, even a friendly one, are a dreadful scourge to any people," a Connecticut soldier wrote from Pennsylvania. "You cannot imagine what devastation and distress mark their steps." British and American armies marched back and forth across New Jersey, forcing Patriot and Loyalist families to flee their homes to escape arrest—or worse. Soldiers and partisans looted farms for food or political revenge. Wherever the armies went, disorderly troops harassed and raped women and girls. When British warships sailed up the Potomac River, women and children fled from Alexandria, Virginia, and "stowed themselves into every Hut they can get, out of the reach of the Enemys canon" and troops.

The war became a bloody partisan conflict. Patriots formed Committees of Safety that collected taxes, sent food and clothing to the Continental army, and imposed fines or jail sentences on those who failed to support the cause. In New England mobs of Patriot farmers beat suspected Tories and destroyed their property. "Every Body submitted to our Sovereign Lord the Mob," a Loyalist preacher lamented. In some areas of Maryland, the number of "nonassociators"—those who refused to join either side—was so large that they successfully defied Patriot organizers. "Stand off you dammed rebel sons of bitches," Robert Davis of Anne Arundel County shouted, "I will shoot you if you come any nearer."

Such defiance exposed the weakness of the new state governments, which teetered on the brink of bankruptcy. To feed, clothe, and pay their troops, state officials borrowed gold, silver, or British currency from wealthy individuals. When those funds ran out, Patriot officials were afraid to raise taxes. Instead, individual states printed paper money, issuing $260 million in currency. Because it was printed in huge quantities and was not backed by gold, tax revenues, or mortgages on land, many Americans refused

**Paper Currency**

To symbolize their independent status, the new state governments printed their own currency. Rejecting the English system of pounds and shillings, Virginia used the Spanish gold dollar as the basic unit of currency but included the equivalent in English pounds ($1,200 was £360, a ratio of 3.3 to 1). By 1781, Virginia had printed so much paper money to pay its soldiers and wartime expenses that the value of the currency had depreciated. It now took 40 Virginia paper dollars to buy the same amount of goods as one English pound (a 40-to-1 ratio). American Numismatic Society.

to accept the new currency at its face value. North Carolina's paper money came to be worth so little that even the tax collectors refused it.

The finances of the Continental Congress collapsed too, despite the efforts of the Philadelphia merchant Robert Morris, the government's chief treasury official. The Congress lacked the authority to impose taxes and so depended on funds requisitioned from the states, which frequently paid late or not at all. The Congress therefore borrowed gold from France and encouraged wealthy Americans to purchase Continental bonds. When those funds and other French and Dutch loans were exhausted, the Congress followed the lead of the states and printed $191 million in currency and bills of credit, which quickly declined in value. Unwilling to accept nearly worthless currency, farmers refused to sell their crops, even to the Continental army. Military morale crumbled, causing some Patriot leaders to doubt that the rebellion could succeed.

Fears reached their peak during the winter of 1777. While Howe's army partook of warm lodgings and ample food in Philadelphia, Washington's army retreated twenty miles to the west to Valley Forge, where about 12,000 soldiers and hundreds of camp followers suffered horribly. "The army . . . now begins to grow sickly," a surgeon confided to his diary. "Poor food—hard lodging—cold weather—fatigue—nasty clothes—nasty cookery. . . . Why are we sent here to starve and freeze?" Nearby farmers refused to help. Some were pacifists—Quakers and German sectarians—unwilling to support either side. Others looked out for their families, hoarding grain in hopes of higher prices or accepting only the gold and silver offered by British quartermasters. "Such a dearth of public spirit, and want of public virtue," Washington lamented, distressed that few Patriots were upholding republican ideas, but to no effect. By spring, 1,000 hungry soldiers had vanished into the countryside and another 3,000 had died from malnutrition and disease. One winter at Valley Forge took as many American lives as had two years of fighting.

In this dark hour Baron von Steuben raised the self-respect and readiness of the American army. A former Prussian military officer, von Steuben was one of a handful of republican-minded foreign aristocrats who aided the American cause. To counter falling morale, he instituted a system of drill and maneuver and encouraged officers to become more professional in their demeanor. Thanks to von Steuben, the smaller Continental army that emerged from Valley Forge in the spring of 1778 was a much tougher and better-disciplined force.

# The Path to Victory, 1778–1783

Wars are often won by astute diplomacy and the War of Independence was no exception. The Patriots' prospects improved dramatically in 1778, when the United States formed a military alliance with France, the most powerful European nation. The alliance brought the Americans money, troops, and supplies and changed the conflict from a colonial rebellion to an international war.

## The French Alliance

France and America were unlikely partners. France was Catholic and a monarchy; the United States was Protestant and a federation of republics. From 1689 to 1763 the two peoples had been military enemies, and New Englanders had recently forced the French population of Acadia (Nova Scotia) into exile. However, the Comte de Vergennes, the French foreign minister, was determined to avenge the loss of Canada to Britain. In 1776 he persuaded King Louis XVI to extend a secret loan to the rebellious colonies and supply them with much-needed gunpowder. Early in 1777 Vergennes opened negotiations with Benjamin Franklin and other American diplomats. When news of the American victory at Saratoga reached Paris in December 1777, Vergennes sought a formal alliance with the Continental Congress.

Franklin and his associates craftily exploited the rivalry between France and Britain to win an explicit commitment to American independence. The Treaty of Alliance of February 1778 specified that once France entered the war against Great Britain, neither partner would sign a separate peace before the "liberty, sovereignty, and independence" of the United States were ensured. In return, the American diplomats pledged that their government would recognize any French conquests in the West Indies. The alliance gave new life to the Patriots' cause. "There has been a great change in this state since the news from France," a Patriot soldier reported from Pennsylvania. Farmers—"mercenary wretches," he called them—"were as eager for Continental Money now as they were a few weeks ago for British gold."

The alliance bolstered the confidence of the Continental Congress. Acting now with purpose, the Congress addressed the demands of the officer corps. Most officers came from the upper ranks of society and had used their own funds to equip themselves and sometimes their men; in return they demanded lifetime military pensions at half pay. John Adams condemned the officers for "scrambling for rank and pay like apes for nuts," but General Washington urged Congress to grant the pensions, warning the lawmakers that "the salvation of the cause depends upon it." Congress reluctantly granted the officers half pay after the war, but only for seven years.

Meanwhile, the war was becoming increasingly unpopular in Britain. Radical agitators and republican-minded artisans supported American demands for greater rights and campaigned for domestic political reforms, such as the elimination of "rotten boroughs" (small voting districts controlled by wealthy men) and greater representation for cities in Parliament. The landed gentry protested increases in the land tax, and merchants condemned new levies on carriages, wine, and imported goods. "It seemed we were to be taxed and stamped ourselves instead of inflicting taxes and stamps on others," a British politician complained.

But George III still vowed to crush the rebellion. If America won independence, he warned Lord North, "the West Indies must follow them. Ireland would soon follow the same plan and be a separate state, then this island would be reduced to itself, and soon would be a poor island indeed." Following the British defeat at Saratoga, the king moderated his stance. To head off an American alliance with

France, he authorized North to seek a negotiated settlement. In February 1778 North persuaded Parliament to repeal the Tea and Prohibitory Acts and, in an amazing concession, to renounce its power to tax the colonies. Opening discussions with the Continental Congress, the prime minister proposed a return to the constitutional "condition of 1763," before the Sugar and Stamp Acts. The Patriots, now allied with France and seeking independence, rejected the overture.

## War in the South

The French alliance expanded the war but did not bring it to a rapid conclusion. When France entered the conflict in June 1778, it sent its naval forces to the West Indies in hopes of capturing Barbados, Jamaica, or another rich sugar island. Spain, which joined the war against Britain in 1779, also had its own agenda: it wanted to regain Florida and Gibraltar. The Patriot cause was now caught up in a web of European territorial quarrels and diplomatic intrigue.

Beset by many enemies on many fronts, the British ministry revised its American strategy. It decided to use its army to recapture the rich tobacco- and rice-growing colonies of Virginia, the Carolinas, and Georgia and then rely on local Loyalists to hold them. The British could count on the allegiance of Scottish Highlanders in North Carolina and hoped to recruit other Loyalists from the ranks of the Regulators, the enemies of the low-country Patriot planters (see Chapter 4). The ministry also planned to exploit the racial divisions in the South. In 1776 over 1,000 slaves had fought for Lord Dunmore under the banner "Liberty to Slaves!"; a new British military offensive might prompt thousands more to flee from their Patriot owners or to rise in rebellion. South Carolina could not raise an army to defend itself, its representative told the Continental Congress, "by reason of the great proportion of citizens necessary to remain at home to prevent insurrection among the Negroes." When the Congress suggested that South Carolina raise 3,000 black troops, the state assembly overwhelmingly rejected the proposal.

Implementing Britain's southern military strategy became the responsibility of Sir Henry Clinton. After moving the main British army to secure quarters in New York City, Clinton launched a successful seaborne attack on Savannah, Georgia, in December 1778. Mobilizing hundreds of blacks to unload and transport supplies, Clinton moved inland and captured Augusta early in 1779. By the end of the year, Clinton's forces and local Loyalists controlled Georgia, and 10,000 troops were poised for an assault on South Carolina (Map 6.2).

During most of 1780 British forces marched from victory to victory. In May Clinton laid siege to Charleston, South Carolina, and forced the surrender of General Benjamin Lincoln and his garrison of 5,000 troops. Then Lord Cornwallis assumed control of the British forces and marched into the countryside. In August, at the battle of Camden, Cornwallis defeated an American force commanded by General Horatio Gates, the hero of Saratoga. Only 1,200 Patriot militiamen joined Gates at Camden—a fifth of the number at Saratoga—and many of them panicked. As Cornwallis took

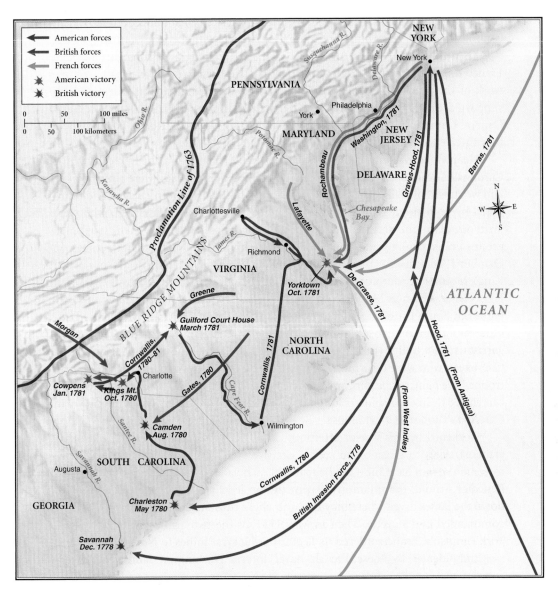

**MAP 6.2 The War in the South, 1778–1781**

The British ministry's southern strategy started well. British forces captured Savannah in December 1778, took control of Georgia during 1779, and vanquished Charleston in May 1780. Over the next eighteen months, brutal warfare conducted by small bands of irregular troops raged in the interior of the Carolinas and ended in a stalemate between British forces and their Loyalist supporters and the American army and militia. Hoping to break the deadlock, in 1781 British General Charles Cornwallis carried the battle into Virginia. A Franco-American army led by Washington and Lafayette, aided by the French fleet under Admiral de Grasse, surrounded Cornwallis's forces on the Yorktown peninsula and forced their surrender.

control of South Carolina, hundreds of African Americans fled to freedom in British-controlled Florida, while hundreds more found refuge with the British army.

Then the tide of battle turned. The Dutch declared war against Britain, and France finally dispatched troops to America. The French decision was partly the work of the Marquis de Lafayette, a republican-minded aristocrat who had long supported the American cause. In 1780 Lafayette persuaded Louis XVI to send General Comte de Rochambeau and 5,500 men to Newport, Rhode Island, where they threatened British forces in New York City.

Meanwhile, Washington dispatched General Nathanael Greene to recapture the Carolinas. Greene faced a difficult task. His troops, he reported, "were almost naked and we subsist by daily collections and in a country that has been ravaged and plundered by both friends and enemies." To make use of local militiamen, who were "without discipline and addicted to plundering," Greene divided them into small groups under strong leaders and unleashed them on less-mobile British forces. In October 1780 a militia force of Patriot farmers defeated a regiment of Loyalists at King's Mountain, South Carolina, taking about 1,000 prisoners. Led by the "Swamp Fox," General Francis Marion, American guerrillas won a series of small but fierce battles in South Carolina. Then, in January 1781, General Daniel Morgan led another American force to a bloody victory at Cowpens, South Carolina. But Loyalist garrisons and militia units remained powerful, assisted by the well-organized Cherokees, who were determined to protect their lands from American settlers and troops. "We fight, get beaten, and fight again," General Greene declared doggedly. In March 1781, Greene's soldiers fought Cornwallis's seasoned army to a draw at North Carolina's Guilford Court House.

Weakened by this **war of attrition**, Cornwallis decided to concede the southernmost states to Greene and seek a decisive victory in Virginia. Aided by reinforcements from New York, the British general invaded the Tidewater region. There Benedict Arnold, the infamous Patriot traitor, led British troops in raids up and down the James River, where they met only slight resistance from an American force commanded by Lafayette. Then in May 1781, as the two armies sparred near the York Peninsula, France ordered its fleet from the West Indies to North America.

Emboldened by these French naval forces, Washington launched a well-coordinated attack. Feinting an assault on New York City, he secretly marched General Rochambeau's army from Rhode Island to Virginia, where it joined his Continental army. Simultaneously, the French fleet massed off the coast, establishing control of Chesapeake Bay. By the time the British discovered Washington's audacious plan, Cornwallis was surrounded, his 9,500-man army outnumbered two to one on land and cut off from reinforcement or retreat by sea. Abandoned by the British navy, Cornwallis surrendered at Yorktown in October 1781.

The Franco-American victory at Yorktown broke the resolve of the British government. "Oh God! It is all over!" Lord North exclaimed when he heard the news. Isolated diplomatically in Europe, stymied militarily in America, and lacking public support at home, the British ministry gave up active prosecution of the war.

## The Patriot Advantage

Angry members of Parliament demanded an explanation. How could mighty Britain, victorious in the Great War for Empire, be defeated by a motley colonial army? The ministry blamed the military leadership, pointing with some justification to a series of blunders. Why had Howe not ruthlessly pursued Washington's army in 1776? How could Howe and Burgoyne have failed to coordinate the movement of their armies in 1777? Why didn't British generals make better use of the 55,000 Tories and thousands of Native American allies after 1778? Why had Cornwallis marched deep into the Patriot-dominated state of Virginia in 1781?

While criticizing these blunders, historians have emphasized the high odds against British success, given the broad support in America for the rebel cause. Although only a third of the white colonists were zealous Patriots, another third supported the war effort by paying taxes and joining the militia. Moreover, the Patriots had experienced politicians who commanded public support and, in George Washington, an inspired leader of the Continental army. An astute politician, Washington deferred to the civil authorities and thereby won respect and support from the Congress and the state governments. Confident of his own abilities, he recruited outstanding military officers to instill discipline in the fledgling Continental army and turn it into a respectable fighting force.

Finally, Washington also had a greater margin for error than the British generals did because Patriots controlled local governments. At crucial moments, they could mobilize the rural militia to assist his Continental army. Alone, the Patriot militia lacked the organization necessary to defeat the British army. However, in combination with the Continental forces, it proved potent, providing the margin of victory at Saratoga in 1777 and forcing Cornwallis from the Carolinas in 1781. In the end the American people decided the outcome. Preferring Patriot rule, they refused to support Loyalist forces or accept occupation by the British army. Consequently, while the British won many military victories, they achieved little. Once the rebels had the financial and military support of France, they could reasonably hope for a victory, such as that at Yorktown, that would end the conflict.

## Diplomatic Triumph

After Yorktown diplomats took two years to conclude the war. Peace talks began in Paris in April 1782, but the French and Spanish stalled because they still hoped for a major naval victory or territorial conquest. Their delaying tactics infuriated the American diplomats—Benjamin Franklin, John Adams, and John Jay. Fearing that France might sacrifice American interests, the Patriot diplomats negotiated secretly with the British, prepared if necessary to sign a separate peace. The British ministry was also eager for a quick settlement because Parliament no longer supported the war and officials feared the loss of a rich West Indian sugar island.

Exploiting the rivalry between Britain and France, the American diplomats secured peace on very favorable terms. In the Treaty of Paris, signed in September 1783, Great Britain formally recognized the independence of its seaboard colonies. While retaining Canada, Britain also relinquished its claims to lands south of the Great Lakes and east of the Mississippi River and promised to withdraw British garrisons "with all convenient speed." Leaving the pro-British Indian peoples in the trans-Appalachian west to their fate, the British negotiators did not insist on a separate Indian territory. "In endeavouring to assist you," a Wea Indian complained to a British general, "it seems we have wrought our own ruin."

Other treaty provisions were equally favorable to the American side. They granted Americans fishing rights off Newfoundland and Nova Scotia, forbade the British from "carrying away any negroes or other property," and guaranteed freedom of navigation on the Mississippi to both British subjects and American citizens "forever." In return, the American government allowed British merchants to pursue legal claims for prewar debts and to encourage the state legislatures to return confiscated property to Loyalists and grant them citizenship.

In the Treaty of Versailles, signed at the same time as the Treaty of Paris, Britain made peace with France and Spain. Neither American ally gained very much. Spain reclaimed Florida from Britain but failed to regain the strategic fortress of Gibraltar, while France's only territorial gain was the Caribbean island of Tobago. Moreover, the war had quadrupled France's national debt, and six years later cries for tax relief and political liberty would spark the French Revolution. Only Americans profited handsomely from the treaties, which gave them independence from Britain and opened the trans-Appalachian west for settlement.

# Republicanism Defined and Challenged

From the moment they became revolutionary republicans, Americans began to define their new social order. In the Declaration of Independence, Thomas Jefferson invoked John Locke, the philosopher of private liberty, in declaring a universal human right to "Life, Liberty, and the pursuit of Happiness." But Jefferson and many other Americans also lauded "republican virtue," an enlightened quest for the public good. As the New Hampshire constitution phrased it, "Government [was] instituted for the common benefits, protection, and security of the whole community." The tension between individual self-interest and the public interest would shape the future of the new nation.

## *Republican Ideals under Wartime Pressures*

Simply put, a republic is a state with a representative system of government. For many Americans, republicanism also meant a community-oriented outlook. "The word republic" in Latin, wrote Thomas Paine, "means the public good," which all citizens have a duty to secure. "Every man in a republic is public property," asserted the Philadelphia Patriot Benjamin Rush, who eventually extended the notion to include women as well. "His time and talents—his youth—his manhood—his old age—nay more, life, all belong to his country." Reflecting this sense of community, members of the Continental Congress praised the militiamen who fought and fell at Lexington and Concord, Saratoga and Camden. And they applauded Henry Laurens of South Carolina when he condemned as a "total loss of virtue" the demand by Continental army officers for lifetime pensions. Raised as gentlemen, officers should be exemplars of virtue who gave freely to the republic.

However, the hardships of war undermined selfless idealism. Unruly Continental troops stationed at Morristown, New Jersey, in the winters of 1779 and 1780 mutinied, unwilling any longer to endure low pay and sparse rations. To restore military authority Washington ordered the execution of several mutineers but urged Congress to pacify the soldiers with back pay and new clothing. Later in the war, dissident officers at Newburgh, New York, talked of a military coup and Washington had to use his personal authority to thwart a dangerous challenge to Congress's authority.

Economic distress likewise tested the republican virtue of ordinary citizens. The British naval blockade cut supplies of European manufactures and disrupted the New England fishing industry. British occupation of Boston, New York, and Philadelphia trimmed domestic trade and manufacturing. As unemployed shipwrights, dock laborers, masons, coopers, and bakers deserted the cities and drifted into the countryside, New York City's population declined from 21,000 residents in 1774 to less than half that number by the war's end. In the Chesapeake, the British blockade deprived tobacco planters of European markets and forced them to cultivate grain, which could be sold to the contending armies. All across the land farmers and artisans adapted to a war economy.

Faced with a shortage of goods and constantly rising prices, government officials requisitioned military supplies directly from the people. In 1776 Connecticut officials called on the citizens of Hartford for 1,000 coats and 1,600 shirts and assessed smaller towns on a proportionate basis. In 1777 Connecticut officials again pressed the citizenry to provide shirts, stockings, and shoes for their Continental units. Soldiers added personal pleas. After losing "all the shirts except the one on my back" during the Battle of Long Island in 1776, Captain Edward Rogers told his wife that "the making of cloath . . . must go on. . . . I must have shirts and stockings & a jacket sent me as soon as possible & a blankit."

Patriot women responded to this challenge by increasing production of homespun cloth. One Massachusetts town produced 30,000 yards of homespun, while women in Elizabeth, New Jersey, promised "upwards of 100,000 yards of linnen and woolen cloth." Other women assumed the burdens of farm production while their men were away at war. Some went into the fields, plowing, harvesting, and loading grain, while others supervised hired laborers or slaves and acquired a taste for making decisions. "We have sow'd our oats as you desired," Sarah Cobb Paine wrote to her absent husband. "Had I been master I should have planted it to Corn." Taught

**Mobilizing for War**

This 1779 woodcut illustrated a poem by Molly Guttridge, a Daughter of Liberty in Marblehead, Massachusetts, and used a military image to symbolize the wartime contributions of American women. Although only a few Patriot women disguised themselves as men and fought in the war, hundreds more traveled with the Continental army and provided the troops with food and support. Most important, thousands of women ran farms in the absence of their soldier-husbands.

New-York Historical Society.

from childhood to value the welfare of their fathers, brothers, and husbands above their own, women were expected to act "virtuously" and often did so. Their wartime efforts not only maintained farm output but also boosted self-esteem and prompted some women to expect greater rights in the new republican society.

Despite the women's efforts, goods remained in short supply and prices rose sharply. Hard-pressed consumers decried merchants and traders as "enemies, extortioners, and monopolizers" and called for government regulation. But in 1777, when a convention of New England states imposed price ceilings, many farmers and artisans refused to sell their goods at the set prices. In the end, a government official admitted, consumers had to pay the higher market prices "or submit to starving."

The struggle over regulation came to a head in Philadelphia. Following the British withdrawal in 1778, artisans and laborers forced the municipal government to establish a Committee on Prices. Invoking the traditional concept of the "just price," the committee set rates for thirty-two commodities and urged citizens to act with "republican virtue." However, Patriot financier Robert Morris and most merchants condemned the price controls and espoused "classical liberal" ideas of free trade. They argued that regulation would encourage farmers to hoard their crops, whereas allowing prices to rise would bring more goods to market. As Benjamin Franklin put it, price controls were "contrary to the nature of commerce."

Nonetheless, most Philadelphians favored "fair" trade rather than "free" trade—at least in principle. At a town meeting in August 1779, over 2,000 Philadelphians voted for regulation, and fewer than 300 opposed it. In practice, however, many artisan-republicans—shoemakers, tanners, and bakers—found that they could not support their families on fixed prices and so refused to abide by them.

Spiraling inflation posed a severe challenge to all American families. By 1778 so much currency had been printed that a family needed $7 in Continental bills to buy goods worth $1 in gold or silver. As the ratio steadily escalated—to 42 to 1 in 1779, to 100 to 1 in 1780, and to 146 to 1 in 1781—it sparked social upheaval. In Boston a mob of women accused merchant Thomas Boyleston of hoarding goods, "seazd him by his Neck," and forced him to sell his wares at the traditional prices. In rural Ulster County, New York, women demanded that the Patriot Committee of Safety take steps to lower food prices; otherwise, they said, "their husbands and sons shall fight no more." To restore the value of Continental currency, the Congress asked the states to allow their citizens to pay taxes in depreciated Continental bills (with $40 in paper money counting as $1 in specie). This plan redeemed $120 million in Continental bills, but at the end of the war speculators still held $71 million in currency in the hope that the government would eventually redeem it at face value. "Private Interest seemed to predominate over the public weal," a leading Patriot complained.

Ultimately, this currency inflation transferred most of the costs of the war to ordinary Americans. Tens of thousands of farmers and artisans received Continental bills in return for supplies and thousands of soldiers took them as pay—only to find that the currency literally depreciated in their pockets. Every time they kept a paper dollar for a week, the money lost value and could buy less, thereby imposing a hidden "currency tax" on them. Each individual tax was small—a few pennies on each dollar they handled. But taken together—as millions of dollars changed hands multiple times—these currency taxes paid the huge cost of the war.

### The Loyalist Exodus

As the war turned in favor of the Patriots, more than 100,000 Loyalists emigrated to the West Indies, Canada, and Britain. Relatively few of the more prominent refugees found happiness in exile in England; the majority complained of "their uneasy abode in this country of aliens." Many refugees suffered severe financial losses. John Tabor Kempe, the last royal attorney general of New York, sought £65,000 sterling (about $5 million today) in compensation from the British government but received only £5,000. The great mass of Loyalist refugees got nothing, and many lamented the loss of their old lives. Watching "sails disappear in the distance," an exiled Loyalist woman in Nova Scotia had "such a feeling of loneliness come over me that . . . I sat down on the damp moss with my baby on my lap and cried bitterly."

Some angry Patriots demanded that the state governments seize the property of wealthy Loyalists and distribute it to needy Americans. However, most Patriot leaders argued that confiscation would be contrary to individual rights and the republican principle of legal equality. In Massachusetts, officials cited the state's constitution of 1780, which declared that every citizen should be protected "in the enjoyment of his life, liberty, and property, according to the standing laws." Consequently, the new republican governments did not promote a social revolution. They confiscated only a small amount of Loyalist property and usually sold it to the highest bidder, who was often a wealthy Patriot rather than a yeoman or a propertyless foot soldier. In a few cases confiscation did produce a democratic result. In North Carolina about half the new owners of Loyalist lands were small-scale farmers. And on the former Philipse manor in New York many Patriot tenants used their hard-earned savings to buy the seized land. When Philipse tried to reclaim his land, former tenants told him they had "purchased it with the price of their best blood" and "will never become your vassals again." But in general the revolutionary upheaval did not drastically alter the structure of rural society.

Social turmoil was greater in the cities, as Patriot merchants replaced Tories at the top of the economic ladder. In Massachusetts the Lowell, Higginson, Jackson, and Cabot families moved their trading enterprises to Boston to fill the vacuum created by the departure of the Loyalist Hutchinson and Apthorp clans. In Philadelphia, small-scale Patriot traders stepped into the vacancies created by the collapse of Anglican and Quaker mercantile firms. The War of Independence replaced a tradition-oriented economic elite—one that invested its profits from trade in real estate and became landlords—with a group of entrepreneurial-minded republican merchants who promoted new trading ventures and domestic manufacturing.

## The Problem of Slavery

Slavery revealed an enormous contradiction in the Patriots' republican ideology. "How is it that we hear the loudest yelps for liberty among the drivers of Negroes?" the British author Samuel Johnson chided the rebellious white Americans, a point some Patriots took to heart. "I wish most sincerely there was not a Slave in the province," Abigail Adams confessed to her husband, John. "It always appeared a most iniquitous Scheme to me—to fight ourselves for what we are daily robbing and plundering from those who have as good a right to freedom as we have."

In fact, the white Patriots' struggle for independence raised the prospect of freedom for enslaved Africans. As the war began, a black preacher in Georgia told his fellow slaves that King George III "came up with the Book [the Bible], and was about to alter the World, and set the Negroes free." Similar rumors circulated among slaves in Virginia and the Carolinas and prompted thousands of African Americans to flee behind British lines. Two neighbors of Richard Henry Lee, the Virginia Patriot, lost "every slave they had in the world," as did many other planters. When the British army evacuated Charleston, more than 6,000 former slaves went with them; another 4,000 left from Savannah. All told, some 30,000 blacks may have fled their owners. Hundreds of black Loyalists settled permanently in Canada. Over 1,000 others, poorly treated by British officials and settled on inferior land in Nova Scotia, sought a better life in the abolitionist settlement in Sierra Leone, West Africa.

**Symbols of Slavery—and Freedom**

The scar on the forehead of this black woman, who was widely known as "Mumbet," underlined the cruelty of slavery. Winning emancipation through a legal suit in Massachusetts, she chose a name befitting her new status: Elizabeth Freeman. This watercolor, by Susan Sedgwick, was painted in 1811. Massachusetts Historical Society.

Yet thousands of African Americans decided to serve the Patriot cause. Eager to raise their social status, free blacks in New England volunteered for military service in the First Rhode Island Company and the Massachusetts "Bucks." In Maryland a large number of slaves took up arms for the Patriot cause in return for a promise of freedom. Throughout the Chesapeake region slaves struck informal bargains with their Patriot masters by trading loyalty in wartime for a promise of eventual liberty. In 1782 the Virginia assembly passed an act allowing **manumission** (liberation); within a decade planters had freed 10,000 slaves.

The Quakers took the lead in condemning slavery. Beginning in the 1750s the Quaker evangelist John Woolman had urged Friends to free their slaves, and during the war many did so. Rapidly growing Christian evangelical churches, notably the Methodists and the Baptists, also advocated emancipation and admitted both enslaved and free blacks to their congregations. In 1784 a conference of Virginia Methodists declared that slavery was "contrary to the Golden Law of God on which hang all the Law and Prophets."

Enlightenment philosophy also worked to undermine slavery and racism. John Locke had argued that ideas were not innate but stemmed from a person's experiences in the world. Accordingly, Enlightenment thinkers suggested that the oppressive conditions of slavery, not inherent inferiority, accounted for the debased situation of

Africans in the Western Hemisphere. As one Enlightenment-influenced American put it, "A state of slavery has a mighty tendency to shrink and contract the minds of men." Anthony Benezet, a Quaker philanthropist who funded a school for blacks in Philadelphia, defied popular opinion in declaring that African Americans were "as capable of improvement as White People."

These new religious and intellectual currents sparked legal change. In 1784, judicial rulings abolished slavery in Massachusetts and, over the next twenty years, every state north of Delaware enacted legislation providing for the gradual end of slavery. However, these gradual emancipation laws compensated white owners by requiring more years—even decades—of servitude. For example, the New York Emancipation Act of 1799 granted freedom to slave children only when they reached the age of twenty-five. As late as 1810, almost 30,000 blacks in the northern states—nearly a fourth of their African American residents—were still enslaved. Emancipation came slowly because whites feared competition for jobs and the prospect of race melding. To keep the races separate, in 1786 Massachusetts reenacted an old law prohibiting whites from marrying blacks, Indians, or mulattos (see Voices from Abroad, "The Character of Northern Slavery," p. 191).

The tension between the republican values of liberty and property was greatest in the South, where slaves made up 30 to 60 percent of the population and represented a huge financial investment. Some Chesapeake tobacco planters, moved by religious principles or oversupplied with workers, allowed blacks to buy their freedom through paid work as artisans or laborers. Manumission and self-purchase gradually brought freedom to a third of the African American residents of Maryland. However, in 1792 the Virginia legislature made manumission more difficult. Following the lead of Thomas Jefferson, who owned more than 100 slaves, the Virginia legislators argued that slavery was a "necessary evil" required to maintain white supremacy and the luxurious planter lifestyle. Resistance to freedom for blacks was even greater in North Carolina, where the legislature condemned Quaker manumissions as "highly criminal and reprehensible." The rice-growing states of South Carolina and Georgia rejected emancipation out of hand (Map 6.3).

The debate over emancipation among southern whites ended in 1800, when Virginia authorities thwarted an uprising planned by the enslaved artisan Gabriel Prosser and hanged him and thirty of his followers. "Liberty and equality have brought the evil upon us," a letter to the *Virginia Herald* proclaimed, for such doctrines are "dangerous and extremely wicked in this country, where every white man is a master, and every black man is a slave." To preserve their privileged social position, southern whites redefined republicanism so that it applied only to the "master race."

## A Republican Religious Order

The demand for greater liberty unleashed by the republican revolution of 1776 also forced Patriot lawmakers to devise new relationships between church and state. During the colonial era only the Quaker- and Baptist-controlled governments of

## VOICES FROM ABROAD

# The Character of Northern Slavery

### ALEXANDER COVENTRY

When Alexander Coventry migrated from Scotland to New York in 1785, he began to record his daily experiences in a journal. The following selections provide insight into the condition of New York's rural African Americans, most of whom were slaves owned by farmers of Dutch descent. Coventry's comments suggest both the exploitation inherent in the system of slavery and the opportunities open to northern blacks to run away, form interracial liaisons, and bargain over the conditions of their work.

2 February 1787 Rode through the Cocksaxie settlement. . . . The houses are substantially built of Lime-stone, and are generally 1½ stories high; the barns are capacious. . . . Cocksaxie farmers are supposed to be the most opulent in the state. Their fertile soil, and its convenience to market, being much in their favor. The tact [area of land] is almost exclusively inhabited by the low Dutch . . . and each farmer has a number of Negro slaves . . . who did all the work on the farm, and in the house. . . . Although the blacks were slaves, yet I feel warranted in asserting that the laboring class in no country lived more easy, were better clothed and fed, or had more of life, than these slaves.

2 April 1787 [Went with] William Van Valkenburg to see his brother John, who has received a stab in his thigh about 5 inches deep. He received the wound from a negro, whom his former master and John went to take. The negro and his wench had run away, and escaped into Boston state (Massachusetts) where negroes are free.

9–11 April 1789 Van Curen's negro Cuff came here and wanted W.C. [William Coventry, Alexander's cousin] to buy him . . . but Van Curen and W.C. could not agree, therefore I told him if the negro would agree to live with me, I would buy him. He asked 77 pounds. I offered 76 pounds. We tossed up and he won. . . . I asked Cuff if he would live with me. He said he would; he helped to drive the cows home to fodder. . . . Cuff wanted two days next week to keep Paas [Easter Sunday]. I told him to return on Wednesday morning, which he said he would do.

4 April 1790 While foddering, Thursday, before sunrise, a man and woman passed, the man was black, and asked the road to Hudson. Heard since that it was a negro run off with a white woman.

21 December 1791 Went over to Jacobus Legat's to see whether he would sell his Wench, Cuff's wife. Legat offered her, with her youngest child for £45. I offered him £40 and so we parted [without a sale].

3 February 1792 Cornelius Van Curen here; wants to buy Cuff back again, but Cuff won't go to him again.

SOURCE: Alexander Coventry, *Memoirs of an Emigrant: The Journal of Alexander Coventry, M.D.* (Albany: Albany Institute of History and Art, 1978).

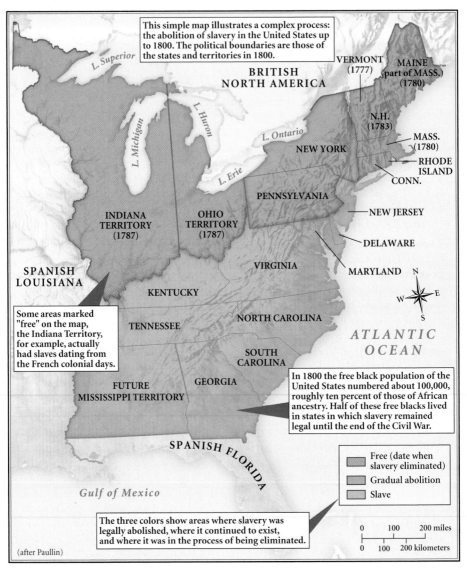

This simple map illustrates a complex process: the abolition of slavery in the United States up to 1800. The political boundaries are those of the states and territories in 1800.

Some areas marked "free" on the map, the Indiana Territory, for example, actually had slaves dating from the French colonial days.

In 1800 the free black population of the United States numbered about 100,000, roughly ten percent of those of African ancestry. Half of these free blacks lived in states in which slavery remained legal until the end of the Civil War.

The three colors show areas where slavery was legally abolished, where it continued to exist, and where it was in the process of being eliminated.

Free (date when slavery eliminated)
Gradual abolition
Slave

0    100    200 miles
0    100    200 kilometers

(after Paullin)

**MAP 6.3 The Status of Slavery, 1800**

In 1775 racial slavery was legal in every British American colony. By the time the American states achieved their independence in 1783, most African Americans in New England had also become free. By 1800 nearly all of the states north of Maryland had provided for the gradual abolition of slavery, but the process was slow and not completed until the 1830s. After the Revolution, some slave owners in the Chesapeake region also manumitted their slaves, leaving only the whites of the Lower South firmly committed to racial bondage.

Pennsylvania and Rhode Island had repudiated the idea of an **established church**. Then in 1776 James Madison and George Mason used Enlightenment principles to undermine the traditional commitment to a state-supported church in Virginia. They persuaded the state's constitutional convention to issue a Declaration of Rights guaranteeing all Christians the "free exercise of religion." To win broad support for the war, the Virginia Anglican elite accepted the legitimacy of the dissenting Presbyterian and Baptist churches that they had previously persecuted. Indeed, in 1778 Virginia Anglicans launched their own revolution by severing ties with the hierarchy of the Church of England and creating the Protestant Episcopal Church of America.

After the Revolution an established church and compulsory religious taxes were no longer the norm in the United States. Baptists in particular opposed the use of taxes to support religion. In Virginia their political influence prompted lawmakers to reject a bill supported by George Washington and Patrick Henry, which would have imposed a general tax to fund all Christian churches. Instead, in 1786 the Virginia legislature enacted Thomas Jefferson's Bill for Establishing Religious Freedom, which made all churches equal before the law and granted direct financial support to none. In New York and New Jersey the sheer number of churches—Episcopalian, Presbyterian, Dutch Reformed, Lutheran, and Quaker, among others—prevented legislative agreement on an established church or compulsory religious taxes. In New England Congregationalism remained the official state church until the 1830s, but state laws allowed Baptists and Methodists to pay religious taxes to their own churches.

However, even in Virginia, the separation of church and state was never complete. Many Americans believed that firm connections between church and state were necessary to promote morality and respect for authority. "Pure religion and civil liberty are inseparable companions," a group of North Carolinians advised their minister. "It is your particular duty to enlighten mankind with the unerring principles of truth and justice, the main props of all civil government." Accepting this premise, most state governments provided churches with indirect aid by exempting their property and ministers from taxation.

Freedom of conscience proved equally difficult to achieve. In Virginia, Jefferson's Bill for Establishing Religious Freedom prohibited religious requirements for political and civil officeholding, but other states continued to deny full citizenship to those who dissented from the doctrines of Protestant Christianity. The North Carolina constitution of 1776 disqualified from public office any citizen "who shall deny the being of God, or the Truth of the Protestant Religion, or the Divine Authority of the Old or New Testament." New Hampshire's constitution contained a similar provision until 1868.

Americans influenced by the Enlightenment and by evangelical Protestantism condemned such religious restrictions but for different reasons. Leading American intellectuals, including Thomas Jefferson and Benjamin Franklin, argued that God had given humans the power of reason so that they could determine moral truths for themselves. To protect society from "ecclesiastical tyranny," they demanded complete freedom of conscience. Many evangelical Protestants also wanted religious liberty, but their goal was to protect their churches from the government. The New England minister Isaac Backus warned Baptists not to incorporate their churches or accept public funds because that might lead to state control. In Connecticut a devout Congregationalist welcomed voluntarism (the voluntary funding of churches by their members) because it allowed the laity to control the clergy, thereby furthering "the principles of republicanism."

In religion as in politics, independence provided American leaders with the opportunity to fashion a new institutional order. In both cases they repudiated the hierarchical ways of the past—monarchy and establishment—in favor of a republican alternative. These choices reflected the increased influence of ordinary citizens, who had fought and financed the long, difficult military struggle, and wanted a voice in the new republican political and religious institutions. As a wealthy Virginia planter had warned in April 1776, a successful revolt against British rule would assist yeomen to promote "their darling Democracy."

## TIMELINE

| | | | |
|---|---|---|---|
| 1775 | Battle of Concord (April 19) | | Severe inflation of paper currency begins |
| | Second Continental Congress meets in Philadelphia (May) | 1778 | Franco-American alliance (February) |
| | Battle of Bunker Hill | | Lord North seeks political settlement; Congress rejects negotiations |
| | Congress creates Continental army | | |
| | Congressional moderates submit Olive Branch petition; king rejects it | | British begin southern strategy; capture Savannah (December) |
| | Lord Dunmore's proclamation offers freedom to slaves and servants (November) | 1780 | Sir Henry Clinton seizes Charleston (May) |
| | American invasion of Canada | | French army lands in Rhode Island |
| 1776 | Patriots and Loyalists skirmish in the South | 1781 | Lord Cornwallis invades Virginia (April); surrenders at Yorktown (October) |
| | Thomas Paine publishes *Common Sense* (January) | | Large-scale Loyalist emigration |
| | Declaration of Independence (July 4) | | Partial redemption of Continental currency at 40 to 1 |
| | Howe forces Washington to retreat from New York and New Jersey | 1782 | Virginia passes law allowing slave manumission (reversed in 1792) |
| | Virginia Declaration of Rights | | |
| 1777 | Patriot women become important in war economy | 1783 | Treaty of Paris (September 3) officially ends war |
| | Howe occupies Philadelphia (September) | 1786 | Virginia enacts Bill for Establishing Religious Freedom |
| | Gates defeats Burgoyne at Saratoga (October) | | |
| | Continental army suffers at Valley Forge during winter | 1800 | Gabriel Prosser organizes slave rebellion in Virginia |

# For Further Exploration

In *Angel in the Whirlwind: The Triumph of the American Revolution* (1997), Benson Bobrick presents the break with England as a grand epic stretching from the French and Indian War to Washington's inauguration. Gordon Wood, *The Radicalism of the American Revolution* (1992), offers a more scholarly account of these years. A compelling fictional account of the life of Tom Paine is Howard Fast, *Citizen Tom Paine* (1943). Pauline Maier, *American Scripture: Making the Declaration of Independence* (1997), explains the background of the Declaration and shows how it has been redefined over the past two centuries. For some vivid firsthand accounts of the military conflict, see John C. Dann, ed., *The Revolution Remembered: Eyewitness Accounts of the War for Independence* (1980). James L. Stokesbury, *A Short History of the American Revolution* (1991), suggests parallels between the British defeat and the American failure in Vietnam. Colin G. Calloway, *The American Revolution in Indian Country: Crisis and Diversity in Native American Communities* (1995), traces the Revolution's impact on the native peoples, while Robin Blackburn, *The Overthrow of Colonial Slavery, 1776–1848* (1988), shows how it aided the decline of racial bondage in the Western Hemisphere. Sylvia R. Frey, *Water from the Rock: Black Resistance in a Revolutionary Age* (1991), traces the impact of the Revolution on African Americans and their adaptations of republican ideology and Christian beliefs. In *Liberty's Daughters: The Revolutionary Experience of American Women, 1750–1800* (1980), Mary Beth Norton portrays both the continuities and the changes in women's lives.

*Liberty! The American Revolution* (PBS video; 6 hours) and the companion Web site, at <http:/www.pbs.org/liberty>, cover the war and the making of the Constitution. The Virtual Marching Tour of the Philadelphia Campaign 1777, at <http://www.ushistory.org/brandywine/index.html>, offers an interesting multimedia view of Howe's attack on Philadelphia and subsequent events. A fine, data-rich source on the black experience is Africans in America: Revolution, at <http://www.pbs.org/wgbh/aia/part2/title.html>; other parts of this site cover the entire African American experience. To explore the political philosophy of Thomas Jefferson, log on to Thomas Jefferson: On Politics & Government, at <http://etext.virginia.edu/jefferson/quotations>, a site that is conveniently arranged by topic.

---

For definitions of key terms boldfaced in this chapter, see the glossary at the end of the book.

To assess your mastery of the material covered in this chapter, see the Online Study Guide at **bedfordstmartins.com/henrettaconcise**.

For map resources and primary documents, see **bedfordstmartins.com/henrettaconcise**.

# Chapter 7

# THE NEW POLITICAL ORDER
## 1776–1800

Idolatry to Monarchs, and servility to Aristocratical Pride, was never so totally eradicated from so many minds in so short a time.

JOHN ADAMS, 1776

Like an earthquake, the American Revolution shook the foundations of the European monarchical order, and its aftershocks were felt far into the nineteenth century. By "creating a new republic based on the rights of [the] individual, the North Americans introduced a new force into the world," the eminent German historian Leopold von Ranke bluntly advised the king of Bavaria in 1854. Indeed, the new ideology of republicanism might cost the monarch his throne:

> This was a revolution of principle. Up to this point, a king who ruled by the grace of God had been the center around which everything turned. Now the idea emerged that power should come from below [from the people]. . . .

Previous republican revolutions—such as that of the Puritan Commonwealth in England in the 1650s—had ended in political chaos and military rule, and many Europeans expected the new American states to experience the same fate. However, General George Washington stunned the political leaders of Europe in 1783 when he voluntarily left public life to return to his plantation. "Tis a Conduct so novel," the American painter John Trumbull reported from London, that it is "inconceivable to People [here]." Washington's voluntary retirement bolstered the authority of elected Patriot leaders, who were firmly committed to fashioning representative republican government.

This great task absorbed the energy and intellect of an entire generation. Between 1776 and 1800 Americans wrote new state and federal constitutions and devised a system of politics that was responsive to the popular will. Many political leaders worried that the result was too democratic. When a bill was introduced into a state legislature, grumbled conservative Ezra Stiles, every elected official "instantly thinks how it will affect his constituents" rather than its impact on the welfare of the entire public. What Stiles criticized as irresponsible self-interest, most ordinary Americans welcomed. For the first time the interests of middling citizens were represented in the halls of government, and the monarchs of Europe trembled.

# Creating Republican Institutions, 1776–1787

Once independence became the goal, Patriots had to decide how to allocate political power among themselves. "Which of us shall be the rulers?" asked a Philadelphia newspaper. The question was complex: Where would power reside, in the national government or the states? Who would control the new republican institutions, traditional elites or average citizens?

## *The State Constitutions: How Much Democracy?*

In May 1776 the Continental Congress urged Americans to suppress royal authority and establish new governing institutions. Most states quickly complied. Within six months Virginia, Maryland, North Carolina, New Jersey, Delaware, and Pennsylvania had written new constitutions, and Connecticut and Rhode Island had transformed their colonial charters into republican documents by deleting references to the king. "Constitutions employ every pen," an observer noted.

However, republicanism meant more than ousting the king. The Declaration of Independence had stated the principle of popular sovereignty: that governments derive "their just powers from the consent of the governed." In the heat of revolution many Patriots gave this clause a democratic twist. In North Carolina the back-country farmers of Mecklenburg County instructed their delegates to the state's constitutional convention to "oppose everything that leans to aristocracy or power in the hands of the rich and chief men exercised to the oppression of the poor." In Virginia, voters elected a new assembly that, an observer remarked, "was composed of men not quite so well dressed, nor so politely educated, nor so highly born" as colonial era legislatures.

This democratic impulse received its fullest expression in Pennsylvania, thanks to a coalition of Scots-Irish farmers, Philadelphia artisans, and Enlightenment-influenced intellectuals. The Pennsylvania Constitution of 1776 abolished property owning as a test of citizenship and granted taxpaying men the right to vote and hold office. It also created a unicameral (one-house) legislature with complete power. There was no upper house, and no governor exercised veto power. Other constitutional provisions mandated an extensive system of elementary education and protected citizens from imprisonment for debt. Pennsylvania's democratic constitution alarmed many leading Patriots, who believed officeholding should be restricted to "men of learning, leisure and easy circumstances." From Boston John Adams denounced Pennsylvania's unicameral legislature as "so democratical that it must produce confusion and every evil work." "Remember," Adams continued, "democracy

### The American Star

The portraits of kings and queens had traditionally served as icons or symbols of their monarchical nations. This idealized portrait of Washington, by the American artist John Coles Jr., follows this custom on the occasion of the death of the great American general and political leader. The Roman goddess Minerva, wise in the ways of peace and skilled in the arts of war, holds Washington's portrait, as a Revolutionary Era soldier and the American goddess Columbia lament his death.

The Metropolitan Museum of Art. Gift of Edgar William and Bernice Chrysler Garbisch, 1964 (64.309.6).

FOR MORE HELP ANALYZING THIS IMAGE, see the Online Study Guide at **bedfordstmartins. com/henrettaconcise**.

never lasts long. It soon wastes, exhausts, and murders itself." Along with other conservative Patriots, Adams feared that ordinary citizens would use their numerical advantage to tax the rich: "If you give [democrats] the command or preponderance in the . . . legislature, they will vote all property out of the hands of you aristocrats. . . ."

To counter the appeal of the Pennsylvania Constitution, Adams published his *Thoughts on Government* (1776). In his treatise Adams adapted the British Whig theory of mixed government (in which power was shared by the king, lords, and commons) to a republican society. To preserve liberty, his system dispersed authority by assigning the different functions of government—lawmaking, administering, and judging—to separate institutions. Legislatures would make the laws while the executive and the judiciary would enforce them. Adams also called for a bicameral (two-house) legislature in which the upper house would be composed of substantial property owners; its role would be to check the power of popular majorities in the lower house. As a further curb on democracy, he proposed an elected governor with the power to veto laws and an appointed—not elected—judiciary to review them.

Leading Patriots endorsed Adams's scheme for elected bicameral legislatures because it preserved representative government while restricting popular power.

However, they hesitated to give the veto power to governors because they recalled the arbitrary conduct of royal governors and had no wish to enhance the power of the executive. However, in line with Adams's suggestion, most states retained traditional property qualifications for voting. In New York 90 percent of white men could vote in elections for the assembly, but only 40 percent had enough property to vote for the governor and the upper house. The most flagrant use of property to maintain the power of the elite occurred in South Carolina, where the 1778 constitution required candidates for governor to have a debt-free estate of £10,000 (about $600,000 today), senators to be worth £2,000, and assemblymen to own property valued at £1,000. These provisions ruled out officeholding for about 90 percent of white men.

Nonetheless, post-Revolutionary politics had a distinctly democratic flavor. The legislature emerged as the dominant branch of government, and state constitutions apportioned seats on the basis of population, which gave farmers in rapidly growing western areas the fair representation they had long demanded. Indeed, backcountry pressure prompted some legislatures to move the state capital from merchant-dominated seaports such as New York City and Philadelphia to inland cities such as Albany and Harrisburg. Even conservative South Carolina moved its capital inland, from Charleston to Columbia.

Moreover, new sorts of political leaders now predominated in many state legislatures. Rather than electing their social "betters" to office, ordinary citizens increasingly chose men of "middling circumstances" who knew "the wants of the poor." By the mid-1780s middling farmers and urban artisans controlled the lower houses in most northern states and formed a sizable minority in southern assemblies. These middling men took the lead in opposing the collection of back taxes and other measures that tended "toward the oppression of the people."

The political legacy of the Revolution was complex. Only in Pennsylvania and Vermont were radical Patriots able to take power and create democratic institutions. Yet everywhere representative legislatures had more power, and the day-to-day politics of electioneering and interest-group bargaining became much more responsive to the demands of average citizens.

The extraordinary excitement of the Revolutionary era also tested the dictum that only men could engage in politics. While men continued to control all public institutions—legislatures, juries, government offices—upper-class women entered political debate and filled their letters and diaries (and undoubtedly their conversations) with opinions on public issues. "The men say we have no business [with politics]," Eliza Wilkinson of South Carolina complained in 1783. "They won't even allow us liberty of thought, and that is all I want." (See American Voices, "The Status of Women," p. 200.)

These American women did not insist on complete civic equality with men but on the elimination of certain restrictive customs and laws. Thus, Abigail Adams demanded equal legal rights for married women; she pointed out that under existing common law, wives could not own most forms of property and could not enter into contracts or initiate lawsuits without their husbands' action. "Men would be

## AMERICAN VOICES

# The Status of Women

### ABIGAIL AND JOHN ADAMS

*M**ost American women of European descent accepted the subordinate status of their sex; it was the way life had always been and, many believed, the way God intended it to be. Yet, the rhetoric of liberty and equality prompted a few women, including Abigail Adams, the wife of the prominent Massachusetts Patriot John Adams, to challenge men's dominant position. However, as this exchange between the Adamses suggests, most of these challenges were very tentative and very brief.*

*March 31, 1776, Abigail Adams to John Adams*

I long to hear that you have declared an independancy [from Britain] — and by the way in the new Code of Law . . . be more generous and favorable to [the Ladies] than your ancestors. Do not put such unlimited power into the hands of Husbands. Remember all Men would be tyrants if they could. If perticuliar care and attention is not paid to the Ladies we are determined to foment a Rebellion, and will not hold ourselves bound by any Laws in which we have no voice, or Representation. . . .

*April 14, 1776, John Adams to Abigail Adams*

As to your extraordinary Code of Laws, I cannot but laugh. We have been told that our Struggle [for independence] has loosened the bonds of Government every where. That Children and Apprentices were disobedient — that schools and Colledges were grown turbulent — that Indians slighted their Guardians and Negroes grew insolent to their Masters. But your letter was the first Intimation that another Tribe more numerous and powerful than all the rest were grown discontented. . . .

Depend on it, We know better than to repeal our Masculine System. Altho they are in full Force, . . . in Practice you know We are the subjects. We have only the Name of Masters, and rather than give up this, which would compleatly subject Us to the Despotism of the Peticoat, I hope General Washington, and all our brave Heroes would fight. . . .

*May 7 and August 14, 1776, Abigail Adams to John Adams*

Notwithstanding all your wise Laws and Maxims we have it in our power not only to free ourselves but to subdue our Masters, and without violence to throw both your natural and legal authority at our feet. . . .

I most sincerely wish that some more liberal plan might be laid or executed for the Benefit of the rising Generation, and that our new constitution may be distinguished for Learning and Virtue. If we mean to have Heroes, Statesmen and Philosophers, we should have learned women. The world would laugh at me, and accuse me of vanity, But you I know have a mind too enlarged and liberal. . . . If much depends as is allowed upon the early Education of youth and the first principles which are instilld take the deepest root, great benifit must arise from litirary accomplishments in women.

SOURCE: Lyman H. Butterfield, ed., *Adams Family Correspondence*, 4 vols. (Cambridge: Harvard University Press, 1963), 1: 370, 382–83, 402–3; 2: 94.

tyrants" if they continued to hold such power over women, Adams declared to her husband, criticizing him and other Patriots for "emancipating all nations" from monarchical despotism while "retaining absolute power over Wives."

Most men paid little attention to women's requests, and most husbands remained patriarchs who dominated their households. Even young men who embraced the republican ideal of **"companionate" marriage** did not support reform of the common law or a public role for their wives and daughters. With the partial exception of New Jersey, which until 1807 granted the vote to unmarried and widowed women of property, women remained second-class citizens, unable to participate directly in American political life.

The republican quest for an educated citizenry allowed advances by some American women. In her 1779 essay "On the Equality of the Sexes," Judith Sargent Murray argued that men and women had an equal capacity for memory and that women had a superior imagination. She conceded that most women were inferior to men in judgment and reasoning, but only because of a lack of training: "We can only reason from what we know," Murray argued, and most women had been denied "the opportunity of acquiring knowledge." However, in the 1790s the attorney general of Massachusetts declared that girls had an equal right to schooling under the state constitution. With greater access to public elementary schools and

**Judith Sargent (Murray), Age Nineteen**

The well-educated daughter of a wealthy Massachusetts merchant, Judith Sargent enjoyed a privileged childhood. However, she endured a difficult seventeen-year marriage to John Stevens, who ultimately went bankrupt, fled from his creditors, and died in the West Indies. In 1788 she wed the Reverend John Murray, who became a leading American Universalist. Her portrait, painted around 1771 by the renowned artist John Singleton Copley, captures Sargent's skeptical view of the world, an outlook that enabled her to question customary gender roles.

Terra Museum of American Art, Chicago, Illinois. Daniel J. Terra Collection.

the rapid creation of girls' academies (private high schools), many young women became literate and knowledgeable. By 1850 as many women as men in the northeastern states would be able to read and write, and literate women would again challenge their subordinate legal and political status.

## The Articles of Confederation

As the Patriots moved toward independence in 1776, they envisioned a central government with limited powers. Carter Braxton of Virginia thought the Continental Congress should have the power to "regulate the affairs of trade, war, peace, alliances, &c." but "should by no means have authority to interfere with the internal police [governance] or domestic concerns of any Colony."

This intensely state-oriented outlook informed the Articles of Confederation, passed by Congress in November 1777. The first national constitution, the Articles provided for a loose confederation in which "each state retains its sovereignty, freedom, and independence" as well as all powers and rights not "expressly delegated" to the United States. Still, the Articles gave the Confederation government considerable authority; it could declare war and peace, make treaties with foreign nations, adjudicate disputes between the states, borrow and print money, and requisition funds from the states "for the common defense or general welfare." These powers were exercised by a central legislature, Congress, in which each state had one vote regardless of its wealth or population. Important laws needed approval by at least nine of the thirteen states, and changes in the Articles required unanimous consent. In the Confederation government, there was no separate executive and no judiciary.

Because of disputes over western lands, some states did not ratify the Articles until 1781. States such as Virginia, Massachusetts, and Connecticut claimed that their royal charters gave them boundaries that stretched westward to the Pacific Ocean. States without western claims, such as Maryland and Pennsylvania, refused to accept the Articles until the land-rich states relinquished their claims to the Congress. Threatened by Cornwallis's army in 1781, Virginia finally agreed to give up its land claims, and Maryland, the last holdout, then ratified the Articles (Map 7.1).

This formal approval of the Articles was anticlimactic. During the previous four years Congress had exercised de facto constitutional authority as it raised the Continental army and negotiated with foreign nations. Nonetheless, the Confederation government had a major weakness because the state legislatures were slow to contribute to its support and it lacked the authority to impose taxes. By 1780 the Confederation was nearly bankrupt. Facing imminent disaster, General Washington called urgently for a national system of taxation, warning Patriot leaders that otherwise "our cause is lost."

In response, nationalist-minded members of Congress tried to expand the Confederation's authority. Robert Morris, who became superintendent of finance in 1781, persuaded Congress to charter the Bank of North America, a private institution in Philadelphia, in hopes that its notes could stabilize the inflated

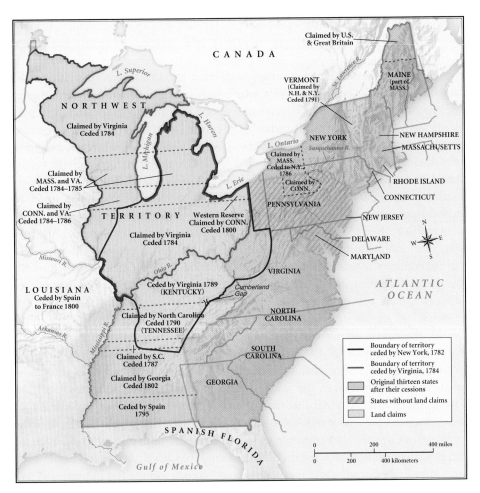

## MAP 7.1 The Confederation and Western Land Claims

The Confederation Congress resolved the conflicting land claims of the states by creating a "national domain" west of the Appalachian Mountains. Between 1781 and 1802 all of the seaboard states with western land claims ceded them to the national government. In the Northwest Ordinances, the Confederation Congress divided the domain north of the Ohio River into territories, opened them to settlement by citizens from all the states, and set up democratic procedures by which they could join the Union.

FOR MORE HELP ANALYZING THIS MAP, see the Online Study Guide at **bedfordstmartins.com/henrettaconcise**.

Continental currency. Morris also developed a comprehensive financial system that handled army expenditures, apportioned war expenses among the states, and centralized the foreign debt. He hoped that the consciousness of a "national" debt would underline the Confederation's need for an import duty. But some state legislatures refused to increase the Confederation's powers, which required the unanimous consent of the states. Both Rhode Island and New York rejected Morris's proposal for an import duty of 5 percent. His state had opposed similar British-imposed duties, the New York representative told Morris, and would not accept them from Congress.

To raise revenue, Congress strongly asserted the Confederation's title to the lands of the trans-Appalachian West, which were much in demand by farmers and speculators. In 1783 Congress began negotiations with Indian tribes, hoping to persuade them that the Treaty of Paris had extinguished their land rights. Congress also sought payment from the white squatters— "white savages," John Jay called them— who had illegally settled on unoccupied land. Given the natural barrier of the Appalachian Mountains, many members of Congress feared that western settlers might set up separate republics and then ally themselves with Spain in order to export their crops via the Mississippi River and Spanish-controlled Louisiana. The danger was real: in 1784 settlers in what is now eastern Tennessee organized the new state of Franklin. To preserve its authority over the West, Congress refused to recognize Franklin or to admit it to the Confederation. Instead, the delegates directed the states of Virginia, North Carolina, and Georgia to administer the process of creating new states south of the Ohio River, a decision that indirectly encouraged the expansion of slavery into that vast region.

To deal with lands north of the Ohio River, Congress issued three important ordinances. The Ordinance of 1784, written by Thomas Jefferson, called for the division of the region into territories and the admission of a territory as a state as soon as its population equaled that of the smallest existing state. To deter squatters, the Land Ordinance of 1785 required that the regions be surveyed before settlement and, to allow this work to be done quickly, mandated a grid surveying system that ignored the contours of the land. The ordinance also specified a minimum price of $1 per acre and required that half of the townships be sold in single blocks of 23,040 acres each, which only large-scale investors and speculators could afford, and the rest in parcels of 640 acres each, which only well-to-do farmers could manage to buy (Map 7.2).

Finally, the Northwest Ordinance of 1787 provided for the creation of the territories that would eventually become the states of Ohio, Indiana, Illinois, Michigan, and Wisconsin. Reflecting the Enlightenment beliefs of Jefferson and other Patriots, the ordinance prohibited slavery in those territories and earmarked funds from land sales for the support of schools. It also specified that Congress would appoint a governor and judges to administer a new territory; once there were 5,000 free adult men in residence, they could elect a territorial legislature. When the population reached 60,000, the legislature could write a republican constitution and apply to join the Confederation on a basis of complete equality with the existing states.

The land ordinances of the 1780s were a great and enduring achievement. They provided for the orderly settlement of the West while reducing the prospect of secessionist movements and preventing the emergence of dependent "colonies." The ordinances also added a new "western" dimension to the national identity. The United States was no longer confined to thirteen governments on the eastern seaboard. It had space to expand.

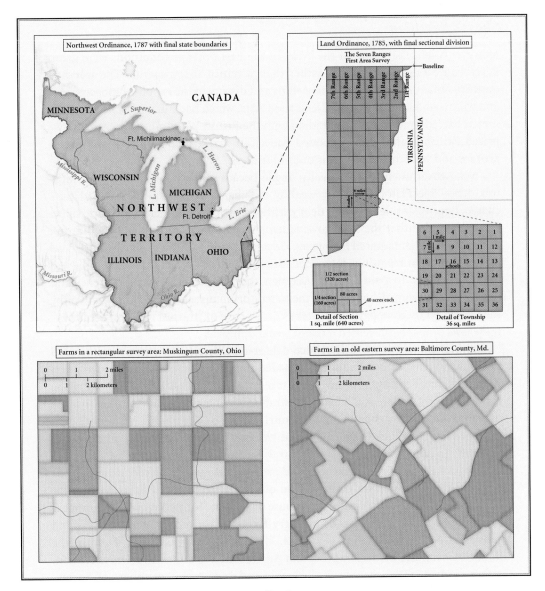

## MAP 7.2 Land Division in the Northwest Territory

Throughout the Northwest Territory, government surveyors imposed a rectangular grid on the landscape, regardless of the local topography. The use of a grid reflected both the influence of Enlightenment conceptions of regularity and rationality and the desire to survey the land quickly to deter squatters from settling on it illegally. Congress specified that half of the townships be sold in huge blocks of 23,040 acres each, which ensured their purchase by land speculators, and the rest in substantial parcels of 640 acres each, which only well-to-do farmers could afford. The right-angled property lines in Muskingum County, Ohio (lower left), contrasted sharply with those in Baltimore County, Maryland (lower right), where—as in most of the eastern and southern states—boundaries followed the contours of the land.

## Shays's Rebellion

However bright the future of the West, in the East postwar conditions were grim. Peace had brought a recession rather than a return to prosperity. The war had destroyed many American merchant ships and disrupted the export of tobacco, rice, and wheat. And now the British Navigation Acts, which had nurtured colonial commerce, barred Americans from trading with the British West Indies. Moreover, low-priced British manufactures flooded American markets and drove many urban artisans and wartime textile firms out of business.

State governments were equally fragile because they were saddled with large war debts. Speculators—mostly wealthy merchants and landowners—had purchased huge quantities of state debt certificates for far less than their face value. They demanded that the state governments redeem the bonds quickly and at full value, a policy that required high taxes. However, yeomen farmers and artisans, hard hit by the postwar recession, demanded tax relief, and most state legislatures followed their sentiments. To assist indebted yeomen, they printed more paper currency and passed laws allowing debtors to pay their creditors in installments. Although wealthy men deplored these stopgap measures as destructive of "the just rights of creditors," these laws probably prevented a major social upheaval.

In Massachusetts, the lack of such debtor-relief legislation provoked an armed uprising. Merchants and creditors persuaded the Massachusetts legislature to repay the state's war debt by imposing high taxes and to deter inflation by halting the issuance of paper currency. When cash-strapped farmers could not pay their private debts, creditors threatened them with court suits. Debtor Ephraim Wetmore heard that merchant Stephan Salisbury "would have my Body Dead or Alive in case I did not pay." In response, residents of central and western counties called extralegal meetings in 1786 to protest the taxes and property seizures and to demand the abolition of imprisonment for debt, the end of property qualifications for officeholding, and the elimination of the upper house of the state legislature. To back up these radical political demands, bands of angry farmers—including men of status and substance—closed the courts by force. "[I] had no Intensions to Destroy the Publick Government," declared Captain Adam Wheeler, a former town selectman; rather, he had rioted to prevent "Valuable and Industrious members of Society [being] dragged from their families to prison [because of their debts], to the great damage . . . [of] the Community at large." The resistance gradually grew into a full-scale revolt led by Captain Daniel Shays, a former Continental army officer.

As a struggle against taxes imposed by a distant government, Shays's Rebellion resembled colonial resistance to the British Stamp Act. To drive home that point, members of Shays's army placed twigs from pine trees in their hats, just as the Continental army had done. "The people have turned against their teachers the doctrines which were inculcated to effect the late revolution," complained the conservative Massachusetts political leader Fisher Ames. However, some men who were radical Patriots in 1776 also condemned the Shaysites. "Those Men, who . . . would lessen the

Weight of Government lawfully exercised must be Enemies to our happy Revolution and Common Liberty," charged onetime revolutionary Samuel Adams. To put down the rebellion, the Massachusetts legislature passed the Riot Act, outlawing illegal assembly. With financing from eastern merchants, Governor James Bowdoin equipped a formidable fighting force and called for additional troops from the Continental Congress. In the end, Shays's army fell victim to freezing weather and inadequate supplies during the winter of 1786–87, and Bowdoin's military force easily dispersed the rebels.

Shays's Rebellion provided graphic proof that the costs of war and the fruits of independence were not being shared evenly. Middling Patriot families who had endured wartime shortages and sacrifices felt they had exchanged one tyranny for another. Angry Massachusetts voters turned Governor Bowdoin out of office, and debt-ridden farmers in New York, northern Pennsylvania, Connecticut, and New Hampshire also closed courthouses and demanded economic relief. British officials in Canada predicted the imminent demise of the United States, and many Americans feared for the fate of their republican experiment. Events in Massachusetts, declared nationalist Henry Knox, formed "the strongest arguments possible" for the creation of "a strong general government."

# The Constitution of 1787

From the moment of its creation, the Constitution was a controversial document, praised by advocates as a solution to the nation's economic woes and condemned by critics as a perversion of republicanism. Simply put, the issue was whether the institutions of self-government could function successfully only on the state level or could be adapted to govern a vast nation. This debate, begun in 1787, would not be finally resolved until the Civil War.

## The Rise of a Nationalist Faction

Money questions—debts, taxes, and **tariffs**—dominated the postwar political agenda. Some men, mostly those who had served the Confederation government as military officers, diplomats, and officials, looked at these problems from a "national" perspective and became advocates of a stronger central government. Thus, General Washington, financier Robert Morris, and diplomats Benjamin Franklin, John Jay, and John Adams demanded that Congress be given the power to control foreign commerce and impose tariffs. However, key commercial states in the North—New York, Massachusetts, Pennsylvania—resisted national tariffs in order to protect local merchants and state-imposed levies on imported goods. Most southern planters also opposed tariffs because they wanted to import British textiles and ironware at the lowest possible prices.

Nonetheless, some southern planters joined the nationalist faction because they feared the financial policies of the state governments. Legislatures in Virginia and other southern states had responded to the economic hard times of the 1780s by lowering taxes. Such measures troubled wealthy creditors because they diminished public revenue and delayed the redemption of state debts. Taxpayers were being led to believe they would "never be compelled to pay" the public debt, lamented Charles Lee of Virginia, a wealthy bondholder. Private creditors had similar complaints against state governments that enacted laws that "stayed" (delayed) the payment of debts. "While men are madly accumulating enormous debts, their legislators are making provisions for their non-payment," complained a South Carolina creditor. To these nationalists, the democratic majorities in the state legislatures constituted a grave threat to republican government.

In 1786 James Madison and other nationalists persuaded the Virginia legislature to call a special commercial convention to discuss tariff and taxation policies. However, only five state governments sent delegates to the meeting in Annapolis, Maryland; undeterred by their small numbers, the twelve delegates called for another meeting in Philadelphia to undertake an even broader review of the Confederation government. Spurred on by Shays's Rebellion, nationalists in Congress secured a resolution supporting the Philadelphia convention and calling for a revision of the Articles of Confederation "adequate to the exigencies of government." "Nothing but the adoption of some efficient plan from the Convention," a fellow nationalist wrote to James Madison, "can prevent anarchy first & civil convulsions afterwards."

### The Philadelphia Convention

In May 1787, fifty-five delegates arrived in Philadelphia, representing every state except Rhode Island, whose legislature opposed any increase in central authority. Most delegates were men of property: merchants, slaveholding planters, or "monied men." There were no artisans, backcountry settlers, or tenants, and only a single yeoman farmer.

Some delegates, such as Benjamin Franklin of Pennsylvania, had been early advocates of independence while others, including George Washington and Robert Morris, had risen to prominence during the war. Several important Patriots missed the convention. John Adams and Thomas Jefferson were abroad, as the American ministers to Britain and France, respectively. The Massachusetts legislature declined to send radical Samuel Adams, and his fellow firebrand from Virginia, Patrick Henry, refused to attend because he favored a strictly limited national government and "smelt a rat." Their absence allowed capable young nationalists to set the agenda of the convention. Arguing that decisions of the convention would "decide for ever the fate of Republican Government," James Madison insisted on an increase in national authority, while Alexander Hamilton demanded a strong central government that would protect the republic from "the imprudence of democracy."

The delegates elected Washington as the presiding officer and, to forestall popular opposition, decided to deliberate in secret. This secrecy encouraged the delegates to exceed their mandate to revise the Articles of Confederation and to consider the Virginia Plan, a scheme for a powerful national government devised by James Madison. Madison, just thirty-six years old, had arrived in Philadelphia determined to fashion a new political order run by men of high character. A graduate of Princeton, he had read classical and modern political theory and served in both the Confederation Congress and the Virginia assembly. Once an optimistic Patriot, Madison had grown increasingly discouraged as his experience in the Virginia legislature revealed the "narrow ambition" of many elected state officials.

Madison's Virginia Plan differed from the Articles of Confederation in three crucial respects. First, it rejected state sovereignty in favor of the "supremacy of national authority." The central government would have the power not only to "legislate in all cases to which the separate States are incompetent" but also to overturn state laws. Second, the plan called for a national government to draw authority directly from the entire people and to exercise direct power on them. As Madison explained, it would bypass the state governments, and operate directly "on the individuals composing them." Third, the plan created a three-tier national government in which the people would elect only the lower house of the legislature. The lower house would name the members of the upper house, and then both houses of the legislature would select the executive and judiciary.

From a political perspective Madison's plan had two fatal flaws. First, the provision allowing the national government to veto state laws raised the ire of state politicians and many ordinary citizens. Second, the great powers assigned to the lower house of the legislature, whose membership was based on population, greatly increased the influence of the large states. Delegates from small states immediately rejected this provision; as a Delaware delegate put it, Madison's scheme would allow the populous states to "crush the small ones whenever they stand in the way of their ambitious or interested views."

Delegates from the smaller states rallied behind a plan devised by William Paterson, a delegate from New Jersey. The New Jersey Plan, as it came to be called, strengthened the Confederation by giving it the power to raise revenue, control commerce, and make binding requisitions on the states. But it preserved the states' control over their own laws and guaranteed their equality: each state would have one vote in a unicameral legislature, as in the existing Confederation. Delegates from the populous states vigorously opposed this voting provision. Finally, after a month of debate, a bare majority of the states agreed to take Madison's Virginia Plan as the basis of discussion.

This decision raised the prospect of a dramatically new constitutional system and prompted two New York representatives—Robert Yates and John Lansing—to accuse the delegates of exceeding their mandate and to leave the convention. During the hot, humid summer of 1787 the remaining delegates met six days a week, debating high principles and discussing practical details. Experienced and realistic politicians, they knew that their plan had to be acceptable to existing political interests and powerful social groups. Pierce Butler of South Carolina invoked a classical Greek precedent: "We must follow the example of Solon, who gave the Athenians not the best government he could devise but the best they would receive."

Representation remained the central problem. To satisfy both large and small states the Connecticut delegates suggested that the upper house, the Senate, would always have two members from each state, while seats in the lower chamber, the House of Representatives, would be apportioned on the basis of population, as determined every ten years by a national census. After bitter debate, this "Great Compromise" was accepted, but only reluctantly; to some delegates from populous states it seemed less a compromise than a victory for the smaller states.

Other state-related issues were quickly settled by restricting (or leaving ambiguous) the extent of central authority. Some delegates opposed establishing national courts within the states, warning that "the states will revolt at such encroachments." The convention therefore defined the judicial power of the United States in broad terms, vesting it "in one supreme Court" and leaving the new national legislature to decide whether to establish lower courts within the states. The convention also refused to require voters in national elections to be landowners. "Eight or nine states have extended the right of **suffrage** beyond the freeholders [landowners]," George Mason of Virginia pointed out. "What will people there say if they should be disfranchised?" The convention also placed the selection of the president in an electoral college chosen on a state-by-state basis and specified that state legislatures, not the voters at large, would elect members of the U.S. Senate. By giving states an important role in the new constitutional system, the delegates encouraged their citizens to accept a reduction in state sovereignty.

Slavery hovered in the background of the delegates' debates, rarely discussed but always present. When the issue arose, speakers divided along regional lines. Speaking for many northerners Gouverneur Morris of New York condemned slavery as "a nefarious institution" and hoped for its eventual demise. Reflecting the outlook of Chesapeake planters, who already owned ample numbers of slaves, George Mason of Virginia called for an end to the Atlantic slave trade. However, rice-growing planters from South Carolina and Georgia insisted that slave imports must continue; otherwise their states "shall not be parties to the Union." At their insistence the delegates denied Congress the power to regulate immigration until 1808 (at which time Congress abolished the slave trade).

For the sake of national unity, the delegates likewise treated other slavery-related issues as political rather than moral questions. To protect the property of southern slave owners, they agreed to a "fugitive" clause that allowed masters to reclaim enslaved blacks (or white indentured servants) who took refuge in other states. To mollify antislavery sentiment in the northern states, the delegates did not give slavery national legal recognition by explicitly mentioning it in the Constitution (which spoke instead of citizens and "all other Persons"). They also refused southern demands to count slaves and citizens equally in determining states' representation in Congress. Instead, they counted a slave as three-fifths of a free person for purposes of representation and taxation.

Having allayed the concerns of small states and slave states, the delegates created a powerful procreditor national government. The finished document made the Constitution and all national legislation the "supreme" law of the land. It gave the national government broad powers over taxation, military defense, and external

**Gouverneur Morris, Federalist Statesman**

Morris almost became a Loyalist because he was a snob who liked privilege and feared the people. ("The mob begins to think and reason," he once noted with disdain.) He became a Federalist for similar reasons, helped to write the Philadelphia Constitution and, after 1793, strongly supported the Federalist Party.

National Portrait Gallery, Smithsonian Institution / Art Resource, NY.

commerce as well as the authority to make all laws "necessary and proper" to implement those and other provisions. To protect creditors and establish the fiscal integrity of the new government, the Constitution mandated that the United States honor the existing **national debt**. Finally, it restricted the ability of state governments to assist debtors by forbidding the states to issue money or enact "any Law impairing the Obligation of Contracts."

The proposed Constitution was not a "perfect production," Benjamin Franklin admitted on September 17, 1787, as he urged the forty-one delegates still present to sign it. Yet, the great diplomat confessed his astonishment at finding "this system approaching so near to perfection as it does." His colleagues apparently agreed; all but three signed the document.

## The People Debate Ratification

The procedures for ratifying the new Constitution were as controversial as its contents. The delegates refused to submit the Constitution to the state legislatures for their unanimous consent, as required by the Articles of Confederation, because they knew that Rhode Island (and perhaps a few other states) would reject it. So they arbitrarily specified that the Constitution would go into effect when ratified by special conventions in nine of the thirteen states. Because of its nationalist sympathies, the Confederation Congress winked at this extralegal procedure; surprisingly, so too did most state legislatures, which promptly called the ratification conventions.

As the great constitutional debate began, the nationalists seized the initiative with two bold moves. First, they called themselves Federalists, suggesting that they favored a loose, decentralized system of government and obscuring their quest for a strong central authority. Second, they launched a coordinated pamphlet and newspaper campaign lauding the proposed Constitution.

The opponents of the Constitution, who became known as Antifederalists, had diverse backgrounds and motives. Some, like Governor George Clinton of New York, feared losing their power at the state level. Others were rural democrats who pointed out that the federal Constitution, unlike most state constitutions, lacked a declaration of individual rights. As smallholding farmers, they also worried that the powerful central government would be run by an aristocracy of wealth. "These lawyers and men of learning and monied men expect to be managers of this Constitution," worried a Massachusetts farmer, "and get all the power and all the money into their own hands and then they will swallow up all of us little folks . . . just as the whale swallowed up Jonah." Giving substance to these fears, Melancton Smith of New York argued that the large electoral districts prescribed by the Constitution would bring wealthy upper-class men into office, whereas the smaller districts used in state elections usually produced legislatures "composed principally of respectable yeomanry."

Well-educated Americans with a traditional republican outlook also opposed the new system. To keep government "close to the people," they wanted the nation to remain a collection of small sovereign republics tied together only for trade and defense—not the "United States" but the "States United." Citing the French political philosopher Montesquieu, these Antifederalists argued that republican institutions were best suited to cities or small states—a localist outlook that shaped American political thinking well into the twentieth century. "No extensive empire can be governed on republican principles," declared James Winthrop of Massachusetts. Patrick Henry predicted the Constitution would re-create the worst features of British rule: high taxes, an oppressive bureaucracy, a standing army, and a "great and mighty President . . . supported in extravagant munificence."

In New York, where ratification was hotly contested, James Madison, John Jay, and Alexander Hamilton countered these arguments in a series of eighty-five essays collectively called *The Federalist*. Although not widely read at the time outside of New York City (only a few of the essays were reprinted in newspapers elsewhere), *The Federalist* was subsequently recognized as a classic work of political theory. Its authors stressed the need for a strong government to conduct foreign affairs and denied that it would foster domestic tyranny. Citing Montesquieu's praise for mixed government (and drawing on John Adams's *Thoughts on Government*), Madison, Jay, and Hamilton pointed out that national authority would be divided among a president, a bicameral legislature, and a judiciary. Each branch of government would "check and balance" the others, thus preserving liberty.

Indeed, in *The Federalist*, No. 10, Madison made a significant contribution to political theory by denying that republicanism was suited only to small states. It was "sown in the nature of man," Madison wrote, that individuals would seek power and form factions to advance their interests. Indeed, "a landed interest, a manufacturing interest, a mercantile interest, a moneyed interest, with many lesser interests, grow up of necessity in civilized nations." He argued that a free society should not suppress those groups but rather prevent any one of them from becoming dominant—an end best achieved in a large republic. "Extend the sphere," Madison concluded, "and you take in a greater variety of parties and interests; you make it less probable that a majority of the whole will have a common motive to invade the rights of other citizens."

The delegates who debated these issues in the state ratification conventions included untutored farmers and middling artisans as well as educated gentlemen. Generally, backcountry representatives were Antifederalists; whereas those from the seacoast were Federalists. In Pennsylvania, Philadelphia merchants and artisans combined with Federalist-oriented commercial farmers to ratify the Constitution. Other early Federalist successes came in the less populous states of Delaware, New Jersey, Georgia, and Connecticut, where delegates hoped a strong national government would offset the power of large neighboring states (Map 7.3).

The Constitution's first real test came in January 1788 in Massachusetts, one of the most populous states and a hotbed of Antifederalist sentiment. Influential Patriots, including Samuel Adams and Governor John Hancock, opposed the new constitution, as did many former followers of Daniel Shays. But Boston artisans, who wanted tariff protection from British imports, supported ratification, and Federalist leaders assured delegates that the new government would consider a national bill of rights. By a close vote of 187 to 168, the Federalists carried the day.

Spring brought new Federalist victories in Maryland and South Carolina, and when New Hampshire narrowly ratified the Constitution in June, the required nine states had approved it. Still, the essential states of Virginia and New York had not yet acted, and it took the powerful arguments advanced in *The Federalist* and the promise of a national bill of rights to carry the day. The Constitution won ratification in Virginia, by 89 to 79, and that success carried the Federalists to victory in New York by the even smaller margin of 30 to 27. Suspicious of centralized power, the yeomen of North Carolina and Rhode Island ratified only in 1789 and 1790, respectively.

Ratification of the Constitution ended Antifederalist agitation and temporarily limited the resistance to centralized authority by the democratically and independently inclined state legislatures. "A decided majority" of the New Hampshire assembly had opposed the "new system," reported Joshua Atherton, but accepted the outcome, saying, "It is adopted, let us try it." In Virginia, Antifederalist firebrand Patrick Henry likewise vowed to "submit as a quiet citizen" and fight for amendments "in a constitutional way."

Working against great odds, the Federalists had created a national republic and partly restored an elitist system of political authority. To celebrate their victory Federalists organized great processions in the seaport cities. By marching in an orderly fashion—in conscious contrast to the riotous Revolutionary mobs—Federalist-minded citizens affirmed their allegiance to a self-governing republican community. To endow their regime with moral legitimacy, marching Federalists

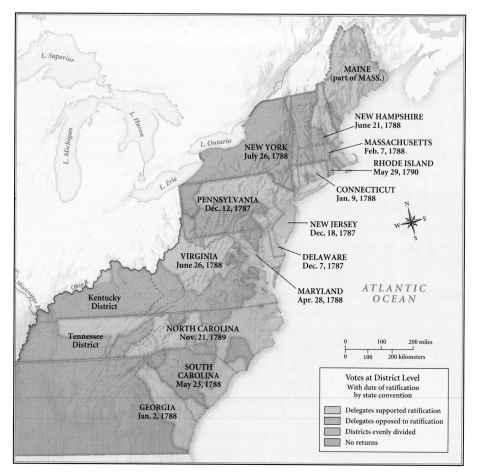

**MAP 7.3 Ratifying the Constitution of 1787**

In 1907 the geographer Owen Libby mapped the votes of members of the state conventions that ratified the Constitution. His map shows that most delegates from seaboard or commercial farming districts favored the Constitution, while those from backcountry areas opposed it. Subsequent research has confirmed Libby's socioeconomic interpretation of this voting pattern in North and South Carolina and Massachusetts; however, other factors influenced delegates in other states, such as Georgia, where the Constitution was ratified by delegates from all regions.

placed a copy of the Constitution on an "altar of liberty" float, using sacred symbolism to lay the foundations for a secular **"civil religion"** of American nationality.

## The Federalists Implement the Constitution

The Constitution expanded the dimensions of American political life because voters could now elect national as well as local and state officials. The Federalists swept the election of 1788, placing forty-four supporters in the first House of

Representatives; only eight Antifederalists won election. As expected, members of the electoral college chose George Washington as president. John Adams received the second highest number of electoral votes and became vice president.

Washington, the military savior of his country, became its political father as well. At fifty-seven he was a man of great personal dignity and influence. Instinctively cautious, Washington generally followed the administrative practices of the Confederation and asked Congress to reestablish the existing executive departments: foreign affairs (state), finance (treasury), and war. However, he made one important innovation. The Constitution specified that the president could appoint major officials with the consent of the Senate, but Washington insisted that only he—and not the Senate—could remove them, thus ensuring the chief executive's control over the bureaucracy. To head the Department of State Washington chose Thomas Jefferson, a fellow Virginian and an experienced diplomat. For secretary of the treasury he turned to Alexander Hamilton, a lawyer and wartime military aide. The new president designated Jefferson, Hamilton, and Secretary of War Henry Knox as his cabinet, or advisory body.

The Constitution had created a Supreme Court but left the establishment of the rest of the national court system to Congress. Because the Federalists wanted national institutions to act directly on individual citizens, they enacted the Judiciary Act in 1789 that created a federal district court in each state. The act provided three circuit courts to hear appeals from the districts, with the Supreme Court having the final say. The Judiciary Act also permitted appeals to the Supreme Court of federal legal issues that arose in state-run courts, ensuring that national (and not state) judges would decide the meaning of the Constitution.

The Federalists kept their promise to add a declaration of rights to the Constitution. James Madison, who had been elected to the House of Representatives, submitted a list of nineteen amendments to the first Congress, and ten of them were approved by that Congress and ratified by the states in 1791. These ten amendments, which became known as the Bill of Rights, safeguarded certain fundamental personal liberties, such as freedom of speech and religion, and mandated various legal procedures that protected the individual, such as trial by jury. By addressing Antifederalists' concerns about the potentially oppressive power of the national government, the amendments secured the legitimacy of the new Constitution.

# The Political Crisis of the 1790s

The final decade of the century brought fresh political challenges. The Federalists divided into two irreconcilable factions over financial policy, and this split widened further because of the ideological impact of the French Revolution. During these struggles, Alexander Hamilton and Thomas Jefferson offered contrasting visions of the American future. Would the United States remain, as Jefferson preferred, an agricultural nation in which local and state governments were predominant? Or, as Hamilton advised, would it use the authority of the national government to stimulate trade and industry?

## Hamilton's Financial Program

One of George Washington's most important decisions was his choice of Alexander Hamilton as secretary of the treasury. An ambitious self-made man of great charm and intelligence, Hamilton had served as Washington's personal aide during the war. He married into the Schuyler family of rich and influential Hudson River Valley landowners, and during the 1780s became a leading lawyer in New York City. As a delegate to the Philadelphia convention, Hamilton condemned the "amazing violence and turbulence of the democratic spirit" and called for an authoritarian government headed by a president with nearly monarchical powers.

As treasury secretary Hamilton devised bold policies to enhance the national authority and favor wealthy financiers and seaport merchants. He outlined his plans in three path-breaking and interrelated reports to Congress: on public credit (January 1790), on a national bank (December 1790), and on manufactures (December 1791).

The financial and social implications of Hamilton's "Report on the Public Credit" made it instantly controversial. The report called for Congress to "redeem" at face value the millions of dollars in securities issued by the Confederation. Intended to bolster the government's credit, this plan also provided excessive profits to speculators. For example, the Massachusetts merchant firm of Burrell & Burrell had paid about $600 for Confederation notes with a face value of $2,500; their redemption at full value would bring an enormous profit of $1,900. Equally controversial, Hamilton proposed to pay the Burrells and other Confederation note holders with new government-issued, interest-bearing securities that could be bought and sold—thereby creating a permanent national debt.

Hamilton's plan for a permanent national debt owned by wealthy families reawakened Radical Whig and republican fears. Speaking for the Virginia House of Burgesses, Patrick Henry condemned this plan "to erect, and concentrate, and perpetuate a large monied interest" and warned that it would prove "fatal to the existence of American liberty." Challenging the morality of Hamilton's proposal, James Madison asked Congress to pay part of the redemption fee to the original owners— the thousands of shopkeepers, farmers, and soldiers who had accepted Confederation securities during the dark days of the war and who had then been forced by hard times to sell them to speculators. But finding the original owners would have been difficult, and nearly half the members of the House of Representatives owned Confederation securities and would personally profit from Hamilton's plan. Melding practicality with self-interest, the House rejected Madison's innovative proposal.

Hamilton then advanced a second proposal that favored wealthy creditors, a plan by which the national government would take over ("assume") the war debts of the states. Rumors of this plan unleashed a flurry of speculation and some governmental corruption. Before Hamilton's announcement, Assistant Secretary of the Treasury William Duer bought up the depreciated war bonds of southern states; if Congress approved the assumption plan, Duer and his speculator associates would reap an enormous profit. Concerned members of Congress condemned such speculation and pointed out that some state legislatures had already levied high taxes to pay off their war debts. Responding to that argument, Hamilton modified his plan to reimburse those states. Other representatives from Virginia and Maryland argued that assumption would further enhance the already excessive powers of the national government. To quiet their fears about a runaway central government, the treasury chief backed their bid to locate the permanent national capital along the banks of the Potomac—where they could easily watch its operations. Such astute political bargaining gave Hamilton the votes he needed in the House of Representatives to enact his assumption plan.

In December 1790 Hamilton issued a second report asking Congress to charter a national financial institution, the Bank of the United States. The bank would be jointly owned by private stockholders and the national government. Hamilton argued that the bank, by making loans to merchants, handling government funds, and issuing financial notes, would provide a respected currency for the specie-starved American economy and make the new national debt easier to fund. These benefits persuaded Congress to enact Hamilton's bank bill and send it to the president for approval.

At this critical juncture Secretary of State Thomas Jefferson joined ranks with Madison against Hamilton's financial initiatives. Jefferson had condemned the shady dealings in southern war bonds and the "corrupt squadron of paper dealers" who had arranged them. Now he charged that Hamilton's scheme for a national bank was unconstitutional. "The incorporation of a Bank," Jefferson told President Washington, was not a power "delegated to the United States by the Constitution." Giving a *strict* interpretation to the national charter, Jefferson maintained that the central government had only the limited powers explicitly assigned to it. In response, Hamilton articulated a *loose* interpretation, noting that Article 1, Section 8, empowered Congress to make "all Laws which shall be necessary and proper" to carry out the Constitution's provisions. Washington agreed with his treasury secretary and signed the legislation creating the bank.

Hamilton turned now to the final element of his financial system: a national revenue to pay the annual interest on the permanent debt. In 1792, at Hamilton's insistence, the Congress imposed a variety of domestic excise taxes, including a duty on whiskey distilled in the United States. But the revenue from those taxes was a mere $1 million a year. To raise another $4–5 million the treasury secretary proposed to raise tariffs on foreign imports. Although Hamilton's "Report on Manufactures" (1791) urged the nation to become self-sufficient in such goods, he did not ask Congress to impose high protective tariffs that would aid American

**Two Visions of America**

Thomas Jefferson and Alexander Hamilton confront each other in these portraits, as they did during the political battles of the 1790s. Jefferson was pro-French, Hamilton pro-British. Jefferson favored farmers and artisans; Hamilton supported merchants and financiers. Jefferson believed in democracy and rule by legislative majorities; Hamilton argued for a strong executive and for judicial review. But in 1800 Hamilton's support for Jefferson in his postelection struggle with Aaron Burr, whom Hamilton detested, secured the presidency for his longtime political foe.

Jefferson, by Rembrandt Peale, © White House Historical Association / Photo by National Geographic Society; Yale University Art Gallery, Mabel Brady Garven Collection.

manufacturers by excluding foreign products. Instead, Hamilton settled for a modest increase in customs duties, a revenue tariff that would allow trade and provide income for the national government.

Hamilton's scheme worked brilliantly. As American trade increased, customs revenue rose steadily (providing about 90 percent of the U.S. government's income from 1790 to 1820) and allowed the treasury to pay for the redemption and assumption programs. In less than two years Hamilton had devised a strikingly modern fiscal system that provided the new national government with financial stability.

## Jefferson's Agrarian Vision

Hamilton paid a high price for this success. Even before Washington began his second four-year term in 1793, Hamilton's financial measures had split the Federalists who wrote and ratified the Constitution into two irreconcilable factions. Most northern Federalists adhered to the political alliance led by Hamilton and most southerners to a rival group headed by Madison and Jefferson. By the elections of 1794 the two factions had acquired names. Hamilton's supporters retained their original name: Federalists; Madison's and Jefferson's supporters called themselves Democratic-Republicans or simply Republicans.

The southern planters and western farmers who became Republicans rejected Hamilton's economic and social philosophy, and Thomas Jefferson spoke for them. Well read in architecture, natural history, scientific farming, and political theory, Jefferson embraced the optimistic spirit of the Enlightenment and believed in the "improvability of the human race." But he knew that progress was not inevitable and deplored both the long-standing speculative practices of merchants and financiers and the emerging social divisions of an industrial economy. Having seen the masses of propertyless laborers in the manufacturing regions in Britain, Jefferson had concluded that workers who depended on wages lacked the economic independence required to sustain a republic.

Consequently, Jefferson's vision of the American future was agrarian and democratic. Although he had grown up (and remained) a privileged slave owner, Jefferson pictured a West without slavery and settled by productive yeomen farm families. His vision took form in his *Notes on the State of Virginia* (1785): "Those who labor in the earth are the chosen people of God," he wrote. Their grain and meat would feed European nations, which "would manufacture and send us in exchange our clothes and other comforts" in an international division of labor similar to that proposed by the Scottish economist Adam Smith in *The Wealth of Nations* (1776).

Turmoil in Europe created new opportunities for American farmers and brought Jefferson's vision closer to reality. The French Revolution began in 1789, and four years later France's new republican government went to war against a British-led coalition of monarchical states. As warfare disrupted European farming, wheat prices leaped from 5 to 8 shillings a bushel and remained high for twenty years, bringing substantial profits to export-minded Chesapeake and Middle Atlantic farmers. Simultaneously, a boom in the export of raw cotton, fueled by the invention of the cotton gin and mechanization of cloth production in Britain (see Chapter 10), boosted the economy of Georgia and South Carolina. As Jefferson had hoped, European markets brought prosperity to American farmers and planters.

### The French Revolution Divides Americans

American merchants profited even more handsomely from the European war. President Washington issued a Proclamation of Neutrality, which allowed U.S. citizens to trade with both sides. As neutral carriers, American ships claimed the right to pass through the British naval blockade along the French coastline and soon took over the lucrative sugar trade between France and its West Indian islands. The American merchant fleet increased dramatically from 355,000 tons in 1790 to more than 1.1 million tons in 1808. Commercial earnings rose spectacularly, averaging

$20 million annually in the 1790s—twice the value of cotton and tobacco exports. Northern shipowners provided work for thousands of shipwrights, sail makers, laborers, and seamen by investing in new vessels. Hundreds of carpenters, masons, and cabinetmakers in the major seaports of Boston, New York, and Philadelphia likewise found work building warehouses and fashionable "Federal-style" town houses for newly affluent merchants. In Philadelphia, a European visitor reported, "a great number of private houses have marble steps to the street door, and in other respects are finished in a style of elegance."

Even as they prospered from the European struggle, Americans argued passionately over its ideologies. Most Americans had welcomed the French Revolution of 1789 because it abolished feudalism and established a constitutional monarchy. But the creation of the democratic French republic in 1792 and the execution of King Louis XVI the following year divided public opinion. Many American artisans praised the egalitarianism of the radical French Jacobins and followed their example by addressing each other as "citizen" and by founding political clubs modeled on the radical democratic societies in Paris—the controversial Jacobin clubs. But Americans with strong religious beliefs condemned the new French regime for abandoning Christianity in favor of atheism. Wealthy Americans likewise denounced Robespierre and his radical republican followers for executing King Louis XVI, 3,000 of his aristocratic supporters, and 14,000 other citizens.

These ideological conflicts sharpened the debate over Hamilton's economic policies and even helped to foment a domestic insurrection. In 1794 farmers in western Pennsylvania mounted the Whiskey Rebellion to protest Hamilton's excise tax on spirits, which had raised the price—and thus cut the demand—for the corn whiskey they bartered for eastern manufactures. Like the Sons of Liberty of 1765 and the Shaysites of 1786, the whiskey rebels attacked both local tax collectors and the authority of a distant government. However, these protesters also waved banners proclaiming the French revolutionary slogan, "Liberty, Equality, and Fraternity!" To suppress these radical-minded dissenters, uphold national authority, and deter secessionist movements along the frontier, President Washington raised an army of 12,000 troops that soon dispersed the whiskey rebels.

Britain's maritime strategy also widened the growing political divisions in the United States. In November 1793 the Royal Navy began to prey on American ships bound for France from the West Indies and eventually seized more than 250 vessels and their cargoes of sugar. Seeking to resolve this controversy though diplomacy, President Washington dispatched John Jay to Britain. Jay returned in 1795 with a controversial treaty requiring the U.S. government to make "full and complete compensation" to British merchants for all pre–Revolutionary War debts owed by American citizens. The treaty also acknowledged Britain's right to remove French property from neutral ships, overturning the American merchants' claim that "free ships make free goods." In return, the agreement allowed American merchants to submit claims of illegal seizure to arbitration and, more importantly,

**An Anti-French Cartoon**

A five-headed monster, representing the leaders of France under the Directory, demands a bribe ("Money, Money, Money") from American diplomats. Federalists used the bribery incident— named the XYZ Affair for the three anonymous French agents who asked for the bribe—to whip up anti-French sentiment in the United States and to launch an undeclared naval war.
Huntington Library.

required the British to remove their military garrisons from the Northwest Territory and to end their aid to the Indians there. Jefferson and other Republicans attacked Jay's Treaty as too conciliatory, and the Senate ratified it only by the bare two-thirds majority required by the Constitution. However, as long as Hamilton and his Federalist allies were in power, the United States would have a pro-British foreign policy.

## The Rise of Political Parties

The appearance of Federalists and Republicans marked a new stage in American politics. Although colonial legislatures had often divided into temporary factions based on family alliances, ethnicity, or region, they lacked well-organized parties.

The new state and national constitutions made no provision for organized political bodies; indeed, most Americans considered parties unnecessary and dangerous. Following classical republican principles, they wanted voters and legislators to act independently and in the interest of the entire public. Thus, Senator Pierce Butler of South Carolina criticized his congressional colleagues as "men scrambling for partial advantage, State interests, and in short, a train of narrow, impolitic measures."

Political parties appeared, however, because the financial and ideological conflicts of the 1790s divided the political elite and the revolutionary ideology of popular sovereignty drew average citizens into politics. The resulting contest for votes created a competitive—and divisive—party system. Most merchants, creditors, and urban artisans favored Federalist policies, as did wheat-exporting slaveholders in the Tidewater districts of the Chesapeake. The emerging Republican coalition was more diverse. It included not only southern tobacco and rice planters and debt-conscious western farmers but also Germans and Scots-Irish in the southern backcountry and subsistence-oriented eastern farmers.

Party identity crystallized during the election of 1796. To prepare for the election, Federalist and Republican leaders called legislative caucuses in Congress and conventions in the states to discuss policies and nominate candidates. To mobilize the citizenry the parties organized public festivals and processions, with the Federalists celebrating Washington's achievements and the Republicans invoking the egalitarian principles of the Declaration of Independence.

Federalist candidates triumphed in the 1796 election, winning a majority in Congress and electing John Adams as the new president. Adams continued Hamilton's pro-British foreign policy and reacted sharply when the French navy seized American merchant ships. When the French foreign minister Talleyrand solicited a loan and a bribe from American diplomats to stop the seizures, Adams charged that Talleyrand's agents, whom he dubbed X, Y, and Z, had insulted American honor. Responding to the "XYZ Affair," the Federalist-controlled Congress cut off trade with France in 1798 and authorized American privateers to seize French ships. Party conflict, which had begun over Hamilton's financial policies, now extended to foreign affairs.

## Constitutional Crisis, 1798–1800

For the first time in American history (but not the last) a controversial foreign policy prompted domestic protest and governmental repression. As the United States fought an undeclared maritime war against France, pro-Republican and anti-British immigrants from Ireland vehemently attacked Adams's foreign policy. A Philadelphia Federalist pamphleteer responded in kind: "Were I president, I would hang them for otherwise they would murder me" (see Voices from Abroad, "Peter Porcupine Attacks Pro-French Americans," p. 223). To silence their critics, the Federalists enacted a series of coercive measures in 1798. The Naturalization Act

## VOICES FROM ABROAD

# Peter Porcupine Attacks Pro-French Americans

## WILLIAM COBBETT

*The Democratic-Republican followers of Thomas Jefferson declared that "he who is an enemy to the French Revolution, cannot be a firm republican." William Cobbett, a British journalist who settled in Philadelphia and wrote under the pen name "Peter Porcupine," contested this definition of republicanism. A strong supporter of the Federalist Party, Cobbett attacked its opponents in caustic and widely read pamphlets and newspaper articles. Here he evokes the horrors of the Terror in France, during which thousands of aristocrats and ordinary citizens were executed, and warns that the triumph of Radical Republicanism would bring the same fate to the United States.*

France is a republic, and . . . this word outweighs, in the estimation of some persons (I wish I could say they were few in number), all the horrors that have been and that can be committed in that country. One of these modern republicans will tell you that he does not deny that hundreds of thousands of innocent persons have been murdered in France; that the people have neither religion nor morals; . . . that its riches, along with millions of the best of the people, are gone to enrich and aggrandize its enemies. . . . But at the end of all this, he will tell you that it must be happy, because it is a republic. . . . Such a sentiment is characteristic of a mind locked up in a savage ignorance.

Shall we say that these things never can take place among us? . . . We are not what we were before the French revolution. Political projectors from every corner of Europe, troublers of society of every description, . . . have taken shelter in these States.

We have seen the guillotine toasted. . . . And what would the reader say, were I to tell him of a Member of Congress, who wished to see one of these murderous machines employed for lopping off the heads of the French, permanent in the State-house yard of the city of Philadelphia?

If these men of blood had succeeded in plunging us into a war; if they had once got the sword into their hands, they would have mowed us down like stubble. The word Aristocrat would have been employed to as good account here, as ever it had been in France. We might, ere this, have seen our places of worship turned into stables; we might have seen the banks of the Delaware, like those of the Loire, covered with human carcasses, and its waters tinged with blood. . . .

I know the reader will start back with horror. His heart will tell him that it is impossible. But, once more, let him look at the example before us. The attacks on the character and conduct of the aged Washington, have been as bold, if not bolder, than those which led to the downfall of the unfortunate French Monarch [Louis XVI, executed in 1793]. Can it then be imagined, that, had they possessed the power, they wanted the will to dip their hands in his blood?

SOURCE: William Cobbett, *Peter Porcupine in America*, ed., David A. Wilson (Ithaca: Cornell University Press, 1994), 150–54.

lengthened the residency requirement for American citizenship from five to four-teen years; the Alien Act authorized the deportation of foreigners; and the Sedition Act prohibited the publication of ungrounded or malicious attacks on the president or Congress. "He that is not for us is against us," thundered the Federalist *Gazette of the United States.* Prosecutors arrested more than twenty Republican newspaper editors and politicians, accused them of sedition, and won convictions and jail sentences against some of them.

The Federalists' repressive actions created a constitutional crisis. Republicans charged that the Sedition Act violated the First Amendment's prohibition against "abridging the freedom of speech, or of the press." However, they did not appeal to the Supreme Court, both because the Court's power to review congressional legislation had not been established and because the Court was packed with Federalists. Instead, Madison and Jefferson looked to the state legislatures to rem-edy unconstitutional laws. At their urging, in 1798 the Kentucky and Virginia legislatures declared the Alien and Sedition Acts to be "unauthoritative, void, and of no force." The resolutions set forth a **"states' rights"** interpretation of the Constitution by arguing that the states had a "right to judge" the legitimacy of national laws.

The debate over the Sedition Act set the stage for the election of 1800. Jefferson, once opposed in principle to political parties, now saw them as a valuable way "to watch and relate to the people" the activities of an oppressive government. As Republicans strongly supported Jefferson's bid for the presidency, President Adams reevaluated his foreign policy. Adams was a complicated man who was easily offended but had great personal strength and determination. Rejecting Hamilton's advice to declare war against France (and benefit from an upsurge in patriotism), Adams put country ahead of party and entered into diplomatic negotiations that ended the fighting.

Nonetheless, the election of 1800 was the first "dirty" political campaign. The Federalists attacked Jefferson's character, branding him an irresponsible pro-French radical, "the arch-apostle of irreligion and free thought," and both parties changed state election laws to favor their candidates. A low Federalist turnout in Virginia and Pennsylvania and the three-fifths rule for slave representation (which boosted the electoral votes in the southern states) gave Jefferson a narrow 73 to 65 victory over Adams in the electoral college. But the Republican electors also gave seventy-three votes to Aaron Burr of New York, who was Jefferson's vice presiden-tial running mate. Because both Republican candidates had the same number of votes, the Constitution specified that the House of Representatives would choose between them.

Ironically, the arch-Federalist aristocrat Alexander Hamilton ushered in a more democratic era. For thirty-five ballots, Federalists in the House of Representatives blocked Jefferson's election. Then Hamilton intervened. Calling Burr an "embryo Caesar" and the "most unfit man in the United States for the office of president," he persuaded key Federalists to permit Jefferson's selection. The Federalists' concern for political stability also played a role. As Senator James Bayard of Delaware explained, "It was admitted on all hands that we must risk the Constitution and a Civil War or take Mr. Jefferson."

Jefferson called the election the "Revolution of 1800," and so it was. The bloodless transfer of power demonstrated that governments elected by the people could be changed in an orderly way, even in times of bitter partisan conflict. In his inaugural address in 1801 Jefferson praised this achievement, declaring: "We are all Republicans, we are all Federalists." Defying the predictions of European conservatives, the new republican constitutional order of 1776 had survived a quarter century of economic and political turmoil.

## TIMELINE

| | | | |
|---|---|---|---|
| **1776** | Pennsylvania approves a democratic constitution<br><br>John Adams, *Thoughts on Government*<br><br>Propertied women allowed to vote in New Jersey (retracted in 1807) | **1789** | George Washington inaugurated as first president<br><br>Judiciary Act establishes federal court system<br><br>Outbreak of French Revolution |
| **1777** | Articles of Confederation (ratified 1781) | **1790** | Hamilton wins Congress's approval of redemption and assumption |
| **1779** | Judith Sargent Murray, "On the Equality of the Sexes" (published in 1790) | **1791** | Bill of Rights ratified |
| **1780s** | Postwar commercial recession increases creditor-debtor conflicts in the states | **1792** | Mary Wollstonecraft, *A Vindication of the Rights of Woman* |
| **1781** | Confederation Congress charters Bank of North America | **1793** | French create republic and execute King Louis XVI<br><br>Madison and Jefferson found Republican Party<br><br>War between Britain and France; Washington's Proclamation of Neutrality |
| **1784–1785** | Political and Land Ordinances outline settlement policy for new states | | |
| **1785** | Thomas Jefferson, *Notes on the State of Virginia* | | |
| **1786** | Commercial convention in Annapolis, Maryland<br><br>Shays's Rebellion roils Massachusetts | **1794** | Whiskey Rebellion in western Pennsylvania |
| **1787** | Northwest Ordinance<br><br>Constitutional convention in Philadelphia | **1795** | Jay's Treaty with Great Britain creates controversy |
| **1787–1788** | States hold ratification conventions<br><br>John Jay, James Madison, and Alexander Hamilton write *The Federalist* essays | **1798** | Alien, Sedition, and Naturalization Acts<br><br>Kentucky and Virginia Resolutions contest national authority |
| | | **1800** | Jefferson elected president in "Revolution of 1800" |

# For Further Exploration

For a lively, drama-filled retelling of the Constitutional Convention, see Catherine Drinker Bowen's *Miracle at Philadelphia: The Story of the Constitutional Convention, May to September 1787* (1966). Jack Rakove's *Original Meanings: Politics and Ideas in the Making of the Constitution* (1996) is a more complex analysis that shows the divergent perspectives of the framers and how they compromised their differences. A fine study of the opponents of the new constitution is Saul Cornell's *The Other Founders: The Antifederalists and the American Dissenting Tradition* (1999). Michael Kammen, *A Machine That Would Go by Itself: The Constitution in American Culture* (1986), explains the changing reputation of the founding document, while David Waldstreicher, *In the Midst of Perpetual Fetes: The Making of American Nationalism, 1776–1820* (1997), presents a fascinating analysis of the links between public celebrations and the emergence of an American national identity.

James Roger Sharp offers an engaging study of the near disintegration of the new nation in the 1790s in *American Politics in the Early Republic: The New Nation in Crisis* (1993). A detailed study of one of the major crises of these years, Thomas P. Slaughter's *The Whiskey Rebellion* (1986), shows how this uprising reflected the localistic, antitax outlook of the Revolutionary era. Rosemarie Zagarri suggests the impact of republicanism on women and provides a concise biography of an important Patriot in *A Woman's Dilemma: Mercy Otis Warren and the American Revolution* (1995). See also Linda Kerber, *No Constitutional Right to Be Ladies: Women and the Obligations of Citizenship* (1999).

The strong political and leadership abilities of the first president are a central theme of William Martin's fictionalized biography *Citizen Washington* (1999). William Martin also wrote the documentary *George Washington: The Man Who Wouldn't Be King* (PBS video, 1 hour). Additional material, including Washington's published correspondence, is available online at The Papers of George Washington, <http://www.virginia.edu/gwpapers/>. For more information on Thomas Jefferson consult the PBS Web site Thomas Jefferson, at <http://www.pbs.org/jefferson>, which contains information on the documentary (PBS video, 3 hours), transcripts of interviews with Jeffersonian scholars, and a good collection of documents relating to Jefferson's personal and public life.

---

For definitions of key terms boldfaced in this chapter, see the glossary at the end of the book.

To assess your mastery of the material covered in this chapter, see the Online Study Guide at **bedfordstmartins.com/henrettaconcise**.

For map resources and primary documents, see **bedfordstmartins.com/henrettaconcise**.

# Chapter 8

## THE DYNAMICS OF WESTERN SETTLEMENT AND EASTERN CAPITALISM
### 1790–1820

Once we became an independent people it was as much a law of
nature that this [expansion to the west] should become our
pretension as that the Mississippi should flow to the sea.

JOHN QUINCY ADAMS

"It is a country in flux," a French aristocrat observed of the United
States in 1799, and "that which is true today as regards its population, its establishments, its prices, its commerce will not be true six months from now." Indeed, by
1800, the American republic was poised to begin a period of dynamic westward
expansion and eastern economic development that would soon change its very
character. "If movement and the quick succession of sensations and ideas constitute
life," another French observer wrote a few decades later, "here one lives a hundred
fold more than elsewhere; here, all is circulation, motion, and boiling agitation."

Circulation and motion were especially evident along the western frontier. As
early as 1766, a white observer had noted that "the thirst after Indian lands, is
become almost universal." After 1783, when the Treaty of Paris gave Americans
access to the trans-Appalachian West, hundreds of thousands of extraordinarily
self-confident farmers trekked into the interior with little or no regard for Indian
land rights. As western land speculator George Washington put it, the Sons of
Liberty became "the lords and proprietors of a vast tract of continent."
Unfortunately for Washington's Federalist Party, the votes of these western farmers
bolstered the political ascendancy of Republican president Thomas Jefferson and
his western-oriented policies. To provide even more land for American farmers,
Jefferson doubled the country's size through the Louisiana Purchase in 1803. "[No]
territory can be too large," declared Dr. David Ramsay of South Carolina, "for a
people, who multiply with such unequalled rapidity."

As Republican policy in the West encouraged homesteading, state legislatures in the East promoted banking, manufacturing, and commercial expansion. This stimulus from state governments unleashed a cumulative process of capitalist-financed economic growth. "Experiment follows experiment; enterprise follows enterprise," a European traveler noted, and "riches and poverty follow." Of the two, riches were the more apparent. Beginning around 1800 per capita income in the United States increased by more than 1 percent per year—over 30 percent in a single generation. By the 1820s the nation was well on its way to becoming a republic that was continental in scope and **capitalist** in character.

# Westward Expansion

Many generations past, Shawnee diplomats told American officials in 1803, their ancestors had gazed out into the Atlantic Ocean and seen a strange object. "At first they took it for a great bird, but they soon found it to be a monstrous canoe filled with . . . white people." Soon thereafter, the Indian emissaries continued, the white people robbed the Shawnees of their wisdom and then "usurped their land," purchasing it with goods that "were more the property of the Indians than the white people because the knowledge which enabled them to manufacture these goods actually belonged to the Shawnees."

Whatever the truth of this legend, by 1803 the expansionist-minded American republic clearly threatened the Shawnees and other native peoples. In 1790 the first national census counted only 200,000 Americans living west of the Appalachian Mountains, out of a total population of 3.9 million. Thirty years later, no fewer than 2 million slaves and citizens (of a total of 9.6 million) inhabited nine new states and three new territories west of the Appalachians. The country was moving west at an astonishing pace.

## Native American Resistance

In the Treaty of Paris of 1783 Great Britain relinquished its claims to the trans-Appalachian region and, as one British statesman put it, left the Indian nations "to the care of their [American] neighbours." *Care* was hardly the right term, given that some influential Americans wanted to exterminate the native peoples. "Cut up every Indian Cornfield and burn every Indian town," proclaimed William Henry Drayton of South Carolina, so that their "nation be extirpated and the lands become the property of the public." Others, including Henry Knox, President Washington's first secretary of war, favored assimilating the Indians into American society. Knox proposed the division of commonly held tribal lands among individual Indian families, who would become citizens of the various states. Most Indians rejected these policies and continued to view themselves as members of a particular clan or tribe. A few Native American leaders raised the notion of a broader, pan-Indian identity, but without much success.

**Treaty Negotiations at Greenville**

In 1785 the Shawnee, Chipewyan, Ottawa, Miami, and other tribes formed the Western Confederacy to prevent white settlement north of the Ohio River. The American victory at the Battle of Fallen Timbers (1794) opened up the region for white farmers. However, the Treaty of Greenville (1795) recognized many Indian rights because, as the artist suggests, it was negotiated between relative equals. Note the height and stately bearing of the Indian leaders and their placement in the picture slightly in front of the American officers.

Unknown, *Treaty of Greenville*, n.d., Chicago Historical Society.

Not surprisingly, the major struggle between Indians and whites concerned land rights. Invoking the Paris treaty and viewing Britain's Indian allies as conquered peoples, the United States government asserted its ownership of the trans-Appalachian West. Native Americans rejected this claim and pointed out that they had not signed the treaty and had never been conquered. Brushing aside those arguments, U.S. commissioners used military threats to force pro-British Iroquois peoples—the Mohawks, Onondagas, Cayugas, and Senecas—to relinquish much of their land in New York and Pennsylvania in the Treaty of Fort Stanwix (1784). New York officials and land speculators used liquor and bribes to take title to millions of additional acres and confined the once-powerful Iroquois to relatively small reservations.

American negotiators employed similar tactics farther to the west. In 1785 they induced the Chipewyans, Delawares, Ottawas, and Wyandots to sign away most of the future state of Ohio. The tribes quickly repudiated the agreements, claiming—justifiably—that they were made under duress. Those peoples, along with the Shawnees, Miamis, and Potawatomis, formed the Western Confederacy to defend themselves. Led by Little Turtle, a Miami chief, they crushed American expeditionary forces commanded by General Harmar in 1790 and General St. Clair in 1791.

Fearing an alliance between the Western Confederacy and the British in Canada, President Washington doubled the size of the U.S. Army and ordered General "Mad Anthony" Wayne to lead a new expedition. In August 1794 Wayne defeated the Indians in the Battle of Fallen Timbers (near present-day Toledo, Ohio). Nevertheless, in 1795 the Western Confederacy forced a compromise peace in the Treaty of Greenville (Ohio). American negotiators acknowledged Indian ownership of the land, and the members of the confederacy agreed to place themselves "under the protection of the United States, and no other Power whatever." In practice, this agreement eventually brought the transfer of millions of acres of Indian land to the U.S. government. Indeed, during the Greenville negotiations the Indians ceded ownership of most of Ohio and various strategic areas along the Great Lakes, including Detroit and the future site of Chicago (Map 8.1). These American advances prompted Britain to reduce its trade with the Indian peoples and, in Jay's Treaty of 1795, to reaffirm its (still unfulfilled) obligation under the Treaty of Paris to remove its military garrisons from the region.

The Greenville Treaty sparked a wave of American migration. By 1805 the two-year-old state of Ohio had more than 100,000 residents. Thousands more farm families moved into the future states of Indiana and Illinois and sparked new conflicts with native peoples over land and hunting rights. As a Delaware Indian declared, "The Elks are our horses, the buffaloes are our cows, the deer are our sheep, & the whites shan't have them."

To alleviate these tensions the U.S. government encouraged Native Americans to become farmers and assimilate into white society. The goal, as one Kentucky Protestant minister put it, was to make the Indian "a farmer, a citizen of the United States, and a Christian." Some Indians embraced Christian teachings while retaining many ancestral values. To view themselves as individuals, as the Europeans demanded, meant repudiating the clan, the essence of Indian life. Consequently, most Native Americans resisted assimilation. As a Munsee prophet put it, "There are two ways to God, one for the whites and one for the Indians." To preserve their traditional cultures, many Indian peoples drove out white missionaries and forced Christianized Indians to participate in tribal rites. A few Indian leaders tried to find a middle path. Among the Senecas of New York the prophet Handsome Lake promoted traditional pagan ceremonies that gave thanks to the earth, plants, animals, water, and sun. But his teachings also included some Christian elements, such as a belief in heaven and hell, which he used to deter his followers from drinking alcohol, gambling, and practicing witchcraft. Handsome Lake's doctrines divided the tribe into hostile religious factions. More conservative Senecas, led by Chief Red Jacket, condemned Indians who accepted white

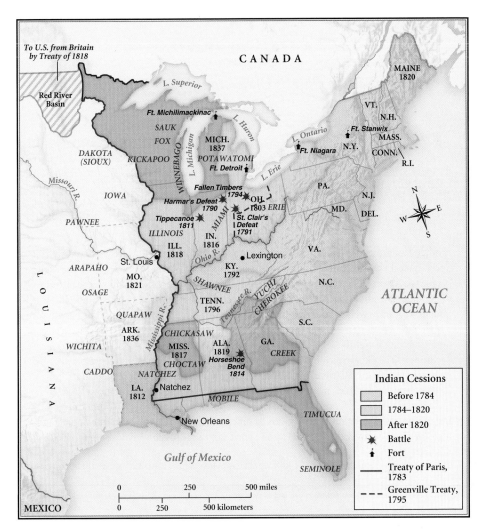

**MAP 8.1 Indian Cessions and State Formation, to 1840**

By virtue of the Treaty of Paris of 1783 with Britain, the United States claimed sovereignty over the entire trans-Appalachian West. The Western Indian Confederacy contested this claim, which the U.S. government upheld by military force. By 1840 Native American peoples had been forced by armed diplomacy to move west of the Mississippi River. White settlers occupied their lands, formed territorial governments, and eventually entered the Union as members of separate—and equal—states. Gradually, the trans-Appalachian region emerged as an important economic and political force.

ways, and they demanded a return to ancestral customs (see American Voices, "A Seneca Chief's Understanding of Religion," p. 232).

Most Indians also rejected the efforts of American missionaries to place agriculture in the hands of men. Among Eastern Woodland peoples, women had traditionally been responsible for growing staple foods; partly as a result, they controlled the inheritance

## AMERICAN VOICES

# A Seneca Chief's Understanding of Religion

### RED JACKET

*The Seneca chief Red Jacket (c. 1758–1830) acquired his name during the Revolutionary War, when he fought for the British "redcoats" to protect his people from the threat posed by American settlers. Although reconciled to American rule, Red Jacket strongly adhered to Indian values and opposed attempts by missionaries to convert the Iroquois people to Christianity. In 1805 he explained why to a group of missionaries, whom he addressed as "Brother."*

Brother: Continue to listen. You say that you are sent to instruct us how to worship the Great Spirit agreeably to his mind; and, if we do not take hold of the religion which you white people teach, we shall be unhappy hereafter. You say that you are right, and we are lost. How do we know this to be true? We understand that your religion is written in a book. If it was intended for us as well as you, why has not the Great Spirit given to us, and not only to us, but why did He not give to our forefathers, the knowledge of the book, with the means of understanding it rightly?

Brother: The Great Spirit has made us all, but he has made a great difference between his white and red children. He has given us different complexions and different customs. To you He has given the arts [i.e., manufacturing]. To these He has not opened our eyes. We know these things to be true. Since He has made a great difference between us in other things, why may we not conclude that He has given us different religion according to our understanding? The Great Spirit does right. He knows what is best for his children; we are satisfied.

SOURCE: David J. Rothman and Sheila Rothman, eds., *Sources of the American Social Tradition* (New York: Basic Books, 1975), 182.

of cultivation rights and exercised considerable political power. In fact, among the Shawnees, women "war chiefs" had the authority to dispatch war parties and order the torture of captives. Nor were Indian men interested in becoming farmers; when hunting was no longer possible, they turned to the grazing of cattle and sheep.

### Migration and the Changing Farm Economy

Native American resistance did not halt the advance of white farmers and planters, who poured across the Appalachians and moved along the Atlantic coastal plain in search of fertile lands. This migratory upsurge brought financial rewards to many settlers and transformed the American farm economy.

Between 1790 and 1820 two great streams of migrants moved out of the southern states. One stream, composed primarily of white tenant farmers and struggling yeomen families, flocked through the Cumberland Gap into Kentucky and Tennessee. They were fleeing the depleted soils and planter elite of the Chesapeake region and hoped to prosper by growing cotton and hemp, which were in great demand. "Boundless settlements open a door for our citizens to run off and leave us," a worried eastern landlord lamented in the *Maryland Gazette*, "depreciating all our landed property and disabling us from paying taxes."

Many migrants to Kentucky and Tennessee were poor, without ready cash to buy land. To gain title to farmland, they invoked the "the ancient cultivation law" articulated earlier by the North Carolina Regulators (see Chapter 4). In their view, poor settlers had a customary right "from time out of Mind" to occupy "back waste vacant Lands" sufficient "to provide a subsistence for themselves and their posterity." The Virginia government, which administered the Kentucky Territory, had a more elitist and capitalist vision. Although it allowed poorer settlers to purchase up to 1,400 acres of land at reduced prices, it also sold or granted estates of 20,000 to 200,000 acres to scores of wealthy individuals and partnerships. Consequently, when Kentucky became a state in 1792, a handful of speculators owned one-fourth of the state, while half the adult white men owned no land and lived as squatters or tenant farmers.

Meanwhile, a second stream of southern migrants from the Carolinas, dominated by slave-owning planters and their enslaved African American workers, moved along the coastal plain of the Gulf of Mexico. At first, these planters set up new slave plantations in the interior of Georgia and South Carolina. Then they moved into the Old Southwest—the future states of Alabama, Mississippi, and Louisiana, taking some slaves with them and importing more from Africa. Between 1776 and 1808, when Congress cut off the Atlantic slave trade, these planters bought about 115,000 Africans. The American black population grew even more through reproduction and increased from half a million in 1775 to 1.8 million in 1820.

Although many African Americans still toiled in tobacco and rice fields of the Chesapeake and South Carolina, many more planted and picked a new crop: cotton. Beginning around 1750, technological innovations such as water-powered spinning jennies and weaving mules boosted European textile production and greatly increased the demand for raw wool and cotton. Responding to the demand for cotton, South Carolina and Georgia planters began growing the crop and American inventors—including Connecticut-born Eli Whitney—developed machines (called gins) that efficiently extracted the seeds from the strands of cotton. The cotton boom financed the rapid settlement of Alabama and Mississippi. In a single year a government land office in Huntsville, Alabama, sold $7 million of uncleared land, and the two states entered the Union in 1817 and 1819, respectively.

As southern whites and blacks moved into the trans-Appalachian West and the Gulf Coast, a third stream of migrants flowed out of the overcrowded communities of New England. Previous generations of yeomen farm families from Massachusetts and Connecticut had moved north and east, settling New Hampshire, Vermont, and Maine. Now farmers throughout New England were on the move, this time to the West. Seeking land for their children, thousands of parents packed their wagons

**Slave Auction in Charleston, South Carolina, 1833**

As one slave departs with his new master (far right), the auctioneer tries to interest the assembled planters in his next sale item, a black family. The artist, a British Canadian named Henry Byam Martin, showed his disdain for these proceedings in the sketch itself (compare the family's dignified bearing with the planters' slouching postures) and in its sarcastic title: *The Land of the Free and the Home of the Brave*. National Archives of Canada.

with tools and household goods and migrated into New York. By 1820 nearly 800,000 New England migrants lived in a string of settlements that stretched from Albany to Buffalo. Thousands more moved on to Ohio and Indiana.

This vast migration was organized not by governments or joint-stock companies but by the settlers themselves, who often moved in large groups linked by family and religion. As a traveler reported from central New York, "The town of Herkimer is entirely populated by families come from Connecticut. We stayed at Mr. Snow's who came from New London with about ten male and female cousins." When 176 residents of Granville, Massachusetts, moved to Ohio, they were led by the minister and elders of their Congregational church. Throughout this region — known as the Old Northwest — many "new" communities were actually old communities that had moved inland.

In New York, as in Kentucky, well-connected speculators snapped up much of the best land. In the 1780s the financier Robert Morris acquired 1.3 million acres in the Genesee region of central New York, where the Wadsworth family also bought thousands of acres and tried to set up a manorial regime like that in the Hudson Valley. To attract tenants, the Wadsworths leased farms rent-free for the first seven years, after which they charged rents. Many New England yeomen preferred to sign agreements with the Holland Land Company, a Dutch-owned syndicate of speculators. Holland Land contracts allowed settlers to buy the land as they worked it, but high interest rates and the lack of markets initially mired thousands of these aspiring freeholders in debt. As one pioneer recalled, "In the early years, there was none but a home market and that was mostly barter—it was so many bushels of wheat for a cow; so many bushels for a yoke of oxen."

As western farmers exported wheat to pay their debts, they forced changes in eastern agriculture. Unable to compete against low-priced western grains, farmers in New England switched to potatoes, which were high yielding and nutritious. To compensate for the lost labor of sons and daughters, Middle Atlantic farmers replaced metal-tipped wooden plows with cast-iron models that dug deeper and required a single yoke of oxen instead of two or three. Such technological improvements allowed them to maintain production levels even with fewer laborers.

Easterners also took advantage of the progressive farming methods publicized by wealthy British agricultural reformers. "Improvers" in Pennsylvania doubled the average yield per acre by rotating their crops and planting nitrogen-rich clover to offset nutrient-hungry crops of wheat and corn. Yeomen farmers diversified production by raising sheep and selling the wool to textile manufacturers. Many farmers adopted a year-round planting cycle, sowing wheat in the winter for market sale and corn in the spring for animal fodder. Women and girls milked the family cows and made butter and cheese for sale in the growing towns and cities.

In this new agricultural economy families worked harder and longer, but their efforts were rewarded with higher output and a better standard of living. Whether hacking fields out of western forests or carting manure to replenish eastern soils, farm families increased their productivity. Westward migration had boosted the entire American economy.

### The Transportation Bottleneck

America's geography threatened to cut short this economic advance. Although water transport was the quickest and cheapest way to get goods to market, no rivers cut through the Appalachian Mountains. Improved inland trade therefore became a high priority for the new state governments, which actively encouraged transportation ventures. Between 1793 and 1812 the Pennsylvania legislature granted fifty-five corporate charters to private turnpike companies, and Massachusetts chartered over a hundred. Turnpike companies built gravel roads that significantly reduced transport costs and charged tolls for their use. State governments and private entrepreneurs constructed even more cost-efficient waterways by dredging rivers to make them navigable and constructing short canals to bypass waterfalls or rapids. By 1816 the United States had about 100 miles of canals, but only three of these artificial waterways were more than 2 miles long and none breached the great Appalachian barrier. Only after 1819, when the Erie Canal connected the central counties of New York to the Hudson River, could inland farmers easily sell their produce in eastern markets (see Chapter 10).

**Hop Picking, by Lucy Sheldon, 1801**

Work was nothing new for rural women and children, who had always labored about the farm. What was different after 1800 was the growing number of outworkers, landless or poor families who worked for shopkeepers and manufacturers. In this somewhat romanticized watercolor by a schoolgirl at the Litchfield Female Academy in Connecticut, a young couple and their children pick hops, which they will deliver to a storekeeper or local brewer to be made into beer. Litchfield Historical Society.

For western farmers the great streams that connected to the Mississippi River represented the great hope. Western settlers paid premium prices for land near the Ohio, Tennessee, and Mississippi Rivers, and speculators bought up property in growing towns along their banks: Cincinnati, Louisville, Chattanooga, and St. Louis. Western farmers and merchants built barges to float cotton, surplus grain, and meat down this great river system to the port of New Orleans, which by 1815 was handling about $5 million in agricultural products yearly.

However, many settlers in the trans-Appalachian West lacked access to these waterways and had to be self-sufficient. "A noble field of Indian corn stretched away into the forest on one side," an English visitor to an isolated Ohio farm noted,

> and immediately before the house was a small potato garden, with a few peach and apple trees. The woman told me that they spun and wove all the cotton and woollen garments of the family, and knit all the stockings; her husband, though not a shoemaker by trade, made all the shoes. She manufactured all the soap and candles they use.

Self-sufficiency meant a low standard of living. As late as 1840 per capita income in the Old Northwest was only 70 percent of the national average.

Despite these financial hardships and transportation bottlenecks, white Americans continued to migrate westward. They knew it would take a generation to clear land; build houses, barns, and roads; and plant orchards. Yet they were confident that their sacrifices and the expanding canal and road system would yield future security for themselves and their children. The humble achievements of thousands of yeomen and tenant families slowly transformed the landscape, turning forests into farms and crossroads villages into bustling communities.

# The Republicans' Political Revolution

Agricultural expansion was a central policy of the Republican Party and accounted for much of its appeal. From 1801 to 1825 three Republicans from Virginia— Thomas Jefferson, James Madison, and James Monroe—served two terms each as president. Supported by voters in the new western states and strong majorities in Congress, this "Virginia Dynasty" completed what Jefferson called the Revolution of 1800 by reversing many Federalist policies and actively supporting a policy of westward expansion. The movement of American settlers onto lands claimed by Indian peoples, Spain, and Britain, together with maritime disputes in the Atlantic, precipitated the War of 1812.

## *The Jeffersonian Presidency*

Thomas Jefferson was an accomplished statesman, an insightful political philosopher, and a superb politician. On assuming the presidency in 1801 Jefferson became the first chief executive to serve in the District of Columbia, the new national capital. However, his administration did not begin with a clean slate. A dozen years of Federalist presidents had filled the national judiciary with their appointees, including the formidable John Marshall of Virginia, who presided over the Supreme Court. To perpetuate Federalist power, the outgoing Congress passed a new Judiciary Act in 1801. The act created sixteen new judgeships and six additional circuit courts, which President Adams filled with "midnight appointments" just before he left office. The Federalists "have retired into the judiciary as a stronghold," Jefferson complained, "and from that battery all the works of Republicanism are to be beaten down and destroyed."

Jefferson's fears were quickly realized. In 1798, Republican-dominated legislatures in Kentucky and Virginia had repudiated the Alien and Sedition Acts and claimed the authority to determine the constitutionality of national laws (see Chapter 7). However, the Constitution stated that "the judicial Power shall extend to all Cases . . . arising under this Constitution [and] the Laws of the United States" and implied that the Supreme Court held the power of constitutional review. This important issue came to the fore when James Madison, the new secretary of state, refused to deliver the commission appointing William Marbury, one of Adams's midnight appointees, as a justice of the peace in the District of Columbia. Marbury petitioned the Supreme Court to compel delivery under the terms of the Judiciary Act of 1789. However, in *Marbury v. Madison* (1803), Chief Justice Marshall ruled that, while Marbury had a right to the commission, the Court did not have power under the Constitution to enforce that right. More important, in reaching this decision by voiding a section of the Judiciary Act of 1789, Marshall asserted the Court's power of **judicial review**. "It is emphatically the province and duty of the judicial department to say what the law is," Marshall declared, directly repudiating the Republican view that the state legislatures had that authority.

Despite this setback, Jefferson and the Republicans used their newfound national power to reverse many Federalist policies. Charging the Federalists with grossly expanding the national government's size and power, Jefferson mobilized the Republican Congress to shrink it back. When the Alien and Sedition Acts expired in 1801, the Congress branded the acts as politically motivated and unconstitutional and refused to reenact them. It also amended the Naturalization Act to permit resident aliens to become citizens after five years. But the new president governed tactfully. Although Jefferson secured repeal of the Judiciary Act, thereby ousting forty of Adams's "midnight appointees," he allowed competent Federalist bureaucrats to retain their jobs. Apart from the midnight appointees, he removed only 69 of 433 Federalist officeholders during his eight years as chief executive.

In foreign affairs Jefferson faced an immediate crisis. During the 1790s the Barbary States of North Africa had systematically raided merchant ships in the Mediterranean and, like many European states, Federalist officials had paid an annual bribe ("tribute") to protect American vessels. Initially Jefferson reversed this policy and refused to pay these bribes. When the Barbary "pirates" renewed their assaults, he ordered the U.S. Navy to retaliate. However, Jefferson wanted to avoid all-out war, which would increase taxes and the national debt, and so he negotiated a diplomatic settlement that reduced the tribute payment.

In domestic matters Jefferson set a clearly Republican course. He abolished all internal taxes, including the excise tax that had sparked the Whiskey Rebellion of 1794. Addressing his party's fears of a military coup, Jefferson reduced the size of the permanent army. He tolerated the economically important Bank of the United States (which he had condemned as unconstitutional in 1791) but chose as his secretary of the treasury Albert Gallatin, a fiscal conservative who believed that the national debt was "an evil of the first magnitude." By carefully controlling expenditures and using customs revenues to redeem government bonds, Gallatin reduced the debt from $83 million in 1801 to $45 million in 1808. With Jefferson and Gallatin at the helm, the nation was no longer run in the interests of northeastern creditors and merchants.

## Jefferson and the West

Long before he became president, Jefferson championed the settlement of the West. He celebrated the yeoman farmer in *Notes on the State of Virginia* (1785), wrote one of the Confederation's western land ordinances, and strongly supported Pinckney's Treaty of 1795, which allowed settlers in the Mississippi River Valley to export crops through the Spanish-held port of New Orleans.

As president, Jefferson worked to increase the flow of settlers to the West. In 1796 a Federalist-dominated Congress had made it more difficult for migrating families to buy a farm in the national domain by doubling the minimum price to $2 per acre. To populate the West with yeomen farm families, the Republicans in Congress passed laws in 1800 and 1804 reducing the minimum allotment first to 320 and then to 160 acres. Eventually the Land Act of 1820 cut the minimum purchase to 80 acres and the price to $1.25 per acre, enabling a farmer with only $100 in cash to buy a western farm.

International events challenged Jefferson's vision of the West as a limitless source of land for American farmers. In 1799 Napoleon Bonaparte seized power in France and began an ambitious campaign to establish a French empire both in Europe and in America. In 1801 Napoleon coerced Spain into signing a secret treaty that returned to France its former colony of Louisiana. A year later he directed Spanish officials in Louisiana to restrict American access to New Orleans, thus violating the terms of Pinckney's Treaty. Meanwhile, Napoleon planned an invasion to restore French rule in Haiti (then called Saint-Domingue), a rich sugar island seized in 1793 by rebellious black slaves led by Toussaint L'Ouverture.

Napoleon's aggressive actions prompted Jefferson to question his party's pro-French foreign policy. "The day that France takes possession of New Orleans," the president warned, "we must marry ourselves to the British fleet and nation." To avoid hostilities with France Jefferson instructed Robert R. Livingston, the American minister in Paris, to negotiate the purchase of New Orleans. Simultaneously, Jefferson sent James Monroe to Britain to seek its assistance in case of war with France.

Jefferson's diplomacy yielded a magnificent prize: the entire territory of Louisiana. By 1802 the French invasion of Haiti was faltering in the face of disease and determined black resistance, a new war threatened in Europe, and Napoleon feared an American invasion of Louisiana. Acting with characteristic decisiveness, the French ruler offered to sell not only New Orleans but also the entire territory of Louisiana for $15 million (about $450 million today). "We have lived long," Livingston remarked to Monroe as they concluded the Louisiana Purchase, "but this is the noblest work of our lives."

The Louisiana Purchase forced the president to reconsider his "strict" interpretation of the Constitution. Jefferson had always maintained that the national government possessed only the powers "expressly" delegated to it in the Constitution. Because there was no constitutional provision for adding new territory, Jefferson pragmatically accepted a "loose" interpretation and used the treaty-making powers in the Constitution to complete the deal with France.

A scientist as well as a statesman, Jefferson wanted detailed information about the physical features of the new territory, its plant and animal life, and its native peoples. In 1804 he sent his personal secretary, Meriwether Lewis, to explore the region with William Clark, an army officer. Aided by Indian guides, Lewis and Clark and their group of American soldiers and frontiersmen traveled up the Missouri River, across the Rocky Mountains, and (venturing beyond the bounds of the Louisiana Purchase) down the Columbia River to the Pacific Ocean. After two years they returned with the first maps of the immense wilderness and vivid accounts of its natural resources and inhabitants.

Although the Louisiana Purchase was a stunning accomplishment that doubled the size of the nation, it brought a new threat. New England Federalists, fearing that western expansion would diminish the power of their states and their party, talked openly of leaving the Union. Because Alexander Hamilton refused to support their plan for a separate Northern Confederacy, the secessionists turned to Aaron Burr, the ambitious vice president. When Hamilton accused Burr of participating in a conspiracy to destroy the Union, Burr challenged him to a pistol duel. To uphold his aristocratic sense of "honor," Hamilton accepted the dare and died by gunshot in the illegal confrontation.

This tragic event propelled Burr into yet another secessionist scheme. As his vice presidential term ended in 1805, Burr moved west to avoid prosecution. There he conspired with General James Wilkinson, the military governor of the Louisiana Territory. Their plan remains a mystery, but it probably involved either the capture of territory in New Spain or a rebellion to establish Louisiana as a separate nation headed by Burr. However, Wilkinson betrayed Burr and arrested the former vice president as he led an armed force down the Ohio River. In a highly politicized trial presided over by Chief Justice John Marshall, the jury acquitted Burr of treason. The verdict was less important than the dangers to national unity that it revealed. The Republicans' policy of western expansion had increased party conflict and generated secessionist schemes in both New England and the West.

## Conflict with Britain and France

As the Napoleonic Wars ravaged Europe between 1802 and 1815, they endangered American commerce because neither Britain nor France respected the neutrality of American merchant vessels. Napoleon imposed the "Continental System" on European ports controlled by France and ordered the seizure of neutral ships that had stopped in Britain. For its part, the British ministry set up a naval blockade that stopped ships carrying goods to Europe, including American vessels filled with sugar and molasses from the French West Indies. The British navy also searched American ships for British deserters and impressed (forced) them back into service in the Royal Navy. Between 1802 and 1811 British officers seized nearly eight thousand sailors, including many American citizens. In 1807 American resentment against impressment turned to outrage when a British warship attacked the U.S. Navy vessel *Chesapeake*, killing or wounding twenty-one men and seizing four alleged deserters. "Never since the battle of Lexington have I seen this country in such a state of exasperation as at present," Jefferson declared.

To protect American interests while avoiding war Jefferson pursued a policy of peaceful coercion. Working closely with Secretary of State James Madison, the president devised the Embargo Act of 1807, which prohibited American ships from leaving their home ports until Britain and France repealed their restrictions on U.S. trade. Though the embargo was a creative diplomatic measure—an economic weapon similar to the nonimportation movements of the 1760s—it overestimated the dependence of France and Britain on American shipping and underestimated resistance from New England merchants, who feared it would ruin them.

Indeed, the embargo was a disaster for the American economy. Exports plunged from $108 million in 1806 to $22 million in 1808, which hurt farmers as well as merchants and prompted Federalists to demand its repeal. "Would to God," exclaimed one Federalist, "that the Embargo had done as little evil to ourselves as it has done to foreign nations."

Despite discontent over the embargo, voters elected Republican James Madison to the presidency in 1808. As a powerful advocate for the Constitution, the architect of the Bill of Rights, and a prominent congressman and party leader, Madison had served the nation well. However, John Beckley, a loyal Republican, worried that Madison was "too timid and indecisive as a statesman" and events proved him correct. Acknowledging the embargo's failure, Madison replaced it with a series of new economic restrictions, none of which persuaded France and Britain to respect America's neutral rights. "The Devil himself could not tell which government, England or France, is the most wicked," an exasperated congressman declared.

Republican congressmen from the West—the future "war hawks" of 1812—thought Britain was the major offender and pointed in particular to its assistance to the Indians in the Ohio River Valley. Bolstered by British guns and supplies, in 1809 the Shawnee chief Tecumseh [ta-CUM-sa], assisted by his brother, the prophet Tenskwatawa [tens-QUA-ta-wa], revived the Western Confederacy. Their goal was to unite the Indian peoples and exclude whites from all lands west of the Appalachian Mountains. Republican expansionists in Congress condemned British support of Tecumseh and threatened to invade Canada. In 1811, following a series of clashes between settlers and the Western Confederacy, William Henry Harrison, the governor of the Indiana Territory, led an army against Tenskwatawa's village of Prophetstown (on the Wabash River in present-day Indiana). Fending off the confederacy's warriors at the Battle of Tippecanoe, Harrison burned the village to the ground.

Henry Clay of Kentucky, the new Speaker of the House of Representatives, and John C. Calhoun, a rising young congressman from South Carolina, pushed Madison toward war with Great Britain. Like other western Republicans, they favored the acquisition of new territory in British Canada and Spanish Florida. They also hoped that war would discredit the Federalists and their pro-British foreign policy. With national elections approaching, Madison demanded British respect for American sovereignty in the West and neutral rights on the Atlantic.

When the British did not respond quickly, Madison asked Congress for a declaration of war. In June 1812 a sharply divided Senate voted 19 to 13 for war, and the House of Representatives concurred, 79 to 49.

The underlying causes of the War of 1812 have been much debated. Officially, the United States went to war because of violations of its neutral rights: the seizure of merchant ships and the impressment of American sailors. But the Federalists who represented merchants' and seamen's interests in Congress voted against the war declaration, and in the election of 1812, voters in New England and the Middle Atlantic states cast their ballots (and 89 electoral votes) for the Federalist candidate for president, De Witt Clinton of New York. Madison amassed most of his 128 electoral votes in the South and West, where voters strongly supported the war. Because of this regional split, many historians argue that the conflict was actually "a western war with eastern labels."

## The War of 1812

The War of 1812 was a near disaster for the United States, both militarily and politically. Predictions of an easy advance into British Canada ended quickly when an American invasion force had to beat a hasty retreat back to Detroit. But Americans stayed on the offensive in the West. Commodore Oliver Hazard Perry defeated a small British flotilla on Lake Erie, and in October 1813 General William Henry Harrison invaded Canada and triumphed over a combined British and Indian force at the Battle of the Thames, killing Tecumseh, who had become a general in the British army. Another American expedition burned York (present-day Toronto) and then quickly withdrew.

Political divisions prevented a major invasion of Canada in the East. New Englanders opposed the war and prohibited their militias from fighting outside their states. Boston merchants and banks declined to lend money to the federal government, making the war difficult to finance. In Congress Daniel Webster, a dynamic young representative from New Hampshire, led Federalist opposition to higher taxes and tariffs and to the national conscription of state militiamen.

Partly because of these domestic political conflicts, the tide of battle gradually turned in Britain's favor. Initially American privateers captured scores of British merchant vessels but the Royal Navy soon seized the initiative. By 1813 British shipping moved in relative safety and a flotilla of British warships harassed American shipping and threatened seaport cities along the Atlantic coast. In 1814 a British fleet sailed up Chesapeake Bay and British troops stormed ashore to attack Washington City, in the new federal district, where they burned U.S. government buildings. Then the troops advanced on Baltimore but were repulsed at Fort McHenry. After two years of warfare the United States was stalemated along the Canadian frontier and on the defensive in the Atlantic, with its new capital city in ruins. The only positive news came from the Southwest. There a rugged slave-owning planter named Andrew Jackson led an army of militiamen from Tennessee to victory over the British-supported Creek Indians in the Battle of Horseshoe Bend (1814) and forced the Indians to cede 23 million acres of land (Map 8.2).

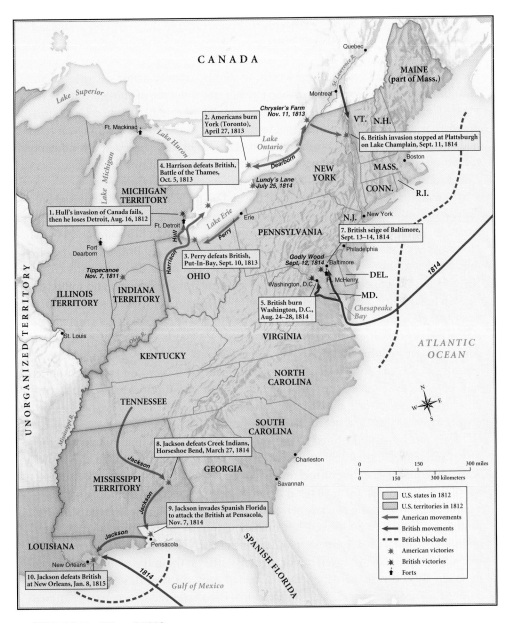

**MAP 8.2 The War of 1812**

Unlike the War for Independence, the War of 1812 had few large-scale military campaigns. In 1812 and 1813, most fighting took place along the Canadian border, as American armies and naval forces attacked British targets with mixed success (#1–4). The British took the offensive in 1814, launching a successful raid on Washington and Baltimore but suffering heavy losses when they invaded the United States along Lake Champlain (#5–7). Near the Gulf of Mexico, American forces moved from one success to another, as General Andrew Jackson defeated the pro-British Creek Indians at the Battle of Horseshoe Bend and, in the major battle of the war, routed an invading British army at New Orleans (#8–10).

American military setbacks strengthened opposition to the war in New England. In 1814 Federalists in the Massachusetts legislature called for a convention "to lay the foundation for a radical reform in the National Compact," and New England Federalists met in Hartford, Connecticut, to discuss strategy. Some delegates to the Hartford convention proposed secession by their states, but the majority favored revising the Constitution. To end Virginia's domination of the presidency, the delegates proposed a constitutional amendment that would limit the office to a single four-year term and rotate it among citizens from different states. They also suggested amendments restricting commercial embargoes to sixty days and requiring a two-thirds majority in Congress to declare war, prohibit trade, or admit a new state to the Union.

As a minority party in Congress and the nation, the Federalists could prevail only if the war continued to go badly—a very real prospect. In the late summer of 1814 an American naval victory on Lake Champlain narrowly averted a British invasion of the Hudson River Valley. A few months later, thousands of seasoned British troops landed outside New Orleans and threatened to cut American trade down the Mississippi River. The United States was under military pressure from both north and south.

Fortunately for the young American republic, Britain wanted peace. The twenty-year struggle against France had sapped its wealth and energy, and so it entered into negotiations with the United States in Ghent, Belgium. At first the American commissioners—John Quincy Adams, Albert Gallatin, and Henry Clay—demanded territory in Canada and Florida, and British diplomats insisted on an Indian buffer state between the United States and Canada. Ultimately, both sides realized that these objectives were not worth the costs of prolonged warfare. The Treaty of Ghent, signed on Christmas Eve 1814, restored the prewar borders of the United States.

This result hardly justified three years of fighting, but a final military victory lifted Americans' morale. Before news of the Treaty of Ghent reached the United States, newspaper headlines proclaimed an "ALMOST INCREDIBLE VICTORY!! GLORIOUS NEWS": on January 8, 1815, General Andrew Jackson's troops (including a contingent of French-speaking black Americans, the Corps d'Afrique) crushed the British forces attacking New Orleans. The Americans fought from carefully constructed breastworks and rained "grapeshot and cannister bombs" on the massed British formations. The British lost seven hundred men, with two thousand wounded or taken prisoner. By contrast the Americans sustained only thirteen dead and fifty-eight wounded. The victory made Jackson a national hero, redeemed the nation's battered pride, and, together with the coming of peace, undercut the Hartford convention's demands for a significant revision of the Constitution.

As Jackson emerged as a war hero, John Quincy Adams also rose to national prominence for his diplomatic efforts at Ghent and his successes as secretary of state under President James Monroe (1817–1825). The son of Federalist president John Adams, John Quincy had joined the Republican Party before the war. In 1817 Adams negotiated the Rush-Bagot Treaty with Great Britain, which limited both nations' naval forces on the Great Lakes; the following year he won an agreement setting the forty-ninth parallel as the border between the Louisiana Purchase and British Canada. Then in the Adams-Onís Treaty of 1819, he persuaded Spain to cede Florida to the United States. In return the American government took responsibility for its citizens' financial claims against Spain, renounced Jefferson's earlier claim that Spanish Texas was part of the Louisiana Purchase, and agreed on a compromise boundary between New Spain and the state of Louisiana, which had entered the Union in 1812 (Map 8.3). Finally, at Adams's behest in 1823, President Monroe warned Spain and other European powers not to interfere in the affairs of the former Spanish colonies in Latin America that had revolted and established independent republics. In announcing this new foreign policy (which thirty years later, became known as the Monroe Doctrine) the president declared that the American continents were not "subject for further colonization" by the nations of Europe. In return, he reiterated the policy of the United States "not to interfere in the internal concerns" of European nations. Thanks to Adams, the United States had taken a significant diplomatic initiative and gained undisputed possession of nearly all the land south of the forty-ninth parallel and east of the Rocky Mountains.

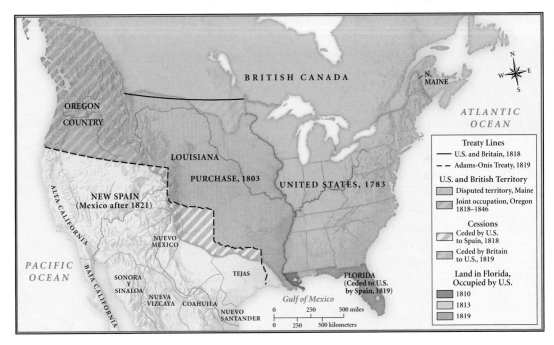

**MAP 8.3 Defining the National Boundaries, 1800–1820**

After the War of 1812 Secretary of State John Quincy Adams negotiated treaties with Great Britain and Spain that defined the boundaries of the Louisiana Purchase with British Canada to the north and New Spain (which in 1821 became the independent nation of Mexico) to the south and west. These treaties eliminated the threat of border wars with neighboring states for a generation, providing the United States with a much-needed period of peace and security.

FOR MORE HELP ANALYZING THIS MAP, see the Online Study Guide at **bedfordstmartins.com/henrettaconcise**.

# The Capitalist Commonwealth

The increasing size of the American republic was matched by the growth of its economic institutions and wealth. Before 1790 the United States was an agricultural society that was dependent on Britain for markets, credit, and manufactured goods. Over the next generation the nation developed a more diverse economy as rural Americans became manufacturers, bankers supplied credit to expand trade, and merchants developed regional markets.

This new American economic order had an increasingly capitalist character. Some capitalist features, such as the private ownership of property and the development of a market economy, were legacies of the colonial era. However, after independence men who owned "capital"—landlords, bankers, and entrepreneurs—played an increasingly prominent role in political and financial life.

## *Banks, Manufacturing, and Markets*

America was "a Nation of Merchants," a British visitor reported from Philadelphia in 1798, who were "keen in the pursuit of wealth in all the various modes of acquiring it." And acquire it they did by exploiting the opportunities for spectacular profits during the decades of warfare in Europe (1793–1815). Entrepreneurs such as the fur trader John Jacob Astor and the merchant Robert Oliver became the nation's first millionaires. Oliver started in Baltimore as an agent for Irish linen merchants and then opened his own mercantile firm. Exploiting the wartime shipping boom, he reaped enormous profits in the West Indian coffee and sugar trades. Migrating from Germany to New York in 1784, Astor became wealthy by carrying furs from the Pacific Northwest to markets in China.

To finance such mercantile enterprises Americans needed a banking system. Before 1776 ambitious colonists found it difficult to raise money. Farmers relied on government-sponsored land banks for loans, while merchants arranged partnerships, borrowed funds from other merchants, or obtained credit from British suppliers. Then in 1781 Philadelphia merchants persuaded the Confederation Congress to charter the Bank of North America to provide short-term commercial loans; in 1784 traders in Boston and New York founded similar institutions to finance their transactions. "Our monied capital has so much increased from the Introduction of Banks, & the Circulation of the Funds," the Philadelphia merchant William Bingham boasted in 1791, "that the Necessity of Soliciting Credits from England will no longer exist, & the Means will be provided for putting in Motion every Specie of Industry."

That same year Congress chartered the First Bank of the United States. The bank issued notes and made commercial loans, and its profits averaged a handsome 8 percent annually. Responding to the demand for commercial credit, by 1805 the bank had branches in eight major cities. Despite these successes, the bank did not survive. Jeffersonian Republicans, who were suspicious of corruption by monied men, accused the bank of encouraging "a consolidated, energetic government supported by public creditors, speculators, and other insidious men lacking in public spirit of any kind." When the bank's twenty-year charter expired in 1811, President Madison did not seek its renewal, and so merchants, artisans, and farmers petitioned their state legislatures to charter new banks. By 1816, there were 246 state-chartered banks with $68 million in banknotes in circulation.

However, many state banks were shady operations that issued notes without adequate specie reserves and made ill-advised loans to insiders. These banking policies were one cause of the Panic of 1819, a financial crisis sparked by a sharp drop in world agricultural prices. As farm prices and income abruptly dropped by 30 percent, many farmers could not pay their debts to local storekeepers, wholesale merchants, and state banks. The result was a massive wave of bankruptcies. By 1821, those state banks that were still solvent had only $45 million in circulation and court dockets were crowded with thousands of legal suits, as creditors tried to save their businesses by suing their debtors. The panic gave Americans their first taste of the **business cycle**—the periodic expansion and contraction of profits and employment that is an inherent part of a capitalist market economy.

The Panic of 1819 also revealed that artisans and yeomen as well as merchants now depended on regional or national markets. Before 1790 most artisans in New England and the Middle Atlantic region sold their handicrafts locally or bartered them with neighbors. For example, John Hoff of Lancaster, Pennsylvania, exchanged his fine wooden-cased clocks for a dining table, a bedstead, and labor on his small farm. But other artisans—shipbuilders in seacoast towns, iron smelters in Pennsylvania and Maryland, and shoemakers in Lynn, Massachusetts—sold their products in far-flung markets. Indeed, merchant-entrepreneurs had developed a rural-based manufacturing system similar to the European outwork, or putting-out, system (see Chapter 1). These enterprising merchants bought raw materials from farmers, hired workers in other farm families to manufacture goods, and then sold finished products in regional or national markets. When a French traveler visited central Massachusetts in 1795, he found "almost all these houses . . . inhabited by men who are both cultivators and artisans; one is a tanner, another a shoemaker, another sells goods, but all are farmers."

By the 1820s thousands of New England farm families made shoes, brooms, palm-leaf hats, and tinware—baking pans, cups, utensils, lanterns. Merchants shipped these products to cities and slave plantations, while New England peddlers, equipped "with a horse and a cart covered with a box or with a wagon," blanketed the South and acquired a reputation as crafty, hard-bargaining "Yankees."

This economic advance stemmed primarily from innovations in organization and marketing rather than in technology. Water-powered machines—the product of the Industrial Revolution in Britain—were adopted slowly in America. In the 1780s merchants built small textile mills along the waterways of New England and the Middle Atlantic states. They hired workers and installed water-powered machines that carded and combed wool—and later cotton—into long strands. Until 1820, the

**The Yankee Peddler, c. 1830**

Even in 1830 most Americans lived too far from market towns to go there regularly to buy needed goods. Instead, farm families, such as this relatively prosperous one depicted by an unknown artist, purchased most of their tinware, clocks, textiles, and other manufactures from peddlers, often from New England, who traveled far and wide in small horse-drawn vans such as that pictured in the doorway. Collection IBM Corporation, Armonk, NY.

FOR MORE HELP ANALYZING THIS IMAGE, see the Online Study Guide at **bedfordstmartins.com/henrettaconcise**.

outwork system handled the next steps in the textile manufacturing process. Wage-earning farm women and children spun the strands into yarn on foot-driven spinning wheels, and men in other households used foot-powered looms to weave the yarn into cloth. In his "Letter on Manufactures" (1810) Secretary of the Treasury Albert Gallatin estimated that there were 2,500 outwork weavers in New England. A decade later more than 12,000 household workers in the New England region wove woolen cloth, which was then pounded flat and given a smooth finish in water-powered fulling mills. Thus, even before textile production was centralized in factories, the nation had a profitable and expanding system of manufacturing (see Chapter 10).

The penetration of the market economy into rural areas motivated farmers to produce more goods. Ambitious farm families switched from growing crops to raising livestock; they sold meat to city markets, sent cattle hides to the booming shoe industry, and used the milk from dairy cows to make butter and cheese for market sale. "Along the whole road from Boston, we saw women engaged in making cheese," a Polish traveler reported from central Massachusetts in 1798. Hatmaking emerged as another new industry. "Straw hats and Bonnets are manufactured by many families," a Maine official commented, while another observer estimated that "probably 8,000 females" in the vicinity of Foxborough, Massachusetts, braided rye straw into hats for market sale. Other farm families raised sheep and sold raw wool to textile manufacturers. Processing these raw materials brought new businesses to many farming towns. In 1792 Concord, Massachusetts, had one slaughterhouse and five small tanneries; a decade later the town boasted eleven slaughterhouses and six large tanneries.

As the rural economy turned out more goods, it significantly altered the environment. Foul odors from stockyards and tanning pits now wafted over Concord and many other leather-producing towns, and each year tanners cut down thousands of acres of hemlock trees and used their bark in processing leather. The multiplication of livestock—dairy cows, cattle, and especially sheep—brought the destruction of even more trees as farmers created vast new pastures and meadows. By the mid-nineteenth century, most of the forests in southern New England and eastern New York were gone, leaving a barren visual landscape. "The hills had been stripped of their timber," the New York *Catskill Messenger* noted, "so as to present their huge, rocky projections." Scores of textile milldams now dotted New England's rivers, altering their flow and making it difficult for fish to reach their upriver spawning grounds. Even as the income of many farmers rose, the quality of their natural environment deteriorated.

The new capitalist-run market economy had other drawbacks. Rural parents and their children now worked longer and harder as they made yarn, hats, and brooms during the winter and carried on their regular farming chores during the warmer seasons. Perhaps more important, these farm families lost some of their economic independence. Instead of working solely for themselves, they toiled as part-time wage earners for merchants and manufacturers. Many families stopped making their own textiles and shoes and bought them with the cash or store credit they had earned. Thus, the new market system decreased the self-sufficiency of families and communities even as it made them more productive and prosperous. The tide of change was unstoppable.

## Public Policy: The Commonwealth System

Throughout the nineteenth century state governments were the most important political institutions in the United States. They enacted legislation affecting all aspects of civil and criminal affairs, collected and spent most tax revenue, and oversaw county, city, and town officials. Consequently, state governments had a much greater impact on the day-to-day lives of Americans than did the national government.

Beginning in the 1790s state legislatures devised an American plan of mercantilism, known to historians as the commonwealth system (because its goal was to increase the "common wealth" of the society). Just as the British Parliament had promoted the imperial economy through the Navigation Acts, state legislatures enacted measures to stimulate commerce and economic development. In particular, they granted corporate charters to private businesses to build roads, bridges, and canals; they intended these enterprises to be "of great public utility," as the act establishing the Massachusetts Bank put it. Thus, in 1794 the Pennsylvania legislature chartered the Lancaster Turnpike Company to lay a graded gravel road between Lancaster and Philadelphia, a distance of sixty-five miles. The venture was expensive—nearly $500,000 (about $8 million today)—but the road made a modest profit for the investors and greatly enhanced the regional economy. "The turnpike is finished," a farm woman noted, "and we can now go to town at all times and in all weather." A boom in turnpike construction soon connected dozens of inland market centers to seaport cities.

By 1800 state governments had granted more than three hundred corporate charters. These charters often included a grant of limited liability that made it easier to attract investors; if the business failed, the personal assets of the shareholders could not be seized to pay the corporation's debts. Most transportation charters also included the power of eminent domain; this provision allowed turnpike, bridge, and canal corporations to force the sale of privately owned land along their routes at reasonable prices. State legislatures also aided capitalist flour millers and textile manufacturers whose dams flooded adjacent farmland. In Massachusetts, the Mill Dam Act of 1795 required farmers to accept "fair compensation" for their lost acreage.

To some critics such uses of state power by private companies ran contrary to republicanism, "which does not admit of granting peculiar privileges to any body of men." Charters not only violated the "equal rights" of all citizens, opponents argued, but also restricted the sovereignty of the people. As a Pennsylvanian put it, "Whatever power is given to a corporation, is just so much power taken from the State" and its citizens. Nonetheless, state courts consistently upheld corporate charters and routinely approved grants of eminent domain to private corporations. "The opening of good and easy internal communications is one of the highest duties of government," declared a New Jersey judge.

The state-based mercantilism of the commonwealth system soon encompassed much more than transportation. Following the embargo of 1807, which cut off goods and credit from Europe, New England states awarded charters to two hundred iron-mining, textile-manufacturing, and banking firms, and the Pennsylvania legislature granted more than eleven hundred. Thus by 1820 innovative state governments had created a new political economy: the commonwealth system that used state incentives to encourage business and improve the general welfare.

### Federalist Law: John Marshall and the Supreme Court

Both Federalists and Republicans endorsed the commonwealth idea, but in different ways. Federalists supported Alexander Hamilton's program of national mercantilism: a funded debt, tariffs, and a central bank. Jeffersonian Republicans generally preferred the state-based commonwealth system. However, following the War of 1812 some Republicans advocated national economic initiatives. As Speaker of the House of Representatives in 1816, Republican Henry Clay of Kentucky won legislation creating the Second Bank of the United States and persuaded President Madison to sign it. In the following year Clay won passage of the Bonus Bill, sponsored by Representative John C. Calhoun of South Carolina, which would have established a national fund for roads and other internal improvements. But many Republicans believed that such internal improvements exceeded the powers delegated to the national government and welcomed Madison's veto of the Bonus Bill.

The difference between Federalist and Jeffersonian Republican conceptions of public policy emerged during John Marshall's tenure on the Supreme Court. Appointed chief justice by President John Adams in January 1801, Marshall was a committed Federalist who dominated the Court until 1822 and then upheld nationalist principles until his death in 1835. Marshall's success stemmed not from a mastery of legal principles and doctrines but from the power of his logic and the force of his personality. By winning the support of Joseph Story and other nationalist-minded Republican judges, Marshall shaped the evolution of the Constitution. Three principles formed the basis of his jurisprudence: a commitment to judicial authority, the supremacy of national over state legislation, and a traditional, static view of property rights.

**John Marshall, by Chester Harding, c. 1830**

Even at age seventy-five, John Marshall (1755–1835) had a commanding personal presence. Upon becoming chief justice of the U.S. Supreme Court in 1801, Marshall elevated the Court from a minor department of the national government to a major institution in American legal and political life. His decisions dealing with judicial review, contract rights, the regulation of commerce, and national banking permanently shaped the character of American constitutional law. Boston Athenaeum.

After Marshall proclaimed the power of judicial review in *Marbury v. Madison*, the doctrine evolved slowly. Before 1850 state courts voided relatively few laws and not until the *Dred Scott* decision in 1857 would the Supreme Court void another law passed by Congress (see Chapter 13).

However, the Marshall Court frequently overturned state laws that infringed on the national Constitution. Its jurisprudence on federal-state relations was most eloquently expressed in *McCulloch v. Maryland* (1819). When Congress created the Second Bank of the United States in 1816, it allowed the bank to set up branches in the various states. To preserve the competitive position of its state-chartered banks, the Maryland legislature imposed an annual tax of $15,000 on notes issued by the Baltimore branch office of the Second Bank. In response, the Second Bank contested the constitutionality of the Maryland law and claimed that it infringed on the powers of the national government. To make their case, lawyers for the state of Maryland invoked Jefferson's argument that Congress lacked the constitutional authority to charter a national bank. Even if such a bank could be created, the lawyers argued, Maryland had a right to tax its activities within the state.

Marshall and the nationalist-minded Republicans on the Court firmly rejected both arguments. The Second Bank was constitutional, said the chief justice, because it was "necessary and proper," given the national government's responsibility to control currency and credit. Like Alexander Hamilton, Marshall adopted a loose construction of the Constitution. If the goal of a law is "legitimate [and] . . . within the scope of the Constitution," he wrote, then "all means which are appropriate" to secure that goal are also constitutional, even if they are not explicitly mentioned. As for Maryland's right to tax the national bank, the chief justice stated that "the power to tax involves the power to destroy" and suggested that Maryland's bank tax would render the national government "dependent on the states"—an outcome that "was not intended by the American people" who ratified the Constitution.

The Marshall Court asserted the dominance of national statutes over state legislation again in *Gibbons v. Ogden* (1824). This decision struck down a monopoly that the New York legislature had granted to Aaron Ogden for steamboat passenger service across the Hudson River to New Jersey. Asserting that the Constitution gave the federal government the authority to regulate interstate commerce, the chief justice sided with Thomas Gibbons, who held a federal license to transport people and goods between the two states.

Marshall also used the Constitution to uphold his view of property rights. During the 1790s Thomas Jefferson and other Republicans had celebrated the primacy of statute (or "positive") law enacted by "the will of the supreme power, which is the will of THE PEOPLE." In response, Federalist judges and politicians warned that popular sovereignty would lead to "tyranny of the majority" if state legislatures enacted statutes that infringed on the property rights of wealthy citizens. To prevent this outcome, Federalist lawyers asserted that judges had the power to void laws that violated traditional common-law principles or were contrary to "natural law" or "natural rights" (see Chapter 4).

Marshall shared the goal of protecting individuals' property from the acts of popularly-elected legislatures and invoked the contract clause of the Constitution to do it. The contract clause (in Article 1, Section 10, on p. D-13) prohibits the states from passing any law "impairing the obligation of contracts." The delegates at the Philadelphia convention included the clause to overturn state legislation that prevented creditors from seizing the lands and goods of debtors. In *Fletcher v. Peck* (1810), Marshall expanded the clause to defend other property rights by broadly defining *contract* to include the grants and charters made by the state governments. The case involved a large grant of land made by the Georgia legislature to the Yazoo Land Company. When a new legislature canceled the grant, alleging fraud and bribery, speculators who had already purchased Yazoo lands appealed to the Supreme Court to uphold their titles. Marshall ruled that the legislative grant was a contract that could not subsequently be abridged. This far-reaching decision safeguarded "vested" property rights and, by protecting out-of-state investors, promoted the development of a national capitalist economy.

The Court extended its defense of vested property rights even further in *Dartmouth College v. Woodward* (1819). Dartmouth College was a private institution in New Hampshire established by a charter granted by King George III. In 1816 the Republican-dominated legislature enacted a statute that converted the college into a public university. The Dartmouth trustees opposed this legislation and engaged Daniel Webster to plead their case. A renowned constitutional lawyer as well as a leading Federalist politician, Webster cited the Court's decision in *Fletcher v. Peck* and argued that the royal charter constituted a contract that could not be altered by the New Hampshire legislature. The Supreme Court agreed and upheld the rights of the college. Marshall's triumph seemed complete. Important Federalist principles, such as judicial review and corporate property rights, had been permanently incorporated into the American legal system (see Voices from Abroad, "Law and Lawyers in the United States," p. 254).

Even as Marshall announced the *Dartmouth* and *McCulloch* decisions in 1819, the political fortunes of his Federalist Party were in severe decline. Nationalist-minded Republicans had won the allegiance of many Federalist voters in the East, while the pro-farmer policies of Jeffersonian Republicans commanded the support of most western settlers and southern planters. "No Federal character can run with success," Gouverneur Morris of New York lamented, and the election results of 1818 bore out his pessimism. Following the election Republicans outnumbered Federalists 37 to 7 in the Senate and 156 to 27 in the House of Representatives. Westward expansion and the transformation in American government begun by Jefferson's Revolution of 1800 had brought the demise of the Federalists and the end of the First Party System.

**VOICES FROM ABROAD**

# Law and Lawyers in the United States

## ALEXIS DE TOCQUEVILLE

*A French aristocrat and lawyer, Alexis de Tocqueville came to the United States to study its innovative prison system. Instead he wrote* Democracy in America *(1835), a comprehensive and astute analysis of the dynamic society and political system of the United States. Here Tocqueville argues that the raw vigor of American democracy was restrained by the ingrained conservatism of men of the law, who dominated the political system.*

The political activity that pervades the United States must be seen in order to be understood. No sooner do you set foot upon American ground than you are stunned by a kind of tumult . . . everything is in motion around you; here the people of one quarter of a town are met to decide upon the building of a church; there the election of a representative is going on. . . .

The political agitation of American legislative bodies, which is the only one that attracts the attention of foreigners, is a mere episode, or a sort of continuation, of that universal movement which originates in the lowest classes of the people and extends successively to all the ranks of society. . . .

In visiting the Americans and studying their laws, we perceive that the authority they have entrusted to the members of the legal profession, and the influence that these individuals exercise in the government, are the most powerful existing security against the excesses of democracy. . . . Men who have made a special study of the laws derive from [that] occupation certain habits of order, a taste for formalities, and a kind of instinctive regard for the regular connection of ideas, which naturally render them very hostile to the revolutionary spirit and the unreflecting passions of the multitude. . . .

[Moreover,] the government of democracy is favorable to the political power of lawyers; for when the wealthy, the noble, and the prince are excluded from the government, the lawyers take possession of it, in their own right, as it were, since they are the only men of information and sagacity, beyond the sphere of the people, who can be the object of popular choice. . . .

Lawyers belong to the people by birth and interest, and to the aristocracy by habit and taste; they may be looked upon as the connecting link between the two great classes of society. . . . When the American people are intoxicated by passion or carried away by the impetuosity of their ideas, they are checked and stopped by the almost invisible influence of their legal counselors.

As most public men are legal practitioners, they introduce the customs and technicalities of their profession into the management of public affairs. The jury extends this habit to all classes. The language of the law thus becomes, in some measure, a vulgar tongue . . . so that at last the whole people contract the habits and the tastes of the judicial magistrate.

SOURCE: Alexis de Tocqueville, *Democracy in America*, ed., Philip Bradley (New York: Vintage, 1945), 1: 283–90.

The decline of the Federalists and of party politics prompted contemporary observers to dub James Monroe's two terms as president (1817–1825) the "Era of Good Feeling." Actually, political harmony was more apparent than real because the Republican Party was now divided into a National faction and a Jeffersonian (or state-oriented) faction. The two groups fought bitterly over the issue of federal support for internal improvement projects such as roads and canals. As the aging Jefferson himself complained about the National Republicans, "You see so many of these new republicans maintaining in Congress the rankest doctrines of the old federalists." This division in the ranks of the Republican Party would soon produce a Second Party System—in which national-minded Whigs faced off against state-focused Democrats (see Chapter 11). One cycle of American politics and economic debate had ended and another was about to begin.

## TIMELINE

| Year | Event | Year | Event |
|------|-------|------|-------|
| 1783 | Treaty of Paris gives Americans access to the trans-Appalachian West | 1801–1807 | Treasury Secretary Albert Gallatin reduces national debt |
| 1787 | Northwest Ordinance | | Seizures of American ships by France and Britain |
| 1790s | State mercantilism: states grant corporation charters | 1803 | Louisiana Purchase; Lewis and Clark expedition |
| | Entrepreneurs build turnpikes and short canals | | Marshall asserts judicial review in *Marbury v. Madison* |
| | Merchants create a rural outwork system | 1807 | Embargo Act cripples American shipping |
| 1790–1791 | Little Turtle defeats American armies in Northwest Territory | | Congress bans importation of slaves |
| 1791 | First Bank of the United States founded; charter expires in 1811 | 1809 | Tecumseh and Tenskwatawa mobilize Indians |
| 1792 | Kentucky joins Union; Tennessee follows (1796) | 1810 | *Fletcher v. Peck* extends contract clause |
| 1794 | Battle of Fallen Timbers | 1810s | Expansion of slavery into Old Southwest |
| 1795 | Treaty of Greenville recognizes Indian land rights | 1811 | Battle of Tippecanoe |
| | Massachusetts Mill Dam Act promotes textile industry | 1812–1815 | War of 1812 |
| | Pinckney's Treaty with Spain allows U.S. use of Mississippi River | 1817–1825 | Era of Good Feeling during Monroe's presidency |
| 1801 | Spain secretly restores Louisiana to France | 1819 | Adams-Onís Treaty annexes Florida and defines Texas boundary |
| | John Marshall becomes chief justice of the Supreme Court | | *McCulloch v. Maryland* enhances power of national government |
| | | | *Dartmouth College v. Woodward* protects property rights |

# For Further Exploration

Gregory Evans Dowd, *A Spirited Resistance: The North American Indian Struggle for Unity, 1745–1815* (1992), presents a fine survey of the Indian peoples, while Gregory Nobles, *American Frontiers: Cultural Encounters and Continental Conquest* (1997), traces the course of American expansion to the west. Two fine studies of cultural interaction are Theda Perdue, *Cherokee Women: Gender and Culture Change, 1700–1835* (1998) and William G. McLoughlin, *Cherokee Renascence in the New Republic* (1986).

Ralph Louis Ketcham's *Presidents above Party: The First American Presidency, 1789–1829* (1984) portrays the evolving political ideology of the early republic, while Gore Vidal's *Burr: A Novel* (1973) offers an entertaining narrative of the life and times of Aaron Burr. Donald R. Hickey, *The War of 1812: A Forgotten Conflict* (1989), places the conflict in an economic and diplomatic context. R. Kent Newmyer, *The Supreme Court under Marshall and Taney* (1968), concisely analyzes early constitutional development, and Jack Larkin, *The Reshaping of Everyday Life, 1790–1840* (1997), demonstrates the impact of economic change on material culture.

*Lewis and Clark: The Journey of the Corps of Discovery* (PBS video, 4 hours) tells the story of the initial exploration by white Americans of the Louisiana Purchase; the companion Web site, at <http://www.pbs.org/lewisandclark/>, contains a rich body of material on the explorers and the Indian peoples of the region. The Chickasaw Historical Research Page, at <http://home.flash.net/~kma/>, contains letters written by or about Chickasaw Indians between 1792 and 1849, the texts of more than thirty treaties, and other documents.

The Duel (PBS video, 1 hour) reenacts the confrontation between Alexander Hamilton and Aaron Burr, while A Century of Lawmaking for a New Nation, at <http://memory.loc.gov/ammem/amlaw/lawhome.html>, part of the Library of Congress's American Memory project, contains congressional documents and debates, including discussions of the Northwest Ordinance, the ban on slave imports, the embargo of 1807, and the decision for war in 1812. The site also contains information and maps of Indian land cessions from 1784 to 1894. For access to American Journeys: Eyewitness Accounts of Early American Exploration and Settlement, consult the documents and images compiled by the Wisconsin Historical Society at <http://www.americanjourneys.org/>.

---

For definitions of key terms boldfaced in this chapter, see the glossary at the end of the book.

To assess your mastery of the material covered in this chapter, see the Online Study Guide at **bedfordstmartins.com/henrettaconcise**.

For map resources and primary documents, see **bedfordstmartins.com/henrettaconcise**.

# Chapter 9

# THE QUEST FOR A REPUBLICAN SOCIETY 1790–1820

[Societies and] governments are republican only in proportion as they embody the will of their people.

THOMAS JEFFERSON, 1813

**B**y the 1820s a sense of optimism pervaded white American society. "The temperate zone of North America already exhibits many signs that it is the promised land of civil liberty, and of institutions designed to liberate and exalt the human race," a Kentucky judge declared in a Fourth of July speech. Indeed, many Americans took it as a sign of divine favor that both John Adams and Thomas Jefferson died on July 4, 1826, the fiftieth anniversary of their experiment in republican government. Americans had good reason to feel fortunate. Despite periods of political conflict and economic turmoil, white Americans still lived in a self-governing society that was free from both arbitrary taxes and an oppressive church. Moreover, many citizens now considered themselves "republicans" not simply in their constitutional system of representative government but also in their political behavior, social outlook, and cultural habits.

Yet Americans defined republicanism in different ways. Many citizens in the North subscribed to "democratic republicanism." This ideology encouraged individuals to aspire to greater equality in politics and within the family, though they often fell short of this goal. In the South many whites shared these democratic aspirations, but their society was so sharply divided along the lines of class and race that such ideals were impossible to sustain. Consequently, southern leaders gradually devised an aristocratic-republican ideology that better described their hierarchical and deferential society. Yet a third vision of American republicanism appeared in the wake of the Second Great Awakening, the massive religious revival that swept through the nation during the first half of the nineteenth century. For the many Americans—white and black, southern and northern—who embraced this religious vision, the United States was both a great experiment in republican government and the seedbed of a new Christian civilization that would redeem the world.

# Democratic Republicanism

After independence, leading Americans advocated a political system based on the principle of "ordered liberty," which in practice meant rule by the traditional elite. White men of modest means soon repudiated this elitist outlook and embraced a democratic republican outlook that celebrated political equality and social mobility. Many citizens also redefined the nature of the family and of education by seeking more egalitarian marriages and more affectionate ways of rearing and educating their children.

## *Social and Political Equality for White Men*

Between 1780 and 1820 hundreds of well-educated Europeans visited the United States and declared, almost unanimously, that the American republic embodied a social order that was genuinely different and more just than that of their homelands. In his famous *Letters from an American Farmer* (1782), the French-born essayist St. Jean de Crèvecoeur wrote that European society was composed "of great lords who possess everything, and of a herd of people who have nothing." America, by contrast, had "no aristocratical families, no courts, no kings, no bishops."

The absence of a hereditary aristocracy encouraged Americans to condemn inherited social privilege and to extol the republican legal equality of all free men. "The law is the same for everyone both as it protects and as it punishes," noted one European traveler. Yet Americans willingly accepted social divisions based on personal achievement. As individuals used their "talents, integrity, and virtue" to amass wealth, they gained a higher social standing, a result that astounded some Europeans. "In Europe to say of someone that he rose from nothing is a disgrace and a reproach," remarked an aristocratic Polish visitor. "It is the opposite here. To be the architect of your own fortune is honorable. It is the highest recommendation."

Some Americans from long-distinguished families questioned the morality of a social order based on mobility and financial success. "The aristocracy of Kingston [New York] is more one of money than any village I have ever seen," complained Nathaniel Booth, whose family had once ruled Kingston but had lost its prominence. "Man is estimated by dollars," he lamented; "what he is worth determines his character and his position at once." For most white men such a system meant the opportunity to better themselves.

By the 1810s republicanism also meant voting rights for all free white men. As early as 1776 the state constitutions of Pennsylvania and Vermont allowed all taxpayers to vote. This provision opened up political participation to propertyless young men who paid a "poll" (or head) tax and artisans who did not own land but paid an occupational tax. By 1810 Maryland and South Carolina had extended the vote to all adult white men, and the new states of Indiana (1816), Illinois (1818),

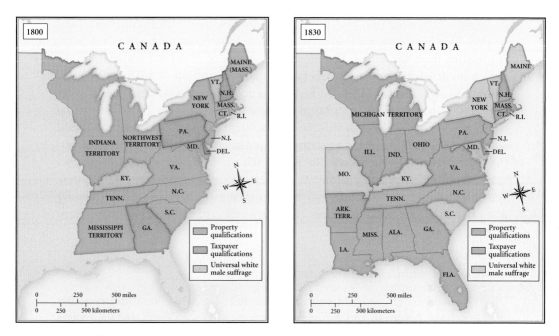

**MAP 9.1 The Expansion of Voting Rights for White Men, 1800–1830**

Between 1800 and 1830 the United States moved steadily toward political democracy for white men. Many existing states revised their constitutions, replacing property ownership with taxpaying or militia service as a qualification for voting. Some new states in the West extended suffrage to all adult white men. As parties sought votes from a broader electorate, the tone of politics became more open and competitive—swayed by the interests and values of ordinary people.

and Alabama (1819) provided for a broad male franchise in their constitutions. Within another decade fifteen states allowed all white male taxpayers to vote, and another seven instituted universal white manhood suffrage. Only three states retained property qualifications for voting (Map 9.1).

The expansion of suffrage changed the tone of politics. Most conservative politicians accepted popular rule but insisted that voters should elect men of high social status. As Samuel Stone put it, the Federalist ideal was "a speaking aristocracy in the face of a silent democracy." However, Americans increasingly refused to vote for politicians who flaunted their high social status by wearing "top boots, breeches, and shoe buckles," their hair in "powder and queues." Instead, voters elected men who dressed simply and endorsed democracy, even if those leaders favored policies that benefited those with substantial wealth.

As legislators eliminated property qualifications for voting by white men, they erected barriers for women and black men. During the colonial period, few white women or free blacks voted; regardless of their wealth, custom and prejudice ruled out their participation in public affairs. Now state officials wrote customary racial and gender exclusions into law. In 1802 Ohio disfranchised African Americans, and in 1821 New York retained property-holding requirements for black voters while eliminating them for whites. The most striking case of racial and sexual discrimination occurred in New Jersey, where the state constitution of 1776 had granted suffrage to all property holders. As Federalists and Republicans competed for votes after 1800, they challenged political custom by encouraging property-owning single women and widows to vote. Sensing a threat to the male-centered political world, in 1807 the New Jersey legislature limited full citizenship (and therefore voting rights) to white men only. To justify the exclusion of women, legislators invoked both biology and custom. As one letter to a newspaper put it, "Women, generally, are neither by nature, nor habit, nor education, nor by their necessary condition in society fitted to perform this duty with credit to themselves or advantage to the public."

## Toward a Republican Marriage System

The controversy over gender in politics replicated the debate over authority within the household. European and American husbands had long dominated their wives and controlled the family's property. But as John Adams had lamented in 1776, the revolutionary doctrine of political equality had "spread where it was not intended" and encouraged some white women to speak out on public matters and to demand control of their finances. These women insisted that their subordinate social position was at odds with the republican ideology of equal natural rights. Patriarchy was not a "natural" rule but only a social contrivance, argued the Patriot author and historian Mercy Otis Warren; making men the heads of households was justified only "for the sake of order in families."

Economic and cultural changes also eroded customary paternal authority. Traditionally, landowning fathers had arranged their children's marriages to ensure the economic well-being of themselves and their wives during old age. As land holdings shrank in long-settled rural communities, yeomen fathers could no longer bequeath substantial farms and had less influence over their children's selection of spouses. Young men and women began to choose their own partners, influenced by the new cultural attitude of **sentimentalism**.

Sentimentalism originated in Europe as part of the Romantic movement of the late eighteenth century and spread quickly among all classes of American society. Sentimentalism celebrated the importance of "feeling"—that is, a physical, sensuous appreciation of God, nature, and other human beings. This new sensibility found many forms of expression. It dripped from the pages of German and English literary works, fell from the lips of actors in popular tear-jerking melodramas, and infused the emotional rhetoric of revivalist preachers.

As the passions of the heart overwhelmed the cool logic of the mind, a new marriage system appeared. Parents had always considered physical attraction and emotional compatibility as they arranged marriages for their children, but they were concerned primarily with the personal character and financial resources of a prospective son- or daughter-in-law. However, after 1800 magazines encouraged marriages "contracted from motives of affection, rather than of interest," and many young people sought a spouse who was, as Eliza Southgate of Maine put it, "calculated to promote my happiness."

As young people arranged their own marriages, fathers became paternalists who tried to protect the interests of their children. To guard against free-spending sons-in-law, wealthy fathers placed their daughters' inheritances in legal trusts— out of their husbands' control. As a Virginia planter wrote to his lawyer, "I rely on you to see the property settlement properly drawn before the marriage, for I by no means consent that Polly shall be left to the Vicissitudes of Life."

In theory, the new republican ideal of companionate marriage gave wives "true equality, both of rank and fortune," with their husbands, as one Boston man suggested. However, husbands continued to occupy a privileged position because of deeply ingrained cultural habits and because the legal system still gave them control of the family's property. The new marriage system also discouraged parents from becoming too involved in their children's married lives and made young wives more dependent on their husbands than their mothers had been. In addition, governments accepted no obligation to prevent domestic abuse; as a lawyer noted, women who would rather "starve than submit" to the orders of their husbands were left to their fate. The marriage contract "is so much more important in its consequences to females than to males," a young man at the Litchfield Law School in Connecticut astutely observed in 1820, "for besides leaving everything else to unite themselves to one man, they subject themselves to his authority. He is their all—their only relative—their only hope."

Young adults who chose partners unwisely were severely disappointed when their spouses failed as providers or faithful companions, and a few sought divorces. Before 1800 most petitioners for divorce charged their spouses with neglect, abandonment, or adultery—serious offenses against the moral order of society. After 1800 emotional grounds dominated divorce petitions. One woman complained that her husband had "ceased to cherish her," while a man grieved that his wife had "almost broke his heart." Reflecting these changed cultural values, some states expanded the legal grounds for divorce to include personal cruelty and drunkenness.

### Republican Motherhood

In all societies, marriage has many purposes: it channels sexuality, facilitates the inheritance of property, and, by creating strong family and kinship ties, eases the rearing of children. Traditionally, most American women had focused their lives on family duties: working in the home or on the farm and bearing and nurturing children. However, by the 1790s the birthrate in the northern seaboard states was dropping dramatically. In the farm village of Sturbridge, Massachusetts, women who had married before 1750 gave birth on average to eight or nine children, whereas women who married around 1810 had only about six. In the growing seaport cities, native-born white women bore an average of only four children.

The United States was one of the first countries in the world to experience this sharp decline in the birthrate—what historians have termed the "demographic transition." There were several causes. Beginning in the 1790s thousands of young men migrated to the trans-Appalachian West; their departure left some women without partners for life and delayed marriage for many more. Women who married later in life had fewer children. In addition, thousands of white American couples in the middling classes of society deliberately limited the size of their families. Fathers favored smaller families so that they could provide each of their children with an adequate inheritance; mothers, affected by new ideas of individualism and self-achievement, were no longer willing to spend all of their active years bearing and rearing children. After having four or five children, such couples used birth control or abstained from sexual intercourse. Women's lives changed as well because of new currents in Christian social thought. Traditionally, most religious writers had viewed women as morally inferior to men—as sexual temptresses or witches—but by 1800, Protestant ministers were blaming men for sexual and social misconduct. This shift reflected both the numerical dominance of women in many churches (as men devoted their energies to business affairs) and new intellectual currents. Christian moralists now claimed that modesty and purity were inherent in women's nature and made them uniquely qualified to educate the spirit.

Reflecting this sentiment, political leaders called on women to become dedicated "republican wives" and "republican mothers" who would correctly shape the characters of American men. In his *Thoughts on Female Education* (1787), the Philadelphia physician Benjamin Rush argued that a young woman should receive intellectual training so that she would be "an agreeable companion for a sensible man" and ensure "his perseverance in the paths of rectitude." Rush also called for loyal "republican mothers" who would instruct "their sons in the principles of liberty and government."

Christian ministers readily embraced the idea of **republican motherhood**. "Preserving virtue and instructing the young are not the fancied, but the real 'Rights of Women,'" the Reverend Thomas Bernard told the Female Charitable Society of Salem, Massachusetts. He urged his audience to dismiss the public roles for women, such as voting and officeholding, advocated by English activist Mary Wollstonecraft and others. Instead, women should be content to care for their children, a responsibility that gave them "an extensive power over the fortunes of man in every generation." Although Bernard wanted women to remain in their traditional domestic sphere, he campaigned to enhance its value. A few ministers envisioned a public role for women based on their domestic virtues. As South Carolina minister Thomas Grimké asserted, "Give me a host of educated pious mothers and sisters and I will revolutionize a country, in moral and religious taste."

**Republican Motherhood**

Art often reveals the cultural values of the time. In this 1795 painting, the artist James Peale, brother of the famous portraitist Charles Willson Peale, depicts himself with his wife and children. The mother stands in the foreground, offering advice to her eldest daughter, while her husband stands to the rear, pointing to the other children. The father, previously the center of attention in family portraits during the colonial era (see p. 101), now gives pride of place to his wife and offspring. Pennsylvania Academy of the Fine Arts, Philadelphia.

## Raising and Educating Republican Children

Republican social thought altered assumptions about inheritance and childrearing. Under English common law, property owned by a father who died without a will passed to his eldest son, a practice known as primogeniture. However, legislators in most American states enacted statutes that required such estates to be divided equally among all the offspring. Most American parents supported these statutes because they had already begun to treat their children as equals.

Foreign visitors believed that republican ideology encouraged American parents to relax parental discipline and give their children greater freedom. Because of the "general ideas of Liberty and Equality engraved on their hearts," suggested a Polish aristocrat who traveled around the United States in 1800, American children had "scant respect" for their parents. Several decades later a British traveler stood dumbfounded as an American father excused his son's "resolute disobedience" with a smile and the remark, "a sturdy republican, sir." The traveler guessed that American parents encouraged such independence to assist young people to "go their own way" in the world.

However, these relatively permissive childrearing habits were not universal. Foreign visitors interacted primarily with well-to-do Americans, who were often members of Episcopal or Presbyterian churches. These parents often followed the teachings of rationalist-minded religious writers influenced by John Locke and other Enlightenment thinkers. For such authors, children were "rational creatures" who should be encouraged to act correctly by means of praise, advice, and reasoned restraint. The parents' role was to develop the children's consciences and stress self-discipline so that young people would learn to control their own behavior and to think and act responsibly. This rationalist mode of childrearing became the preference among families in the rapidly expanding middle class.

By contrast, many yeomen and tenant farmers influenced by the Second Great Awakening (see p. 277) raised their children by following the precepts of authoritarian-minded ministers and authors. Many evangelical Baptists and Methodists believed that infants were "full of the stains and pollution of sin" and needed strict rules and harsh discipline. Fear was a "useful and necessary principle in family government," the minister John Abbott advised parents; a child "should submit to your authority, not to your arguments or persuasions." Abbott told parents to instill humility in children and to teach them to subordinate their personal desires to God's will.

The values transmitted within families were crucial because until the 1820s most education still took place within the household. In New England, locally funded public schools provided most boys and some girls with basic instruction in reading and writing. Among whites in other regions, about a quarter of the boys and perhaps 10 percent of the girls attended privately funded schools or had personal tutors. Even in New England only a small fraction of the men and almost no women went on to grammar (high) school. Only 1 percent of men graduated from college.

In the 1790s Bostonian Caleb Bingham, an influential textbook author, called for "an equal distribution of knowledge to make us emphatically a 'republic of letters.'" Thomas Jefferson and Benjamin Rush separately proposed ambitious schemes for a comprehensive system of primary and secondary schooling, followed by college attendance for young men. They also advocated the establishment of a university in which distinguished scholars would lecture on law, medicine, theology, and political economy.

To ordinary citizens such educational proposals smacked of elitism. Farmers, artisans, and laborers looked to schools for basic instruction in the "three Rs": reading, 'riting, and 'rithmetic. They supported public funding only for elementary education because their teenage children had to work and could not attend secondary schools or colleges. "Let anybody show what advantage the poor man receives from colleges," an anonymous "Old Soldier" wrote to the Maryland *Gazette*. "Why should they support them, unless it is to serve those who are in affluent circumstances, whose children can be spared from labor, and receive the benefits?"

Although many state constitutions encouraged legislatures to support education, few state governments acted until the 1820s. Then a new generation of reformers, led primarily by merchants and manufacturers, successfully campaigned to raise standards by certifying qualified teachers and appointing state superintendents of education. To encourage self-discipline and individual enterprise in the students, the reformers chose textbooks, such as *The Life of George Washington* by "Parson" Mason Weems, that praised honesty and hard work and condemned gambling, drinking, and laziness. Believing that patriotic instruction would foster shared cultural ideals, they also required the study of American history. As a New Hampshire schoolboy named Thomas Low recalled, "We were taught every day and in every way that ours was the freest, the happiest, and soon to be the greatest and most powerful country of the world."

The author Noah Webster championed the goal of American intellectual greatness. Asserting that "America must be as independent in *literature* as she is in politics," he called on his fellow citizens to detach themselves "from the dependence on foreign opinions and manners, which is fatal to the efforts of genius in this country." Webster's *Dissertation on the English Language* (1789) introduced American spelling (such as *labor* for the British *labour*) and defined words according to American usage. His "blue-backed speller," first published in 1783, sold 60 million copies over the next half century and helped give Americans of all backgrounds a common vocabulary and grammar. "None of us was 'lowed to see a book," an enslaved African American recalled, "but we gits hold of that Webster's old blueback speller and we . . . studies [it]."

Despite Webster's efforts, a republican American literary culture was slow to develop. Ironically, the most accomplished and successful writer in the new republic was Washington Irving, an elitist-minded Federalist. His essays and histories, including *Salmagundi* (1807) and *Diedrich Knickerbocker's History of New York* (1809), had substantial American sales and won fame abroad. Impatient with the slow pace of American literary development, Irving lived in Europe for seventeen years, drawn to its aristocratic manners and intense intellectual life.

Apart from Irving, no American author was well known in Europe or, indeed, in the United States. "Literature is not yet a distinct profession with us," Thomas Jefferson told an English friend. "Now and then a strong mind arises, and at its intervals from business emits a flash of light. But the first object of young societies is bread and covering." Not until the 1830s and 1840s would American-born authors achieve a professional identity and, in the works of Ralph Waldo Emerson and novelists of the American Renaissance, make a significant contribution to the great literature of Western society (see Chapter 12).

# Aristocratic Republicanism and Slavery

Both in theory and in practice, republicanism in the South differed significantly from that in the North. Republican authors had long identified political tyranny as a major threat to liberty, and southern planters, who feared governmental interference with their property in slaves, were especially aware of this danger. To prevent despotic rule by demagogues or radical-minded legislatures, they wanted authority to rest in the hands of incorruptible men of "virtue." Indeed, many affluent and well-educated planters saw themselves as the practical embodiment of this ideal. Some consciously cast themselves as republican aristocrats. "The planters here are essentially what the nobility are in other countries," declared James Henry Hammond of South Carolina. "They stand at the head of society & politics . . . [and form] an aristocracy of talents, of virtue, of generosity and courage."

## The North and South Grow Apart

European visitors to the new American republic agreed that the South formed a distinct society but were much less positive than Hammond about its character. New England was home to religious "fanaticism," according to a British observer, but "the lower orders of citizens" there had "a better education, are more intelligent, and better informed" than those he met in the South. "The state of poverty in which a great number of white people live in Virginia" surprised the Marquis de Chastellux, and other visitors to the South commented on the rude manners, heavy drinking, and lack of a strong work ethic they found there. White tenant farmers and small freeholders seemed only to have a "passion for gaming at the billiard table, a cock-fight or cards," and many planters squandered their wealth in extravagant living while their slaves suffered bitter poverty.

Some southerners admitted that slavery corrupted their society and contributed to the ignorance and poverty of the mass of the white population. Thus, a South Carolina merchant linked slavery to a weak work ethic: "Where there are Negroes a White Man despises to work, saying what, will you have me a Slave and work like a Negroe?" For their part, wealthy planters wanted a compliant labor force that was content with the drudgery of agricultural work. Consequently, they trained most of their slaves as field hands (allowing only a few to learn the arts of the blacksmith, carpenter, or bricklayer), and did little to provide ordinary whites with elementary instruction in reading or arithmetic. In 1800 the political leaders of Essex County, Virginia, spent about twenty-five cents per person for local government, including schooling, while their counterparts in Acton, Massachusetts, expended about one dollar per person. This difference in support for education mattered: by the 1820s nearly all native-born men and women in New England could read and write, while over one-third of white southerners lacked these basic intellectual skills.

Slavery quickly found its way into national politics. At the Philadelphia convention in 1787 the delegates had accepted the existence of slavery and, to secure

**The Internal Slave Trade**

Mounted whites escort a convoy of slaves from Virginia to Tennessee in Lewis Miller's *Slave Trader, Sold to Tennessee* (1853). For white planters, the trade was a lucrative one because it pumped money into the declining Chesapeake economy and provided fresh workers for the expanding plantations of the cotton belt. For blacks it was a traumatic journey, a new Middle Passage, that broke up families and long-settled slave communities. Abby Aldrich Rockefeller Folk Art Center.

ratification of the constitution in the South, inserted clauses to deal with fugitive slaves and slave imports (see Chapter 7). Southerners immediately sought additional protection for slavery and won approval in the second session of the new national legislature of James Madison's resolution that "Congress have no authority to interfere in the emancipation of slaves, or in the treatment of them within any of the States."

Nonetheless, slavery remained a contested issue. Slave revolts in Haiti during the 1790s brought a flood of white refugees to the United States and prompted congressional debates about diplomatic relations with the island's new black government. Simultaneously, northern political leaders assailed the British impressment of American sailors as just "as oppressive and tyrannical as the slave trade" and demanded the end of both. When Congress prohibited legal American participation in the Atlantic slave trade in 1808, northern representatives called for the regulation of the interstate trade in slaves and the emancipation of illegally imported slaves. In response, southern leaders mounted a defense of their labor system. "A large majority of people in the Southern states do not consider slavery as even an evil," declared one congressman. And the South's political clout—especially its domination of the presidency and the Senate—ensured that the national government would continue to protect slavery.

Thus, American diplomats vigorously—and successfully—demanded compensation for slaves freed by the British during the War of 1812, and Congress enacted legislation upholding the property rights of slave owners in the District of Columbia.

Political conflict over slavery increased as the northern states gradually emancipated their African American laborers and the South expanded its slave-based agricultural economy into the lower Mississippi Valley. Antislavery advocates had hoped that African bondage would "die a natural death" following the demise of the Atlantic slave trade and the decline of the tobacco economy. But their hopes faded as the cotton boom increased the demand for slaves, and Louisiana (1812), Mississippi (1817), and Alabama (1819) joined the Union with state constitutions permitting slavery.

In 1817 the founders of the American Colonization Society, who included President James Monroe and Speaker of the House Henry Clay, acknowledged the baneful effects of the southern labor system. As Clay explained, racial bondage had placed his state of Kentucky "in the rear of our neighbors ... in the state of agriculture, the progress of manufactures, the advance of improvement, and the general prosperity of society." Slavery had to end and, the colonization society argued, the freed slaves had to be sent back to Africa. Emancipation without removal, Clay predicted, "would be followed by instantaneous collisions between the two races, which would break out into a civil war that would end in the extermination or subjugation of the one race or the other." To prevent racial conflict, the society would encourage southern planters to emancipate their slaves—who now numbered nearly 1.5 million people—and would arrange for their resettlement in Africa.

The American Colonization Society was a dismal failure. Few planters freed their slaves and, despite appeals to wealthy individuals, churches, and state governments, the society was able to purchase freedom for only a few hundred slaves. Equally important, most free blacks rejected colonization. They agreed with Bishop Richard Allen of the African Methodist Episcopal Church that "this land which we have watered with our tears and our blood is now our mother country." Three thousand African Americans met in Philadelphia's Bethel Church to condemn colonization and to claim citizenship; their goal was to advance in American society using "those opportunities ... which the Constitution and the laws allow to all." Lacking significant support from either blacks or whites, the society transported only 6,000 African Americans to Liberia, a colony it established on the west coast of Africa.

## Toward a New Southern Social Order

Colonization failed in part because the South was changing in ways that encouraged the expansion of slavery. In 1780 the western boundary of the plantation system ran through the middle of Georgia; by 1820 the plantation frontier stretched through the middle of Louisiana. That advance of six hundred miles doubled the geographic area cultivated by slave labor. Moreover, many of the workers on the newly established cotton and sugar plantations were African-born slaves. Between 1780 and 1808 nearly 250,000 Africans were added to the southern workforce—a total that equaled the number of slaves imported into Britain's mainland settlements during the entire colonial period.

Despite this influx of new African workers, the demand for labor in the Southwest far exceeded the supply. "The Negro business is a great object with us," one merchant declared, because "the Planter will . . . sacrifice every thing to attain Negroes." To satisfy this demand, merchants and planters looked to the Chesapeake region, which now had a surplus of enslaved laborers. Between 1790 and 1820 whites relocated to the Southwest more than 150,000 African Americans from Maryland, Virginia, and parts of North and South Carolina. Some of these forced migrants—perhaps as many as one-half—moved with relatives and friends when their owners sold their old holdings and began new plantations on the fertile plains of Alabama, Mississippi, and Louisiana (Map 9.2).

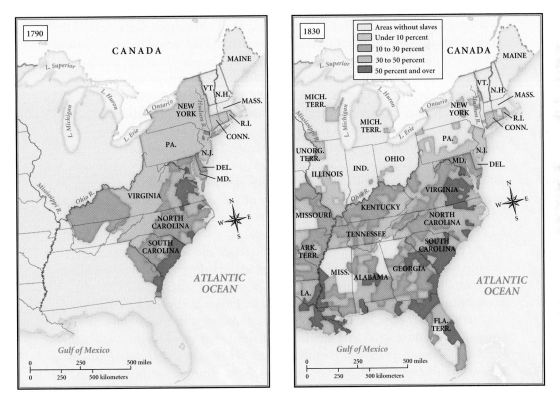

**MAP 9.2 Distribution of the Slave Population in 1790 and 1830**

The cotton boom prompted a great forced migration of enslaved African Americans from their eighteenth-century communities to the Old Southwest. In 1790, most slaves lived and worked on the tobacco plantations of the Chesapeake and in the rice and indigo areas of South Carolina. By 1830, tens of thousands of slaves were laboring on the cotton and sugar lands of the lower Mississippi Valley and on cotton plantations in Georgia and Florida.

FOR MORE HELP ANALYZING THIS MAP, see the Online Study Guide at **bedfordstmartins.com/henrettaconcise**.

However, many planters remained on their estates in Maryland, Virginia, the Carolinas, and Georgia and reaped impressive profits by selling their "surplus" workers to slave traders. For African American families, separation became a common experience. "I am Sold to a man by the name of Peterson a trader," lamented a Georgia slave. "My Dear wife for you and my Children my pen cannot Express the griffe I feel to be parted from you all." Some of these slaves lost touch with their families forever. "Dey sole [sold] my sister Kate," Anna Harris remembered decades later, ". . . and I ain't seed or heard of her since." The profits to be gained by planting cotton in the Southwest and selling enslaved laborers from the Southeast doomed both the colonization movement and many long-established African American communities.

Westward movement also changed the character of white society. Following the tobacco and rice revolutions around 1700 (see Chapter 3), a wealthy planter elite exercised considerable political power. However, in tobacco-growing areas, slave owning became broadly diffused. During the 1770s, about 60 percent of the white families in the Chesapeake region owned at least one African American worker and benefited directly from slavery. By 1820, however, a much smaller proportion of white southern families owned slaves, and the percentage continued to fall. In Alabama in 1830, only 30 percent of the voters owned slaves and most slaves were the property of wealthy men. Like the rice-growing plantations in South Carolina and Georgia, the cotton plantations in the lower Mississippi Valley were large-scale operations that used dozens of enslaved black workers. Their wealthy and influential owners dominated society and gave an aristocratic-republican definition to politics. In Alabama, a majority of the state's elected officials owned more than 20 African Americans, and one-quarter of the legislators held more than 50. "Inequality is the fundamental law of the universe," proclaimed one southern politician. "Slavery does indeed create an aristocracy."

As cotton production was consolidated in fewer and fewer hands, some white yeomen sold their land and became the tenants of wealthy planter-landlords. Other white families in plantation regions scraped by on small farms, growing foodstuffs for sustenance and a few bales of cotton for cash. Influenced by the patriarchal ideology of the planter class, the husbands in these households asserted traditional male authority over their wives and children and ruled their small worlds with a firm hand. Other yeomen families retreated into the backcountry near the Appalachian Mountains, where they struggled to maintain their economic independence and to control local county governments. Owning hilly farms of fifty to one hundred acres, these families grew some cotton but primarily raised corn and livestock, especially hogs. Their goal was modest: to preserve their holdings and secure enough new land to set up all of their children as small-scale farmers.

In the new southwestern economy, prosperity was limited primarily to the shrinking minority of the white population that owned plantations and slaves. The cotton revolution had undercut the democratic prospects of the Revolutionary era and powered the expansion of aristocratic-republican plantation society.

## Slave Society and Culture

As wealthy planters solidified their rule over a class-divided society, African Americans created a distinct and increasingly homogeneous rural culture. A major cause of this homogeneity was the end of the transatlantic slave trade in 1808, which gradually created a slave population that was virtually all American born. Even in South Carolina—after 1776 a major point of entry for imported slaves—only 20 percent of the black inhabitants in 1820 had been born in Africa. The rapid movement of slavery into the Mississippi Valley also reduced cultural differences among slaves. Thus, the Gullah dialect spoken by migrants from the Carolina low country gradually died out on the cotton plantations of Alabama and Mississippi, replaced by the black English spoken by slaves from the Chesapeake.

Even as the black population became more homogeneous, African cultural influence remained important. At least one-third of the slaves who entered the United States between 1776 and 1809 were from the Congo region of west-central Africa, and they brought their culture with them. As the traveler Isaac Holmes reported in 1821, "In Louisiana, and the state of Mississippi, the slaves . . . dance for several hours during Sunday afternoon. The general movement is in what they call the Congo dance." Similar descriptions of blacks who "danced the Congo and sang a purely African song to the accompaniment of . . . a drum" appeared as late as 1890.

African Americans also continued to respect African incest taboos and shunned marriage between cousins. On the Good Hope plantation in South Carolina, nearly half of the slave children born between 1800 and 1857 were related by blood to one another, yet only one marriage had taken place between cousins. Because southern state legislatures and law courts prohibited legal marriages between slaves (so they could be sold without breaking a legal bond), African Americans devised their own rituals. Following African custom, many couples symbolized their married state by jumping over a broomstick together in a public ceremony. Christian slaves were often married by a white or black preacher, but these rites rarely ended with the customary phrase "until death do you part." Knowing that black marriages often ended through sale, one white minister blessed the couple "for so long as God keeps them together." To maintain their cultural identity, recently imported slaves often gave their children African names. Males born on Friday were often called Cuffee—the name of that day in several West African languages. Although most Chesapeake slaves chose names of British origin, they named sons after fathers, uncles, or grandfathers and daughters after grandmothers. Like incest rules and marriage rituals, this intergenerational sharing of names solidified kinship ties.

By forming stable families and strong communities, African Americans tried to create a sense of order in the harsh and arbitrary world of slavery. Some groups won substantial control over their lives. During the Revolutionary era, blacks in the rice-growing lowlands of South Carolina asserted the right to labor by the **task** rather than to work under constant supervision. Each day these task-workers had to complete a precisely defined job—for example, turn over a quarter acre of land, hoe half an acre, or pound seven mortars of rice. By working hard, many finished their tasks "by one or two o'clock in the afternoon," a Methodist preacher reported, and had "the rest of the day for themselves, which they spend in working their own private fields . . . planting rice, corn, potatoes, tobacco &c. for their own use and profit." These private efforts provided slaves with better clothes and food, but few African Americans enjoyed a comfortable standard of living (see American Voices, "A Child Learns the Meaning of Slavery," p. 273).

A few blacks, such as Gabriel and Martin Prosser in Virginia (1800), plotted mass uprisings and murders, and others, such as Denmark Vesey in South Carolina (1822), may have done so as well. But in most areas blacks numbered less than half the population, and everywhere they lacked the strong institutions—such as the communes of free peasants or serfs in Europe—needed to organize a successful rebellion. Moreover, whites were well armed, unified, and militant.

Escape was equally problematic. Blacks in the Lower South could seek freedom in Spanish Florida until 1819, when the United States annexed that territory. Even then, hundreds of blacks continued to flee to Florida, where they intermarried with the Seminole Indians. Elsewhere in the South small groups of escaped slaves eked out a meager existence in deserted marshy areas or in mountain valleys. Given these limited options, most slaves had no choice but to build the best possible lives for themselves on the plantations where they lived.

### The Free Black Population

Between 1790 and 1820 the number of free blacks rose steadily from 8 percent of the African American population to about 13 percent, but few were truly free. One-third of all free blacks—some 50,000 in 1810—lived in the North, where they were treated as second-class citizens. In rural areas free blacks worked as farm laborers or tenant farmers; in towns and cities they toiled as domestic servants, laundresses, or day laborers. Only a small minority of free African Americans owned land. "You do not see one out of a hundred . . . that can make a comfortable living, own a cow, or a horse," a traveler in New Jersey noted. In addition, blacks were usually forbidden to vote, attend public schools, or sit next to whites in churches. Of the states admitted to the Union between 1790 and 1821, only Vermont and Maine extended the vote to free blacks, and they could testify against whites in court only in Massachusetts. The federal government did not allow free African Americans to work for the postal service, claim public lands, or hold a U.S. passport.

Nonetheless, a few African Americans were able to make full use of their talents, and some achieved great distinction. The mathematician and surveyor Benjamin Banneker published an almanac and helped lay out the new national capital in the District of Columbia. Joshua Johnston, a skilled painter, won praise for his portraiture, and merchant Robert Sheridan acquired a small fortune from his business enterprises. More impressive and enduring were the community institutions created by this first generation of free African Americans. Throughout the North they founded

## AMERICAN VOICES

# A Child Learns the Meaning of Slavery

## JACOB STROYER

*Jacob Stroyer, born into slavery in South Carolina, was emancipated and became a minister in Salem, Massachusetts, and an abolitionist. In* My Life in the South *(1885), he relates a dramatic incident that revealed his family's subordinate and powerless status as slaves.*

Father had a surname, Stroyer, which he could not use in public, as the surname Stroyer would be against the law; he was known only by the name of William Singleton, because that was his master's name. . . . Mother's name was Chloe. She belonged to Colonel M. R. Singleton too; she was a field hand, and was never sold, but her parents once were. . . .

Father . . . used to take care of horses and mules. I was around with him in the barnyard when but a small boy; of course that gave me an early relish for the occupation of hostler, and soon I made known my preference to Colonel Singleton, who was a sportsman and had fine horses. . . . Hence I was allowed to be numbered among those who took care of the fine horses, and learned to ride. . . .

It was not long after I had entered my new work before they put me upon the back of a horse which threw me to the ground almost as soon as I reached his back. . . . When I got up there was a man standing near with a switch in hand, and he immediately began to beat me. . . . This was the first time I had been whipped by anyone except Mother and Father, so I cried out in a tone of voice as if I would say, this is the first and last whipping you will give me when Father gets hold of you.

When I got away from him I ran to Father with all my might, but soon my expectation was blasted, as Father very coolly said to me, "Go back to your work and be a good boy, for I cannot do anything for you." But that did not satisfy me, so I went on to Mother with my complaint and she came out to the man who whipped me. He was a groom, a white man whom master hired to train his horses . . . [and] he took a whip and started for her, and she ran from him, talking all the time. . . .

Then the idea first came to me that I, with my dear father and mother and the rest of my fellow Negroes, was doomed to cruel treatment through life and was defenseless. . . .

One day, about two weeks after Boney Young and Mother had the conflict, he . . . gave me a first-class flogging. That evening when I went home to Father and Mother, I said to them, "Mr. Young is whipping me too much now; I shall not stand it. I shall fight him." Father said to me, "You must not do that, because if you do he will say that your mother and I advised you to do it, and it will make it hard for your mother and me, as well as yourself. You must do as I told you my son. . . . I can do nothing more than pray to the Lord to hasten the time when these things shall be done away."

SOURCE: Linda R. Monk, ed., *Ordinary Americans: U.S. History through the Eyes of Everyday People* (Alexandria, VA: Close Up Publications, 1994), 71–72.

**Captain Absalom Boston**

Absalom Boston was born in 1785 on the island of Nantucket, the heart of the American whaling industry. A member of a community of free black whalers manumitted from slavery by their Quaker owners, Boston went to sea at age fifteen. By the age of thirty he had used his earnings to become the proprietor of a public inn. In 1822, Boston became the first black master with an all-black crew to undertake a whaling voyage from Nantucket. In later years he became an important leader of the island's black community, serving as a trustee of the African School.
Nantucket Historical Association.

schools, mutual-benefit organizations, and fellowship groups, often with the title Free African Society. Discriminated against by white Protestants, they formed their own congregations and a new religious denomination—the African Methodist Episcopal (AME) Church, headed by Bishop Richard Allen. These institutions gave free African Americans a sense of cultural, if not political, autonomy.

Most free blacks who lived in slave states resided in the Upper South—some 110,000 in 1810. In Maryland a quarter of the black population was free; in Delaware free blacks outnumbered slaves by three to one. But their freedom was fragile. Free blacks accused of crimes were often denied a jury trial, and those charged with vagrancy were sometimes forced back into slavery. To prove their free status, African Americans had to carry manumission documents, which might not protect them from kidnapping and sale. Yet the shortage of skilled workers in southern cities created opportunities, and blacks became the backbone of the region's urban workforce. African American carpenters, blacksmiths, barbers, butchers, and shopkeepers played prominent roles in the economies of Baltimore, Richmond, Charleston, and New Orleans and in the social life of their black residents.

As a privileged group among African Americans, free blacks felt loyalty both to the welfare of their families, which often meant assimilating white culture, and to their race, which meant identifying with the great mass of enslaved African Americans. Some well-to-do free blacks, particularly the mulatto offspring of white masters and black women, drew apart from common black laborers and field hands and adopted the outlook of the planter class. In Charleston and New Orleans a few free African Americans even owned slaves.

However, most free African Americans acknowledged their unity with the enslaved population and saw blacks as one people. "We's different [from whites] in color, in talk and in 'ligion and beliefs," as one put it. Knowing their own liberty was not secure as long as slavery existed, free blacks sought freedom for all those of African ancestry. Free blacks in the South—who were often the offspring of white planters—aided fugitive slaves, while northern blacks supported the antislavery movement. In the rigid caste system of American race relations, free blacks stood as symbols of hope to enslaved African Americans and as omens of danger to the majority of whites.

## The Missouri Crisis

The success of their campaign against the Atlantic slave trade encouraged northern reformers to rid American society of slave labor. In 1818 Congressman Nathaniel Macon of North Carolina warned southerners that radical-minded members of the "colonizing bible and peace societies" hoped to use the national government "to try the question of emancipation." In fact, a major national conflict over slavery came even more quickly than Macon had anticipated. When Missouri applied for admission to the Union as a slave state in 1819, Congressman James Tallmadge of New York proposed a ban on the importation of slaves into Missouri and the gradual emancipation of its black inhabitants. When Missouri whites rejected Tallmadge's proposals, the northern majority in the House of Representatives blocked the territory's admission to the Union.

Southerners were horrified. "It is believed by some, & feared by others," Alabama senator John Walker reported from Washington, that Tallmadge's amendment was "merely the entering wedge and that it points already to a total emancipation of the blacks." The outlook for the South was grim. "You conduct us to an awful precipice, and hold us over it," Mississippi congressman Christopher Rankin warned his northern colleagues. To underline their commitment to slavery, southerners used their power in the Senate (where they held half the seats) to withhold statehood from Maine, which was seeking to separate itself from Massachusetts.

In the ensuing debate, southerners advanced three constitutional arguments. First, raising the principle of "equal rights," they argued that Congress could not impose conditions on Missouri that it had not imposed on other territories seeking statehood. Second, they suggested that slavery was an internal affair that fell under the sovereignty of the state governments. Finally, they maintained that Congress had no authority to infringe on the property rights of individual slaveholders. Going beyond these constitutional issues, southern leaders abandoned their traditional argument that slavery was a "necessary evil" and now championed it as a "positive good." "Christ himself gave a sanction to slavery," declared Senator William Smith of South Carolina. "If it be offensive and sinful to own slaves," a prominent Mississippi Methodist added, "I wish someone would just put his finger on the place in Holy Writ."

Controversy raged for two years before Henry Clay of Kentucky put together a series of political agreements known collectively as the Missouri Compromise. The compromise allowed Maine to enter the Union as a free state in 1820 and Missouri to follow as a slave state in 1821. By admitting both states, the agreement preserved the existing balance in the Senate between North and South and set a precedent for future additions to the Union. To mollify antislavery sentiment in the House of Representatives, southern congressmen accepted legislation that prohibited slavery in the rest of the Louisiana Purchase north of latitude 36°30′, the southern boundary of Missouri (Map 9.3).

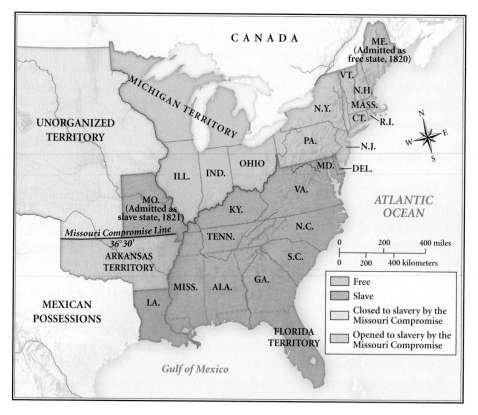

**MAP 9.3 The Missouri Compromise, 1820–1821**

The Missouri Compromise resolved for a generation the issue of slavery in the lands of the Louisiana Purchase. The agreement prohibited slavery north of the Missouri Compromise line (36°30′ north latitude), with the exception of the state of Missouri. To maintain an equal number of senators from free and slave states in the U.S. Congress, the compromise provided for the nearly simultaneous admission to the Union of Maine and Missouri.

As in the Constitutional Convention of 1787, white politicians had given first priority to the Union by devising ways to handle the perilous issue of slavery. But the task had become more difficult. The Philadelphia delegates had resolved sectional differences in two months. Congress took two years to work out the Missouri Compromise, and, because slavery had become an intensely debated political issue, there was no guarantee that it would work. The fate of the western lands, the Union, and the black race were now inextricably intertwined and raised the specter of civil war. As the aging Thomas Jefferson exclaimed during the Missouri crisis, "This momentous question, like a fire-bell in the night, awakened and filled me with terror."

# Protestant Christianity as a Social Force

Throughout the colonial era, religion played a significant role in American life. However, beginning in 1790 a series of religious **revivals** planted the values of evangelical Protestant Christianity deep in the national character and gave a spiritual definition to American republicanism. The revivals also changed the lives of women and blacks. Thousands of African Americans absorbed the faith of white Baptists and Methodists and created a distinctive and powerful institution—the black Christian church. Evangelical Christianity likewise created new public roles for women, especially in the North, and set in motion a long-lasting movement for social reform.

## The Second Great Awakening

The revivals that began around 1790 were much more complex than those of the First Great Awakening. In the 1740s most revivals had occurred in existing congregations; fifty years later they took place both in churches and frontier camp meetings and often led to the creation of new denominations.

In the new American republic, the churches that prospered were those that preached spiritual equality and governed themselves in a relatively democratic fashion. Because bishops and priests dominated the Roman Catholic Church, it attracted few converts among Protestants, who preferred Luther's doctrine of the priesthood of all believers. The unchurched—the great number of nonreligious Americans—likewise shunned Catholicism because they feared clerical power. Likewise, few ordinary native-born Americans joined the Episcopal Church (created by former members of the Church of England) because it had a hierarchical structure similar to that of Catholicism and was dominated by its wealthiest members. The Presbyterian Church was more popular, in part because its members elected laymen to the synods (congresses) which determined doctrine and practice. The Methodist and Baptist Churches attracted even more Americans because most of their preachers were fervent evangelists and promoted an egalitarian religious culture marked by communal singing and emotional services.

A continuous wave of revivalism fueled the expansion of Protestant Christianity. Beginning in the 1790s Baptists and Methodists evangelized the cities and the backcountry of New England. A new sect of Universalists, who repudiated the Calvinist doctrine of predestination and preached universal salvation, attracted thousands of converts, especially in Massachusetts and northern New England. After 1800 enthusiastic camp-meeting revivals swept the frontier regions of South Carolina, Kentucky, Tennessee, and Ohio.

When frontier preachers got together at a revival meeting, the atmosphere was electrifying. James McGready, a Scots-Irish Presbyterian preacher, "could so array hell before the wicked," an eyewitness reported, "that they would tremble and Quake, imagining a lake of fire and brimstone yawning to overwhelm them." James Finley described the Cane Ridge, Kentucky, revival of 1802:

> The noise was like the roar of Niagara. The vast sea of human beings seemed to be agitated as if by a storm. I counted seven ministers, all preaching at one time, some on stumps, others on wagons. . . . Some of the people were singing, others praying, some crying for mercy.

Through such revivals, Baptist and Methodist preachers reshaped the spiritual landscape of the South and the Old Southwest. Because of their emotional message and promise of religious fellowship, revivalists were particularly successful in attracting the unchurched and geographically mobile families who had few social ties in their new communities. With the assistance of black ministers, they began to implant evangelical Protestant Christianity among African Americans as well (see Voices from Abroad, "A Camp Meeting in Indiana," p. 279).

The Second Great Awakening changed the denominational makeup of American religion. The leading churches of the colonial period—the Congregationalists, Episcopalians, and Quakers—grew slowly through natural increase while Methodist and Baptist churches expanded in spectacular fashion by seeking converts and soon became the nation's largest religious denominations. In New England and the Middle Atlantic states, pious evangelical women supplemented the work of preachers and lay elders by holding prayer meetings and providing material aid and spiritual comfort to poorer members of congregations. In the South and West, Baptist and Methodist preachers traveled constantly. A Methodist minister followed a circuit, "riding a hardy pony or horse . . . with his Bible, hymn-book, and Discipline." These "circuit riders" established new churches by searching out devout families, bringing them together for worship, and then appointing lay elders to lead the congregation and enforce moral discipline until the circuit-riding preacher returned.

Evangelical ministers copied the "practical preaching" techniques of George Whitefield and other eighteenth-century revivalists. To attract converts, preachers adopted theatrical gestures and a flamboyant style, threw away their stodgy written sermons, and spoke in plain language. "Preach without papers" and emphasize piety

# A Camp Meeting in Indiana

## FRANCES TROLLOPE

*Frances Trollope, the mother of the English novelist Anthony Trollope, lived during the late 1820s in Cincinnati, where she owned a bazaar that sold European goods. Unsuccessful as a storekeeper, she won great acclaim as the author of* Domestic Manners of the Americans *(1832), a critical study of life in the United States. Here she provides her readers with a vivid description of a revivalist meeting in Indiana around 1830.*

We reached the ground about an hour before midnight. . . . The spot chosen was the verge of an unbroken forest, where a space of about twenty acres appeared to have been partially cleared for the purpose. Tents of different sizes were pitched very near together in a circle round the cleared space. . . .

Four high frames, constructed in the form of altars, were placed at the four corners of the inclosure; on these were supported layers of earth and sod, on which burned immense fires of blazing pine-wood. On one side a rude platform was erected to accommodate the preachers, fifteen of whom attended this meeting, and . . . preached in rotation, day and night, from Tuesday to Saturday.

When we arrived, the preachers were silent; but we heard issuing from nearly every tent mingled sounds of praying, preaching, singing, and lamentation. . . . [One of the tents contained a] . . . close-packed circle of men and women who knelt on the floor. Out of about thirty persons thus placed, perhaps half a dozen were men. One of these [was] a handsome-looking youth of eighteen or twenty. . . . His arm was encircling the neck of a young girl who knelt beside him, with her hair hanging dishevelled upon her shoulders, and her features working with the most violent agitation; soon after they both fell forward on the straw, as if unable to endure in any other attitude the burning eloquence of a tall grim figure in black, who, standing erect in the center, was uttering with incredible vehemence an oration that seemed to hover between praying and preaching. . . .

One tent was occupied exclusively by Negroes. They were all full-dressed, and looked exactly as if they were performing a scene on a stage. . . . The men were in snow white pantaloons, with gay colored linen jackets. One of these, a youth of coal-black comeliness, was preaching with the most violent gesticulations. . . .

At midnight, a horn sounded through the camp, which, we were told, was to call the people from private to public worship; and . . . about two thousand persons assembled.

One of the preachers began in a low nasal tone, and, like all other Methodist preachers, assured us of the enormous depravity of man. . . . Above a hundred persons, nearly all females, came forward, uttering howlings and groans so terrible that I shall never cease to shudder when I recall them. They appeared to drag each other forward, and on the word being given, "let us pray," they fell on their knees. . . .

SOURCE: Frances Trollope, *Domestic Manners of the Americans* (London: Whittaker, Treacher and Co., 1832), 139–42.

### A Baptist Ceremony

Unlike many other Christian churches, which practiced infant baptism, Baptists reserved this sacred ceremony for adults who had been born again by the infusion of God's grace. Some Baptist congregations, such as the one depicted in this 1819 painting, required complete immersion in water, symbolizing the cleansing of all sins. Such communal practices, along with an egalitarian atmosphere and an intense religiosity, attracted tens of thousands of converts and quickly made the Baptists one of the largest American denominations. Chicago Historical Society.

FOR MORE HELP ANALYZING THIS IMAGE, see the Online Study Guide at **bedfordstmartins.com/henrettaconcise.**

rather than theology, advised one minister, "seem earnest & serious; & you will be listened to with Patience, & Wonder."

In the South evangelical religion was initially a disruptive force. By proclaiming the spiritual equality of all people—women and blacks as well as white men—it incurred the wrath of husbands and planters. In response Methodist and Baptist preachers adapted the social content of their religious message so that it upheld the authority of yeomen patriarchs and slave-owning planters. "We hold that a Christian slave must be submissive, faithful, and obedient," a Methodist conference proclaimed, while a Baptist minister declared that a man was naturally at "the head of the woman." Ultimately Christian republicanism in the South added a sacred dimension to the ideology of aristocratic republicanism.

But this was not the case among blacks. After the family, the religious community was the most important institution among slaves, and initially most blacks maintained the practices of their African homeland. "At the time I first went to Carolina," remembered Charles Ball, an escaped slave, "there were a great many African slaves in the country. . . . Many of them believed there were several gods [and] I knew several . . . Mohamedans [Muslims]."

When the First Great Awakening swept through the Upper South after 1750, only a few blacks joined Christian churches. The first major wave of African American conversions to Christianity occurred only in the mid-1780s along the James River in Virginia.

Subsequently, white evangelical Baptists and Methodists won the conversion of hundreds of slaves and free blacks, who adapted the teachings of the Protestant churches to their own needs. Black Christians generally envisioned God as a warrior who had liberated the Jews, his chosen people. Their "cause was similar to the Israelites'," Martin Prosser told his fellow slave conspirators as they plotted rebellion in Virginia in 1800. "I have read in my Bible where God says, if we worship him, . . . five of you shall conquer a hundred and a hundred of you a hundred thousand of our enemies." Confident of their special relationship with God, slaves prepared themselves spiritually for emancipation, the first step in their journey to the Promised Land.

Consequently, black Christians generally ignored the doctrines of original sin and predestination as well as biblical passages that encouraged unthinking obedience to authority. When a white minister urged slaves in Liberty County, Georgia, to obey their masters, "one half of my audience deliberately rose up and walked off." Slaves identified not only with the powerful Father-God but also with his persecuted Savior-Son, whose suffering helped them endure the manifest injustice of their own lives. Black Christianity thus developed as a complex mixture of stoical endurance and emotional fervor, and encouraged slaves to affirm their spiritual equality with whites.

Like African Americans, whites responded more positively to certain Christian doctrines than to others. The Calvinist preoccupation with human depravity and weakness had profoundly shaped the sensibilities of many colonial-era writers, teachers, and statesmen. By the early nineteenth century, most Protestant ministers placed greater stress on human ability and individual free will. In New England many educated and affluent Congregationalists, influenced by Enlightenment thought, placed increasing emphasis on the power of human reason. Rejecting the concept of the Trinity—Father, Son, and Holy Spirit—they worshiped an indivisible and "united" God; hence they took the name of Unitarians. "The ultimate reliance of a human being is, and must be, on his own mind," argued the famous Unitarian minister William Ellery Channing, "for the idea of God is the idea of our own spiritual nature, purified and enlarged to infinity."

Other New England Congregationalists likewise abandoned the Calvinist outlook of their Puritan ancestors. Although Lyman Beecher, the preeminent Congregationalist clergyman, continued to believe that humans had a natural tendency to sin, he affirmed the capacity of all men and women to choose God and to be saved. In emphasizing the free will of the believer and the possibility of universal salvation, Beecher testified to the growing confidence in the power of human action and the increasing democratic and capitalistic spirit of the age.

Reflecting this optimistic outlook, the minister Samuel Hopkins linked individual salvation to religious benevolence. Benevolence was the practice of disinterested virtue. According to the New York Presbyterian minister John Rodgers, fortunate individuals who had received God's grace had a duty "to dole out charity to their poorer brothers and sisters." Heeding this message, pious merchants founded the New York Humane Society and other charitable organizations. By the 1820s so many devout Protestant men and women had embraced benevolent reform that conservative church leaders warned against the pursuit of secular goals, such as the prevention of pauperism, to the neglect of spiritual matters. This criticism underlined a key element of the new religious outlook: its emphasis on improving society. It was her belief, the social reformer Lydia Maria Child later recalled, that "the only true church organization [is] when heads and hearts unite in working for the welfare of the human-race."

Unlike the First Great Awakening of the 1740s, which split churches into factions, the Second Great Awakening fostered cooperation among the denominations. Religious leaders founded five interdenominational societies between 1815 and 1826: the American Education Society (1815), the American Bible Society (1816), the American Sunday School Union (1824), the American Tract Society (1824), and the American Home Missionary Society (1826). Although based in eastern cities—New York, Boston, and Philadelphia—they ministered to a national congregation. Each year the societies dispatched hundreds of missionaries to small towns and rural villages and distributed tens of thousands of religious pamphlets.

The growing unity among Protestants had a galvanizing effect, as men and women scattered across the expanding nation saw themselves as part of a single religious movement that could change the course of history (Map 9.4). "I want to see our state evangelized," declared one pious layman who lived along the Erie Canal (where the fires of revivalism were so hot and so frequent that it was known as the "Burned-Over District"): "Suppose the great State of New York in all its physical, political, moral, commercial, and pecuniary resources should come over to the Lord's side. Why it would turn the scale and could convert the world. I shall have no rest until it is done."

Because the Second Awakening aroused such pious enthusiasm in thousands of Americans, religion became a central force in political life. On July 4, 1827, the Reverend Ezra Stiles Ely called on the members of the Seventh Presbyterian Church in Philadelphia to begin a "Christian party in politics." Ely's sermon, "The Duty of Christian Freemen to Elect Christian Rulers," proclaimed a religious goal for the American republic—an objective that Thomas Jefferson and John Adams would

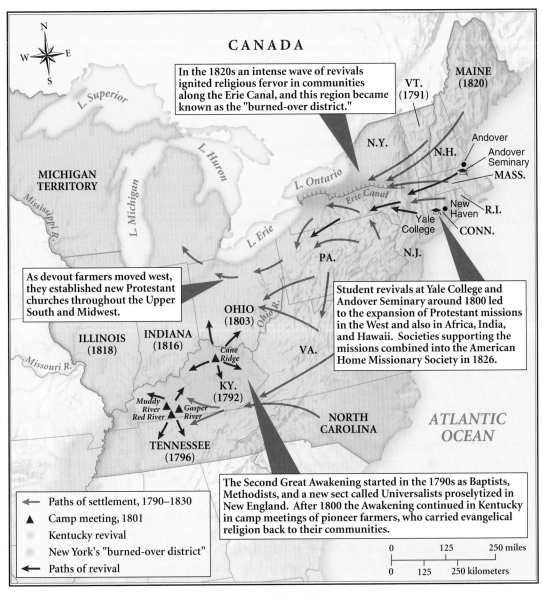

In the 1820s an intense wave of revivals ignited religious fervor in communities along the Erie Canal, and this region became known as the "burned-over district."

As devout farmers moved west, they established new Protestant churches throughout the Upper South and Midwest.

Student revivals at Yale College and Andover Seminary around 1800 led to the expansion of Protestant missions in the West and also in Africa, India, and Hawaii. Societies supporting the missions combined into the American Home Missionary Society in 1826.

The Second Great Awakening started in the 1790s as Baptists, Methodists, and a new sect called Universalists proselytized in New England. After 1800 the Awakening continued in Kentucky in camp meetings of pioneer farmers, who carried evangelical religion back to their communities.

← Paths of settlement, 1790–1830
▲ Camp meeting, 1801
Kentucky revival
New York's "burned-over district"
← Paths of revival

| 0 | 125 | 250 miles |
| 0 | 125 | 250 kilometers |

**MAP 9.4 The Second Great Awakening, 1790–1860**

The awakening lasted for decades and invigorated churches in every part of the nation. However, the revivals in Kentucky and in New York State were particularly intense and influential. As thousands of farm families migrated to the West, they carried with them the fervor generated by the Cane Ridge revival in Kentucky in 1802 and the religious wildfires that swept through the "Burned-Over District" along the Erie Canal in New York between 1825 and 1835.

have found strange if not troubling. The two recently deceased founders had believed that America's mission was to spread political republicanism. In contrast Ely urged the United States to become an evangelical Christian nation dedicated to religious conversion at home and abroad: "All our rulers ought in their official capacity to serve the Lord Jesus Christ."

## Women's New Religious Roles

The upsurge in religious enthusiasm provided women with new opportunities to demonstrate their piety and even to found new sects. Mother Ann Lee organized the Shakers in Britain and in 1774 migrated to America, where she attracted numerous recruits; by the 1820s Shaker communities dotted the American countryside from New Hampshire to Kentucky and Indiana (see Chapter 12). Jemima Wilkinson, a young Quaker woman in Rhode Island, led a less successful religious movement. In 1776, stirred by reading the sermons of George Whitefield, Wilkinson had a vision that she had died and been reincarnated as Christ. Repudiating her birth name, Wilkinson declared herself to be the Publick Universal Friend and preached a new gospel, which blended the Calvinist warning of "a lost and guilty, gossiping, dying World" with Quaker-inspired plain dress, pacifism, and abolitionism. Wilkinson's charisma initially won scores of converts, but her radical personal lifestyle and teachings brought a rapid end to her sect.

Far more important than these religious experiments were the activities undertaken by women in mainstream churches. To give but a few examples, in New Hampshire women managed more than fifty local "cent" societies that raised funds for the Society for Promoting Christian Knowledge. Evangelical women in New York City founded the Society for the Relief of Poor Widows. And young Quaker women in Philadelphia ran the Society for the Free Instruction of African Females.

Women became active in religion and charitable work partly because they were excluded from other spheres of public life and partly because ministers relied increasingly on women to do the work of the church. After 1800 over 70 percent of the members of New England Congregational churches were female, and ministers acknowledged their numerical predominance by ending long-standing practices such as gender-segregated prayer meetings. Indeed, evangelical Methodist and Baptist preachers actively encouraged mixed praying. "Our prayer meetings have been one of the greatest means of the conversion of souls," a minister in central New York reported in the 1820s, "especially those in which brothers and sisters have prayed together."

Far from leading to sexual promiscuity, as critics feared, these new practices promoted greater moral self-discipline. Believing in female virtue, many young women and the men who courted them now postponed sexual intercourse until after marriage—a form of self-restraint uncommon in the eighteenth century. In Hingham,

Massachusetts, and many other New England towns, more than 30 percent of the women who married between 1750 and 1800 had borne a child within eight months of their wedding day. By the 1820s the proportion had dropped to 15 percent.

As women exercised their new spiritual authority, men scrutinized their behavior and tried to curb their power. Evangelical Baptist churches that had once stressed spiritual equality now denied women the right to vote on church affairs or to offer testimonies of faith before the congregation. Such activities, declared one layman, were "directly opposite to the apostolic command in Cor[inthians] xiv, 34, 35, 'Let your women learn to keep silence in the churches.'" "Women have a different *calling*," claimed another, "That they *be chaste, keepers at home* is the Apostle's direction." Seizing on that role, by the 1820s mothers throughout the United States had founded local maternal associations to encourage Christian childrearing. Newsletters such as *Mother's Magazine* were widely read in hundreds of small towns and villages and gave women a sense of shared purpose and identity.

Religious activism also advanced female education. Churches established scores of seminaries and academies where girls from the middling classes received sound intellectual and moral instruction. Emma Willard, the first American advocate of higher education for women, opened the Middlebury Female Seminary in Vermont in 1814 and later founded girls' schools in Waterford and Troy, New York.

## TIMELINE

| | | | |
|---|---|---|---|
| **1782** | St. Jean de Crèvecoeur publishes *Letters from an American Farmer* | | Chesapeake blacks adopt Protestant beliefs |
| **1787** | Benjamin Rush writes *Thoughts on Female Education* | **1807** | New Jersey excludes propertied women from suffrage |
| **1790s** | Parents limit family size as farms shrink<br>Second Great Awakening expands church membership<br>Ministers encourage "republican motherhood" | **1810s** | Expansion of suffrage for men<br>Spread of evangelical Baptists and Methodists<br>Slavery defended as a "necessary evil"<br>Growth of cotton South and domestic slave trade |
| **1800** | Gabriel Prosser plots a slave rebellion in Virginia | | Five states join union: Louisiana (1812), Indiana (1816), Mississippi (1817), Illinois (1818), Alabama (1819) |
| **1800s** | Rise of sentimentalism and of companionate marriages<br>Women's religious activism; founding of female academies<br>Religious benevolence sparks social reform | **1819–1821** | Conflict over admission of Missouri as a slave state ends with Missouri Compromise |
| | | **1820s** | Reform of public education<br>Women become schoolteachers |

Beginning in the 1820s women educated in these seminaries and academies displaced men as public-school teachers. Because educated women had few other opportunities for paid employment, they accepted lower pay than men would. Female schoolteachers earned from $12 to $14 per month with room and board—less than a farm laborer. However, as schoolteachers women had an acknowledged place in public life, a goal that had been beyond their reach in colonial and Revolutionary times.

Just as the ideology of democratic republicanism had expanded voting rights and the political influence of ordinary men in the North, so the values of Christian republicanism had bolstered the public authority of middling women. The Second Great Awakening made Americans a fervently Protestant people. Along with republican and capitalist values, this religious impulse—embodied in the shared experience of hundreds of thousands of Americans between the 1770s and the 1820s—formed the core of an emerging national identity, even as the citizens of the North and the South defined republicanism and economic progress in distinctly different ways.

# For Further Exploration

For an intimate portrayal of family life on the Maine frontier, see Laurel Thatcher Ulrich, *A Midwife's Tale: The Life of Martha Ballard* (1990), which has also been made into a PBS dramatic documentary, *A Midwife's Tale* (1.5 hours). Additional materials on Ballard's experiences and women's lives are available on the Web at <http://www.pbs.org/amex/midwife> and <http://www.DoHistory.org>. Jan Lewis's *The Pursuit of Happiness: Family and Values in Jefferson's Virginia* (1983) explores the domestic and emotional lives of the paternalistic slave-owning gentry of the late eighteenth century in the Upper South, while Stephanie McCurry's *Masters of Small Worlds: Yeomen Households, Gender Relations, and the Political Culture of the Antebellum South Carolina Low Country* (1995) offers a brilliant analysis of yeomen families. Two recent studies of slave owners are William Kauffman Scarborough, *Masters of the Big House: Elite Slaveholders of the Mid-Nineteenth-Century South* (2003), and James David Miller, *South by Southwest: Planter Emigration and Identity in the Slave South* (2002).

Two stimulating analyses of the changing character of slavery and African American society are Ira Berlin, *Generations of Captivity: A History of African-American Slaves* (2003) and Peter Kolchin, *American Slavery, 1619–1877* (1993). Douglas R. Egerton, *Gabriel's Rebellion: The Virginia Slave Conspiracies of 1800 and 1802* (1995), traces the political and economic causes of Gabriel's movement and its near success. For primary documents that illustrate the ways in which African Americans acquired and transformed Protestant Christianity, log on to Documenting the American South: The Church in the Southern Black Community, at <http://docsouth.unc.edu/church/index.html>.

In *The Democratization of American Christianity* (1987) Nathan Hatch traces the impact of evangelical Protestantism on the life and politics of the early republic. Other fine overviews of American religion which offer dramatic portraits of revivalists, such as Charles

Grandison Finney, and explore the many links between religious enthusiasm and social reform are Mark A. Noll, *America's God: From Jonathan Edwards to Abraham Lincoln* (2003), and Bernard Weisberger, *They Gathered at the River* (1958). The Library of Congress offers a fine collection of material under Religion and the Founding of the American Republic at <http://www.loc.gov/exhibits/religion/>.

---

For definitions of key terms boldfaced in this chapter, see the glossary at the end of the book.

To assess your mastery of the material covered in this chapter, see the Online Study Guide at **bedfordstmartins.com/henrettaconcise**.

For map resources and primary documents, see **bedfordstmartins.com/henrettaconcise**.

---

# Part Three

## ECONOMIC REVOLUTION AND SECTIONAL STRIFE

### 1820–1877

| ECONOMY | SOCIETY | GOVERNMENT |
|---|---|---|
| The Economic Revolution Begins | A New Class Structure Emerges | Creating a Democratic Polity |
| **1820** ▸ Waltham textile factory (1814) <br> Erie Canal completed (1825); market economy expands | ▸ Business class emerges <br> Rural women and girls recruited as factory workers | ▸ Spread of universal white male suffrage <br> Rise of Jackson and Democratic Party |
| **1830** ▸ Protective tariffs aid owners and workers <br> Panic of 1837 <br> U.S. textile makers outcompete British | ▸ Mechanics form craft unions <br> Depression shatters labor movement | ▸ Anti-Masonic movement <br> Whig Party formed (1834); Second Party System emerges |
| **1840** ▸ Irish immigrants join labor force <br> *Commonwealth v. Hunt* (1842) legalizes unions <br> Manufacturing expands | ▸ Working-class districts emerge in cities <br> Irish and German immigration accelerates | ▸ Log Cabin campaign mobilizes voters <br> Antislavery parties: Liberty and Free-Soil |
| **1850** ▸ Surge of cotton output in South and of railroads in the North and Midwest <br> Panic of 1857 | ▸ Expansion of farm society into Midwest and Far West <br> Free labor ideology justifies inequality | ▸ Whig Party disintegrates; Republican Party founded (1854): Third Party System begins |
| **1860** ▸ Republicans enact policy agenda: Homestead Act, railroad aid, high tariffs, national banking | ▸ Emancipation Proclamation (1863) <br> Free blacks struggle for control of land | ▸ Thirteenth Amendment (1865) ends slavery <br> Fourteenth Amendment (1868) extends legal and political rights |
| **1870** ▸ Panic of 1873 | ▸ Rise of sharecropping in the South | ▸ Fifteenth Amendment extends vote to black men (1870) |

| CULTURE | SECTIONALISM |
|---|---|
| **Reforming People and Institutions** | **From Compromise to Civil War and Reconstruction** |
| ▶ American Colonization Society (1817)<br><br>Benevolent reform movements<br><br>Revivalist Charles Finney | ▶ Missouri Compromise (1820)<br><br>David Walker's *Appeal to the Colored Race* (1829) |
| ▶ Joseph Smith founds Mormonism<br><br>Female Moral Reform Society (1834)<br><br>Temperance crusade expands | ▶ Nullification crisis (1832)<br><br>W. L. Garrison forms American Anti-Slavery Society (1833) |
| ▶ Fourierist and other communal settlements founded<br><br>Seneca Falls convention (1848) | ▶ Texas annexation, Mexican War, and Wilmot Proviso (1846) increase sectional conflict |
| ▶ Harriet Beecher Stowe's *Uncle Tom's Cabin* (1852)<br><br>Anti-immigrant nativist movement | ▶ Compromise of 1850<br><br>Kansas-Nebraska Act (1854) and Bleeding Kansas<br><br>*Dred Scott* decision (1857) |
| ▶ U.S. Sanitary Commission and American Red Cross founded | ▶ South Carolina leads secession movement (1860)<br><br>Confederate States of America (1861–1865) |
| ▶ Freed African Americans create schools and churches | ▶ Compromise of 1877 ends Reconstruction |

In America, a French visitor remarked in 1839, "all is circulation, motion, and boiling agitation. Enterprise follows enterprise [and] riches and poverty follow." Indeed, the society was changing in basic ways. In 1820 the United States was predominately an agricultural nation; by 1877 it boasted one of the world's most powerful manufacturing economies. This profound transformation affected every aspect of life in the northern and midwestern states and brought important changes to the agricultural states of the south as well. Indeed, the growing social and cultural differences among the regions was an important cause of the political divisions which led ultimately to the tragedy of the Civil War.

**ECONOMY** Two revolutions in industrial production and the market system transformed the nation's economy. Factory owners used high-speed machines and a new system of labor discipline to boost production, and enterprising merchants employed a recently built network of canals and railroads to create a vast national market. The manufacturing sector produced an ever-increasing share of the country's wealth: from less than 5 percent in 1820 to more than 30 percent in 1877.

**SOCIETY** The new economic system spurred the creation of a class-based society. A wealthy elite of merchants, manufacturers, bankers, and other entrepreneurs emerged at the top of the social order and tried to maintain social stability through a paternalistic program of benevolent reform. However, a rapidly growing urban middle class created a distinct material and religious culture and spearheaded movements for radical social reform. Equally striking, an increasing number of propertyless workers, many of them immigrants from Germany and Ireland, now labored for wages and lived at the edge of poverty in urban ghettos.

**GOVERNMENT** Economic expansion and social diversity combined with the growth of political parties to create a more open, democratic polity. Farmers, workers, and entrepreneurs turned increasingly to government to seek improved transportation, shorter workdays, and special corporate charters. Catholic immigrants from Ireland and Germany also entered the political arena in order to protect their religion and culture from attacks by nativists and reformers. Led by Andrew Jackson, the Democratic Party advanced the interests of southern planters, farmers, and urban workers. It carried through a democratic political and constitutional revolution that cut governmental aid to financiers, merchants, and business corporations. To contend with the Democrats, the Whig Party (and, beginning in the 1850s, the Republican Party) devised an interrelated program of economic development, moral reform, and individual social mobility. This party competition engaged the energies of the electorate and unified the fragmented social order.

**CULTURE** During these decades, a series of reform movements, many with religious roots and goals, swept across America. Dedicated men and women preached the gospel of temperance, observance of Sunday, prison reform, and dozens of other causes. Some Americans pursued their social dreams in utopian communities, but most reformers worked within society. Two interrelated groups—abolitionists and women's rights activists—demanded radical changes in the existing social order: the immediate end of slavery and the overthrow of the patriarchal legal and political order. As southern planters increasingly defended slavery as a "positive good," antislavery advocates turned to political action. During the 1840s and 1850s, they campaigned for free soil in the western territories and alleged that a "slave power conspiracy" threatened free labor and republican values throughout the nation.

**SECTIONALISM** These economic, political, and cultural changes sharpened sectional divisions: the North developed into an urbanizing and industrializing society based on free labor, whereas the South remained a rural, slaveholding society dependent on the production of cotton. Following the Mexican War (1846–1848), northern and southern politicians could not agree on the issue of permitting slavery in the vast territories seized from Mexico. The election of Republican Abraham Lincoln prompted the secession of the South from the Union and, thereafter, civil war. The conflict became a total war, a struggle between two societies as well as two armies. Because of new technology and the mass mobilization of armies, the two sides endured unprecedented casualties and costs before the North emerged victorious.

The fruits of victory were substantial. During Reconstruction, the Republican Party ended slavery, imposed its economic policies and constitutional doctrines on the nation, and began to extend full democratic rights to the former slaves. Faced by massive resistance from white Southerners, northern leaders lacked the will to undertake the fundamental transformation of the economic and political order of the South required to provide African Americans with the full benefits of freedom.

# Chapter 10

# THE ECONOMIC REVOLUTION
## 1820–1860

Ten years ago we had *nothing*—now we have *everything*.

THE CATSKILL (N.Y.) RECORDER, 1828

$I$n 1804 life suddenly turned grim for eleven-year-old Chauncey Jerome of Connecticut. Following the death of his father, Jerome was hired out as an indentured servant to a farmer. Knowing that few farmers "would treat a poor boy like a human being," Jerome bought out his indenture by taking a job making dials for clocks and eventually ended up as a journeyman for clockmaker Eli Terry. A manufacturing wizard, Terry had designed an enormously popular desk-model clock with brass parts and turned Litchfield, Connecticut, into the clock-making center of the United States. Jerome followed in Terry's footsteps and in 1816 set up his own clock business. By organizing work more efficiently and using new machines that made interchangeable metal parts, Jerome drove down the price of a simple clock from $20 to $5 and then to less than $2. By the 1840s he was selling his clocks in England, the center of the Industrial Revolution; two decades later his workers were turning out two hundred thousand clocks a year, clear testimony to American enterprise. Together the Industrial Revolution and the Market Revolution created a new economy. By 1860 the United States was not only the world's leading exporter of cotton and wheat but also the third-ranked manufacturing nation behind Britain and France.

A European immigrant, Francis Grund, captured a key feature of Chauncey Jerome's experience and the American economic revolution. "Business is the very soul of an American: the fountain of all human felicity," Grund observed. "It is as if all America were but one gigantic workshop, over the entrance of which there is the blazing inscription, 'No admission here, except on business.'" Stimulated by the intensely work-oriented culture of early-nineteenth-century America, tens of thousands of artisan-inventors like Eli Terry and Chauncey Jerome propelled the country into a new economic era. As the editor of *Niles' Weekly Register* in Baltimore put it, there was an "almost universal ambition to get forward."

Not all Americans embraced the new ethic of enterprise, and many who did failed to share in the new prosperity. The spread of industry and commerce created a class-divided society that challenged the founders' vision of an agricultural republic with few distinctions of wealth. As the philosopher Ralph Waldo Emerson warned in 1839, "The invasion of Nature by Trade with its Money, its Credit, its Steam, [and] its Railroad threatens to . . . establish a new, universal Monarchy."

# The Coming of Industry: Northeastern Manufacturing

Industrialization came to the United States around 1790, as merchants and manufacturers reorganized work routines and built new factories. The rapid construction of turnpikes, canals, and railroads by state governments and private entrepreneurs allowed these manufactures to be sold throughout the land. Thanks to these innovations in production and transportation, the average per capita wealth of Americans increased by nearly 1 percent per year—30 percent over the course of a generation. Goods that once had been luxury items became part of everyday life.

## *Division of Labor and the Factory*

This impressive gain in living standards stemmed initially from changes in the organization of work. Consider the shoe industry. Traditionally, New England shoemakers worked in small wooden shacks called "ten-footers," where they turned leather hides into finished shoes and boots. During the 1820s and 1830s the merchants and manufacturers of Lynn, Massachusetts, took over the shoe industry by increasing output through an outwork system and a **division of labor**. The employers hired semiskilled journeymen and set them to work in large shops cutting the leather into soles and uppers. They sent out the upper sections to women shoe binders in dozens of Massachusetts towns who sewed in fabric linings. The manufacturers then had other journeymen assemble the shoes and return them to the central shop for inspection and packing. The new system turned an employer into a powerful "shoe boss" and eroded workers' control over their labor. "I guess you won't catch me to do that little thing again," vowed one woman shoe binder. Whatever the cost to workers, the division of labor dramatically increased the output of shoes and cut their price.

For products that were not suited to the outwork system, entrepreneurs created the modern factory, which concentrated production under one roof and divided the work into specialized tasks. For example, in the 1830s Cincinnati merchants built slaughterhouses that subdivided the process of butchering hogs into specific tasks. A simple system of overhead rails moved the hog carcasses past workers who split the animals, removed various organs, and trimmed the carcasses into pieces. Then packers stuffed the cuts of pork into barrels and pickled them to prevent spoilage. The Cincinnati system was so efficient and quick—sixty hogs per hour—that by the 1840s the city became known as "Porkopolis."

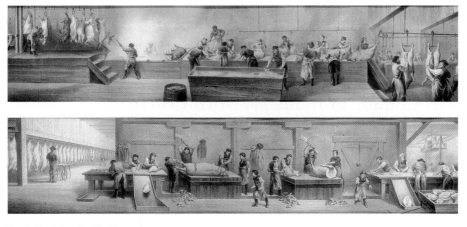

**Pork Packing in Cincinnati**

The only form of modern technology in this Cincinnati pork-packing plant was the overhead pulley system that carried hog carcasses past the workers. The plant's efficiency came from organization: a division of labor in which each worker performed a specific task. Such plants pioneered the design of the moving assembly lines that reached a high level of sophistication in the early twentieth-century automobile factories of Henry Ford. Cincinnati Historical Society.

Some factories boasted impressive new technology. The prolific Delaware inventor Oliver Evans built a highly automated flour mill driven by waterpower. His machinery lifted the grain to the top of the mill, cleaned the grain as it fell into hoppers, ground it into flour, conveyed the flour back to the top of the mill, and then cooled the flour during its descent into barrels. Evans's factory, remarked one observer, "was as full of machinery as the case of a watch." It needed only six men to mill one hundred thousand bushels of grain a year.

By the 1830s, factory owners used newly improved stationary steam engines to power their mills and manufactured new types of products. Previously, factories mainly processed agricultural goods—pork, leather, wool, and cotton; subsequently they fabricated metal goods and parts. Cyrus McCormick of Chicago used power-driven conveyor belts to assemble reaping machines, and Samuel Colt built an assembly line in Hartford, Connecticut, to produce his invention—the "six-shooter" revolver, as it became known. Such technological advances alarmed a team of British observers: "The contriving and making of machinery has become so common in this country, and so many heads and hands are at work with extraordinary energy, that . . . it is to be feared that American manufacturers will become exporters not only to foreign countries, but even to England."

## The Textile Industry and British Competition

British textile manufacturers were particularly worried about American competition. To protect its industrial leadership, the British government prohibited the export of textile machinery and the emigration of **mechanics** who knew how to build it. However, lured by high wages or offers of partnerships, thousands of British mechanics disguised themselves as ordinary laborers and set sail for the United States. By 1812 there were more than 300 British mechanics at work in the Philadelphia area alone.

Samuel Slater was the most important of the immigrants. Slater came to America in 1789 after working for Richard Arkwright, the inventor of the most advanced British machinery for spinning cotton. He reproduced Arkwright's innovations in merchant Moses Brown's cotton mill in Providence, Rhode Island; its opening in 1790 marks the advent of the American Industrial Revolution.

In competing with British mills, American manufacturers had the advantage of an abundance of natural resources. The nation's farmers produced a wealth of cotton and wool, and its rivers provided a cheap source of energy. As rivers cascaded downhill from the Appalachian foothills to the Atlantic coastal plain, they were easily harnessed to run power machinery. From Massachusetts to Delaware, industrial villages and towns sprang up along these waterways, dominated by massive textile mills—some as large as 150 feet long, 40 feet wide, and four stories high.

Nevertheless, British textile producers easily undersold their American competitors. Thanks to cheap shipping and low interest rates in Britain, they could import raw cotton from the United States, manufacture it into cloth, and sell it in America at a bargain price. Moreover, the well-established British companies could engage in cutthroat competition by slashing prices sharply to drive the new American firms out of business. The most important British advantage was cheap labor. Britain had a larger population—about 12.6 million in 1810 compared with 7.3 million Americans—and thousands of landless laborers who were willing to take low-paying factory jobs.

To offset these British advantages American entrepreneurs won assistance from the federal government. In 1816 Congress passed a tariff that protected manufacturers from low-cost imports of cotton cloth. In 1824 a new tariff levied a tax of 35 percent on imported iron products, higher-grade woolen and cotton textiles, and various agricultural products, and the rate rose to 50 percent in 1828. But in 1833, under pressure from southern planters, western farmers, and urban consumers—who wanted inexpensive imports—Congress began to reduce tariffs (see Chapter 11) and some American textile firms went bankrupt.

American producers used two other strategies to compete with their British rivals. First, they improved on British technology. In 1811 Francis Cabot Lowell, a wealthy Boston merchant, toured British textile mills. A charming young man, he flattered his hosts by asking many questions and secretly made detailed drawings of power machinery. Paul Moody, an experienced American mechanic, then copied the machines and made improvements. In 1814 Lowell joined with merchants Nathan Appleton and Patrick Tracy Jackson to form the Boston Manufacturing Company. Raising the staggering sum of $400,000, they built a textile plant on the Charles River in Waltham, Massachusetts. The Waltham factory was the first in America to perform all the operations of cloth making under one roof. Thanks to Moody's improvements, Waltham's power looms operated at higher speeds than British looms and needed fewer workers.

The second American strategy was to find less expensive workers. In the 1820s the Boston Manufacturing Company pioneered a labor system that became known as the "Waltham plan." The company recruited thousands of farm girls and women to work as textile operatives and provided them with boardinghouses and cultural activities such as evening lectures. To reassure anxious parents, the mill owners enforced strict curfews, prohibited alcoholic beverages, and required regular church attendance. At Lowell (1822), Chicopee (1823), and other sites in Massachusetts and New Hampshire, the company built new cotton factories based on the Waltham plan; other Boston-owned firms quickly followed suit.

By the early 1830s more than 40,000 New England women worked in textile mills primarily because (an observer noted) the wages were "more than could be obtained by the hitherto ordinary occupation of housework." Lucy Larcom became a textile operative at the age of eleven so that she would not be "a trouble or burden or expense" to her widowed mother. Other women operatives used their wages to pay off their fathers' farm mortgages, send their brothers to school, or accumulate a dowry for themselves. A few just had a good time. Susan Brown, a Lowell weaver,

**Mill Girl, c. 1850**

This fine daguerreotype (an early form of photography) shows a neatly dressed textile worker about twelve years old. The harsh working conditions in the mill have taken a toll on her spirit and body: the young girl's eyes and mouth show little joy or life and her hands are rough and swollen. She probably worked either as a knotter, tying broken threads on spinning jennies, or a warper, straightening out the strands of cotton or wool as they entered the loom. Jack Naylor Collection.

spent half of her earnings on food and lodging and the rest on plays, concerts, lectures, and a two-day excursion to Boston. Like most textile operatives, Brown soon tired of the monotony and never-ending rigor of factory labor—twelve hours a day, six days a week. After eight months she quit, lived at home for a spell, and then moved to another mill. Whatever the hardships, waged work gave young women a new sense of freedom and autonomy. "Don't I feel independent!" a mill worker wrote to her sister. "The thought that I am living on no one is a happy one indeed to me" (see American Voices, "Early Days at Lowell," p. 298).

The owners of the Boston Manufacturing Company were even happier. By combining improved technology, female labor, and tariff protection, they could undersell their British rivals. Their textiles were also cheaper than those manufactured in New York and Pennsylvania, where farmworkers were better paid than in New England and textile wages consequently were higher. Manufacturers in those states remained in business by using advanced technology to produce higher-quality cloth. Even Thomas Jefferson, the great champion of yeoman farming, was impressed. "Our manufacturers are now very nearly on a footing with those of England," he noted in 1825.

### American Mechanics and Technological Innovation

By the 1820s American-born craftsmen had replaced British immigrants at the cutting edge of technological innovation. Although few of these mechanics had a formal education, they now claimed respect as "men professing an ingenious art." In 1837 one such inventor, Richard Garsed, fashioned improvements that nearly doubled the speed of the power looms in his father's factory. By 1846 Garsed had patented a cam and harness device that allowed machines to weave fabrics such as damask (which contains elaborate designs).

In the Philadelphia region the most important inventors came from the remarkable Sellars family. Samuel Sellars Jr. invented a machine for twisting worsted woolen yarn. His son John devised more efficient ways of using waterpower to run the family's sawmills and built a machine to weave wire sieves. John's sons and grandsons built machine shops that turned out riveted leather fire hoses, paper-making equipment, and eventually locomotives. In 1824 the Sellars family and other mechanics founded the Franklin Institute in Philadelphia. Named after Benjamin Franklin, whom the mechanics admired for his scientific accomplishments and idealization of hard work, the Franklin Institute published a journal; provided high-school-level instruction in mechanics, chemistry, mathematics, and mechanical drawing; and organized annual fairs to exhibit new products. Craftsmen in Ohio and other states soon established their own mechanics' institutes, which disseminated technical knowledge and encouraged innovation. Around 1820 the United States Patent Office issued about two hundred patents on new inventions each year, mostly to gentlemen and merchants. By 1860 it was awarding four thousand patents annually, mostly to mechanics from modest backgrounds.

# Early Days at Lowell

## LUCY LARCOM

*L* *ucy Larcom (1824–1893) went to work in a textile mill in Lowell, Massachusetts, when she was eleven years old and remained there for a decade. She then migrated to Illinois with her sisters and a great tide of other New Englanders. In later life Larcom became a teacher and a writer; in her autobiography she described the contradictory impact of industrial labor— confining and yet liberating—on the lives of young women from farms and rural villages.*

I never cared much for machinery. The buzzing and hissing and whizzing of pulleys and rollers and spindles and flyers around me often grew tiresome. I could not see into their complications, or feel interested in them. But in a room below us we were sometimes allowed to peer in through a sort of blind door at the great waterwheel that carried the works of the whole mill. It was so huge we could only watch a few of its spokes at a time, and part of its dripping rim, moving with a slow, measured strength through the darkness that shut it in. It impressed me with something of the awe which comes to us in thinking of the great Power which keeps the mechanism of the universe in motion. . . .

We did not call ourselves ladies. We did not forget that we were working girls, wearing coarse aprons suitable to our work, and that there was some danger of our becoming drudges. I know that sometimes the confinement of the mill became very wearisome to me. In the sweet June weather I would lean far out of the window, and try not to hear the unceasing clash of sound inside. Looking away to the hills, my whole stifled being would cry out

*Oh, that I had wings!*

Still I was there from choice, and

*The prison unto which we doom*
*ourselves,*
*No prison is.*

I regard it as one of the privileges of my youth that I was permitted to grow up among these active, interesting girls, whose lives were not mere echoes of other lives, but had principle and purpose distinctly their own. Their vigor of character was a natural development. The New Hampshire girls who came to Lowell were descendants of the sturdy backwoodsmen who settled that State scarcely a hundred years before. Their grandmothers had suffered the hardships of frontier life. . . . Those young women did justice to their inheritance. They were earnest and capable; ready to undertake anything that was worth doing. My dreamy, indolent nature was shamed into activity among them. They gave me a larger, firmer ideal of womanhood. . . .

Country girls were naturally independent, and the feeling that at this new work the few hours they had of every-day leisure were entirely their own was a satisfaction to them. They preferred it to going out as "hired help." It was like a young man's pleasure in entering upon business for himself. Girls had never tried that experiment before, and they liked it. It brought out in them a dormant strength of character which the world did not previously see.

SOURCE: Lucy Larcom, *A New England Girlhood* (Boston: Houghton Mifflin, 1889), 153–55, 181–83, 196–200.

American craftsmen facilitated the rapid spread of the Industrial Revolution by pioneering the development of machine tools—machines for making other machines. Mechanics in the textile industry invented lathes, planers, and boring machines that turned out standardized parts for new spinning jennies and weaving looms. Moreover, the new jennies and looms were precise enough in design and construction to operate at higher speeds than British equipment.

Technological innovation swept through the rest of American manufacturing. In 1832 the mechanics employed by Samuel W. Collins in his Connecticut ax-making company built a vastly improved die-forging machine—a device that pressed and hammered hot metal into dies, or cutting forms. Using this machine, a worker could now make three hundred ax heads a day, as opposed to twelve using the old methods. In Richmond, Virginia, Welsh- and American-born mechanics made similar technical advances at the Tredegar Iron Works. The firearms industry witnessed major innovations. To produce thousands of guns for the federal government, Eli Whitney and his coworkers in Connecticut developed machine tools that produced interchangeable, precision-crafted parts. After Whitney's death his partner, John H. Hall, an engineer at the federal armory at Harpers Ferry, Virginia, built lathes to fashion gun stocks and an array of machine tools to work metal: turret lathes, milling machines, and precision grinders. Soon many manufacturers were using these machine tools to produce complicated manufacturing equipment with great speed, at low cost, and in large quantities.

With this expansion in the availability of machines, the American Industrial Revolution came of age. The sheer volume of output caused some products—Remington rifles, Singer sewing machines, and Yale locks—to become household names in the United States and abroad. After showing their machine-tooled goods at the Crystal Palace Exhibition in London in 1851 (the first major international display of industrial goods), Remington, Singer, and other American businesses built factories in Great Britain and soon dominated many European markets.

## Wage Workers and the Labor Movement

As the Industrial Revolution gathered momentum, it changed the nature of work and of workers' lives. Each decade, more and more Americans took jobs as wage-earning workers who had little security of employment or control over their working conditions.

Some wageworkers labored as journeymen in one of the traditional artisan crafts. These carpenters, stonecutters, masons, and cabinetmakers had specialized skills and a strong sense of craft identity. Consequently, they were able to form unions and bargain with their master-artisan employers. The journeymen's main concern was the increasing length of the workday, which kept them from their families and from educational opportunities. During the eighteenth century the workday in the building trades had averaged about twelve hours, including breaks for meals. By the 1820s masters were demanding a longer day during the summer, when it stayed light longer, while paying journeymen the old daily rate. In response, 600 carpenters in Boston went on strike in 1825, demanding a ten-hour workday, 6 A.M. to 6 P.M., with an hour each for breakfast and lunch. Although the Boston protest failed, in 1827 journeymen carpenters in Philadelphia won a similar strike and then joined the Mechanics' Union of Trade Associations. This citywide organization of fifty unions and 10,000 Philadelphia wageworkers demanded "a just balance of power . . . between all the various classes." To secure this goal, in 1828 the Philadelphia artisans founded the Working Men's Party, which campaigned for the abolition of banks, equal taxation, and a universal system of public education. By the mid-1830s building-trades workers had won a ten-hour workday from many employers and from the federal government at the Philadelphia navy yard.

Artisans whose occupations were threatened by industrialization were less successful. As aggressive entrepreneurs and machine technology changed the nature of production, shoemakers, hatters, printers, furniture makers, and weavers faced declining incomes, unemployment, and loss of status. To avoid the regimentation of factory work some artisans in these trades moved to small towns or set up specialized shops. In New York City, 800 highly skilled cabinetmakers owned small shops that made fashionable or custom-made furniture. In status and income they outranked a much larger group of 3,200 semitrained workers—derogatively called "botches"—who labored for wages in large factories making cheap, mass-produced tables and chairs. The new industrial system had divided the traditional artisan class into two groups: self-employed craftsmen and wage-earning workers.

In many industries wage earners banded together to form unions and bargain for better pay and working conditions. However, under English and American common law, such organizations were illegal—"a government unto themselves," in the words of a Philadelphia judge—because they interfered with an employer's authority over his "servant" and prevented other workers from hiring out for whatever wages they wished. Despite such legal obstacles, unions sprang up. In 1830 in Lynn, Massachusetts, journeymen shoemakers founded a Mutual Benefit Society, which quickly spread to other shoemaking centers. "The division of society into the producing and nonproducing classes," the journeymen explained, had made workers like themselves into a mere "commodity" whose labor could be bought and sold without regard for their welfare. As another group of workers put it, "The capitalist has no other interest in us, than to get as much labor out of us as possible. We are hired men, and hired men, like hired horses, have no souls." In 1834 local unions from Boston to Philadelphia formed the National Trades' Union, the first regional union of different trades.

Union leaders criticized the new industrial order by articulating an artisan-republican ideology that celebrated the labor and autonomy of working people. Pointing out that wage earners were becoming "slaves to a monied aristocracy," they condemned the new outwork and factory systems in which "capital and labor stand opposed." To restore a just society in which workers could "live as comfortably as others," they proposed a **labor theory of value**. This theory stated that the price of a good should reflect the labor required to make it and that most of the money from its sale should go to the producer (and not merchants and factory owners). Appealing to the spirit of the American Revolution, which had destroyed the aristocracy of birth, they called for a new revolution to destroy the aristocracy of capital. Armed with this artisan-republican ideology, in 1836 union men organized nearly fifty strikes for higher wages.

Women textile operatives were equally active. Competition in the cotton textile industry was fierce because the output of textiles grew faster than demand and prices fell. As profits declined, employers reduced workers' wages and imposed more stringent work rules. In 1828 women mill workers in Dover, New Hampshire, struck against new rules and won some relief; six years later more than 800 Dover women walked out to protest wage cuts. In Lowell, Massachusetts, 2,000 women operatives backed a strike by withdrawing their savings from an employer-owned bank. "One of the leaders mounted a pump," the *Boston Transcript* reported, "and made a flaming . . . speech on the rights of women and the iniquities of the 'monied aristocracy.'" When conditions did not improve, young New England women refused to enter the mills, and impoverished Irish (and later French Canadian) immigrants took their places.

By the 1850s workers faced the threat of unemployment. As machines produced more goods, the supply of manufactures exceeded the demand for them and prompted employers to lay off workers. One episode of overproduction preceded the Panic of 1857—a financial crisis sparked by speculative investments in railroads that went bankrupt—and resulted in a major recession. Unemployment rose to 10 percent, reminding Americans of the social costs of the new—and otherwise very successful—system of industrial production.

# The Market Revolution

As American factories and farms turned out more goods, merchants and legislators created faster and cheaper ways to get those products to consumers. Beginning in the 1820s they constructed a massive system of canals and roads that linked the Atlantic coast states with one another and with the new states in the trans-Appalachian West. This transportation system set in motion both a **Market Revolution** and a great migration of people. By 1860 nearly one-third of the nation's citizens lived in the Midwest (the five states carved out of the Northwest Territory—Ohio, Indiana, Illinois, Michigan, and Wisconsin—along with Missouri, Iowa, and Minnesota), where they created a complex society and economy that increasingly resembled that of the Northeast.

## Migration to the Southwest and the Midwest

As vast numbers of men and women migrated to the West, they abandoned farms and homes in the countryside of the Carolinas, Vermont, and New Hampshire.

Some migrant families sought enough land to settle their children on nearby farms and re-create traditional rural communities. Others were more entrepreneurial and hoped for greater profits from the fertile soil of the western territories. By 1840 about 5 million people lived west of the Appalachians.

As in the past the new pioneers migrated in three great streams. In the South plantation owners met the voracious demand for raw cotton by expanding production into Louisiana, Mississippi, and Alabama. "The Alabama Fever rages here with great violence," a North Carolina planter remarked, "and has carried off vast numbers of our Citizens." Subsequently, planters pushed on to Missouri (admitted in 1821) and Arkansas (1836).

Small-scale farmers from the Upper South, especially Virginia and Kentucky, formed another migrant stream as they crossed the Ohio River into the Northwest Territory. Some of these settlers were fleeing planter-dominated slave states. In a free community, thought Peter Cartwright, a Methodist lay preacher from southwestern Kentucky, "I would be entirely clear of the evil of slavery . . . [and] could raise my children to work where work was not thought a degradation." These southerners introduced corn and hog farming into Ohio, Indiana, and Illinois.

A third throng of migrants poured out of the overcrowded communities of New England. Thousands of settlers flowed first into upstate New York and then into the fertile farmlands of the Great Lakes basin, where they set up wheat farms in northern Ohio, northern Illinois, Michigan (admitted in 1837), Iowa (1846), and Wisconsin (1848) (Map 10.1).

To meet the demand for cheap farmsteads, in 1820 Congress reduced the price of federal land from $2.00 an acre to $1.25—just enough to cover the cost of the survey and sale. For $100 a farmer could buy eighty acres, the minimum required under federal law. By 1860 the population center of American society had shifted significantly to the west.

## The Transportation Revolution Forges Regional Ties

To enhance the "common wealth" of their citizens, the federal and state governments chartered private companies to build toll-charging turnpikes in well-populated areas and subsidized road construction in the West. The most significant feat was the National Road, which started in Cumberland, Maryland, passed Wheeling (then in Virginia) in 1818, crossed the Ohio River in 1833, and reached Vandalia, Illinois, in 1839. The National Road and other interregional highways carried migrants and their heavily loaded wagons to the West and herds of livestock destined for eastern markets. However, such long-distance road travel was slow and expensive.

To carry wheat, corn, and manufactured goods to far-flung markets, Americans developed a water-borne transportation system of unprecedented size, complexity, and cost. When the New York legislature approved the building of the Erie Canal in 1817, no artificial waterway in the United States was longer than 28 miles—a reflection of the huge capital cost and the lack of American engineering expertise.

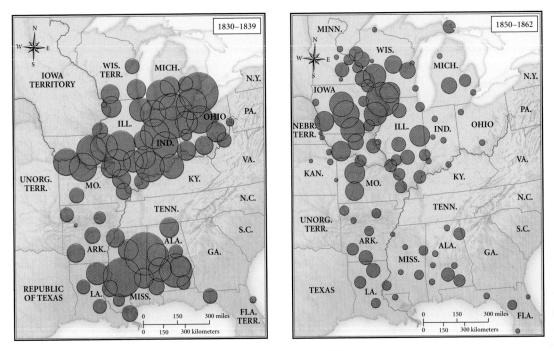

**MAP 10.1 Western Land Sales, 1830–1839 and 1850–1862**

The federal government set up offices to sell farmsteads to western settlers. During the 1830s the offices sold huge amounts of land in the corn and wheat belt of the Old Northwest (Ohio, Indiana, Illinois, and Michigan) and the cotton belt of the Old Southwest (especially Alabama and Mississippi). By the 1850s most government land sales were in the upper Mississippi River Valley (particularly Iowa and Wisconsin). Each circle centers on a government land office and depicts the relative amount of land sold at that office.

The New York project had three things in its favor: the vigorous support of New York City merchants, who wanted access to western markets; the backing of New York's governor, De Witt Clinton, who persuaded the legislature to finance the waterway from tax revenues, tolls, and bond sales to foreign investors; and the relative gentleness of the terrain west of Albany. Even so, the task was enormous. Workers—many of them Irish immigrants—had to dig out millions of cubic yards of soil, quarry thousands of tons of rock to build the huge locks that raised and lowered boats, and construct vast reservoirs to ensure a steady supply of water.

The first great engineering project in American history, the Erie Canal altered the ecology and the economy of an entire region. As towns and farming communities sprang up along the waterway, residents cut down millions of trees to provide wood for building, hemlock bark for tanning leather, and land for growing wheat and corn. Cows and sheep foraged on pastureland once occupied by forests, deer, and bears, and spring rains caused massive erosion of the denuded landscape. As one traveler noted, "the hills had been stripped of their timber so as to present their huge, rocky projections."

**Building the Erie Canal**

The success of the Erie Canal prompted the construction by 1860 of a vast canal system that was the precursor of the national railroad network of the late nineteenth century and the interstate highway system of the late twentieth century. Tens of thousands of workers—many of them Irish immigrants and free blacks—dug out thousands of miles of canals by hand and, with the aid of the simple hoists shown here, built hundreds of stone locks. The unknown artist who sketched this scene was more interested in the scale of the project than in the personalities of the faceless laborers who undertook this dangerous work. In the marshes near Syracuse, New York, a thousand workers fell ill with fever and many died.

Miriam and Ira D. Wallach Division of Art, Prints and Photographs. The New York Public Library. Astor, Lenox and Tilden Foundations.

The Erie Canal was an instant success. The first section, a stretch of 75 miles, opened in 1819 and immediately generated enough revenue to repay its cost. When the canal was completed in 1825, a 40-foot-wide ribbon of water stretched 364 miles from the Lake Erie port of Buffalo to Albany, where it joined the Hudson River for a 150-mile trip to New York City. After a trip on the canal, the novelist Nathaniel Hawthorne suggested that its water "must be the most fertilizing of all fluids, for it causes towns with their masses of brick and stone, their churches and theaters, their business and hubbub, their luxury and refinement, their gay dames and polished citizens, to spring up."

The Erie Canal brought prosperity to central and western New York by carrying wheat and meat to eastern cities and foreign markets. One-hundred-ton freight barges pulled by two horses moved along the canal at a steady 30 miles a day, cutting transportation costs and greatly accelerating the flow of goods. In 1818 the mills in Rochester had processed 26,000 barrels of flour; ten years later their output soared to 200,000 barrels and in 1840 to 500,000 barrels. Northeastern manufacturers used the canal to ship clothing, boots, and agricultural equipment to farm families throughout the Great Lakes basin and the Ohio Valley. In payment, the farmers sent grain, cattle, and hogs as well as raw materials (such as leather, wool, and hemp) to the East.

The spectacular benefits of the Erie Canal prompted a national canal boom. Civic and business leaders in Philadelphia and Baltimore proposed waterways to link their cities to the West. Copying New York's fiscal innovations, they persuaded their state governments to invest directly in canal companies or force state-chartered banks to do so. They also won state guarantees for canal bonds to encourage British and Dutch investors to buy them. Indeed, foreign investors provided almost three-quarters of the $400 million invested in canals by 1840. These waterways connected the Midwest with the great port cities of New York, Philadelphia, and Baltimore (via the Erie, Pennsylvania, and Chesapeake and Ohio Canals) and New Orleans (via the Ohio and Mississippi Rivers) (Map 10.2).

The steamboat, another product of the industrial age, ensured the success of the western transportation system. The engineer-inventor Robert Fulton had built the first American steamboat, the *Clermont*, which he navigated up the Hudson River in 1807. However, the first steamboats could not navigate shallow western rivers. During the 1820s engineers broadened the hulls of these boats, thereby enlarging their cargo capacity and giving them a shallower draft. The improved steamboats cut in half the cost of upstream river transport and, along with the canals, dramatically increased the flow of goods, people, and news into the interior. In 1830 a traveler or a letter from New York could go by water to Buffalo or Pittsburgh in less than a week and to Detroit or St. Louis in two weeks. Thirty years earlier the same journeys had taken twice as long.

The national government played a key role in the creation of this interregional system of transportation and communication. Following the passage of the Post Office Act of 1792, the mail network grew rapidly—to eight hundred post offices by 1800 and more than eight thousand by 1830—and safely carried thousands of letters and millions of dollars of banknotes from one end of the country to the other. The Supreme Court, headed by John Marshall, likewise encouraged interstate trade by striking down state restrictions on commerce. In the crucial case of *Gibbons v. Ogden* (1824) the Court voided a New York law that created a monopoly on steamboat travel into New York City and established the paramount authority of the federal government over interstate commerce (see Chapter 8). This decision meant that no local or state monopolies—or tariffs—would impede the flow of goods, services, and news across the nation.

Another product of industrial technology—the railroad—linked the Northeast and the Midwest. In 1852 canals carried twice the tonnage transported by railroads; within a decade, track mileage had increased dramatically and railroads became the main carriers of freight. Serviced by a vast network of locomotive and

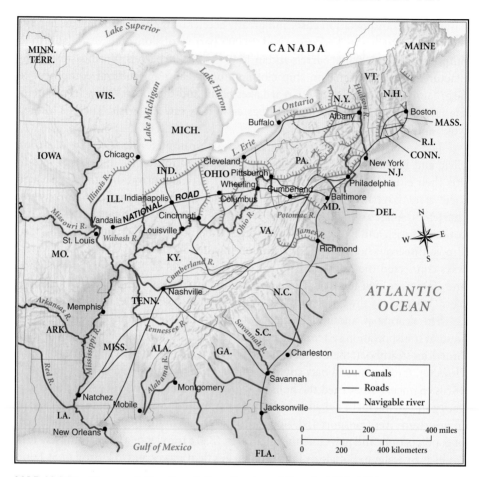

**MAP 10.2 The Transportation Revolution: Roads and Canals, 1820–1850**

By 1850 the United States had an efficient transportation system with three distinct parts. One system, composed of short canals and navigable rivers, carried cotton, tobacco, and other products from the up-country of the southern seaboard states into the Atlantic commercial system. A second system, centered on the Erie, Chesapeake and Ohio, and Pennsylvania Mainline Canals, linked the major seaport cities of the Northeast to the vast trans-Appalachian region. Finally, a set of regional canals in the Old Northwest connected most of the Great Lakes region to the Ohio and Mississippi Rivers and New Orleans.

FOR MORE HELP ANALYZING THIS MAP, see the Online Study Guide at **bedfordstmartins.com/henrettaconcise**.

freight-car repair shops, the Erie Railroad, the Pennsylvania Railroad, and other long-distance carriers connected the Atlantic ports—New York, Philadelphia, and Boston—with the Great Lakes cities of Cleveland and Chicago. As the railroad boom of the 1850s extended lines into the countryside and lowered the cost of

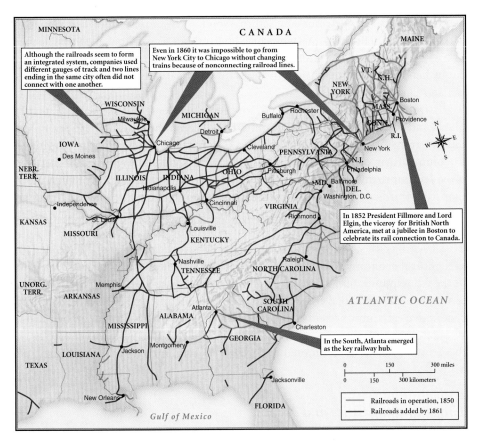

Although the railroads seem to form an integrated system, companies used different gauges of track and two lines ending in the same city often did not connect with one another.

Even in 1860 it was impossible to go from New York City to Chicago without changing trains because of nonconnecting railroad lines.

In 1852 President Fillmore and Lord Elgin, the viceroy for British North America, met at a jubilee in Boston to celebrate its rail connection to Canada.

In the South, Atlanta emerged as the key railway hub.

Railroads in operation, 1850
Railroads added by 1861

**MAP 10.3 Railroads of the North and South, 1850–1860**

In the decade before the Civil War, entrepreneurs in the Northeast and the Midwest laid thousands of miles of new railroad lines, which provided those regions with extensive and dense transportation systems that stimulated economic development. The South built a much simpler system. In all regions, railroad companies used different track gauges, which hindered the efficient flow of traffic.

shipping grain to market, settlers established 250,000 new farms (covering 19 million acres) on the prairie lands of the midwestern states (Map 10.3).

Many of the first migrants to the Midwest came from New England and relied on manufactured goods made in Britain or in the Northeast. They bought high-quality shovels and spades fabricated at the Delaware Iron Works, axes forged in Connecticut factories, and steel horseshoes manufactured in Troy, New York. By the 1830s midwestern entrepreneurs were producing these and other goods. As a blacksmith in Grand Detour, Illinois, John Deere made his first steel plow out of old saws in 1837; ten years later he opened a factory in Moline, Illinois, that used **mass-production** techniques. Deere's steel plows were stronger than the cast-iron models developed earlier in New York by Jethro Wood. Other midwestern companies—McCormick and Hussey—mass-produced self-raking reapers that allowed a farmer to harvest twelve acres of grain a day (rather than the two or three acres he could cut by hand) and vastly increased the amount of wheat available for export to eastern and European markets.

Extraregional trade also linked southern planters to northeastern textile plants and foreign markets. This commerce bolstered the wealth of the South but did not transform its economic and social order. Southern investors continued to commit their capital to land and slaves, which yielded high profits and also provided impressive increases in output. By the 1840s the South produced more than two-thirds of the world's cotton and accounted for almost two-thirds of American exports. However, except in Richmond, Virginia, and a few other places, planters did not invest their cotton profits in local manufacturing industries. Lacking cities, factories, and highly trained workers, the South remained an agricultural economy that provided high living standards only to the 25 percent of the white population who owned plantations and slaves. By 1860 the southern economy generated an average annual per capita income of $103, while the more productive economic system of the Northeast created an average income of $141. The national system of commerce left unchanged the agricultural character of the South even as it promoted a diversified economy in the Northeast and Midwest.

## The Growth of Cities and Towns

The expansion of industry and trade led to a dramatic increase in the American urban population. In 1820 there were only 58 towns with more than 2,500 inhabitants; by 1840 there were 126 urban centers, located mostly in the Northeast and Midwest. During those two decades the total number of city dwellers grew fourfold, from 443,000 to 1,844,000.

The most rapid growth occurred in the new industrial towns that sprang up along the fall line (the point at which rivers began a rapid descent to the coastal plain). In 1822 the Boston Manufacturing Company built a complex of mills in the sleepy Merrimack River village of East Chelmsford, Massachusetts, and quickly transformed it into the bustling textile factory town of Lowell. Hartford, Connecticut; Trenton, New Jersey; and Wilmington, Delaware, also became urban centers, as mill owners exploited the waterpower of their rivers and recruited workers from the countryside.

Western commercial cities such as New Orleans, Pittsburgh, Cincinnati, and Louisville grew almost as rapidly. These cities expanded because of their location at points where goods were transferred from one mode of transport, such as canal boats or farmers' wagons, to another, such as steamboats or sailing vessels. As the midwestern population grew during the 1830s and 1840s, St. Louis and Detroit also emerged as dynamic centers of commerce. Their merchants and bankers developed the marketing, provisioning, and financial services that were essential to farmers and small-town merchants in the surrounding countryside.

Within a few decades these midwestern commercial hubs—joined by Buffalo, Cleveland, and Chicago—became manufacturing centers as well. Maximizing these cities' locations as key junctions for railroad lines and steamboats, entrepreneurs built docks, warehouses, flour mills, and packing plants and provided work for hundreds of artisans and factory laborers. In 1846 Cyrus McCormick moved his reaper factory from western Virginia to Chicago to be closer to his midwestern customers. St. Louis and Chicago were the fastest-growing boom towns and by 1860 had become the nation's third and fourth largest cities, respectively, after New York and Philadelphia.

The old Atlantic seaports—Boston, Philadelphia, Baltimore, Charleston, and especially New York City—remained important for their foreign commerce and, increasingly, as centers of finance and manufacturing. The New York metropolis grew at a phenomenal rate; between 1820 and 1860 its population quadrupled to more than 800,000 as tens of thousands of German and Irish immigrants poured into the city. Drawing on the abundant supply of labor, New York became a center of small-scale manufacturing and the ready-made clothing industry, which relied on the labor of thousands of low-paid seamstresses. "The wholesale clothing establishments are . . . absorbing the business of the country," a "Country Tailor" complained to the New York *Tribune*, "casting many an honest and hardworking man out of employment [and allowing] . . . the large cities to swallow up the small towns."

New York's growth stemmed primarily from its dominant position in foreign and domestic trade. It had the best harbor in the United States and, thanks to the Erie Canal, was the best gateway to the interior for manufactures and the best outlet for shipments of western grain. Exploiting the city's prime location, in 1818 four Quaker merchants founded the Black Ball Line, which carried cargo, people, and mail on a regular schedule between New York and the European ports of Liverpool, London, and Le Havre. New York merchants likewise dominated trade with the newly independent Latin American nations of Brazil, Peru, and Venezuela. New York–based traders took over the cotton trade by offering finance, insurance, and shipping to export merchants in southern ports. By 1840 the port of New York handled almost two-thirds of foreign imports into the United States, almost half of all foreign trade, and much of the immigrant traffic.

# Changes in the Social Structure

The Industrial and Market Revolutions improved the material lives of many Americans by enabling them to live in larger houses, cook on iron stoves, and wear better-made clothes. But the new economic order created distinct social classes: a wealthy industrial and commercial elite, a substantial urban middle class, and a mass of propertyless wage earners. By creating a class-divided society, industrialization posed a momentous challenge to American republican ideals.

## The Business Elite

Before industrialization, white Americans were members of various ranks, with "notable" families ruling over the "lower orders." However, in rural society the different ranks shared a common culture: gentlemen farmers talked easily with yeomen about crop yields, while their wives conversed about the art of quilting. In the South humble tenants and aristocratic slave owners shared the same amusements: gambling, cockfighting, and horse racing. Rich and poor attended the same Quaker meetinghouse or Presbyterian church. "Almost everyone eats, drinks, and dresses in the same way," a European visitor to Hartford, Connecticut, reported in 1798, "and one can see the most obvious inequality only in the dwellings."

The Industrial Revolution shattered this traditional order and created a fragmented society composed of distinct regions, classes, and cultures. Thus, the new economic system pulled many Americans into large cities, thereby accentuating the differences between rural and urban life. Moreover, it made a few city residents—the business elite of merchants, manufacturers, bankers, and landlords—very rich. In 1800 the top 10 percent of the nation's families owned about 40 percent of the wealth; by 1860 the wealthiest 10 percent owned nearly 70 percent. In large cities—New York, Chicago, Baltimore, New Orleans—the richest 1 percent of the population held more than 40 percent of all tangible property—such as land and buildings—and an even higher share of intangible property—such as stocks and bonds.

Government tax policies facilitated this accumulation of wealth. The U.S. Treasury raised most of its revenue from tariffs—taxes on imported goods such as textiles that were purchased mostly by ordinary citizens. State and local governments also favored the wealthier classes. They usually taxed real estate (farms, city lots, and buildings) and tangible personal property (such as furniture, tools, and machinery) but almost never taxed the stocks and bonds owned by the rich or the inheritances they passed on to their children.

Cities that were once relatively homogenous took on an increasingly fragmented character. Over time the wealthiest families consciously set themselves apart from the rest of the population. They dressed in well-tailored clothes, rode in fancy carriages, and lived in expensively furnished houses tended by butlers, cooks, and other servants. The women no longer socialized with those of lesser wealth, and the men no longer labored side by side with their journeymen. Instead, they became managers and directors and used trusted subordinates to issue orders to hundreds of factory operatives. Increasingly merchants, manufacturers, and bankers chose to live in separate residential areas, often at the edge of the city. The desire for greater privacy by privileged families and the massive flow of immigrants into other districts created cities that were divided geographically along the lines of class, race, and ethnicity.

## The Middle Class

Standing between wealthy owners at one end of the urban social spectrum and non-propertied wage earners at the other was a growing middle class—the product of the Market Revolution. As a Boston printer explained, the bulk of the "middling class" was made up of "the farmers, the mechanics, the manufacturers, the traders, who carry on professionally the ordinary operations of buying, selling, and exchanging merchandize." Other members of the middle class came from various professional groups—building contractors, lawyers, and surveyors—who suddenly found their services in great demand and financially profitable. Middle-class business owners, employees, and professionals were most numerous in the Northeast, where in the 1840s they numbered about 30 percent of the population, but they could be found even in the agrarian South. In 1854 in the boom town of Oglethorpe, Georgia (population 2,500), there were no fewer than eighty "business houses" and eight hotels.

The growing size, wealth, and cultural influence of the middle class stemmed from a dramatic rise in urban prosperity. Between 1830 and the Panic of 1857, the per capita income of Americans increased by about 2.5 percent a year, a remarkable rate never since matched. This surge in income, along with the availability of inexpensive mass-produced goods, facilitated the creation of a distinct middle-class, urban culture. Middle-class husbands earned enough to support their families and saved about 15 percent of their income, which they used to buy a well-built house in a "respectable part of town." They purchased handsome clothes and drove about town in smart carriages. Relieved from the burden of labor, their wives became purveyors of culture as they bought books and pianos as well as commodious furniture for their front parlors. Rather than hiring servants to perform menial tasks, middle-class families turned to the new industrial technology. They outfitted their residences with furnaces that heated water for bathing and for radiators that warmed entire rooms; cooking stoves with ovens; and treadle-operated sewing machines. Urban families could keep their perishable food in iceboxes, which ice-company wagons filled periodically, and buy many varieties of packaged goods. As early as 1825 the Underwood Company of Boston was marketing well-preserved Atlantic salmon in jars.

If material comfort was one distinguishing mark of the middle class, moral and mental discipline was another. To pass on their status to their children, successful parents usually provided them with a high school education (in an era when most white children received only five years of schooling). Ambitious parents were equally concerned with their children's character and stressed discipline, morality, and hard work. Many American Protestants had long believed that diligent work in an earthly "calling" was a duty owed to God. Now the business elite and the middle class gave this idea a secular twist. They celebrated work as the key to a higher standard of living for the nation and social mobility for the individual.

**Middle-Class Family Life, 1836**

The family of Azariah Caverly boasted many of the amenities of middle-class life—handsome clothes, finely decorated furniture, and a striking floor covering. Underlining the social conventions of the time, the husband and his son hold a newspaper and a square, symbolizing the worlds of commerce and industry, while the wife and her daughter are pictured next to a Bible, indicating their domestic and moral vocations. New York State Historical Association, Cooperstown, NY.

FOR MORE HELP ANALYZING THIS IMAGE, see the Online Study Guide at **bedfordstmartins.com/henrettaconcise**.

Benjamin Franklin gave classical expression to the secular work ethic in his *Autobiography*, which was published in full in 1818 and immediately found a huge audience. Heeding Franklin's suggestion that an industrious man would become a rich one, tens of thousands of young American men worked hard, saved their money, adopted temperate habits, and practiced honesty in their business dealings. Countless magazines, children's books, self-help manuals, and novels taught the same lessons. The ideal of the **"self-made man"** became a central theme of American popular culture. Just as a rural-producer ethic had united the social ranks in pre-1800 America, this new goal of personal achievement tied together the upper and middle classes of the new industrializing society. Knowing that many affluent families had risen from modest beginnings, middle-class men and women took them as models and shunned the rapidly increasing numbers of working families who owned nothing and struggled just to survive.

## Urban Workers and the Poor

As thoughtful business leaders surveyed their society, they concluded that the old yeoman ideal of independent producers no longer seemed possible. "Entire independence ought not to be wished for," Ithamar A. Beard, the paymaster of the Hamilton Manufacturing Company, told a mechanics' association in 1827. "In large manufacturing towns, many more must fill subordinate stations and must be under the immediate direction and control of a master or superintendent, than in the farming towns."

Beard had a point. In 1840 all of the nation's slaves and about half of its native-born free workers were laboring for others rather than for themselves. The bottom 10 percent of the white wage earners consisted of casual workers—those hired on a short-term basis for the most arduous jobs. Poor women washed clothes, while their husbands and sons carried lumber and bricks for construction projects, loaded ships, and dug out dirt and stones to build canals. When they could find work, these men earned "their dollar *per diem*," an "Old Inhabitant" wrote to the *Baltimore American*, but he cautioned that those workers could never save enough "to pay rent, buy fire wood and eatables" when the harbor froze up. During business depressions they bore the brunt of unemployment, and even in the best of times their jobs were temporary and dangerous.

Other laborers had greater security of employment, but few were prospering. In Massachusetts in 1825 the daily wage of an unskilled worker was about two-thirds that of a mechanic; two decades later it was less than half as much. The 18,000 native-born and immigrant women who made men's clothing in New York City in the 1850s earned less than $80 a year. Such meager wages barely paid for food and rent, so many wage earners were unable to take advantage of the rapidly falling prices of manufactured goods. Only the most fortunate working-class families could afford to educate their children, buy an apprenticeship for their sons, or accumulate small dowries so that their daughters could marry men with better prospects. Most families sent their children out to work, and the death of a parent often threw the survivors into dire poverty. As a charity worker noted, "What can a bereaved widow do, with 5 or 6 little children, destitute of every means of support but what her own hands can furnish (which in a general way does not amount to more than 25 cents a day)."

Over time, their poverty forced these urban workers to move into dilapidated housing or undesirable neighborhoods. Single men and women lived in crowded boardinghouses, while families jammed themselves into tiny apartments in the basements and attics of small houses. As immigrants poured into the nation after 1840, urban populations soared and developers squeezed more and more dwellings and foul-smelling outhouses onto a single lot. Venturing into the slums of New York City in the 1850s, shocked state legislators found gaunt, shivering people with "wild ghastly faces" living amid "hideous squalor and deadly effluvia, the dim, undrained courts oozing with pollution, the dark, narrow stairways, decayed with age, reeking with filth, overrun with vermin."

Living in such distressing conditions, many wage earners turned to the dubious solace of alcohol. Beer and rum had long been standard fare in many American rituals: patriotic ceremonies, work breaks, barn raisings, and games. But during the 1820s the consumption of intoxicating beverages and alcoholism throughout the population reached new heights. Heavy drinking killed Daniel Tomkins, vice president under James Monroe, and undermined Henry Clay's bid for the presidency. It had an equally devastating impact on urban wage earners. While Methodist artisans and ambitious craft workers "swore off" liquor to protect their work skills, health, and finances, other workers began to drink heavily on the job—and not just during the traditional 11 A.M. and 4 P.M. "refreshers." As a baker recalled, "One man was stationed at the window to watch, while the rest drank." Long before the arrival of spirit-drinking Irish and beer-drinking German immigrants, there were grogshops on almost every block in working-class districts. These saloons became focal points of disorder. Unrestrained drinking by young men led to fistfights, brawls, and robberies; the urban police forces, consisting of low-paid watchmen and untrained constables, were unable to contain the lawlessness.

### The Benevolent Empire

The disorder among native-born urban wage earners sparked concern among well-to-do Americans. Inspired by the religious ideal of benevolence, they created a number of organizations that historians refer to collectively as the **"Benevolent Empire."** During the 1820s Congregational and Presbyterian ministers united with like-minded merchants and their wives to launch a program of social regulation. Their purpose, announced leading Presbyterian minister Lyman Beecher, was to restore "the moral government of God." The reformers introduced new forms of moral discipline into their own lives and tried to infuse them into the lives of working people as well. They would regulate popular behavior—by persuasion if possible, by law if necessary.

Although the Benevolent Empire targeted age-old evils such as drunkenness, prostitution, and crime, its methods were new. Instead of relying on church sermons and moral suasion by community leaders, the reformers set out to institutionalize charity and systematically combat evil. They established large-scale organizations, such as the Prison Discipline Society and the American Society for the Promotion of Temperance, among many others. Each organization had a managing staff, a network of hundreds of chapters and thousands of volunteer members, and a newspaper.

Often working in concert, these benevolent groups set out to improve society. First, they encouraged people to lead well-disciplined lives by campaigning for temperance and regular habits. They persuaded local governments to ban carnivals of drink and dancing, such as Negro Election Day (mock festivities in which African Americans symbolically took over the government), which had been enjoyed by whites as well as blacks. Second, they devised new institutions to assist dependent people and control those whom they considered threats to society. Reformers provided homes of refuge for abandoned children and asylums for insane individuals, who previously had been confined by their families in attics and cellars. They also campaigned to end corporal punishment and to rehabilitate criminals in new penitentiaries designed to modify antisocial behavior.

Women were an important part of the Benevolent Empire. Since the 1790s upper-class women had sponsored charitable organizations such as the Society for the Relief of Poor Widows with Small Children, founded in New York by Isabella Graham, a devout Presbyterian widow. Her daughter Joanna Bethune set up other charitable institutions, including the Orphan Asylum Society and the Society for the Promotion of Industry, which found jobs for hundreds of poor women as spinners and seamstresses.

Some reformers believed that the greatest threat to the "moral government of God" was the decline of the traditional Sabbath. As commerce increased, merchants and storekeepers conducted business on Sundays and urban saloons provided drink and entertainment. To halt such activities, in 1828 Lyman Beecher and other ministers formed the General Union for Promoting the Observance of the Christian Sabbath. General Union chapters—replete with women's auxiliaries—sprang up from Maine to the Ohio Valley. To rally Christians to their cause, the General Union demanded repeal of a law Congress had enacted in 1810 allowing mail to be transported—though not delivered—on Sunday. Its members also boycotted shipping companies that did business on the Sabbath and campaigned for municipal laws forbidding games and festivals on the Lord's day.

The program of the Benevolent Empire aroused controversy. Workers who labored twelve or fourteen hours a day for six days a week refused to spend their one day of leisure in meditation and prayer. Shipping company managers demanded that the Erie Canal provide lockkeepers on Sundays and joined those Americans who argued that using laws to enforce a particular set of moral beliefs was "contrary to the free spirit of our institutions." When some evangelical reformers proposed to teach Christianity to slaves, many white southerners were outraged. Such popular resistance or indifference limited the success of the Benevolent Empire.

## Revivalism and Reform

The Presbyterian minister Charles Grandison Finney found a new way to propagate religious values among Americans. Finney was not part of the traditional religious elite. Born into a poor farming family in Connecticut, he hoped to join the new middle class as a lawyer. But in 1823 Finney underwent an intense conversion experience and decided to become a minister. Beginning in towns along the Erie Canal, the young minister conducted emotional revival meetings that stressed conversion rather than instruction and discipline. Repudiating traditional Calvinist beliefs, he maintained that God would welcome any sinner who submitted to the Holy Spirit. Finney's ministry drew on—and greatly accelerated—the Second Great Awakening, the wave of Protestant revivalism that had begun after the Revolution (see Chapter 9).

**Charles Finney, Evangelist
(1792–1875)**

When this portrait was painted in 1834, Finney was forty-two years old and at the height of his career as an evangelist. Handsome and charismatic, Finney had just led a series of enormously successful revivals in Rochester, New York, and other cities along the Erie Canal. In 1835 he established a theology department at the newly founded Oberlin College in Ohio, where he helped train a genera-tion of ministers and served as its president from 1851 to 1866.

Oberlin College Archives.

Finney's message that "God has made man a moral free agent" who could choose salvation was particularly attractive to members of the new middle class, who had already chosen to improve their material lives. But he became famous for converting those at the ends of the social spectrum: the haughty rich, who had placed themselves above God, and the abject poor, who seemed lost to drink and sloth. Finney celebrated their common fellowship in Christ and identified them spiritually with pious middle-class respectability.

Finney's most spectacular triumph came in 1830, when he moved his revivals from small towns to Rochester, New York, now a major milling and commercial city on the Erie Canal. Preaching every day for six months and promoting group prayer meetings in family homes, he won over the influential merchants and manufactur-ers of Rochester, who pledged to reform their lives and those of their workers. They promised to attend church, give up intoxicating beverages, and work hard. To encourage their employees to follow suit, wealthy businessmen founded a Free Presbyterian church—"free" because members did not have to pay for pew space. Other evangelical Protestants founded similar churches to serve transient canal la-borers, and pious businessmen set up a savings bank to encourage thrift among the working classes. Meanwhile, Finney's wife, Lydia, and other pious middle-class women carried the Christian message to the wives of the unconverted, set up Sunday schools for poor children, and formed the Female Charitable Society to as-sist the unemployed.

Finney's efforts to create a harmonious community of morally disciplined Christians were not completely successful. Skilled workers who belonged to strong crafts organizations—boot makers, carpenters, stonemasons, and boat builders—argued that they needed higher wages and schools more urgently than sermons and prayers. And Finney's revival seldom attracted poor people, especially the Irish Catholic immigrants who had recently begun arriving in Rochester and other northeastern cities and who hated Protestants as religious heretics and as their political oppressors in Ireland.

Ignoring this resistance, revivalists from New England to the Midwest copied Finney's evangelical message and techniques. In New York City, the wealthy silk merchants Arthur and Lewis Tappan founded a magazine, *The Christian Evangelist*, which promoted Finney's ideas. The revival swept through Pennsylvania, North Carolina, Tennessee, and Indiana where, a convert reported, "you could not go upon the street and hear any conversation, except upon religion." The success of the revival "has been so general and thorough," concluded a Presbyterian general assembly, "that the whole customs of society have changed."

The **temperance movement** proved to be the most effective arena for evangelical social reform. In 1832 evangelicals gained control of the American Temperance Society; soon the society boasted two thousand chapters and more than 200,000 members. The society employed the methods that had worked so well in the revivals—group confession and prayer, a focus on the family and the spiritual role of women, and sudden, emotional conversion—and took them into every northern town and southern village. On one day in New York City in 1841, more than 4,000 people took the temperance "pledge." All across the land, the consumption of spirits fell dramatically, from five gallons per person in 1830 to two gallons in 1845 (see American Voices, "The Vice of Intemperance," p. 318).

Evangelical reformers celebrated religion as the moral foundation of the American work ethic. Laziness and drinking could not be cured by following Benjamin Franklin's method of self-discipline, they argued; rather, people had to experience the profound change of heart achieved through religious conversion. This evangelical message fostered individual enterprise and moral discipline not only among middle-class Americans but also among many wage earners. Thus, religion and the ideology of social mobility served as powerful cement that held society together in the face of the disarray created by the market economy, industrial enterprise, and cultural diversity.

## Immigration and Cultural Conflict

Cultural diversity stemmed in part from a vast wave of immigrants. Between 1840 and 1860 about 2 million Irish, 1.5 million Germans, and 750,000 Britons poured into the United States. Most immigrants avoided the South because they opposed slavery, shunned blacks, or feared competition from enslaved workers. Many German migrants settled in the midwestern states of Wisconsin, Iowa, and Missouri. Other

**AMERICAN VOICES**

## The Vice of Intemperance

### JOHN GOUGH

*John Gough (1817–1886) was twelve years old when his impoverished English parents shipped him to New York City, where he found work as a bookbinder—and eventually turned to drink. In 1842, at age twenty-five, Gough converted to temperance. For the next four decades he used his eloquence as a lecturer—and his considerable talents as an actor—to command high fees and persuade thousands to join the temperance movement. The following selection is taken from his* Autobiography *(1869).*

Will it be believed that I again sought refuge in rum? Yet so it was. Scarcely had I recovered from the fright, than I sent out, procured a pint of rum, and drank it all in less than an hour. And now came upon me many terrible sensations. Cramps attacked me in my limbs, which racked me with agony; and my temples throbbed as if they would burst. . . . Then came on the drunkard's remorseless torturer—delirium tremens, in all its terrors, attacked me. For three days I endured more agony than pen could describe, even were it guided by the mind of Dante. . . . I was at one time surrounded by millions of monstrous spiders, that crawled slowly over every limb, whilst the beaded drops of perspiration would start to my brow, and my limbs would shiver until the bed rattled. . . . All at once, whilst gazing at a frightful creation of my distempered mind, I seemed struck with sudden blindness. I knew a candle was burning in the room, but I could not see it—all was so pitchy dark. . . . And then the scene would change: I was falling—falling swiftly as an arrow—far down into some terrible abyss. . . .

By the mercy of God, I survived this awful seizure; and when I rose, a weak, broken-down man, and surveyed my ghastly features in the glass, I thought of my mother, and asked myself how I had obeyed the instructions received from her lips, and to what advantage I had turned the lessons she taught me. I remembered her countless prayers and tears. . . . Oh! how keen were my rebukes; and, in the excitement of the moment, I resolved to lead a better life, and abstain from the accursed cup.

For about a month, terrified by what I had suffered, I adhered to my resolution; then my wife came home, and, in my joy at her return, I flung my good resolutions to the wind, and, foolishly fancying that I could now restrain my appetite, which had a whole month remained in subjugation, I took a glass of brandy. That glass aroused the slumbering demon, who would not be satisfied by so tiny a libation. Another and another succeeded, until I was again far advanced in the career of intemperance. The night of my wife's return, I went to bed intoxicated.

SOURCE: David Brion Davis, ed., *Antebellum American Culture: An Interpretive Anthology* (Lexington, MA: Heath, 1979), 402–3.

Germans and most of the Irish settled in the Northeast, where by 1860 they accounted for nearly one-third of white adults.

The immigrants were a diverse lot. The British were primarily Protestant and relatively prosperous; their ranks included many trained professionals, propertied farmers, and skilled workers. Many German immigrants also came from property-owning farming and artisan families and could afford to buy land in America. The poorest migrants were Irish peasants and laborers, who were fleeing a famine caused by severe overpopulation and a devastating blight on the potato crop. Arriving in dire poverty, the Irish settled in the cities of New England and New York and took low-paying jobs in factories and construction projects and as servants in private residences. Many Irish families lived in crowded tenements with primitive sanitation systems and were the first to die in epidemics. In the summer of 1849 a cholera epidemic took the lives of thousands of poor immigrants in St. Louis and New York City.

In times of hardship and sorrow, immigrants turned to their churches. Many Germans and virtually all the Irish were Catholics, and they fueled the growth of the Catholic Church. In 1840 there were sixteen Catholic dioceses and seven hundred churches in the United States; by 1860 the number had increased to forty-five dioceses and twenty-five hundred churches. Under the guidance of their priests and bishops, Catholics built an impressive network of institutions—charitable societies, orphanages, militia companies, parochial schools, and political organizations—that helped them maintain both their religion and their Irish or German identity.

Because of the Protestant religious fervor stirred up by the Second Great Awakening, Catholic immigrants met with widespread hostility. A rash of anti-Catholic publications greeted the first Irish immigrants in the 1830s. One of the most militant critics of Catholicism was the artist and inventor Samuel F. B. Morse (who would later make the first commercial adaptation of the telegraph). In 1834 Morse published *Foreign Conspiracy against the Liberties of the United States*, which warned of a Catholic threat to American republican institutions. Morse believed that Catholic immigrants would obey the dictates of Pope Pius IX, who had condemned republicanism as a false political ideology based on the sovereignty of the people rather than on the sovereignty of God. Republican-minded Protestants of many denominations shared Morse's fears, and *Foreign Conspiracy* became their textbook.

The social tensions stemming from industrialization also intensified anti-Catholic sentiment. Unemployed Protestant mechanics and factory workers joined mobs that attacked Catholics and accused them of taking jobs and driving down wages; other Protestants organized Native American Clubs, which called for limits on immigration, the restriction of public office to native-born citizens, and the exclusive use of the Protestant version of the Bible in public schools. Social reformers often supported the anti-Catholic movement for reasons of public policy—to prevent the diversion of tax resources to Catholic schools and to oppose rowdyism by drunken Irish men. These cultural conflicts hurt the labor movement because many Protestant wage earners felt they had more in common with their Protestant employers than with their Catholic coworkers.

In many northeastern cities, religious and cultural conflicts led to violence. In 1834 in Charlestown, Massachusetts, a quarrel between Catholic laborers repairing a convent owned by the Ursuline order of nuns and Protestant workers in a neighboring brickyard turned into a full-scale riot and the burning of the convent. In Philadelphia violence erupted in 1844 when the Catholic bishop persuaded public school officials to use both Catholic and Protestant versions of the Bible. Anti-Irish rioting incited by the city's Native American Clubs lasted for two months and escalated into open warfare between Protestants and the Pennsylvania militia.

Even as economic revolution brought prosperity to many Americans, it divided the society along class lines and, by encouraging the influx of immigrants, created new ethnic and religious tensions. Differences of class and culture now split the North in much the same way that race and class had long divided the South. To address these divisive economic and social issues, Americans looked increasingly to the political system, which was becoming increasingly democratic. Indeed, the resulting tension between social inequality and political democracy would soon become an enduring, and troubling, part of American life.

## T I M E L I N E

| | | | |
|---|---|---|---|
| 1782 | Oliver Evans develops automated flour mill | 1824 | Congress levies protective tariffs; increases rates in 1828 |
| 1790 | Samuel Slater opens spinning mill in Providence, Rhode Island | | *Gibbons v. Ogden* promotes interstate trade |
| 1793 | Eli Whitney manufactures cotton gins | 1830s | Emergence of western commercial cities |
| | | | Labor movement gains strength |
| 1807 | Robert Fulton launches the *Clermont*, the first American steamboat | | Class-segregated cities |
| | | | Growth of temperance movement |
| 1810s | Cotton kingdom begins in Old Southwest | | Creation of middle-class culture |
| | | 1830 | Charles Grandison Finney begins Rochester revival |
| 1814 | Boston Manufacturing Company opens cotton mill in Waltham, Massachusetts | 1837 | Panic of 1837 |
| 1817 | Erie Canal begun; completed in 1825 | | John Deere invents steel plow |
| 1820 | Minimum federal land price reduced to $1.25 per acre | 1839 | European financial crisis begins four-year depression in United States |
| 1820s | New England women become textile operatives | 1840s | Irish and German immigration; ethnic riots |
| | Building-trade workers seek ten-hour workday | 1850s | Expansion of railroads in Northeast and Midwest |
| | Rise of Benevolent Empire | | Rise of machine-tool industry |
| 1821 | End of Panic of 1819; fifteen-year boom begins | 1857 | Financial panic after fourteen-year boom |

# For Further Exploration

Stuart Weems Bruchey, *Enterprise: The Dynamic Economy of a Free People* (1990), offers a panoramic history of America's economy. An important study is Charles G. Sellers's, *The Market Revolution: Jacksonian America, 1815–1846* (1991), which focuses on social and cultural change and underlines the tensions between market capitalism and democratic politics. David Freeman Hawke, *Nuts and Bolts of the Past: A History of American Technology, 1776–1860* (1988), offers an entertaining account of eccentric inventors and technical progress. Sites that explore the impact of technology include The Eli Whitney Museum & Workshop at <http://www.eliwhitney.org/> and The City Transformed: Railroads and Their Influence on the Growth of Chicago in the 1850s at <http://hcs.harvard.edu/~dreyfus/history.html>.

Stephen Aron, *How the West Was Lost: The Transformation of Kentucky from Daniel Boone to Henry Clay* (1996), explores the drama of economic and political conflict in the trans-Appalachian West, while Peter Way, *Common Labor: Workers and the Digging of North American Canals, 1780–1860* (1993), describes the deprivation and anger experienced by the men who dug the western canals. For material on New York's Erie Canal, go to <http://www.canals.state.ny.us/culture/history/>.

The appearance of a new urban society forms the background of Stuart M. Blumin's study, *The Emergence of the Middle Class: Social Experience in the American City, 1760–1900* (1989). A fine study of urban disorder is David Grimsted's *American Mobbing* (1998). In *Home and Work: Housework, Wages, and the Ideology of Labor in the Early Republic* (1990), Jeanne Boydston takes a critical look at the impact of the Market Revolution and urban life on women's lives. For a woman textile operative's first-hand account of mill life, see <http://www.fordham.edu/halsall/mod/robinson-lowell.html>. W. J. Rorabaugh, *The Alcoholic Republic, an American Tradition* (1979), describes a society awash in liquor and the efforts of the temperance reformers to do something about it.

For more about the settlement of the Great Lakes region, log on to Pioneering the Upper Midwest: Books from Michigan, Minnesota, and Wisconsin, 1820–1910 at <http://memory.loc.gov/ammem/umhtml/umhome.html>, for the full text of first-person accounts, biographies, and promotional literature from the collections of the Library of Congress.

---

For definitions of key terms boldfaced in this chapter, see the glossary at the end of the book.

To assess your mastery of the material covered in this chapter, see the Online Study Guide at **bedfordstmartins.com/henrettaconcise**.

For map resources and primary documents, see **bedfordstmartins.com/henrettaconcise**.

# Chapter 11

# A DEMOCRATIC REVOLUTION
## 1820–1844

Of the two great parties, . . . I should say that one [the Democratic Party or the Democracy] has the best cause . . . for free trade, for wide suffrage. . . . The other [the Whig Party] has the best men [but is] . . . merely defensive of property. It vindicates no right, it aspires to no real good. . . .

RALPH WALDO EMERSON, "ESSAY ON POLITICS," 1844

**I**f some Americans were critical of their political parties and republican institutions, they had strong allies among visiting Europeans. "The gentlemen spit, talk of elections and the price of produce, and spit again," Mrs. Frances Trollope reported in *Domestic Manners of the Americans* (1832). In her view American politics was the sport of party hacks who reeked of "whiskey and onions." Other European visitors likewise found little to celebrate. Harriet Martineau was "deeply disgusted" by the "clap-trap of praise and pathos" uttered by a leading Massachusetts politician, while Basil Hall could only shake his head in astonishment at the shallow arguments, the "conclusions in which nothing was concluded," that were advanced by the inept "farmers, shopkeepers, and country lawyers" who sat in the New York assembly.

The verdict was unanimous and negative. "The most able men in the United States are very rarely placed at the head of affairs," concluded the French aristocrat Alexis de Tocqueville in *Democracy in America* (1835), a result he ascribed to the character of democracy itself. Ordinary citizens ignored important issues of policy, refused to elect their intellectual superiors to office, and willingly assented to "the clamor of a mountebank [a charismatic fraud] who knows the secret of stimulating [their] tastes."

The European visitors were witnesses to the unfolding of the American democratic revolution. In the early years of the nation, the ruling ideology had been *republicanism*, rule by property-owning "men of TALENTS and VIRTUE." By the 1820s and 1830s, the watchword was *democracy*, which in practice meant rule by popularly elected party politicians. "That the majority should govern was a fundamental maxim in all free governments," declared Martin Van Buren, the most talented of the new breed of middle-class professional politicians who had taken over the halls of government. The new party politicians often pursued selfish goals, but by uniting ordinary Americans in "election fever" and party organizations, they held together a social order increasingly fragmented by the economic revolution.

# The Rise of Popular Politics, 1820–1829

Expansion of the **franchise** was the most dramatic expression of the democratic revolution. As early as the 1810s some states ended property qualifications for voting and brought nearly every male farmer and wage earner into the political arena. Nowhere else in the world did ordinary men have so much power; in England, the Reform Bill of 1832 extended the vote to only 600,000 out of 6 million English men—a mere 10 percent.

## *The Decline of the Notables and the Rise of Parties*

The American Revolution weakened the deferential society of the colonial era, but it did not overthrow it. Families in the low and middle ranks continued to accept the leadership of their social "betters," and wealthy notable men—northern landlords, slave-owning planters, and seaport merchants—dominated the political system. As former Supreme Court Justice John Jay put it in 1810, "Those who own the country are the most fit persons to participate in the government of it." Local notables managed elections by building up an "interest": lending money to small farmers, giving business to storekeepers, and treating their tenants to rum at election time. An outlay of $20 for refreshments, remarked one poll watcher, "may produce about 100 votes." Martin Van Buren, whose father was a tavern keeper, knew from personal experience that this gentry-dominated system excluded men without wealth and "powerful family connections" from running for office.

Smallholding farmers and ambitious laborers in the Midwest and Southwest launched the first challenges to the traditional political order. In Ohio, a traveler reported, "no white man or woman will bear being called a servant." Reflecting this social egalitarianism, the constitutions of the new states of Indiana (1816), Illinois (1818), and Alabama (1819) prescribed a broad male franchise and voters usually elected middling men to local and state offices. A well-to-do migrant in Illinois noted with surprise that the man who plowed his fields "was a colonel of militia, and a member of the legislature." Once in public office, men from modest backgrounds enacted laws that restricted imprisonment for debt, kept taxes low, and allowed farmers to claim "squatters' rights" to unoccupied land.

To deter migration to the West and unrest at home, the notables who ran state legislatures in the East grudgingly accepted a broader franchise. In 1810 in Maryland, reformers condemned property qualifications as a "tyranny" that endowed "one class of men with privileges which are denied to another" and won a broad franchise. By the mid-1820s only a few states—North Carolina, Virginia, Rhode Island—required the ownership of freehold property for voting. Many states had instituted universal white manhood suffrage, and others, such as Ohio and Louisiana, excluded only the relatively few men who did not pay taxes or serve in the militia. Moreover, between 1818 and 1821 Connecticut, Massachusetts, and New York wrote new constitutions that reapportioned legislative districts on the basis of population and made local governments more democratic by mandating the election (rather than the appointment) of judges and justices of the peace.

Democratic politics was contentious and often corrupt. Powerful entrepreneurs and speculators—both notables and self-made men—demanded government assistance for their business enterprises and paid bribes to legislators to get it. Bankers sought state charters and opposed limits on interest rates, while land speculators demanded the eviction of squatters and the building of roads and canals. Other Americans turned to politics to advance religious and cultural causes. In 1828 evangelical Presbyterians in Utica, New York, called for a town ordinance to restrict Sunday entertainment. In reply, a member of the local Universalist church (a free-thinking Protestant denomination) denounced such coercive reforms and called for "Religious Liberty."

The appearance of political parties encouraged debate on issues of government policy. Revolutionary era Americans had condemned political "factions" and "parties" as antirepublican and refused to give them constitutional status. But as the power of notables waned, political parties became more prominent. By the 1820s the parties were highly disciplined organizations managed by professional politicians, who were often middle-class lawyers and journalists. Some observers compared the parties to the mechanical innovations of the Industrial Revolution. Like a well-designed textile loom, they were "machines" that wove the diverse interests of social and economic groups into an elaborate tapestry—a coherent legislative program.

Martin Van Buren of New York was the chief architect of the emerging system of party government. Between 1817 and 1821 the "Little Magician" created the first statewide **political machine**, the Albany Regency; a decade later he organized the first nationwide political party, the Jacksonian Democrats. Van Buren repudiated the republican principle that political parties were dangerous to the common wealth and argued that the opposite was true: "All men of sense know that political parties are inseparable from free government" because they check the government's "disposition to abuse power . . . [and curb] the passions, the ambition, and the usurpations" of potential tyrants.

One key to Van Buren's success in New York was his systematic use of the *Albany Argus* and other party newspapers to promote a platform and drum up the vote. **Patronage** was even more important. The Albany Regency's control of the legislature gave Van Buren and his followers a greater "interest" than the notables—some six thousand appointments to New York's legal bureaucracy of judges, justices of the peace, sheriffs, deed commissioners, and coroners. Finally, Van Buren insisted on party discipline and required state legislators to follow the dictates of a party meeting, or cau-cus. On one crucial occasion, Van Buren persuaded seventeen legislators to "magnani-mously sacrifice individual preferences for the general good" and honored them at a banquet where they were treated with "something approaching divine honors."

## The Election of 1824

The advance of political democracy undermined the old system of national politics and the power of the leading notables who ran it. The aristocratic Federalist Party virtually disappeared, and the Republican Party broke up into competing factions. As the election of 1824 approached, no fewer than five candidates, all calling them-selves Republicans, campaigned for the presidency. Three were veterans of President James Monroe's cabinet: Secretary of State John Quincy Adams, the son of former president John Adams; Secretary of War John C. Calhoun; and Secretary of the Treasury William H. Crawford. The fourth candidate was Henry Clay of Kentucky, the dynamic Speaker of the House of Representatives, and the fifth was General Andrew Jackson, now a senator from Tennessee. When a caucus of Republicans in Congress selected Crawford as the "official" nominee, the other candidates refused to accept that result.

Instead, they introduced democracy to national politics by seeking popular support. Because of democratic reforms, eighteen of the twenty-four states used popular elections (rather than a vote of the state legislature) to choose members of the electoral college. The battle was closely fought. Thanks to his diplomatic suc-cesses as secretary of state (see Chapter 8), John Quincy Adams enjoyed national recognition and, because of his Massachusetts origins, commanded the electoral votes of New England. Henry Clay framed his candidacy around domestic issues. As a congressman, Clay promoted the **American System**, an integrated program of na-tional economic development that relied on the Second Bank of the United States to regulate state banks and advocated the use of tariff revenues to build roads and canals. Clay's nationalistic program was popular in the West, which needed trans-portation improvements, but sharply criticized in the South, which relied on rivers to carry its cotton to market and did not have manufacturing industries to protect. William Crawford of Georgia, an ideological heir of Thomas Jefferson, spoke for the South. Fearing the "consolidation" of political power in Washington, Crawford and other "Old Republicans" denounced the American System. Recognizing Crawford's appeal in the South, John C. Calhoun of South Carolina withdrew from the presi-dential race and endorsed Andrew Jackson.

As the hero of the Battle of New Orleans, Jackson benefited from the wave of nationalistic pride that flowed from the War of 1812. Born in the Carolina back-country, Jackson had settled in Nashville, Tennessee, where he formed ties to influ-ential families through marriage and his career as an attorney and slave-owning cotton planter. His rise from common origins fit the tenor of the new democratic age and his reputation as a "plain solid republican" attracted voters in all regions.

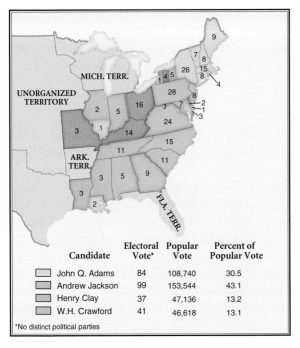

| Candidate | Electoral Vote* | Popular Vote | Percent of Popular Vote |
|---|---|---|---|
| John Q. Adams | 84 | 108,740 | 30.5 |
| Andrew Jackson | 99 | 153,544 | 43.1 |
| Henry Clay | 37 | 47,136 | 13.2 |
| W.H. Crawford | 41 | 46,618 | 13.1 |

*No distinct political parties

**MAP 11.1 Presidential Election of 1824**

Regional ties decided the presidential election of 1824. John Quincy Adams captured every electoral vote in New England and most of those in New York. Henry Clay carried Ohio and Kentucky, the most populous trans-Appalachian states, and William Crawford took the southern states of Virginia and Georgia. Only Andrew Jackson claimed a national constituency, winning Pennsylvania and New Jersey in the East, Indiana and Illinois in the Midwest, and most of the South. Only about 356,000 Americans voted, about 27 percent of the eligible adult white male electorate. In contrast, nearly 1.2 million American men cast ballots in 1828.

Still, Jackson's strong showing in the election surprised most political leaders. The Tennessee senator received 99 votes in the electoral college; Adams garnered 84 votes; Crawford, who suffered a stroke during the campaign, won 41; and Clay finished with 37 (Map 11.1). Since no candidate received an absolute majority, the Constitution specified that the House of Representatives would choose the president from among the three leading contenders. This procedure hurt Jackson because many congressmen rebelled at the thought of a rough-hewn "military chieftain" in the White House and worried he might become a political tyrant. Personally out of the race, Henry Clay used his influence as Speaker of the House to thwart Jackson's election. When the House met in February 1825, Clay had assembled a coalition of congressmen from New England and the Ohio Valley that voted Adams into the presidency. Adams showed his gratitude by appointing Clay as secretary of state, the traditional steppingstone to the presidency.

**John Quincy Adams (1767–1848)**

This famous daguerreotype of the former president, taken about 1843 by Philip Haas, conveys his rigid personality and high moral standards. These personal attributes hindered Adams's effectiveness as the nation's chief executive but contributed to his success as an antislavery congressman from Massachusetts in the 1830s and 1840s.

Metropolitan Museum of Art. Gift of I. N. Phelps Stokes, Edward S. Hawes, Alice Mary Hawes, Marion Augusta Hawes.

Clay's appointment was a politically fatal mistake for both men. John C. Calhoun accused Adams of using "the power and patronage of the Executive" to thwart the popular will. Jackson's many supporters likewise suspected that Clay had made a deal with Adams to become secretary of state. Condemning this "corrupt bargain," they vowed that Clay would never become president.

## The Last Notable President: John Quincy Adams

As president, Adams called for bold national leadership. "The moral purpose of the Creator," he told Congress, was to use the president and every other public official to "improve the conditions of himself and his fellow men." Adams called for the establishment of a national university in Washington, extensive scientific explorations in the Far West, and a uniform standard of weights and measures. Most important of all, he embraced Henry Clay's American System of national economic development: (1) a protective tariff to stimulate manufacturing, (2) federally subsidized roads and canals to aid commerce, and (3) a national bank to control credit and provide a uniform currency.

Manufacturers, entrepreneurs, and market-oriented farmers in the Northeast and Midwest welcomed Adams's policies. However, they won little support among southern planters, who opposed protective tariffs, and smallholding farmers, who feared powerful banks. From his deathbed Thomas Jefferson condemned Adams for promoting "a single and splendid government of [a monied] aristocracy . . . riding and ruling over the plundered ploughman and beggared yeomanry."

Other politicians objected to the American System on constitutional grounds. In 1817 President Madison had vetoed a Bonus Bill that would have used the national government's income from the Second Bank of the United States to fund improvement projects in the various states. Such projects, Madison had argued, were the sole responsibilities of the states, a sentiment that was widely shared. Declaring his allegiance to the constitutional "doctrines of the Jefferson School," Martin Van Buren joined the Old Republicans in defeating most national subsidies for roads and canals. Congress approved only a few of Adams's proposals for internal improvements, such as a short extension of the National Road from Wheeling, Virginia, into Ohio.

The most far-reaching battle of the Adams administration came over tariffs. The Tariff of 1816 placed high duties on imports of cheap English cotton cloth, thereby allowing New England textile producers to dominate that market. In 1824 Adams and Clay supported a new tariff that protected manufacturers in New England and Pennsylvania against imports of more expensive woolen and cotton textiles as well as iron goods. When Van Buren and the Jacksonians took control of Congress in 1826, they wanted higher tariffs on imported raw materials, such as wool and hemp. Their goal was to win the support of farmers in New York, Ohio, and Kentucky for Jackson's presidential candidacy in 1828. The tariff had become a prisoner of politics. "I fear this tariff thing," remarked Thomas Cooper of South Carolina, "by some strange mechanical contrivance . . . it will be changed into a machine for manufacturing Presidents, instead of broadcloths, and bed blankets." Disregarding southern opposition, northern Jacksonians joined with the supporters of Adams and Clay to enact the Tariff of 1828, which raised duties on raw materials, textiles, and iron goods.

The new tariff enraged the South. As the world's cheapest producer of raw cotton, the South did not need a protective tariff. Moreover, by raising the price of British manufactures, the tariff cost southern planters about $100 million a year. Planters could either buy higher-cost American textiles and iron goods, thus enriching northeastern businesses and workers, or highly taxed British goods, thus paying the cost of the national government. The new tariff was "little less than legalized pillage" declared an Alabama legislator, a "Tariff of Abominations."

## "The Democracy" and the Election of 1828

Ignoring the Jacksonians' support for the tariff, most southerners blamed President Adams for the new act. They also criticized Adams's Indian policy. A deeply moralistic man, the president had supported the land rights of Native Americans against expansionist-minded southern whites. In 1825 U.S. commissioners had secured a treaty from one Creek faction that ceded the tribe's lands in Georgia to the United States.

When the Creek National Council repudiated the treaty as fraudulent, Adams called for new negotiations. In response Governor George M. Troup attacked the president as a "public enemy . . . the unblushing ally of the savages" and persuaded Congress to pass legislation that extinguished the Creeks' land titles and forced most Creeks to leave the state.

Elsewhere in the nation Adams's primary weakness was his increasingly out-of-date political style. The last notable to serve in the White House, he acted the part: aloof, moralistic, paternalistic. When Congress rejected his activist economic policies, Adams questioned the wisdom of the people and advised elected officials not to be "palsied by the will of our constituents." Ignoring his waning popularity, the president did not use patronage to reward his supporters and allowed hostile federal officials to remain in office. Rather than "run" for reelection in 1828, Adams "stood" for it, telling supporters, "If my country wants my services, she must ask for them."

Martin Van Buren and the professional politicians handling Andrew Jackson's campaign had no reservations about "running" for the presidency. Now a U.S. senator from New York, Van Buren re-created the old Jeffersonian coalition by uniting northern farmers and artisans (the "plain Republicans of the North") with the southern slave owners and smallholding farmers who had voted for the Virginia Dynasty. John C. Calhoun, Jackson's vice-presidential running mate, brought his South Carolina allies into Van Buren's party, and Jackson's close friends in Tennessee rallied voters in the Old Southwest. At Van Buren's direction, state politicians orchestrated a massive newspaper campaign; in New York fifty newspapers declared their support for Jackson on the same day. Local Jacksonians organized mass meetings, torchlight parades, and barbecues to celebrate their candidate's frontier origins and his rise to fame. Old Hickory—the nickname came from the toughest American hardwood tree—was a "natural" aristocrat, a self-made man. "Jackson for ever!" was their cry.

Initially the Jacksonians called themselves Democratic Republicans, but as the campaign wore on, they became Democrats or "the Democracy." The name conveyed their message. As Jacksonian Thomas Morris told the Ohio legislature, the republic had been corrupted by legislative gifts of corporate charters that gave "a few individuals rights and privileges not enjoyed by the citizens at large." Morris promised that his party would destroy such "artificial distinction in society" and ensure rule by the majority—the Democracy. As Jackson himself declared, "Equality among the people in the rights conferred by government" was the "great radical principle of freedom."

Jackson's message of equal rights and popular rule appealed to many social groups. His hostility to business corporations and to Clay's American System won support among northeastern artisans and workers who felt threatened by industrialization. In the Southeast and the Midwest, Old Hickory's well-known animus toward Native Americans reassured white farmers who favored Indian removal. Although Jackson won votes from Pennsylvania ironworkers and New York farmers because of the controversial Tariff of Abominations, he remained popular in the South by declaring his personal preference for a "judicious" tariff.

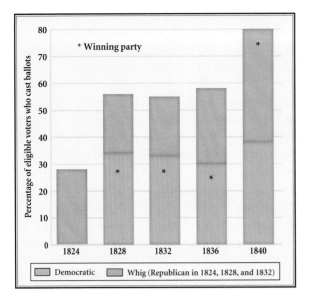

**FIGURE 11.1 Changes in Voting Patterns, 1824–1840**

Because of the return of two-party competition, voter participation soared in the critical presidential elections of 1828 and 1840.

The Democrats' commitment to popular democracy carried Jackson into office. In 1824 only about a fourth of the eligible electorate had voted; in 1828 more than half went to the polls, and they voted overwhelmingly for the senator from Tennessee (Figure 11.1). Jackson received 178 of 261 electoral votes and became the first president from a western state. As the president-elect traveled to Washington, an English visitor noted, he "wore his hair carelessly but not ungracefully arranged, and in spite of his harsh, gaunt features looked like a gentleman and a soldier." However, the massive outpouring of popular support for Jackson frightened men of wealth and influence. As the ex-Federalist and corporate lawyer Daniel Webster warned his clients, the new president would "bring a breeze with him. Which way it will blow, I cannot tell [but] . . . my fear is stronger than my hope." Watching an unruly crowd clamber over the elegant furniture in the White House to shake the hand of the newly inaugurated president, Supreme Court Justice Joseph Story could only lament that "the reign of King 'Mob' seemed triumphant" (see American Voices, "Republican Majesty and Mobs," p. 331).

# The Jacksonian Presidency, 1829–1837

American-style political democracy—a broad franchise, a disciplined political party, and policies tailored to specific social groups—ushered Andrew Jackson into office. Subsequently, Jackson used his popular mandate to enhance the authority of the president over that of Congress, to destroy the nationalistic American System of Adams and Clay, and to ordain a new ideology for the Democracy. An Ohio supporter outlined Jackson's vision: "the Sovereignty of the People, the Rights of the States, and a Light and Simple Government."

**AMERICAN VOICES**

~

# Republican Majesty and Mobs

MARGARET BAYARD SMITH

*W*hen Andrew Jackson ascended to the presidency in 1829, he threatened the established political system by questioning the legitimacy of a powerful central government and calling for democracy and "equal rights." Writing to her son, the Washington socialite Margaret Bayard Smith revealed a mixture of pride and anxiety about the new president and the coming of popular democracy.

The inauguration . . . was one grand whole—an imposing and majestic spectacle. . . . Thousands and thousands of people, without distinction of rank, collected in an immense mass around the Capitol, silent, orderly, and tranquil, with their eyes fixed on the front of the Capitol, waiting the appearance of the president. . . . The door from the Rotunda opens, preceded by the marshall surrounded by the judges of the Supreme Court, the old man [President Jackson] with his grey hair, that crown of glory, advances, bows to the people, who greet him with a shout that rends the air. The cannon, from the heights around from Alexandria and Fort Washington, proclaim the [oath of office] he has taken and all the hills around reverberate the sound. It was grand; it was sublime! An almost breathless silence succeeded and the multitude was still—listening to catch the sound of his voice. . . .

After reading his speech, the oath was administered to him by the chief justice. The marshall presented the Bible. The president took it from his hand, pressed his lips to it, laid it reverently down, then bowed again to the people. Yes, to the people in all their majesty—and had the spectacle closed here, even Europeans must have acknowledged that a free people, collected in their might, silent and tranquil, restrained solely by a moral power, without a shadow around of military force, was majesty, rising to sublimity, and far surpassing the majesty of kings and princes, surrounded with armies and glittering in gold. . . .

[But at the White House reception that followed,] what a scene did we witness!! The majesty of the people had disappeared, and a rabble, a mob . . . scrambling, fighting, romping . . . [crowded around] the president, [who,] after having literally been nearly pressed to death . . . escaped to his lodgings at Gadsby's. Cut glass and bone china to the amount of several thousand dollars had been broken in the struggle to get refreshments. . . .

God grant the people do not put down all rule and rulers. I fear . . . as they have been found in all ages and countries where they get power in their hands, that of all tyrants, they are the most ferocious, cruel, and despotic. The . . . rabble in the president's house brought to my mind descriptions I had read of the mobs in the Tuileries and at Versailles [during the French Revolution].

SOURCE: M. B. Smith to J. B. H. Smith, March 1829, Smith Family Correspondence, Library of Congress, in Linda R. Monk, ed., *Ordinary Americans: U.S. History through the Eyes of Ordinary People* (Alexandria, VA: Close Up Foundation, 1993), 49–50.

## Jackson's Agenda: Patronage and Policy

To decide policy, Jackson relied primarily on an informal group of advisors, his so-called Kitchen Cabinet. Its most influential members were Francis Preston Blair of Kentucky, who edited the *Washington Globe*; Amos Kendall, also from Kentucky, who helped Jackson write his public addresses; Roger B. Taney of Maryland, who became attorney general, treasury secretary, and then chief justice of the United States; and, the most influential, Secretary of State Martin Van Buren.

Following Van Buren's example in New York, Jackson used patronage to create a loyal and disciplined national party. He insisted on rotation in office: when a new administration came to power, bureaucrats would have to leave government service and return "to making a living as other people do." Dismissing the argument that rotation would lessen expertise, Jackson suggested that most public duties were "so plain and simple that men of intelligence may readily qualify themselves for their performance." William L. Marcy, a New York Jacksonian, put it more bluntly: government jobs were like the spoils of war, and "to the victor belong the spoils of the enemy." Using the **spoils system**, Jackson dispensed government jobs to aid his friends and win support for his legislative program.

Jackson's main priority was to destroy the American System. As Henry Clay noted apprehensively, the new president wanted "to cry down old constructions of

**President Andrew Jackson, 1830**

The new president came to Washington with a well-deserved reputation as an aggressive Indian fighter and dangerous military chieftain. But in the "official" portrait of 1830 he appears "presidential"—his dress and posture (and the artist's composition) creating an image of a calm and deliberate statesman. Subsequent events would show that Jackson had not lost his hard-edged personality. Library of Congress.

the Constitution . . . to make all Jefferson's opinions the articles of faith of the new Church." Declaring that the "voice of the people" called for "economy in the expenditures of the Government," Jackson rejected national support for transportation projects, which he also opposed on constitutional grounds. In 1830 he vetoed four internal improvement bills, including an extension of the National Road, because they amounted to "an infringement of the reserved powers of states." Then Jackson turned his attention to two complex and equally controversial parts of the American System: protective tariffs and the national bank.

## The Tariff and Nullification

The Tariff of 1828 had helped Jackson win the presidency, but it saddled him with a major political crisis. Fierce opposition to the tariff arose in South Carolina, where white planters suffered from chronic insecurity. South Carolina was the only state with an African American majority—56 percent of the population in 1830—and its slave owners, like the sugar planters in the West Indies, lived in fear of a black rebellion. They also worried about the legal abolition of slavery. The British Parliament had promised to end slavery in the West Indies (and did so in August 1833), and South Carolina planters worried that the U.S. government might do the same. "If the general government shall continue to stretch their powers," a southern congressman had warned as early as 1818, antislavery societies "will undoubtedly put them to try the question of emancipation." To sidetrack this possibility, South Carolina politicians tried to limit the power of the central government and chose the tariff as their target.

The crisis began in 1832 when high-tariff congressmen ignored southern warnings that they were "endangering the Union" and reenacted the Tariff of Abominations. In response, leading South Carolinians called a state convention in November, which boldly adopted an Ordinance of Nullification. The ordinance declared the tariffs of 1828 and 1832 null and void, forbade the collection of those duties in South Carolina after February 1, 1833, and threatened secession if federal bureaucrats tried to collect them.

South Carolina's act of **nullification** rested on the constitutional arguments developed in a tract of 1828, *The South Carolina Exposition and Protest*. Written anonymously by Vice President John C. Calhoun, the *Exposition* challenged the legitimacy of majority rule. "Constitutional government and the government of a majority are utterly incompatible," Calhoun wrote. "An unchecked majority is a despotism." To devise a mechanism to check the power of congressional majorities, Calhoun turned to the arguments advanced by Jefferson and Madison in the Kentucky and Virginia Resolutions of 1798. Developing a constitutional theory that states' rights advocates would use well into the twentieth century, Calhoun maintained that the U.S. Constitution had been ratified by citizens meeting in state conventions. Consequently, he argued, a state convention could decide if a congressional law was unconstitutional and declare it null and void within the state's borders.

Although Jackson wanted to limit the reach of the national government, he denounced this radical redefinition of the existing constitutional system: "Our Federal Union—it must be preserved," he declared in 1830. Two years later, the president's response to South Carolina's Nullification Ordinance was equally direct. Jackson declared that nullification violated the Constitution and was "unauthorized by its spirit . . . and destructive of the great object for which it was formed." "Disunion by armed force is treason," he warned. At Jackson's request, Congress passed a Force Bill early in 1833 that authorized the president to use military force to compel South Carolina to obey national laws. Simultaneously, Jackson addressed the South's objections to high import duties by winning passage of a Tariff Act that gradually reduced rates. By 1842, tariffs would revert to the modest rates of 1816, thereby eliminating another part of Clay's American System.

The compromise worked. Having won a gradual reduction in duties, the South Carolina convention rescinded its nullification of the tariff (while defiantly nullifying the Force Bill). Jackson was satisfied. He had upheld the principle that no state could nullify a law of the United States, a position that Abraham Lincoln would embrace in defense of the Union during the secession crisis of 1861.

## The Bank War

In the middle of the tariff crisis, Jackson faced another major challenge from the political supporters of the Second Bank of the United States. Founded in Philadelphia in 1816, the bank was a privately managed institution that held a twenty-year charter from the federal government, which owned 20 percent of its stock. The bank's most important role was to stabilize the nation's money supply. Most American money consisted of notes and bills of credit—in effect, paper money—issued by state-chartered banks. The banks promised to redeem the notes on demand with "hard" money—that is, gold or silver coins (also known as specie). By collecting those notes and regularly demanding specie, the Second Bank kept the state banks from issuing too much paper money.

During the prosperous 1820s, the Second Bank had maintained monetary stability by closing reckless state banks and restraining expansion-minded bankers in the western states. This tight-money policy pleased bankers and entrepreneurs in Boston, New York, and Philadelphia, whose capital investments were underwriting economic development. However, most ordinary Americans did not understand the regulatory role of the Second Bank and feared its ability to force bank closures, which left them holding worthless paper notes. New York bankers also opposed the Second Bank because they resented the financial clout wielded by its arrogant president, Nicholas Biddle. "As to mere power," Biddle boasted, "I have been for years in the daily exercise of more personal authority than any President habitually enjoys." Fearing Biddle's influence, some state bankers wanted the specie owned by the federal government to be deposited in their institutions rather than in the Second Bank. Others, including friends of Jackson in Nashville, wanted to escape supervision by any central bank.

However, it was a political miscalculation by the Second Bank's political allies that brought about its downfall. In 1832 Jackson's opponents in Congress, led by Henry Clay and Daniel Webster, persuaded Biddle to seek an early extension of the bank's charter. They commanded enough votes in Congress to enact the required legislation and hoped to lure Jackson into a veto that would split the Democrats just before the 1832 elections.

Jackson turned the tables on Clay and Webster. He vetoed the bill that rechartered the bank and issued a masterful veto message that blended constitutional arguments with class rhetoric and patriotic fervor. Adopting Jefferson's position, Jackson declared that Congress had no constitutional authority to charter a national bank, which was "subversive of the rights of the States." Using the populist republican rhetoric of the American Revolution, he then attacked the Second Bank as "dangerous to the liberties of the people." Indeed, it was a nest of special privilege and monopoly power that promoted "the advancement of the few at the expense of . . . farmers, mechanics, and laborers." Finally, the president evoked national patriotism by pointing out that British aristocrats owned much of the bank's stock; any such powerful institution should be "purely American," he declared.

**Jackson Destroys the Bank**

In this political cartoon Jackson proudly orders the withdrawal of "Public Money" from the privately run Second Bank of the United States. Crushed by the subsequent collapse of the bank are its director Nicholas Biddle, depicted as the Devil, wealthy British and American investors, and the newspapers that supported Biddle during the bank war. Standing behind the president is "Major Jack Downing," the pseudonym for Seba Smith, a pro-Jackson humorist. Library of Congress.

FOR MORE HELP ANALYZING THIS IMAGE, see the Online Study Guide at **bedfordstmartins.com/henrettaconcise**.

Jackson's attack on the bank carried him to victory in the election of 1832. He jettisoned Calhoun as a running mate because of the South Carolinian's support for nullification and Calhoun's refusal to support Peggy Eaton, a cabinet wife accused of sexual improprieties. As his new vice president, Jackson chose his longtime political ally Martin Van Buren. Together Old Hickory and Little Van overwhelmed Henry Clay, who headed the National Republican ticket, by 219 to 49 electoral votes. Jackson's most fervent supporters were eastern workers and western farmers, whose lives had been disrupted by falling wages or price fluctuations and who blamed their fate on the Second Bank. "All the flourishing cities of the West are mortgaged to this money power," charged Jacksonian senator Thomas Hart Benton of Missouri. "They may be devoured by it at any moment." But just as many Jacksonians had prospered during a decade of strong economic growth. Along with thousands of middle-class Americans—lawyers, clerks, shopkeepers, artisans—they wanted equal opportunity to rise in the world and cheered Jackson's attacks on privileged corporations.

Early in 1833, Jackson called on Roger B. Taney, a strong opponent of corporate privilege, to launch a new assault on the Second Bank, which still had four years left on its original charter. Assuming control of the Treasury Department, Taney withdrew the government's gold and silver from the Second Bank and deposited it in state institutions, which critics called Jackson's "pet banks." To justify this abrupt (and probably illegal) act, Jackson claimed that his own reelection represented "the decision of the people against the bank" and gave him a mandate to destroy it. This was the first time a president had claimed that victory at the polls allowed him to act independently of Congress.

The "bank war" escalated into an all-out political battle. In March 1834 Jackson's opponents in the Senate passed Henry Clay's resolution censuring the president and warning of executive tyranny: "We are in the midst of a revolution, hitherto bloodless, but rapidly descending towards a total change of the pure republican character of the Government, and the concentration of all power in the hands of one man." Jackson was not deterred by widespread opposition in Congress. "The Bank is trying to kill me but I will kill it," he vowed to Van Buren. And so he did. When the Second Bank's national charter expired in 1836, Jackson prevented its renewal.

Jackson had destroyed both national banking—the creation of Alexander Hamilton—and the American System of protective tariffs and internal improvements favored by John Quincy Adams and Henry Clay. The result was a profound reduction in the purview and the powers of the national government. "All is gone," observed a Washington newspaper correspondent. "All is gone, which the General Government was instituted to create and preserve."

## Indian Removal

The status of the Native American peoples posed an equally complex political problem. By the late 1820s white voices throughout the western states and territories were calling for the resettlement of Indians west of the Mississippi River. Many easterners who were sympathetic to the native peoples also favored resettlement.

Removal to the West seemed the only way to protect Indian societies from alcoholic degradation, economic sharp dealing, and cultural decline.

However, most Indians had no wish to leave their ancestral lands. The Old Southwest was home to the so-called Five Civilized Tribes: the Cherokees and Creeks in Georgia, Tennessee, and Alabama; the Chickasaws and Choctaws in Mississippi and Alabama; and the Seminoles in Florida. During the War of 1812 Andrew Jackson had forced the Creeks to relinquish millions of acres. But Indian peoples still controlled vast tracts and, led by the mixed-blood offspring of white traders and Indian women, strongly resisted removal. Growing up in a bicultural world, many mixed-bloods knew the political ways of whites and some emulated the lifestyle of southern planters. James Vann, a Georgia Cherokee, owned more than twenty black slaves, two trading posts, and a gristmill. Forty other Cherokee mixed-blood families owned a total of more than a thousand African American slaves. To protect their property and the lands of their people, the mixed-bloods promoted a strong Indian identity. Sequoyah, a mixed blood, developed a system of writing for the Cherokee language, and in 1827 mixed-blood Cherokees introduced a new charter of government modeled directly on the U.S. Constitution. Full-blooded Cherokees, who made up 90 percent of the population, resisted many of the mixed-bloods' cultural and political innovations but were equally determined to retain their ancestral lands. "We would not receive money for land in which our fathers and friends are buried," one chief declared. "We love our land; it is our mother."

The Cherokees' preferences carried no weight with the Georgia legislature. In 1802 Georgia had given up its western land claims in return for a federal promise to extinguish Indian landholdings in the state. Now it demanded the fulfillment of that promise. Having spent his military career fighting Indians and seizing their lands, Jackson gave full support to Georgia. On assuming the presidency, he withdrew the federal troops that had protected Indian enclaves there and in Alabama and Mississippi. The states, he declared, were sovereign within their borders.

Jackson then pushed through Congress the Indian Removal Act of 1830. The act granted money and lands in present-day Oklahoma and Kansas to Native American peoples who would give up their ancestral holdings (see American Voices, "A Sacred Reverence for Our Lands," p. 338). To persuade Indians to move, government officials promised that they could live on the new lands, "they and all their children, as long as grass grows and water runs." When Chief Black Hawk and his Sauk and Fox followers refused to move from rich farmland in western Illinois in 1832, Jackson sent troops to expel them. Rejecting Black Hawk's offer to surrender, the American army pursued him into the Wisconsin Territory and, in the brutal eight-hour Bad Axe Massacre, killed 850 of Black Hawk's 1,000 warriors. Over the next five years American diplomatic pressure and military power forced seventy Indian peoples to sign treaties and move west of the Mississippi (Map 11.2).

Meanwhile, the Cherokees had carried their case to the Supreme Court, where they claimed the status of a "foreign nation." In *Cherokee Nation v. Georgia* (1831)

# A Sacred Reverence for Our Lands

## BLACK HAWK

*B*  *lack Hawk (1767–1838), or Makataimeshekiakiak in his native language, was a chief of the Sauk and Fox peoples. In 1833 he dictated his life story to a government interpreter, and a young newspaper editor published it. Here Black Hawk describes the coming of white settlers to his village, near present-day Rock Island, Illinois, and his decision to resist removal to lands west of the Mississippi River.*

We had about eight hundred acres in cultivation. The land around our village . . . was covered with bluegrass, which made excellent pasture for our horses. . . . The rapids of Rock river furnished us with an abundance of excellent fish, and the land, being good, never failed to produce good crops of corn, beans, pumpkins, and squashes. We always had plenty—our children never cried with hunger, nor our people were never in want. Here our village had stood for more than a hundred years.

[In 1828] Nothing was now talked of but leaving our village. Ke-o-kuck [the principal chief] had been persuaded to consent to . . . remove to the west side of the Mississippi. . . . [I] raised the standard of opposition to Ke-o-kuck, with full determination not to leave my village. . . . I was of the opinion that the white people had plenty of land and would never take our village from us. . . .

During the [following] winter, I received information that three families of whites had arrived at our village and destroyed some of our lodges, and were making fences and dividing our corn-fields for their own use. . . . I requested them [to remove, but some weeks later] we came up to our village, and found that the whites had not left it— but that others had come, and that the greater part of our corn-fields had been enclosed. . . . Some of the whites permitted us to plant small patches in the fields they had fenced, keeping all the best ground for themselves. . . . The white people brought whiskey into our village, made people drunk, and cheated them out of their homes, guns, and [beaver] traps!

That fall [1829] I paid a visit to the agent, before we started to our hunting grounds. . . . He said that the land on which our village stood was now ordered to be sold to individuals; and that, when sold, our right to remain, by treaty, would be at an end, and that if we returned next spring, we would be forced to remove! I refused . . . to quit my village. It was here, that I was born—and here lie the bones of many friends and relatives. For this spot I felt a sacred reverence, and never could consent to leave it, without being forced therefrom.

SOURCE: David Jackson, ed., *Black Hawk: An Autobiography* (Urbana: University of Illinois Press, 1964), 88–90, 95–97, 111–13.

**Black Hawk (1767–1838)**

This portrait of Black Hawk, by Charles Bird King, shows the Indian leader as a young warrior, wearing a medal commemorating an early-nineteenth-century agreement with the U.S. government. Later, in 1830, when Congress approved Andrew Jackson's Indian Removal Act, Black Hawk mobilized Sauk and Fox warriors to protect ancestral lands in Illinois. "It was here, that I was born—and here lie the bones of many friends and relatives," the aging chief declared. "I . . . never could consent to leave it." Newberry Library.

Chief Justice John Marshall denied their claim to an independent national existence. Speaking for a majority of the justices, Marshall declared that Indian peoples were "domestic dependent nations." However, in *Worcester v. Georgia* (1832) Marshall sided with the Cherokees against Georgia. Voiding Georgia's extension of state law over the Cherokee, he held that Indian nations were "distinct political communities, having territorial boundaries, within which their authority is exclusive . . . [and this is] guaranteed by the United States."

Rather than guaranteeing the Cherokees' territory, the U.S. government took it from them. After negotiating a removal treaty with a minority Cherokee faction, American officials insisted that all Cherokees abide by it. However, only 2,000 of the 17,000 Cherokees had departed by the deadline of May 1838, and Martin Van Buren, who had succeeded Jackson as president, ordered General Winfield Scott to enforce the treaty. Scott's army rounded up about 14,000 Cherokees and forcibly marched them 1,200 miles to the new Indian Territory, an arduous journey they remembered as the Trail of Tears. Along the way 3,000 Indians died of starvation and exposure. After the Creeks, Chickasaws, and Choctaws moved west of the Mississippi, the only remaining Indian people in the Old Southwest were the Seminoles. Aided by runaway slaves who had married into the tribe, the Seminoles fought a successful guerrilla war during the 1840s and retained their lands in Florida. They were the exceptions. The national government had forced the removal of most eastern Indian peoples.

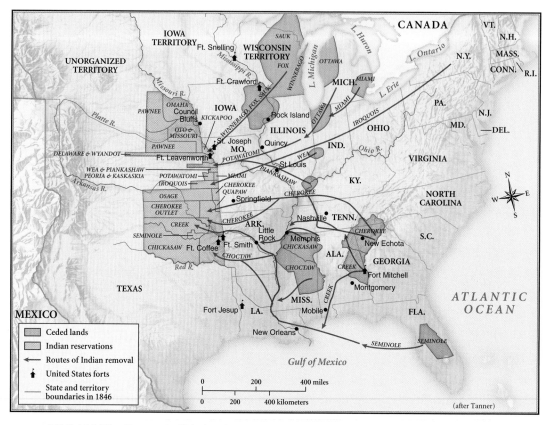

**MAP 11.2 The Removal of Native Americans, 1820–1843**

Beginning in the 1820s the U.S. government coerced scores of Native American peoples to sign treaties that exchanged Indian lands in the East for money and designated tracts in the West. During the 1830s the government used military force to expel the Cherokees, Chickasaws, Choctaws, Creeks, and many Seminoles from their ancestral homes in the Old Southeast and resettle them on reservations in the present-day states of Oklahoma and Kansas.

FOR MORE HELP ANALYZING THIS MAP, see the Online Study Guide at **bedfordstmartins.com/henrettaconcise**.

## The Jacksonian Impact

Jackson's legacy, like that of every great president, was complex and rich. Thus, he permanently expanded the authority of the nation's chief executive. Using the rhetoric of popular sovereignty, Jackson asserted that "the President is the direct representative of the American people." Assuming that role during the nullification crisis, he upheld national authority by threatening the use of military force. At the same time, Jackson purposefully curbed the reach of national power. By undermining Clay's American System, he reinvigorated the Jeffersonian tradition of a limited and frugal central government.

As Jackson and his Democratic Party achieved political ascendancy, they infused many American institutions with their principles. Following John Marshall's death, Jackson appointed Roger B. Taney as chief justice of the Supreme Court. During his long tenure (1835–1864), Taney persuaded the Court to give constitutional legitimacy to Jackson's policies of antimonopoly and states' rights. In the landmark case *Charles River Bridge Co. v. Warren Bridge Co.* (1837), Taney declared that a legislative charter did not necessarily bestow a monopoly. Consequently, the legislature could promote the general welfare by chartering a competing bridge company. As Taney put it, "While the rights of private property are sacredly guarded, we must not forget that the community also has rights." This decision challenged John Marshall's interpretation of the contract clause of the Constitution in *Dartmouth College v. Woodward* (1819), which had emphasized the binding nature of public charters (see Chapter 8). By limiting the property claims of existing canal and turnpike companies, the decision opened the way for legislatures to charter railroads that would provide a cheaper and more efficient transportation system.

Other decisions by the Taney Court placed limits on Marshall's nationalistic interpretation of the commerce clause by enhancing the regulatory role of state governments. For example, in *Mayor of New York v. Miln* (1837) the Taney Court ruled that New York State could use its "police power" to inspect the health of arriving immigrants. The Jacksonian Court also restored to the states some of the economic powers they had exercised before 1787. In *Briscoe v. Bank of Kentucky* (1837) the Court ruled that issuance of currency by a bank owned and controlled by the state of Kentucky did not violate the provision of the U.S. Constitution (Article 1, Section 10, on p. D-13) that prohibits states from issuing "bills of credit."

Jacksonian Democrats in the various states mounted their own constitutional revolutions. Between 1830 and 1860 twenty states called conventions to revise their basic charters. Most states extended the vote to all white men and reapportioned their legislatures on the basis of population. The revised constitutions also brought government "near to the people" by mandating the election, rather than the appointment, of most public officials—including sheriffs, justices of the peace, and judges.

Just as Jackson had destroyed the American System and its program of national government subsidies, so his disciples in the states undermined the "commonwealth" philosophy of using chartered corporations and state funds to promote economic development. Most Jacksonian-era constitutions prohibited states from granting exclusive charters to corporations or extending loans and credit guarantees to private businesses. "If there is any danger to be feared in . . . government," declared a New Jersey Democrat, "it is the danger of associated wealth, with special privileges." The revised state constitutions also protected taxpayers by setting strict limits on state debts and encouraging judges to enforce them. As a New York reformer put it, "We will not trust the legislature with the power of creating indefinite mortgages on the people's property."

"The world is governed too much," the Jacksonians proclaimed, as they condemned government-granted special privileges and embraced a small-government, laissez-faire outlook. The first American "populists," they celebrated the power of ordinary people to make decisions in the marketplace and the voting booth.

# Class, Culture, and the Second Party System

The rise of the Democracy and Jackson's tumultuous presidency sparked the creation in the mid-1830s of a second national party—the Whigs—and a new party system. For the next two decades Whigs and Democrats competed fiercely for votes. Many evangelical Protestants became Whigs, while most Catholics and nonevangelical Protestants joined the Democrats. By debating issues of economic policy, class power, and moral reform, party politicians offered Americans a clear choice between rival political ideologies and programs.

## *The Whig Worldview*

The Whig Party began in 1834, when a group of congressmen banded together to oppose Andrew Jackson's policies and his high-handed, "kinglike" conduct. They took the name Whigs to identify themselves with the pre-Revolutionary American and British parties—also called Whigs—that had opposed the arbitrary actions of British monarchs. The Whigs accused "King Andrew I" of violating the Constitution by creating a "spoils system" and increasing presidential authority. Jackson's "executive usurpation," they charged, undermined government by elected legislators, who were the true representatives of the sovereign people.

Initially the Whigs were a diverse group, a "heterogeneous mass" drawn from various political factions and outlooks. However, led by Senators Webster of Massachusetts, Clay of Kentucky, and Calhoun of South Carolina, the Whigs gradually elaborated a distinct vision. Their goal, like that of the Federalists of the 1790s, was a political world dominated by men of ability and wealth; unlike the Federalists, the Whig elite would be chosen by talent, not birth.

The Whigs celebrated the role played by enterprising entrepreneurs. "This is a country of self-made men," they boasted, pointing to the relative absence of permanent distinctions of class and status among the white citizens of the United States. Embracing the Industrial Revolution, northern Whigs welcomed the investments of "moneyed capitalists" which provided the poor with jobs, "bread, clothing and homes." Whig congressman Edward Everett told a Fourth of July crowd in Lowell, Massachusetts, that there was a "holy alliance" among laborers, owners, and governments. Many workers agreed, especially those holding jobs in the New England textile factories and Pennsylvania iron mills that benefited from state subsidies and protective tariffs. To ensure continued economic progress, Everett and other northern Whigs called for a return to the American System of Henry Clay and John Quincy Adams.

BORN TO COMMAND.

OF VETO MEMORY.

HAD I BEEN CONSULTED.

KING ANDREW THE FIRST.

### A Whig Cartoon

Attacking the president as "KING ANDREW THE FIRST," this political cartoon accuses Andrew Jackson of acting arbitrarily, like a monarch, and trampling on the principles of the Constitution. It emphasizes Jackson's contempt for Congress, expressed in his vetoes of legislation on banking and internal improvements. Seeking to turn democratic fervor and popular sovereignty to the advantage of the Whig Party, the caption asked: "Shall he reign over us, or shall the PEOPLE RULE?"

New-York Historical Society.

Support for the Whigs in the South rested on the appeal of specific policies rather than agreement with the Whigs' social vision. Some southern Whigs were wealthy planters who invested in railroads and banks or sold their cotton to New York merchants. The majority were yeomen whites who wanted to break the grip over state politics held by low-country planters, most of whom were Democrats. In addition, some states' rights Democrats in Virginia and South Carolina became Whigs because, like John C. Calhoun, they condemned Andrew Jackson's crusade against nullification.

Like Calhoun, most southern Whigs did not share their party's enthusiasm for high tariffs and social mobility. Indeed, Calhoun argued that the northern Whig ideal of equal opportunity was contradicted not only by slavery, which he considered a fundamental American institution, but also by the wage-labor system of industrial capitalism. "There is and always has been in an advanced state of wealth and civilization a conflict between labor and capital," Calhoun argued in 1837. He urged slave owners and factory owners to unite against their common foe: the working class composed of enslaved blacks and propertyless whites.

Most northern Whigs rejected Calhoun's class-conscious vision. "A clear and well-defined line between capital and labor" might fit the slave South or class-ridden European societies, Daniel Webster conceded, but in the North "this distinction grows less and less definite as commerce advances." Webster focused on the growing size and affluence of the northern middle class. Indeed, in the election of 1834 the Whigs won a majority in the House of Representatives by appealing to evangelical Protestants and upwardly mobile groups—the prosperous farmers, small-town merchants, and skilled industrial workers in New England, New York, and the new communities along the Great Lakes.

Many Whigs had previously supported the Anti-Masonic Party, a powerful but short-lived political movement of the late 1820s. As the name implies, Anti-Masons opposed the Order of Freemasonry, a secret deistic and republican organization that began in eighteenth-century Europe. The order spread rapidly in America and attracted political leaders—including George Washington, Henry Clay, and Andrew Jackson—and ambitious businessmen. By the mid-1820s there were 20,000 Masons in New York State alone, organized into 450 local lodges. Following the kidnapping and murder of William Morgan, a New York Mason who had threatened to reveal the order's secrets, the order fell into disrepute. Thurlow Weed, a Rochester newspaper editor, spearheaded an Anti-Masonic political party that attacked Masonry as a secret aristocratic fraternity and ousted its members from local and state offices.

The Whigs recruited Anti-Masons by endorsing their values of temperance, equality of opportunity, and evangelical moralism. Throughout the Northeast and Midwest, Whig politicians advocated legal curbs on the sale of alcohol and supported local by-laws that preserved Sunday as a day of worship. The Whigs also won congressional seats in the Ohio and Mississippi Valleys, where farmers, bankers, and shopkeepers favored Henry Clay's policies for governmental subsidies for roads, canals, and bridges.

In the election of 1836 the Whig Party faced Martin Van Buren, the architect of the Democratic Party and Jackson's handpicked successor. Van Buren denounced the American System and warned that its revival would undermine the rights of the states and create an oppressive system of "consolidated government." Positioning himself as a defender of individual rights, Van Buren likewise opposed the plans of Whigs and moral reformers to use governmental power to impose temperance and abolish slavery. "The government is best which governs least" became his motto.

To oppose Van Buren, the Whigs ran four regional candidates. Their plan was to garner enough electoral votes to throw the contest into the House of Representatives. However, the Whig tally—73 electoral votes collected by William Henry Harrison of Ohio, 26 by Hugh L. White of Tennessee, 14 by Daniel Webster of Massachusetts, and 11 by W. P. Mangum of Georgia—fell far short of Van Buren's 170 votes. Still, the size of the popular vote for the four Whig candidates— 49 percent of the total—showed that the party's message of economic improvement and moral uplift appealed not only to middle-class Americans but also to farmers and workers with little or no property. For the next two decades, Whigs and Democrats dominated American political life.

## Labor Politics and the Depression of 1837–1843

As the Democratic and Whig Parties battled for supremacy, they faced a challenge from the Working Men's Parties that had sprung up in fifteen states between 1827 and 1833. Rising prices and stagnant wages had lowered the standard of living of many urban artisans and wage earners. Increasingly aware of what they called "the glaring inequality of society," workers organized for political action. "Past experience teaches us that we have nothing to hope from the aristocratic orders of society," declared the New York Working Men's Party. It vowed "to send men of our own description, if we can, to the Legislature at Albany" and to pass laws that would put an end to private banks, chartered monopolies, and imprisonment for debt. In Philadelphia, the Working Men's Party demanded higher taxes on the wealthy and, in 1834, persuaded the Pennsylvania legislature to authorize free, tax-supported schools to assist workers' children to advance into the propertied classes.

Artisan republicanism—workers' independence—was the core ideology of Working Men's Parties. Their goal was a society in which (as the radical thinker Orestes Brownson put it) there would be no dependent wage earners and "all men will be independent proprietors, working on their own capitals, on their own farms, or in their own shops." This vision prompted many artisan-republicans to join Jacksonian Democrats in demanding equal rights and attacking chartered corporations. "The only safeguard against oppression," argued William Leggett, a leading member of the New York Loco-Foco (Equal Rights) Party, "is a system of legislation which leaves to all the free exercise of their talents and industry." At first the Working Men's Parties prospered at the polls, but divisions over policy and voter apathy soon took a toll. By the mid-1830s most politically active workers had joined the Democratic Party, which they urged to oppose protective tariffs and to tax the stocks and bonds of wealthy capitalists.

Even as they campaigned for a more egalitarian society, workers formed unions to bargain for higher wages for themselves. Employers responded by attacking the union movement. In 1836 clothing manufacturers in New York City agreed not to hire workers belonging to the Society of Journeymen Tailors and circulated a list—a so-called **blacklist**—of its members. The employers also brought lawsuits to overturn **closed-shop agreements** that required them to hire only union members. They argued that such contracts violated both the common law and legislative statutes that prohibited "conspiracies" in restraint of trade.

Judges usually agreed with the employers. In 1835 the New York Supreme Court found that a shoemakers' union in Geneva had illegally caused "an industrious man" to be "driven out of employment." "It is important to the best interests of society that the price of labor be left to regulate itself," the Court declared. When a court in New York City upheld a conspiracy verdict against a tailors' union, a crowd of 27,000 people demonstrated outside city hall, and tailors circulated handbills proclaiming that the "Freemen of the North are now on a level with the slaves of the South." In 1836, such popular demonstrations prompted juries to acquit shoemakers in Hudson, New York, carpet makers in Thompsonville, Connecticut, and plasterers in Philadelphia of similar conspiracy charges.

At this juncture the Panic of 1837 threw the American economy—and the union movement—into disarray. The panic began when the Bank of England, hoping to boost the faltering British economy, sharply curtailed the flow of money and credit to the United States. For the previous decade and a half, British manufacturers and investors had provided southern planters with credit to expand cotton production and had purchased millions of dollars of the canal bonds issued by northern states. Suddenly deprived of British funds, American planters, merchants, and canal corporations had to withdraw specie from domestic banks to pay their foreign loans and commercial debts. Moreover, because the Bank of England refused credit to brokers to buy cotton, the price of raw cotton in the South collapsed from 20 cents a pound to 10 cents or less.

Falling cotton prices and the drain of gold and silver set off a general financial crisis. On May 8 the Dry Dock Bank of New York City closed its doors. Panicked depositors quickly withdrew more than $2 million in gold and silver coins from other New York banks, which forced them to suspend all specie payments. Within two weeks every bank in the United States stopped trading specie and curtailed credit, which sent the economy into a steep decline. "This sudden overthrow of the commercial credit and honor of the nation" had a "stunning effect," observed Henry Fox, the British minister in Washington. "The conquest of the land by a foreign power could hardly have produced a more general sense of humiliation and grief."

A second, longer-lasting economic downturn began in 1839. Following the Panic of 1837, state governments increased their investments in canals and other transportation ventures. As more and more bonds to finance these ventures were sold in Europe, bond prices fell sharply and sparked a four-year-long international financial crisis. The crisis engulfed state governments, which were unable to meet the substantial interest payments on their bonds. Nine states defaulted on their obligations to foreign creditors, which undermined the confidence of European investors and cut the flow of capital to the United States. Bumper crops drove down cotton prices even further, bringing more bankruptcies.

The American economy fell into a deep depression. By 1843 canal construction had dropped 90 percent and prices nearly 50 percent. Unemployment reached almost 20 percent of the workforce in seaports and industrial centers. Minister Henry Ward Beecher described a land "filled with lamentation . . . its inhabitants wandering like bereaved citizens among the ruins of an earthquake, mourning for children, for houses crushed, and property buried forever."

By creating a surplus of unemployed workers, the depression devastated the labor movement. In 1837, six thousand masons, carpenters, and other building-trades workers lost their jobs in New York City, depleting union membership and destroying unions' bargaining power. By 1843 most local unions and all the national labor organizations had disappeared, along with their newspapers.

However, two events improved the long-term prospects of the labor movement. The first was a major legal success. In *Commonwealth v. Hunt* (1842), Massachusetts chief justice Lemuel Shaw upheld the rights of workers to form unions and enforce a closed shop. Shaw, one of the great jurists of the nineteenth century, overturned common-law precedents by ruling that a union was not an inherently illegal organization and could strike to enforce a closed shop. Courts in many states accepted Shaw's opinion, but judges (who were mostly Whigs) found other methods, such as **court injunctions**, to restrict strikes. Labor's second success was political. Continuing Jackson's effort to recruit workers to the Democratic Party, President Van Buren signed an executive order in 1840 setting a ten-hour day for federal employees. This victory showed that the outcome of workers' struggles—like conflicts over tariffs, banks, and internal improvements—depended not only on economic factors but also on political decisions.

### *"Tippecanoe and Tyler Too!"*

The depression had a major impact on politics because many Americans blamed the Democrats for their economic woes. In particular, they derided Jackson for destroying the Second Bank and for issuing the Specie Circular of 1836, which required western settlers to use gold and silver coins to pay for land purchases. Not realizing that specie shipments to Britain (to pay off past debts) were the main cause of the financial panic, the Whigs blamed Jackson's policies.

The public turned its anger on Van Buren, who took office just as the panic began. Ignoring the pleas of influential bankers, the new president refused to revoke the Specie Circular or take other actions to reverse the downturn. Holding to his philosophy of limited government, Van Buren advised Congress that "the less government interferes with private pursuits the better for the general prosperity." As a major depression took hold in 1839, this laissez-faire outlook commanded less and less political support. Worse, Van Buren's major piece of economic legislation, the Independent Treasury Act of 1840, actually delayed recovery. The act pulled federal specie out of Jackson's "pet banks" (which had used it to back loans) and placed it in government vaults (where it did no economic good at all).

Determined to exploit Van Buren's weakness, the Whigs organized their first national convention in 1840 and nominated William Henry Harrison of Ohio for president and John Tyler of Virginia for vice president. A military hero of the Battle of Tippecanoe and the War of 1812, Harrison was well advanced in age (sixty-eight) and had little political experience. But the Whig leaders in Congress, Clay and Webster, simply wanted a president who would rubber-stamp their program for protective tariffs and a national bank. An unpretentious, amiable man, Harrison told voters that Whig policies were "the only means, under Heaven, by which a poor industrious man may become a rich man without bowing to colossal wealth."

Panic and depression stacked the political cards against Van Buren, but the contest turned as much on style as on substance. It became the great "log cabin"

**The Log Cabin Campaign, 1840**

During the Second Party System, politics became more responsive to the popular will as ordinary people voted for candidates who shared their values and lifestyles. The barrels of hard cider surrounding this homemade campaign banner evoke the drink of the common man, while the central image falsely portrays William Henry Harrison as a poor and simple frontier farmer.
New-York Historical Society.

campaign—the first occasion on which two well-organized parties competed for the loyalties of a mass electorate and created a new style of festive political celebrations. Whig pamphleteering, songfests, parades, and well-orchestrated mass meetings drew new voters into the political arena. Whig speakers assailed "Martin Van Ruin" as a manipulative politician with aristocratic tastes—a devotee of fancy wines and elegant clothes, as indeed he was. With less candor they praised Harrison, whose father was a wealthy planter who had signed the Declaration of Independence, as a self-made man who lived in a simple log cabin and enjoyed hard cider, a drink of the common people.

The Whigs boosted their electoral hopes by welcoming women to their festivities. Previously women had been excluded not only from voting and jury duty but also from marching in political parades. Jacksonian Democrats celebrated politics as a "manly" affair and denounced women who ventured into the political arena as "public" women—the prostitutes who plied their trade in theaters and other public places. However, the Whigs recognized that women from Yankee families, a core Whig constituency, had already entered American public life through religious revivalism, the temperance movement, and other benevolent activities. In October 1840 Daniel Webster addressed a mass meeting of 1,200 Whig women and praised their support for the Whig programs for moral reform. "This way of making politicians of their women is something new under the sun," noted one Democrat, worried that it would bring more Whig men to the polls. Indeed, more than 80 percent of the eligible male voters cast ballots in 1840 (up from less than 60 percent in 1832 and 1836). Heeding the Whig slogan "Tippecanoe and Tyler Too," they voted Harrison into the White House and gave the Whigs a majority in Congress.

The Whigs' joy was short-lived. One month after his inauguration Harrison died of pneumonia, and the nation got "Tyler Too." The new president, John Tyler of Virginia, had joined the Whigs to oppose Jackson's stance against nullification. On economic issues Tyler shared Jackson's hostility to the Second Bank and the American System. Consequently, he vetoed bills that would have raised tariffs and created a new national bank. Also like Jackson, Tyler favored the rapid settlement of the West. He approved the Preemption Act of 1841, which allowed cash-poor settlers to stake a free claim to 160 acres of federal land. By building a house and farming the land, they could buy the property later at a set price of $1.25 an acre.

The split between Tyler and the Whigs allowed the Democrats to regroup. The party vigorously recruited supporters among subsistence farmers in the North and smallholding planters in the South. It cultivated the votes of the urban working class and was particularly successful among Irish and German Catholic immigrants—whose numbers had increased rapidly during the 1830s—by supporting their demands for religious and cultural freedom. Thanks to these recruits, the Democrats remained the majority party in most parts of the nation. Their program of equal rights, states' rights, and cultural liberty was more attractive than the Whig platform of economic nationalism, moral reform, and individual mobility.

The continuing struggle between Whigs and Democrats, each claiming to speak for "the people," completed the democratic revolution that European visitors found so troubling. The new system perpetuated many problematic political customs—denying women, Indians, and most African Americans an effective voice in public life—and introduced a few more dubious practices, such as the spoils system and a coarser standard of public debate. Yet the United States now boasted universal suffrage for white men as well as a highly organized system of representative government that was responsive to ordinary citizens. In their scope and significance these political initiatives matched the economic advances of the Industrial and Market Revolutions.

## T I M E L I N E

| | | | |
|---|---|---|---|
| **1810s** | State constitutions revised to expand voting rights for white men<br><br>Martin Van Buren creates a disciplined party in New York | **1833** | Force Bill and compromise Tariff Act |
| | | **1834** | Whig Party formed by Henry Clay, John C. Calhoun, and Daniel Webster |
| **1825** | John Quincy Adams elected president by House; advocates Henry Clay's American System | **1835** | Roger Taney named Supreme Court chief justice |
| | | **1837** | *Charles River Bridge Co. v. Warren Bridge Co.* weakens legal position of chartered monopolies<br><br>Panic of 1837 ends long period of economic expansion |
| **1827** | Philadelphia Working Men's Party organized | | |
| **1828** | "Tariff of Abominations" raises duties on imported materials and manufactures<br><br>*The South Carolina Exposition and Protest* challenges legitimacy of national legislation and majority rule | **1838** | Trail of Tears: thousands of Cherokees die on forced march to new Indian Territory |
| | | **1839** | American borrowings spark international financial crisis and four-year economic depression |
| **1830** | Andrew Jackson vetoes extension of National Road<br><br>Congress enacts Jackson's Indian Removal Act | **1840** | Van Buren finally wins Independent Treasury Act<br><br>Whig victory in "log cabin" campaign |
| **1831** | *Cherokee Nation v. Georgia* denies Indians' claim of national independence | **1841** | John Tyler succeeds William Henry Harrison as president<br><br>Preemption Act promotes purchase of federal land |
| **1832** | Expulsion of Sauk and Fox peoples; Bad Axe Massacre by American troops<br><br>Jackson vetoes the rechartering of the Second Bank<br><br>South Carolina asserts intention to nullify Tariffs of 1828 and 1832<br><br>*Worcester v. Georgia* upholds political autonomy of Indian peoples | **1842** | *Commonwealth v. Hunt* legitimates trade unions |

# For Further Exploration

George Dangerfield, *The Era of Good Feelings* (1952), is the classic study of American politics between 1815 and 1828. Two concise and well-written surveys of the Jacksonian era are Harry L. Watson, *Liberty and Power: The Politics of Jacksonian America* (1990), which emphasizes the importance of republican ideology and the Market Revolution, and Daniel Feller, *The Jacksonian Promise: America, 1815–1840* (1995), which underlines its tremendous optimism. In *The Idea of a Party System* (1969), Richard Hofstadter lucidly explains the traditional opposition to parties and their triumphant entry into American politics. The Internet Public Library has material on the election of 1824, the John Quincy Adams administration, and links to primary sources at <http://www.ipl.org/div/potus/jqadams.html>.

Robert V. Remini, *The Life of Andrew Jackson* (1988), highlights Jackson's triumphs without neglecting his shortcomings. The brutal impact of Jackson's Indian policy is brought to life in Robert J. Conley, *Mountain Windsong: A Novel of the Trail of Tears* (1992) and two studies by historians: Sean Michael O'Brien, *In Bitterness and in Tears: Andrew Jackson's Destruction of the Creeks and Seminoles* (2003) and John Buchanan, *Jackson's Way: Andrew Jackson and the People of the Western Waters* (2001). Major L. Wilson, *The Presidency of Martin Van Buren* (1984), provides a shrewd assessment of the man and his policies. The ideology and politics of the laboring population is the focus of Sean Wilentz, *Chants Democratic: New York City and the Rise of the American Working Class, 1788–1850* (1986).

Alexis de Tocqueville's classic, *Democracy in America* (1835), should be sampled for its insights into the character of American society and political institutions. The book is available online accompanied by an excellent exhibit and collection of essays at <http://xroads.virginia.edu/~hyper/detoc/home.html>. For a brief treatment of the life of Andrew Jackson and some of his important state papers, log on to the Revolution to Reconstruction site at the University of Groningen in the Netherlands at <http://odur.let.rug.nl/~usa/P/aj7/aj7.htm>. For material on the Cherokees, see the Web site prepared by Ken Martin, a tribal member of the Cherokee Nation of Oklahoma, <http://cherokeehistory.com/>, and also <http://www.rosecity.net/tears/>, which has links to articles, primary sources, and other Web sites.

---

For definitions of key terms boldfaced in this chapter, see the glossary at the end of the book.

To assess your mastery of the material covered in this chapter, see the Online Study Guide at **bedfordstmartins.com/henrettaconcise**.

For map resources and primary documents, see **bedfordstmartins.com/henrettaconcise**.

# Chapter 12

# RELIGION AND REFORM
## 1820–1860

A peaceable man can hardly venture to eat or drink, . . . to correct his
child or kiss his wife, without obtaining the permission . . . of some
moral or other reform society.

ORESTES BROWNSON, 1838

"The spirit of reform is in every place," the children of legal reformer
David Dudley Field wrote in their handwritten monthly *Gazette* in 1842:

> The labourer with a family says "reform the common schools"; the merchant
> and the planter say, "reform the tariff"; the lawyer "reform the laws," the politi-
> cian "reform the government," the abolitionist "reform the slave laws," the
> moralist "reform intemperance," . . . the ladies wish their legal privileges ex-
> tended, and in short, the whole country is wanting reform.

Like many Americans, the young Field children sensed that the political whirlwind
of the 1830s had transformed the way people thought about themselves as individuals and as a society. Suddenly, thousands of men and women, inspired by the optimistic enthusiasm of the Second Great Awakening and democratic spirit of the age,
believed they could improve not just their personal lives but society as a whole. Some
dedicated themselves to the cause of reform. Beginning as an antislavery advocate,
William Lloyd Garrison went on to embrace women's rights, pacifism, and the abolition of prisons. Such individuals, the Unitarian minister Henry W. Bellows warned,
were obsessed, pursuing "an object, which in its very nature is unattainable—the
perpetual improvement of the outward condition."

Many obstacles stood in the way of the reformers' quest for a better society. The
American social order was rigidly divided by race and gender as well as by wealth and
religious belief. Moreover, recent social changes imposed new burdens on some individuals even as they enhanced the standard of living for many others. Most strikingly, the new market economy encouraged greater discipline, both at work and in
family life. Planters forced enslaved African Americans to labor in organized gangs,
and factory managers prescribed strict routines for factory operatives. Moreover, the

first wave of American "social improvers," the benevolent reformers of the 1820s, celebrated the extension of discipline over all phases of life. To solve the nation's ills, they championed regular church attendance, temperance, and the strict moral codes of the evangelical churches.

Then in the 1830s and 1840s a more radical wave of reform spilled out of these conservative religious channels and threatened to submerge traditional values and institutions. The new reformers were mostly middle-class northerners and midwesterners. They propounded a bewildering assortment of radical ideals—extreme individualism, common ownership of property, the immediate emancipation of slaves, and sexual equality—and demanded immediate action to satisfy their visions. Although they formed a small minority of the American population, the reformers launched intellectual and cultural debate that won the attention, if not the respect, of the majority. As a fearful southerner saw it, the goal of the reformers was a world in which there would be "No-Marriage, No-Religion, No-Private Property, No-Law and No-Government."

# Individualism

The reform movement reflected the actual social conditions and intellectual currents of American life. In 1835 Alexis de Tocqueville coined a new word, *individualism,* to describe the lives of native-born white Americans. In his view, Americans were "no longer attached to each other by any tie of caste, class, association, or family" and so lived in a more solitary world than most Europeans did. Unlike Tocqueville, an aristocrat who feared the disintegration of society, the New England transcendentalist Ralph Waldo Emerson (1803–1882) celebrated this liberation of the individual from traditional social and institutional constraints. Emerson's vision of individual freedom—balanced by a sense of personal responsibility—influenced thousands of ordinary Americans and a generation of important artists and writers.

### Emerson and Transcendentalism

Emerson was the leading spokesman for **transcendentalism**, an intellectual movement rooted in the religious soil of New England. Its first advocates were spiritually inclined young men, often Unitarian ministers from well-to-do New England families, who questioned the constraints of their Puritan heritage. For inspiration they turned to Europe and a new conception of self and society known as *Romanticism.* Romantic thinkers, such as the English poet Samuel Taylor Coleridge, rejected the ordered, rational world of the eighteenth-century Enlightenment. Instead they tried to capture the passionate aspects of the human spirit and gain deeper insights into the mysteries of existence. Drawing on the ideas of the German philosopher Immanuel Kant, English romantics and Unitarian radicals tried to go beyond rational thought and the world experienced through the senses of sight and sound

**The Founder of Transcendentalism**

As this painting of Ralph Waldo Emerson by an unknown artist indicates, the young New England philosopher was an attractive man, his face brimming with confidence and optimism. Because of his radiant personality and incisive intellect, Emerson deeply influenced dozens of influential writers, artists, and scholars and enjoyed great success as a lecturer among the emerging middle class. The Metropolitan Museum of Art, bequest of Chester Dale, 1962 [64.97.4].

and touch. By tapping mysterious intuitive powers people could "transcend" the limits of ordinary existence and gain mystical knowledge of ultimate and eternal things.

As a Unitarian minister, Emerson already stood outside the mainstream of American Protestantism. Unlike most Christians, Unitarians held that God was a single being and not a trinity of Father, Son, and Holy Spirit. In 1832 Emerson took a more radical step by resigning his Boston pulpit and rejecting all organized religion. Moving to Concord, Massachusetts, he gradually articulated the philosophy of transcendentalism. In a series of influential essays Emerson focused on what he called "the infinitude of the private man," the idea of the radically free individual.

The young philosopher saw people as being trapped in inherited customs and institutions. They wore the ideas of earlier times—the tenets of New England Calvinism, for example—as a kind of "faded masquerade" and needed to shed those values and practices. "What is a man born for but to be a Reformer, a Remaker of what man has made?" he asked. For Emerson, an individual could be remade only by discovering his or her own "original relation with Nature," an insight that would produce a mystical union with the "currents of Universal Being." The ideal setting for such a transcendent discovery was solitude under an open sky, among nature's rocks and trees.

Emerson's genius lay in his capacity to translate such abstract ideas into examples that made sense to ordinary middle-class Americans. His essays and lectures suggested that all nature was saturated with the presence of God—a pantheistic spiritual outlook that departed from traditional Christian doctrine. Emerson also warned his readers that the new market society was diverting the nation's spiritual energy into a preoccupation with work, profits, and the consumption of factory-made goods. "Things are in the saddle," Emerson wrote, "and ride mankind."

The transcendentalist message of self-realization reached hundreds of thousands of people, primarily through Emerson's writings and lectures. Public lectures had become a spectacularly successful way of spreading information and fostering discussion among the middle classes. Beginning in 1826 the American Lyceum promoted "the general diffusion of knowledge" by organizing lecture tours by hundreds of poets, preachers, scientists, and reformers. Named in honor of the place where the ancient Greek philosopher Aristotle taught, the Lyceum became an important cultural institution in the North and Midwest (but not in the South, where popular education had a lower priority and apologists for slavery discouraged the free discussion of ideas). In 1839, nearly 150 local Lyceums in Massachusetts invited lecturers to their towns to speak to more than 33,000 subscribers. The most popular lecturer on the Lyceum circuit, Emerson gave 1,500 lectures in more than 300 towns in twenty states.

Emerson's essays celebrated individuals who rejected traditional social restraints but acted as self-disciplined and responsible members of society. And, in fact, his writings spoke directly to the personal experience of many mid-nineteenth-century middle-class Americans, who had left the farms of their ancestors and made their own way in the urban world. Charles Grandison Finney's widely known account of his religious conversion underscored the appeal of Emerson's ideas and values. Finney pictured his conversion as a mystical union of an individual, alone in the woods, with God. And, like Emerson, Finney stressed the need to transcend the constraints and doctrines of the past. As the revivalist put it, "God has made man a moral free agent," endowing individuals with the ability—and the responsibility—to determine their spiritual fate.

### Emerson's Literary Influence

Emerson took as one of his tasks the remaking of American literature. In an address entitled "The American Scholar" (1837) the philosopher issued a literary declaration of independence from the "courtly muse" of Old Europe. He urged American writers to celebrate democracy and individual freedom and find inspiration not in the lives of kings and aristocrats but in ordinary experiences: "the ballad in the street; the news of the boat; the glance of the eye; the form and gait of the body."

A young New England intellectual, Henry David Thoreau (1817–1862) heeded Emerson's call by turning to the American environment for inspiration. In 1845, depressed by his beloved brother's death, Thoreau turned away from society and embraced the natural world. He built a cabin at the edge of Walden Pond near Concord, Massachusetts, and lived alone there for two years. In 1854 he published *Walden, or Life in the Woods*, an account of his spiritual search for meaning beyond the artificiality of "civilized" life:

> I went to the woods because I wished to live deliberately, to front only the essential facts of life, and see if I could not learn what it had to teach, and not, when I came to die, discover that I had not lived.

Although Thoreau's book had little impact during his lifetime, *Walden* has become an essential text of American literature and an inspiration to those who reject the dictates of society. Its most famous metaphor provides an enduring justification for independent thinking: "If a man does not keep pace with his companions, perhaps it is because he hears a different drummer." Beginning from this premise, Thoreau advocated social nonconformity and civil disobedience against unjust laws.

As Thoreau sought independence and self-realization for men, Margaret Fuller (1810–1850) explored the possibilities of freedom for women. Born into a wealthy Boston family, Fuller mastered six languages, read broadly in the classic works of literature, and educated her four siblings. While teaching in a school for girls, she became interested in Emerson's ideas and in 1839 began a transcendental "conversation," or discussion group, for educated Boston women. Soon Fuller was editing the leading transcendentalist journal, the *Dial*, and in 1844 she published *Woman in the Nineteenth Century*, which proclaimed that a "new era" was coming in the relations between men and women.

Fuller's philosophy began with the transcendental belief that women, like men, had a mystical relationship with God that gave them identity and dignity. Every woman therefore deserved psychological and social independence—the ability "to grow, as an intellect to discern, as a soul to live freely and unimpeded." "We would have every arbitrary barrier thrown down," she wrote, and "every path laid open to Woman as freely as to Man." Embracing that vision, Fuller became the literary critic of the New York *Tribune* and traveled to Italy to report on the Revolution of 1848. Her adventurous life led to an early death; returning to the United States, she drowned in a shipwreck. Nonetheless, Fuller's example and writings inspired a rising generation of women writers and reformers.

Another writer who responded to Emerson's call was the poet Walt Whitman (1819–1892). When Whitman first encountered Emerson, he had been "simmering, simmering." Then Emerson "brought me to a boil." Whitman worked as a teacher, a journalist, an editor of the *Brooklyn Eagle*, and an influential publicist for the Democratic Party. But poetry was the "direction of his dreams." In *Leaves of Grass*, first published in 1855 and constantly revised and expanded for almost four decades afterward, he recorded in verse his efforts to pass a number of "invisible boundaries": between solitude and community, between prose and poetry, and even between the living and the dead. A wild, exuberant poem in both form and content, *Leaves of Grass* self-consciously violated every poetic rule and every canon of respectable taste. At the center of *Leaves of Grass* is the individual—the figure of the poet, "I, Walt." He begins alone: "I celebrate myself, and sing myself." But because he has an Emersonian "original relation" with nature, Whitman claims not solitude but perfect communion with others: "For every atom belonging to me as good belongs to you." Whitman celebrates democracy as well as himself by seeking a profoundly intimate, mystical relationship with a mass audience. For Emerson, Thoreau, and Fuller, the individual had a divine spark. For Whitman the individual had expanded to become divine and democracy assumed a sacred character.

The transcendentalists were not naive optimists. Whitman wrote about human suffering with passion, and Emerson's accounts of transcendence were tinged with anxiety. "I am glad," he once said, "to the brink of fear." Thoreau had a gloomy judgment of everyday life: "The mass of men lead lives of quiet desperation." Still, such dark murmurings were muted in their work, overshadowed by triumphant and expansive assertions that nothing was impossible for an individual who could break free from tradition, law, and other social restraints.

Emerson's writings also influenced two great novelists, Nathaniel Hawthorne and Herman Melville, who had more pessimistic outlooks. Both sounded powerful warnings that unfettered egoism could destroy individuals and those around them. Hawthorne's most brilliant exploration of the theme of excessive individualism appeared in his novel *The Scarlet Letter* (1850). The two main characters, Hester Prynne and Arthur Dimmesdale, challenge their seventeenth-century New England community in the most blatant way—by committing adultery and producing a child. The result of their assertion of individual freedom from social discipline and responsibility is not liberation but degradation—a profound sense of personal guilt and condemnation by the community.

Herman Melville explored the limits of individualism in even more extreme and tragic terms and emerged as a scathing critic of transcendentalism. He made his most powerful statement in *Moby-Dick* (1851), the story of Captain Ahab's obsessive hunt for a mysterious white whale that ends in death not only for Ahab but also for all but one member of his crew. Here the quest for spiritual meaning in nature brings death, not transcendence, because Ahab, the liberated individual, lacks inner discipline and self-restraint.

*Moby-Dick* was a commercial failure. The middle-class audience that was the primary target of American publishers refused to follow Melville into the dark, dangerous realms of individualism gone mad. Readers also were unenthusiastic about Thoreau's advocacy of civil disobedience during the Mexican War and Whitman's boundless claims of a mystical union between the man of genius and the democratic masses. What American readers emphatically preferred were the more modest examples of individualism offered by Emerson and Finney—personal improvement through spiritual awareness and self-discipline.

## Brook Farm

To escape the constraints of life in America's emerging market society, transcendentalists and other radical reformers created ideal communities, or utopias. They hoped that these planned societies, which organized life in new ways, would allow their members to realize their spiritual and moral potential. The most important transcendentalist communal experiment was Brook Farm, founded just outside Boston in 1841. By opting out of the competition and tension of urban society, its members hoped to develop their minds and souls and to inspire a new social order.

The intellectual life at Brook Farm was electric. Hawthorne lived there for a time and later used the setting for his novel *The Blithedale Romance* (1852). All the major transcendentalists, including Emerson, Thoreau, and Fuller, were residents or frequent visitors. A former member recalled that they "inspired the young with a passion for study, and the middle-aged with deference and admiration, while we all breathed the intellectual grace that pervaded the atmosphere." If Brook Farm provided intellectual bliss, it offered few economic rewards. To escape the unpredictable boom-and-bust cycle of a market economy, the Brook Farmers sought to become self-sufficient in food and to exchange their surplus milk, vegetables, and hay for nonagricultural goods. However, its first members were ministers, teachers, writers, and students who had few farming skills, and only the cash payments of intellectually inclined residents kept the enterprise afloat. Following a devastating fire in 1846, the organizers disbanded and sold the farm.

After the failure of Brook Farm, the Emersonians abandoned their quest for a new system of social organization. Most transcendentalists accepted the brute reality of the emergent industrial order and tried to reform it, especially through the education of workers. However, the passion of the transcendentalists for individual freedom and social progress lived on in the movement to abolish slavery, which many of them actively supported.

# Communalism

Even as Brook Farm collapsed, thousands of Americans joined other communal settlements in the rural areas of the Northeast and Midwest (Map 12.1). Most communalists were ordinary farmers and artisans who were seeking refuge and security during the seven-year economic depression that began with the Panic of 1837. However, these rural utopias were also symbols of social protest and experimentation. By prescribing the common ownership of property and devising unconventional forms of marriage and family life, the communalist leaders challenged the legitimacy of acquisitive capitalist values and traditional gender roles.

## *The Shakers*

The Shakers were the first successful American communal movement. In 1770 Ann Lee Stanley (Mother Ann), a young cook in Manchester, England, had a vision that she was an incarnation of Christ and that Adam and Eve had been banished from

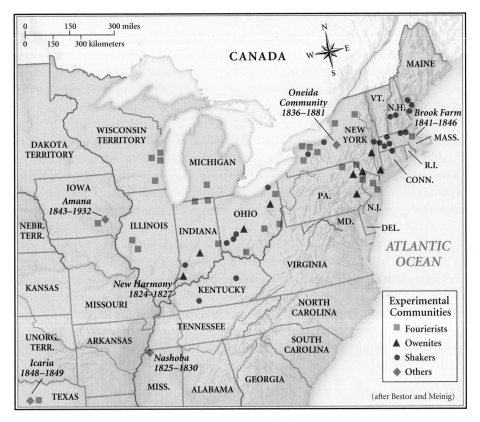

**MAP 12.1 Major Communal Experiments before 1860**

Some experimental communities settled along the frontier, but the vast majority chose relatively secluded areas in well-settled regions of the North and West. Because of their opposition to slavery, communalists avoided the South. Most secular experiments failed within a few decades, as the founders lost their reformist enthusiasm or died off; religious communities—such as the Shakers and the Mormons—were longer lived.

the Garden of Eden because of their sexual lust. Four years later she led a band of eight followers to America, where they established a church near Albany, New York. Because of the ecstatic dances that were part of their worship, the sect became known as "Shaking Quakers" or, more simply, "Shakers." After Mother Ann's death in 1784, the Shakers venerated her as the Second Coming of Christ, withdrew from the profane world, and formed strictly run religious communities. Members embraced the common ownership of property, accepted strict oversight by the church, and pledged to abstain from alcohol, tobacco, politics, and war. Shakers also repudiated marriage and sexual pleasure. Their commitment to celibacy followed Mother Ann's testimony against "the lustful gratifications of the flesh as the source and foundation of human corruption."

The Shakers' theology was as radical as their social thought. They held that God was "a dual person, male and female," and that Mother Ann represented God's female element. These doctrines underpinned their efforts to eliminate arbitrary distinctions of authority between the sexes. They placed community governance in the hands of both women and men—the eldresses and elders. However, in other respects Shakers maintained a traditional division of labor between the sexes.

Beginning in 1787 Shakers founded twenty communities, mostly in New England, New York, and Ohio. Their agriculture and crafts, especially furniture making, acquired a reputation for quality that enabled most of these communities to become self-sustaining and even comfortable. Thanks to this economic success and their ideology of sexual equality, Shaker communities attracted more than three thousand converts during the 1830s, with women outnumbering men more than two to one. They welcomed blacks as well as whites; to Rebecca Cox Jackson, an African American seamstress from Philadelphia, the Shakers seemed to be "loving to live forever." Because the Shakers disdained sexual intercourse and had no children of their own, they had to rely on converts and the adoption of young orphans to replenish their numbers. As these sources dried up in the 1840s and 1850s, the communities stopped growing and eventually began to decline. By the end of the nineteenth century most Shaker communities had disappeared, leaving as their material legacy a distinctive and much-imitated furniture style.

**The Shaker Community at Poland Hill, Maine (detail)**

Like all Shaker communities, the settlement at Poland Hill, Maine, painted by Joshua H. Bussell around 1850, was built on a regular gridlike plan. There was a large dwelling for communal living, surrounded by various workshops and farm buildings. The design of the architecture, like that of Shaker furniture, was plain and sparse.

Collection of the United Society of Shakers, Sabbathday Lake, ME.

FOR MORE HELP ANALYZING THIS IMAGE, see the Online Study Guide at **bedfordstmartins.com/ henrettaconcise**.

## The Fourierist Phalanxes

One cause of the Shakers' decline was the rise during the 1840s of the American Fourierist movement. Charles Fourier (1777–1837) was a French utopian reformer who devised an eight-stage theory of social evolution that predicted the imminent decline of individualism and capitalism. As interpreted by Arthur Brisbane, Fourier's leading American disciple, Fourierism would allow the completion of "our great political movement of 1776" by eliminating the "menial and slavish system of Hired Labor or Labor for Wages." In the place of capitalist waged labor, men and women would work cooperatively in communities called phalanxes. The members of a phalanx would be its shareholders; they would own all its property in common, including stores and a bank as well as a school and a library.

Fourier and Brisbane saw the phalanx as a practical, more humane alternative to a society based on private property and capitalist values, and one that would liberate women as well as men. "In society as it is now constituted," Brisbane wrote, "Woman is subjected to unremitting and slavish domestic duties." In the "new Social Order . . . based upon Associated households" women's domestic labor would be shared with men.

Brisbane skillfully promoted Fourier's ideas in his influential book *The Social Destiny of Man* (1840), a regular column in Horace Greeley's New York *Tribune*, and hundreds of lectures, many of them in towns along the Erie Canal. Fourierist ideas found a receptive audience among educated farmers and craftsmen, who yearned for economic stability and communal solidarity in the wake of the Panic of 1837. During the 1840s Brisbane and his followers started nearly one hundred cooperative communities, mostly in western New York and the midwestern states of Ohio, Michigan, and Wisconsin. However, most of these communities quickly collapsed because of internal disputes over work responsibilities and social policies. Just as the rise of Fourierism underscored the social dislocation caused by the economic depression, so its collapse showed the difficulty of establishing a utopian community in the absence of charismatic leaders or a compelling religious vision.

## John Humphrey Noyes and the Oneida Community

The radical minister John Humphrey Noyes (1811–1886) was both charismatic and deeply religious. He ascribed the Fourierists' failure to the absence of the strong religious ethic required for sustained altruism and cooperation and praised the Shakers as the true "pioneers of modern Socialism." The Shakers' marriageless society likewise appealed to Noyes and inspired him to create a community that defined sexuality and gender roles in radically new ways.

Noyes was a well-to-do graduate of Dartmouth College in New Hampshire who joined the ministry because of the inspired preaching of Charles Finney. Dismissed from his Congregational church for holding unorthodox beliefs, Noyes turned to perfectionism. Perfectionism was an evangelical movement that began in the 1830s and attracted thousands of religiously minded New Englanders who had moved to New York and Ohio. Perfectionists believed that the Second Coming of Christ had already occurred and that people could therefore aspire to sinless perfection in their earthly lives. Unlike most perfectionists (who lived conventional personal lives), Noyes believed that the major barrier to achieving this ideal state was marriage, which did not exist in heaven and should not exist on earth. "Exclusiveness, jealousy, quarreling have no place at the marriage supper of the Lamb," Noyes wrote. Like the Shakers, Noyes wanted to liberate individuals from sin by reforming relations between men and women. However, instead of Shaker celibacy, Noyes and his followers embraced complex marriage—all the members of his community were married to one another.

Noyes's marriage system reflected growing concern over the legal and cultural constraints on women's lives. He rejected monogamy partly because he wished to free women from being regarded as the property of their husbands, as they were by custom and by common law. To give women the time and energy to become full and equal participants in economic and social life, Noyes urged them to avoid multiple pregnancies. He asked men to assist this effort by avoiding orgasm during intercourse. To raise the children of his followers, Noyes set up communal nurseries that were run by both sexes. To symbolize sexual equality, Noyes's women followers cut their hair short and wore pantaloons under calf-length skirts.

In the late 1830s Noyes established a community based on complex marriage near his hometown of Putney, Vermont. When local opposition to his unorthodox sexual practices became intense, Noyes moved his followers to an isolated settlement in Oneida, New York. By the mid-1850s about two hundred people were living at Oneida, and it became financially successful when the inventor of a highly successful steel animal trap joined the community. With the profits acquired by selling those traps, Oneida diversified into the production of silverware. After Noyes fled to Canada in 1879 to avoid prosecution for adultery, the community abandoned complex marriage and founded a joint-stock silver manufacturing company, the Oneida Community, Ltd., which remained a well-known and prosperous enterprise well into the twentieth century.

As with the Shakers and Fourierists, the historical significance of Noyes and the Oneidians does not lie in their numbers, which were small, or in their fine crafts. Rather, these communities were important because, in a dramatically more radical fashion than Emerson and the transcendentalists, they questioned traditional customs and repudiated the class divisions and sexual norms of the emergent capitalist society. They stood as countercultural blueprints for a more egalitarian social order.

## The Mormon Experience

The Shakers and the Oneidians challenged marriage and family life—two of the most deeply rooted institutions—but their small communities aroused little hostility. The

Mormons, members of the Church of Jesus Christ of Latter-day Saints, provoked much more animosity because of their different, but equally controversial, doctrines and their success in attracting thousands of members.

Like many social movements of the era, Mormonism emerged from the religious ferment among families of Puritan descent who lived along the Erie Canal. The founder of the Mormon Church was Joseph Smith (1805–1844), a vigorous, powerful individual. Born in Vermont to a poor farming and shopkeeping family, he moved at the age of ten to Palmyra in central New York. In a series of religious experiences that began in 1820, Smith came to believe that God had singled him out to receive a special revelation of divine truth. In 1830 he published *The Book of Mormon*, which he claimed to have translated from ancient hieroglyphics on gold plates shown to him by an angel named Moroni. *The Book of Mormon* told the story of ancient civilizations from the Middle East that had migrated to the Western Hemisphere and of the visit of Jesus Christ, soon after the Resurrection, to one of them.

Smith proceeded to organize the Church of Jesus Christ of Latter-day Saints. Seeing himself as a prophet to a sinful, excessively individualistic society, Smith revived traditional social doctrines, such as patriarchal authority within the family. Like many Protestant ministers, he also encouraged practices that were central to individual success in the age of capitalist markets and factories—frugality, hard work, and entrepreneurial enterprise. Unlike most other nineteenth-century ministers, Smith placed great emphasis on a communal framework that would protect the Mormon "New Jerusalem" from individualism and rival religious doctrines. His goal was a church-directed society that would inspire moral perfection.

Smith struggled for years to establish a secure home for his new religion. Facing persecution from anti-Mormons, Smith and his growing congregation trekked west, eventually settling in Nauvoo, Illinois, a town they founded on the Mississippi River (Map 12.2). By the early 1840s Nauvoo had become the largest utopian community in the United States, with 30,000 inhabitants. The rigid discipline and secret rituals of the Mormons—along with their prosperity, hostility to other sects, and bloc voting in Illinois elections—fueled resentment among their neighbors. This resentment turned to overt hostility when Smith refused to abide by any Illinois law that he did not approve, asked Congress to turn Nauvoo into a separate federal territory, and declared himself a candidate for president of the United States (see American Voices, "An Illinois 'Jeffersonian' Attacks the Mormons," p. 365).

Moreover, Smith claimed to have received a new revelation that justified polygamy—the practice of a man having more than one wife at one time. When a few leading Mormon men took several wives, they sparked a vigorous debate within the Mormon community and enraged Christians in neighboring towns and villages. In 1844 Illinois officials arrested Smith and charged him with treason for allegedly conspiring with foreign powers to create a Mormon colony in Mexican territory. An anti-Mormon mob stormed the jail in Carthage, Illinois, where Smith and his brother were being held, and murdered them.

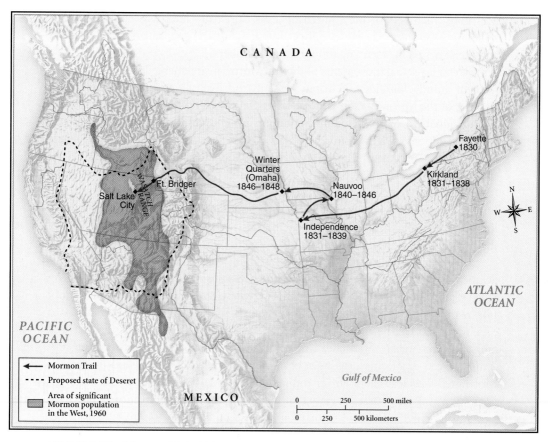

**MAP 12.2 The Mormon Trek, 1830–1848**

Because of their unorthodox religious views and communal solidarity, Mormons faced hostility first in New York and then in Missouri and Illinois. Following the murder of Joseph Smith, Brigham Young led the polygamist faction of Mormons into lands thinly populated by Native American peoples. From Omaha, the migrants followed the path of the Oregon Trail to Fort Bridger and then struck off to the Southwest, settling in Mexican territory along the Wasatch Range in the basin of the Great Salt Lake in present-day Utah.

Led by Brigham Young, a contingent of Mormons fled from these religious conflicts by leaving the United States. In 1846 Young guided more than 10,000 people across the Great Plains into Mexican territory, where they settled in the Great Salt Lake Valley in present-day Utah. Using communal labor and an elaborate irrigation system based on communal water rights, the Mormon pioneers transformed the region. They quickly spread planned agricultural communities along the base of the Wasatch mountain range. Many Mormons who rejected polygamy remained in the United States. Led by Smith's son, Joseph Smith III, they formed the Reorganized Church of Jesus Christ of Latter-day Saints and settled throughout the Midwest.

## AMERICAN VOICES

# An Illinois "Jeffersonian" Attacks the Mormons

*T*he corporate solidarity of the Mormons enraged many Illinois residents, who feared both the political power of Mormons' large and nearly independent city-state at Nauvoo and the military might of the two-thousand-strong "Legion" commanded by Joseph Smith. In 1844 a mob led by "respectable citizens" assassinated Smith and his brother, and some Illinois residents—such as the author of this letter to the Warsaw Signal, a newspaper in a town near Nauvoo—called for the forcible expulsion of the Mormons.

Mr. Editor,
... It is a low pitiable contemptable kind of electioneering, that old Tom Jefferson would have been ashamed of—when a body of men acting under the garb of religion (as the Mormons themselves say they are) shall decide our elections and act together as a body politically, we might as well bid a final farewell to our liberties and the common rights of man.

Now Sir, under all these circumstances, it is high time that every individual should come out and clearly define the position that he occupies. I too am an Anti-Mormon both in principle and in practice.... Mr. Editor when I speak harshly of the Mormons, I wish it to be perfectly understood I do not mean every individual that advocates the Mormon cause. By no means; that there are some good, law-abiding peaceable citizens belonging to the Mormon profession I verily believe ... but I am opposed to them because of the unprincipled manner in which the leaders of that fanatical sect, set at defiance the laws of the land ... (as was the case in Missouri) claiming to be the chosen people of God; not subject to the laws of the state in any respect whatever, and receiving revelations direct from Heaven almost daily commanding them to take the property of the older citizens of the county and confiscate it to the use of the Mormon church....

It was for the commission of such deeds together with deeds ten fold more dark and damning in their nature that finally led to their expulsion from that state, and one of the brightest pages in the history of Missouri is that, on which is written "Governor Boggs's exterminating order" directing that the lawless rabble should be driven beyond the limits of the state....

Strange to tell, yet such is the fact, they have commenced nearly the same operation here that they did in Missouri ... they have attempted to subsidize the press, thereby attempting to corrupt the very fountains of public virtue,—they have went [sic] into the legislative halls and attempted to bribe the representatives of the people ... and made them their tools.

They have in short, by a long series of high handed outrages ... forfeited all claims (if any they ever had) to confidence and respect, and ought justly to receive the condemnation of every individual, not only in this community, but in this nation.

SOURCE: David Brion Davis, *Antebellum America: An Interpretive Anthology* (University Park: Pennsylvania State University Press, 1997), 226–27.

**A Mormon Man and His Wives**

During the 1840s various groups of Americans—including Shakers, Fourierists, and women's rights advocates—challenged traditional definitions of gender roles and of marriage. Generally, these groups sought to free women from restrictive customs and their husbands' authority. Conversely, the Mormons who migrated to Utah hoped to preserve traditional patriarchal authority and, through the practice of polygamy, to extend it. However, only a minority of Mormon men in Utah had more than one wife, and only a few had as many as this homesteader. Library of Congress.

When the United States acquired Mexico's northern territories in 1848 (see Chapter 13), the Salt Lake Mormons petitioned Congress to create a vast new state, Deseret, that stretched from present-day Utah to the Pacific coast (Map 12.2). Instead, Congress set up the much smaller Utah Territory in 1850 and named Brigham Young as territorial governor. In 1858 President James Buchanan responded to pressure from Protestant Christians to eliminate polygamy by removing Young from the governorship and sending a small army to Salt Lake City. However, the "Mormon War" proved bloodless. Fearing that the forced abolition of the "domestic institution" of polygamy would serve as a precedent for ending slavery, Buchanan pursued a prosouthern policy and withdrew the troops.

Mormons had succeeded where other social experiments and utopian communities had failed. By endorsing the private ownership of property and encouraging individualistic economic enterprise, they became prosperous contributors to the new market society. However, Mormon leaders resolutely used strict religious controls to create patriarchal families and disciplined communities, reaffirming traditional values inherited from the eighteenth century. This blend of economic innovation, social conservatism, and hierarchical leadership created a wealthy church with a strong missionary impulse.

# Abolitionism

Abolitionism was more widespread than Mormonism and just as controversial. Abolitionists' demands for the immediate end to racial slavery led to fierce political debates, riots, and sectional conflict. Like other reform movements, abolitionism drew on the religious energy and ideas generated by the Second Great Awakening. Early-nineteenth-century reformers had criticized human bondage as contrary to republicanism and liberty. Now abolitionists condemned slavery as a sin and saw it as their moral duty to end this violation of God's law.

## *Uplift, Race-Equality, and Rebellion*

During the first decades of the nineteenth century, leading African Americans in the North advocated policies of social uplift. They encouraged free blacks to "elevate" themselves through education, temperance, moral discipline, and hard work and, by securing "respectability," to assume a position of equality with the white citizenry. To promote that goal, black leaders such as James Forten, a Philadelphia sail maker; Prince Hall, a Boston barber; and ministers Hosea Easton and James Allen founded an array of churches, schools, and self-help associations. Capping off this effort in 1827, John Russwurm and Samuel D. Cornish of New York published the first African American newspaper, *Freedom's Journal*.

The black quest for respectability elicited a violent response from whites in Boston, Pittsburgh, and many other northern cities. Refusing to accept African Americans as their social equals, white mobs terrorized black communities. In Cincinnati, white mobs were so violent and destructive that they prompted several hundred African Americans to flee to Canada.

Responding to these attacks in 1829, David Walker published a stirring pamphlet: *An Appeal . . . to the Colored Citizens of the World*. Walker was a free black from North Carolina who had moved to Boston, where he sold secondhand clothes and *Freedom's Journal*. A self-educated man, Walker studied the speeches of Thomas Jefferson and, seeking to place racial slavery in a coherent historical context, devoured volumes of history. His *Appeal* ridiculed the religious pretensions of slaveholders, justified slave rebellion, and in biblical language warned white Americans that the slaves would revolt if justice was delayed. "We must and shall be free," he told white Americans. "And woe, woe, will be it to you if we have to obtain our freedom by fighting. . . . Your DESTRUCTION is at hand, and will be speedily consummated unless you REPENT." Within a year Walker's pamphlet had gone through three printings and, carried by black merchant seamen, had begun to reach free African Americans in the South.

In 1830 Walker and other African American activists called a national convention in Philadelphia. The delegates did not endorse Walker's radical call for revolt but made collective equality for all blacks—enslaved as well as free—their fundamental demand. This new generation of African American leaders focused on "race-equality" rather than individual uplift and respectability. They urged free blacks to use every legal means to break "the shackles of slavery" and improve the condition of their race.

As Walker was predicting violent black rebellion from Boston, Nat Turner, a slave in Southampton County, Virginia, staged a bloody slave revolt—a coincidence that had far-reaching consequences. As a child Turner had taught himself to read and had hoped to be emancipated, but a new master forced him into field work and another new master separated him from his wife. Turner became deeply spiritual and, in a religious vision, "the Spirit" told him that "Christ had laid down the yoke he had borne for the sins of men, and that I should take it on and fight against the Serpent, for the time was fast approaching when the first should be last and the last should be first." Taking an eclipse of the sun as an omen, Turner and a handful of relatives and close friends decided to meet the masters' terror with a terror of their own. In August 1831 Turner and his followers rose in rebellion and killed almost sixty whites. Turner hoped that a vast army of slaves would rally to his cause but he mustered only sixty men, and the white militia quickly dispersed his poorly armed force. Whites took their revenge. One company of cavalry killed forty blacks in two days and put the heads of fifteen on poles to warn "all those who should undertake a similar plot." After hiding for nearly two months Turner was captured and hanged, still identifying his mission with that of the Savior. "Was not Christ crucified?" he asked.

Deeply shaken by Nat Turner's Rebellion, the Virginia assembly debated a bill providing for gradual emancipation and colonization. When the representatives rejected the bill by a vote of 73 to 58, the possibility that southern planters would legislate an end to slavery faded forever. Instead, the southern states toughened their slave codes, limited the movement of blacks, and prohibited anyone from teaching slaves to read. They would meet Walker's radical *Appeal* with radical measures of their own.

## Garrison and Evangelical Abolitionism

The prospect of a bloody racial revolution prompted a cadre of evangelical Christians in the North and Midwest to launch a moral crusade to abolish slavery. Many Quakers—and some pious Methodists and Baptists—had already freed their own slaves and advocated the gradual emancipation of all blacks. Beginning in 1831, radical Christian abolitionists demanded that southerners free their slaves immediately. The issue was absolute: if the slave owners did not allow slaves their God-given status as free moral agents, they faced revolution in this world and damnation in the next. "The conviction that SLAVERY IS A SIN is the Gibraltar of our cause," declared abolitionist Wendell Phillips.

The most uncompromising abolitionist leader was William Lloyd Garrison (1805–1879). A Massachusetts-born printer, Garrison had worked in Baltimore

## William Lloyd Garrison, c. 1835

As this portrait suggests, William Lloyd Garrison was an intense and righteous man. In 1831 his hatred of slavery prompted Garrison to demand its immediate end, thereby beginning the abolitionist movement. Believing the U.S. Constitution upheld slavery, he publicly burned a copy, declaring, "So perish all compromises with tyranny." Garrison's attack on slavery led him eventually on a passionate quest to destroy all institutions and cultural practices that prevented individuals—whites as well as blacks, women as well as men—from discovering their full potential.

during the 1820s with Quaker Benjamin Lundy, the publisher of the *Genius of Universal Emancipation*. In 1830 Garrison went to jail, convicted of libeling a New England merchant engaged in the domestic slave trade. The following year Garrison moved to Boston, founded his own antislavery weekly, *The Liberator*, and spearheaded the formation of the New England Anti-Slavery Society.

From the outset *The Liberator* took a radical stance, demanding the immediate abolition of slavery without reimbursement to slaveholders. In pursuing this goal, Garrison declared, "I will not retreat a single inch—AND I WILL BE HEARD." He lived up to his word—winning attention as he accused the American Colonization Society of trying to perpetuate slavery and assailed the U.S. Constitution as "a covenant with death, an agreement with Hell," because of its implicit acceptance of racial bondage.

Theodore Dwight Weld, another leading abolitionist, came to the movement from the religious revivals of the 1830s. The son of a Congregationalist minister and inspired by Charles Finney, Weld advocated temperance and educational reform before turning to abolitionism. He told northern Presbyterians and Congregationalists that all Americans bore moral responsibility for slavery and encouraged students at Lane Theological Seminary in Cincinnati to form an antislavery society. Buttressed by the theological arguments he advanced in *The Bible against Slavery* (1837), Weld's crusade gathered force. Working closely with Weld were Angelina Grimké, whom he married in 1838, and her sister, Sarah. The Grimkés had left their father's South Carolina slave plantation, converted to Quakerism, and taken up the abolitionist cause in Philadelphia.

Weld and the Grimkés provided the abolitionist movement with a mass of evidence in *American Slavery as It Is: Testimony of a Thousand Witnesses* (1839). The book set out to answer a simple question—"What is the actual condition of the slaves in the United States?"—with evidence from southern newspapers and first-hand testimonies. In her testimonial, Angelina Grimké told of a treadmill that slave owners used for punishment: "One poor girl, [who was] sent there to be flogged, and who was accordingly stripped naked and whipped, showed me the deep gashes on her back—I might have laid my whole finger in them—large pieces of flesh had actually been cut out by the torturing lash." The book sold over 100,000 copies in its first year.

In 1833 Weld and Garrison met in Philadelphia with sixty abolitionists, black and white, and established the American Anti-Slavery Society. The society received financial support from Arthur and Lewis Tappan, wealthy silk merchants in New York City. Women abolitionists established separate organizations, such as the Philadelphia Female Anti-Slavery Society, founded by Lucretia Mott in 1833, and the Anti-Slavery Conventions of American Women, formed by a network of local societies in the late 1830s. The women's societies raised money for *The Liberator* and carried the movement to the farm villages and rural areas of the Midwest, where they distributed abolitionist literature and collected tens of thousands of signatures on antislavery petitions.

Abolitionist leaders developed a three-pronged plan of attack, beginning with an appeal to public opinion. To foster public opposition to slavery, they adopted the tactics of the religious revivalists: large rallies led by stirring speakers and home visits by local agents of the movement. The abolitionists also used the latest techniques of mass communication. Assisted by new steam-powered printing presses, the American Anti-Slavery Society distributed more than 100,000 pieces of literature in 1834. In 1835 the society launched its "great postal campaign," which flooded the nation, including the South, with a million abolitionist pamphlets.

The abolitionists' second tactic was to assist the African Americans who fled from slavery. Blacks who lived near a free state had the greatest chance of success, but fugitives from plantations deeper in the South received aid from the "underground railroad," an informal network of whites and free blacks in Richmond, Charleston, and other southern cities. In Baltimore, a free African American sailor lent his identification papers to the future abolitionist Frederick Douglass, who used them to escape to New York. Some escaped slaves, such as Harriet Tubman, returned repeatedly to the South, risking reenslavement or death to help others escape. As Tubman wrote, "I should fight for . . . liberty as long as my strength lasted, and when the time came for me to go, the Lord would let them take me." Thanks to the "railroad," by the 1840s about a thousand African Americans reached freedom in the North each year.

There they faced an uncertain future because whites did not favor civic equality for African Americans. In fact, six northern and midwestern states changed their constitutions to deny the franchise to free blacks. Moreover, the Fugitive Slave Law (1793) allowed masters and hired slave catchers to capture suspected fugitives and carry them back to bondage. To thwart these efforts, white abolitionists and free blacks in northern cities formed mobs that seized recaptured slaves and drove slave catchers out of town.

The third element of the abolitionists' program was to seek support among state and national legislators. In 1835 the American Anti-Slavery Society encouraged its members to bombard Congress with petitions demanding the abolition of slavery in the District of Columbia, an end to the domestic slave trade, and a ban on the admission of new slave states. By 1838 petitions with nearly 500,000 signatures had arrived in Washington.

This agitation drew thousands of deeply religious farmers and small-town proprietors to abolitionism. The number of local abolitionist societies grew from about two hundred in 1835 to nearly two thousand by 1840—when they had nearly 200,000 members, including many leading transcendentalists. Emerson condemned American society for tolerating slavery; Thoreau was even more assertive. Seeing the Mexican War (see Chapter 13) as an attempt to extend slavery, in 1846 he refused to pay his taxes and submitted to arrest. Two years later Thoreau published "Resistance to Civil Government," an essay urging individuals to resist the state and follow a higher moral law.

## Opposition and Internal Conflict

Despite these successes, abolitionists remained a small minority. Perhaps 10 percent of northerners and midwesterners strongly supported the movement; another 20 percent were sympathetic to its goals. Its opponents were more numerous and equally aggressive. Men of wealth feared that the attack on slave property might become a general assault on all property rights; tradition-minded clergymen condemned the public roles assumed by abolitionist women; and northern merchants and textile manufacturers supported the southern planters who supplied them with cotton. Northern wage earners feared that freed slaves would work for subsistence wages and take their jobs. Finally, whites almost universally opposed the prospect of "amalgamation"—racial mixing and intermarriage—that Garrison seemed to support by encouraging meetings of black and white abolitionists of both sexes.

Motivated by such sentiments, northern antiabolitionists turned to violent mob actions, which were often led or instigated by "gentlemen of property and standing." In 1833 a mob of fifteen hundred New Yorkers stormed a church in search of Garrison and Arthur Tappan. Another white mob swept through

Philadelphia's African American neighborhoods, clubbing and stoning residents and destroying homes and churches. In 1835 in Utica, New York, a group of lawyers, merchants, and bankers broke up an abolitionist convention and beat several delegates. Two years later in Alton, Illinois, a mob shot and killed an abolitionist editor, Elijah P. Lovejoy. By pressing the issues of emancipation and equality, the abolitionists revealed the extent of racial prejudice in the North and the near impossibility of creating a biracial middle class of "respectable" whites and blacks. Indeed, their initiative had heightened race consciousness and encouraged whites—and blacks—to identify across class lines with those of their own race.

Racial solidarity was especially strong in the South, where whites reacted to abolitionism by banning the movement and demanding that northern states do the same. The Georgia legislature offered a $5,000 reward to anyone who would kidnap Garrison and bring him south to be tried for inciting rebellion. In Nashville, vigilantes whipped a northern college student for distributing abolitionist pamphlets, and in Charleston a mob attacked the post office and destroyed sacks of abolitionist mail. After 1835 southern postmasters simply refused to deliver mail suspected to be of abolitionist origin.

Politicians joined the fray. President Andrew Jackson was a longtime slave owner and a firm supporter of the southern social order. In 1835 he asked Congress to restrict the use of the mails by abolitionist groups. Congress did not comply, but in 1836 the House of Representatives adopted the so-called gag rule. Under this informal rule, which remained in force until 1844, antislavery petitions were automatically tabled when they were received so that they could not become the subjects of debate in the House (Map 12.3).

Assailed by racists from the outside, abolitionists were also divided among themselves over issues of gender. Many antislavery clergymen opposed an activist social role for women and condemned the Grimké sisters and other abolitionist women for lecturing to mixed-sex audiences. However, Garrison had broadened his reform agenda to include pacifism, the abolition of prisons, and women's rights. Arguing that "our object is universal emancipation, to redeem women as well as men from a servile to an equal condition," he demanded that the American Anti-Slavery Society support women's rights. At the society's convention in 1840 Garrison insisted on equal participation by women and precipitated a split with more conservative abolitionists. Women's rights advocates, such as Abby Kelley, Lucretia Mott, and Elizabeth Cady Stanton, remained with Garrison in the American Anti-Slavery Society, and proclaimed the common interests of enslaved blacks and free white women.

Garrison's opponents founded a new organization, the American and Foreign Anti-Slavery Society, which received financial backing from Lewis Tappan and focused its energies on ending slavery. Some of its members mobilized their churches to oppose racial bondage and others turned to electoral politics. In 1840 they established the Liberty Party, which nominated James G. Birney for president. Birney was a former Alabama slave owner who had been converted to abolitionism by Theodore Weld and

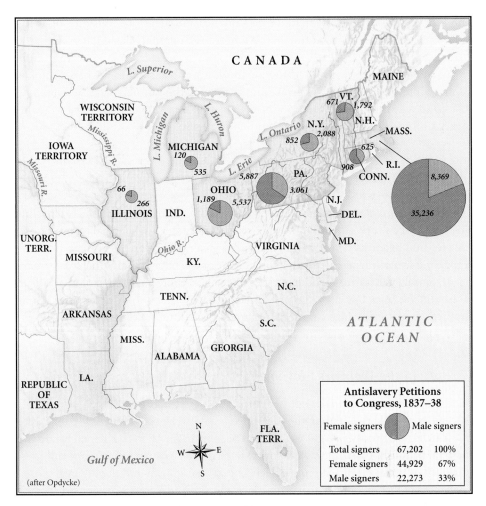

**MAP 12.3 Women and Antislavery, 1837–1838**

Beginning in the 1830s, abolitionists and antislavery advocates dispatched dozens of petitions to Congress, which, to avoid sectional conflict, refused to discuss them. Women made up two-thirds of the 67,000 people signing the petitions submitted in 1837–1838, which suggests not only their influence in the antislavery movement but also the extent of female organizations and social networks.

<small>FOR MORE HELP ANALYZING THIS MAP, see the Online Study Guide at **bedfordstmartins.com/henrettaconcise**.</small>

had founded an antislavery newspaper in Cincinnati. Birney and the Liberty Party argued that the Constitution did not recognize slavery and, consequently, that slaves became automatically free when they entered areas of federal authority, such as the District of Columbia and national territories. However, Birney won few votes in the election of 1840, and the future of political abolitionism appeared dim.

Coming hard on the heels of popular violence in the North and governmental suppression in the South, these schisms and electoral failures stunned the abolitionist movement. By melding the energies and ideas of thousands of evangelical Protestants, moral reformers, and transcendentalists, it had raised the banner of antislavery to new heights. Indeed, the very strength of the abolitionist movement had now aroused the hostility of a substantial majority of the nation's white population. "When we first unfurled the banner of *The Liberator*," Garrison admitted, ". . . it did not occur to us that nearly every religious sect, and every political party would side with the oppressor."

# The Women's Rights Movement

The prominence of women among the abolitionists was the product of a broad shift in American culture. After 1800 women played an increasingly active role in public life, joining religious revivals and reform movements such as the temperance crusade. As a consequence of this activism, issues of gender—sexual behavior, marriage, family authority—suddenly became significant not only among radical communal groups but also among ordinary citizens. The public activities of abolitionist women crystallized these issues and made some reformers into women's rights activists, who argued for complete equality with men.

## *Origins of the Women's Movement*

"Don't be afraid, not afraid, fight Satan; stand up for Christ; don't be afraid." So spoke Mary Walker Ostram on her deathbed in 1859. Her religious convictions were as firm at the age of fifty-eight as they had been in 1816, when she helped found the first Sabbath School in Utica, New York. Married to a lawyer-politician but childless, Ostram had devoted her life to evangelical Presbyterianism and the benevolent social reform that it helped to spawn. Her minister, Philemon Fowler, celebrated Ostram as a "living fountain" of faith, an exemplar of "Women's Sphere of Influence" in the world.

Such a public presence was hard won and still contested. Even as Reverend Fowler heaped praise on Ostram, he reiterated Revolutionary era precepts that women should limit their political role to that of "republican mothers" who would instruct "their sons in the principles of liberty and government." As Fowler put it, women inhabited a "**separate sphere**" and had no place in "the markets of trade, the scenes of politics and popular agitation, the courts of justice and the halls of legislation. Home is her peculiar sphere and members of her family her peculiar care."

But Ostram and many other middle-class women had transcended these rigid boundaries by joining in the Second Great Awakening. Such spiritual activities bolstered their authority within the household and gave them influence over many areas of family life, including the timing of pregnancies. Publications such as

*Godey's Lady's Book* and Catharine Beecher's *Treatise on Domestic Economy* (1841) taught women how to make their homes more efficient and alerted them to threats to their lives of middle-class domesticity. To protect their homes and husbands from the dangers of alcoholic excess, many farm women joined the Independent Order of Good Templars, a temperance organization that granted them full membership and sought to safeguard family life.

Some women used their newfound religious authority to increase their public activities, especially in the area of moral reform. In 1834 a group of middle-class New York women founded the Female Moral Reform Society and elected Lydia Finney, the wife of the evangelical minister Charles Finney, as its president. Its goals were to end prostitution, redeem fallen women, and protect single women from moral corruption. Rejecting the sexual double standard, the society demanded chastity for men as well as for women. By 1840 it had grown into a national association, with 555 chapters and 40,000 members throughout the North and Midwest. Employing only women as its agents, the society provided moral guidance for factory girls, seamstresses, and female servants who lived away from their families. Society members visited brothels, where they sang hymns, offered prayers, searched for runaway girls, and noted the names of clients. They also founded homes of refuge for prostitutes and won the passage of laws in Massachusetts and New York regulating men's sexual behavior and making seduction a crime.

Other women turned their energies to the improvement of almshouses, asylums, hospitals, and jails, all of which grew in number in the 1830s and 1840s. The Massachusetts reformer Dorothea Dix led these efforts and persuaded many state legislatures to expand state-run hospitals to accommodate mentally ill women rather than jail them with criminals. Other female reformers likewise solicited governmental support for their endeavors. In New York in 1849 the Female Guardian Society secured legal authority to take charge of the children of "dissipated and vicious parents" and to supervise their upbringing and education.

Both as reformers and as teachers, northern women transformed public education. From Maine to Wisconsin women vigorously supported the movement led by Horace Mann to increase the number of elementary schools and improve their quality. As secretary of the newly created Massachusetts Board of Education from 1837 to 1848, Mann lengthened the school year; established teaching standards in reading, writing, and arithmetic; and improved instruction by recruiting well-educated women as teachers. The intellectual leader of the new corps of women educators was Catharine Beecher, who founded academies for young women in Hartford and Cincinnati. In widely read publications Beecher argued that "energetic and benevolent women" were better qualified than men to impart moral and intellectual instruction to the young. By the 1850s most teachers were women both because local school boards heeded Beecher's arguments and because women could be paid less than men could.

## Abolitionism and Women

Women had long played an active part in the antislavery movement (Map 12.3). During the Revolutionary era, Quaker women in Philadelphia established schools for freed slaves, and Baptist and Methodist women in the Upper South endorsed religious arguments against slavery. One of the first abolitionists recruited by William Lloyd Garrison was Maria W. Stewart, an African American, who spoke to mixed audiences of men and women in Boston in the early 1830s. As the abolitionist movement mushroomed, scores of white women delivered lectures condemning slavery and thousands more conducted home "visitations" to win converts to their cause.

Women abolitionists were acutely aware of the special horrors of slavery for their sex. In her autobiography, *Incidents in the Life of a Slave Girl*, the black abolitionist Harriet Jacobs described forced sexual relations with her white owner: "I cannot tell how much I suffered in the presence of these wrongs." As Jacobs and other female slaves testified, such sexual assaults were compounded by cruel treatment at the hands of their masters' wives, who were enraged by their husbands' promiscuity. In her best-selling novel, *Uncle Tom's Cabin* (1852), Harriet Beecher Stowe charged that among the greatest moral failings of slavery was the degradation of slave women.

As abolitionist women assailed slavery and sexual oppression, many men challenged their right to participate in public debate. In response, activist women rejected the subordinate status of their sex. The most famous were Angelina and Sarah Grimké, who had become antislavery lecturers. When some Congregationalist clergymen demanded in 1836 that they cease lecturing to mixed male and female audiences, Sarah Grimké turned to the Christian Bible for justification: "The Lord Jesus defines the duties of his followers in his Sermon on the Mount . . . without any reference to sex or condition," she wrote. "Men and women are CREATED EQUAL! They are both moral and accountable beings and whatever is right for man to do is right for woman." In a debate with Catharine Beecher (who wanted women to exercise power primarily as wives, mothers, and schoolteachers), Angelina Grimké pushed the argument beyond religion by invoking Enlightenment principles to claim equal civic rights for women:

> It is a woman's right to have a voice in all the laws and regulations by which she is governed, whether in Church or State. . . . The present arrangements of society, on these points are a violation of human rights, a rank usurpation of power, a violent seizure and confiscation of what is sacredly and inalienably hers.

By 1840 female abolitionists were asserting that traditional gender roles amounted to the "domestic slavery" of women. "How can we endure our present marriage relations," asked Elizabeth Cady Stanton, since they give woman "no charter of rights, no individuality of her own?" As another female reformer put it, "the radical difficulty . . . is that women are considered as *belonging* to men" (see American Voices, "A Farm Woman Defends the Grimké Sisters," p. 377). Drawn into

# A Farm Woman Defends the Grimké Sisters

### KEZIAH KENDALL

*T*he Grimké sisters' lecture tour of New England on behalf of abolitionism sparked a huge outcry from orthodox ministers and social conservatives, who questioned the propriety of women assuming public roles and speaking to "mixed" audiences of men and women. In a lecture titled "The Legal Rights of Women," Simon Greenleaf, Royall Professor of Law at Harvard College, added his voice to those advocating a restricted role for women. Replying to Greenleaf, Keziah Kendall—possibly the fictional creation of a contemporary women's rights advocate—sent the following letter to her local newspaper.

My name is Keziah Kendall. I live not many miles from Cambridge, on a farm with two sisters, one older, one younger than myself. I am thirty two. Our parents and only brother are dead—we have a good estate—comfortable house—nice barn, garden, orchard &c and money in the bank besides. . . . Under these circumstances the whole responsibility of our property, not less than twenty five thousand dollars rest upon me.

Well—our milkman brought word when he came from market that you were a going to lecture on the legal rights of women, and so I thought I would go and learn. Now I hope you wont think me bold when I say, I did not like that lecture much . . . [because] there was nothing in it but what every body knows. . . .

What I wanted to know, was good reasons for some of those laws that I cant account for. . . . One Lyceum lecture that I heard in C[ambridge] stated that the Americans went to war with the British, because they were taxed without being represented in Parliament. Now we [women] are taxed every year to the full amount of every dollar we possess— town, county, state taxes—taxes for land, for movable [property], for money and all. Now I don't want to [become a legislative] representative . . . any more than I do to be a "constable or a sheriff," but I have no voice about public improvements, and I don't see the justice of being taxed any more than the "revolutionary heroes" did.

Nor do I think we are treated as Christian women ought to be, according to the Bible rule of doing to others as you would others should do unto you. . . . Another thing . . . women have joined the Antislavery societies, and why? Women are kept for slaves as well as men—it is a common cause, deny the justice of it, who can! To be sure I do not wish to go about lecturing like the Misses Grimkie, but I have not the knowledge they have, and I verily believe that if I had been brought up among slaves as they were . . . I should run the venture of your displeasure, and that of a good many others like you.

SOURCE: Dianne Avery and Alfred S. Konefsky, "The Daughters of Job: Property Rights and Women's Lives in Mid-Nineteenth-Century Massachusetts," *Law and History Review* 10 (Fall 1992): 323–56.

public life by abolitionism, thousands of northern women had become firm advocates of greater rights not only for enslaved African Americans but also for themselves.

## The Program of Seneca Falls and Beyond

During the 1840s women's rights activists devised a pragmatic program of reform. While championing full civil equality for women, they did not challenge the institution of marriage or even the conventional division of labor within the family. Rather, they tried to strengthen the legal rights of married women, especially with respect to property. This initiative won crucial support from affluent men, who wanted to protect their wives' assets in case their own businesses went into bankruptcy in the volatile economy of mid-nineteenth-century America. By giving property rights to their married daughters, fathers also hoped to protect them (and their inheritances) from irresponsible, spendthrift sons-in-law. Such considerations prompted legislatures in three states—Mississippi, Maine, and Massachusetts—to enact Married Women's Property Acts between 1839 and 1845. In New York, women activists won a more comprehensive statute (1848), which gave a woman full legal control over the property she brought to a marriage and became the model for similar laws in fourteen other states.

To advance the nascent women's movement, Elizabeth Cady Stanton and Lucretia Mott, who had become friends at the World Anti-Slavery Convention in London in 1840, organized a gathering in the small town of Seneca Falls in central New York in 1848. Seventy women activists and thirty men attended the meeting, which devised a rousing manifesto for women's equality. Taking the republican ideology of the Declaration of Independence as a starting point, the attendees declared that "all men and women are created equal." "The history of mankind is a history of repeated injuries and usurpations on the part of man toward woman," their Declaration of Sentiments continued, "having in direct object the establishment of an absolute tyranny over her." To persuade Americans to right this long-standing wrong, the activists resolved to "use every instrumentality within our power ... [to] employ agents, circulate tracts, petition the State and National legislatures, and endeavor to enlist the pulpit and the press on our behalf." By staking out claims for equality for women in public life, the Seneca Falls reformers repudiated the idea that "separate spheres" for men and women was the natural order of society.

Most men dismissed the Seneca Falls Declaration as nonsense, and many women repudiated the activists and their message. Writing in her diary, one small-town mother and housewife lashed out at the female reformer who "aping mannish manners ... wears absurd and barbarous attire, who talks of her wrongs in harsh tone, who struts and strides, and thinks that she proves herself superior to the rest of her sex."

Nonetheless, the women's rights movement attracted a growing number of supporters. In 1850 the activists convened the first national women's rights convention in Worcester, Massachusetts, and hammered out a program of action. Local and state conventions of women called on churches to revise concepts of female inferiority in their theology. Addressing state legislatures, they proposed laws that would guarantee the custody rights of mothers in the event of divorce or the husband's death, and ensure that married women could institute lawsuits and testify in court. Finally, and above all else, they began a concerted campaign to win the vote for women. The national women's rights convention of 1851 declared that suffrage was "the corner-stone of this enterprise, since we do not seek to protect woman, but rather to place her in a position to protect herself."

The struggle for legislation required leaders who had talents as organizers and lobbyists. The most prominent political operative was Susan B. Anthony (1820–1906). Anthony came from a Quaker family and as a young woman had been active in temperance and antislavery efforts. Her experience in those movements,

## Sojourner Truth

Few women had as interesting a life as Sojourner Truth. Born as "Isabella" in Dutch-speaking rural New York about 1797, she labored as a slave until 1827. Following a religious vision, Isabella moved to New York City, learned English, and worked for deeply religious—and ultimately fanatical—Christian merchants. In 1843, seeking further spiritual enlightenment, she took the name "Sojourner Truth" and left New York. After briefly joining the Millerites (who believed the world would end in 1844), Truth became famous as a forceful speaker on behalf of abolitionism and women's rights. This illustration, showing Truth addressing an antislavery meeting, suggests her powerful personal presence. Miriam and Ira D. Wallach Division of Art, Prints and Photographs, the New York Public Library.

Anthony explained, had taught her "the great evil of woman's utter dependence on man." In 1851 she joined the movement for women's rights. Working closely with Elizabeth Cady Stanton, Anthony created a network of political "captains," all women, who relentlessly lobbied the legislature in New York and other states. In 1860 her efforts culminated in a New York law granting women the right to collect and spend their own wages (which fathers or husbands previously could insist on controlling), to bring suit in court, and, if widowed, to acquire full control of the property they had brought to the marriage. Such successes laid the basis for more aggressive reform attempts after the Civil War.

The attack by women's rights activists against the traditional legal and social prerogatives of husbands, like the abolitionists' assault on the power and property of southern slaveholders, prompted many Americans to fear that social reform might not perfect their society but destroy it instead. The various movements for reform, begun with such confidence and religious zeal, had raised legal and political issues that threatened the fabric of society and the unity of the nation.

## T I M E L I N E

| | | | |
|---|---|---|---|
| 1829 | David Walker's *Appeal . . . to the Colored Citizens* encourages slave rebellion | 1841 | Transcendentalists found Brook Farm, a utopian community |
| 1830 | Joseph Smith publishes *The Book of Mormon* | | Dorothea Dix promotes hospitals for the insane |
| 1831 | William Lloyd Garrison founds *The Liberator* | 1844 | Margaret Fuller publishes *Woman in the Nineteenth Century* |
| | Nat Turner's uprising in Virginia | 1845 | Henry David Thoreau withdraws to Walden Pond |
| 1832 | Ralph Waldo Emerson rejects organized religion and embraces transcendentalism | 1846 | Mormon followers of Brigham Young trek to Salt Lake |
| 1833 | American Anti-Slavery Society founded | 1848 | John Humphrey Noyes founds Oneida Community |
| 1834 | New York Female Moral Reform Society created | | Seneca Falls convention proposes women's equality |
| 1835 | Abolitionists launch mail campaign; antiabolitionists riot against them | 1850 | Nathaniel Hawthorne publishes *The Scarlet Letter* |
| 1836 | House of Representatives adopts gag rule on antislavery petitions | 1851 | Herman Melville's *Moby-Dick* |
| | Grimké sisters defend public roles for women | 1852 | Harriet Beecher Stowe writes *Uncle Tom's Cabin* |
| 1840 | Liberty Party runs James G. Birney for president | | Walt Whitman issues first edition of *Leaves of Grass* |
| 1840s | Fourierist communities founded in Midwest | 1858 | The "Mormon War" over polygamy |

# For Further Exploration

Ronald Walters, *American Reformers, 1815–1860* (1978), offers a succinct discussion of the major antebellum reform movements. Robert H. Abzug, *Cosmos Crumbling: American Reform and the Religious Imagination* (1994), demonstrates the religious roots of the reform impulse. David S. Reynolds, *Walt Whitman's America: A Cultural Biography* (1995), is a comprehensive study of the poet and nineteenth-century society. Charles Capper, *Margaret Fuller: An American Romantic Life* (1992), illuminates Fuller's intellectual milieu. Fuller inspired the character of Zenobia in Nathaniel Hawthorne's *The Blithedale Romance* (1852), which reflects his life at Brook Farm and touches on many issues (and fads) of the day, including communalism and mesmerism. For a fine Web site on transcendentalism, log on to <http://www.vcu.edu/engweb/transcendentalism/>. A provocative study of religious utopianism gone mad is Paul E. Johnson and Sean Wilentz, *The Kingdom of Matthias: A Story of Sex and Salvation in Nineteenth-Century America* (1995).

James B. Stewart, *Holy Warriors: The Abolitionists and American Slavery* (1976), places the Garrisonian movement in a broad social context. See also Mark Perry, *Lift Up Thy Voice: The Grimké Family's Journey from Slaveholders to Civil Rights Leaders* (2001). Stephen B. Oates, *The Fires of Jubilee: Nat Turner's Fierce Rebellion* (1975), explores the life of the insurrectionist, while materials including *The Confessions of Nat Turner* are available at <http://docsouth.unc.edu/turner/menu.html>. *The Narrative of the Life of Frederick Douglass, An American Slave, Written by Himself* (1845) is a literary masterpiece. For antiabolitionism, see the probing studies by Leonard L. Richards, *"Gentlemen of Property and Standing": Anti-Abolition Mobs in Jacksonian America* (1970), and David Roediger, *The Wages of Whiteness* (1995). For many resources on slavery and abolition, see the PBS Africans in America site: <http://www.pbs.org/wgbh/aia/part4/>.

Mary Ryan, *Women in Public: Between Banners and Ballots, 1825–1880* (1990), explores the limits on women's civic activities, and Eleanor Flexner, *Century of Struggle* (1959), narrates the history of the women's movement. The PBS video directed by Ken Burns, *Not for Ourselves Alone: The Story of Elizabeth Cady Stanton and Susan B. Anthony* (3 hours), offers insight into the first generation of activists. See also the National Park Service Web site for Seneca Falls: <http://www.nps.gov/wori/>.

---

For definitions of key terms boldfaced in this chapter, see the glossary at the end of the book.

To assess your mastery of the material covered in this chapter, see the Online Study Guide at **bedfordstmartins.com/henrettaconcise**.

For map resources and primary documents, see **bedfordstmartins.com/henrettaconcise**.

# Chapter 13

# THE CRISIS OF THE UNION
## 1844–1860

This government was made by our fathers, by white men for the benefit of white men and their posterity forever.

STEPHEN DOUGLAS, 1858

**D**uring the 1850s crusaders for temperance and antislavery faced off against defenders of traditional rights. The resulting struggle was especially intense in South Carolina. When temperance activists demanded a "Maine law" to prohibit the sale of intoxicants, Randolph Turner was outraged: any such "legislation upon Liquor would cast a shade on my character which as a Caucassian [*sic*] and a white man, I am not willing to bear." A candidate for the South Carolina assembly, Turner vowed to shoulder his musket and, along with "hundreds of men in this district, . . . fight for individual rights, as well as State Rights."

In Washington, South Carolina congressman Preston Brooks battled for "Southern Rights." In an inflammatory speech in 1856, Senator Charles Sumner of Massachusetts denounced the South and accused Senator Andrew P. Butler of South Carolina of having taken "the harlot slavery" as his mistress. Outraged by Sumner's verbal attack on his uncle, Brooks accosted the Massachusetts senator at his desk and beat him unconscious with a walking cane. As these events unfolded in Washington, Axalla Hoole of South Carolina and other proslavery migrants in the Kansas Territory leveled their guns at an armed force of abolitionist settlers. Passion and violence had replaced political compromise as the hallmark of American public life.

The immediate cause of the political violence of the 1850s was the geographic expansion that began with the admission of Texas to the Union in 1845 and the acquisition of vast territories from Mexico in 1848. The ultimate causes were more complex and stemmed from the growing economic and cultural differences between the northern and southern states. By midcentury these sectional disparities were keenly felt, especially in the South. White southerners feared the North's increasing wealth, political power, and moral righteousness, John C. Calhoun explained in 1850, especially its "long-continued agitation of the slavery question."

382

A massive surge of population to the West accentuated the importance of those divisions. To many Americans it was the nation's "manifest destiny" to extend republican institutions to the Pacific Ocean. But whose republican institutions: the aristocratic traditions and practices of the slaveholding South or the more democratic customs and culture of the reform-minded North and Midwest? The answer to this question would determine the future of the nation.

# Manifest Destiny

Shaken by the crisis over Missouri (see Chapter 9), the two major political parties shunned policies that would spark another confrontation over slavery. This policy worked as long as the geographic boundaries of the United States remained unchanged, but by the 1840s the people of the nation were again on the move.

## The Mature Cotton Economy, 1820–1860

Between 1820 and 1860 the white planters in the South grew rich and powerful as they developed a cotton economy. By 1840 the American South produced over two-thirds of the world's supply of raw cotton—1.5 million bales (at 500 pounds per bale) each year. Smallholding white families accounted for hundreds of thousands of bales of the prized fiber, but most cotton came from large plantations employing slave labor. As *Hunt's Merchants' Magazine* noted in 1855, "The whole Commerce of the world turns upon the product of slave labor." To increase output, profit-conscious slave owners in the upland regions of South Carolina and Georgia and the fertile plains of Alabama and Mississippi devised a new **gang-labor system**. Previously planters had either supervised their workers sporadically or assigned a daily quota and let them work at their own pace. Now masters with twenty or more slaves organized disciplined teams, or "gangs," supervised by black "drivers" or white overseers. They instructed drivers and overseers to use the lash to work the gangs at a steady pace, clearing and plowing the land or hoeing and picking cotton. A traveler glimpsed two gangs returning from work in Mississippi:

> First came, led by an old driver carrying a whip, forty of the largest and strongest women I ever saw together; they were all in a simple uniform dress of a bluish check stuff, the skirts reaching little below the knee; . . . they carried themselves loftily, each having a hoe over the shoulder, and walking with a free, powerful swing.

Next marched the plow hands with their mules, "the cavalry, thirty strong, mostly men, but a few of them women." Finally, "a lean and vigilant white overseer, on a brisk pony, brought up the rear." By 1860 nearly two million enslaved African Americans were laboring along an arc of fertile land—the "black belt"—sweeping from Mississippi through Georgia, and the South's annual cotton output had surged dramatically to 4 million bales.

The slaveholding elite who owned great plantations and scores of slaves thought of themselves as aristocrats and acted accordingly. They married their children to one another, and their sons and daughters became commercial and cultural leaders—the men working as planters, merchants, lawyers, newspaper editors, and ministers and the women hosting plantation balls and church bazaars. To confirm their status, leading planters lived extravagantly. John Henry Hammond, a leading South Carolina politician, built a Greek Revival mansion with a center hall fifty-three feet by twenty feet, its floor embellished with stylish Belgian tiles and expensive Brussels carpets. "Once a year, like a great feudal landlord," a guest recounted, Hammond "gave a fete or grand dinner to all the country people."

The planters justified their rule in moral terms. Ignoring the old defense of slavery as a "necessary evil," southern apologists now argued that slavery was a "positive good" that allowed a civilized lifestyle for leading whites and provided tutelage for genetically inferior Africans. Southern ministers pointed out that the Hebrews, God's chosen people, had owned slaves and that Jesus Christ had never condemned slavery. As Hammond told a British abolitionist in 1845: "What God ordains and Christ sanctifies should surely command the respect and toleration of man." Some defenders of slavery depicted planters and their wives as aristocratic models of "disinterested benevolence," who provided food and housing for their workers and cared for them in old age (see American Voices, "A Slaveholding Woman's Diary," p. 385).

Although elite planters encouraged ambitious men to buy slaves and grow rich, southern politics and society remained deeply divided along the lines of class and geography. Wealthy planters used their political influence to exempt slave property from taxation and to shift the tax burden to backcountry yeomen farmers, by imposing land taxes by acreage rather than by value. Planters also enacted laws that forced yeomen to "fence in" their livestock and spared themselves the cost of building fences around their fields. Finally, planter-dominated legislatures forced all white men—whether they owned slaves or not—to serve in the patrols and militias that deterred black uprisings. Defending such onerous regulations, John Henry Hammond told his poor white neighbors that "in a slave country every freeman is an aristocrat."

Planters worried constantly that enslaved African Americans—a majority of the population throughout the "black belt"—would rise in rebellion. In theory, a master had virtually unlimited power over his slaves, who were subject to his discipline and could be bought and sold as if they were horses. As Justice Thomas Ruffin of the North Carolina Supreme Court wrote in a decision in 1829, "The power of the master must be absolute to render the submission of the slave perfect."

However, in practice, African American resistance limited the masters' power. Slaves slowed the pace of work by feigning illness and losing or breaking tools. Some blacks challenged their owners' authority by insisting that people be sold "in families." One Maryland slave, faced with transport to Mississippi and separation from his wife,

# A Slaveholding Woman's Diary

## MARY BOYKIN CHESNUT

*In response to Harriet Beecher Stowe's* Uncle Tom's Cabin *(1852) and Republican celebrations of free labor, proslavery advocate George Fitzhugh wrote* Sociology for the South; or, the Failure of Free Society *(1857). Fitzhugh depicted slavery as a benevolent institution and contrasted the planters' concern for their workers with the factory owners' indifference toward their wage laborers. Mary Boykin Chesnut (1823–1886), wife of South Carolina senator James Chesnut, held a more complex view of slavery. While Chesnut believed that blacks were innately inferior and that southern women were benevolent, she hated slavery because it oppressed the women of both races. During the Civil War Chesnut recorded her views in notes and later revised them into a beautifully written diary.*

March 18, 1861 . . . I wonder if it be a sin to think slavery a curse to any land. [Massachusetts senator Charles] Sumner said not one word of this hated institution which is not true. Men and women are punished when their masters and mistresses are brutes and not when they do wrong—and then we live surrounded by prostitutes. . . . God forgive us, but ours is a monstrous system and wrong. . . . Like the patriarchs of old our men live all in one house with their wives and their concubines, and the mulattoes one sees in every family exactly resemble the white children—and every lady tells you who is the father of all the mulatto children in everybody's household, but those in her own she seems to think drop from the clouds, or pretends so to think. Good women we have . . . the purest women God ever made. Thank God for my countrywomen—alas for the men! . . .

November 27, 1861 . . . Now what I have seen of my mother's life, my grandmother's, my mother-in-law's: These people were educated at Northern schools mostly—read the same books as their Northern condemners, the same daily newspapers, the same Bible—have the same ideas of right and wrong—are highbred, lovely, good, pious—doing their duty as they conceive it. They live in negro villages. They do not preach and teach hate as a gospel and the sacred duty of murder and insurrection, but they strive to ameliorate the condition of these Africans in every particular. . . . These women are more troubled by their duty to negroes, have less chance to live their own lives in peace than if they were African missionaries. They have a swarm of blacks about them as children under their care—not as Mrs. Stowe's fancy paints them, but the hard, unpleasant, unromantic, undeveloped savage Africans. And they hate slavery worse than Mrs. Stowe. . . .

    We are human beings of the nineteenth century—and slavery has to go, of course. All that has been gained by it goes to the North and to negroes. The slave-owners, when they are good men and women, are the martyrs. And as far as I have seen, the people here are quite as good as anywhere else. I hate slavery.

SOURCE: C. Vann Woodward, *Mary Chesnut's Civil War* (New Haven: Yale University Press, 1981), 29–30, 245–46.

"neither yields consent to accompany my people, or to be exchanged or sold," his owner reported. Masters ignored such resistance at their peril because the slave (or his relatives) might retaliate by setting fire to houses and barns, poisoning his food, or destroying crops or equipment. Such worries, as well as critical scrutiny by abolitionists, prompted many masters to resort less frequently to the lash and to use positive incentives of food and other privileges to manage their laborers. Slavery was never a regime of equality, but over the first half of the nineteenth century, masters and their now-American-born slaves devised rules and rituals that reduced the extent of day-to-day violence. Even as slavery evolved, it remained central to the southern social order, and white planters and politicians wanted to extend its sway across the continent.

## The Independence of Texas

By the 1830s settlers from the Ohio Valley and the South had carried both yeoman farming and plantation slavery into Arkansas and Missouri. Between those states and the Rocky Mountains stretched the semiarid lands of the Great Plains, which an army explorer, Major Stephen H. Long, described as the Great American Desert, "almost wholly unfit for cultivation." Consequently, settlers looking for land turned south toward the Mexican province of Texas.

Texas had long been occupied primarily by Indian peoples. The Spanish government in Mexico had used Texas as a buffer zone against the French prior to the Louisiana Purchase of 1803; afterward the province became a shield against the United States. Although some American adventurers settled in Texas, the Adams-Onís Treaty of 1819 guaranteed Spanish sovereignty over the region.

After winning independence from Spain in 1821, the Mexican government used lavish land grants to encourage both Mexicans and Americans to move to Texas. One early grantee was American Moses Austin, who created an aristocratic-like landed estate occupied by tenants and smallholders: "one great family who are under my care." His son, Stephen F. Austin, later acquired about 180,000 acres, which he sold to incoming Americans. By 1835 about 27,000 white Americans and their 3,000 African American slaves were raising cotton and cattle in eastern and central Texas; they far outnumbered the 3,000 Mexican residents, most of whom lived in the southwestern towns of Goliad and San Antonio (Map 13.1).

As the Mexican government asserted greater political control over Texas in the mid-1830s, the Americans split into two groups. A "peace party," led by Stephen Austin and other longtime settlers, sought more autonomy for the province, while the "war party," led by recent migrants from Georgia, demanded independence. Austin won significant concessions from Mexican authorities, but the new national-minded president, General Antonio López de Santa Anna, nullified these measures. When Santa Anna appointed a military commandant for Texas, the war party provoked a rebellion that most of the American settlers ultimately supported. On March 2, 1836, the American rebels proclaimed the independence of Texas and adopted a constitution legalizing slavery.

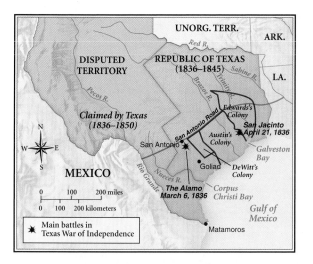

**MAP 13.1 American Settlements in Texas, 1821–1836**

During the 1820s Mexican authorities granted huge tracts of land in the province of Texas to Stephen F. Austin and other American *empresarios* (land entrepreneurs who were expected to encourage immigration). By 1835 Austin had issued land titles to more than 1,000 families, who grew cotton and exported it from Galveston and other Gulf ports. By the mid-1830s, there were nearly 30,000 Americans in Texas. They far outnumbered Mexican settlers, who lived primarily in the town of Goliad and areas to the south.

Santa Anna vowed to put down the rebellion. On March 6 his army wiped out the rebel garrison defending the Alamo in San Antonio and then took control of Goliad. Santa Anna thought he had crushed the rebellion, but New Orleans and New York newspapers romanticized the heroism of the Texans and the deaths at the Alamo of folk heroes Davy Crockett and Jim Bowie. Drawing on anti-Catholic rhetoric, the newspapers described the Mexicans as tyrannical butchers in the service of the pope. Hundreds of American adventurers, lured by offers of land grants, flocked to Texas to join the rebel army. Led by General Sam Houston, the Texas rebels routed the Mexicans in the Battle of San Jacinto in April 1836. Thereafter, the Mexican government abandoned efforts to reconquer Texas but refused to accept its status as an independent republic.

The Texans quickly voted by plebiscite for annexation by the United States, but Presidents Andrew Jackson and Martin Van Buren refused to act. They knew that adding Texas as a slave state would divide the Democratic Party and the nation and almost certainly lead to war with Mexico.

## The Push to the Pacific: Oregon and California

The annexation of Texas became a more pressing issue in the 1840s, as American expansionists developed continental ambitions. The term **Manifest Destiny** captured those dreams. As John L. O'Sullivan, the editor of the *Democratic Review* who coined

SIEGE OF THE ALAMO.

**Assault on the Alamo**

After a thirteen-day siege, on March 6, 1836, a Mexican army of 4,000 stormed the small mission in San Antonio, Texas. "The first to climb were thrown down by bayonets . . . or by pistol fire," reported a Mexican officer. Only a half hour of continuous assaults gave the attackers control of the wall. This contemporary woodcut shows the fierceness of the battle, which took the lives of all 250 American defenders; the Mexicans suffered 1,500 dead or wounded. Archives Division, Texas State Library.

FOR MORE HELP ANALYZING THIS IMAGE, see the Online Study Guide at **bedfordstmartins.com/henrettaconcise**.

the term in 1845, put it, "Our manifest destiny is to overspread the continent allotted by Providence for the free development of our yearly multiplying millions." Underlying the rhetoric of Manifest Destiny was a sense of American cultural and racial superiority; "inferior" peoples—Native Americans and Mexicans—were to be brought under American dominion, taught republicanism, and converted to Protestantism.

Already many residents of the Ohio River Valley were casting their eyes westward to the fertile valleys of the Oregon Country. This region stretched along the Pacific Coast from the border with Mexican California to the border with Russian Alaska. Since 1818 a British-American convention had allowed both British and Americans to settle anywhere in the disputed region. The British-run Hudson's Bay Company developed a lucrative fur trade north of the Columbia River, while several hundred Americans settled to the south, mostly in the Willamette Valley. On the basis of this settlement, the United States claimed the zone between California and the Columbia River.

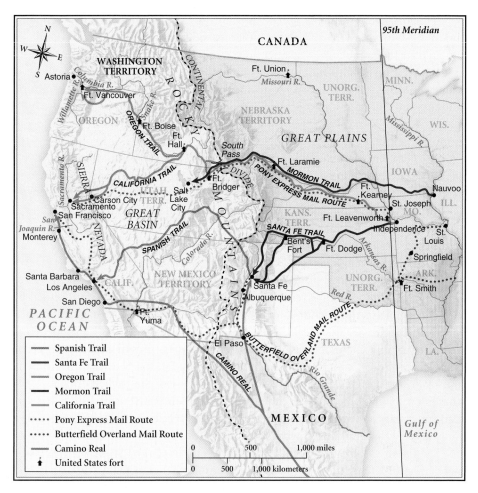

**MAP 13.2 Routes to the West, 1835–1860**

By the 1840s a variety of trails spanned the arid zone between the ninety-fifth meridian and the Pacific Coast. From the south, El Camino Real linked Mexico City to the California coast, Santa Fe, and the breakaway province of Texas. From the east, the Santa Fe, Oregon, California, and Mormon Trails carried tens of thousands of Americans from departure points on the Mississippi and Missouri Rivers to new communities in Utah and along the Pacific Coast. By the 1860s both the Pony Express and the Butterfield Overland Mail provided reliable communication between the eastern states and California.

In 1842 American interest in Oregon increased dramatically. The U.S. Navy published a glowing report of fine harbors in the Puget Sound, which was welcome news to New England merchants plying the China trade. In the same year a party of a hundred settlers journeyed along the Oregon Trail that fur traders and explorers had blazed through the Great Plains and the Rocky Mountains. Their reports from Oregon told of a mild climate and fertile soil (Map 13.2).

"Oregon fever" suddenly raged. In May 1843 a thousand men, women, and children — with more than a hundred wagons and five thousand oxen and cattle — gathered in Independence, Missouri, for the six-month trek to Oregon. The migrants were mostly farming and trading families from Missouri, Kentucky, and Tennessee. Overcoming flooding streams, dust storms, dying livestock, and encounters with Indians, they reached the Willamette Valley, after a journey of 2,000 miles. During the next two years another 5,000 people reached Oregon, and the numbers continued to grow.

By 1860 about 350,000 Americans had braved the Oregon Trail. More than 34,000 of them died in the effort, mostly from disease and exposure; only 400 deaths came from Indian attacks. The walking migrants wore three-foot-deep paths and their wagons carved five-foot-deep ruts across sandstone formations in southern Wyoming — tracks that are visible today. Women found the trail especially difficult because it exaggerated the authority of their husbands and added the labor of driving wagons and animals to their traditional chores.

Some pioneers ended up in the Mexican province of California. They left the Oregon Trail at the Snake River, trudged down the California Trail, and settled in the interior along the Sacramento River. Lying at the northern edge of Spain's American empire, California had been settled by the Spanish only in the 1770s, when they built a chain of religious missions and forts (presidios) along the coast (see Chapter 8). To promote California's development, the Mexican government took over the Franciscan-run missions and liberated the 20,000 Indians who worked on them. Some mission Indians rejoined their Native American tribes but many intermarried with mestizos (Mexicans of mixed Spanish and Indian ancestry) and worked as laborers and cowboys on large cattle ranches.

The rise of cattle ranching linked California to the United States. New England merchants dispatched dozens of agents to buy leather and tallow for use in the booming Massachusetts boot and shoe industry. Many of those resident agents married into the families of the elite Mexicans — the Californios — and adopted their dress, manners, outlook, and Catholic religion. A crucial exception was Thomas Oliver Larkin, the most successful merchant in the coastal town of Monterey. Larkin worked closely with Mexican ranchers, but he remained an American citizen and plotted for the peaceful annexation of California to the United States. Like Larkin, American migrants in the Sacramento Valley had no desire to assimilate into Mexican society. Many were squatters or held land grants of dubious legality and hoped for eventual annexation by the United States. However, these settlers numbered only about 700 in the early 1840s, compared with the coastal population of 7,000 Mexicans and 300 American traders.

## The Fateful Election of 1844

The election of 1844 determined the American government's western policy. Since 1836 some southern leaders had advocated the territorial expansion of slavery, but their plans had been thwarted by cautious party politicians and northern abolitionists. Now southerners sensed a British threat to their ambitions. There were rumors that Britain wanted the Mexican government to cede California in payment for large debts owed to British investors. Southern leaders also believed that Britain was encouraging Texas to remain independent and had designs on Spanish Cuba, which some southerners wanted to annex. To thwart such British schemes, southern expansionists demanded the immediate annexation of Texas.

At this crucial moment "Oregon fever" and Manifest Destiny altered the political and diplomatic landscape in the North. In 1843 Americans in the Ohio Valley and the Great Lakes states organized "Oregon conventions" that called for an end to joint occupation of the region. In July, Democrat and Whig politicians met in a bipartisan national convention and demanded that the United States seize Oregon all the way to 54°40′ north latitude, the southern limit of Russian Alaska.

With northern Democrats demanding expansion in Oregon, southern Democrats could champion the annexation of Texas. Moreover, they had the support of President John Tyler. Disowned by the Whigs because of his opposition to Henry Clay's nationalist economic program, Tyler hoped to win reelection in 1844 as a Democrat. To curry favor among expansionists, Tyler proposed to annex Texas and seize all of Oregon. In April 1844 Tyler and John C. Calhoun, his new secretary of state, sent to the Senate a treaty to annex Texas. Two rival presidential candidates, Democrat Martin Van Buren and Whig Henry Clay, quickly declared their opposition. Knowing that annexation would raise the issue of slavery and divide the nation, they persuaded the Senate to defeat the treaty.

Texas and Oregon became the central issues in the election of 1844. The Democrats passed over Tyler, whom they did not trust, and Van Buren, whom southerners despised for his opposition to annexation. They selected Governor James K. Polk of Tennessee, a slave owner who favored annexation. Unimpressive in appearance, Polk was a man of iron will and boundless ambition for the nation. "Fifty-four forty or fight!" became the patriotic cry of his expansionist campaign.

The Whigs nominated Henry Clay, who again championed his American System of internal improvements, high tariffs, and national banking. Clay initially dodged the issue of Texas but ultimately indicated support for annexation. His evasive position disappointed thousands of northern Whigs and Democrats who opposed any expansion of slavery. Rather than vote for Clay, they voted for James G. Birney of the Liberty Party. Birney garnered less than 3 percent of the national vote but won enough support among Whigs in New York to cause Clay to lose that state. By taking New York's 36 electoral votes, Polk won the presidency by a margin of 170 to 105 in the electoral college.

Following Polk's victory, Democrats in Congress called for the immediate annexation of Texas. Unable to secure the needed two-thirds majority in the Senate to ratify a treaty with the Republic of Texas, they approved annexation by a joint resolution of Congress, which required only a majority vote in each house. Polk's strategy of linking Texas and Oregon had put him in the White House and Texas in the Union.

# War, Expansion, and Slavery, 1846–1850

Texas was just the beginning. Polk wanted American control over all Mexican territory between Texas and the Pacific Ocean and was prepared to go to war to get it. What he consciously ignored was the major crisis over slavery that would be unleashed by his expansionist dreams.

## The War with Mexico, 1846–1848

Since gaining independence, Mexico had not prospered. Its stagnant economy yielded few surpluses and modest tax revenues, which were quickly devoured by interest payments on foreign debts and a bloated government bureaucracy. The distant northern provinces of California and New Mexico contributed little to the national economy and, with a Spanish-speaking population of only 75,000 in 1840, remained sparsely settled. Nonetheless, Mexican officials vowed to preserve their nation's historical territories; when the breakaway Republic of Texas entered the American Union on July 4, 1845, Mexico broke off diplomatic relations with the United States.

Nonetheless, President Polk set into motion his plans to acquire Mexico's far northern provinces. To intimidate the Mexican government, he ordered General Zachary Taylor and an American army of 2,000 soldiers to occupy disputed lands between the Nueces River (the historical southern boundary of Texas) and the Rio Grande, which the Republic of Texas had claimed as its border with Mexico (see Map 13.1). Simultaneously Polk launched a secret diplomatic initiative. He sent John Slidell to Mexico City with instructions to win acceptance of the Rio Grande boundary and buy the Mexican provinces of New Mexico and California, paying as much as $30 million. When Slidell arrived in December 1845, Mexican officials refused to see him.

Anticipating the failure of Slidell's mission, Polk had already embarked on an alternative plan. He hoped to foment a revolution in California that, as in Texas, would lead to an independent republic and a request for annexation. In October 1845 Secretary of State James Buchanan told merchant Thomas O. Larkin, now the U.S. consul in the port of Monterey, to encourage influential Mexican residents to declare independence and support peaceful annexation. To add military muscle, Polk ordered American naval commanders to seize San Francisco Bay and California's coastal towns in case of war with Mexico. The president also had the War Department dispatch Captain John C. Frémont and an "exploring" party of heavily armed soldiers into Mexican territory. By December 1845 Frémont had reached California's Sacramento Valley.

Events now moved quickly toward war. Polk ordered General Taylor toward the Rio Grande to incite an armed response by Mexico. "We were sent to provoke a fight," an American officer recalled, "but it was essential that Mexico should commence it." When the armies clashed near the Rio Grande in May 1846, Polk called for war. Taking liberties with the truth, the president declared that Mexico "has passed the boundary of the United States, has invaded our territory, and shed American blood upon the American soil." Ignoring Whig pleas for a negotiated settlement, the Democratic majority in Congress voted for war, a decision that was greeted with great popular acclaim. To avoid a simultaneous conflict with Britain, Polk retreated from his campaign pledge of "fifty-four forty or fight" and accepted a British proposal to divide the Oregon Country at the forty-ninth parallel.

American forces in Texas quickly established their military superiority. Zachary Taylor's army crossed the Rio Grande, occupied Matamoros, and after a fierce six-day battle in September 1846, took the interior Mexican town of Monterrey. Two months later a U.S. naval squadron in the Gulf of Mexico seized Tampico, Mexico's second most important port. By the end of 1846 the United States controlled much of northeastern Mexico (Map 13.3).

Fighting had also broken out in California. In June 1846 naval commander John Sloat landed 250 marines in Monterey and declared that California "henceforward will be a portion of the United States." Almost simultaneously American settlers in the interior staged a revolt and, supported by Frémont's forces, captured the town of Sonoma. To cement these victories, Polk ordered army units to capture Santa Fe in New Mexico and then march to California. Despite stiff Mexican resistance, American forces secured control of California early in 1847.

Polk expected that these American victories would end the war, but he had underrated the Mexicans' national pride and the determination of President Santa Anna. Santa Anna took the offensive and attacked the depleted units of Zachary Taylor at Buena Vista in February 1847. Only superior artillery enabled Taylor to hold the American line in northeastern Mexico.

To bring Santa Anna to terms, Polk accepted General Winfield Scott's plan to strike deep into the heart of Mexico. In March 1847 Scott captured the port of Veracruz and began the 260-mile march to Mexico City. Leading Scott's 14,000 troops was a cadre of talented West Point officers who would become famous in the Civil War: Robert E. Lee, George Meade, and P. G. T. Beauregard. Scott's troops crushed Santa Anna's forces at Cerro Gordo and Churubusco and seized Mexico City in September 1847. A new Mexican government agreed to make peace with the United States.

## A Divisive Victory

Initially many Americans viewed the war with Mexico as a noble struggle to extend American republican institutions, but the conflict soon divided the nation. A few Whigs, such as Charles Francis Adams of Massachusetts (the son of President John Quincy Adams) and Joshua Giddings of Ohio, opposed the war from the beginning on moral grounds. Known as "conscience Whigs," they warned of a southern conspiracy to add new slave states in the West, undermine the Jeffersonian ideal of a yeoman freeholder society, and ensure permanent control of the federal government by slaveholding Democrats. These antislavery Whigs grew bolder after the elections of 1846 gave their party control of Congress.

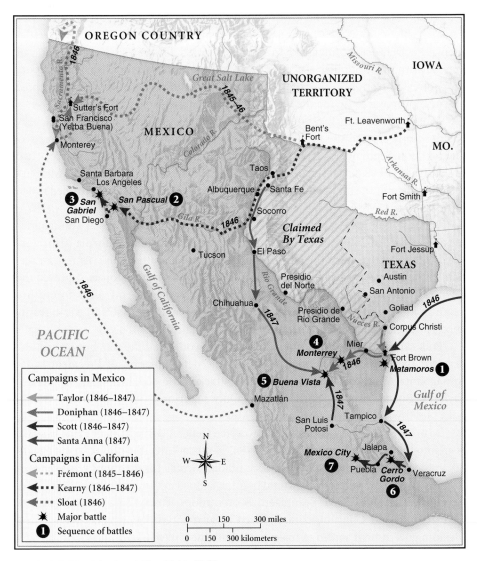

**MAP 13.3 The Mexican War, 1846–1848**

Departing from Fort Leavenworth in present-day Kansas, American forces commanded by Captain John C. Frémont and General Stephen Kearney defeated Mexican armies in California in 1846 and early 1847. Simultaneously U.S. armies under General Zachary Taylor and Colonel Alfred A. Doniphan won victories over General Santa Anna's forces far to the south of the Rio Grande. Then in mid-1847 General Winfield Scott mounted a successful attack on Mexico City, ending the war.

Polk's expansionist policy also split the Democrats into sectional factions. As early as 1839 Democratic senator Thomas Morris of Ohio had warned that "the power of slavery is aiming to govern the country, its Constitutions and laws." In August 1846 David Wilmot, a Democratic congressman from Pennsylvania, took up that refrain. To limit the spread of slavery, Wilmot proposed to prohibit the institution in any territories acquired from Mexico. This measure, known as the Wilmot Proviso, rallied antislavery northerners. In the House of Representatives, the northern Democratic allies of Martin Van Buren joined forces with antislavery Whigs to pass the proviso. The Senate, dominated by southerners and proslavery northern Democrats, killed it.

Fervent Democratic expansionists became even more aggressive. Polk, Secretary of State Buchanan, and Senators Stephen A. Douglas of Illinois and Jefferson Davis of Mississippi called for the United States to take Mexican territory south of the Rio Grande. However, to avoid a longer war and the assimilation of a huge number of Mexicans, John C. Calhoun and other southern leaders insisted that the United States should acquire only California and New Mexico, the most sparsely populated areas of Mexico.

To reunify the Democratic Party, Polk accepted Calhoun's policy. In February 1848 Polk signed the Treaty of Guadalupe Hidalgo, in which the United States agreed to pay Mexico $15 million in return for more than one-third of its territory: Texas, New Mexico, and California. The Senate ratified the treaty in March 1848.

The passions aroused by the war dominated the election of 1848. The Senate's rejection of the Wilmot Proviso prompted antislavery advocates to revive Thomas Morris's charge of a massive "Slave Power" conspiracy. To thwart any such plan, thousands of ordinary northerners joined a new "**free-soil**" movement. "The curse of slavery," Abijah Beckwith of Herkimer County in New York told his grandson, "threatens the general and equal distribution of our lands into convenient family farms." For Beckwith and other yeomen farmers, slavery was an institution of "aristocratic men" and a threat to the liberties of "the great mass of the people."

The free-soilers abandoned the Liberty Party's focus on the sinfulness of slavery and the natural rights of African Americans. Like Beckwith, they depicted slavery as a threat to republican institutions and white yeoman farming. This shift in emphasis led the radical abolitionist William Lloyd Garrison to denounce free-soil doctrine as racist "whitemanism." However, Frederick Douglass, the foremost black abolitionist, endorsed the movement as the best means of confronting the South and overthrowing slavery. Indeed, the Wilmot Proviso's call for free soil was the first antislavery proposal to attract broad popular support. Hundreds of women in the Great Lakes states joined female free-soil organizations formed by the American and Foreign Anti-Slavery Society.

The conflict over slavery took a toll on Polk and the Democratic Party. Opposed by free-soilers and exhausted by his rigorous dawn-to-midnight work regime, Polk declined to run for a second term and died three months after leaving office. In his place the Democrats nominated Senator Lewis Cass of Michigan, an avid expansionist who had advocated buying Cuba, annexing Mexico's Yucatán Peninsula, and taking all of Oregon. To maintain party unity, Cass was deliberately vague on the question of slavery in the West. He promoted a new idea—squatter sovereignty—that would allow settlers in each territory to determine its status as free or slave. Cass's political ingenuity failed to hold the party together. Demanding unambiguous opposition to the expansion of slavery, some northern Democrats joined the newly formed Free-Soil Party, which nominated Martin Van Buren for president. To attract Whig votes, the Free-Soil Party chose conscience Whig Charles Francis Adams as its candidate for vice president.

To keep their party intact, the Whigs nominated General Zachary Taylor. Taylor was a Louisiana slave owner, but he had not taken a position on the charged issue of slavery in the territories. Equally important, the general's military exploits had made him a popular hero. Known as "Old Rough and Ready," Taylor possessed a common touch that had won him the affection of his troops. "Our Commander on the Rio Grande," wrote Walt Whitman, "emulates the Great Commander of our revolution"—George Washington.

In 1848, as in 1840, running a military hero worked for the Whigs. Taylor took 47 percent of the popular vote against 42 percent for Cass. However, he won a majority in the electoral college (163 to 127) only because the Free-Soil ticket of Van Buren and Adams deprived the Democrats of enough votes in New York to cost Cass that state and the presidency. The bitter debate over the Wilmot Proviso had fractured the Democratic Party in the North and changed the dynamics of American politics.

## 1850: Crisis and Compromise

Even before President Zachary Taylor took office, events in California sparked a major political crisis. In January 1848 workmen building a mill for John A. Sutter in the Sierra Nevada foothills in northern California discovered flakes of gold. Sutter was a Swiss immigrant who arrived in California in 1839, became a Mexican citizen, and established an estate in the Sacramento Valley. He tried to keep the discovery a secret, but by May Americans who had already migrated to Monterey and San Francisco were pouring into the foothills. When President Polk confirmed the discovery in December, the gold rush was on. By January 1849 sixty-one crowded ships had left from northeastern ports to sail around Cape Horn to San Francisco, and by May, twelve thousand wagons had crossed the Missouri River, also bound for the gold fields. In 1849 alone more than 80,000 migrants—the "forty-niners"—arrived in California.

The rapid influx of settlers revived the national debate over free soil. The forty-niners, who lived in crowded, chaotic towns and mining camps, demanded the formation of a territorial government to protect their lives and property. To avoid an extended debate over slavery, President Taylor advised the Californians to apply for statehood immediately, and in November 1849 they ratified a state constitution that prohibited slavery. Taylor wanted to attract Free-Soilers and northern Democrats into the Whig Party and urged Congress to admit California as a free state.

The swift victory of the antislavery forces in California alarmed southern politicians. The admission of California as a free state would prevent the expansion of slavery to the Pacific and raise the number of free states in the Senate to sixteen, as opposed to fifteen slave states. Fearing that the South would be placed at a permanent disadvantage in Congress, southerners decided to block California's admission unless the federal government guaranteed the future of slavery.

**California Gold Prospectors**

Beginning in 1849, thousands of fortune seekers from all parts of the world converged on the California gold fields. By 1852 the state had 200,000 residents, including 25,000 Chinese, many of whom toiled in the gold fields as wage laborers. Working at the head of the Auburn Ravine in 1852, these prospectors are using a primitive technique—panning—to separate gold from sand and gravel. California State Library.

The resulting political impasse produced passionate debates in Congress and four distinct positions with respect to slavery in the territories. On the verge of death, John C. Calhoun took his usual extreme stance. He asserted the right of states to secede from the Union and proposed a constitutional amendment that would permanently balance the political power of the North and the South. Calhoun also advanced the radical doctrine that Congress had no constitutional authority to regulate slavery in the territories. This argument ran counter to a half century of practice. In 1787 Congress had prohibited slavery in the Northwest Territory, and in the Missouri Compromise of 1820 it had extended this ban to most of the Louisiana Purchase.

Calhoun's assertion that the territories were open to slavery won support in the Deep South, but many southerners favored a second—more moderate—position: an extension of the Missouri Compromise line to the Pacific Ocean. Such an extension would guarantee slave owners access to some western territory, including a separate state in southern California. Some northern Democrats, including former secretary of state James Buchanan, also favored this means of resolving the crisis.

A third alternative was squatter sovereignty, the idea advanced by Lewis Cass in 1848 and now championed by Democratic senator Stephen Douglas of Illinois. Douglas called his plan "**popular sovereignty**" to emphasize its roots in republican ideology, and it had considerable appeal. Popular sovereignty would place decisions about slavery in the hands of local settlers and their territorial governments and remove the explosive issue from national politics. However, popular sovereignty was a vague and slippery concept. Could residents accept or ban slavery when a territory was first organized or only when a territory had enough people to frame a constitution and apply for statehood?

Moreover, antislavery advocates were unwilling to accept any plan for California that might involve the expansion of slavery in the territories. Senator Salmon P. Chase of Ohio, elected by a Democratic–Free-Soil coalition, and Senator William H. Seward, a New York Whig, urged federal authorities to restrict slavery within its existing boundaries and then extinguish it completely. Condemning slavery as "morally unjust, politically unwise, and socially pernicious" and invoking "a higher law than the Constitution," Seward demanded bold action to protect freedom, "the common heritage of mankind."

Standing on the brink of disaster, senior politicians desperately sought a compromise. Assisted by Millard Fillmore, who became president in 1850 on the death of Zachary Taylor, Whig leaders Henry Clay and Daniel Webster and Democrat Stephen A. Douglas devised a package of six laws known collectively as the Compromise of 1850. To mollify the South, the Compromise included a new Fugitive Slave Act that enlisted federal magistrates in the task of returning runaway slaves. To satisfy the North, the legislation admitted California as a free state, resolved a boundary dispute between New Mexico and Texas in favor of New Mexico, and abolished the slave trade (but not slavery) in the District of Columbia. Finally, the Compromise organized the rest of the lands acquired from Mexico into the territories of New Mexico and Utah on the basis of popular sovereignty (Map 13.4).

The Compromise averted a secession crisis in 1850—but only barely. At one point the governor of South Carolina declared that there was not "the slightest doubt" that his state would secede from the Union. He and other "fire-eaters" in Georgia, Mississippi, and Alabama organized special conventions to ensure "Southern Rights" through secession. To persuade these conventions to support the Compromise, moderate southern politicians agreed to support secession in the future if Congress abolished slavery anywhere or refused to grant statehood to a territory with a proslavery constitution. Political wizardry had solved the immediate constitutional crisis but not the underlying issue of slavery.

# The End of the Second Party System, 1850–1858

The architects of the Compromise of 1850 hoped it would last for at least a generation, but their optimism was quickly dashed. Demanding freedom for fugitive slaves and free soil in the West, antislavery northerners refused to accept the Compromise, and expansionist-minded southerners plotted to extend slavery into the West and the Caribbean. The resulting disputes destroyed the Second Party System and deepened the crisis of the Union.

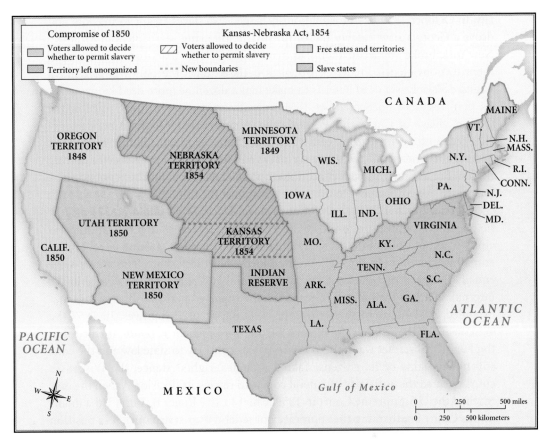

**MAP 13.4 The Compromise of 1850 and the Kansas-Nebraska Act of 1854**

Vast territories were at stake in the contest over the extension of slavery. The Compromise of 1850 resolved the status of lands in the Far West: California would be a free state, and the settlers of the Utah and New Mexico Territories would vote for or against slavery (the doctrine of popular sovereignty). The decision in 1854 to use popular sovereignty to decide the fate of slavery in the Kansas and Nebraska Territories sparked a bitter local war and revealed a fatal flaw in the doctrine.

FOR MORE HELP ANALYZING THIS MAP, see the Online Study Guide at **bedfordstmartins.com/henrettaconcise**.

## Resistance to the Fugitive Slave Act

The Fugitive Slave Act proved the most controversial element of the Compromise. Under its terms federal magistrates in the northern states determined the status of alleged runaway slaves. The law denied accused blacks jury trials and even the right to testify. Using its provisions, southern owners reenslaved about two hundred fugitives (as well as some free northern blacks).

The plight of runaways and the appearance of slave catchers in the North and Midwest aroused popular hostility, and free blacks and abolitionists defied the new law. In October 1850 Boston abolitionists helped two slaves escape to freedom and drove a Georgia slave catcher out of town. The following year rioters in Syracuse, New York, broke into a courthouse to free a fugitive slave. Abandoning his commitment to nonviolence, Frederick Douglass declared that "the only way to make a Fugitive Slave Law a dead letter is to make half a dozen or more dead kidnappers." As if in response, in September 1851 a deadly confrontation took place in the Quaker village of Christiana, Pennsylvania. About twenty African Americans exchanged gunfire with a group of slave catchers from Maryland, killing two of them. Federal authorities indicted thirty-six blacks and four whites for treason for defying the law. But a Pennsylvania jury acquitted one defendant, and northern public opinion forced the government to drop charges against the rest.

Harriet Beecher Stowe's abolitionist novel *Uncle Tom's Cabin* (1852) magnified northern opposition to the Fugitive Slave Act. By translating the moral principles of abolitionism into heartrending personal situations, Stowe's novel evoked empathy and outrage throughout the North. Northern state legislatures were equally incensed that the act allowed the federal government to intervene in the internal affairs of their states. In response, they enacted personal-liberty laws that extended legal rights to their citizens, including accused fugitives. In 1857 the Wisconsin Supreme Court went even further. In *Ableman v. Booth*, it ruled that the Fugitive Slave Act was void in Wisconsin as contrary to state law and the constitutional rights of its citizens. Taking a "states' rights" stance, the Wisconsin court rejected the authority of federal courts to review its decision. When the case reached the U.S. Supreme Court in 1859, Chief Justice Roger B. Taney led a unanimous Court in affirming the supremacy of federal over state courts—a position that has stood the test of time—and upheld the constitutionality of the Fugitive Slave Act. By that time popular opposition in the North had made it nearly impossible to catch fugitive blacks. As Frederick Douglass had hoped, the act had become a "dead letter."

### The Political System in Decline

The conflict over slavery split both major political parties along sectional lines and stymied creative political leadership. The Whigs, weakened by the death of Henry Clay, chose General Winfield Scott, another hero of the war with Mexico, as their presidential candidate in 1852. However, many southern Whigs refused to support Scott because northern Whigs refused to support slavery. The Democrats were equally divided. Southerners wanted a candidate who would support Calhoun's position that all territories should be open to slavery. But northern and midwestern Democrats advocated popular sovereignty, as did the three leading candidates—Lewis Cass of Michigan, Stephen Douglas of Illinois, and James Buchanan of Pennsylvania. Ultimately, the party settled on a compromise nominee, Franklin Pierce of New Hampshire, a congenial man reputed to be sympathetic to the South.

The Democrats' cautious strategy paid off, and they swept the election. Pleased by the admission of California as a free state, Martin Van Buren and many other Free-Soilers voted for Pierce, reuniting the Democratic Party. Conversely, the election fragmented the Whig Party into sectional wings; it would never again wage a national campaign.

As president, Pierce pursued an expansionist foreign policy. To assist northern merchants, he sent a mission to Japan to negotiate a commercial treaty. To mollify southern expansionists, he revived Polk's plan to annex extensive Mexican territories south of the Rio Grande. When Mexico rejected this initiative, Pierce settled for the purchase of a narrow slice of land that would assist his negotiator, James Gadsden, to build a southern-based transcontinental rail line.

Pierce's most dramatic, and most ill-fated, foreign policy initiative came in the Caribbean. Southern expansionists had previously funded three clandestine military expeditions to Cuba, where they hoped to prod sugar-producing slave owners to declare independence from Spain and join the United States. In 1853, Pierce covertly supported a new Cuban expedition and, to assist this venture, threatened war with Spain over the seizure of an American ship. When northern Democrats in Congress refused to support this aggressive diplomacy, Pierce and Secretary of State William L. Marcy had to back down. Still determined to seize Cuba, Marcy tried to buy the island from Spain. When that scheme also failed, Marcy arranged for American diplomats in Europe to inform Pierce, in the so-called Ostend Manifesto of 1854, that the United States would be justified "by every law, human and Divine" in seizing Cuba. Leaked to the press by antiexpansionists, the publication of the Ostend Manifesto revived northern fears of a "Slave Power" conspiracy and halted planter dreams of carving out an empire for slavery in the Caribbean.

### The Kansas-Nebraska Act and the Rise of New Parties

In 1854 a new struggle over westward expansion inflamed sectional divisions. Because the Missouri Compromise prohibited new slave states in the Louisiana Purchase north of 36°30', southern senators had delayed the political organization of that area. But westward-looking residents of the Ohio River Valley and the Upper South demanded its settlement. Senator Stephen A. Douglas of Illinois became their spokesman, partly because he supported the construction of a transcontinental railroad linking Chicago to California. In 1854 Douglas introduced a bill to extinguish Native American rights on the central Great Plains and organize a large free territory to be called Nebraska.

Douglas's bill conflicted with the plans of southern politicians who wanted to extend slavery throughout the Louisiana Purchase and wanted a southern city — New Orleans, Memphis, or St. Louis — to serve as the eastern terminus of a transcontinental railroad. To win southern support for the organization of Nebraska, Douglas made two major concessions. First, he amended his bill so that it explicitly repealed the Missouri Compromise and organized the region on the basis of popular sovereignty. Second, Douglas agreed to the formation of two new territories, Nebraska and

Kansas. This provision would give southern planters the opportunity to settle Kansas and, using popular sovereignty, eventually make it a slave state (see Map 13.4). To win support of this scheme by northern congressmen, Douglas argued that Kansas was not suited to plantation agriculture and would become a free state. After weeks of bitter debate, the Senate enacted the Kansas-Nebraska Act. When sixty-six northern Democrats in the House of Representatives defied party policy to vote against the act, Pierce used patronage and persuasion to get twenty-two members to change their votes, and the measure squeaked through.

The Kansas-Nebraska Act had disastrous consequences for the American political system because it destroyed the Whig Party and nearly wrecked the Democratic Party. Denouncing the act as "part of a great scheme for extending and perpetuating supremacy of the slave power," northern Whigs and "anti-Nebraska" Democrats abandoned their respective parties. They joined with Free-Soilers and abolitionists in a new Republican Party, which vowed to ban slavery from the territories. Although the Republican Party was a coalition of diverse groups, its founders shared a common philosophy. They opposed slavery because it degraded manual labor by enslaving blacks and driving down the wages and working conditions of free whites. And they celebrated the moral virtues of a society based on "the middling classes who own the soil and work it with their own hands." Abraham Lincoln, an Illinois Whig who became a Republican, articulated the party's vision of social mobility. "There is no permanent class of hired laborers among us," he argued, and every man had a chance to become a property owner. In the face of increasing class divisions in the industrializing North and Midwest, Lincoln and his fellow Republicans asserted the values of republican freedom and individual enterprise.

The Republicans faced severe competition from another new party, the American, or "Know-Nothing," Party. The American Party had its origins in the anti-immigrant and anti-Catholic organizations of the 1840s (see Chapter 10). In 1850 these secret societies banded together as the Order of the Star-Spangled Banner, and the following year they formed the American Party. The secrecy-conscious members often replied "I know nothing" to outsiders' questions, thus giving the party its nickname, but its program was far from secret. Know-Nothings hoped to unite native-born Protestants against the "alien menace" of Irish and German Catholics, prohibit further immigration, and institute literacy tests for voting. In 1854 the Know-Nothings gained control of the state governments of Massachusetts and Pennsylvania and, allied with the Whigs, commanded a majority in the U.S. House of Representatives. The emergence of a major party led by nativists suddenly became a real possibility.

Moreover, the Kansas-Nebraska Act had created yet another political crisis. In 1854 thousands of settlers rushed into the Kansas Territory, putting Douglas's theory of popular sovereignty to the test. On the side of slavery, Senator David R. Atchison of Missouri organized residents to cross into Kansas and vote in crucial elections there. Opposing him was the abolitionist New England Emigrant Aid Society, which dispatched hundreds of free-soilers to Kansas. In March 1855 the Pierce administration stepped into the fray by accepting the legitimacy of the territorial legislature sitting in

Lecompton, Kansas, which had been elected primarily by border-crossing Missourians and had adopted proslavery legislation. However, the majority of Kansas residents favored free soil and refused allegiance to the Lecompton government.

In May 1856 both sides turned to violence. A proslavery gang, seven hundred strong, sacked the free-soil town of Lawrence, destroying two newspaper offices, looting stores, and burning down buildings (see American Voices, "'Bleeding Kansas': A Southern View," p. 404). The attack enraged John Brown, a fifty-six-year-old abolitionist from New York and Ohio, whose free-state militia force arrived too late to save the town. Brown was a complex man with a checkered financial past. Despite a long record of failed businesses, Brown had an intelligence and a moral intensity that won the trust of influential people. Taking vengeance for the sack of Lawrence, he and a few followers murdered and mutilated five proslavery settlers. We must "strike terror in the hearts of the proslavery people," Brown declared. The southerners' sack of Lawrence and the "Pottawatomie massacre," as Brown's killings became known, began a guerrilla war in Kansas that took about two hundred lives.

## The Election of 1856 and Dred Scott

The violence in Kansas dominated the presidential election of 1856. The two-year-old Republican Party counted on anger over "Bleeding Kansas" to boost its fortunes. The party's platform denounced the Kansas-Nebraska Act and, alleging a "Slave Power" conspiracy, insisted that the federal government prohibit slavery in all the territories. Its platform also called for federal subsidies for transcontinental railroads, reviving an element of the Whig economic program that was popular among midwestern Democrats. For president the Republicans nominated Colonel John C. Frémont, a Free-Soiler famous for his role in the conquest of California.

The American Party also entered the election with high hopes, but it quickly split into sectional factions over Kansas. The southern faction of the American Party nominated former Whig president Millard Fillmore. The Republicans cleverly maneuvered the northern faction of the American Party into endorsing Frémont, and they won the votes of Know-Nothing workingmen by emphasizing anti-Catholic nativism and high tariffs on foreign manufactures. As a Pennsylvania Republican put it, "Let our motto be, protection to everything American, against everything foreign." In New York, Republicans assumed the mantle of reform by shaping their policies "to cement into a harmonious mass . . . all of the Anti-Slavery, Anti-Popery and Anti-Whiskey" voters.

The Democrats reaffirmed their support for popular sovereignty and the Kansas-Nebraska Act and nominated James Buchanan of Pennsylvania. A tall, dignified figure of sixty-four, Buchanan was an experienced but unimaginative politician. Drawing upon his party's organizational strength and the loyalty of Democratic voters, Buchanan won the three-way race, amassing 174 votes in the electoral college and winning the popular vote—1.8 million votes (45 percent) to 1.3 million (33 percent) for Frémont. However, Buchanan took only five free states

**AMERICAN VOICES**

## "Bleeding Kansas": A Southern View

### AXALLA JOHN HOOLE

*Early in 1856 Axalla John Hoole and his bride left South Carolina to build a new life in the Kansas Territory (K.T.). These letters from Hoole to his family show that things did not go well from the start and gradually got worse; after eighteen months the Hooles returned to South Carolina. A Confederate militia captain during the Civil War, Axalla Hoole died in the Battle of Chickamauga in September 1863.*

Kansas City, Missouri, Apl. 3d., 1856. The Missourians . . . are very sanguine about Kansas being a slave state & I have heard some of them say it shall be . . . but generally speaking, I have not met with the reception which I expected. Everyone seems bent on the Almighty Dollar, and as a general thing that seems to be their only thought. . . . [T]he supper bell has rung and I must close. Give my love to [the family] and all the Negroes. . . .

Lecompton, K.T., Sept. 12, 1856. I have been unwell ever since the 9th of July. . . . I thought of going to work in a few days, when the Abolitionists broke out and I have had to stand guard of nights when I ought to have been in bed, took cold which . . . caused diarrhea. . . . Betsie is well. . . . I am now in Lecompton, almost all of the Proslavery party between this place and Lawrence are here. We brought our families here, as we thought that we would be better able to defend ourselves. . . .

Lane [and a force of abolitionists] came against us last Friday (a week ago to-day). As it happened we had about 400 men with two cannon—we marched out to meet him, though we were under the impression at the time that we had 1,000 men. We came in gunshot of each other, but the regular [U.S. Army] soldiers came and interfered, but not before our party had shot some dozen guns, by which it is reported that five of the Abolitionists had been killed or wounded. We had strict orders . . . not to fire until they made the attack, but some of our boys would not be restrained. I was a rifleman and one of the skirmishers, but did all that I could to restrain our men though I itched all over to shoot myself. . . .

July the 5th., 1857. I fear, Sister, that [our] coming here will do no good at last, as I begin to think that this will be made a Free State at last. 'Tis true we have elected Proslavery men to draft a state constitution, but I feel pretty certain, if it is put to a vote of the people, it will be rejected, as I feel pretty confident that they have a majority here at this time. The South has ceased all efforts, while the North is redoubling her exertions. We nominated a candidate for Congress last Friday—Ex-Gov. Ransom of Michigan. I must confess I have not much faith in him, tho he professes to hate the abolitionists bitterly. . . . If we had nominated a Southern man, he would have been sure to have been beaten. . . .

SOURCE: William Stanley Hoole, ed., "A Southerner's Viewpoint of the Kansas Situation, 1856–1857," *Kansas Historical Quarterly* 3 (1934): 43–65, 149–71, passim.

(as opposed to eleven for Frémont), and a small shift of the popular vote to Frémont in Illinois and Pennsylvania would have given him the presidency. Fillmore, the candidate of the southern faction of the American Party, won 21 percent of the national vote but only 8 electoral votes.

The dramatic restructuring of parties was now apparent (Map 13.5). With the splintering of the Know-Nothings, the Republicans had replaced the Whigs as the second major party. Moreover, because they had no support in the South, a Republican victory in the next presidential election might prompt the southern states to withdraw from the Union. The fate of the republic hinged on the ability of President Buchanan to defuse the passions of the past decade and devise a way of protecting free soil in the West and slavery in the South.

Events—and his own values and weaknesses—conspired against Buchanan. During the election, the Supreme Court considered the case of *Dred Scott v. Sandford*, which raised the controversial issue of Congress's constitutional authority to regulate slavery in the territories. Scott was an enslaved African American who had lived for a time with his owner, an army surgeon, in the free state of Illinois and at Fort Snelling, then in the Wisconsin Territory, where the Northwest Ordinance (1787) prohibited slavery. In his suit Scott claimed that his residence in a free state and a free territory had made him free. Partly as result of Buchanan's pressure on several northern justices, seven of the nine members of the Court agreed that Scott

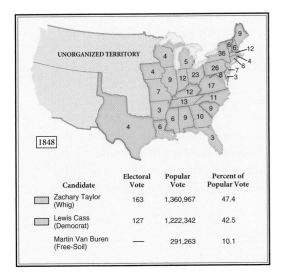

| Candidate | Electoral Vote | Popular Vote | Percent of Popular Vote |
|---|---|---|---|
| Zachary Taylor (Whig) | 163 | 1,360,967 | 47.4 |
| Lewis Cass (Democrat) | 127 | 1,222,342 | 42.5 |
| Martin Van Buren (Free-Soil) | — | 291,263 | 10.1 |

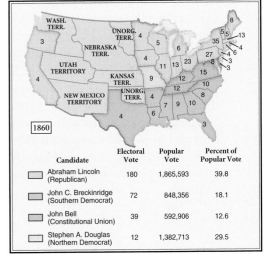

| Candidate | Electoral Vote | Popular Vote | Percent of Popular Vote |
|---|---|---|---|
| Abraham Lincoln (Republican) | 180 | 1,865,593 | 39.8 |
| John C. Breckinridge (Southern Democrat) | 72 | 848,356 | 18.1 |
| John Bell (Constitutional Union) | 39 | 592,906 | 12.6 |
| Stephen A. Douglas (Northern Democrat) | 12 | 1,382,713 | 29.5 |

**MAP 13.5 Political Realignment, 1848–1860**

In the presidential election of 1848, both Whigs and Democrats won electoral votes in most parts of the nation. Then the political conflict over slavery and the Compromise of 1850 destroyed the Whig Party in the South. As the only nationwide party, the Democrats won easily over the Whigs in 1852 and, because of the split between Republicans and Know-Nothings, in 1856 as well. However, by 1860 a new regionally based party system had taken shape and would persist for the next seventy years, with Democrats dominant in the South and Republicans in the Northeast and Midwest.

remained a slave. But the judges were unable to agree on the legal issues, and each justice wrote a separate opinion.

Chief Justice Roger B. Taney of Maryland composed the most influential opinion. He declared that Negroes, whether enslaved or free, could not be citizens of the United States, and that Scott therefore had no right to sue in federal court. That argument was controversial enough, since free blacks could be citizens of a state, which presumably gave them access to the federal courts. But Taney proceeded to make two even more controversial points. First, he endorsed John C. Calhoun's argument regarding the Fifth Amendment. Because the amendment prohibited "takings" of property without due process of law, Taney ruled that Congress could not deny southern citizens the right to take their slave property into the territories and own it there. Consequently, the chief justice concluded, the provisions of the Northwest Ordinance and the Missouri Compromise that prohibited slavery had never been constitutional. Second, Taney declared that Congress could not give to territorial governments any powers that Congress itself did not possess. Since Congress had no authority to prohibit slavery in a territory, neither did a territorial government. Taney thereby endorsed Calhoun's interpretation of popular sovereignty: only when settlers wrote a constitution and requested statehood could they prohibit slavery.

In a single stroke a Democrat-dominated Supreme Court had declared the Republicans' antislavery platform to be unconstitutional, a decision the Republicans could never accept. Led by Senator William H. Seward of New York, they accused the Supreme Court and President Buchanan of participating in the "Slave Power" conspiracy.

Buchanan then added new fuel to the raging constitutional fire. In early 1858 he recommended the admission of Kansas as a slave state under the Lecompton constitution, although its legitimacy was widely questioned. Angered that Buchanan would not permit a referendum on the Lecompton constitution, Stephen Douglas, the most influential Democratic senator, broke with the president and persuaded Congress to deny statehood to Kansas. (Kansas would enter the Union as a free state in 1861.) By pursuing a proslavery agenda—first in the *Dred Scott* decision and then in Kansas—Buchanan had helped to split his party and the nation.

# Abraham Lincoln and the Republican Triumph, 1858–1860

The crisis of the Union intensified as the Democratic Party fragmented and the Republicans gained support in the North. Abraham Lincoln emerged as the pivotal figure in American politics, the only Republican leader whose policies and temperament might have saved the Union. But few southerners trusted Lincoln, and the prospect of his election to the presidency gave new life to the southern secessionists who had threatened to leave the Union since 1850.

## Lincoln's Political Career

The middle-class world of storekeepers, lawyers, and entrepreneurs in the small towns of the Ohio River Valley shaped Lincoln's early career. He came from an impoverished yeoman farm family that had moved from Kentucky, where Lincoln was born in 1809, to Indiana and then to Illinois. In 1831 Lincoln rejected his father's life as a subsistence farmer and became a store clerk in New Salem, Illinois. Socially ambitious, Lincoln sought entry into the middle class by joining the New Salem Debating Society, reading Shakespeare, and studying law.

Lincoln's ambition was "a little engine that knew no rest," his closest associate remarked. Admitted to the bar in 1837, Lincoln moved to Springfield, the new state capital. There he met Mary Todd, the cultured daughter of a Kentucky banker; they married in 1842. The couple was a picture in contrasts. Her tastes were aristocratic; his were humble. She was volatile in temperament; he had an easygoing manner but suffered bouts of depression that tried her patience and tested his character. Entering political life, Lincoln served four terms as a Whig in the Illinois assembly, where he promoted education, state banking, and canals and railroads.

In 1846 the rising lawyer-politician won election to Congress, which was bitterly divided over the Wilmot Proviso. Lincoln had long felt that human bondage was unjust but did not believe that the federal government had the constitutional authority to tamper with slavery in the South. To exclude slavery from the territories, he voted for the Wilmot Proviso. Lincoln also proposed that Congress enact legislation for the gradual (and therefore compensated) emancipation of slaves in the District of Columbia. He argued that such measures—firm opposition to the expansion of slavery, gradual emancipation, and the colonization of freed slaves in Africa—was the only practical way to address the issue. However, both abolitionists and proslavery activists derided these pragmatic policies and Lincoln lost his bid for reelection. Dismayed, he withdrew from politics and developed a lucrative legal practice representing railroads and manufacturers.

Lincoln returned to the political fray after the passage of Stephen Douglas's Kansas-Nebraska Act. Attacking Douglas's doctrine of popular sovereignty, Lincoln reaffirmed his position on slavery. He would not threaten the institution in the states where it existed but would use national authority to exclude it from the territories. Confronting the moral issue, Lincoln declared that if the nation was to uphold its republican ideals, then it must eventually cut out slavery like a "cancer."

Abandoning the Whig Party in favor of the Republicans, Lincoln quickly emerged as their leader in Illinois. Campaigning for the U.S. Senate against Stephen Douglas in 1858, Lincoln alerted his audiences to the dangers of the "Slave Power." He warned that the proslavery Supreme Court might soon declare that the Constitution "does not permit a state to exclude slavery from its limits," just as it had decided (in *Dred Scott*) that "neither Congress nor the territorial legislature can do it." In that event, he continued, "we shall awake to the reality . . . that the Supreme Court has made Illinois a slave state." The prospect of slavery spreading into the North informed Lincoln's famous "House Divided" speech. Quoting from the Bible, "A house divided against itself cannot stand," he predicted a crisis: "I believe this government cannot endure permanently half slave and half free. . . . It will become all one thing, or all the other."

The contest in Illinois attracted national interest because of Douglas's prominence and Lincoln's reputation as a formidable speaker. During a series of seven debates, Douglas declared his support for white supremacy and attacked Lincoln for supporting "negro equality." Put on the defensive by Douglas's racial tactics, Lincoln advocated economic opportunity for blacks but not equal political rights. He asked how Douglas could accept the *Dred Scott* decision (which protected slave owners' property in the territories) and yet advocate popular sovereignty (which asserted settlers' power to exclude slavery). Douglas responded with the so-called Freeport Doctrine, which suggested that the residents could exclude slavery simply by not adopting a law to protect it. Although Douglas's Freeport statement pleased neither proslavery advocates nor abolitionists, the Democrats won a narrow victory over the Republicans in Illinois, and the state legislature reelected Douglas to the U.S. Senate.

**Abraham Lincoln and Stephen Douglas, 1860**

When Douglas and Lincoln squared off in the presidential election of 1860, they distributed thousands of silk campaign ribbons bearing their portraits and signatures. The well-known photographer Matthew Brady took their pictures and retouched the images to make them more flattering—smoothing out Lincoln's gaunt and well-lined face and slimming down Douglas's ample cheeks.

Collection of Janice L. and David J. Frent.

## The Party System Fragments

The debates with Douglas gave Lincoln a national reputation, while the election of 1858 gave the Republican Party control of the House of Representatives. In the wake of these Republican gains, southern Democrats divided into two groups. Moderates, such as Senator Jefferson Davis of Mississippi, who were known as Southern Rights Democrats, continued to seek political commitments to protect slavery. However, radical southern leaders, such as Robert Barnwell Rhett of South Carolina and William Lowndes Yancey of Alabama, repudiated the Union and actively promoted secession. Radical antislavery northerners played into their hands. Senator William Seward of New York declared that freedom and slavery were locked in "an irrepressible conflict" and the militant abolitionist John Brown suggested what that might mean. In October 1859, Brown led eighteen heavily armed black and white men in a raid on the federal arsenal at Harpers Ferry, Virginia. Brown hoped to secure arms, lead a slave rebellion, and establish a separate African American state in the South.

Republican leaders disavowed Brown's unsuccessful raid, but Democrats called his plot "a natural, logical, inevitable result of the doctrines and teachings of the Republican party." Brown was charged with treason, sentenced to death, and hanged—only to be praised by reformer Henry David Thoreau as "an angel of light." Horrified by northern admiration of Brown, southerners looked to the future with fear. "The aim of the present black republican organization is the destruction of the social system of the Southern States, without regard to consequences," warned one newspaper.

Nor could the South count on the Democratic Party to protect its interests. At the party convention in April 1860, northern Democrats rejected Jefferson Davis's program to protect slavery in the territories, so the delegates from eight southern states quit the meeting. At a second Democratic convention in Baltimore, northern and western delegates nominated Stephen Douglas for president; meeting separately, southern Democrats nominated John C. Breckinridge of Kentucky.

With the Democrats divided, the Republicans sensed victory. They courted white voters by opposing both slavery and racial equality: "Missouri for white men and white men for Missouri," declared that state's Republican platform. The national Republican convention chose Lincoln as its presidential candidate because his position on slavery was more moderate than that of the best-known Republicans, Senator William H. Seward of New York and Salmon P. Chase of Ohio, who demanded its abolition. Lincoln also conveyed a compelling egalitarian image that appealed to smallholding farmers and wage earners. And Lincoln's home territory—the rapidly growing Midwest—was crucial in the competition between Democrats and Republicans.

The Republican strategy succeeded. Lincoln received only 40 percent of the popular vote but won a majority in the electoral college by carrying every northern and western state except New Jersey. Douglas took 30 percent of the total vote, but won electoral votes only in Missouri and New Jersey. Breckinridge captured every state in the Deep South as well as Delaware, Maryland, and North Carolina, while John Bell, a former Tennessee Whig who was the nominee of the compromise-seeking Constitutional Union Party, carried the Upper South states where the Whigs had been strongest: Kentucky, Tennessee, and Virginia.

The Republicans had united the Northeast, the Midwest, and the Far West behind free soil and had seized national power. A revolution was in the making. Slavery had permeated the American federal republic for so long and so thoroughly that southerners had come to see it as part of the constitutional order—an order now under siege. To many southerners it seemed time to think carefully about the meaning of Lincoln's words of 1858 that the Union must "become all one thing, or all the other."

## T I M E L I N E

| | | | |
|---|---|---|---|
| 1820s | Expansion of cattle raising in Mexican California | | California, New Mexico, and Texas to the United States |
| 1821 | Mexico wins independence from Spain | 1850 | Compromise of 1850 seeks to preserve the Union |
| 1836 | Texas proclaims independence from Mexico | | Fugitive Slave Act rejected by northern abolitionists |
| 1842 | Overland migration to Oregon begins | 1851 | American (Know-Nothing) Party formed |
| 1844 | Policy toward Texas and Oregon dominates presidential election | 1852 | Harriet Beecher Stowe publishes *Uncle Tom's Cabin* |
| 1845 | John O'Sullivan coins term *Manifest Destiny* | 1854 | Ostend Manifesto seeks to expand slavery by acquiring Cuba |
| | Texas admitted to Union as a slave state | | Kansas-Nebraska Act tests policy of popular sovereignty |
| | John Slidell's diplomatic mission to Mexico fails | | Republican Party formed |
| 1846 | United States declares war on Mexico | 1856 | "Bleeding Kansas" undermines popular sovereignty |
| | Treaty with Britain divides Oregon Country at forty-ninth parallel | | |
| | Wilmot Proviso prohibiting slavery in newly acquired territories approved by House but not by Senate | 1857 | *Dred Scott v. Sandford* allows slavery in the territories |
| | | 1858 | James Buchanan backs Lecompton constitution |
| 1847 | American troops under General Winfield Scott capture Mexico City | | Lincoln-Douglas debates |
| 1848 | Gold discovered in California | 1860 | Abraham Lincoln elected president in four-way contest |
| | Free-Soil Party organized | | |
| | In Treaty of Guadalupe Hidalgo Mexico cedes its provinces of | | |

# For Further Exploration

Patricia Nelson Limerick, *The Legacy of Conquest: The Unbroken Past of the American West* (1989), provides a sharply written interpretation of the struggle among individuals, groups, and nations for control of the West. First-Person Narratives of California's Early Years, 1849–1900 are available through the Library of Congress at <http://lcweb2.loc.gov/ammem/cbhtml/cbhome.html>. A fine video documentary, *The West* (6 hours), by Ken Burns and Stephen Ives has a useful Web site—New Perspectives on the West, at <http://www.pbs.org/thewest>—that includes a good collection of maps, biographical essays, original documents, and images. For the early history of Texas, see <http://www.tsl.state.tx.us/treasures/>. The PBS documentary *The U.S.-Mexican War* (4 hours) and its Web site, at <http://www.pbs.org/usmexicanwar>, view the war both from the American and the Mexican perspectives and draw on the expertise of historians from each country.

David Potter, *The Impending Crisis, 1848–1861* (1976), presents a lucid account of the political history of the pre–Civil War years. Two recent works, John Patrick Daly, *When Slavery Was Called Freedom: Evangelicalism, Proslavery, and the Causes of the Civil War* (2002), and Leonard L. Richards, *The Slave Power: The Free North and Southern Domination, 1780–1860* (2000), offer a broad cultural analysis of the sectional conflict.

For an eloquent discussion of the ideology and politics of the Republican Party, see Eric Foner, *Free Soil, Free Labor, Free Men* (1970). Michael Holt's *The Political Crisis of the 1850s* (1978) shows how the loss of morale among voters and the collapse of the Second Party System allowed sectional rivalries to engulf the nation in war. For an incisive treatment of Lincoln's personal and political life, see Stephen Oates, *With Malice Toward None: A Life of Abraham Lincoln* (1977). For Lincoln's speech on the *Dred Scott* decision, refer to <http://www.usconstitution.com/AbrahamLincolnonDredScottDecision.htm>; the justices' opinions in the case can be read at <http://odur.let.rug.nl/~usa/D/1851-1875/dredscott/dredxx.htm>. Uncle Tom's Cabin and American Culture: A Multi-Media Archive, at <http://jefferson.village.virginia.edu/utc/>, is an extremely rich Web site that explores the literary and cultural context of the time through essays, original documents, and recordings of minstrel music.

---

For definitions of key terms boldfaced in this chapter, see the glossary at the end of the book.

To assess your mastery of the material covered in this chapter, see the Online Study Guide at **bedfordstmartins.com/henrettaconcise**.

For map resources and primary documents, see **bedfordstmartins.com/henrettaconcise**.

# Chapter 14

# TWO SOCIETIES AT WAR
## 1861–1865

Our fathers made this country, we their children are to save it.

ENLISTEE, TWELFTH OHIO REGIMENT, UNION ARMY, 1861

"What a scene it was," the Union soldier Elisha Hunt Rhodes wrote in his diary in July 1863 as the battle of Gettysburg ended. "Oh the dead and the dying on this bloody field." The passions kindled by southern rights and northern reformism had already inspired thousands of men to die in battle, and the slaughter would continue for two more years. "What is this all about?" asked Confederate lieutenant R. M. Collins at the end of another gruesome battle. "Why is it that 200,000 men of one blood and tongue . . . [should be] seeking one another's lives? We could settle our differences by compromising and all be at home in ten days." But there was no compromise—not in 1863 nor even in 1865.

To explain why Southerners seceded and then fought the war to the bitter end is not simple, but racial slavery is an important part of the answer. For political leaders in the South, the Republican victory in 1860 presented a clear and immediate danger to the slave-owning republic that had existed since 1776. Lincoln was elected without a single electoral vote from the South, and Southerners knew that his Republican Party would prevent the extension of slavery into the territories.

Moreover, they did not believe Lincoln when he promised not "directly or indirectly, to interfere with the institution of slavery in the States where it exists." "The mission of the Republican party," a southern newspaper declared, was "to meddle with everything—to meddle with the domestic institutions of other States, and to meddle with family arrangements in their own states—to overthrow Democracy, Catholicism and Slavery." Soon, a southern senator warned, "cohorts of Federal office-holders, Abolitionists, may be sent into [our] midst" to mobilize the African American population. The result would be bloody slave revolts and racial intermixture—by which was meant relations between black men and white women, as white owners had already fathered untold numbers of children by their black women slaves. "Better, far better! [to] endure all horrors of civil war," insisted a Confederate recruit from Virginia, "than to see the dusky sons of Ham leading the fair daughters of the South to the altar." To preserve black slavery and the supremacy of white men, radical southern leaders embarked on the dangerous journey of secession.

Lincoln and the North would not let them go in peace. Living in a world still ruled by kings and princes, northern leaders believed that the failure of the American Union might destroy for all time the prospect of a republican government based on constitutional procedures, majority rule, and democratic elections. "We cannot escape history," the new president eloquently declared. "We shall nobly save, or meanly lose, the last best hope of earth." A young Union army recruit from Ohio put the issue more simply: "If our institutions prove a failure . . . of what value will be house, family, or friends?"

And so came the Civil War. Called the "War between the States" by Southerners and the "War of the Rebellion" by Northerners, the struggle continued until the great issues of the Union and slavery had been finally resolved. The cost was incredibly high: more lives lost than in all the nation's subsequent wars and a century-long legacy of bitterness between the triumphant North and the vanquished South.

# Secession and Military Stalemate, 1861–1862

Following Lincoln's election in November 1860, secessionist fervor swept through the Deep South, and the future of the Union appeared dim. Henry Clay and Daniel Webster, architects of the great sectional agreements of the past, had died and lesser men now sat in Congress. Nonetheless, veteran Washington politicians did not give up. In the four months before Lincoln's election, they struggled to forge a new compromise that (like those of 1787, 1821, and 1850) would preserve the Union.

## Choosing Sides

The movement toward secession was most rapid in South Carolina—the home of John C. Calhoun, nullification, and the Southern Radical movement. Robert Barnwell Rhett and other "fire-eaters" had called for secession ever since the crisis of 1850 and, with Lincoln's election, their goal was suddenly within reach. On December 20 a special state convention voted unanimously to dissolve "the union now subsisting between South Carolina and other States."

Moving quickly, fire-eaters elsewhere in the Deep South called similar conventions and mobilized vigilante groups and militia units to suppress local Unionists and prepare for war. In early January, amid an atmosphere of public celebration, Mississippi enacted a secession ordinance. Within a month Florida, Alabama, Georgia, Louisiana, and Texas had also left the Union (Map 14.1). In early February the jubilant secessionists met in Montgomery, Alabama, to proclaim a new nation—the Confederate States of America. Adopting a provisional constitution, the delegates named Jefferson Davis of Mississippi, a former U.S. senator and secretary of war, as its interim president.

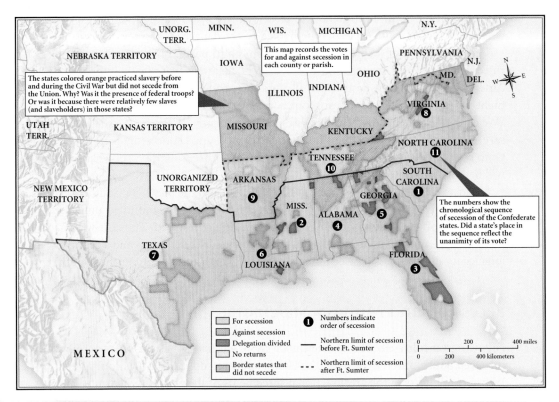

**MAP 14.1 The Process of Secession, 1860–1861**

The states of the Lower South, which had the highest concentration of slaves, led the secessionist movement. After the attack on Fort Sumter, the states of the Upper South joined the Confederacy. Yeomen farmers in Tennessee and the backcountry of Alabama, Georgia, and Virginia opposed secession but, except in the future state of West Virginia, initially rallied to the Confederate cause. Consequently, the South entered the Civil War with a relatively united white population.

Secessionist fervor was less intense in the eight slave states of the Upper South (Virginia, Delaware, Maryland, North Carolina, Kentucky, Tennessee, Missouri, and Arkansas), where there were fewer slaves and yeomen farmers had greater political power. Yeomen had long resented the authority claimed by the slave-owning gentry, and some actively opposed it. In the 1850s, Hinton Helper of North Carolina roused the "Non-slaveowners of the South! farmers, mechanics and workingmen," and warned them that "the slaveholders, the arrogant demagogues whom you have elected to offices of honor and profit, have hoodwinked you." Influenced partly by such sentiments, in January 1861 the legislatures of Virginia and Tennessee refused to join the secessionist movement. Seeking a compromise, Upper South leaders proposed federal guarantees for slavery in the states where it existed.

Meanwhile, the Union government floundered. In his final message to Congress in December 1860, President Buchanan declared secession illegal but denied that the federal government had the authority to restore the Union by force. South Carolina viewed Buchanan's message as an implicit recognition of its independence and demanded the surrender of Fort Sumter, a federal garrison in Charleston harbor. To test the secessionists' resolve, Buchanan ordered the resupply of the fort by an unarmed merchant ship. When the South Carolinians fired on the ship, Buchanan showed his own lack of resolve by refusing to order the navy to escort it into the harbor.

Instead, Buchanan urged Congress to find a compromise. The scheme proposed by Senator John J. Crittenden of Kentucky, an aging follower of Henry Clay, received the most support. Crittenden's plan had two parts. The first part, which won congressional approval, called for a constitutional amendment that would permanently protect slavery from federal interference in any state where it already existed. Crittenden's second provision called for the westward extension of the Missouri Compromise line (36°30′ north latitude) to the California border. Slavery would be barred north of the line and protected to the south, including any territories "hereafter acquired."

On Lincoln's instructions, congressional Republicans rejected this part of Crittenden's plan. The president-elect was firmly committed to the doctrine of free soil and feared this compromise would simply encourage the South to embark on new imperialist adventures in the Caribbean and Latin America. Crittenden's plan, Lincoln charged, would be "a perpetual covenant of war against every people, tribe, and State owning a foot of land between here and Tierra del Fuego [the southern tip of South America]."

In his inaugural address in March 1861, Lincoln carefully balanced a call for reconciliation with a firm commitment to the Union. He promised to safeguard slavery where it existed and to ensure free soil in the territories. Most important, Lincoln stated that the Union was "perpetual"; consequently, the secession of the Confederate states was illegal and acts of violence in support of their action constituted insurrection. He clearly declared his intention to enforce federal law throughout the Union and—of particular relevance to Fort Sumter—to continue to "hold, occupy, and possess" federal property in the seceded states and "to collect duties and imposts" there. If force was necessary to preserve the Union, Lincoln—like Andrew Jackson during the nullification crisis—promised to use it. The choice was the South's: return to the Union or face war.

The South's decision came quickly. The garrison at Fort Sumter urgently needed food and medicine. Upholding his promise to defend federal property, Lincoln dispatched a relief expedition and assured the Confederate government of its peaceful mission. However, Jefferson Davis and associates wanted a military confrontation to turn the wavering Upper South against the North and win foreign support for the Confederate cause. Davis demanded the surrender of the fort and, when Major Robert Anderson refused, the Confederate forces opened fire and forced a capitulation on April 14. The next day Lincoln called 75,000 state militiamen into federal service for ninety days to put down an insurrection "too powerful to be suppressed by the ordinary course of judicial proceedings." All talk of compromise was past.

Northerners responded to Lincoln's call to arms with wild enthusiasm. Asked to provide thirteen regiments of volunteers, Republican governor William Dennison of Ohio sent twenty. Many northern Democrats declared their support for the Union cause. "Every man must be for the United States or against it," Stephen Douglas declared. "There can be no neutrals in this war, only patriots—or traitors."

The white residents of the Upper South now had to choose between the Union and the Confederacy, and their decision was crucial. Those eight states accounted for two-thirds of the South's white population, more than three-fourths of its industrial production, and well over half of its food and fuel. They were home to many of the nation's best military leaders, including Colonel Robert E. Lee of Virginia, a career officer whom veteran general Winfield Scott recommended to Lincoln to lead the new Union army. And they were geographically strategic. Kentucky, with its 500-mile border on the Ohio River, was essential to the movement of troops and supplies. Maryland was vital to the Union's security because it surrounded the nation's capital on the north.

The weight of history decided the outcome in Virginia, the original home of American slavery. Three days after the fall of Fort Sumter, a Virginia convention voted to secede by a margin of 88 to 55, with the dissenters drawn mainly from the yeoman-dominated northwestern counties. Elsewhere, Virginia whites rallied to the Confederate cause. "The North was the aggressor," declared lawyer William Poague as he enlisted in an artillery unit. "The South resisted her invaders." Refusing Scott's offer of the Union command, Robert E. Lee resigned from the army. "Save in defense of my native state," Lee told Scott, "I never desire again to draw my sword." Arkansas, Tennessee, and North Carolina quickly joined Virginia in the Confederacy.

Lincoln moved aggressively to hold the rest of the Upper South. In May he ordered General George B. McClellan to take control of northwestern Virginia to secure the railway line between Washington and the Ohio Valley. In October, voters in that yeoman region overwhelmingly approved the formation of a breakaway territory, West Virginia, which was admitted to the Union in 1863. Unionists easily carried the day in Delaware but not in Maryland, where slavery was well entrenched. A pro-Confederate mob attacked Massachusetts troops marching between railroad stations in Baltimore, causing the war's first combat deaths: four soldiers and twelve civilians. When secessionists destroyed railroad bridges and telegraph lines, Lincoln ordered the military occupation of Maryland and the arrest of Confederate sympathizers, including state legislators. He released them only in November 1861, after Unionists gained control of the Maryland government.

In the west, Lincoln was equally energetic and resourceful. To win Missouri (and control of trade and communications along the Missouri and upper Mississippi Rivers), Lincoln mobilized the German American militia; in July, it defeated a force of Confederate sympathizers commanded by the governor. Despite continuing raids by Confederate guerrilla bands, the Union retained control of the state (see Voices from Abroad, "German Immigrants and the Civil War within Missouri," p. 417). In Kentucky, secessionist and Unionist sentiment was evenly balanced, so Lincoln moved cautiously. When Unionists took control of the state government in August, Lincoln ordered federal troops to halt Kentucky's thriving trade

**VOICES FROM ABROAD**

# German Immigrants and the Civil War within Missouri

## ERNEST DUVEYIER DE HAURANNE

*T*ens of thousands of Germans migrated to Missouri and other midwestern states after 1840, and as the following letter by the Frenchman Ernest Duveyier de Hauranne indicates, most of them supported the Union cause. Hauranne traveled widely, and his letters home offer an intelligent commentary on American politics and society during the Civil War.

St. Louis, September 12, 1864

Missouri is to all intents and purposes a rebel state, an occupied territory where the Federal forces are really nothing but a garrison under siege. . . . Party quarrels here are poisoned by class hatreds. . . . The old Anglo-French families, attached to Southern institutions, harbor a primitive, superstitious prejudice in favor of slavery. Conquered now, but full of repressed rage, they exhibit the implacable anger peculiar to the defenders of lost causes. . . .

The more recent German population is strongly abolitionist. They have brought to the New World the instincts of European democracy, together with its radical attitudes and all-or-nothing doctrines. Ancient precedents and worn-out laws matter little to them. They have not studied history and have no respect for hallowed injustices; but they do have, to the highest degree, that sense of moral principle which is more or less lacking in American democracy. They aren't afraid of revolution: to destroy a barbarous institution they would, if necessary, take an axe to the foundations of society.

Furthermore, their interests coincide with their principles. . . . The immigrant arrives poor and lives by his work. A newcomer, having nothing to lose and caring little for the interests of established property owners, sees that the subjection of free labor to the ruinous competition of slave labor must be ended. At the same time, his pride rebels against the prejudice attached to work in a land of slavery; he wants to reestablish its value. . . .

There is no mistaking the hatred the two parties, not to say the two peoples, have for each other. . . . The Federal government sent General [John C.] Frémont here as army commander and dictator. . . . An abolitionist and a self-made man, he put himself firmly at the head of the German party, determined to crush the friends of slavery. He formed an army of Germans who are completely devoted to their chief. . . .

[However,] bands of guerrillas hold the countryside, where they raid as much as they please; politics serves as a fine pretext for looting. Their leaders are officers from the army of the South who receive their orders from the Confederate government. . . . These "bushwackers," who ordinarily rob indiscriminately, maintain their standing as political raiders by occasionally killing some poor, inoffensive person. . . . You can see what emotions are still boiling in this region that is supposed to be pacified.

SOURCE: Ernest Duveyier de Hauranne, *A Frenchman in Lincoln's America* (Chicago: Lakende Press, 1974), 305–9.

with the Confederacy and to defend the state. In September, Illinois volunteers under the command of the relatively unknown Brigadier General Ulysses S. Grant crossed the Ohio River and drove out an invading Confederate force. Of the eight states of the Upper South, Lincoln had kept four (Delaware, Maryland, Kentucky, and Missouri) and a portion of a fifth (western Virginia) in the Union.

### Setting War Aims and Devising Strategies

At his inauguration in February 1861, Jefferson Davis called on the people of the Confederacy to defend its independence. He identified the Confederates' cause with that of the American revolutionaries: like their grandfathers, white Southerners were fighting against tyranny and for the "sacred right of self-government." As Davis put it, the Confederacy sought "no conquest, no aggrandizement . . . ; all we ask is to be let alone." The decision to focus on the defense of the Confederacy and not to seek western territories gave the South a strategic advantage: it needed only a military stalemate to guarantee independence. Ignoring opposition to slavery among potential European allies, the Confederate constitution explicitly stated that "No . . . law denying or impairing the right of property in negro slaves shall be passed," and vice president Alexander Stephens ruled out any plan for gradual emancipation. In Stephens's view, the Confederacy's "cornerstone rests upon the great truth that the Negro is not equal to the white man, that slavery—subordination to the superior race—is his natural or normal condition."

Lincoln made his first major statement on Union goals and strategy in a speech to Congress on July 4, 1861. He portrayed secession as an attack on popular government, which was America's great contribution to world history, and tested "whether a constitutional republic, or a democracy . . . [can] maintain its territorial integrity against its domestic foe." Convinced that the Union had to crush the rebellion, Lincoln rejected General Winfield Scott's plan to use economic sanctions and a naval blockade to persuade the Confederates to return to the Union. Instead, the president insisted on an aggressive military strategy and a policy of unconditional surrender.

The president hoped that a quick strike against the Confederate capital of Richmond, Virginia, would end the rebellion. He therefore dispatched General Irvin McDowell and an army of 30,000 men to attack P. G. T. Beauregard's force of 20,000 troops at Manassas, a rail junction thirty miles southwest of Washington. In July, McDowell launched a strong assault near Manassas Creek (also called Bull Run), but panic swept through his troops during a Confederate counterattack. For the first time Union soldiers heard the hair-raising rebel yell. "The peculiar corkscrew sensation that it sends down your backbone under these circumstances can never be told," one Union veteran wrote. "You have to feel it." McDowell's troops retreated in disarray to Washington, along with the many civilians who had come to observe the battle.

The rout of the Union army at Bull Run made it clear that the rebellion would not be easily crushed. Lincoln replaced McDowell with General George B. McClellan and enlisted an additional million men, who would serve for three years in the newly created Army of the Potomac. A cautious military engineer, McClellan spent the winter of 1861 training the recruits, and early in 1862 he launched a major offensive. With great logistical skill, the Union general transported 100,000 troops by boat down the Potomac River and put them ashore on the peninsula between the York and James Rivers (Map 14.2). Ignoring Lincoln's advice to "strike a blow" quickly, McClellan

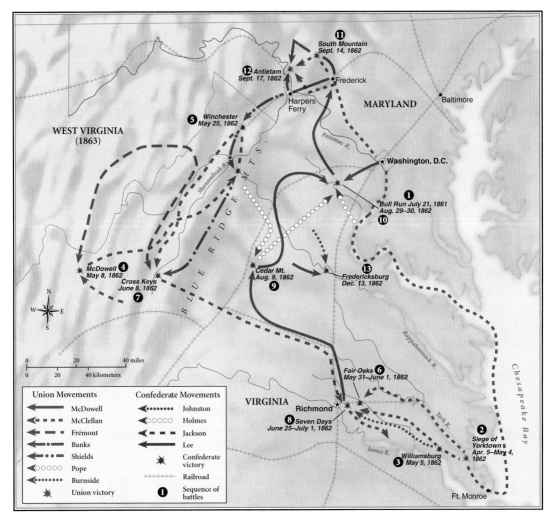

**MAP 14.2 The Eastern Campaigns of 1862**

Many of the great battles of the Civil War took place in the 125 miles between the Union capital of Washington and the Confederate capital of Richmond. During 1862, Confederate generals Robert J. "Stonewall" Jackson and Robert E. Lee secured defensive victories that safeguarded the Confederate capital (# 3, 6, 8 and 13) and launched offensive strikes against Union forces that guarded Washington (# 1, 4, 5, 7, 9, and 10). They also suffered a defeat—at Antietam, in Maryland—that was almost fatal (#12). As was often the case in the Civil War, the victors in these battles were either too bloodied or too timid to exploit their advantage.

advanced slowly toward the South's capital. His deliberate tactics allowed the Confederates to mount a counterstroke. To relieve the pressure on Richmond, a Confederate army under Thomas J. ("Stonewall") Jackson marched rapidly north up the Shenandoah Valley in western Virginia and threatened Washington. Lincoln recalled 30,000 troops from McClellan's army to protect the Union's capital, but Jackson, a brilliant general, tied down the larger Union forces. Then Jackson returned quickly to Richmond and the main Confederate army commanded by General Robert E. Lee. Lee launched a ferocious attack that lasted for seven days (June 25–July 1), suffering 20,000 casualties to the Union's 10,000. When McClellan failed to exploit the Confederates' weakness and requested fresh troops, Lincoln ordered the withdrawal of the Army of the Potomac, and Richmond remained secure.

Seeking victories that would humiliate Lincoln's government, Lee went on the offensive. Joining with Jackson in northern Virginia, he routed Union troops in the Second Battle of Bull Run (August 1862) and then struck north through western Maryland, where he met with near disaster. When Lee divided his force—sending Jackson to capture Harpers Ferry in West Virginia—a copy of his orders fell into McClellan's hands. The Union general again failed to exploit his advantage. He delayed his attack against Lee's depleted army, thereby allowing it to occupy a strong defensive position behind Antietam Creek, near Sharpsburg, Maryland. Outnumbered 87,000 to 50,000, Lee desperately fought off McClellan's attacks. Just as Union regiments were about to overwhelm his right flank, Jackson's troops arrived, saving the Confederates from a major defeat. Appalled by the number of Union casualties, McClellan let Lee retreat to Virginia.

The fighting at Antietam was savage. A Wisconsin officer described his men as "loading and firing with demoniacal fury and shouting and laughing hysterically." At a critical point in the battle, a sunken road—nicknamed Bloody Lane—was filled with Confederate bodies two and three deep, and the attacking Union troops knelt on "this ghastly flooring" to shoot at the retreating Confederates. The battle at Antietam on September 17, 1862, remains the bloodiest single day in U.S. military history. Together, the Confederate and Union dead numbered 4,800 and the wounded 18,500, of whom 3,000 soon died. (In comparison, there were 6,000 American casualties on D-Day, which began the invasion of Nazi-occupied France in World War II.)

In public, Lincoln declared Antietam a victory, but privately he declared that McClellan should have fought Lee to the finish. A masterful organizer of men and supplies, McClellan lacked the stomach for an all-out attack. Dismissing McClellan as his main commander, Lincoln began a long search for an effective replacement. His first choice was Ambrose E. Burnside, who proved to be more daring but less competent than his predecessor. In December, after heavy losses in futile attacks against well-entrenched Confederate forces at Fredericksburg, Virginia, Burnside resigned his command and Lincoln replaced him with Joseph ("Fighting Joe") Hooker. As 1862 ended, the Confederates had reason to be content: the war in the East was stalemated.

In the West, Union commanders had been more successful (Map 14.3). Their goal was to control the Ohio, Mississippi, and Missouri Rivers, and thereby divide the

**Fields of Death**

Fought with mass armies and new weapons, the Civil War took a huge toll in human lives. This grisly photograph depicts a thin slice of the battlefield at Antietam, Maryland, where, in September 1862, nearly 8,000 Union and Confederate soldiers lost their lives and another 15,000 suffered wounds. Library of Congress.

FOR MORE HELP ANALYZING THIS IMAGE, see the Online Study Guide at **bedfordstmartins.com/henrettaconcise**.

Confederacy and reduce the mobility of its armies. Thanks to Kentucky's refusal to join the rebellion, the Union already dominated the Ohio River Valley. In 1862, the Union army launched a series of highly innovative land and water operations to gain control of the Tennessee and Mississippi Rivers as well. In the North, General Ulysses S. Grant used riverboats clad with iron plates to take Fort Henry on the Tennessee River and Fort Donelson on the Cumberland. Grant then moved south along the Tennessee to seize critical railroad lines. On April 6, a Confederate army led by Albert Sidney Johnston and P. G. T. Beauregard caught Grant by surprise near a small log church named Shiloh. In the ensuing battle, Grant relentlessly committed troops (and took huge casualties) until he forced a Confederate withdrawal. As the fighting ended, Grant looked out over a large field "so covered with dead that it would have been possible to walk over the clearing in any direction, stepping on dead bodies, without a foot touching the ground." The cost in lives was high, but Lincoln was pleased. "What I want . . . is generals who will fight battles and win victories."

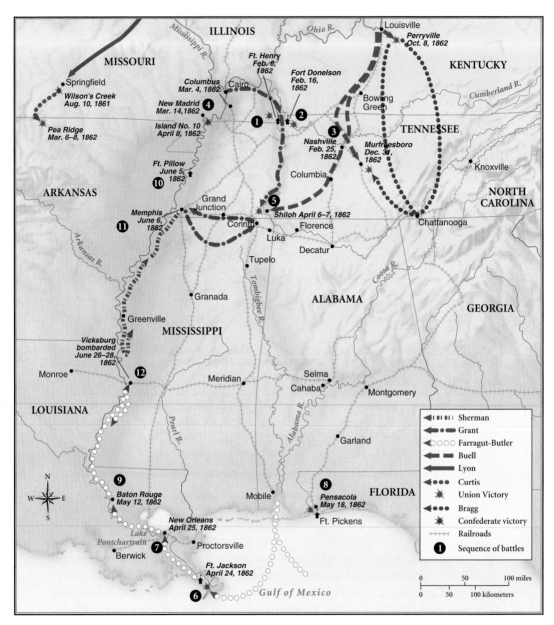

**MAP 14.3 The Western Campaigns, 1861–1862**

As the Civil War intensified in 1862, Union and Confederate military and naval forces fought to control the great valleys of the Ohio, Tennessee, and Mississippi Rivers. From February through April of 1862, Union armies moved south through western Tennessee (#1, 2, 3, and 5). By the end of June, Union naval forces controlled the Mississippi River north of Memphis (#4, 10, and 11) and from the Gulf of Mexico to Vicksburg (#6, 7, 9, and 12). These military and naval victories gave the Union control of crucial transportation routes, kept Missouri in the Union, and carried the war to the borders of the states of the Deep South.

Three weeks later Union naval forces commanded by David G. Farragut struck the Confederacy from the Gulf of Mexico and captured New Orleans. The Union now held the South's financial center and largest city as well as a major base for future naval operations. Union victories in the West had significantly undermined Confederate strength in the Mississippi Valley.

# Toward Total War

The military carnage in 1862 made it clear that the war would be long and costly. After Shiloh, Grant later noted, he "gave up all idea of saving the Union except by complete conquest." The conflict became a **total war**—arraying the entire resources of the two societies against each other. Aided by the Republican Party and a talented cabinet, Lincoln skillfully organized an effective central government. Jefferson Davis was less successful in harnessing the resources of the South because the eleven states of the Confederacy remained deeply suspicious of centralized rule.

## *Mobilizing Armies and Civilians*

Initially, patriotic fervor filled both armies with eager volunteers. The widowed mother of nineteen-year-old Elisha Hunt Rhodes of Pawtuxet, Rhode Island, sent her son to war, saying, "My son, other mothers must make sacrifices and why should not I?" The call for soldiers was especially successful in the South, which had a strong military tradition, an ample supply of trained officers, and a culture that stressed duty and honor. "Would you, My Darling, . . . be willing to leave your Children under such a [despotic Union] government?" James B. Griffin of Edgefield, South Carolina, asked his wife. "No—I know you would sacrifice every comfort on earth, rather than submit to it." However, enlistments fell off as potential recruits learned of the realities of mass warfare: heavy losses to epidemic diseases in the camps and wholesale death on the battlefields. Both governments soon faced the necessity of forced enlistment.

The Confederacy was the first to act. In April 1862, after the bloody battle at Shiloh, the Confederate Congress imposed the first legally binding draft in American history. One law extended existing enlistments for the duration of the war; another required three years of military service from men between the ages of eighteen and thirty-five. In September, after the heavy casualties at Antietam, the age limit was raised to forty-five. The Confederate draft had two loopholes, both controversial. First, it exempted one white man—the planter, a son, or an overseer—for each twenty slaves and so allowed some whites on large plantations to avoid military service. Second, drafted men could hire substitutes. Before this provision was repealed in 1864, the price for a substitute had risen to $300 in gold, about three times the annual wages of a skilled worker. Laborers and yeomen farmers angrily complained that it was "a rich man's war and a poor man's fight."

Consequently, some Southerners refused to serve. Because the Confederate constitution vested sovereignty in the individual states, the Confederate government lacked the power to compel military service. Strong governors such as Joseph Brown of Georgia and Zebulon Vance of North Carolina simply ignored Davis's first draft call in early 1862. Elsewhere state judges issued writs of **habeas corpus** (a legal process designed to protect people from arbitrary arrest) and ordered the Confederate army to release protesting draftees. However, the Confederate Congress overrode the judges' authority to free conscripted men and enabled the government to keep substantial armies in the field well into 1864.

The Union government acted more ruthlessly toward potential foes and reluctant citizens. To prevent sabotage and resistance to the war effort, Lincoln suspended habeas corpus and over the course of the war imprisoned about 15,000 Confederate sympathizers without trial. The president also extended martial law to civilians, which subjected them to military courts rather than local juries if they discouraged enlistments or resisted the draft. These firm policies had the desired effect. When the Militia Act of 1862 set local recruitment quotas, states and towns enticed volunteers with cash bounties and eventually signed up nearly a million men. As in the South, wealthy men could avoid military service by providing a substitute or paying a $300 commutation, or exemption, fee.

The Enrollment Act of 1863 raised quotas and was strongly opposed by recent immigrants from Germany and Ireland, who protested that it was not their war. Northern Democrats seized upon this issue. They accused Lincoln of drafting poor whites to win freedom for blacks, who would flood into the cities and take their jobs. In July 1863, the immigrants' hostility to the draft and to African Americans brought violence to the streets of New York City. For five days Irish and German workers ran rampant, burning draft offices, sacking the homes of influential Republicans, and attacking the police. The rioters lynched and mutilated a dozen African Americans, drove hundreds of black families from their homes, and burned down the Colored Orphan Asylum. Lincoln rushed in Union troops, fresh from the battle of Gettysburg, who killed over a hundred rioters and suppressed the insurrection.

The Union government's commitment to total war won greater support among native-born, middle-class citizens. In 1861, prominent New Yorkers established the United States Sanitary Commission to provide medical services and prevent the spread of epidemic diseases. Through its network of 7,000 local auxiliaries, the sanitary commission collected clothing, food, and medicine and recruited battlefield nurses and doctors for the Union Army Medical Bureau. Despite such measures, dysentery, typhoid, and malaria spread through the camps, as did childhood viruses such as mumps and measles, to which many rural men had not developed immunity. Diseases and infections killed about 250,000 Union soldiers, about twice the number who died in combat. Still, better sanitation and high-quality food kept the mortality rate among Union troops significantly below that of soldiers in nineteenth-century European wars. Confederate soldiers were less fortunate. Thousands of women volunteered as nurses,

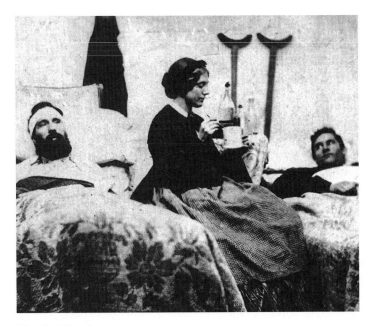

**Hospital Nursing**

Working as nurses in battlefront hospitals, thousands of Union and Confederate women gained firsthand experience of the horrors of war. A sense of calm prevails in this behind-the-lines Union hospital in Nashville, Tennessee, as nurse Anne Belle tends to the needs of soldiers recovering from their wounds. Most Civil War nurses served as unpaid volunteers and spent time cooking and cleaning for their patients as well as tending their injuries. U.S. Army Military History Institute.

but the Confederate health system was poorly organized. Thousands of southern soldiers contracted scurvy because of the lack of vitamin C in their diets, and they died from camp diseases at higher rates than did Union soldiers.

Women took a leading role in the sanitary commission and other wartime agencies. As superintendent of female nurses, Dorothea Dix became the first woman to receive a major federal appointment. Dix successfully combated the prejudice against women providing medical treatment to men and thereby opened a new occupation to women. Thousands of educated Union women joined the war effort as clerks in the expanding government bureaucracy, while in the South women staffed the efficient Confederate postal service. Indeed, in both sections millions of women assumed new economic responsibilities and worked with far greater intensity. They took over many farm tasks previously done by men and filled jobs not only in schools and offices but also in textile, clothing, and shoe factories. A number of women even took on military duties as spies, scouts, and (disguising themselves as men) soldiers. As the nurse Clara Barton, who later founded the American Red Cross, recalled, "At the war's end, woman was at least fifty years in advance of the normal position which continued peace would have assigned her."

## Mobilizing Resources

Wars are usually won by the side with superior resources and economic organization, and in this regard the Union entered the war with a distinct advantage. With nearly two-thirds of the population of the nation, two-thirds of the railroad mileage, and almost 90 percent of the industrial output, the North's economy was far superior to the South's. The North had an especially great advantage in the manufacture of cannon and rifles because many of its arms factories were equipped for mass production.

However, the Confederate position was far from weak. Virginia, North Carolina, and Tennessee had substantial industrial capacity. Richmond, with its Tredegar Iron Works, was an important manufacturing center, and in 1861 the Confederacy transported the gun-making machinery from the U.S. armory at Harpers Ferry to Richmond. The production of the Richmond armory, the purchase of Enfield rifles from Britain, and the capture of 100,000 Union guns enabled the Confederacy to provide every infantryman with a modern rifle-musket by 1863.

Moreover, with 9 million people, the Confederacy could mobilize enormous armies. Although more than one-third of that number were slaves, their masters kept them in the fields, producing food for the army and cotton for export. In fact, Confederate leaders counted on "King Cotton" to provide the revenue to purchase clothes, boots, blankets, and weapons from abroad. They also counted on cotton as a diplomatic weapon that would persuade Britain, which depended on the South to supply its textile factories, to grant diplomatic recognition and provide military aid. However, British manufacturers had stockpiled raw cotton, and when those stocks ran out, they found new sources in Egypt and India. Nonetheless, the South's hope was partially fulfilled. Although the British government never recognized the independence of the Confederacy, it recognized the rebel government as a belligerent power with the right under international law to borrow money and purchase weapons. Thus, the odds did not necessarily favor the Union, despite its superior resources.

To mobilize the resources of the North, Lincoln and the Republicans enacted a program of government-assisted national economic development that far surpassed the American System advocated by Henry Clay and the Whig Party. First, the Republicans raised tariffs to win the political support of northeastern manufacturers and laborers, who feared competition from cheaper foreign goods. Then Secretary of the Treasury Salmon P. Chase secured national banking legislation that forced thousands of local banks to accept federal charters and regulations. This integrated banking system was far more effective in raising capital and controlling inflation than earlier efforts by the First and Second Banks of the United States had been. Finally, the Lincoln administration implemented Clay's program for a nationally financed system of internal improvements. In 1862 the Republican Congress chartered the Union Pacific and Central Pacific companies to build a transcontinental railroad line and assisted them with lavish subsidies. In addition the Republicans provided northern farmers with "free land" in the West. The Homestead Act of 1862 gave heads of families or individuals age twenty-one or older the title to 160 acres of public land after five years of residence. This economic program won the allegiance of many Northerners to the Republican Party and bolstered the Union's ability to fight the war.

The Confederate government had a much less coherent economic policy. True to its states' rights philosophy, the Confederacy initially left most economic matters in the hands of the state governments. As the realities of total war became clear, the Davis administration took some extraordinary measures: it built and operated shipyards, armories, foundries, and textile mills; commandeered food and scarce raw materials such as coal, iron, copper, and lead; requisitioned slaves to work on fortifications; and exercised direct control over foreign trade. Ordinary southern citizens increasingly resented and resisted these governmental measures. To sustain the war effort, the Confederacy increasingly counted on white solidarity: Jefferson Davis warned whites that a Union victory would destroy slavery "and reduce the whites to the degraded position of the African race."

For both sides, the cost of fighting a total war was enormous. In the Union, government spending shot up from less than 2 percent of gross national product to about 15 percent. To meet those expenses, the Republicans established a powerful modern state that raised money in three ways. First, the government increased tariffs on consumer goods and imposed direct taxes on business corporations, large inheritances, and incomes. These levies paid for about 20 percent of the cost of the war. The sale of treasury bonds financed another 65 percent. Led by Jay Cooke, a Philadelphia banker, the treasury used newspaper advertisements and 2,500 subagents to persuade nearly a million northern families to buy war bonds. In addition the National Banking Acts of 1863 and 1864 forced most banks to purchase treasury bonds.

The Union paid the remaining cost of the war by printing paper money. The Legal Tender Act of 1862 authorized the issue of $150 million in treasury notes—which soon became known as greenbacks—and required the public to accept them as legal tender. As with the "Continentals" issued during the War of Independence, these treasury notes were not backed by specie; unlike the Continentals, this paper was printed in relatively limited amounts and so did not depreciate disastrously in value. By imposing broad-based taxes, borrowing from the middle classes, and creating a national monetary system, the Union government had created the financial foundations of a modern nation-state.

The financial demands on the South were just as great, but it lacked a powerful central government that could tax and borrow. The Confederate Congress fiercely opposed taxes on cotton exports and slaves, the most valuable property of wealthy planters, and urban middle-class and yeomen farm families often refused to pay their taxes. Consequently, the Confederacy covered less than 5 percent of its expenditures through taxation. The government paid for another 35 percent by borrowing, although wealthy planters and foreign bankers were increasingly wary of investing in Confederate bonds that might never be redeemed.

Thus, the Confederacy had to finance about 60 percent of its expenses with unbacked paper money. The flood of currency created a spectacular inflation; by 1865 prices had risen to ninety-two times their 1861 level. As the vast supply of money (and shortages of goods) caused food prices to soar, riots broke out in more than a dozen southern cities and towns. In Richmond several hundred women broke into bakeries, crying, "Our children are starving while the rich roll in wealth." As inflation rose, Southerners increasingly refused to accept Confederate money, sometimes with serious consequences. When South Carolina store clerk Jim Harris rejected the Confederate notes presented by a group of soldiers, they raided his storehouse and "robbed it of about five thousand dollars worth of goods." Army supply officers did the same and offered payment in worthless IOUs. Fearing a strong government and high taxation, the Confederacy ended up violating the property rights of its citizens to sustain the war effort.

# The Turning Point: 1863

By 1863 the Lincoln administration had created a complex war machine and a coherent financial system. "Little by little," the young diplomat Henry Adams noted at his post in London, "one began to feel that, behind the chaos in Washington power was taking shape; that it was massed and guided as it had not been before." Slowly but surely, the tide of the struggle shifted toward the Union.

## Emancipation

From the beginning of the conflict, antislavery Republicans demanded their party make abolition—as well as restoration of the Union—a central goal. Because slave-grown crops sustained the Confederacy, they argued for abolition on military as well as moral grounds. As Frederick Douglass put it, "Arrest that hoe in the hands of the Negro, and you smite the rebellion in the very seat of its life." Initially, Lincoln downplayed these demands for black freedom: "[I]f I could save the Union without freeing any slave, I would do it," he told Horace Greeley of the New York *Tribune*. However, as war casualties mounted, Lincoln and some Republican leaders began to redefine the conflict as a struggle against slavery—the cornerstone of southern society.

Nonetheless, it was enslaved African Americans who forced the issue by seizing freedom for themselves. Exploiting the disorder of wartime, tens of thousands of slaves left their plantations and sought refuge behind Union lines. When three slaves reached the camp of General Benjamin Butler in Virginia in May 1861, he labeled them "contraband of war" and refused to return them. His term stuck, and within a few months a thousand "contrabands" were camping with Butler's army. To define their status and undermine the Confederate war effort, in August 1861 Congress passed a Confiscation Act, which authorized the seizure of all property—including slaves—used to support the rebellion.

Radical Republicans—Treasury Secretary Salmon Chase, Senator Charles Sumner of Massachusetts, and Representative Thaddeus Stevens of Pennsylvania—now saw a way to use wartime legislation to end slavery. A longtime congressman and an uncompromising foe of slavery, Stevens was a masterful politician who was adept at fashioning legislation that could win majority support. In April 1862 Stevens and his Radical allies persuaded Congress to end slavery in the District of Columbia by providing compensation for owners. In June, Congress outlawed slavery in the federal territories (finally enacting the Wilmot Proviso of 1846) and in July passed a second Confiscation Act. This far-reaching legislation overrode the property rights of Confederate slave owners, declaring "forever free" all fugitive slaves and all slaves captured by the Union army. Emancipation had become an instrument of war.

Lincoln built upon the Radicals' initiative. In July 1862 he prepared a general proclamation of emancipation and, viewing the battle of Antietam as "an indication of the Divine Will," issued it on September 22, 1862. Invoking the president's responsibility as commander in chief to suppress the rebellion, the proclamation abolished slavery in all states that still remained out of the Union on January 1, 1863. The rebel states had a hundred days in which to preserve slavery by renouncing secession. None chose to do so.

The proclamation was politically astute. Because Lincoln wanted to avoid hostility from slave owners in the Union-controlled border states, such as Maryland and Missouri, and because he had only limited power as commander in chief over areas not in the rebellion, the proclamation left slavery intact in those states. It also left slavery untouched in the areas occupied by Union armies—western and central Tennessee, western Virginia, and southern Louisiana, including New Orleans. Consequently, the Emancipation Proclamation did not actually free a single slave. Yet, as the abolitionist Wendell Phillips perceived, Lincoln's proclamation had moved the institution of slavery to "the edge of Niagara," where it would soon be swept over the brink. Indeed, advancing Union troops became agents of liberation. "I became free in 1863, in the summer, when the yankees come by and said I could go work for myself," Jackson Daniel of Maysville, Alabama, recalled. "I was farming after that [and also] . . . making shoes." The conflict was no longer simply a struggle to preserve the Union but, as Lincoln put it, a war of "subjugation" in which "the old South is to be destroyed and replaced by new propositions and ideas."

As a war aim, emancipation was controversial. In the Confederacy, Jefferson Davis labeled it the "most execrable measure recorded in the history of guilty man," while in the North it produced a backlash among white voters. During the congressional election of 1862, the Democrats denounced emancipation as unconstitutional, warned of slave uprisings, and claimed that a "black flood" would wash away the jobs of northern workers. Democrat Horatio Seymour won the governorship of New York by declaring that if abolition was a goal of the war, the South should not be conquered. Other Democrats swept to victory in Pennsylvania, Ohio, and Illinois, and the party gained thirty-four seats in Congress. However, the Republicans still held a twenty-five-seat majority in the House and had gained five seats in the Senate. Lincoln refused to retreat. On New Year's Day 1863 he signed the Emancipation Proclamation. To reassure Northerners, Lincoln urged slaves to "abstain from all violence" and justified emancipation as an "act of justice." "If my name ever goes into history," he said, "it was for this act."

## Vicksburg and Gettysburg

The fate of the proclamation would depend on the success of Union armies and the Republican Party. The outlook was not encouraging. Not only had Democrats registered gains in the election of 1862 but there was also increased popular support for a negotiated peace. Two brilliant victories by Lee, whose army defeated Hooker's forces at Fredericksburg (December 1862) and Chancellorsville, Virginia (May 1863), caused further erosion of northern support for the war.

At this critical juncture General Grant mounted a major offensive in the West designed to split the Confederacy in two. Grant drove south along the west bank of the Mississippi and then moved his troops across the river near Vicksburg, Mississippi, where he defeated two Confederate armies and laid siege to the city. After repelling Union assaults for six weeks, the exhausted and starving Vicksburg garrison surrendered on July 4, 1863. Five days later Union forces took Port Hudson, Louisiana, and established Union control of the Mississippi River. Grant had taken 31,000 prisoners, cut off Louisiana, Arkansas, and Texas from the rest of the Confederacy, and prompted hundreds of slaves to desert their plantations.

Grant's initial advance down the Mississippi prompted an argument over strategy among Confederate leaders. Jefferson Davis and other politicians wanted to send reinforcements to Vicksburg and dispatch troops to Tennessee to draw Grant out of Mississippi. But General Robert E. Lee, buoyed by his recent victories over Hooker, favored a new invasion of the North, which might draw Union armies to the east, thereby relieving the pressure on Vicksburg, or give the Confederacy a major victory that would undermine northern support for the war.

Lee won out. In June 1863 he maneuvered his army north through Maryland into Pennsylvania. The Union's Army of the Potomac moved along with him, positioning itself between Lee and the federal capital of Washington. Early in July the two great armies met by accident at Gettysburg, Pennsylvania, in what became a decisive confrontation (Map 14.4). On the first day of battle, July 1, Lee drove the Union's advance guard to the south of town. General George G. Meade, who had just taken over command of the Union forces from Hooker, placed his troops in well-defended hilltop positions and called up reinforcements. By the morning of the second day Meade had 90,000 troops to Lee's 75,000. Aware that he was outnumbered but bent on victory, Lee ordered assaults on both of Meade's flanks but failed to turn them. General Richard B. Ewell, assigned to attack the Union right, was unwilling to risk his men in an all-out assault, and General Longstreet, on the Union left, could not dislodge Meade's forces from a hill known as Little Round Top.

On July 3, Lee decided on a frontal assault against the center of the Union lines. He recognized the danger of this tactic but he had enormous confidence in his troops and thought they could inflict a crushing defeat on the North. After the heaviest

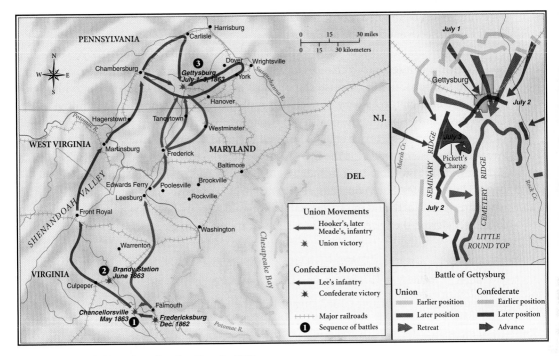

**MAP 14.4 Lee Invades the North, 1863**

After Lee's victory at Chancellorsville and Brandy Station in May and June of 1863 (#1 and 2), the Confederate forces moved northward, constantly shadowed by the Union army. In early July the two armies met accidentally near Gettysburg, Pennsylvania. In the ensuing battle (#3), the Union army, commanded by General George Meade, emerged victorious, primarily because it was much larger than the Confederate force and held well-fortified positions along Cemetery Ridge, which gave its units a major tactical advantage.

artillery barrage of the war, Lee ordered 14,000 men under General George E. Pickett to take Cemetery Ridge. Anticipating this attack, Meade had reinforced the center of his line with artillery and his best troops. When Pickett's men charged across a mile of open terrain, they were met by massive fire from artillery and rifle-muskets; thousands were killed, wounded, or captured. As the three-day battle ended, Lee had suffered 28,000 casualties, one-third of the Army of Northern Virginia, while 23,000 of Meade's soldiers lay killed or wounded. Shocked by the bloodletting, Meade allowed the remaining Confederate soldiers to escape. "As it is," Lincoln brooded, "the war will be prolonged indefinitely."

Nonetheless, Gettysburg was a great Union victory and, in combination with the triumph at Vicksburg, represented a major turning point in the conflict. Never again would a southern army invade the North. In the fall of 1863, Republicans reaped the political gains by sweeping state and local elections in Pennsylvania, Ohio, and New York. In the South the military setbacks accentuated war weariness. The Confederate elections of 1863 went sharply against the politicians who supported Jefferson Davis.

A few members of the new Confederate Congress and many ordinary citizens criticized the ineffectiveness of the war effort.

Vicksburg and Gettysburg also transformed the balance of diplomatic power and ended the Confederacy's chances of winning foreign recognition and acquiring advanced weapons. In 1862 British shipbuilders had supplied the Confederacy with an ironclad cruiser, the *Alabama*, which had sunk or captured more than a hundred Union merchant ships, and the delivery of two more ironclad cruisers was imminent. News of the Union victories changed everything, and Charles Francis Adams, the American minister, persuaded the British government to impound the ships. Britain did not want to risk Canada or its merchant marine by provoking the military might of the United States. Such concerns, along with Britain's increasing reliance on cheap wheat from the North and the strong opposition to slavery by British workers and reformers, deterred the government from supporting the Confederacy.

# The Union Victorious, 1864–1865

While the Union victories of 1863 meant that the South could not achieve a decisive military triumph, the Confederacy could still realistically hope for a stalemate on the battlefield and a negotiated peace. Lincoln faced the daunting alternative of winning an overwhelming victory or losing the support of the northern voters.

## Soldiers and Strategy

Two developments allowed the Union to prosecute the war with continued vigor and eventually to prevail: the enlistment of African American soldiers and the emergence of capable and determined generals.

As early as 1861, free African Americans and fugitive slaves had tried to enlist in the Union army, and the black abolitionist Frederick Douglass had embraced their cause: "Once let the black man get upon his person the brass letters, 'U.S.' . . . a musket on his shoulder and bullets in his pockets, and there is no power on earth which can deny that he has earned the right to citizenship in the United States." The prospect of citizenship for blacks frightened many northern whites, and most Union generals doubted that former slaves would make good soldiers. Consequently, the Lincoln administration initially refused to consider blacks for military service. Nonetheless, by 1862 free and contraband blacks had formed regiments in South Carolina, Louisiana, and Kansas and were eager to join the fighting.

The Emancipation Proclamation changed popular thinking and military policy. If blacks were to benefit from a Union victory, some northern whites argued, they should share in the fighting and dying. The valor exhibited by the first African American regiments also influenced northern opinion. In January 1863 Thomas Wentworth Higginson, the white abolitionist commander of the black First South Carolina Volunteers, wrote a glowing newspaper account of its military prowess: "No officer in this regiment now doubts that the key to the successful prosecution of the

**Black Soldiers in the Union Army**

Determined to end racial slavery, tens of thousands of African Americans volunteered for service in the Union army in 1864 and 1865, boosting the northern war effort at a critical time. These proud soldiers were members of the 107th Colored Infantry, stationed at Fort Corcoran near Washington, D.C. In January 1865 their regiment participated in the daring capture of Fort Fisher, which protected Wilmington, North Carolina, the last Confederate port open to blockade-runners. Library of Congress.

war lies in the unlimited employment of black troops." In July the heroic, but costly, attack on Fort Wagner, South Carolina, by another black regiment, the Fifty-fourth Massachusetts Infantry, convinced many Union officers of the value of black soldiers. The War Department authorized their enlistment, and as white resistance to conscription increased, the Lincoln administration recruited as many African Americans as it could. Without black soldiers, the president suggested in the autumn of 1864, "we would be compelled to abandon the war in three weeks." By the spring of 1865, there were nearly 200,000 African American soldiers and sailors.

Military service did not end racial discrimination. Black soldiers served under white officers in segregated regiments and were used primarily to build fortifications, garrison forts, and guard supply lines. At first they were paid less than white soldiers ($10 versus $13 per month) and won equal pay only by threatening to lay down their arms. Despite such treatment African Americans volunteered for military service in disproportionate numbers and diligently served the Union cause. They knew they were fighting for freedom and the possibility of a new social order. "Hello, Massa," said one black soldier to his former master, who had been taken prisoner. "Bottom rail on top dis time." The worst fears of the secessionists had come true: through the agency of the Union army, blacks had risen in a great rebellion against slavery.

As African Americans joined the army's ranks, Lincoln finally found a capable commanding general. In March 1864 Lincoln placed General Ulysses S. Grant in charge of all the Union armies and created a unified structure of command. From then on, the president would determine general strategy and Grant would decide how best to implement it. Lincoln directed Grant to advance simultaneously against all the major Confederate forces, a strategy Grant had long favored. Both the general and the president wanted a decisive victory before the election of 1864.

As the successful western campaigns of mid-1863 showed, Grant understood how to fight a modern war—a war relying on industrial technology and directed at an entire society. At Vicksburg he had besieged an entire city and forced its surrender. Then, in November 1863, he had used railroad transport to charge to the rescue of a Union army near Chattanooga, Tennessee, and drive back an invading Confederate army. Moreover, Grant was willing to accept heavy casualties in assaults on strongly defended positions. The attempts of earlier Union commanders "to conserve life" through cautious tactics had prolonged the war, Grant argued. Such aggressive methods earned Grant a reputation as a butcher both of his own men and of enemy armies, which he pursued relentlessly.

In May 1864 Grant ordered major new offensives on two fronts. Personally taking charge of the 115,000-strong Army of the Potomac, he set out to destroy Lee's force of 75,000 troops in Virginia. Simultaneously he instructed General William Tecumseh Sherman, who shared his views on warfare, to invade Georgia and take Atlanta. As Sherman prepared for battle, he wrote that "all that has gone before is mere skirmish. The war now begins."

Grant advanced toward Richmond, hoping to force Lee to fight in open fields, where the Union's superior manpower and artillery could prevail. Remembering his tactical errors at Gettysburg, Lee remained in strong defensive positions and attacked only when he held an advantage. The Confederate general seized such opportunities twice and won narrow victories in early May at the battles of the Wilderness and Spotsylvania Court House. Despite heavy losses at Cold Harbor, Grant drove on. His attacks severely eroded Lee's forces, which suffered 31,000 casualties, but Union losses were even higher at 55,000 men (Map 14.5).

The fighting took a heavy psychological toll. "Many a man has gone crazy since this campaign began from the terrible pressure on mind and body," observed a Union captain. As the morale and health of the soldiers declined, many deserted. In June Grant laid siege to Petersburg, an important railroad center near Richmond. Protracted trench warfare, which foreshadowed that of World War I, made the spade as important as the sword. Union and Confederate soldiers built complex networks of trenches, tunnels, and artillery emplacements for almost fifty miles around Richmond and Petersburg. Invoking the intense imagery of the Bible, an officer described the continuous artillery firing and sniping as "living night and day within the 'valley of the shadow of death.'" The stress was especially great for the outnumbered Confederate troops, who spent months in the muddy, sickening trenches without rotation to the rear.

As time passed, Lincoln and Grant felt pressures of their own. The enormous casualties and continued military stalemate threatened Lincoln with defeat in the November election. The outlook for the Republicans worsened in July 1864, when

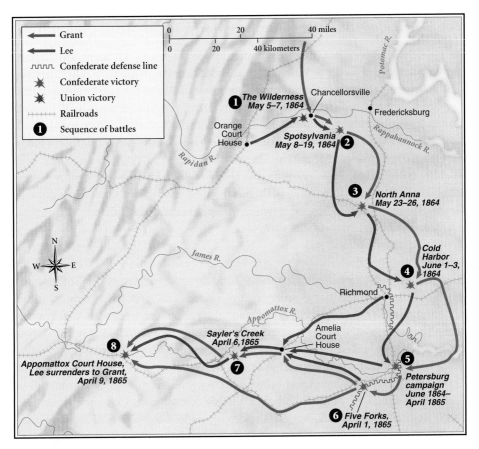

**MAP 14.5 The Closing Virginia Campaign, 1864–1865**

Beginning in May 1864, General Ulysses Grant launched an all-out campaign against Richmond. By threatening General Robert E. Lee's lines of supply from Richmond, Grant attempted to lure him into open battle. Lee avoided a major test of strength. Instead, he retreated to defensive positions and inflicted heavy casualties on the Union attackers at the Wilderness, Spotsylvania, North Anna, and Cold Harbor (#1–4). From June 1864 to April 1865, the two armies faced each other across defensive fortifications outside Petersburg (#5), a protracted siege broken finally by Grant's flanking maneuver at Five Forks (#6). Lee's surrender followed shortly.

a raid near Washington by Jubal Early's cavalry forced Grant to divert his best troops from the Petersburg campaign. To punish farmers in the Shenandoah Valley, who had provided a base for Early and food for Lee's army, Grant ordered General Philip H. Sheridan to turn the region into "a barren waste." Sheridan's troops conducted a scorched-earth campaign and destroyed grain supplies, barns, farming implements, and gristmills. Such terrorism went beyond the military norms of the day; most officers regarded civilians as noncombatants and feared that punishing them would erode military discipline. However, Grant's practice of carrying the war to Confederate civilians was changing the definition of conventional warfare.

## The Election of 1864 and Sherman's March to the Sea

As the siege at Petersburg dragged on, the president's hopes for reelection increasingly depended on General William Tecumseh Sherman in Georgia. Sherman had gradually penetrated to within about thirty miles of Atlanta, a great railway hub at the heart of the Confederacy. Although his army outnumbered that of General Joseph E. Johnston by 90,000 to 60,000 men, Sherman avoided a direct attack and slowly pried the Confederates out of one defensive position after another. Finally, on June 27 at Kennesaw Mountain, Sherman engaged Johnston in a set battle, only to suffer 3,000 casualties while inflicting about 600. By late July the Union general had laid siege to Atlanta on the north, but the next month brought little gain. Like Grant, Sherman seemed bogged down in a hopeless campaign.

Meanwhile, the presidential campaign of 1864 was well under way. In June a Republican convention attended by both Republicans and Unionist Democrats resisted the attempt of dissidents to prevent Lincoln's renomination. They endorsed the president's war strategy, demanded the unconditional surrender of the Confederacy, and called for a constitutional amendment to abolish slavery. Attempting to attract border-state voters to their party, Lincoln and the Republican leadership gave it a new name, the National Union Party, and chose as Lincoln's vice presidential running mate Andrew Johnson, a slave owner and a Unionist Democrat from Tennessee.

The Democratic convention met in late August and nominated General George B. McClellan, whom Lincoln had twice removed from military commands — first for an excess of caution and then for his opposition to emancipation. Like McClellan, the Democratic delegates rejected freedom for blacks and condemned Lincoln's uncompromising repression of domestic dissent. However, they split into two camps over the issue of continuing the war. By threatening to leave the convention, the "Peace Democrats" forced through a platform calling for "a cessation of hostilities" and a constitutional convention to restore peace. Although personally a "War Democrat," McClellan promised if elected to recommend an immediate armistice and a peace convention. Rejoicing in "the first ray of real light I have seen since the war began," Confederate vice president Alexander Stephens declared that if Atlanta and Richmond held out, then Lincoln could be defeated and northern Democrats persuaded to accept an independent Confederacy.

However, on September 2, 1864, Atlanta fell to Sherman's army. In a stunning move, the Union general pulled his troops from the trenches and swept around the city and destroyed its rail links to the rest of the Confederacy. Fearing that Sherman would be able to trap his army, Hood abandoned the city. "Atlanta is ours, and fairly won," Sherman telegraphed Lincoln, sparking 100-gun salutes and wild Republican celebrations in northern cities. A deep pessimism settled over the Confederacy. In her diary Mary Chesnut, a slave-owning plantation mistress, confessed that she "felt as if all were dead within me, forever" and foresaw the end of the Confederacy: "We are going to be wiped off the earth." Acknowledging the dramatically changed military situation, McClellan repudiated the Democratic peace platform, and dissident

Republicans abandoned efforts to dump Lincoln. Instead, the Republican Party went on the offensive. Its newspapers charged that McClellan was still a peace candidate and that Peace Democrats were "copperheads" (poisonous snakes) who were hatching treasonous plots.

Sherman's success in Georgia gave Lincoln a clear-cut victory in November. The president received 55 percent of the popular vote and won 212 of 233 electoral votes. Republicans captured 145 of the 185 seats in the House of Representatives and increased their Senate majority to 42 of 52 seats. Many of those victories came from the votes of Union troops, most of whom wanted the war to continue until the Confederacy met every Union demand, including emancipation.

Legal emancipation was already under way at the edges of the South. In 1864 Maryland and Missouri amended their constitutions to free their slaves, and the three occupied states of Tennessee, Arkansas, and Louisiana followed suit. Abolitionists still worried that the Emancipation Proclamation, which was based on the president's wartime powers, would lose its force at the end of the war and that some states would reestablish slavery. Urged on by Lincoln, the Republican-dominated Congress took a major step to guarantee black freedom. On January 31, 1865, it approved the Thirteenth Amendment, which prohibited slavery throughout the United States, and sent it to the states for ratification. Slavery was nearly dead.

Thanks to William Tecumseh Sherman, the Confederacy was nearly dead as well. After the capture of Atlanta, Sherman decided on a bold strategy. Rather than follow the retreating Confederate army northward into Tennessee, he proposed to move south and "cut a swath through to the sea." To persuade Lincoln and Grant to approve his unconventional plan to cut his supply links and live off the land, Sherman pointed out that his march would devastate Georgia and score a major psychological victory. It would be "a demonstration to the world, foreign and domestic, that we have a power [Jefferson] Davis cannot resist" (Map 14.6).

Sherman carried out the concept of "hard war" that he and Sheridan had pioneered: destruction of the enemy's economic resources and will to resist. "We are not only fighting hostile armies," Sherman wrote, "but a hostile people, and must make old and young, rich and poor, feel the hard hand of war." He left Atlanta in flames and, during his three-hundred-mile march to the sea, consumed or demolished everything in his path. A Union veteran wrote that "[we] destroyed all we could not eat, stole their niggers, burned their cotton & gins, spilled their sorghum, burned & twisted their R.Roads and raised Hell generally." The havoc so demoralized Confederate soldiers that many deserted their units and fled home to protect their farms and families (see American Voices, "Sherman's March through Georgia," p. 439). When Sherman reached Savannah, Georgia, in mid-December, the 10,000 Confederate defenders left without a fight.

In February 1865 Sherman invaded South Carolina, both to link up with Grant at Petersburg and punish the state where secession had begun. His troops cut a comparatively narrow swath across the state but completely ravaged the countryside. After capturing South Carolina's capital, Columbia, they burned the business district, most churches, and the wealthiest residential neighborhoods. "This disappointment to me

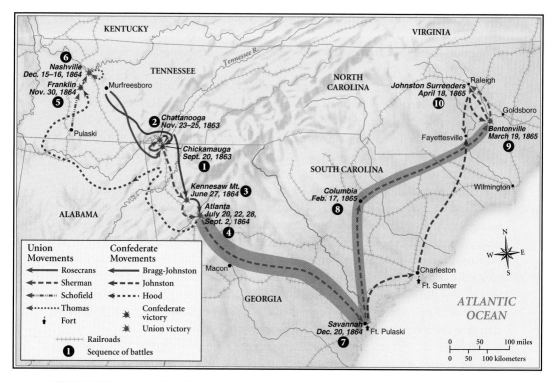

**MAP 14.6 Sherman's March through the Confederacy, 1864–1865**

The Union victory (#2) in November 1863 at Chattanooga, Tennessee, was almost as critical as the victories in July at Gettysburg and Vicksburg because it opened up a route of attack into the heart of the Confederacy. In mid-1864 General William Tecumseh Sherman advanced on the railway hub of Atlanta (#3 and 4). After finally taking the city in September 1864, Sherman relied on other Union armies to repulse General John B. Hood's invasion of Tennessee (#5 and 6). Sherman swept on to Savannah in a devastating "March to the Sea" (#7) and then in 1865 cut a swath through the Carolinas (#8, 9, and 10).

<small>FOR MORE HELP ANALYZING THIS MAP, see the Online Study Guide at **bedfordstmartins.com/henrettaconcise**.</small>

is extremely bitter," lamented Jefferson Davis. By March Sherman had reached North Carolina and was on the verge of linking up with Grant and crushing Lee's army.

Grant's war of attrition had already exposed an internal Confederate weakness: rising class resentment on the part of poor whites. Long angered by the "twenty-negro" exemption from military service given to slave owners and fearing that the Confederacy was doomed, ordinary southern farmers resisted military service. "It is no longer a reproach to be known as a deserter," a Confederate officer in South Carolina complained as early as 1863. "I am now going to work instead of to the war," declared David Harris, a backcountry farmer. "I think I will like it the best." By early 1865 the Confederacy had so few new recruits that its leaders decided to take an extreme measure: arming the slaves. Urged on by Lee, the Confederate Congress voted to enlist black soldiers and Davis issued an executive order granting freedom

# Sherman's March through Georgia

## DOLLY SUMNER LUNT

"We must make old and young, rich and poor, feel the hard hand of war," General William Tecumseh Sherman wrote to General Grant late in 1864, as he signaled his intention to carry the war to the civilian population of the South. A few weeks later Dolly Sumner Lunt of Covington, Georgia, found out what Sherman meant. Born in Maine in 1817, Dolly Sumner came south to teach school, married a slave owner, and following his death, ran the family's plantation. Her wartime journal describes its destruction by Sherman's army.

November 19, 1864

Slept in my clothes last night, as I heard that the Yankees went to neighbor Montgomery's on Thursday night at one o'clock, searched his house, drank his wine, and took his money and valuables. As we were not disturbed, I walked after breakfast . . . up to Mr. Joe Perry's, my nearest neighbor, where the Yankees were yesterday. Saw Mrs. Laura [Perry] in the road surrounded by her children . . . looking for her husband. . . . Before we were done talking, up came Joe and Jim Perry from their hiding-place. Jim was very much excited. Happening to turn and look behind, as we stood there, I saw some blue-coats coming down the hill. Jim immediately raised his gun, swearing he should kill them anyhow.

"No, don't" said I, and ran home as fast as I could.

I could hear them cry "Halt! Halt!" and their guns went off in quick succession. Oh God, the time of trial has come. . . .

I hastened back to my frightened servants [slaves] and told them they had better hide, and then went back to the gate to claim protection and a guard. But like demons they [Sherman's troops] rushed in! . . . The thousand pounds of meat in my smokehouse is gone in a twinkling, my flour, my meat, my lard, butter, eggs . . . all gone. My eighteen fat turkeys, hens, chickens . . . are shot down in my yard and hunted as if they were rebels themselves. Utterly powerless I ran out and appealed to the guard.

"I cannot help you, Madam; it is orders." . . .

Sherman himself and a greater portion of his army passed my house that day . . . ; they tore down my garden palings, made a road through my back-yard and lot field . . . desolating my home—wantonly doing it when there was no necessity for it.

Such a day, if I live to the age of Methuselah, may God spare me from ever seeing again!

As night drew its sable curtains around us, the heavens from every point were lit up with flames from burning buildings.

SOURCE: *Eyewitnesses and Others: Readings in American History* (New York: Holt, Rinehart and Winston, 1995), 1: 413–17.

to all blacks who served in the Confederate army. But the war ended too soon to reveal whether any slaves would have fought for the Confederacy.

The symbolic end of the war took place in Virginia. In April 1865 Grant finally gained control of the crucial railroad junction at Petersburg and cut off Lee's supplies. Lee abandoned Richmond and moved west to join Confederate forces in North Carolina. While Lincoln visited the ruins of the Confederate capital, mobbed by joyful ex-slaves, Grant cut off Lee's escape route. On April 9, almost precisely four years after the attack on Fort Sumter, Lee surrendered to Grant at Appomattox Court House, Virginia. By late May, all the Confederate generals had ceased to fight, and the Confederate army and government simply dissolved.

The armies of the Union had destroyed the Confederacy and much of its economy. The South's factories, warehouses, and railroads were in ruins, as were many of its farms and some of its most important cities. Almost 260,000 Confederate soldiers had paid for secession with their lives. The military struggle had preserved the Union and destroyed slavery. But the cost of victory was enormous in money, resources, and lives, with 360,000 Union soldiers dead and hundreds of thousands maimed. The hard and bitter war was over, and a reunited nation turned to the tasks of peace. These were to be equally hard and bitter.

## TIMELINE

| | | | |
|---|---|---|---|
| **1861** | Confederate States of America formed (February 4) | **1863** | Lincoln signs Emancipation Proclamation (January 1) |
| | Abraham Lincoln inaugurated (March 4) | | Union victories at battles of Gettysburg (July 1–3) and Vicksburg (July 4) |
| | Confederates fire on Fort Sumter (April 12) | | |
| | Virginia leads Upper South out of Union (April 17) | | Enrollment Act begins draft in North; riots in New York City (July) |
| | General Benjamin Butler declares runaway slaves "contraband of war" (May) | **1864** | Ulysses S. Grant given command of all Union armies (March) |
| | Confederates rout Union forces at first Battle of Bull Run (July 21) | | Grant advances on Richmond (May) |
| | | | William T. Sherman takes Atlanta (September 2) |
| **1862** | Congress begins to print greenbacks | | Lincoln reelected (November) |
| | Homestead Act provides free land to settlers | | Sherman marches through Georgia (November and December) |
| | Congress gives federal subsidies to transcontinental railroads | **1865** | Congress approves Thirteenth Amendment, which outlaws slavery (January) |
| | Battle of Shiloh advances Union cause in West (April 6–7) | | |
| | Confederacy introduces first draft | | Robert E. Lee surrenders at Appomattox Court House, Virginia (April 9) |
| | Union halts Confederate offensive at Antietam, Maryland (September 17) | | |
| | Lincoln issues preliminary Emancipation Proclamation (September 22) | | Ratification of Thirteenth Amendment |

# For Further Exploration

Charles P. Roland, *An American Iliad: The Story of the Civil War* (1991), is an excellent brief survey, while James M. McPherson, *The Battle Cry of Freedom* (1988), offers a fine synthesis. For a lucid description of the complex mixture of goals, personalities, and circumstances that precipitated the conflict, read Richard Current, *Lincoln and the First Shot* (1963). John Hope Franklin, *The Emancipation Proclamation* (1963), explains the background of Lincoln's edict and its impact.

Nancy Scott Anderson and Dwight Anderson, *The Generals: Ulysses S. Grant and Robert E. Lee* (1988), is a vivid, popular account of their personal histories and military exploits. For scholarly analyses of military matters, consult Mark Grimsley, *The Hard Hand of War: Union Military Policy toward Southern Civilians, 1861–1865* (1995), and Gary W. Gallagher, *The Confederate War: How Popular Will, Nationalism, and Military Strategy Could Not Stave Off Defeat* (1997).

James M. McPherson, *For Cause and Comrades: Why Men Fought in the Civil War* (1997), uses the letters of ordinary soldiers to explain their extraordinary commitment to the cause of the Union and the Confederacy. For experiences of black soldiers told in their own words, see Ira Berlin et al., eds., *Freedom's Soldiers: The Black Military Experience in the Civil War* (1998). Earl J. Hess, *The Union Soldier in Battle: Enduring the Ordeal of Combat* (1997), presents a vivid account of the heat, smell, sounds, and feel of battle, as does Michael Shaara's *Killer Angels* (1974), a masterful novel of the battle of Gettysburg. *Mary Chesnut's Civil War* (1981), edited by C. Vann Woodward, is the diary of a planter's wife that provides an incisive view of southern society.

Civil War photographs from the New-York Historical Society and the Matthew Brady Collection are available at the American Memory project: <http://memory.loc.gov/ammem/ndlpcoop/nhihtml/cwnyhshome.html> and <http://memory.loc.gov/ammem/cwphtml/cwphome.html>. Two award-winning Web sites are "The Valley of the Shadow" at <http://jefferson.village.virginia.edu/vshadow2/>, which traces the history of a northern and a southern community using a multitude of hyperlinked sources—including newspaper, letters, diaries, photographs, and maps—and The Freedmen and Southern Society Project at <http://www.history.umd.edu/Freedmen/home.html>, which captures the drama of war and emancipation in the words of liberated slaves and defeated masters, common folk and political leaders.

---

For definitions of key terms boldfaced in this chapter, see the glossary at the end of the book.

To assess your mastery of the material covered in this chapter, see the Online Study Guide at **bedfordstmartins.com/henrettaconcise**.

For map resources and primary documents, see **bedfordstmartins.com/henrettaconcise**.

# Chapter 15

# RECONSTRUCTION
## 1865–1877

I felt like a bird out of a cage. Amen. Amen. Amen. I could hardly ask
to feel better than I did on that day.

HOUSTON H. HOLLOWAY, A FORMER SLAVE RECALLING

HIS EMANCIPATION IN 1865

In his second inaugural address, President Lincoln spoke of the need to
"bind up the nation's wounds." No one knew better than Lincoln how daunting a
task that would be. Slavery was finished. That much was certain. But what system of
labor should replace plantation slavery? What rights should the freedmen be accorded beyond emancipation? How far should the federal government go to settle
these questions? And, most immediately pressing, on what terms should the rebellious states be restored to the Union?

The last speech Lincoln delivered, on April 11, 1865, demonstrated his grasp of
these issues. Reconstruction, he said, had to be regarded as a practical, not a theo-
retical, problem. It could be solved only if Republicans remained united, even if that
meant compromising on principled differences dividing them, and only if the defeated South gave its consent, even if that meant forgiveness of the South's trans-
gressions. The speech showed, above all, Lincoln's sense of the fluidity of events, of
policy toward the South as an evolving, not a fixed, position.

What course Reconstruction might have taken had Lincoln lived is one of the
unanswerable questions of American history. On April 14, 1865—five days after
Lee's surrender at Appomattox—Lincoln was shot in the head at Ford's Theatre in
Washington by a fanatic actor named John Wilkes Booth. Ironically, Lincoln might
have been spared if the war had dragged on longer, for Booth and his Confederate
associates had originally plotted to kidnap the president to force a negotiated settlement. After Lee's surrender, Booth became bent on revenge. Without regaining
consciousness, Lincoln died on April 15, 1865.

With one stroke John Wilkes Booth had sent Lincoln to martyrdom, hardened
many Northerners against the South, and handed the presidency to a man utterly lacking in Lincoln's moral sense and political judgment, Vice President Andrew Johnson.

# Presidential Reconstruction

The problem of Reconstruction—how to restore rebellious states to the Union—was not addressed by the Founding Fathers. The Constitution does not say which branch of government handles the readmission of rebellious states or, for that matter, even contemplates the possibility of secession. It was an open question whether, upon seceding, the Confederate states had legally left the Union. If so, their reentry surely required legislative action by Congress. If not, if even in defeat they retained their constitutional status, then the terms for restoring them to the Union might be defined as an administrative matter best left to the president. The ensuing battle between the White House and Capitol Hill was one of the fault lines in Reconstruction's stormy history.

## *Lincoln's Approach*

Lincoln, as wartime president, had taken the initiative, offering in December 1863 a general amnesty to all but high-ranking Confederates willing to pledge loyalty to the Union. When 10 percent of a state's 1860 voters had taken this oath, the state would be restored to the Union, provided that it abolished slavery. The Confederate states (save those like Louisiana and Tennessee that were under Union control) rebuffed Lincoln's generous offer, ensuring that the war would have to be fought to the bitter end.

What the Ten Percent Plan also revealed was the rocky road that lay ahead for Reconstruction. In Louisiana, for example, the Unionist government restored under Lincoln's offer employed curfew laws to restrict the movements of the freed slaves and vagrancy regulations to force them back to work. But the Louisiana freedmen fought back. Led by the free blacks of New Orleans, they began to agitate for political rights. No less than their former masters, ex-slaves intended to be actors in the savage drama of Reconstruction.

With the struggle in Louisiana in mind, congressional Republicans proposed a stricter substitute for Lincoln's Ten Percent Plan. The initiative came from the Radical wing of the party—those bent on a stern peace and full rights for the freedmen—but with broad support among more moderate Republicans. The Wade-Davis Bill, passed on July 2, 1864, laid down, as conditions for the restoration of the rebellious states to the Union, an oath of allegiance by a majority of each state's adult white men, new state governments formed only by those who had never carried arms against the Union, and permanent disfranchisement of Confederate leaders. The Wade-Davis Bill served notice that the congressional Republicans were not about to hand over Reconstruction policy to the president.

Rather than openly challenging Congress, Lincoln executed a **pocket veto** of the Wade-Davis Bill by not signing it before Congress adjourned. At the same time he initiated informal talks with congressional leaders aimed at finding common ground. Lincoln's successor, however, had no such inclinations. Andrew Johnson held the view that Reconstruction was the president's prerogative, and by an accident of timing he was free to act on his convictions. Under leisurely rules that went back to the early republic, the 39th Congress elected back in November 1864 was not scheduled to convene until December 1865.

## Johnson Seizes the Initiative

Andrew Johnson was a self-made man from the hills of eastern Tennessee. A Jacksonian Democrat, he saw himself as the champion of the common man. He hated what he called the "bloated, corrupt aristocracy" of the Northeast and was equally disdainful of the southern planters, whom he blamed for the poverty of the South's small farmers. It was the poor whites that he championed, however. Johnson, a slave owner himself, had little sympathy for the enslaved blacks. Johnson's political career had taken him to the U.S. Senate, where he remained when the war broke out, loyal to the Union. After federal forces captured Nashville, Johnson became Tennessee's military governor. The Republicans nominated him for vice president in 1864 in an effort to promote wartime unity and to court the support of southern Unionists.

In May 1865, just a month after Lincoln's death, Johnson launched his own Reconstruction plan. He offered amnesty to all Southerners who took an oath of allegiance to the Constitution, except for high-ranking Confederate officials and wealthy planters. This elite, whom Johnson blamed for secession, could be pardoned only by him. Johnson appointed provisional governors for the southern states and,

**Andrew Johnson**

The president was not an easy man. This photograph of Andrew Johnson (1808–1875) conveys some of the prickly qualities that contributed so centrally to his failure to reach an agreement with Republicans on a moderate Reconstruction program.
Library of Congress.

as conditions for their restoration, required only that they revoke their ordinances of secession, repudiate their Confederate debts, and ratify the Thirteenth Amendment, which abolished slavery. Within months all the former Confederate states had met Johnson's terms and enjoyed functioning, elected governments.

At first Republicans responded favorably. The moderates among them were sympathetic to Johnson's argument that it was up to the states, not the federal government, to define the civil and political rights of the freedmen. Even the Radicals held their fire. They liked the stern treatment of Confederate leaders, and they hoped that the new southern governments would show good faith by generous treatment of the freed slaves.

Nothing of the sort happened. The South lay in ruins. But Southerners held fast to the old order. The newly seated legislatures moved to restore slavery in all but name. They enacted laws—known as **Black Codes**—designed to drive the former slaves back to the plantations. The new governments had mostly been formed by southern Unionists, but when it came to racial attitudes, little distinguished these loyalists from the Confederates. The latter, moreover, soon filtered back into the corridors of power. Despite his hard words against them, Johnson forgave ex-Confederate leaders easily, so long as he got the satisfaction of humbling them when they appealed for pardons.

His perceived indulgence of their efforts to restore white supremacy emboldened the ex-Confederates. They packed the delegations to the new Congress with old comrades—nine members of the Confederate Congress, seven former officials of Confederate state governments, four generals and four colonels, and even the vice president of the Confederacy, Alexander Stephens. This was the last straw for the Republicans.

Under the Constitution, Congress is "the judge of the Elections, Returns and Qualifications of its own Members" (Article 1, Section 5). With this power the Republican majorities in both houses refused to admit the southern delegations when Congress convened in early December 1865, effectively blocking Johnson's Reconstruction program. In response, the southern states backed away from the most flagrant of the Black Codes, replacing them with regulatory ordinances silent on race yet, in practice, applied only to blacks, not to whites. On top of that, a wave of violence erupted across the South against the freedmen. In Tennessee a Nashville paper reported that white gangs "are riding about whipping, maiming and killing all negroes who do not obey the orders of their former masters, just as if slavery existed." Listening to the testimony of officials, observers, and victims, Republicans concluded that the South had embarked on a concerted effort to circumvent the Thirteenth Amendment. The only possible response was for the federal government to intervene.

Back in March 1865, before adjourning, the 38th Congress had established the Freedmen's Bureau to provide emergency aid to ex-slaves during the transition from war to peace. Now in early 1866, under the leadership of the moderate Republican senator Lyman Trumbull, Congress voted to extend the Freedmen's

Bureau's life, gave it direct funding for the first time, and authorized its agents to investigate mistreatment of blacks.

More extraordinary was Trumbull's civil rights bill, declaring all persons born in the United States to be citizens and granting them—without regard to race—equal rights of contract, access to the courts, and protection of person and property. Trumbull's bill nullified all state laws denying citizens equal protection, authorized U.S. attorneys to bring enforcement suits in the federal courts, and provided for fines and imprisonment for violators, including public officials. Provoked by an unrepentant South, even the most moderate Republicans demanded that the federal government assume responsibility for securing the civil rights of the freedmen.

## *Acting on Freedom*

While Congress debated, emancipated slaves acted on their own ideas about freedom. News that their bondage was over left them exultant and hopeful (see American Voices, "Relishing Freedom," p. 447). Freedom meant many things—the end of punishment by the lash, the ability to move around, the reuniting of families, the opportunity to begin schools, to form churches and social clubs, and, not least, to engage in politics. Across the South blacks held mass meetings, paraded, and formed organizations. Topmost among their demands were equality before the law and the right to vote—"an essential and inseparable element of self-government."

First of all, however, came ownership of land, which emancipated blacks believed was the basis for true freedom. In the chaotic final months of the war, as plantation owners fled Union forces, freedmen seized control of plantations where they could. Most famously, General William T. Sherman reserved large coastal tracts in Georgia and South Carolina for liberated slaves and settled them on forty-acre plots. Sherman just didn't want to be bothered with the refugees as his army drove across the Lower South, but the freedmen assumed that Sherman's order meant that the land would be theirs. When the war ended, resettlement became the responsibility of the Freedmen's Bureau, which was charged with feeding and clothing war refugees, distributing confiscated land to "loyal refugees and freedmen," and regulating labor contracts between freedmen and planters. Many black families stayed on their old plantations, awaiting redistribution of the land to them after the war. When the South Carolina planter Thomas Pinckney returned home, his freed slaves told him: "We ain't going nowhere. We are going to work right here on the land where we were born and what belongs to us."

Johnson's amnesty plan, entitling pardoned Confederates to recover property seized during the war, shattered these hopes. In October 1865 Johnson ordered General Oliver O. Howard, head of the Freedmen's Bureau, to restore the plantations on the Sea Islands off the South Carolina coast to their white owners. When Howard reluctantly obeyed, the dispossessed blacks protested: "Why do you take away our lands? You take them from us who have always been true, always true to the Government! You give them to our all-time enemies! That is not right!"

## *Relishing Freedom*

### JOURDON ANDERSON

*F*olklorists have recorded the sly ways that slaves found, even in bondage, for "puttin'
down" their masters. But only in freedom—and beyond reach in a northern state at
*that—could Anderson's sarcasm be expressed so openly, with the jest that his family might con-*
*sider returning if they first received the wages due them, calculated to the dollar, for all those*
*years in slavery. Yet, intermixed with the bitterness and the pride in personal dignity is an ad-*
*mission of affection for "the dear old home" that helps explain why, even after the horror of*
*bondage, ex-slaves often chose to remain in familiar surroundings and even work for their for-*
*mer masters. Anderson's letter, although probably written or edited by a white friend in*
*Dayton, surely is faithful to what the ex-slave wanted to say.*

Dayton, Ohio. August 7, 1865.
To My Old Master, Colonel P. H. Anderson, Big Spring, Tennessee.
Sir:

I got your letter, and was glad to find that you had not forgotten Jourdon, and that you
wanted me to come back and live with you again, promising to do better for me than anybody else can. I have often felt uneasy about you. I thought the Yankees would have hung you
long before this, for harboring Rebs they found at your house. I suppose they never heard
about your going to Colonel Martin's to kill the Union soldier that was left by his company
in their stable. Although you shot at me twice before I left you, I did not want to hear of your
being hurt, and am glad you are still living. It would do me good to go back to the dear old
home again, and see Miss Mary and Miss Martha and Allen, Esther, Green, and Lee. Give my
love to them all, and tell them I hope we will meet in the better world, if not in this. . . .

I want to know particularly what the good chance is you propose to give me. I am doing
tolerably well here. I get twenty-five dollars a month, with victuals and clothing; have a comfortable home for Mandy,—the folks call her Mrs. Anderson,—and the children—Milly,
Jane, and Grundy—go to school and are learning well. . . . We are kindly treated. Sometimes
we overhear others saying, "Them colored people were slaves" down in Tennessee. The children feel hurt when they hear such remarks; but I tell them it was no disgrace in Tennessee
to belong to Colonel Anderson. Many darkeys would have been proud, as I used to be, to call
you master. Now if you will write and say what wages you will give me, I will be better able
to decide whether it would be to my advantage to move back again. . . .

In answering this letter, please state if there would be any safety for my Milly and Jane,
who are now grown up, and both good-looking girls. You know how it was with poor
Matilda and Catherine. I would rather stay here and starve—and die, if it come to that—
than have my girls brought to shame by the violence and wickedness of their young masters. You will also please state if there has been any schools opened for the colored children
in your neighborhood. The great desire of my life now is to give my children an education,
and have them form virtuous habits.

Say howdy to George Carter, and thank him for taking the pistol from you when you
were shooting at me.

From your old servant,
Jourdon Anderson

SOURCE: Stanley I. Kutler, ed., *Looking for America*, 2nd ed. (New York: W. W. Norton, 1979), 2: 4–6.

In the Sea Islands and elsewhere, former slaves resisted efforts to evict them. Led by black veterans of the Union army, they fought pitched battles with plantation owners and bands of ex-Confederate soldiers. Landowners struck back hard. One black veteran wrote from Maryland: "The returned colard Solgers are in Many cases beten, and their guns taken from them, we darcent walk out of an evening. . . . They beat us badly and Sumtime Shoot us." Often aided by federal troops, the local whites generally prevailed in this land war.

As planters prepared for a new growing season, a great battle took shape over the labor system that would replace slavery. Convinced that blacks needed supervision, planters wanted to retain the gang labor of the past, only now with wages replacing the food, clothing, and shelter their slaves had once received. The Freedmen's Bureau, although watchful against exploitative labor contracts, sided with the planters. The main thing, its designers had always felt, was that the bureau not encourage dependency "in the guise of guardianship." Rely upon your "own efforts and exertions," an agent told a large crowd of freedmen in North Carolina, "make contracts with the planters" and "respect the rights of property."

**Wage Labor of Former Slaves**

This photograph, taken in South Carolina shortly after the Civil War, shows former slaves leaving the cotton fields. Ex-slaves were organized into work crews probably not that different from earlier slave gangs, although they now labored for wages and their plug-hatted boss bore little resemblance to the slave drivers of the past. New-York Historical Society.

This was advice given with little regard for the world in which those North Carolina freedmen lived. It was not only their unequal bargaining power they worried about or even that their ex-masters' real desire was to reenslave them under the guise of "free" contracts. In their eyes the condition of wage labor was itself, by definition, debasing. The rural South was not like the North, where working for wages was the norm and qualified a man as independent. In the South, selling one's labor to another—and in particular, selling one's labor to work another's land— implied not freedom, but dependency. "I mean to own my own manhood," responded one South Carolina freedman to an offer of wage work. "I'm going to own my own land."

So the wage issue cut to the very core of the former slaves' struggle for freedom. Nothing had been more horrifying than that as slaves their persons had been the property of others. When a master cast his eye on a slave woman, her husband had no recourse, nor, for that matter, was rape of a slave a crime. In a famous oration celebrating the anniversary of emancipation, the Reverend Henry M. Turner spoke bitterly of the time when his people had "no security for domestic happiness," when "our wives were sold and husbands bought, children were begotten and enslaved by their fathers," and "we therefore were polygamists by virtue of our condition." That was why formalizing marriage was so urgent a matter after emancipation and why, when hard-pressed planters demanded that freedwomen go back into the fields, they resisted so resolutely. If the ex-slaves were to be free as white folk, then their wives could not, any more than white wives, labor for others. "I seen on some plantations," one freedman recounted, "where the white men would . . . tell colored men that their wives and children could not live on their places unless they work in the fields. The colored men [answered that] whenever they wanted their wives to work they would tell them themselves; and if he could not rule his own domestic affairs on that place he would leave it and go someplace else."

The reader will see the irony in this definition of freedom: it assumed the wife's subordinate role and designated her labor the husband's property. But if that was the price of freedom, freedwomen were prepared to pay it. Far better to take a chance with their own men than with their ex-masters.

Many former slaves voted with their feet, abandoning their old plantations and seeking better lives and more freedom in the towns and cities of the South. Those who remained in the countryside refused to work the cotton fields under the hated gang-labor system or negotiated tenaciously over the terms of their labor contracts. Whatever system of labor finally might emerge, it was clear that the freedmen would never settle for anything resembling the old plantation system.

The efforts of former slaves to control their own lives challenged deeply entrenched white attitudes. "The destiny of the black race," asserted one Texan, could be summarized "in one sentence—subordination to the white race." Southern whites, a Freedmen's Bureau official observed, could not "conceive of the negro having any rights at all." And when freedmen resisted, white retribution was swift and often terrible. In Pine Bluff, Arkansas, "after some kind of dispute with some freedmen," whites set fire to their cabins and hanged twenty-four of the inhabitants—men, women, and children. The toll of murdered and beaten blacks mounted into untold thousands. The governments established under Johnson's plan only put the stamp of legality on the pervasive efforts to enforce white supremacy. Blacks "would be *just as well* off with no law at all or no Government," concluded a Freedmen's Bureau agent, as with the justice they got under the restored white rule.

In this unequal struggle, blacks turned to Washington. "We stood by the government when it wanted help," a black Mississippian wrote President Johnson. "Now . . . will it stand by us?"

## Congress versus President

Andrew Johnson was not the man to ask. In February 1866 he vetoed the Freedmen's Bureau bill. The bureau, Johnson charged, was an "immense patronage," showering benefits on blacks never granted to "our own people." Republicans could not muster enough votes to override his veto. A month later, further rebuffing his critics, Johnson vetoed Trumbull's civil rights bill, arguing that federal protection of black civil rights constituted "a stride toward centralization." His racism, hitherto muted, now blazed forth: "This is a country for white men, and by God, as long as I am president, it shall be government for white men."

Galvanized by Johnson's attack on the civil rights bill, the Republicans went into action. In early April they got the necessary two-thirds majorities in both houses and enacted it into law. Passage of the Civil Rights Act was a truly historic event, the first time Congress had prevailed over a presidential veto on a major piece of legislation. Republican resolve was reinforced by news of mounting violence in the South, culminating in three days of rioting in Memphis. Forty-six blacks and two whites were left dead, and hundreds of black homes, churches, and schools were looted and burned. In July an angry Congress renewed the Freedmen's Bureau over a second Johnson veto.

Anxious to consolidate their gains, Republicans moved to enshrine black civil rights in an amendment to the Constitution. The heart of the Fourteenth Amendment was Section 1, which declared that "all persons born or naturalized in the United States" were citizens. No state could abridge "the privileges or immunities of citizens of the United States," deprive "any person of life, liberty, or property, without due process of law," or deny anyone "the equal protection of the laws." These phrases were vague, intentionally so, but they established the constitutionality of the Civil Rights Act and, more important, the basis on which the courts and Congress could erect an enforceable national standard of equality before the law in the states.

For the moment, however, the Fourteenth Amendment was most important for its impact on national politics. With the 1866 congressional elections approaching, Johnson somehow figured he had a winning issue in the Fourteenth Amendment. He urged the states not to ratify it. Months earlier, Johnson had begun to maneuver politically against the Republicans, aiming to build a coalition of white Southerners, northern Democrats, and conservative Republicans under the banner of a new party, National Union. Any hope of launching it, however, was shattered by Johnson's intemperate behavior and by escalating violence in the South. A dissension-ridden National Union convention in July ended inconclusively, and Johnson's campaign against the Fourteenth Amendment became, effectively, a campaign for the Democratic Party.

Republicans responded furiously, unveiling a practice that would become known as "waving the bloody shirt." The Democrats were traitors, charged Indiana governor Oliver Morton, and their party was "a common sewer and loathsome receptacle, into which is emptied every element of treason North and South." In late August Johnson embarked on a disastrous "swing around the circle"—a railroad tour from Washington to Chicago and St. Louis and back—that violated the custom that presidents not campaign personally. Johnson made matters worse by engaging in shouting matches with hecklers and insulting the hostile crowds.

The 1866 congressional elections inflicted a humiliating defeat on Johnson. The Republicans won a three-to-one majority in Congress, so that, to begin with, the Republicans considered themselves "masters of the situation," free to proceed "entirely regardless of [Johnson's] opinions or wishes." As a referendum on the Fourteenth Amendment, moreover, the election registered overwhelming popular support for the civil rights of the former slaves. The Republican Party emerged with a new sense of unity—a unity coalescing not at the center, but on the left, around the unbending program of the Radical minority.

The Radicals represented the abolitionist strain within the Republican Party. Most of them hailed from New England or from the area of the upper Midwest settled by New Englanders. In the Senate they were led by Charles Sumner of Massachusetts and in the House by Thaddeus Stevens of Pennsylvania. For them Reconstruction was never primarily about restoring the Union but about remaking southern society. "The foundations of their institutions . . . must be broken up and relaid," declared Stevens, "or all our blood and treasure will have been spent in vain."

Only a handful went as far as Stevens in demanding that the plantations be treated as "forfeited estates of the enemy" and broken up into small farms for the former slaves. About the need to guarantee the freedmen's civil and political rights, however, there was agreement. In this endeavor Radicals had no qualms about expanding the powers of the national government. "The power of the great landed aristocracy in those regions, if unrestrained by power from without, would inevitably reassert itself," warned Congressman George W. Julian of Indiana. Radicals were aggressively partisan. They regarded the Republican Party as the instrument of God for the regeneration of the South.

At first, in the months after Appomattox, few but the Radicals themselves imagined that so extreme a program had any chance of enactment. Black **suffrage** especially seemed beyond reach, since the northern states themselves (excepting in New England) denied blacks the vote. And yet, as fury mounted against the intransigent South, Republicans became ever more radicalized until, in the wake of the smashing victory of 1866, they embraced the Radicals' vision of a reconstructed South.

# Radical Reconstruction

Afterward, thoughtful Southerners admitted that the South had brought radical Reconstruction on itself. "We had, in 1865, a white man's government in Alabama," remarked the man who had been Johnson's provisional governor, "but we lost it." The state's "great blunder" was not to "have at once taken the negro right under the protection of the laws." Remarkably, the South remained defiant even after the

**Resistance in the South**

This engraving, entitled "If He Is a Union Man or Freedman: Verdict, Hang the D——Yankee and Nigger," appeared in *Harper's Weekly* on March 23, 1867, just as the Reconstruction Act was being adopted. Thomas Nast's cartoon encapsulated the outrage at the South's murderous intransigence that led even moderate Republicans to support radical Reconstruction. Library of Congress.

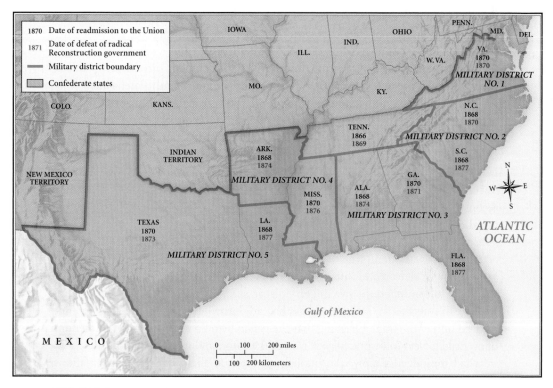

| | |
|---|---|
| 1870 | Date of readmission to the Union |
| 1871 | Date of defeat of radical Reconstruction government |
| —— | Military district boundary |
| ▢ | Confederate states |

IOWA

PENN.

OHIO

MD.

DEL.

IND.

ILL.

W. VA.

VA.
1870
1870

MILITARY DISTRICT
NO. 1

COLO.

KANS.

MO.

KY.

N.C.
1868
1870

NEW MEXICO
TERRITORY

INDIAN
TERRITORY

ARK.
1868
1874

TENN.
1866
1869

MILITARY DISTRICT NO. 2

S.C.
1868
1877

MILITARY DISTRICT NO. 4

MISS.
1870
1876

ALA.
1868
1874

GA.
1870
1871

N
W · E
S

TEXAS
1870
1873

LA.
1868
1877

MILITARY DISTRICT NO. 3

ATLANTIC
OCEAN

MILITARY DISTRICT NO. 5

FLA.
1868
1877

*Gulf of Mexico*

MEXICO

0    100    200 miles
0    100   200 kilometers

**MAP 15.1 Reconstruction**

The federal government organized the Confederate states into five military districts during radical Reconstruction. For each state the first date indicates when that state was readmitted to the Union; the second date shows when radical Republicans lost control of the state government. All the ex-Confederate states rejoined the Union from 1868 to 1870, but the periods of radical rule varied widely. Republicans lasted only a few months in Virginia; they held on until the end of Reconstruction in Louisiana, Florida, and South Carolina.

FOR MORE HELP ANALYZING THIS MAP, see the Online Study Guide at **bedfordstmartins.com/henrettaconcise**.

1866 elections. Every state legislature but Tennessee's rejected the Fourteenth Amendment, mostly by virtual acclamation. It was as if they could not imagine that governments installed under the presidential imprimatur and fully functioning might be swept away. But that, in fact, is just what the Republicans intended to do.

## Congress Takes Command

The Reconstruction Act of 1867, enacted in March by the Republican Congress, organized the South as a conquered land, dividing it into five military districts, each under the command of a Union general (Map 15.1). The price for reentering the Union was granting the vote to the freedmen and disfranchising those of the South's prewar leadership class who had participated in the rebellion. Each military commander was ordered to register all eligible adult males (black as well as white), supervise the election of state conventions, and make certain that the new constitutions contained guarantees of black suffrage. Congress would readmit a state to the Union if its voters ratified the constitution, if that document proved acceptable to Congress, and if the new state legislature approved the Fourteenth Amendment (thus insuring the needed ratification by three-fourths of the states). Johnson vetoed the Reconstruction Act, but Congress overrode the veto (Table 15.1).

The Tenure of Office Act, a companion to the Reconstruction Act, required Senate consent for the removal of any official whose appointment had required Senate confirmation. Congress chiefly wanted to protect Secretary of War Edwin M. Stanton, a Lincoln holdover and the only member of Johnson's cabinet who favored radical Reconstruction. In his position Stanton could do much to frustrate Johnson's anticipated efforts to undermine Reconstruction. The law also required the president to issue all orders to the army through its commanding general, Ulysses S. Grant. In effect, Congress was attempting to reconstruct the presidency as well as the South.

Seemingly defeated, Johnson appointed generals recommended by Stanton and Grant to command the five military districts in the South. But he was just biding his time. In August 1867, after Congress had adjourned, he "suspended" Stanton and replaced him with Grant, believing that the general would act like a good soldier and follow orders. Next Johnson replaced four of the commanding generals. Johnson, however, had misjudged Grant, who publicly objected to the president's machinations. When the Senate reconvened in the fall, it overruled Stanton's suspension. Grant, now an open enemy of Johnson's, resigned so that Stanton could resume his office.

On February 21, 1868, Johnson formally dismissed Stanton. The feisty secretary of war, however, barricaded the door of his office and refused to admit Johnson's appointee. Three days later, for the first time in United States history, House Republicans introduced articles of **impeachment** against a sitting president, employing the power granted the House of Representatives by the Constitution to charge high federal officials with "Treason, Bribery, or other high Crimes and Misdemeanors." The House overwhelmingly approved eleven counts of presidential misconduct, nine of them violations of the Tenure of Office Act.

The case went to the Senate, which acts as the court in impeachment cases, with Chief Justice Salmon P. Chase presiding. After an eleven-week trial, thirty-five senators on May 15 voted for conviction, one vote short of the two-thirds majority required. Seven moderate Republicans broke ranks, voting for acquittal along with twelve Democrats. The dissenting Republicans felt that the Tenure of Office Act was of dubious validity (in fact, the Supreme Court subsequently declared it unconstitutional) and that removing a president for defying Congress was too extreme, too damaging to the constitutional system of checks and balances, even for the sake of punishing Johnson. Despite his acquittal, however, Johnson had been defanged. For the remainder of his term he was powerless to alter the course of Reconstruction.

The impeachment controversy made Grant, already the North's war hero, a Republican hero as well, and he easily won the party's presidential nomination in

**TABLE 15.1 Primary Reconstruction Laws and Constitutional Amendments**

| Law (Date of Congressional Passage) | Key Provisions |
| --- | --- |
| Thirteenth Amendment (January 1865*) | Prohibited slavery |
| Civil Rights Act of 1866 (April 1866) | Defined citizenship rights of freedmen<br>Authorized federal authorities to bring suit against those who violated those rights |
| Fourteenth Amendment (June 1866†) | Established national citizenship for persons born or naturalized in the United States<br>Prohibited the states from depriving citizens of their civil rights or equal protection under the law<br>Reduced state representation in House of Representatives by the percentage of adult male citizens denied the vote |
| Reconstruction Act of 1867 (March 1867‡) | Divided the South into five military districts, each under the command of a Union general<br>Established requirements for readmission of ex-Confederate states to the Union |
| Tenure of Office Act (March 1867) | Required Senate consent for removal of any federal official whose appointment had required Senate confirmation |
| Fifteenth Amendment (February 1869) | Forbade states to deny citizens the right to vote on the grounds of race, color, or "previous condition of servitude" |
| Ku Klux Klan Act (April 1871) | Authorized the president to use federal prosecutions and military force to suppress conspiracies to deprive citizens of the right to vote and enjoy the equal protection of the law |

*Ratified by three-fourths of all states in December 1868.
†Ratified by three-fourths of all states in July 1868.
‡Ratified by three-fourths of all states in March 1870.

1868. In the fall campaign he supported radical Reconstruction, but he also urged reconciliation between the sections. His Democratic opponent, Horatio Seymour, a former governor of New York, almost declined the nomination because he doubted that the Democrats could overcome the stain of disloyalty.

As Seymour feared, the Republicans "waved the bloody shirt," stirring up old wartime emotions against the Democrats to great effect. Grant won about the same share of the northern vote (55 percent) that Lincoln had won in 1864 and received 214 of 294 electoral votes. The Republicans also retained two-thirds majorities in both houses of Congress.

In the wake of their smashing victory, the Republicans quickly produced the last major piece of Reconstruction legislation—the Fifteenth Amendment, which forbade either the federal government or the states from denying citizens the right to vote on the basis of race, color, or "previous condition of servitude." The amendment left room for **poll taxes** and property requirements or literacy tests that might be used to discourage blacks from voting, a necessary concession to northern and western states that already relied on such provisions to keep immigrants and the "unworthy" poor from the polls. A California senator warned that in his state, with its rabidly anti-Chinese sentiment (see Chapter 16), any restriction on that power would "kill our party as dead as a stone."

Despite grumbling by Radical Republicans, the amendment passed without modification in February 1869. Congress required the states still under federal control—Virginia, Mississippi, Texas, and Georgia—to ratify it as a condition for being readmitted to the Union. A year later the Fifteenth Amendment became part of the Constitution.

## Woman Suffrage Denied

If the Fifteenth Amendment troubled some proponents of black suffrage, this was nothing compared to the outrage felt by women's rights advocates. They had fought the good fight for the abolition of slavery for so many years, only to be abandoned when the chance finally came to get the vote for women. All it would have taken was one more word in the Fifteenth Amendment so that the protected categories for voting would have read "race, color, *sex*, or previous condition." Leading suffragists such as Susan B. Anthony and Elizabeth Cady Stanton did not want to hear from Radical Republicans that this was "the Negro's hour" and that women would have to wait for another day. How could suffrage be granted to former slaves, Stanton demanded, but not to them?

In a decisive debate in May 1869 at the Equal Rights Association, the champion of universal suffrage, the black abolitionist Frederick Douglass pleaded for understanding. "When women, because they are women, are hunted down . . . dragged from their homes and hung upon lamp posts . . . when their children are not allowed to enter schools; then they will have an urgency to obtain the ballot equal to our own." Not even all his black sisters agreed. "If colored men get their rights, and not colored women theirs," protested Sojourner Truth, "you see the colored men will be masters over the women, and it will be just as bad as it was before." As for white women in the audience, remarked Frances Harper in support of Douglass, they "all go for sex, letting race occupy a minor position," or worse. In her despair, Elizabeth Cady Stanton lashed out in ugly racist terms against "Patrick and Sambo and Hans and Ung Tung," who were entitled to vote in ignorance even of the Declaration of Independence while the most accomplished of American women remained voteless. Douglass's resolution in support of the Fifteenth Amendment failed, and the Equal Rights convention broke up in acrimony.

At this searing moment a rift opened in the ranks of the women's movement. The majority, led by Lucy Stone and Julia Ward Howe, reconciled themselves to disappointment and accepted the priority of black suffrage. Organized into the American Woman Suffrage Association, these moderates remained allied to the Republican Party, in hopes that once Reconstruction had been settled it would be time for the woman's vote. The Stanton-Anthony group, however, struck out in a new direction. The embittered Stanton declared that woman "must not put her trust in man" in fighting for her rights. The new organization she headed, the New York–based National Woman Suffrage Association, accepted only women, focused exclusively on women's rights, and resolutely took up the battle for a federal woman suffrage amendment.

The fracturing of the women's movement obscured the common ground the two sides shared. Both began to appeal to constituencies beyond the narrow confines of abolitionism and evangelical reform. Both elevated suffrage into the preeminent women's issue. And both were energized for the battles that lay ahead. "If I were to give vent to all my pent-up wrath concerning the subordination of woman," Lydia Maria Child wrote the Republican warhorse Charles Sumner in 1872, "I might frighten *you*. . . . Suffice it, therefore, to say, either the theory of our government is *false*, or women have a right to vote." If radical Reconstruction seemed a barren time for women's rights, in fact it had planted the seeds of the modern feminist movement.

## Republican Rule in the South

Between 1868 and 1871 all the southern states met the congressional stipulations and rejoined the Union. Protected by federal troops and encouraged by northern party leaders, state Republican organizations took hold across the South and won control of the newly established Reconstruction governments. These Republican administrations remained in power for periods ranging from a few months in Virginia to nine years in South Carolina, Louisiana, and Florida. Their core support came from African Americans, who constituted a majority of registered voters in Alabama, Florida, South Carolina, and Mississippi.

Southern white Republicans faced the scorn of Democratic ex-Confederates, who mocked them as **scalawags**—an ancient Scots-Irish term for runty, worthless animals. Whites who had come from the North they denounced as **carpetbaggers**— self-seeking interlopers who carried all their property in cheap suitcases called carpet-bags. Such labels glossed over the actual diversity of these white Republicans.

Some carpetbaggers, while motivated by personal profit, also brought capital and skills. Others were Union army veterans taken with the South—its climate, people, and economic opportunities. And interspersed with the self-seekers were many idealists anxious to advance the cause of emancipation.

The scalawags were even more diverse. Some were former slave owners, ex-Whigs and even ex-Democrats, drawn to Republicanism as the best way to attract northern capital to southern railroads, mines, and factories. But most were yeomen farmers from the backcountry districts who wanted to rid the South of its slaveholding aristocracy. They had generally fought against, or at least refused to support, the Confederacy, believing that slavery had victimized whites as well as blacks. "Now is the time," a Georgia scalawag wrote, "for every man to come out and speak his principles publickly [sic] and vote for liberty as we have been in bondage long enough."

The Democrats' scorn for black political leaders as ignorant field hands was just as false as stereotypes about white Republicans. The first African American leaders in the South came from an elite of free blacks. They were joined by northern blacks who moved south when radical Reconstruction offered the prospect of meaningful freedom. Like their white allies, many were Union army veterans. Some had participated in the antislavery crusade; a number were employed by the Freedmen's Bureau or northern missionary societies. Others had escaped from slavery and were returning home. One of these was Blanche K. Bruce, who had been tutored on the Virginia plantation of his white father. During the war Bruce escaped and established a school for ex-slaves in Missouri. In 1869 he moved to Mississippi, became active in politics, and in 1874 became Mississippi's second black U.S. senator.

As the reconstructed Republican governments of 1867 began to function, this diverse group of ministers, artisans, shopkeepers, and former soldiers reached out to the freedmen. African American speakers, some financed by the Republican Party, fanned out into the old plantation districts and recruited ex-slaves for political roles. Still, few of the new leaders were field hands; most had been preachers or artisans. The literacy of one ex-slave, Thomas Allen, who was a Baptist minister and shoemaker, helped him win election to the Georgia legislature. "In my county," he recalled, "the colored people came to me for instructions, and I gave them the best instructions I could. I took the *New York Tribune* and other papers, and in that way I found out a great deal, and I told them whatever I thought was right."

Although never proportionate to their numbers in the population, black officeholders were prominent across the South. In South Carolina African Americans constituted a majority in the lower house of the legislature in 1868. Three were elected to Congress; another joined the state supreme court. Over the entire course of Reconstruction, twenty African Americans served in state administrations as governor, lieutenant governor, secretary of state, treasurer, or superintendent of education; more than six hundred served as state legislators; and sixteen were congressmen.

The Republicans who took office had ambitious plans for a reconstructed South. They wanted to end its dependence on cotton agriculture and build an entrepreneurial

THE FIRST COLORED SENATOR AND REPRESENTATIVES.

In the 41ˢᵗ and 42ⁿᵈ Congress of the United States.

**African American Congressional Delegation, 1872**

This Currier and Ives lithograph celebrates one of the notable achievements of radical Reconstruction—the representation that ex-slaves won, however briefly, in the U.S. Congress. Hiram Revels of Mississippi, the Senate's first African American member, is seated at the extreme left. Granger Collection.

economy like the North's. They fell far short of achieving this vision but accomplished more than their critics gave them credit for.

The Republicans modernized state constitutions, eliminated property qualification for the vote, and swept out the Black Codes that coerced the freedmen back to the plantation and limited their mobility. Women also benefited from the Republican defense of personal liberty. The new constitutions expanded the rights of married women, enabling them to hold property and earnings independent of their husbands—"a wonderful reform," a Georgia woman wrote, for "the cause of Women's Rights." Republican social programs called for the establishment of hospitals, more humane penitentiaries, and asylums for orphans and the insane. Republican governments built roads in areas where roads had never existed. They poured money into rebuilding the region's railroad network.

To pay for their ambitious programs the Republican governments copied taxes that Jacksonian reformers had earlier introduced in the North—in particular, general property taxes on both real estate and personal wealth. The goal was to make planters pay their fair share and to broaden the tax base. In many plantation counties, former slaves served as tax assessors and collectors, administering the taxation of their one-time owners.

Higher tax revenues never managed to overtake the huge obligations assumed by the Reconstruction governments. State debts mounted rapidly and, as interest payments on bonds fell behind, public credit collapsed. On top of that, much of the spending was wasted or ended up in the pockets of state officials. Corruption was ingrained in American politics, present in the southern states before the Republicans came on the scene, and rampant everywhere in this era, not least in the Grant administration itself. Still, in the free-spending atmosphere of the southern Republican regimes, corruption was especially luxuriant and damaging to the cause of radical Reconstruction.

Nothing, however, could dim the achievement in public education. Here the South had lagged woefully; only Tennessee had a system of public schooling before the Civil War. Republican state governments vowed to make up for lost time, viewing education as the foundation for a democratic order. African Americans of all ages rushed to attend the newly established schools, even when they had to pay tuition. An elderly man in Mississippi explained his hunger for education: "Ole missus used to read the good book [the Bible] to us . . . on Sunday evenin's, but she mostly read dem places where it says, 'Servants obey your masters.' . . . Now we is free, there's heaps of tings in that old book we is just suffering to learn."

The building of schools was part of a larger effort by African Americans to fortify the institutions that had sustained their spirit in the shadow of slavery. Religious belief had struck deep roots in nineteenth-century slave society. Now, in freedom, the African Americans left the white-dominated congregations, where they had been relegated to segregated balconies and denied any voice in church governance, and built churches of their own. These churches joined together to form African American versions of the Southern Methodist and Southern Baptist denominations, including, most prominently, the National Baptist Convention and the African Methodist Episcopal Church. Everywhere the black churches served not only as places of worship but as schools, social centers, and political meeting halls.

Black clerics were community leaders and often political leaders as well. As Charles H. Pearce, a Methodist minister in Florida, declared, "A man in this State cannot do his whole duty as a minister except he looks out for the political interests of his people." Calling forth the special destiny of the ex-slaves as the new "Children of Israel," black ministers provided a powerful religious underpinning for the Republican politics of their congregations.

## The Quest for Land

In the meantime the freedmen were locked in a great economic struggle with their former owners. In 1869 the Republican government of South Carolina had established a land commission empowered to buy property and resell it on easy terms to the landless. In this way about 14,000 black families acquired farms. South

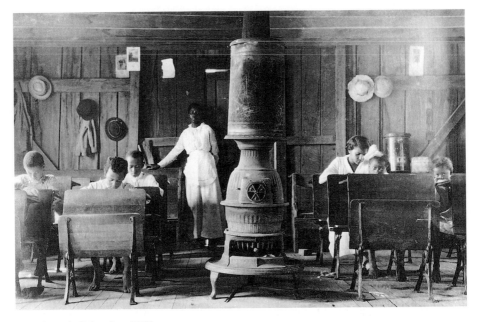

**Freedmen's School, c. 1870**

This rare photograph shows the interior of one of the 3,000 freedmen's schools established across the South after the Civil War. Although many of these schools were staffed by white missionaries, a main objective of northern educators was to prepare blacks to take over the classrooms. The teacher shown here is surely one of the first. Library of Congress.

FOR MORE HELP ANALYZING THIS IMAGE, see the Online Study Guide at **bedfordstmartins.com/henrettaconcise**.

Carolina's land distribution plan showed what was possible, but it was the exception and not the rule. Despite a lot of rhetoric, Republican regimes elsewhere did little to help the freedmen fulfill their dreams of becoming independent farmers. Federal efforts proved equally feeble. The Southern Homestead Act of 1866 offered eighty-acre grants to settlers, limited for the first year to freedmen and southern Unionists. The advantage was mostly symbolic, however, since the public land made available to homesteaders was off the beaten track in swampy, infertile parts of the Lower South. Only about a thousand families succeeded.

There was no reversing President Johnson's order restoring confiscated lands to ex-Confederates. Property rights, it seemed, trumped everything else, even for most Radical Republicans. The Freedman's Bureau, which had earlier championed the land claims of the ex-slaves, now devoted itself to teaching them how to be good agricultural laborers.

While they yearned for farms of their own, most freedmen started out landless and with no option but to work for their former owners. But not, they vowed, under the conditions of slavery—no gang work, no overseers, no fines or punishments, no regulation of their private lives. In certain parts of the agricultural South wage work became the norm—for example, on the great sugar plantations of Louisiana taken over after the war by northern investors. The problem was that cotton planters lacked the money to pay wages, at least not until the crop came in, and sometimes, in lieu of a straight wage, they offered a share of the crop. As a wage, this was a bad deal for the freedmen, but if they could be paid in shares for their work, why could they not pay in shares to rent the land they worked?

This form of land tenantry was already familiar in parts of the white South, and the freedmen now seized on it for the independence it offered them. Planters resisted, believing, as one wrote, that "wages are the only successful system of controlling hands." But, in a battle of wills that broke out all across the cotton South, the planters yielded to "the inveterate prejudices of the freedmen, who desire to be masters of their own time."

Thus there sprang up the distinctive laboring system of cotton agriculture — **sharecropping**, in which the freedmen worked as renters, exchanging their labor for the use of land, house, implements, sometimes seed and fertilizer, typically turning over half to two-thirds of their crops to the landlord (Map 15.2). The sharecropping system joined laborers and the owners of land and capital in a common sharing of risks and returns. But it was a very unequal relationship, given the force of southern law and custom on the white landowner's side and the sharecroppers' dire economic circumstances. Starting out penniless, they had no way of making it through the first growing season without borrowing for food and supplies.

Country storekeepers stepped in. Bankrolled by their northern suppliers, they "furnished" the sharecropper and took as collateral a **lien** on the crop, effectively assuming ownership of the cropper's share and leaving him only the proceeds that remained after his debts had been paid. Once indebted at one store, the sharecropper was no longer free to shop around and became an easy target for exorbitant prices, unfair interest rates, and crooked bookkeeping. As cotton prices declined during the 1870s, more and more sharecroppers failed to settle accounts and fell into permanent debt. And if the merchant was also the landowner, or conspired with the landowner, the debt became a pretext for forced labor, or **peonage**, although evidence now suggests that sharecroppers generally managed to pull up stakes and move on once things became hopeless. Sharecroppers always thought twice about moving, however, because part of their "capital" was being known and well reputed in their home communities. Freedmen who lacked that local standing generally found sharecropping hard going and ended up in the ranks of agricultural laborers.

In the face of so much adversity, black families struggled to better themselves. That it enabled family struggle was, in truth, the saving advantage of sharecropping because it mobilized husbands and wives in common enterprise while shielding both from personal subordination to whites. The wives were doubly blessed. Neither field hands for their ex-masters nor dependent housewives, they became partners laboring side by side with their husbands. The trouble with sharecropping, one planter grumbled, was that "it makes the laborer too independent; he becomes a partner, and has to be consulted." By the end of Reconstruction, about one-quarter of sharecropping families had managed to save enough to rent with cash payments, and eventually black farmers owned about a third of the land they cultivated.

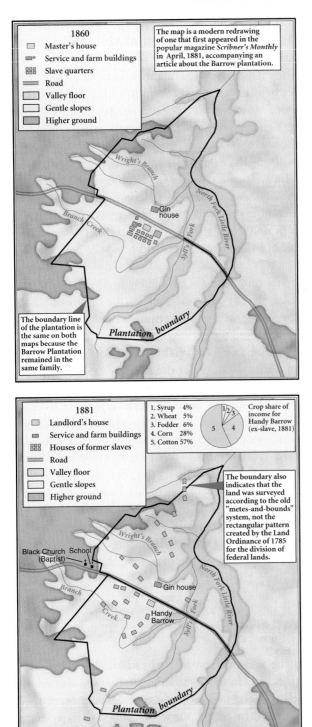

**1860**

☐ Master's house
▭ Service and farm buildings
▦ Slave quarters
══ Road
▭ Valley floor
▭ Gentle slopes
▓ Higher ground

The map is a modern redrawing of one that first appeared in the popular magazine *Scribner's Monthly* in April, 1881, accompanying an article about the Barrow plantation.

*Wright's Branch*

*Branch Creek*

*North Fork Little River*

*Sylt's Fork*

Gin house

The boundary line of the plantation is the same on both maps because the Barrow Plantation remained in the same family.

*Plantation boundary*

**1881**

☐ Landlord's house
▭ Service and farm buildings
▦ Houses of former slaves
══ Road
▭ Valley floor
▭ Gentle slopes
▓ Higher ground

1. Syrup  4%
2. Wheat  5%
3. Fodder  6%
4. Corn  28%
5. Cotton  57%

Crop share of income for Handy Barrow (ex-slave, 1881)

The boundary also indicates that the land was surveyed according to the old "metes-and-bounds" system, not the rectangular pattern created by the Land Ordinance of 1785 for the division of federal lands.

*Wright's Branch*

Black Church (Baptist)   School

*Branch Creek*

*North Fork Little River*

*Sylt's Fork*

Gin house

Handy Barrow

*Plantation boundary*

**MAP 15.2 The Barrow Plantation, 1860 and 1881**

Comparing the 1860 map of this central Georgia plantation with the 1881 map reveals the impact of sharecropping on patterns of black residence. In 1860 the slave quarters were clustered near the planter's house. By 1881 the sharecroppers had scattered across the plantation's 2,000 acres, building cabins on the ridges of land between the low-lying streams. The name Barrow was common among the share-cropping families, which means almost certainly that they had been slaves on the Barrow plantation and that, years after emancipation, they still had not moved on. For all the sharecrop-pers, freedom surely meant hav-ing not only their individual lots and cabins but also the school and church shown on the map.

The battle over the land was by no means unique to the American South. Whenever slavery ended—in Haiti after the slave revolt of 1791, in the British Caribbean by abolition in 1833, in Cuba and Brazil by gradual emancipation during the 1880s—a fierce struggle ensued between planters bent on restoring a gang-labor system and ex-slaves bent on gaining economic autonomy. The outcome of this universal conflict depended on the ex-slaves' access to land. Where vacant land existed, as in British Guiana, or where plantations could be seized, as in Haiti, the ex-slaves became subsistence farmers, and insofar as the Caribbean plantation economy survived without the ex-slaves, it did so by the importation of indentured servants from India and China. Where land could not be had, as in British Barbados or Antigua, the ex-slaves returned to plantation labor as wage-workers, although often in some combination with customary rights to housing and garden plots. The cotton South fit neither of these broad patterns. The freedmen did not get the land, but neither did the planters get field hands. What both got was sharecropping.

The reason for this exceptional outcome was ultimately political. Elsewhere, emancipation almost never meant civil or political equality for the freed slaves. Even in the British islands, where substantial self-government existed, high property qualifications effectively disfranchised the ex-slaves. In the United States, however, hard on the heels of emancipation came civil rights, manhood suffrage, and, for a brief era, a real measure of political power for the freedmen. Sharecropping took shape during Reconstruction, and there was no going back afterward.

For the freedmen sharecropping was not the worst choice; it certainly beat laboring for their former owners. But for southern agriculture the costs were devastating. Sharecropping committed the South inflexibly to cotton because, as a market crop, it alone generated the cash required by landlords and furnishing merchants. Neither soil depletion nor low prices ever enabled sharecroppers to shift away from cotton. And with farms leased year-to-year, neither tenant nor owner had much incentive to improve the property. The crop-lien system lined merchants' pockets with unearned profits that might otherwise have gone into agricultural improvement. The result was a stagnant farm economy, blighting the South's future and condemning it to economic backwardness—a kind of retribution, in fact, for the fresh injustices visited on the people it had once enslaved.

# The Undoing of Reconstruction

Ex-Confederates were blind to the accomplishments of radical Reconstruction. Indeed, no amount of achievement could have persuaded them that it was anything but an abomination, undertaken without their consent and denying them their rightful place in southern society. Led by the planters, ex-Confederates staged a massive counterrevolution—one designed to "redeem" the South and restore them to political power under the banner of the Democratic Party. But the Redeemers could not have succeeded on their own. They needed the complicity of the North. The undoing of Reconstruction is as much about northern acquiescence as it is about southern resistance.

## Counterrevolution

Insofar as they could win at the ballot box, southern Democrats took that route. They worked hard to get ex-Confederates restored to the voting rolls, they appealed to southern patriotism, and they campaigned against black rule as a threat to white supremacy. But force was equally acceptable. Throughout the Deep South, especially where black voters were heavily concentrated, ex-Confederate planters and their supporters organized secret societies and waged campaigns of terror against blacks and their white allies.

Most fearsome was the Ku Klux Klan, which first appeared in 1866 in Tennessee as a paramilitary force under the aegis of Nathan Bedford Forrest, the Confederacy's most decorated cavalry general. By 1870 the Klan was operating almost everywhere in the South as a terrorist organization. The Klan murdered and whipped Republican politicians, burned black schools and churches, and attacked party gatherings (see American Voices, "The Intimidation of Black Voters," p. 466). Such terrorist tactics enabled the Democrats to seize power in Georgia and North Carolina in 1870 and make substantial gains elsewhere.

Congress responded by passing legislation, including the Ku Klux Klan Act of 1871, authorizing federal prosecutions, military force, and martial law to suppress conspiracies to deprive citizens of their political rights and equal protection of the law. In South Carolina, where the Klan was most deeply entrenched, federal troops occupied nine counties, made hundreds of arrests, and drove as many as 2,000 Klansmen from the state.

The Grant administration's assault on the Klan raised the spirits of southern Republicans, but it also emphasized how dependent they were on the federal government. The potency of the Ku Klux Klan Act, a Mississippi Republican wrote, "derived alone from its source" in the federal government. "No such law could be enforced by state authority, the local power being too weak." If they were to prevail over anti-black terrorism, Republicans needed what one carpetbagger described as "steady, unswerving power from without."

But northern Republicans were growing weary of Reconstruction and the endless bloodshed it seemed to produce. Prosecuting Klansmen was an uphill battle. U.S. attorneys usually faced all-white juries and lacked the resources to handle the cases. After 1872 prosecutions began to drop off; many Klansmen received hasty pardons.

In a kind of self-fulfilling prophecy, the unwillingness of the Grant administration to shore up Reconstruction guaranteed that it would fail. Republican governments that were denied federal help found themselves overwhelmed by the massive resistance of their ex-Confederate enemies. Democrats overthrew Republican governments in Texas in 1873, in Alabama and Arkansas in 1874, and in Mississippi in 1875.

# The Intimidation of Black Voters

## HARRIET HERNANDES

*T*he following testimony was given in 1871 by Harriet Hernandes, a black resident of Spartanburg, South Carolina, to the Joint Congressional Select Committee investigating conditions in the South. The terrorizing of black women through rape and other forms of physical violence was among the means of oppression used by the Ku Klux Klan.

**Question:** How old are you?
**Answer:** Going on thirty-four years. . . .
**Q:** Are you married or single?
**A:** Married.
**Q:** Did the Ku-Klux come to your house at any time?
**A:** Yes, sir; twice. . . .
**Q:** Go on to the second time. . . .
**A:** They came in; I was lying in bed. Says he, "Come out here, sir; come out here, sir!" They took me out of bed; they would not let me get out, but they took me up in their arms and toted me out—me and my daughter Lucy. He struck me on the forehead with a pistol, and here is the scar above my eye now. Says he, "Damn you, fall." I fell. Says he, "Damn you, get up." I got up. Says he, "Damn you, get over this fence!" and he kicked me over when I went to get over; and then he went on to a brush pile, and they laid us right down there, both together. They laid us down twenty yards apart, I reckon. They had dragged and beat us along. They struck me right on top of my head, and I thought they had killed me; and I said, "Lord o'mercy, don't, don't kill my child!" He gave me a lick on the head, and it liked to have killed me; I saw stars. He threw my arm over my head so I could not do anything with it for three weeks, and there are great knots on my wrist now.
**Q:** What did they say this was for?
**A:** They said, "You can tell your husband that when we see him we are going to kill him. . . ."
**Q:** Did they say why they wanted to kill him?
**A:** They said, "He voted the radical ticket [slate of candidates], didn't he?" I said, "Yes," that very way. . . .
**Q:** When did [your husband] get back home after this whipping? He was not at home, was he?
**A:** He was lying out; he couldn't stay at home, bless your soul! . . .
**Q:** Has he been afraid for any length of time?
**A:** He has been afraid ever since last October. He has been lying out. He has not laid in the house ten nights since October.
**Q:** Is that the situation of the colored people down there to any extent?
**A:** That is the way they all have to do—men and women both.
**Q:** What are they afraid of?
**A:** Of being killed or whipped to death.
**Q:** What has made them afraid?
**A:** Because men that voted radical tickets they took the spite out on the women when they could get at them.
**Q:** How many colored people have been whipped in that neighborhood?
**A:** It is all of them, mighty near.

SOURCE: Report of the Joint Congressional Select Committee to Inquire into the Condition of Affairs in the Late Insurrectionary States, House Report, 42nd Cong., 2nd sess. (Washington, DC: U.S. Government Printing Office, 1872), vol. 5, South Carolina, December 19, 1871.

**Klan Portrait**

Two armed Klansmen pose in their disguises, which they donned not only to hide their identities but also to intimidate their black neighbors. Northern audiences saw a lithograph based on this photograph in *Harper's Weekly* on December 28, 1868.

Rutherford B. Hayes Presidential Center.

The Mississippi campaign showed all too clearly what the Republicans were up against. As elections neared in 1875, paramilitary groups such as the Rifle Clubs and Red Shirts operated openly. Often local Democrats paraded armed, as if they were militia companies. They identified black leaders in assassination lists called "dead books," broke up Republican meetings, provoked rioting that left hundreds of African Americans dead, and threatened voters. Mississippi's Republican governor, Adelbert Ames, a Congressional Medal of Honor winner from Maine, appealed to President Grant for federal troops, but Grant refused. Ames then contemplated organizing a state militia but ultimately decided against it, believing that only blacks would join and that the state would be plunged into racial war. Brandishing their guns and stuffing the ballot boxes, the Redeemers swept the 1875 elections and took control of Mississippi. Facing impeachment by the new Democratic legislature, Governor Ames resigned his office and returned to the North.

By 1876 Republican governments, backed by token U.S. military units, remained in only three states—Louisiana, South Carolina, and Florida. Elsewhere, the former Confederates were back in power.

## The Acquiescent North

The faltering of Reconstruction stemmed from more than discouragement about prosecuting the Klan, however. Sympathy for the freedman began to wane. The North was flooded with one-sided, often racist reports, such as James M. Pike's *The Prostrate State* (1873), describing extravagant, corrupt Republican rule and South Carolina in the grip of "a mass of black barbarism." The impact of this propaganda could be seen in the fate of the civil rights bill, which Charles Sumner introduced in 1870 at the height of radical Reconstruction. Sumner's bill was a remarkable application of federal power against discrimination in the country, guaranteeing citizens equal access to public accommodation, schools, and jury service. By the time the bill passed in 1875, it had been stripped of its key provisions and was of little account as a weapon against discriminatory treatment of African Americans. The Supreme Court finished the demolition job when it declared the remnant Civil Rights Act unconstitutional in 1883.

The political cynicism that overtook the Civil Rights Act signaled the Republican Party's reversion to the practical politics of earlier days. In many states a second generation took over the party—men like Roscoe Conkling of New York, who treated the Manhattan Customs House, with its regiment of political appointees, as an auxiliary of his organization. Conkling and similarly minded politicos had little enthusiasm for Reconstruction, except as it benefited the Republican Party. As the party lost headway in the South, they abandoned any interest in the battle for black rights. In Washington President Grant presided benignly over this transformation of his party, turning a blind eye on corruption even as it began to lap against the White House.

Grant won a second term overwhelmingly in 1872, capturing 56 percent of the popular vote and every electoral vote against a hapless Horace Greeley, longtime editor of the *New York Tribune* and a warhorse of American reform. But thereafter charges of Republican corruption began to be heard, coming to a head in 1875. The scandal involved the Whiskey Ring, a network of liquor distillers and treasury agents who defrauded the government of millions of dollars of excise taxes on whiskey. The ringleader was a Grant appointee, and Grant's own private secretary, Orville Babcock, had a hand in the thievery. The others went to prison, but Grant stood by Babcock, possibly perjuring himself to save his secretary from jail. The stench of scandal, however, had engulfed the White House.

On top of this the economy had fallen into a severe depression, which was triggered in 1873 by the bankruptcy of the Northern Pacific Railroad and its main investor, Jay Cooke. Both Cooke's privileged role as financier of the Civil War and the generous federal subsidies to the Northern Pacific suggested to many economically pressed Americans that Republican financial manipulation had caused the depression. Grant's administration responded ineffectually, rebuffing the pleas of debtors for relief by increasing the money supply (see Chapter 19).

Among the casualties of the bad economy was the Freedman's Savings and Trust Company, which held the small deposits of thousands of ex-slaves. When the bank failed in 1874, Congress refused to compensate the depositors, and many lost their life savings. In denying their pathetic pleas, Congress was signaling also that Reconstruction had lost its moral claim on the country. National politics had moved on; not the South, but rather concerns about the economy and political fraud absorbed the northern voter as another presidential election approached in 1876.

## The Political Crisis of 1877

Abandoning Grant, the Republicans nominated Rutherford B. Hayes, governor of Ohio, a colorless figure but untainted by corruption or by strong convictions—in a word, a safe man. His Democratic opponent was Samuel J. Tilden, governor of New York, a wealthy lawyer with ties to Wall Street and a reform reputation for his role in cleaning up New York City politics. The Democrat Tilden, of course, favored **home rule** for the South but so, more discreetly, did the Republican Hayes. Reconstruction actually did not figure prominently in the campaign and was mostly subsumed under broader Democratic charges of "corrupt centralism" and "incapacity, waste, and fraud." By now Republicans had essentially written off the South. Not a lot was said about the states still ruled by Reconstruction governments—Florida, South Carolina, and Louisiana.

Once the returns started coming in on election night, however, those three states began to loom very large indeed. Tilden led in the popular vote and, victorious in key northern states, he seemed headed for the White House until sleepless politicians at Republican headquarters realized that if they kept Florida, South Carolina, and Louisiana, Hayes would win by a single electoral vote. Republicans still controlled the state election machinery and, citing Democratic fraud and intimidation, they certified Republican victories. The audacious announcement came forth from Republican headquarters: Hayes had carried Florida, South Carolina, and Louisiana and won the election. Newly elected Democratic officials also sent in electoral votes for Tilden, and, when Congress met in early 1877, it faced two sets of electoral votes from those states.

The Constitution does not provide for this contingency. All it says is that the president of the Senate (in 1877, a Republican) opens the electoral certificates before the House (Democratic) and the Senate (Republican) and that "the Votes shall then be counted" (Article 2, Section 1). Suspense gripped the country. There was talk of inside deals, of a new election, even of a violent coup. Just in case, the commander of the army, General William T. Sherman, deployed four artillery companies in Washington. Finally, Congress appointed an electoral commission to settle the question. The commission included seven Republicans, seven Democrats, and, as the deciding member, David Davis, a Supreme Court justice not known to have fixed party loyalties. Davis, however, disqualified himself by accepting an Illinois seat in the Senate. He was replaced by Republican justice Joseph P. Bradley, and by 8 to 7 the commission awarded the disputed votes to Hayes.

Outraged Democrats had one more trick up their sleeves. They controlled the House, and they stalled a final count of the electoral votes so as to prevent Hayes's inauguration on March 4. But a week before, secret Washington talks had begun between southern Democrats and Ohio Republicans representing Hayes. Everything turned on South Carolina and Louisiana, where rival governments were encamped at the state capitols, with federal soldiers holding the Democrats at bay. Exactly what deal was struck or how involved Hayes himself was will probably never be known, but on March 1 the House Democrats suddenly ended their delaying tactics, the ceremonial counting of votes went forward, and Hayes was inaugurated on schedule. He soon ordered the Union troops back to their barracks, the Republican governors in South Carolina and Louisiana fled the unprotected statehouses, and Democratic claimants took control. Reconstruction had ended.

In 1877 political leaders on all sides seemed ready to say that what Lincoln had called "the work" was complete. But for the former slaves, the work had only begun. Reconstruction turned out to have been a magnificent aberration, a leap beyond what most white Americans actually felt was due their black fellow citizens. Still, something real had been achieved—three rights-defining amendments to the Constitution, some elbow room to advance economically, and, not least, a stubborn confidence among blacks that, by their own efforts, they could lift themselves up. Things would, in fact, get worse before they got better, but the work of Reconstruction was imperishable and could never be erased.

| T I M E L I N E | | | |
|---|---|---|---|
| 1863 | Lincoln announces his Ten Percent Plan | 1868 | Impeachment crisis |
| 1864 | Wade-Davis Bill passed by Congress | | Fourteenth Amendment ratified |
| | Lincoln "pocket" vetoes Wade-Davis Bill | | Ulysses S. Grant elected president |
| 1865 | Freedmen's Bureau established | 1870 | Ku Klux Klan at peak of power |
| | Lincoln assassinated; Andrew Johnson succeeds as president | | Fifteenth Amendment ratified |
| | Johnson implements his restoration plan | 1872 | Grant's reelection |
| 1866 | Civil Rights Act passes over Johnson's veto | 1873 | Panic of 1873 ushers in depression of 1873–1877 |
| | Memphis riots | | |
| | Johnson makes disastrous "swing around the circle"; Democrats defeated in congressional elections | 1875 | Whiskey Ring scandal undermines Grant administration |
| 1867 | Reconstruction Act | 1877 | Compromise of 1877; Rutherford B. Hayes becomes president |
| | Tenure of Office Act | | Reconstruction ends |

# For Further Exploration

The best current book on Reconstruction is Eric Foner's major synthesis, *Reconstruction: America's Unfinished Revolution, 1863–1877* (1988), available also in a shorter version. *Black Reconstruction in America* (1935), by the African American activist and scholar W. E. B. Du Bois, deserves attention as the first book to challenge traditional racist interpretations of Reconstruction and stress the role of blacks in their own emancipation. For the presidential phase of Reconstruction, see Dan T. Carter, *When the War Was Over: The Failure of Self-Reconstruction in the South, 1865–1867* (1985). On the freedmen, Leon F. Litwack, *Been in the Storm So Long: The Aftermath of Slavery* (1979), provides a stirring account. More recent emancipation studies emphasize slavery as a labor system: Julie Saville, *The Work of Reconstruction: From Slave to Wage Laborer in South Carolina, 1860–1870* (1994), and Amy Dru Stanley, *From Bondage to Contract* (1999), which expands the discussion to show what the onset of wage labor meant for freedwomen. Eric Foner, *Nothing But Freedom: Emancipation and Its Legacy* (1983), helpfully places emancipation in a comparative context. William S. McFeely, *Grant: A Biography* (1981), deftly explains the politics of Reconstruction. The emergence of the sharecropping system is explored in Gavin Wright, *Old South, New South* (1986), and Edward Royce, *The Origins of Southern Sharecropping* (1993). On the Compromise of 1877, see C. Vann Woodward's classic *Reunion and Reaction* (1956). Two informative Web sites are <http://womhis.binghampton.edu/intro.htm>, which deals with northern women who assisted the freedpeople, and <http://lcweb2.loc.gov/ammen/aaohtml/aollist.html>, which provides Library of Congress documents and illustrations on African Americans during Reconstruction.

---

For definitions of key terms boldfaced in this chapter, see the glossary at the end of the book.

To assess your mastery of the material covered in this chapter, see the Online Study Guide at **bedfordstmartins.com/henrettaconcise**.

For map resources and primary documents, see **bedfordstmartins.com/henrettaconcise**.

# DOCUMENTS

# The Declaration of Independence

## *The Unanimous Declaration of the Thirteen United States of America*

When in the Course of human events, it becomes necessary for one people to dissolve the political bands which have connected them with another, and to assume among the Powers of the earth, the separate and equal station to which the Laws of Nature and of Nature's God entitle them, a decent respect to the opinions of mankind requires that they should declare the causes which impel them to the separation.

We hold these truths to be self-evident, that all men are created equal, that they are endowed by their Creator with certain unalienable rights, that among these are Life, Liberty, and the pursuit of Happiness. That to secure these rights, Governments are instituted among Men, deriving their just powers from the consent of the governed. That whenever any Form of Government becomes destructive of these ends, it is the Right of the People to alter or to abolish it, and to institute new Government, laying its foundation on such principles and organizing its powers in such form, as to them shall seem most likely to effect their Safety and Happiness. Prudence, indeed, will dictate that Governments long established should not be changed for light and transient causes; and accordingly all experience hath shown, that mankind are more disposed to suffer, while evils are sufferable, than to right themselves by abolishing the forms to which they are accustomed. But when a long train of abuses and usurpations, pursuing invariably the same Object evinces a design to reduce them under absolute Despotism, it is their right, it is their duty, to throw off such Government, and to provide new Guards for their future security. —Such has been the patient sufferance of these Colonies; and such is now the necessity which constrains them to alter their former Systems of Government. The history of the present King of Great Britain is a history of repeated injuries and usurpations, all having in direct object the establishment of an absolute Tyranny over these States. To prove this, let Facts be submitted to a candid world.

He has refused his Assent to Laws, the most wholesome and necessary for the public good.

He has forbidden his Governors to pass Laws of immediate and pressing importance, unless suspended in their operation till his Assent should be obtained; and, when so suspended, he has utterly neglected to attend to them.

He has refused to pass other Laws for the accommodation of large districts of people, unless those people would relinquish the right of Representation in the Legislature, a right inestimable to them and formidable to tyrants only.

He has called together legislative bodies at places unusual, uncomfortable, and distant from the depository of their public Records, for the sole purpose of fatiguing them into compliance with his measures.

He has dissolved Representative Houses repeatedly, for opposing with manly firmness his invasions on the rights of the people.

He has refused for a long time, after such dissolutions, to cause others to be elected; whereby the Legislative powers, incapable of Annihilation, have returned to the People at large for their exercise; the State remaining in the mean time exposed to all the dangers of invasion from without and convulsions within.

He has endeavoured to prevent the population of these States; for that purpose obstructing the Laws of Naturalization of Foreigners; refusing to pass others to encourage their migrations hither, and raising the conditions of new Appropriations of Lands.

He has obstructed the Administration of Justice, by refusing his Assent to Laws for establishing Judiciary powers.

He has made Judges dependent on his Will alone, for the tenure of their offices, and the amount and payment of their salaries.

He has erected a multitude of New Offices, and sent hither swarms of Officers to harass our People, and eat out their substance.

He has kept among us, in times of peace, Standing Armies without the Consent of our legislature.

He has combined with others to subject us to a jurisdiction foreign to our constitution, and unacknowledged by our laws; giving his Assent to their Acts of pretended Legislation:

For quartering large bodies of armed troops among us:

For protecting them, by a mock Trial, from Punishment for any Murders which they should commit on the Inhabitants of these States:

For cutting off our Trade with all parts of the world:

For imposing taxes on us without our Consent:

For depriving us in many cases, of the benefits of Trial by jury:

For transporting us beyond Seas to be tried for pretended offences:

For abolishing the free System of English Laws in a neighbouring Province, establishing therein an Arbitrary government, and enlarging its Boundaries so as to render it at once an example and fit instrument for introducing the same absolute rule into these Colonies:

For taking away our Charters, abolishing our most valuable Laws, and altering fundamentally the Forms of our Governments:

For suspending our own Legislatures, and declaring themselves invested with Power to legislate for us in all cases whatsoever.

He has abdicated Government here, by declaring us out of his Protection and waging War against us.

He has plundered our seas, ravaged our Coasts, burnt our towns, and destroyed the lives of our people.

He is at this time transporting large armies of foreign mercenaries to compleat the works of death, desolation, and tyranny, already begun with circumstances of Cruelty & perfidy scarcely paralleled in the most barbarous ages, and totally unworthy the Head of a civilized nation.

He has constrained our fellow Citizens taken Captive on the high Seas to bear Arms against their Country, to become the executioners of their friends and Brethren, or to fall themselves by their Hands.

He has excited domestic insurrections amongst us, and has endeavoured to bring on the inhabitants of our frontiers, the merciless Indian Savages, whose known rule of warfare, is an undistinguished destruction of all ages, sexes, and conditions.

In every stage of these Oppressions We have Petitioned for Redress in the most humble terms: Our repeated petitions have been answered only by repeated injury. A Prince, whose character is thus marked by every act which may define a Tyrant, is unfit to be the ruler of a free people.

Nor have We been wanting in attention to our British brethren. We have warned them from time to time of attempts by their legislature to extend an unwarrantable jurisdiction over us. We have reminded them of the circumstances of our emigration and settlement here. We have appealed to their native justice and magnanimity, and we have conjured them by the ties of our common kindred to disavow these usurpations, which, would inevitably interrupt our connections and correspondence. They too have been deaf to the voice of justice and of consanguinity. We must, therefore, acquiesce in the necessity, which denounces our Separation, and hold them, as we hold the rest of mankind, Enemies in War, in Peace Friends.

We, therefore, the Representatives of the United States of America, in General Congress, Assembled, appealing to the Supreme Judge of the world for the rectitude of our intentions, do, in the Name, and by Authority of the good People of these Colonies, solemnly publish and declare, That these United Colonies are, and of Right ought to be FREE AND INDEPENDENT STATES; that they are Absolved from all Allegiance to the British Crown, and that all political connection between them and the State of Great Britain, is and ought to be totally dissolved; and that as Free and Independent States, they have full Power to levy War, conclude Peace, contract Alliances, establish Commerce, and to do all other Acts and Things which Independent States may of right do. And for the support of this Declaration, with a firm reliance on the Protection of Divine Providence, we mutually pledge to each other our Lives, our Fortunes, and our sacred Honor.

**John Hancock**

| | | | |
|---|---|---|---|
| **Button Gwinnett** | **George Wythe** | **James Wilson** | **Josiah Bartlett** |
| **Lyman Hall** | **Richard Henry Lee** | **Geo. Ross** | **Wm. Whipple** |
| **Geo. Walton** | **Th. Jefferson** | **Caesar Rodney** | **Saml. Adams** |
| **Wm. Hooper** | **Benja. Harrison** | **Geo. Read** | **John Adams** |
| **Joseph Hewes** | **Thos. Nelson, Jr.** | **Thos. M'Kean** | **Robt. Treat Paine** |
| **John Penn** | **Francis Lightfoot Lee** | **Wm. Floyd** | **Elbridge Gerry** |
| **Edward Rutledge** | **Carter Braxton** | **Phil. Livingston** | **Step. Hopkins** |
| **Thos. Heyward, Junr.** | **Robt. Morris** | **Frans. Lewis** | **William Ellery** |
| **Thomas Lynch, Junr.** | **Benjamin Rush** | **Lewis Morris** | **Roger Sherman** |
| **Arthur Middleton** | **Benja. Franklin** | **Richd. Stockton** | **Sam'el Huntington** |
| **Samuel Chase** | **John Morton** | **Jno. Witherspoon** | **Wm. Williams** |
| **Wm. Paca** | **Geo. Clymer** | **Fras. Hopkinson** | **Oliver Wolcott** |
| **Thos. Stone** | **Jas. Smith** | **John Hart** | **Matthew Thornton** |
| **Charles Carroll**<br>**of Carrollton** | **Geo. Taylor** | **Abra. Clark** | |

# The Articles of Confederation and Perpetual Union

Between the states of New Hampshire, Massachusetts Bay, Rhode Island and Providence Plantations, Connecticut, New York, New Jersey, Pennsylvania, Delaware, Maryland, Virginia, North Carolina, South Carolina, Georgia.*

### ARTICLE 1

The stile of this confederacy shall be "The United States of America."

### ARTICLE 2

Each State retains its sovereignty, freedom and independence, and every power, jurisdiction, and right, which is not by this confederation expressly delegated to the United States, in Congress assembled.

### ARTICLE 3

The said states hereby severally enter into a firm league of friendship with each other for their common defence, the security of their liberties and their mutual and general welfare; binding themselves to assist each other against all force offered to, or attacks made upon them, or any of them, on account of religion, sovereignty, trade, or any other pretence whatever.

### ARTICLE 4

The better to secure and perpetuate mutual friendship and intercourse among the people of the different states in this union, the free inhabitants of each of these states, paupers, vagabonds, and fugitives from justice excepted, shall be entitled to all privileges and immunities of free citizens in the several states; and the people of each State shall have free ingress and regress to and from any other State, and shall enjoy therein all the privileges of trade and commerce, subject to the same duties, impositions, and restrictions, as the inhabitants thereof respectively; provided, that such restrictions shall not extend so far as to prevent the removal of property, imported into any State, to any other State of which the owner is an inhabitant; provided also, that no imposition, duties, or restriction, shall be laid by any State on the property of the United States, or either of them.

If any person guilty of, or charged with treason, felony, or other high misdemeanor in any State, shall flee from justice and be found in any of the United States, he shall, upon demand of the governor or executive power of the State from which he fled, be delivered up and removed to the State having jurisdiction of his offence.

Full faith and credit shall be given in each of these states to the records, acts, and judicial proceedings of the courts and magistrates of every other State.

### ARTICLE 5

For the more convenient management of the general interests of the United States, delegates shall be annually appointed, in such manner as the legislature of each State shall direct, to

---

*This copy of the final draft of the Articles of Confederation is taken from the *Journals,* 9:907–25, November 15, 1777.

meet in Congress, on the 1st Monday in November in every year, with a power reserved to each State to recall its delegates, or any of them, at any time within the year, and to send others in their stead for the remainder of the year.

No State shall be represented in Congress by less than two, nor by more than seven members; and no person shall be capable of being a delegate for more than three years in any term of six years; nor shall any person, being a delegate, be capable of holding any office under the United States, for which he, or any other for his benefit, receives any salary, fees, or emolument of any kind.

Each State shall maintain its own delegates in a meeting of the states, and while they act as members of the committee of the states.

In determining questions in the United States, in Congress assembled, each State shall have one vote.

Freedom of speech and debate in Congress shall not be impeached or questioned in any court or place out of Congress: and the members of Congress shall be protected in their persons from arrests and imprisonments, during the time of their going to and from, and attendance on Congress, except for treason, felony, or breach of the peace.

## ARTICLE 6

No State, without the consent of the United States, in Congress assembled, shall send any embassy to, or receive any embassy from, or enter into any conference, agreement, alliance, or treaty with any king, prince, or state; nor shall any person, holding any office of profit or trust under the United States, or any of them, accept of any present, emolument, office or title, of any kind whatever, from any king, prince, or foreign state; nor shall the United States, in Congress assembled, or any of them, grant any title of nobility.

No two or more states shall enter into any treaty, confederation, or alliance, whatever, between them, without the consent of the United States, in Congress assembled, specifying accurately the purposes for which the same is to be entered into, and how long it shall continue.

No state shall lay any imposts or duties which may interfere with any stipulations in treaties entered into by the United States, in Congress assembled, with any king, prince, or state, in pursuance of any treaties already proposed by Congress to the courts of France and Spain.

No vessels of war shall be kept up in time of peace by any State, except such number only as shall be deemed necessary by the United States, in Congress assembled, for the defence of such State or its trade; nor shall any body of forces be kept up by any State, in time of peace, except such number only as, in the judgment of the United States, in Congress assembled, shall be deemed requisite to garrison the forts necessary for the defence of such State; but every State shall always keep up a well regulated and disciplined militia, sufficiently armed and accoutred, and shall provide, and constantly have ready for use, in public stores, a due number of field pieces and tents, and a proper quantity of arms, ammunition and camp equipage.

No State shall engage in any war without the consent of the United States, in Congress assembled, unless such State be actually invaded by enemies, or shall have received certain advice of a resolution being formed by some nation of Indians to invade such State, and the danger is so imminent as not to admit of a delay till the United States, in Congress assembled, can be consulted; nor shall any State grant commissions to any ships or vessels of war, nor letters of marque or reprisal, except it be after a declaration of war by the United States, in Congress assembled, and then only against the kingdom or state, and the subjects thereof, against which war has been so declared, and under such regulations as shall be established by the United States, in Congress assembled, unless such State be infested by pirates, in which case vessels of war may be fitted out for that occasion, and kept so long as the danger shall continue, or until the United States, in Congress assembled, shall determine otherwise.

## ARTICLE 7

When land forces are raised by any State for the common defence, all officers of or under the rank of colonel, shall be appointed by the legislature of each State respectively, by whom such forces shall be raised, or in such manner as such State shall direct; and all vacancies shall be filled up by the State which first made the appointment.

## ARTICLE 8

All charges of war and all other expences, that shall be incurred for the common defence or general welfare, and allowed by the United States, in Congress assembled, shall be defrayed out of a common treasury, which shall be supplied by the several states, in proportion to the value of all land within each State, granted to or surveyed for any person, as such land and the buildings and improvements thereon shall be estimated according to such mode as the United States, in Congress assembled, shall, from time to time, direct and appoint.

The taxes for paying that proportion shall be laid and levied by the authority and direction of the legislatures of the several states, within the time agreed upon by the United States, in Congress assembled.

## ARTICLE 9

The United States, in Congress assembled, shall have the sole and exclusive right and power of determining on peace and war, except in the cases mentioned in the 6th article; of sending and receiving ambassadors; entering into treaties and alliances, provided that no treaty of commerce shall be made, whereby the legislative power of the respective states shall be restrained from imposing such imposts and duties on foreigners as their own people are subjected to, or from prohibiting the exportation or importation of any species of goods or commodities whatsoever; of establishing rules for deciding, in all cases, what captures on land or water shall be legal, and in what manner prizes, taken by land or naval forces in the service of the United States, shall be divided or appropriated; or granting letters of marque and reprisal in times of peace; appointing courts for the trial of piracies and felonies committed on the high seas, and establishing courts for receiving and determining, finally, appeals in all cases of captures; provided, that no member of Congress shall be appointed a judge of any of the said courts.

The United States, in Congress assembled, shall also be the last resort on appeal in all disputes and differences now subsisting, or that hereafter may arise between two or more states concerning boundary, jurisdiction or any other cause whatever; which authority shall always be exercised in the manner following: whenever the legislative or executive authority, or lawful agent of any State, in controversy with another, shall present a petition to Congress, stating the matter in question, and praying for a hearing, notice thereof shall be given, by order of Congress, to the legislative of executive authority of the other State in controversy, and a day assigned for the appearance of the parties by their lawful agents, who shall then be directed to appoint, by joint consent, commissioners or judges to constitute a court for hearing and determining the matter in question; but, if they cannot agree, Congress shall name three persons out of each of the United States, and from the list of such persons each party shall alternately strike out one, the petitioners beginning, until the number shall be reduced to thirteen; and from that number not less than seven, nor more than nine names, as Congress shall direct, shall, in the presence of Congress, be drawn out by lot; and the persons whose names shall be so drawn, or any five of them, shall be commissioners or judges to hear and finally determine the controversy, so always as a major part of the judges who shall hear the cause shall agree in the determination; and if either party shall neglect to attend at the day appointed, without shewing reasons which Congress shall judge sufficient, or, being present, shall refuse to strike, the Congress shall proceed to nominate three persons out of each State, and the secretary of Congress shall strike in behalf of such party absent or refusing; and the judgment and sentence of the court to be appointed, in the manner before prescribed, shall be final and conclusive; and if any of the parties shall refuse to submit to the authority of such court, or to appear or defend their claim or cause, the court shall nevertheless proceed to pronounce sentence or judgment, which shall, in like manner, be final and decisive, the judgment or sentence and other proceedings begin, in either case, transmitted to Congress, and lodged among the acts of Congress for the security of the parties concerned: provided, that every commissioner, before he sits in judgment, shall take an oath, to be administered by one of the judges of the supreme or superior court of the State where the cause shall be tried, "well and truly to hear and determine the matter in question, according to the best of his judgment, without favour, affection, or hope of reward:" provided, also, that no State shall be deprived of territory for the benefit of the United States.

All controversies concerning the private right of soil, claimed under different grants of two or more states, whose jurisdictions, as they may respect such lands and the states which passed such grants, are adjusted, the said grants, or either of them, being at the same time claimed to have originated antecedent to such settlement of jurisdiction, shall, on the petition of either party to the Congress of the United States, be finally determined, as near as may be, in the same manner as is before prescribed for deciding disputes respecting territorial jurisdiction between different states.

The United States, in Congress assembled, shall also have the sole and exclusive right and power of regulating the alloy and value of coin struck by their own authority, or by that of the respective states; fixing the standard of weights and measures throughout the United States; regulating the trade and managing all affairs with the Indians not members of any of the states; provided that the legislative right of any State within its own limits be not infringed or violated; establishing and regulating post offices from one State to another throughout all the United States, and exacting such postage on the papers passing through the same as may be requisite to defray the expences of the said office; appointing all officers of the land forces in the service of the United States, excepting regimental officers; appointing all the officers of the naval forces, and commissioning all officers whatever in the service of the United States; making rules for the government and regulation of the said land and naval forces, and directing their operations.

The United States, in Congress assembled, shall have authority to appoint a committee to sit in the recess of Congress, to be denominated "a Committee of the States," and to consist of one delegate from each State, and to appoint such other committees and civil officers as may be necessary for managing the general affairs of the United States, under their direction; to appoint one of their number to preside; provided that no person be allowed to serve in the office of president more than one year in any term of three years; to ascertain the necessary sums of money to be raised for the service of the United States, and to appropriate and apply the same for defraying the public expences; to borrow money or emit bills on the credit of the United States, transmitting, every half year, to the respective states, an account of the sums of money so borrowed or emitted; to build and equip a navy; to agree upon the number of land forces, and to make requisitions from each State for in quota, in proportion to the number of white inhabitants in such State; which requisitions shall be binding; and thereupon, the legislature of each State shall appoint the regimental officers, raise the men, and cloathe, arm, and equip them in a soldier-like manner, at the expence of the United States; and the officers and men so cloathed, armed, and equipped, shall march to the place appointed and within the time agreed on by the United States, in Congress assembled; but if the United States, in Congress assembled, shall, on consideration of circumstances, judge proper that any State should not raise men, or should raise a smaller number than its quota, and that any other State should raise a greater number of men than the quota thereof, such extra number shall be raised, officered, cloathed, armed, and equipped in the same manner as the quota of such State, unless the legislature of such State shall judge that such extra number cannot be safely spared out of the same, in which case they shall raise, officer, cloathe, arm, and equip as many of such extra number as they judge can be safely spared. And the officers and men so cloathed, armed, and equipped, shall march to the place appointed and within the time agreed on by the United States, in Congress assembled.

The United States, in Congress assembled, shall never engage in a war, nor grant letters of marque and reprisal in time of peace, nor enter into any treaties or alliances, nor coin money, nor regulate the value thereof, nor ascertain the sums and expences necessary for the defence and welfare of the United States, or any of them: nor emit bills, nor borrow money on the credit of the United States, nor appropriate money, nor agree upon the number of vessels of war to be built or purchased, or the number of land or sea forces to be raised, nor appoint a commander in chief of the army or navy, unless nine states assent to the same; nor shall a question on any other point, except for adjourning from day to day, be determined, unless by the votes of a majority of the United States, in Congress assembled.

The Congress of the United States shall have power to adjourn to any time within the year, and to any place within the United States, so that no period of adjournment be for a longer duration than the space of six months, and shall publish the journal of their proceedings monthly, except such parts thereof, relating to treaties, alliances or military operations, as, in their judgment, require secrecy; and the yeas and nays of the delegates of each State on any question shall be entered on the journal, when it is desired by any delegate; and the delegates of a State, or any of them, at his, or their request, shall be furnished with a transcript of the said journal, except such parts as are above excepted, to lay before the legislatures of the several states.

## ARTICLE 10

The committee of the states, or any nine of them, shall be authorized to execute, in the recess of Congress, such of the powers of Congress as the United States, in Congress assembled, by the consent of nine states, shall, from time to time, think expedient to vest them with; provided, that no power be delegated to the said committee, for the exercise of which, by the articles of confederation, the voice of nine states, in the Congress of the United States assembled, is requisite.

## ARTICLE 11

Canada acceding to this confederation, and joining in the measures of the United States, shall be admitted into and entitled to all the advantages of this union; but no other colony shall be admitted into the same, unless such admission be agreed to by nine states.

## Article 12

All bills of credit emitted, monies borrowed and debts contracted by, or under the authority of Congress before the assembling of the United States, in pursuance of the present confederation, shall be deemed and considered as a charge against the United States, for payment and satisfaction whereof the said United States and the public faith are hereby solemnly pledged.

## Article 13

Every State shall abide by the determinations of the United States, in Congress assembled, on all questions which, by this confederation, are submitted to them. And the articles of this confederation shall be inviolably observed by every State, and the union shall be perpetual; nor shall any alteration at any time hereafter be made in any of them, unless such alteration be agreed to in a Congress of the United States, and be afterwards confirmed by the legislatures of every State.

These articles shall be proposed to the legislatures of all the United States, to be considered, and if approved of by them, they are advised to authorize their delegates to ratify the same in the Congress of the United States; which being done, the same shall become conclusive.

# The Constitution of the United States

We the People of the United States, in Order to form a more perfect Union, establish Justice, insure domestic Tranquility, provide for the common defence, promote the general Welfare, and secure the Blessings of Liberty to ourselves and our Posterity, do ordain and establish this Constitution for the United States of America.

## Article I

*Section 1*

All legislative Powers herein granted shall be vested in a Congress of the United States, which shall consist of a Senate and a House of Representatives.

*Section 2*

The House of Representatives shall be composed of Members chosen every second Year by the People of the several States, and the Electors in each State shall have the Qualifications requisite for Electors of the most numerous Branch of the State Legislature.

No Person shall be a Representative who shall not have attained to the Age of twenty-five Years, and been seven Years a Citizen of the United States, and who shall not, when elected, be an Inhabitant of that State in which he shall be chosen.

Representatives and direct Taxes shall be apportioned among the several States which may be included within this Union, according to their respective Numbers, *which shall be determined by adding to the whole Number of free Persons, including those bound to Service for a Term of Years, and excluding Indians not taxed, three fifths of all other Persons.** The

---

*Note:* The Constitution became effective March 4, 1789. Provisions in italics have been changed by constitutional amendment.

*Changed by Section 2 of the Fourteenth Amendment.

actual Enumeration shall be made within three Years after the first Meeting of the Congress of the United States, and within every subsequent Term of ten Years, in such Manner as they shall by Law direct. The Number of Representatives shall not exceed one for every thirty Thousand, but each State shall have at Least one Representative; and *until such enumeration shall be made, the State of New Hampshire shall be entitled to chuse three, Massachusetts eight, Rhode Island and Providence Plantations one, Connecticut five, New-York six, New Jersey four, Pennsylvania eight, Delaware one, Maryland six, Virginia ten, North Carolina five, South Carolina five, and Georgia three.*

When vacancies happen in the Representation from any State, the Executive Authority thereof shall issue Writs of Election to fill such Vacancies.

The House of Representatives shall chuse their Speaker and other Officers; and shall have the sole Power of Impeachment.

### Section 3

The Senate of the United States shall be composed of two Senators from each State, *chosen by the Legislature thereof,** for six Years; and each Senator shall have one Vote.

*Immediately after they shall be assembled in Consequence of the first Election, they shall be divided as equally as may be into three Classes. The Seats of the Senators of the first Class shall be vacated at the Expiration of the second Year, of the second Class at the Expiration of the fourth Year, and of the third Class at the Expiration of the sixth Year,* so that one-third may be chosen every second Year; *and if Vacancies happen by Resignation, or otherwise, during the Recess of the Legislature of any State, the Executive thereof may make temporary Appointments until the next Meeting of the Legislature, which shall then fill such Vacancies.*†

No person shall be a Senator who shall not have attained to the Age of thirty Years, and been nine Years a Citizen of the United States, and who shall not, when elected, be an Inhabitant of that State for which he shall be chosen.

The Vice President of the United States shall be President of the Senate, but shall have no Vote, unless they be equally divided.

The Senate shall chuse their other Officers, and also a President pro tempore, in the absence of the Vice President, or when he shall exercise the Office of President of the United States.

The Senate shall have the sole Power to try all Impeachments. When sitting for that Purpose, they shall be on Oath or Affirmation. When the President of the United States is tried, the Chief Justice shall preside: And no Person shall be convicted without the Concurrence of two thirds of the Members present.

Judgment in Cases of Impeachment shall not extend further than to removal from Office, and disqualification to hold and enjoy any Office of honor, Trust or Profit under the United States: but the Party convicted shall nevertheless be liable and subject to Indictment, Trial, Judgment and Punishment, according to Law.

### Section 4

The Times, Places and Manner of holding Elections for Senators and Representatives, shall be prescribed in each State by the Legislature thereof, but the Congress may at any time by Law make or alter such Regulations, except as to the Places of Chusing Senators.

---

*Changed by Section 1 of the Seventeenth Amendment.

†Changed by Clause 2 of the Seventeenth Amendment.

The Congress shall assemble at least once in every Year, and such Meeting *shall be on the first Monday in December, unless they shall by Law appoint a different Day.**

### Section 5

Each House shall be the Judge of the Elections, Returns and Qualifications of its own Members, and a Majority of each shall constitute a Quorum to do Business; but a smaller number may adjourn from day to day, and may be authorized to compel the Attendance of absent Members, in such Manner, and under such Penalties, as each House may provide.

Each House may determine the Rules of its Proceedings, punish its Members for disorderly Behavior, and, with the Concurrence of two thirds, expel a Member.

Each House shall keep a Journal of its Proceedings, and from time to time publish the same, excepting such Parts as may in their Judgment require Secrecy; and the Yeas and Nays of the Members of either House on any question shall, at the Desire of one-fifth of those Present, be entered on the Journal.

Neither House, during the Session of Congress, shall, without the Consent of the other, adjourn for more than three days, nor to any other Place than that in which the two Houses shall be sitting.

### Section 6

The Senators and Representatives shall receive a Compensation for their Services, to be ascertained by Law, and paid out of the Treasury of the United States. They shall in all Cases, except Treason, Felony and Breach of the Peace, be privileged from Arrest during their Attendance at the Session of their respective Houses, and in going to and returning from the same; and for any Speech or Debate in either House, they shall not be questioned in any other Place.

No Senator or Representative shall, during the Time for which he was elected, be appointed to any civil Office under the Authority of the United States, which shall have been created, or the Emoluments whereof shall have been increased, during such time; and no Person holding any Office under the United States, shall be a Member of either House during his Continuance in Office.

### Section 7

All Bills for raising Revenue shall originate in the House of Representatives; but the Senate may propose or concur with Amendments as on other Bills.

Every Bill which shall have passed the House of Representatives and the Senate, shall, before it becomes a Law, be presented to the President of the United States; If he approve he shall sign it, but if not he shall return it, with his Objections to that House in which it shall have originated, who shall enter the Objections at large on their Journal, and proceed to reconsider it. If after such Reconsideration two thirds of that House shall agree to pass the Bill, it shall be sent, together with the Objections, to the other House, by which it shall likewise be reconsidered, and if approved by two thirds of that House, it shall become a Law. But in all such Cases the Votes of both Houses shall be determined by Yeas and Nays, and the Names of the Persons voting for and against the Bill shall be entered on the Journal of each House respectively. If any Bill shall not be returned by the President within ten Days (Sundays excepted) after it shall have

---

*Changed by Section 2 of the Twentieth Amendment.

been presented to him, the Same shall be a Law, in like Manner as if he had signed it, unless the Congress by their Adjournment prevent its Return, in which Case it shall not be a Law.

Every Order, Resolution, or Vote to which the Concurrence of the Senate and the House of Representatives may be necessary (except on a question of Adjournment) shall be presented to the President of the United States; and before the Same shall take Effect, shall be approved by him, or being disapproved by him, shall be repassed by two thirds of the Senate and House of Representatives, according to the Rules and Limitations prescribed in the Case of a Bill.

*Section 8*

The Congress shall have Power To lay and collect Taxes, Duties, Imposts and Excises, to pay the Debts and provide for the common Defence and general Welfare of the United States; but all Duties, Imposts and Excises shall be uniform throughout the United States;

To borrow money on the credit of the United States;

To regulate Commerce with foreign Nations, and among the several States, and with the Indian Tribes;

To establish an uniform Rule of Naturalization, and uniform Laws on the subject of Bankruptcies throughout the United States;

To coin Money, regulate the Value thereof, and of foreign Coin, and fix the Standard of Weights and Measures;

To provide for the Punishment of counterfeiting the Securities and current Coin of the United States;

To establish Post Offices and post Roads;

To promote the Progress of Science and useful Arts, by securing for limited Times to Authors and Inventors the exclusive Right to their respective Writings and Discoveries;

To constitute Tribunals inferior to the supreme Court;

To define and punish Piracies and Felonies committed on the high Seas, and Offenses against the Law of Nations;

To declare War, grant Letters of Marque and Reprisal, and make Rules concerning Captures on Land and Water;

To raise and support Armies, but no Appropriation of Money to that Use shall be for a longer Term than two Years;

To provide and maintain a Navy;

To make Rules for the Government and Regulation of the land and naval Forces;

To provide for calling forth the Militia to execute the Laws of the Union, suppress Insurrections and repel Invasions;

To provide for organizing, arming, and disciplining the Militia, and for governing such Part of them as may be employed in the Service of the United States, reserving to the States respectively, the Appointment of the Officers, and the Authority of training the Militia according to the discipline prescribed by Congress;

To exercise exclusive Legislation in all Cases whatsoever, over such District (not exceeding ten Miles square) as may, by Cession of particular States, and the acceptance of Congress, become the Seat of Government of the United States, and to exercise like Authority over all Places purchased by the Consent of the Legislature of the State in which the Same shall be, for the Erection of Forts, Magazines, Arsenals, dock-Yards, and other needful Buildings;—And

To make all Laws which shall be necessary and proper for carrying into Execution the foregoing Powers, and all other Powers vested by this Constitution in the Government of the United States, or in any Department or Officer thereof.

*Section 9*

*The Migration or Importation of such Persons as any of the States now existing shall think proper to admit, shall not be prohibited by the Congress prior to the Year one thousand eight hundred and eight but a tax or duty may be imposed on such Importation, not exceeding ten dollars for each Person.*

The privilege of the Writ of Habeas Corpus shall not be suspended, unless when in Cases of Rebellion or Invasion the public Safety may require it.

No Bill of Attainder or ex post facto Law shall be passed.

No capitation, or other direct, Tax shall be laid, unless in Proportion to the Census or Enumeration herein before directed to be taken.*

No Tax or Duty shall be laid on Articles exported from any State.

No Preference shall be given by any Regulation of Commerce or Revenue to the Ports of one State over those of another: nor shall Vessels bound to, or from, one State, be obliged to enter, clear, or pay Duties in another.

No Money shall be drawn from the Treasury, but in Consequence of Appropriations made by law; and a regular Statement and Account of the Receipts and Expenditures of all public Money shall be published from time to time.

No Title of Nobility shall be granted by the United States: And no Person holding any Office of Profit or Trust under them, shall, without the Consent of the Congress, accept of any present, Emolument, Office, or Title, of any kind whatever, from any King, Prince, or foreign State.

*Section 10*

No State shall enter into any Treaty, Alliance, or Confederation; grant Letters of Marque and Reprisal; coin Money; emit Bills of Credit; make any Thing but gold and silver Coin a Tender in Payment of Debts; pass any Bill of Attainder, ex post facto Law, or Law impairing the Obligation of Contracts, or grant any Title of Nobility.

No State shall, without the Consent of the Congress, lay any Imposts or Duties on Imports or Exports, except what may be absolutely necessary for executing its inspection Laws: and the net Produce of all Duties and Imposts, laid by any State on Imports or Exports, shall be for the Use of the Treasury of the United States; and all such Laws shall be subject to the Revision and Control of the Congress.

No State shall, without the Consent of the Congress, lay any duty of Tonnage, keep Troops, or Ships of War in time of Peace, enter into any Agreement or Compact with another State, or with a foreign Power, or engage in War, unless actually invaded, or in such imminent Danger as will not admit of delay.

## ARTICLE II

*Section 1*

The executive Power shall be vested in a President of the United States of America. He shall hold his Office during the Term of four Years, and, together with the Vice President, chosen for the same Term, be elected, as follows:

Each State shall appoint, in such Manner as the Legislature thereof may direct, a Number of Electors, equal to the whole Number of Senators and Representatives to which the

---

*Changed by the Sixteenth Amendment.

State may be entitled in the Congress; but no Senator or Representative, or Person holding an Office of Trust or Profit under the United States, shall be appointed an Elector.

*The Electors shall meet in their respective States, and vote by Ballot for two Persons, of whom one at least shall not be an Inhabitant of the same State with themselves. And they shall make a List of all the Persons voted for, and of the Number of Votes for each; which List they shall sign and certify, and transmit sealed to the Seat of the Government of the United States, directed to the President of the Senate. The President of the Senate shall, in the Presence of the Senate and House of Representatives, open all the Certificates, and the Votes shall then be counted. The Person having the greatest Number of Votes shall be the President, if such Number be a Majority of the whole Number of Electors appointed; and if there be more than one who have such Majority, and have an equal Number of Votes, then the House of Representatives shall immediately chuse by Ballot one of them for President; and if no Person have a Majority, then from the five highest on the List the said House shall in like Manner chuse the President. But in chusing the President, the Votes shall be taken by States, the Representation from each State having one Vote; a quorum for this Purpose shall consist of a Member or Members from two thirds of the States, and a Majority of all the States shall be necessary to a Choice. In every Case, after the Choice of the President, the Person having the greatest Number of Votes of the Electors shall be the Vice President. But if there should remain two or more who have equal Votes, the Senate shall chuse from them by Ballot the Vice President.**

The Congress may determine the Time of chusing the Electors, and the Day on which they shall give their Votes; which Day shall be the same throughout the United States.

No Person except a natural born Citizen, or a Citizen of the United States, at the time of the Adoption of this Constitution, shall be eligible to the Office of President; neither shall any Person be eligible to that Office who shall not have attained to the Age of thirty five Years, and been fourteen years a Resident within the United States.

In Case of the Removal of the President from Office, or of his Death, Resignation, or Inability to discharge the Powers and Duties of the said Office, the same shall devolve on the Vice President, *and the Congress may by Law provide for the Case of Removal, Death, Resignation, or Inability, both of the President and Vice President, declaring what Officer shall then act as President, and such Officer shall act accordingly, until the Disability be removed, or a President shall be elected.*†

The President shall, at stated Times, receive for his Services a Compensation, which shall neither be increased nor diminished during the Period for which he shall have been elected, and he shall not receive within that Period any other Emolument from the United States, or any of them.

Before he enter on the Execution of his Office, he shall take the following Oath or Affirmation:—"I do solemnly swear (or affirm) that I will faithfully execute the Office of President of the United States, and will to the best of my Ability, preserve, protect and defend the Constitution of the United States."

### Section 2

The President shall be Commander in Chief of the Army and Navy of the United States, and of the Militia of the several States, when called into the actual Service of the United States; he may require the Opinion, in writing, of the principal Officer in each of the executive

---

*Superseded by the Twelfth Amendment.

†Modified by the Twenty-fifth Amendment.

Departments, upon any Subject relating to the Duties of their respective Offices, and he shall have Power to Grant Reprieves and pardons for Offences against the United States, except in Cases of Impeachment.

He shall have Power, by and with the Advice and Consent of the Senate, to make Treaties, provided two thirds of the Senators present concur; and he shall nominate, and by and with the Advice and Consent of the Senate, shall appoint Ambassadors, other public Ministers and Consuls, Judges of the supreme Court, and all other Officers of the United States, whose Appointments are not herein otherwise provided for, and which shall be established by Law: but the Congress may by Law vest the Appointment of such inferior Officers, as they think proper, in the President alone, in the Courts of Law, or in the Heads of Departments.

The President shall have Power to fill up all Vacancies that may happen during the Recess of the Senate, by granting Commissions which shall expire at the End of their next Session.

*Section 3*

He shall from time to time give to the Congress Information of the State of the Union, and recommend to their Consideration such Measures as he shall judge necessary and expedient; he may, on extraordinary Occasions, convene both Houses, or either of them, and in Case of Disagreement between them, with Respect to the Time of Adjournment, he may adjourn them to such Time as he shall think proper; he shall receive Ambassadors and other public Ministers; he shall take Care that the Laws be faithfully executed, and shall Commission all the Officers of the United States.

*Section 4*

The President, Vice President and all civil Officers of the United States, shall be removed from Office on Impeachment for, and Conviction of, Treason, Bribery, or other high Crimes and Misdemeanors.

**ARTICLE III**

*Section 1*

The judicial Power of the United States, shall be vested in one supreme Court, and in such inferior Courts as the Congress may from time to time ordain and establish. The Judges, both of the supreme and inferior courts, shall hold their Offices during good Behaviour, and shall, at stated Times, receive for their Services a Compensation, which shall not be diminished during their Continuance in Office.

*Section 2*

The judicial Power shall extend to all Cases, in Law and Equity, arising under this Constitution, the Laws of the United States, and Treaties made, or which shall be made, under their Authority;—to all Cases affecting Ambassadors, other public Ministers and Consuls;—to all Cases of admiralty and maritime Jurisdiction;—to Controversies to which the United States shall be a Party;—to Controversies between two or more States;—*between a State and Citizens of another State,**—between Citizens of different States;—between Citizens of the

---

*Restricted by the Eleventh Amendment.

same State claiming Lands under Grants of different States, and between a State, or the Citizens thereof, and foreign States, Citizens or Subjects.

In all Cases affecting Ambassadors, other public Ministers and Consuls, and those in which a State shall be Party, the supreme Court shall have original Jurisdiction. In all the other Cases before mentioned, the supreme Court shall have appellate Jurisdiction, both as to Law and Fact, with such Exceptions, and under such Regulations as the Congress shall make.

The trial of all Crimes, except in Cases of Impeachment, shall be by Jury; and such Trial shall be held in the State where said Crimes shall have been committed; but when not committed within any State, the Trial shall be at such Place or Places as the Congress may by Law have directed.

### Section 3

Treason against the United States, shall consist only in levying War against them, or in adhering to their Enemies, giving them Aid and Comfort. No Person shall be convicted of Treason unless on the Testimony of two Witnesses to the same overt Act, or on Confession in open Court.

The Congress shall have Power to declare the Punishment of Treason, but no Attainder of Treason shall work Corruption of Blood, or Forefeiture except during the Life of the Person attainted.

## ARTICLE IV

### Section 1

Full Faith and Credit shall be given in each State to the public Acts, Records, and judicial Proceedings of every other State. And the Congress may by general Laws prescribe the Manner in which such Acts, Records, and Proceedings shall be proved, and the Effect thereof.

### Section 2

The Citizens of each State shall be entitled to all Privileges and Immunities of Citizens in the several States.

A Person charged in any State with Treason, Felony, or other Crime, who shall flee from Justice, and be found in another State, shall on demand of the executive Authority of the State from which he fled, be delivered up, to be removed to the State having Jurisdiction of the Crime.

*No Person held to Service or Labour in one State, under the Laws thereof, escaping into another, shall, in Consequence of any Law or Regulation therein, be discharged from such Service or Labour, but shall be delivered up on Claim of the Party to whom such Service or Labour may be due.** 

### Section 3

New States may be admitted by the Congress into this Union; but no new State shall be formed or erected within the Jurisdiction of any other State; nor any State be formed by the

---

*Superseded by the Thirteenth Amendment.

Junction of two or more States, or parts of States, without the Consent of the Legislatures of the States concerned as well as of the Congress.

The Congress shall have Power to dispose of and make all needful Rules and Regulations respecting the Territory or other Property belonging to the United States; and nothing in this Constitution shall be so construed as to Prejudice any Claims of the United States, or of any particular State.

### Section 4

The United States shall guarantee to every State in this Union a Republican Form of Government, and shall protect each of them against Invasion; and on Application of the Legislature, or of the Executive (when the Legislature cannot be convened) against domestic Violence.

## ARTICLE V

The Congress, whenever two thirds of both Houses shall deem it necessary, shall propose Amendments to this Constitution, or, on the Application of the Legislatures of two thirds of the several States, shall call a Convention for proposing Amendments, which, in either Case, shall be valid to all Intents and Purposes, as Part of this Constitution, when ratified by the Legislatures of three fourths of the several States, or by Conventions in three fourths thereof, as the one or the other Mode of Ratification may be proposed by the Congress; Provided that no Amendment which may be made prior to the Year One thousand eight hundred and eight shall in any Manner affect the first and fourth Clauses in the Ninth Section of the first Article; and that no State, without its Consent, shall be deprived of its equal Suffrage in the Senate.

## ARTICLE VI

All Debts contracted and Engagements entered into, before the Adoption of this Constitution, shall be as valid against the United States under this Constitution, as under the Confederation.

This Constitution, and the Laws of the United States which shall be made in Pursuance thereof; and all Treaties made, or which shall be made, under the Authority of the United States, shall be the supreme Law of the Land; and the Judges in every State shall be bound thereby, any Thing in the Constitution or Laws of any State to the Contrary notwithstanding.

The Senators and Representatives before mentioned, and the Members of the several State Legislatures, and all executive and judicial Officers, both of the United States and of the several States, shall be bound by Oath or Affirmation, to support this Constitution; but no religious Test shall ever be required as a Qualification to any Office or public Trust under the United States.

## ARTICLE VII

The Ratification of the Conventions of nine States shall be sufficient for the Establishment of this Constitution between the States so ratifying the Same.

Done in Convention by the Unanimous Consent of the States present the Seventeenth Day of September in the Year of our Lord one thousand seven hundred and Eighty seven and of the Independence of the United States of America the Twelfth. In Witness whereof We have hereunto subscribed our Names.

**Go. Washington**

President and deputy from Virginia

| New Hampshire | New Jersey | Delaware | North Carolina |
|---|---|---|---|
| John Langdon | Wil. Livingston | Geo. Read | Wm. Blount |
| Nicholas Gilman | David Brearley | Gunning Bedford jun | Richd. Dobbs Spaight |
| | Wm. Paterson | John Dickenson | Hu Williamson |
| Massachusetts | Jona. Dayton | Richard Bassett | |
| Nathaniel Gorham | | Jaco. Broom | South Carolina |
| Rufus King | Pennsylvania | | J. Rutledge |
| | B. Franklin | Maryland | Charles Cotesworth |
| Connecticut | Thomas Mifflin | James McHenry | Pickney |
| Wm. Saml. Johnson | Robt. Morris | Dan. of St. Thos. Jenifer | Pierce Butler |
| Roger Sherman | Geo. Clymer | Danl. Carroll | |
| | Thos. FitzSimons | | Georgia |
| New York | Jared Ingersoll | Virginia | William Few |
| Alexander Hamilton | James Wilson | John Blair | Abr. Baldwin |
| | Gouv. Morris | James Madison, Jr. | |

# Amendments to the Constitution

## AMENDMENT I [1791]*

Congress shall make no law respecting an establishment of religion, or prohibiting the free exercise thereof; or abridging the freedom of speech, or of the press; or the right of the people peaceably to assemble, and to petition the Government for a redress of grievances.

## AMENDMENT II [1791]

A well regulated Militia, being necessary to the security of a free State, the right of the people to keep and bear Arms shall not be infringed.

## AMENDMENT III [1791]

No Soldier shall, in time of peace, be quartered in any house, without the consent of the Owner, nor in time of war, but in a manner to be prescribed by law.

## AMENDMENT IV [1791]

The right of the people to be secure in their persons, houses, papers, and effects, against unreasonable searches and seizures, shall not be violated, and no Warrants shall issue, but upon probable cause, supported by Oath or affirmation, and particularly describing the place to be searched, and the persons or things to be seized.

## AMENDMENT V [1791]

No person shall be held to answer for a capital or otherwise infamous crime, unless on a presentment or indictment of a Grand Jury, except in cases arising in the land or naval forces,

---

*The dates in brackets indicate when the amendments were ratified.

or in the Militia, when in actual service in time of War or public danger; nor shall any person be subject for the same offence to be twice put in jeopardy of life or limb; nor shall be compelled in any criminal case to be a witness against himself, nor be deprived of life, liberty, or property, without due process of law; nor shall private property be taken for public use, without just compensation.

### Amendment VI [1791]

In all criminal prosecutions, the accused shall enjoy the right to a speedy and public trial, by an impartial jury of the State and district wherein the crime shall have been committed, which district shall have been previously ascertained by law, and to be informed of the nature and cause of the accusation; to be confronted with the witnesses against him; to have compulsory process for obtaining witnesses in his favor, and to have the Assistance of Counsel for his defence.

### Amendment VII [1791]

In suits at common law, where the value in controversy shall exceed twenty dollars, the right of trial by jury shall be preserved, and no fact tried by a jury, shall be otherwise reexamined in any Court of the United States, than according to the Rules of the common law.

### Amendment VIII [1791]

Excessive bail shall not be required, nor excessive fines imposed, nor cruel and unusual punishments inflicted.

### Amendment IX [1791]

The enumeration in the Constitution, of certain rights, shall not be construed to deny or disparage others retained by the people.

### Amendment X [1791]

The powers not delegated to the United States by the Constitution, nor prohibited by it to the States, are reserved to the States respectively, or to the people.

### Amendment XI [1798]

The Judicial power of the United States shall not be construed to extend to any suit in law or equity, commenced or prosecuted against one of the United States by Citizens of another State, or by Citizens or subjects of any foreign state.

### Amendment XII [1804]

The Electors shall meet in their respective States and vote by ballot for President and Vice-President, one of whom, at least, shall not be an inhabitant of the same State with themselves; they shall name in their ballots the person voted for as President, and in distinct ballots the person voted for as Vice-President, and they shall make distinct lists of all persons voted for as President, and of all persons voted for as Vice-President, and of the number of votes for each, which lists they shall sign and certify, and transmit sealed to the seat of the government of the United States, directed to the President of the Senate;—the President of the Senate shall, in the presence of the Senate and House of Representatives, open all the certificates and the votes shall then be counted;—The person having the greatest number of votes for President, shall be the President, if such number be a majority of the whole number of Electors appointed; and if no person have such majority, then from the persons having the highest numbers not exceeding three on the list of those voted for as President, the House of Representatives shall choose immediately, by ballot, the President. But in choosing the President, the votes shall be taken by States, the representation from each State having one vote; a quorum for this purpose shall consist of a member or members from two-thirds of the States, and a majority of all the States shall be necessary to a choice. And if the House of Representatives shall not choose a President whenever the right of choice shall devolve upon them, before *the fourth day of March* next following, then the Vice-President shall act as President, as in the case of the death or other constitutional disability of the President.*—The person having the greatest number of votes as Vice-President, shall be the Vice-President, if such number be a majority of the whole number of Electors appointed, and if no person have a majority, then from the two highest numbers on the list, the Senate shall choose the Vice-President; a quorum for the purpose shall consist of two-thirds of the whole number of Senators, and a majority of the whole number shall be necessary to a choice. But no person constitutionally ineligible to the office of President shall be eligible to that of Vice-President of the United States.

## AMENDMENT XIII [1865]

*Section 1*
Neither slavery nor involuntary servitude, except as a punishment for crime whereof the party shall have been duly convicted, shall exist within the United States, or any place subject to their jurisdiction.

*Section 2*
Congress shall have power to enforce this article by appropriate legislation.

## AMENDMENT XIV [1868]

*Section 1*
All persons born or naturalized in the United States, and subject to the jurisdiction thereof, are citizens of the United States and of the State wherein they reside. No State shall make or enforce any law which shall abridge the privileges or immunities of citizens of the United States; nor shall any State deprive any person of life, liberty, or property, without due process of law; nor deny to any person within its jurisdiction the equal protection of the laws.

*Section 2*
Representatives shall be apportioned among the several States according to their respective numbers, counting the whole number of persons in each State, excluding Indians not taxed. But when the right to vote at any election for the choice of electors for President and Vice-President of the United States, Representatives in Congress, the Executive and Judicial officers of a State, or the members of the Legislature thereof, is denied to any of the male inhabitants of such State, being twenty-one years of age, and citizens of the United States, or

---

*Superseded by Section 3 of the Twentieth Amendment.

in any way abridged, except for participation in rebellion, or other crime, the basis of representation therein shall be reduced in the proportion which the number of such male citizens shall bear to the whole number of male citizens twenty-one years of age in such State.

### Section 3
No person shall be a Senator or Representative in Congress, or elector of President and Vice-President, or hold any office, civil or military, under the United States, or under any State, who, having previously taken an oath, as a member of Congress, or as an officer of the United States, or as a member of any State legislature, or as an executive or judicial officer of any State, to support the Constitution of the United States, shall have engaged in insurrection or rebellion against the same, or given aid or comfort to the enemies thereof. Congress may by a vote of two-thirds of each house, remove such disability.

### Section 4
The validity of the public debt of the United States, authorized by law, including debts incurred for payment of pensions and bounties for services in suppressing insurrection or rebellion, shall not be questioned. But neither the United States nor any State shall assume or pay any debt or obligation incurred in aid of insurrection or rebellion against the United States, or any claim for the loss or emancipation of any slave; but all such debts, obligations and claims shall be held illegal and void.

### Section 5
The Congress shall have power to enforce, by appropriate legislation, the provisions of this article.

## AMENDMENT XV [1870]

### Section 1
The right of citizens of the United States to vote shall not be denied or abridged by the United States or by any State on account of race, color, or previous condition of servitude—

### Section 2
The Congress shall have power to enforce this article by appropriate legislation.

## AMENDMENT XVI [1913]
The Congress shall have power to lay and collect taxes on incomes, from whatever source derived, without apportionment among the several States, and without regard to any census or enumeration.

## AMENDMENT XVII [1913]
The Senate of the United States shall be composed of two Senators from each State, elected by the people thereof, for six years; and each Senator shall have one vote. The electors in each State shall have the qualifications requisite for electors of the most numerous branch of the State legislatures.

When vacancies happen in the representation of any State in the Senate, the executive authority of such State shall issue writs of election to fill such vacancies: *Provided,* That the legislature of any State may empower the executive thereof to make temporary appointments until the people fill the vacancies by election as the legislature may direct.

This amendment shall not be so construed as to affect the election or term of any Senator chosen before it becomes valid as part of the Constitution.

## AMENDMENT XVIII [1919]

### Section 1
After one year from the ratification of this article the manufacture, sale, or transportation of intoxicating liquors within, the importation thereof into, or the exportation thereof from the United States and all territory subject to the jurisdiction hereof for beverage purposes is hereby prohibited.

### Section 2
The Congress and the several States shall have concurrent power to enforce this article by appropriate legislation.

### Section 3
This article shall be inoperative unless it shall have been ratified as an amendment to the Constitution by the legislatures of the several States, as provided by the Constitution, within seven years from the date of submission hereof to the States by the Congress.*

## AMENDMENT XIX [1920]
The right of citizens of the United States to vote shall not be denied or abridged by the United States or by any State on account of sex.

Congress shall have power to enforce this article by appropriate legislation.

## AMENDMENT XX [1933]

### Section 1
The terms of the President and Vice-President shall end at noon on the 20th day of January, and the terms of Senators and Representatives at noon on the 3d day of January, of the years in which such terms would have ended if this article had not been ratified; and the terms of their successors shall then begin.

### Section 2
The Congress shall assemble at least once in every year, and such meeting shall begin at noon on the 3d day of January, unless they shall by law appoint a different day.

### Section 3
If, at the time fixed for the beginning of the term of the President, the President elect shall have died, the Vice-President elect shall become President. If a President shall not have been chosen before the time fixed for the beginning of his term, or if the President elect shall have failed to qualify, then the Vice-President elect shall act as President until a President

---

*Repealed by Section 1 of the Twenty-first Amendment.

shall have qualified; and the Congress may by law provide for the case wherein neither a President elect nor a Vice-President elect shall have qualified, declaring who shall then act as President, or the manner in which one who is to act shall be selected, and such person shall act accordingly until a President or Vice-President shall have qualified.

### Section 4

The Congress may by law provide for the case of the death of any of the persons from whom the House of Representatives may choose a President whenever the right of choice shall have devolved upon them, and for the case of the death of any of the persons from whom the Senate may choose a Vice-President whenever the right of choice shall have devolved upon them.

### Section 5

Sections 1 and 2 shall take effect on the 15th day of October following the ratification of this article.

### Section 6

This article shall be inoperative unless it shall have been ratified as an amendment to the Constitution by the legislatures of three-fourths of the several States within seven years from the date of its submission.

## Amendment XXI [1933]

### Section 1

The eighteenth article of amendment to the Constitution of the United States is hereby repealed.

### Section 2

The transportation or importation into any State, Territory, or possession of the United States for delivery or use therein of intoxicating liquors, in violation of the laws thereof, is hereby prohibited.

### Section 3

This article shall be inoperative unless it shall have been ratified as an amendment to the Constitution by conventions in the several States, as provided in the Constitution, within seven years from the date of submission hereof to the States by the Congress.

## Amendment XXII [1951]

### Section 1

No person shall be elected to the office of President more than twice, and no person who has held the office of President, or acted as President, for more than two years of a term to which some other person was elected President shall be elected to the office of the President more than once. But this Article shall not apply to any person holding the office of President when this Article was proposed by the Congress, and shall not prevent any person who may be holding the office of President, or acting as President, during the term within which this Article becomes operative from holding the office of the President or acting as President during the remainder of such term.

*Section 2*
This article shall be inoperative unless it shall have been ratified as an amendment to the Constitution by the legislatures of three-fourths of the several States within seven years from the date of its submission to the States by the Congress.

## Amendment XXIII [1961]

*Section 1*
The District constituting the seat of Government of the United States shall appoint in such manner as the Congress may direct:

A number of electors of President and Vice-President equal to the whole number of Senators and Representatives in Congress to which the District would be entitled if it were a State, but in no event more than the least populous State; they shall be in addition to those appointed by the States, but they shall be considered, for the purposes of the election of President and Vice-President, to be electors appointed by a State; and they shall meet in the District and perform such duties as provided by the twelfth article of amendment.

*Section 2*
The Congress shall have power to enforce this article by appropriate legislation.

## Amendment XXIV [1964]

*Section 1*
The right of citizens of the United States to vote in any primary or other election for President or Vice-President, for electors for President or Vice-President, or for Senator or Representative in Congress, shall not be denied or abridged by the United States or any State by reason of failure to pay any poll tax or other tax.

*Section 2*
The Congress shall have power to enforce this article by appropriate legislation.

## Amendment XXV [1967]

*Section 1*
In case of the removal of the President from office or of his death or resignation, the Vice-President shall become President.

*Section 2*
Whenever there is a vacancy in the office of the Vice-President, the President shall nominate a Vice-President who shall take office upon confirmation by a majority vote of both houses of Congress.

*Section 3*
Whenever the President transmits to the President pro tempore of the Senate and the Speaker of the House of Representatives his written declaration that he is unable to discharge the powers and duties of his office, and until he transmits to them a written declaration to the

contrary, such powers and duties shall be discharged by the Vice-President as Acting President.

### Section 4

Whenever the Vice-President and a majority of either the principal officers of the executive departments or of such other body as Congress may by law provide, transmit to the President pro tempore of the Senate and the Speaker of the House of Representatives their written declaration that the President is unable to discharge the powers and duties of his office, the Vice-President shall immediately assume the powers and duties of the office as Acting President.

Thereafter, when the President transmits to the President pro tempore of the Senate and the Speaker of the House of Representatives his written declaration that no inability exists, he shall resume the powers and duties of his office unless the Vice-President and a majority of either the principal officers of the executive department or of such other body as Congress may by law provide, transmit within four days to the President pro tempore of the Senate and the Speaker of the House of Representatives their written declaration that the President is unable to discharge the powers and duties of his office. Thereupon Congress shall decide the issue, assembling within forty-eight hours for that purpose if not in session. If the Congress, within twenty-one days after receipt of the latter written declaration, or, if Congress is not in session, within twenty-one days after Congress is required to assemble, determines by two-thirds vote of both Houses that the President is unable to discharge the powers and duties of his office, the Vice-President shall continue to discharge the same as Acting President; otherwise, the President shall resume the powers and duties of his office.

## Amendment XXVI [1971]

### Section 1

The right of citizens of the United States, who are eighteen years of age or older, to vote shall not be denied or abridged by the United States or by any state on account of age.

### Section 2

The Congress shall have power to enforce this article by appropriate legislation.

## Amendment XXVII [1992]

No law varying the compensation for services of the Senators and Representatives, shall take effect, until an election of Representatives shall have intervened.

# APPENDIX

## Territorial Expansion

| Territory | Date Acquired | Square Miles | How Acquired |
|---|---|---|---|
| Original states and territories | 1783 | 888,685 | Treaty of Paris |
| Louisiana Purchase | 1803 | 827,192 | Purchased from France |
| Florida | 1819 | 72,003 | Adams-Onís Treaty |
| Texas | 1845 | 390,143 | Annexation of independent country |
| Oregon | 1846 | 285,580 | Oregon Boundary Treaty |
| Mexican cession | 1848 | 529,017 | Treaty of Guadalupe Hidalgo |
| Gadsden Purchase | 1853 | 29,640 | Purchased from Mexico |
| Midway Islands | 1867 | 2 | Annexation of uninhabited islands |
| Alaska | 1867 | 589,757 | Purchased from Russia |
| Hawaii | 1898 | 6,450 | Annexation of independent country |
| Wake Island | 1898 | 3 | Annexation of uninhabited island |
| Puerto Rico | 1899 | 3,435 | Treaty of Paris |
| Guam | 1899 | 212 | Treaty of Paris |
| The Philippines | 1899–1946 | 115,600 | Treaty of Paris; granted independence |
| American Samoa | 1900 | 76 | Treaty with Germany and Great Britain |
| Panama Canal Zone | 1904–1978 | 553 | Hay–Bunau-Varilla Treaty |
| U.S. Virgin Islands | 1917 | 133 | Purchased from Denmark |
| Trust Territory of the Pacific Islands* | 1947 | 717 | United Nations Trusteeship |

*A number of these islands have recently been granted independence: Federated States of Micronesia, 1990; Marshall Islands, 1991; Palau, 1994.

**The Labor Force (thousands of workers)**

| Year | Agricul-ture | Mining | Manufac-turing | Construc-tion | Trade | Other | Total |
|------|------|------|------|------|------|------|------|
| 1810 | 1,950 | 11 | 75 | — | — | 294 | 2,330 |
| 1840 | 3,570 | 32 | 500 | 290 | 350 | 918 | 5,660 |
| 1850 | 4,520 | 102 | 1,200 | 410 | 530 | 1,488 | 8,250 |
| 1860 | 5,880 | 176 | 1,530 | 520 | 890 | 2,114 | 11,110 |
| 1870 | 6,790 | 180 | 2,470 | 780 | 1,310 | 1,400 | 12,930 |
| 1880 | 8,920 | 280 | 3,290 | 900 | 1,930 | 2,070 | 17,390 |
| 1890 | 9,960 | 440 | 4,390 | 1,510 | 2,960 | 4,060 | 23,320 |
| 1900 | 11,680 | 637 | 5,895 | 1,665 | 3,970 | 5,223 | 29,070 |
| 1910 | 11,770 | 1,068 | 8,332 | 1,949 | 5,320 | 9,041 | 37,480 |
| 1920 | 10,790 | 1,180 | 11,190 | 1,233 | 5,845 | 11,372 | 41,610 |
| 1930 | 10,560 | 1,009 | 9,884 | 1,988 | 8,122 | 17,267 | 48,830 |
| 1940 | 9,575 | 925 | 11,309 | 1,876 | 9,328 | 23,277 | 56,290 |
| 1950 | 7,870 | 901 | 15,648 | 3,029 | 12,152 | 25,870 | 65,470 |
| 1960 | 5,970 | 709 | 17,145 | 3,640 | 14,051 | 32,545 | 74,060 |
| 1970 | 3,463 | 516 | 20,746 | 4,818 | 15,008 | 34,127 | 78,678 |
| 1980 | 3,364 | 979 | 21,942 | 6,215 | 20,191 | 46,612 | 99,303 |
| 1990 | 3,186 | 730 | 21,184 | 7,696 | 24,269 | 60,849 | 118,793 |
| 2000 | 3,382 | 524 | 20,256 | 9,591 | 28,140 | 74,998 | 136,891 |

*Source: Historical Statistics of the United States, Colonial Times to 1970 (1975), 139; Statistical Abstract of the United States, 2003, Table 619.*

*Changing Labor Patterns*

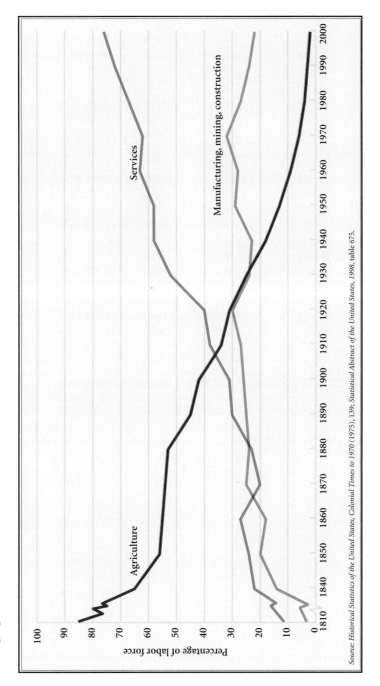

Percentage of labor force

100 90 80 70 60 50 40 30 20 10 0

1810 1820 1830 1840 1850 1860 1870 1880 1890 1900 1910 1920 1930 1940 1950 1960 1970 1980 1990 2000

Services

Manufacturing, mining, construction

Agriculture

*Source: Historical Statistics of the United States, Colonial Times to 1970 (1975), 139; Statistical Abstract of the United States, 1998, table 675.*

**American Population**

| Year | Population | Percent Increase | Year | Population | Percent Increase |
|------|-----------|------------------|------|-----------|------------------|
| 1610 | 350 | — | 1810 | 7,239,881 | 36.4 |
| 1620 | 2,300 | 557.1 | 1820 | 9,638,453 | 33.1 |
| 1630 | 4,600 | 100.0 | 1830 | 12,866,020 | 33.5 |
| 1640 | 26,600 | 478.3 | 1840 | 17,069,453 | 32.7 |
| 1650 | 50,400 | 90.8 | 1850 | 23,191,876 | 35.9 |
| 1660 | 75,100 | 49.0 | 1860 | 31,443,321 | 35.6 |
| 1670 | 111,900 | 49.0 | 1870 | 39,818,449 | 26.6 |
| 1680 | 151,500 | 35.4 | 1880 | 50,155,783 | 26.0 |
| 1690 | 210,400 | 38.9 | 1890 | 62,947,714 | 25.5 |
| 1700 | 250,900 | 19.2 | 1900 | 75,994,575 | 20.7 |
| 1710 | 331,700 | 32.2 | 1910 | 91,972,266 | 21.0 |
| 1720 | 466,200 | 40.5 | 1920 | 105,710,620 | 14.9 |
| 1730 | 629,400 | 35.0 | 1930 | 122,775,046 | 16.1 |
| 1740 | 905,600 | 43.9 | 1940 | 131,669,275 | 7.2 |
| 1750 | 1,170,800 | 29.3 | 1950 | 150,697,361 | 14.5 |
| 1760 | 1,593,600 | 36.1 | 1960 | 179,323,175 | 19.0 |
| 1770 | 2,148,100 | 34.8 | 1970 | 203,235,298 | 13.3 |
| 1780 | 2,780,400 | 29.4 | 1980 | 226,545,805 | 11.5 |
| 1790 | 3,929,214 | 41.3 | 1990 | 248,709,873 | 9.8 |
| 1800 | 5,308,483 | 35.1 | 2000 | 281,421,906 | 13.2 |

*Note:* These figures largely ignore the Native American population. Census takers never made any effort to count the Native American population that lived outside their political jurisdictions and compiled only casual and incomplete enumerations of those living within their jurisdictions until 1890. In that year the federal government attempted a full count of the Indian population: the Census found 125,719 Indians in 1890, compared with only 12,543 in 1870 and 33,985 in 1880.

*Source: Historical Statistics of the United States, Colonial Times to 1970* (1975); *Statistical Abstract of the United States,* 1999; Bureau of the Census, 2001 <http://blue.census.gov/dmd/www/resapport/states/unitedstates.pdf>.

## Presidential Elections

| Year | Candidates | Parties | Percentage of Popular Vote | Electoral Vote | Percentage of Voter Participation |
|---|---|---|---|---|---|
| 1789 | George Washington | No party designations | * | 69 | |
| | John Adams[†] | | | 34 | |
| | Other candidates | | | 35 | |
| 1792 | George Washington | No party designations | | 132 | |
| | John Adams | | | 77 | |
| | George Clinton | | | 50 | |
| | Other candidates | | | 5 | |
| 1796 | John Adams | Federalist | | 71 | |
| | Thomas Jefferson | Democratic-Republican | | 68 | |
| | Thomas Pinckney | Federalist | | 59 | |
| | Aaron Burr | Democratic-Republican | | 30 | |
| | Other candidates | | | 48 | |
| 1800 | Thomas Jefferson | Democratic-Republican | | 73 | |
| | Aaron Burr | Democratic-Republican | | 73 | |
| | John Adams | Federalist | | 65 | |
| | Charles C. Pinckney | Federalist | | 64 | |
| | John Jay | Federalist | | 1 | |
| 1804 | Thomas Jefferson | Democratic-Republican | | 162 | |
| | Charles C. Pinckney | Federalist | | 14 | |
| 1808 | James Madison | Democratic-Republican | | 122 | |
| | Charles C. Pinckney | Federalist | | 47 | |
| | George Clinton | Democratic-Republican | | 6 | |
| 1812 | James Madison | Democratic-Republican | | 128 | |
| | De Witt Clinton | Federalist | | 89 | |
| 1816 | James Monroe | Democratic-Republican | | 183 | |
| | Rufus King | Federalist | | 34 | |
| 1820 | James Monroe | Democratic-Republican | | 231 | |
| | John Quincy Adams | Independent Republican | | 1 | |
| 1824 | John Quincy Adams | Democratic-Republican | 30.5 | 84 | 26.9 |
| | Andrew Jackson | Democratic-Republican | 43.1 | 99 | |
| | Henry Clay | Democratic-Republican | 13.2 | 37 | |
| | William H. Crawford | Democratic-Republican | 13.1 | 41 | |
| 1828 | Andrew Jackson | Democratic | 56.0 | 178 | 57.6 |
| | John Quincy Adams | National Republican | 44.0 | 83 | |
| 1832 | Andrew Jackson | Democratic | 54.5 | 219 | 55.4 |
| | Henry Clay | National Republican | 37.5 | 49 | |
| | William Wirt | Anti-Masonic | 8.0 | 7 | |
| | John Floyd | Democratic | ‡ | 11 | |
| 1836 | Martin Van Buren | Democratic | 50.9 | 170 | 57.8 |
| | William H. Harrison | Whig | | 73 | |
| | Hugh L. White | Whig | | 26 | |
| | Daniel Webster | Whig | 49.1 | 14 | |
| | W. P. Mangum | Whig | | 11 | |
| 1840 | William H. Harrison | Whig | 53.1 | 234 | 80.2 |
| | Martin Van Buren | Democratic | 46.9 | 60 | |

*Prior to 1824, most presidential electors were chosen by state legislators rather than by popular vote.
[†]Before the Twelfth Amendment was passed in 1804, the electoral college voted for two presidential candidates; the runner-up became vice president.
[‡]Percentages below 2.0 have been omitted. Hence the percentage of popular vote might not total 100 percent.

| Year | Candidates | Parties | Percentage of Popular Vote | Electoral Vote | Percentage of Voter Participation |
|------|------------|---------|----------------------------|----------------|-----------------------------------|
| 1844 | **James K. Polk** | Democratic | 49.6 | 170 | 78.9 |
|      | Henry Clay | Whig | 48.1 | 105 | |
|      | James G. Birney | Liberty | 2.3 | 0 | |
| 1848 | **Zachary Taylor** | Whig | 47.4 | 163 | 72.7 |
|      | Lewis Cass | Democratic | 42.5 | 127 | |
|      | Martin Van Buren | Free Soil | 10.1 | 0 | |
| 1852 | **Franklin Pierce** | Democratic | 50.9 | 254 | 69.6 |
|      | Winfield Scott | Whig | 44.1 | 42 | |
|      | John P. Hale | Free Soil | 5.0 | 0 | |
| 1856 | **James Buchanan** | Democratic | 45.3 | 174 | 78.9 |
|      | John C. Frémont | Republican | 33.1 | 114 | |
|      | Millard Fillmore | American | 21.6 | 8 | |
| 1860 | **Abraham Lincoln** | Republican | 39.8 | 180 | 81.2 |
|      | Stephen A. Douglas | Democratic | 29.5 | 12 | |
|      | John C. Breckinridge | Democratic | 18.1 | 72 | |
|      | John Bell | Constitutional Union | 12.6 | 39 | |
| 1864 | **Abraham Lincoln** | Republican | 55.0 | 212 | 73.8 |
|      | George B. McClellan | Democratic | 45.0 | 21 | |
| 1868 | **Ulysses S. Grant** | Republican | 52.7 | 214 | 78.1 |
|      | Horatio Seymour | Democratic | 47.3 | 80 | |
| 1872 | **Ulysses S. Grant** | Republican | 55.6 | 286 | 71.3 |
|      | Horace Greeley | Democratic | 43.9 | 0 | |
| 1876 | **Rutherford B. Hayes** | Republican | 48.0 | 185 | 81.8 |
|      | Samuel J. Tilden | Democratic | 51.0 | 184 | |
| 1880 | **James A. Garfield** | Republican | 48.5 | 214 | 79.4 |
|      | Winfield S. Hancock | Democratic | 48.1 | 155 | |
|      | James B. Weaver | Greenback-Labor | 3.4 | 0 | |
| 1884 | **Grover Cleveland** | Democratic | 48.5 | 219 | 77.5 |
|      | James G. Blaine | Republican | 48.2 | 182 | |
| 1888 | **Benjamin Harrison** | Republican | 47.9 | 233 | 79.3 |
|      | Grover Cleveland | Democratic | 48.6 | 168 | |
| 1892 | **Grover Cleveland** | Democratic | 46.1 | 277 | 74.7 |
|      | Benjamin Harrison | Republican | 43.0 | 145 | |
|      | James B. Weaver | People's | 8.5 | 22 | |
| 1896 | **William McKinley** | Republican | 51.1 | 271 | 79.3 |
|      | William J. Bryan | Democratic | 47.7 | 176 | |
| 1900 | **William McKinley** | Republican | 51.7 | 292 | 73.2 |
|      | William J. Bryan | Democratic; Populist | 45.5 | 155 | |
| 1904 | **Theodore Roosevelt** | Republican | 57.4 | 336 | 65.2 |
|      | Alton B. Parker | Democratic | 37.6 | 140 | |
|      | Eugene V. Debs | Socialist | 3.0 | 0 | |
| 1908 | **William H. Taft** | Republican | 51.6 | 321 | 65.4 |
|      | William J. Bryan | Democratic | 43.1 | 162 | |
|      | Eugene V. Debs | Socialist | 2.8 | 0 | |
| 1912 | **Woodrow Wilson** | Democratic | 41.9 | 435 | 58.8 |
|      | Theodore Roosevelt | Progressive | 27.4 | 88 | |
|      | William H. Taft | Republican | 23.2 | 8 | |
| 1916 | **Woodrow Wilson** | Democratic | 49.4 | 277 | 61.6 |
|      | Charles E. Hughes | Republican | 46.2 | 254 | |
|      | A. L. Benson | Socialist | 3.2 | 0 | |

| Year | Candidates | Parties | Percentage of Popular Vote | Electoral Vote | Percentage of Voter Participation |
|------|-----------|---------|----------------------------|----------------|-----------------------------------|
| 1920 | **Warren G. Harding** | Republican | 60.4 | 404 | 49.2 |
|      | James M. Cox | Democratic | 34.2 | 127 | |
|      | Eugene V. Debs | Socialist | 3.4 | 0 | |
| 1924 | **Calvin Coolidge** | Republican | 54.0 | 382 | 48.9 |
|      | John W. Davis | Democratic | 28.8 | 136 | |
|      | Robert M. La Follette | Progressive | 16.6 | 13 | |
| 1928 | **Herbert C. Hoover** | Republican | 58.2 | 444 | 56.9 |
|      | Alfred E. Smith | Democratic | 40.9 | 87 | |
| 1932 | **Franklin D. Roosevelt** | Democratic | 57.4 | 472 | 56.9 |
|      | Herbert C. Hoover | Republican | 39.7 | 59 | |
| 1936 | **Franklin D. Roosevelt** | Democratic | 60.8 | 523 | 61.0 |
|      | Alfred M. Landon | Republican | 36.5 | 8 | |
| 1940 | **Franklin D. Roosevelt** | Democratic | 54.8 | 449 | 62.5 |
|      | Wendell L. Willkie | Republican | 44.8 | 82 | |
| 1944 | **Franklin D. Roosevelt** | Democratic | 53.5 | 432 | 55.9 |
|      | Thomas E. Dewey | Republican | 46.0 | 99 | |
| 1948 | **Harry S Truman** | Democratic | 49.6 | 303 | 53.0 |
|      | Thomas E. Dewey | Republican | 45.1 | 189 | |
| 1952 | **Dwight D. Eisenhower** | Republican | 55.1 | 442 | 63.3 |
|      | Adlai E. Stevenson | Democratic | 44.4 | 89 | |
| 1956 | **Dwight D. Eisenhower** | Republican | 57.6 | 457 | 60.6 |
|      | Adlai E. Stevenson | Democratic | 42.1 | 73 | |
| 1960 | **John F. Kennedy** | Democratic | 49.7 | 303 | 64.0 |
|      | Richard M. Nixon | Republican | 49.5 | 219 | |
| 1964 | **Lyndon B. Johnson** | Democratic | 61.1 | 486 | 61.7 |
|      | Barry M. Goldwater | Republican | 38.5 | 52 | |
| 1968 | **Richard M. Nixon** | Republican | 43.4 | 301 | 60.6 |
|      | Hubert H. Humphrey | Democratic | 42.7 | 191 | |
|      | George C. Wallace | American Independent | 13.5 | 46 | |
| 1972 | **Richard M. Nixon** | Republican | 60.7 | 520 | 55.5 |
|      | George S. McGovern | Democratic | 37.5 | 17 | |
| 1976 | **Jimmy Carter** | Democratic | 50.1 | 297 | 54.3 |
|      | Gerald R. Ford | Republican | 48.0 | 240 | |
| 1980 | **Ronald W. Reagan** | Republican | 50.7 | 489 | 53.0 |
|      | Jimmy Carter | Democratic | 41.0 | 49 | |
|      | John B. Anderson | Independent | 6.6 | 0 | |
| 1984 | **Ronald W. Reagan** | Republican | 58.4 | 525 | 52.9 |
|      | Walter F. Mondale | Democratic | 41.6 | 13 | |
| 1988 | **George H. W. Bush** | Republican | 53.4 | 426 | 50.3 |
|      | Michael Dukakis | Democratic | 45.6 | 111* | |
| 1992 | **William J. Clinton** | Democratic | 43.7 | 370 | 55.1 |
|      | George H. W. Bush | Republican | 38.0 | 168 | |
|      | H. Ross Perot | Independent | 19.0 | 0 | |
| 1996 | **William J. Clinton** | Democratic | 49 | 379 | 49.0 |
|      | Robert J. Dole | Republican | 41 | 159 | |
|      | H. Ross Perot | Reform | 8 | 0 | |
| 2000 | **George W. Bush** | Republican | 47.9 | 271 | 51.3 |
|      | Albert A. Gore | Democratic | 48.4 | 266† | |
|      | Ralph Nader | Green Party | 2.7 | 0 | |
| 2004 | **George W. Bush** | Republican | 51.0 | 286 | 59.0 |
|      | John F. Kerry | Democratic | 48.0 | 252 | |

*One Dukakis elector cast a vote for Lloyd Bentsen.
†One Gore elector abstained.

# GLOSSARY

This list of terms will help you with the vocabulary of history. Many of these terms refer to broad, enduring concepts that appear not only in your textbook but also in further studies of history and in discussions of current events. The terms appear in bold print at their first use in each volume. The glossary notes the pages on which the terms first appear in bold print. Check the index to look up the terms' uses in other historical eras and different contexts. For definitions and discussions of other unfamiliar words and concepts, consult the book's index or a dictionary.

**affirmative action** Government mandates beginning in the 1970s that required unions, businesses, and educational institutions to make a deliberate effort to achieve a better measure of racial and gender equality in their recruitment and hiring. While the civil rights movement had achieved significant legal and political victories, historic patterns of racial and gender discrimination proved difficult to overcome without the assistance of the government. (p. 930)

**American System** A mercantilist system of national economic development advocated by Henry Clay and supported by John Quincy Adams. It had three interrelated parts: a national bank to manage the financial system; protective tariffs to encourage American industry and provide revenue; and a nationally funded system of internal improvements, such as roads, canals, and railroads. (p. 325)

**anarchism** The advocacy of a stateless society achieved by revolutionary means. Feared for their views, anarchists became the scapegoats for the 1886 Haymarket Square bombing. (p. 527)

**Anglo-Saxonism** A theory widely held in the late nineteenth century that the English-speaking peoples were racially superior and for that reason justified in colonizing and dominating the peoples of less-developed areas of the world. Combined with Social Darwinism, Anglo-Saxonism fueled American expansionism in the late nineteenth century. (p. 636)

**appeasement** Pacifying an enemy by making concessions. In the context of the coming of World War II, it refers specifically to the agreement reached at Munich in 1938 in which England and France agreed to allow Hitler to annex the Sudetenland in exchange for his promise not to take more territory. (p. 782)

**Benevolent Empire** A broad-ranging campaign of moral and institutional reform inspired by evangelical Christian ideals and created by middle-class men and women in the 1820s. "Benevolence" became a seminal concept in American spiritual and social thought during the Second Great Awakening. Promoters of benevolent reform suggested that people who had experienced saving grace should provide charity to the less fortunate. (p. 314)

**bills of exchange** Credit slips that British manufacturers, West Indian planters, and American merchants used to trade among themselves in the eighteenth century. (p. 96)

**Black Codes** Laws passed by southern states after the Civil War denying ex-slaves the civil rights enjoyed by whites and intended to force blacks back to the plantations. (p. 445)

**blacklist** Procedure used by employers throughout the nineteenth century to label and identify workers affiliated with unions. In the 1950s, blacklists were utilized to exclude alleged Communists from jobs in government service, the motion picture business, and many industries and unions. (pp. 345, 835)

**Bolsheviks** Members of Russia's Communist revolutionary party in the early twentieth century. Led by Vladimir Lenin, they took Russia out of the war in early 1917, giving up huge territories to the Germans in the Treaty of Brest-Litovsk. After World War I, Americans often used this term to describe anyone they viewed as radical. (p. 670)

**broker state** An activist government that mediates between contending pressure groups seeking power and benefits. In the United States, Franklin D. Roosevelt's New Deal in the 1930s marked the clear emergence of the broker state. (p. 765)

**business cycle** The periodic rise and decline of business activity characteristic of capitalist-run, market economies. A quest for profit stimulates a level of production that exceeds demand and prompts a decline in output. In the United States, major periods of expansion during 1802–1818, 1824–1836, 1846–1856, 1865–1873, 1896–1914, and 1922–1928 were followed by either relatively short financial panics (1819–1822 and 1857–1860) or extended depressions (1837–1843, 1873–1896, and 1929–1939). (pp. 247, 723)

**capitalism, capitalist** The system of economic production based on the private ownership of property and the contractual exchange for profit of goods, labor, and money (capital). Although some elements of capitalism existed in the United States before 1820, a full-blown capitalist economy and society emerged only with the market revolution of the mid-nineteenth century and reached its pinnacle during the final decades of the century. (p. 228)

**carpetbaggers** A derisive name given by Southerners to Northerners who moved to the South during Reconstruction. Former Confederates despised these Northerners as transient exploiters. Carpetbaggers actually were a varied group, including Union veterans who had served in the South, reformers eager to help the ex-slaves, and others looking for business opportunities. (p. 457)

**caste system** A relatively rigid system of social status based primarily on birth. (p. 29)

**chattel slavery** A system of bondage in which enslaved people have the legal status of property and, hence, may be bought and sold in a manner similar to other forms of property. (p. 50)

**civic humanism** A political and civil outlook that stressed virtuous service to the community and its government. During the Renaissance, this idea of selfless service was thought to be critical in a republic where authority lay in the hands of the citizenry. (p. 19)

**civil religion** A term used to describe the sacred, religious-like allegiance that many Americans gave to their republican political institutions. (p. 214)

**clan** A group of related families who share a common ancestor. In the sixteenth century many native peoples north of the Rio Grande organized their societies around these groups, which often combined to form tribes. (p. 10)

**closed shop** Workplace in which a job seeker had to be a union member to gain employment. In the nineteenth century, the closed shop was favored by craft unions as a method of keeping out incompetent and lower-wage workers and of strengthening their bargaining position with employers. (p. 526)

**closed-shop agreement** A labor contract in which an employer agrees to hire only union members. Many employers strongly opposed such agreements and instituted court cases to have them declared illegal by the judiciary. (p. 345)

**collective bargaining** A process of negotiation between labor unions and employers, particularly favored by the American Federation of Labor (AFL). Led by Samuel Gompers, the AFL accepted the new industrial order, but fought for a bigger share of the profits for the workers. (p. 530)

**collective security** A peacekeeping concept whereby nations ally to protect one another from aggression. The post–World War I League of Nations, in Article X, was the first international body to mandate collective security. Unwillingness to accept Article X contributed to U.S. failure to join the League. In 1945, after World War II, the United States joined the United Nations, thereby agreeing to the principle of collective security. (p. 687)

**Columbian Exchange** The sixteenth-century transfer of agricultural products and diseases among the continents. The foodstuffs of the Western Hemisphere—maize, tomatoes, potatoes, manioc—moved eastward, as did a new variety of syphilis; and African and Eurasian crops, animals, and diseases, particularly smallpox and measles, moved to the Americas. (p. 28)

**common law** Centuries-old body of English law based on custom and judicial interpretation, not legislation, and evolving case by case on the basis of precedent. The common law was transmitted to America along with English settlement and became the foundation of American law at the state and local levels. In the United States, even more than in Britain, the common law gave the courts supremacy over the legislatures in many areas of law. (pp. 142, 611)

**companionate marriage** Reflecting republican ideas, some men and women in the early nineteenth century tried to create marriages based on mutual equality and respect. Although husbands retained significant legal powers, they increasingly viewed their wives as loving partners rather than as inferiors or dependents. (p. 201)

**conservation, conservationist** Advocacy for protection of the natural environment for sustained use. As applied by Theodore Roosevelt at the start of the twentieth century, conservation accepted development of public lands, provided this was in the public interest and not wastefully destructive. In contrast, preservationists valued wilderness in its natural state and were more broadly opposed to development. (p. 613)

**containment** American Cold War policy designed to prevent Soviet expansionism, articulated most forcefully in 1946 by American diplomatic advisor George Kennan. For over forty years, American defense policy was guided by Kennan's argument that the Soviets would stop only when met with "unanswerable force." (p. 820)

**counterinsurgency** A military operation using specially trained forces to defend against guerrilla warfare. The U.S. military created the Green Berets in the early 1960s to fight this type of nontraditional warfare, characteristic of the conflict in Vietnam. (p. 865)

**court injunction** A directive issued by a judge that prohibits certain conduct until a dispute is legally adjudicated. During labor disputes, probusiness judges routinely issued injunctions that prevented labor unions from striking or picketing and imposed stringent penalties against individuals and unions who defied the injunction. (p. 347)

**covert interventions** Secret undertakings by a country in pursuit of foreign-policy goals, as evidenced by the Central Intelligence Agency, started in the 1950s, when operating in the interests of the United States. Knowledge of these acts, like U.S. participation in the overthrow of the government of Guatemala in 1954 and support for the Contras in Nicaragua in the 1980s, was kept from the American people and most members of Congress. (p. 828)

**cultural pluralism** A term coined in 1924 that posits that diversity, especially religious and ethnic diversity, can be a source of strength in a democratic nation and thus cultural differences should be respected and valued. (p. 771)

**deficit spending** High government spending in excess of tax revenues based on the ideas of economist John Maynard Keynes, who proposed in the 1930s that governments should be prepared to go into debt to stimulate a stagnant economy. (p. 764)

**deflation** The sustained decline of prices, generally accompanying an economic depression, but in the United States after the Civil War, the result of rapidly rising productivity, market competition, and a tight money supply. (p. 591)

**Deism, Deist** The belief, popular in the eighteenth century among educated Americans urban artisans, that God made the world but subsequently exerted no influence on it or its people. This doctrine was radical because it repudiated the belief of many Christians that God intervened directly in human affairs. (p. 113)

**deregulation** Process of removing or limiting federal regulatory mechanisms, justified on the basis of promoting competition and streamlining government bureaucracy. President Carter began deregulation in the 1970s, starting with the airline, banking, and communications industries. The process continued under subsequent administrations. (p. 940)

**détente** From the French word for a relaxation of tension, this term was used to signify the new foreign policy of President Nixon, which sought a reduction of tension and hostility between the United States and the Soviet Union and China in the early 1970s. (p. 909)

**direct primary** The selection of party candidates by a popular vote rather than by the party convention, this progressive reform was especially pressed by Robert La Follette, who viewed it as an instrument for breaking the grip of machines on the political parties. In the South, where it was limited to whites, the primary was a means of disfranchising blacks. (p. 604)

**division of labor** A system of manufacture that assigned specific tasks to different workers. It improved efficiency and productivity but also eroded the workers' control over the conditions of labor. This system began around 1800 in the shoe industry and soon became the general practice throughout the manufacturing sector of the economy. (p. 293)

**dollar diplomacy** Policy adopted by President Taft emphasizing the connection between America's economic and political interests overseas. The benefits would flow in both directions. Business would gain from diplomatic efforts in its behalf, while the strengthened American economic presence overseas would give added leverage to American diplomacy. (p. 652)

**domino theory** An American Cold War concept associated with the containment policy that posited that Communist incursions into nations must be stopped before communism spread to neighboring countries and enveloped entire regions. The term was first used by President Eisenhower, who warned of the "falling domino" principle. (p. 820)

**dower, dower right** A legal right originating in medieval Europe and carried to the American colonies that extended to a widow the use of one-third of the family's land and goods during her lifetime. (p. 17)

**enclosure acts** The laws passed in England in the sixteenth century that allowed landowners to fence in the open fields surrounding many peasant villages and set sheep to graze on them. The acts left many peasants without land to cultivate and forced them to work as wage laborers or as wool spinners and weavers. (p. 34)

*encomenderos* Privileged Spanish landholders in America who held land grants from the Spanish crown and the right to collect tribute from the resident Native American population, both in goods and through forced labor. (p. 39)

*encomiendas* Land grants in America given by the Spanish kings to reward conquistadors and others in the sixteenth century. The *encomiendas* also gave the landholders legal control over the native population who lived on or near their estates. (p. 27)

**entitlement programs** Government programs that provide financial benefits to which recipients are entitled by law. Examples include Social Security, Medicare, unemployment compensation, and agricultural price supports. (p. 917)

**established church, establishment** A church that enjoys a government-bestowed preferred legal status. Historically, established churches in Europe and America were supported by public taxes and sometimes were the only legally permitted religious institutions in a nation or colony. (p. 193)

**ethnocultural** Refers to the distinctive social characteristics of immigrants and religious groups, especially in determining their party loyalties and stance on political issues touching personal behavior and public morality. (p. 575)

**fascism** Right-wing antidemocratic totalitarian movements that began in Europe after World War I and which were characterized by strong dictators backed by the military. The dictatorships of Benito Mussolini in Italy, Adolf Hitler in Germany, and Francisco Franco in Spain represent three Fascist states. (p. 766)

**feminism, feminist** Doctrine advanced in the early twentieth century by women activists that women should be equal to men in all areas of life. Earlier women activists and suffragists had accepted the notion of separate spheres for men and women, but feminists sought to overcome all barriers to equality and full personal development. (p. 602)

**fiscal policy** The manipulation of government expenditure and taxation aimed at affecting a nation's allocation of economic resources, the distribution of income, and the level and general growth of economic activity. (p. 868)

**flexible response** A strategy adopted by the Kennedy administration in the early 1960s that called for a military establishment that was prepared to fight any foe—large or small, with conventional or nuclear arms—that was seen as a threat to American interests. (p. 864)

**Fourteen Points** President Wilson proposed these as a basis for peace negotiations at Versailles in 1919. Included in the points were open diplomacy, freedom of the seas, free trade, territorial integrity, arms reduction, national self-determination, and establishment of the League of Nations. (p. 683)

**franchise** The right to vote. It was extended to all adult white males in the 1820s and 1830s by most states, to black men in 1870 by the Fifteenth Amendment to the U.S. Constitution, and to women in 1920 by the Nineteenth Amendment. (p. 323)

**free soil** A political movement of the 1840s that opposed the expansion of slavery in order to allow white farm families to settle the western territories and install democratic republican values and institutions there. The short-lived Free-Soil Party stood for "free soil, free labor, free men," which subsequently became the program of the Republican Party. (p. 395)

**freehold** Property owned in its entirety, without feudal dues or landlord obligations. Freeholders have the legal right to improve, transfer, or sell their property. The first settlers of New England instituted this landholding system in an effort to escape exploitative leaseholds and feudal obligations. (p. 52)

**fundamentalists, fundamentalism** Conservative Protestants who believe in a literal interpretation of the Bible. In the 1920s, fundamentalists opposed modernist Protestants, who tried to reconcile Christianity with Darwin's theory of evolution and recent technological and scientific discoveries. Fundamentalists' promotion of antievolution laws for public schools led to the famous *Scopes* trial of 1925. (p. 713)

**gang-labor system** A system of work discipline used on Southern cotton plantations in the mid-nineteenth century. White overseers or black drivers constantly supervised gangs of enslaved laborers in order to enforce work norms and secure greater productivity. (p. 383)

**general strike** A strike that draws in all the workers in a society, with the intention of shutting the entire system down. Radical groups like the International Workers of the World (IWW), in the early twentieth century, saw the general strike as the means for initiating a social revolution. (p. 533)

**gentry** A class of English men and women who were substantial landholders but lacked the social privileges and titles of nobility that marked the aristocracy. During the Price Revolution of the sixteenth century, the relative wealth and status of the gentry rose while that of the aristocracy declined. (p. 34)

**globalization** As the flow of capital and trade expands, regional economies become more integrated; national political and economic borders become less significant; and multinational corporations dominate world trade. This process began in the 1970s and heated up in the 1990s, in part as a result of the end of the Cold War and the shattering of political barriers that had restrained international trade. (p. 959)

**gold standard** An international monetary standard in which the values of national currencies of participating countries are fixed in terms of gold and, therefore, in terms of each other. (p. 726)

**habeas corpus** A legal writ (Latin for "bring forth the body") used in English common-law courts to force government authorities to justify their arrest and detention of an individual. It was given the status of a formal privilege in the U.S. Constitution

(Art. I, Sec. 9), which also allows its suspension in cases of invasion or insurrection. During the Civil War, Lincoln suspended habeas corpus to stop protests against the draft and disloyal activities. The USA PATRIOT Act (2001) likewise suspends this privilege in cases of suspected terrorism, but the act's constitutional legitimacy has not yet been decided by the courts. (p. 424)

**hegemony** Dominance in global affairs by a nation. The United States and the Soviet Union emerged from World War II as the world's leading powers, each exercising a tremendous influence, or hegemony, within their respective spheres of influence. (p. 718)

**heresy, heresies** Religious doctrines inconsistent with the teaching of an established, official Christian Church. Some of the Crusades between 1096 and 1291 stand as examples of Christians attempting to crush groups spreading these "unauthorized" doctrines. (p. 18)

**home rule** A rallying cry used by southern Democrats painting Reconstruction governments as illegitimate—imposed on the South—and themselves as the only party capable of restoring the South to "home rule." By 1876, northern Republicans were inclined to accept this claim. (p. 469)

**homespun** Yarn and cloth spun and woven by American women and long worn by poor colonists. During political boycotts in the 1760s, the wearing of homespun clothes by higher social classes took on a political meaning. It also substituted for the textiles previously imported from Britain and provided women with the opportunity to contribute directly to the Patriot movement. (p. 148)

**ideology** A systematic philosophy or political theory that purports to explain the character of the social world or to prescribe a set of values or beliefs. (p. 19)

**impeachment** First step in the constitutional process for removing the president from office, in which charges of wrongdoing (articles of impeachment) are passed by the House of Representatives. A trial is then conducted by the Senate to determine whether the impeached president is guilty of the charges. (p. 453)

**indenture, indentured servants** A seventeenth-century labor contract that required service for a period of time in return for passage to North America. Indentures were typically for a term of four or five years, provided room and board in exchange for labor, and granted free status at the end of the contract period. (p. 50)

**indulgences** Certificates granted by the Catholic Church that allegedly pardoned sinners from punishments in the afterlife. In his *Ninety-five Theses*, written in 1517, Martin Luther condemned the sale of indulgences, a common practice among Catholic clergy. (p. 30)

**injunction, court injunction** An order by a judge halting a specified activity by a party to a legal dispute on the grounds that potential injury to the other party would be irreparable. Injunctions are not subject to normal due-process proceedings but are emergency measures instituted prior to the resolution of the dispute. Injunctions were widely used in early-twentieth-century labor disputes. (p. 610)

**isolationism, isolationist** A foreign-policy stance supporting the withdrawal of the United States from involvement with other nations, especially an avoidance of entangling diplomatic relations. The common view of post–World War I U.S. foreign policy is that it was isolationist, but in fact the United States played an active role in world affairs, particularly in trade and finance. (p. 701)

**Jim Crow** A term first heard in antebellum minstrel shows to designate black behavior and used in the age of segregation to designate facilities restricted to blacks, such as Jim Crow railway cars. (p. 585)

**jingoism** This term came to refer to the super-patriotism that took hold during the mid-1890s during the American dispute with Spain over Cuba. Jingoes were enthusiastic about a military solution as a way of showing the nation's mettle and, when diplomacy failed, they got their wish with the Spanish-American War of 1898. (p. 637)

**joint-stock company** A financial arrangement established by the British around 1550 that subsequently facilitated the colonization of North America. These agreements allowed merchants to band together as stockholders, raising large amounts of money while sharing the risks and profits in proportion to their part of the total investment. (p. 44)

**judicial review** The claim by the judiciary that it has the legitimate authority to judge the constitutionality of laws passed by Congress and the state legislatures. This power is implicit in the federal Constitution and was first practiced by the Supreme Court with respect to congressional legislation in *Marbury v. Madison* in 1803. The Court's review of legislation became particularly significant between 1874 and 1937. (p. 238)

**Keynesian economics** Originally developed by John Maynard Keynes in the 1930s, this theory stresses that aggregate (or total) demand for goods and services is the primary determinant of the level of overall economic activity. (p. 764)

**labor theory of value** The belief that the price of a product should reflect the work that went into making it and should be paid mostly to the person who produced it. This idea was popularized by the National Trades' Union and other labor organizations in the mid-nineteenth century. (p. 300)

**laissez-faire** In French, literally "let do" or "leave alone," the term refers to the principle that the less government does, the better, in particular as related to interference with the economy. This was the dominant philosophy of American government in the late nineteenth century and the guiding light of conservative politics in the twentieth. (p. 571)

**liberal consensus** Refers to widespread agreement in the decades of the 1950s and 1960s that government power could be used to stimulate the economy to bring about extensive affluence; protect the rights of disadvantaged minorities; and promote social welfare in general. The liberal consensus supported an optimistic belief in a prosperous, harmonious future that also assumed U.S. world activism to contain communism. (p. 839)

**lien (crop lien)** A legal device enabling a creditor to take possession of the property of a borrower, including the right to have it sold in payment of the debt. Furnishing merchants took such liens on cotton crops as collateral for supplies advanced to sharecroppers during the growing season. This system trapped farmers in a cycle of debt and made them vulnerable to exploitation by the furnishing merchant. (p. 462)

**literacy test** The requirement that an ability to read be demonstrated as a qualification for the right to vote. It was a device easily used by registrars to prevent blacks from voting, whether they could read or not, and was widely adopted across the South beginning with Mississippi in 1890. (p. 577)

**machine tools** Cutting, boring, and drilling machines used to produce standardized metal parts that will then be assembled into products like sewing machines. The development of machine tools by American inventors in the early nineteenth century facilitated the rapid spread of the Industrial Revolution. (p. 523)

**Manifest Destiny** Term coined by John L. O'Sullivan in 1845 describing the idea that Euro-Americans were fated by God to settle the North American continent from the Atlantic to the Pacific and supplant the Native Americans. Adding geographic and secular dimensions to the Second Great Awakening, Manifest Destiny implied that the spread of American republican institutions and Protestant churches across the continent was part of God's plan for the world. With the completion of the westward movement in the late nineteenth century, the focus of "manifest destiny" expanded and began to encompass American overseas expansion. (pp. 387, 636)

**manorial, manorial system** The quasi-feudal system of landholding in the Hudson River Valley in which wealthy landlords leased out thousands of acres to tenant farmers. In return, the tenants owed their landlords rent, a quarter of the value of all improvements, and a number of days of personal service. (p. 69)

**manumission** A word from Latin meaning literally "to release from the hand." The legal act whereby owners relinquished their property rights in slaves. In 1782 the Virginia assembly passed an act allowing manumission and within a decade planters had freed 10,000 slaves. Worried that a large free black population would threaten the institution of slavery, the assembly repealed the law in 1792. (p. 189)

**margin buying** The purchase of stocks or securities with a small down payment while financing the rest with a broker loan. When stock prices started to fall in 1929, brokers requested repayment of such loans; the funds were often not forthcoming, contributing to the crash of the stock market in October of that year. (p. 724)

**Market Revolution** The dramatic increase between 1820 and 1850 in the exchange of goods and services in market transactions. The Market Revolution resulted from the combined impact of the increased output of farms and factories, the entrepreneurial activities of traders and merchants, and the development of a transportation network of roads, canals, and railroads. (p. 301)

**mass production** A system of factory production that, through the use of sophisticated machinery, turns out vast quantities of identical goods at a low cost. In the nineteenth century the textile industry was a pioneer of mass production, which eventually became the standard mode for making consumer goods such as cigarettes, cars, and many electronic items—such as telephones, radios, televisions, and computers. (p. 307)

**matrilineal** A system of family organization in which social identity and property descend through the female line. Children are usually raised by their mother's brother (their uncle), not their biological father. (p. 14)

**mechanics** A term used in the nineteenth century to refer to skilled craftsmen and inventors who built and improved machinery and developed machine tools for industry. They developed a professional identity and established institutes to spread their skills and knowledge. (p. 295)

**mercantilism** A set of policies that regulated colonial commerce and manufacturing for the enrichment of the mother country. These policies insured that the American colonies produced agricultural goods and raw materials, which would then be carried to Britain, where they would be re-exported or made into finished goods. (pp. 20, 70)

**mestizo** A person of mixed blood, the offspring of intermarriage or sexual liaison between white Europeans and native people, usually a white man and an Indian woman. In sixteenth-century Mesoamerica, nearly 90 percent of the Spanish settlers were men who took Indian women as wives or mistresses; the result was a substantial mixed-race population. (p. 29)

**Middle Passage** The brutal sea voyage from Africa to the Americas in the eighteenth and nineteenth centuries during which nearly a million enslaved Africans lost their lives. (p. 80)

**military-industrial complex** A term first used by President Eisenhower in his farewell address in 1961, it refers to the interlinkage of the military and the defense industry that emerged with the arms buildup of World War II and the Cold War and continues to this day. Eisenhower particularly warned against the "unwarranted influence" that the military-industrial complex might exert on public policy. (p. 780)

**Minutemen** In the imperial crisis of the 1770s, colonists reorganized their voluntary militia units so that they were ready to mobilize on short notice. Militiamen formed the core of the armed citizenry army that met the British at Lexington and Concord in 1775. (p. 158)

**modernist movement** A literary and artistic style and movement in the early twentieth century that broke sharply with past traditions and was marked by skepticism and stylistic experimentation. Modernist writers include Gertrude Stein, T. S. Eliot, and John Dos Passos. (p. 716)

**muckrakers** Journalists in the early twentieth century whose stock-in-trade was exposure of the corruption of big business and government. Theodore Roosevelt gave them the name as a term of reproach. The term comes from a character in *Pilgrim's Progress*, a religious allegory by John Bunyan. (p. 599)

**national debt** The financial obligations of the U.S. government for money borrowed from its citizens and foreign investors. Alexander Hamilton thought that the national debt, owed to wealthy Americans, would insure their support for the new national government. For similar reasons, in recent decades the U.S. government encouraged individuals and institutions in crucial foreign nations, such as Saudi Arabia and Japan, to invest billions of dollars in the American national debt. (p. 211)

**national self-determination** This concept holds that nations have the right to be sovereign states with political and economic autonomy. A central component of Woodrow Wilson's World War I Fourteen Points, it challenged the existing colonial empires. The right of national self-determination continues to be invoked by nationalist, usually ethnic, groups, such as the Basques in Spain, the Kurds in Turkey and Iraq, and the Palestinians in Israel. (p. 684)

**nativism** Antiforeign sentiment in the United States that fueled a drive against immigration. Nativism directed at the Chinese led to the 1882 Chinese Exclusion Act. Nativist anxiety about "hyphenated Americans" became particularly strong in the World War I era and led to legislation in 1924 that restricted immigration from Europe by use of a quota system and prohibited all Asian immigrants. (p. 709)

**New Right** Conservative political movement that achieved considerable success beginning in the 1970s, helping to elect Ronald Reagan president in 1980 and enabling the Republican Party to retake both houses of Congress in the 1994 elections.

The New Right has a diverse constituency, including evangelical Christians, concerned primarily about moral issues, and conservatives hostile to federal activism. (p. 938)

**nullification** The constitutional argument that a state could void (nullify) a law enacted by Congress. This idea had its origin in the Kentucky and Virginia Resolutions of 1798, which were drafted by Thomas Jefferson and James Madison, and received its fullest exposition in John C. Calhoun's *Exposition and Protest* in 1828 and South Carolina's attempt at nullifying the tariff in 1832. (p. 333)

**open-door policy** U.S. foreign policy articulated in the Open Door notes sent by the secretary of state in 1899 to Japan, Russia, Germany, and France—all of whom were establishing spheres of influence in China—asking that China remain open to trade on equal terms by all nations. Because it was not participating in the assault on China's territorial integrity, an open door was crucial if the United States was to be assured access to China's large markets. (p. 651)

**outwork** A system of manufacturing, also known as "putting out," used in the English woolen industry. Merchants in the sixteenth and seventeenth centuries bought wool and provided it to landless peasants, who spun and wove it into cloth, which the merchants in turn sold in English and foreign markets. (p. 33)

**patriarchy** A family system in which the father is the dominant authority, usually both by legal right and customary practice. (p. 87)

**patronage** The power of elected officials to grant government jobs. Beginning in the early nineteenth century, politicians systematically used—and abused—patronage to create and maintain strong party loyalties. After 1870, political reformers gradually introduced merit-based civil service systems in the federal and state governments. (pp. 324, 567)

**peasant** A farm laborer who often worked land owned by a landlord. In 1450 Europe, these laborers sometimes owned or leased a small plot in the town and worked collectively with other village laborers on the common lands of the community. (p. 14)

**peonage (debt peonage)** As cotton prices declined during the 1870s, many sharecroppers fell into permanent debt. Merchants often conspired with landowners to make the debt a pretext for forced labor, or peonage. (p. 462)

**pocket veto** Presidential way to kill a piece of legislation without issuing a formal veto. When congressional Republicans passed the Wade-Davis Bill in 1864, a harsher alternative to President Lincoln's restoration plan, Lincoln used this method to kill it by simply not signing the bill and letting it expire after Congress adjourned. (p. 443)

**political machine** Nineteenth-century term for highly organized groups operating within and intending to control political parties. Machines were regarded as antidemocratic by political reformers and were the target especially of Progressive era leaders such as Robert La Follette. The direct primary was the favored antimachine instrument because it made the selection of party candidates the product of a popular ballot rather than conventions that were susceptible to machine control. (pp. 324, 556, 576)

**poll tax** A tax paid for the privilege of voting, used in the South beginning during Reconstruction to disfranchise freedmen. Nationally, the northern states used poll taxes to keep immigrants and others deemed unworthy from the polls. (pp. 455, 584)

**popular sovereignty** The republican principle that ultimate power resides in the hands of the electorate. Following the principle of popular sovereignty, voters directly or indirectly ratify the constitutions of the state and national governments and amendments to those fundamental laws. During the 1850s Congress applied the principle of popular sovereignty to the western lands by enacting legislation giving residents the authority to determine the status of slavery in their territory. (p. 397)

**pragmatism** Philosophical doctrine developed primarily by William James that denied the existence of absolute truths and argued that ideas should be judged by their practical consequences. Problem solving, not ultimate ends, was the proper concern of philosophy, in James's view. Pragmatism provided a key intellectual foundation for progressivism. (p. 599)

**praying towns** Native American settlements in New England that were supervised by Puritan ministers. These seventeenth-century settlements were intended to introduce Indians to Christianity, in part through an Algonquian-language Bible. (p. 61)

**predestination** The idea that God had chosen certain people for salvation even before they were born. This strict belief was preached by John Calvin in the sixteenth century and became a fundamental tenet of Puritan theology. (pp. 30, 55)

**preservationists, preservation** Early-twentieth-century activists, like John Muir, who fought to protect the natural environment from commercial exploitation, particularly in the American West. They should be distinguished from conservationists, who accepted development but on a regulated basis, so as not to be wastefully destructive of the nation's resources. Preservationists were the first to advocate the establishment of national parks like Yellowstone and Yosemite. (p. 613)

**Price Revolution** A term that describes the significance of the high rate of inflation in Europe in the mid-1500s. The inflation resulted from Spain's importation of American gold and silver, which doubled the money supply in Europe, at a time when the population was also increasing. It brought about profound social changes by reducing the political power of the aristocracy and leaving many peasant families on the brink of poverty, setting the stage for a substantial migration to America. (p. 34)

**primogeniture** An inheritance practice by which a family's land was passed on to the eldest son. Although republican-minded Americans of the Revolutionary era felt this practice was unfair, they did not prohibit it. However, most state legislatures passed laws providing that, if the father died without a will, the estate would be distributed equally among his children. (p. 17)

**probate inventory** The inventory of a person's property taken by legal officials at death. These inventories are of great value to historians because they provide detailed lists of personal property, household items, and financial debts and credits. (p. 90)

**Prohibition, prohibitionists** Forbids sale of alcohol by law, thus using legal means to enforce temperance. The Anti-Saloon League, founded in 1893, embarked on a national campaign for Prohibition, which eventually led to the passage of the Eighteenth Amendment, ratified in 1919, which prohibited the "manufacture, sale, or transportation of intoxicating liquors." The Prohibition amendment was repealed in 1933, although some states continued to have Prohibition laws. (p. 680)

**propaganda** The spreading of ideas that support a particular cause. Although this process does not require a distortion of the facts, it usually involves a misrepresentation of the views or policies of one's opponents. During World War I, the U.S. Committee on Public Information, led by George Creel, published literature and sponsored speeches to increase public hostility toward Germany. (p. 662)

**proprietors** Groups of settlers who received land grants from the General Courts of Massachusetts Bay and Connecticut, mostly between 1630 and 1720. The proprietors distributed the land among themselves, usually on the basis of social status and family need. This system encouraged widespread ownership of land. (p. 58)

**pump priming** Term first used during the Great Depression of the 1930s to describe the practice of increased government spending in the hope that it would generate additional economic activity throughout the system. It is the beginning of a process that is supposed to lead to significant economic recovery. (p. 745)

**Radical Whigs** Eighteenth-century faction in the British Parliament that protested against corruption in government, the growing cost of the British empire, and the rise of a wealthy class of government-related financiers. (p. 93)

***reconquista*** The centuries-long campaign by Spanish Catholics to drive North African Moors (Muslim Arabs) from the European mainland. After a long effort to recover their lands, the Spanish defeated the Moors at Granada in 1492 and secured control of all of Spain. (p. 24)

**red-baiting** Tactics used to identify, accuse, or raise suspicion of Communist sympathies. In the 1930s critics of the New Deal charged the Federal Theatre Project with being under the influence of Communists, leading to its termination in 1939. These tactics were also widely evident in the "Red Scares" following World Wars I and II. (p. 775)

**Renaissance** A great revival of classical learning that began in Italy around 1400 and spread after 1500 to northern Europe. Drawing inspiration from ancient Greek and Rome and patronized by wealthy merchants and churchmen, European artists and writers created brilliant works of painting, architecture, and literature. Their work shaped European culture well into the nineteenth century. (p. 18)

**republican motherhood** The idea that the main political role of American women would be to instill the values of patriotic duty and republican virtue in their children and mold them into exemplary citizens. (p. 262)

**republicanism** A political ideology that repudiates rule by kings and princes and celebrates a representative system of government and a virtuous, public-spirited citizenry. Historically, most republics have limited active political participation to those with a significant amount of property. After 1800, the United States became a democratic republic, with widespread participation by white adult men of all social classes. (p. 171)

**restrictive covenant** Limiting clauses in real estate transactions intended to prevent the sale or rental of properties to classes of the population considered "undesirable," such as African Americans, Jews, or Asians. Such clauses were declared unenforceable by the Supreme Court decision in *Shelley v. Kraemer* (1948), but continued to be instituted informally in spite of the ruling. (p. 852)

**revivals, revivalism** An intense outburst of religious enthusiasm, often prompted by the preaching of a charismatic Baptist or Methodist minister. Revivalism swept across the United States in waves between the 1790s and 1850s and imparted a deep religiosity to American culture. Subsequent revivals in the 1880s and 1890 and in the late twentieth century helped to maintain a strong Protestant evangelical culture. (p. 277)

**rotten boroughs** Tiny electoral districts for Parliament whose voters were controlled by wealthy aristocrats or merchants. In the 1760s Radical Whig John Wilkes called for their elimination to make Parliament more representative of the property-owning classes. (p. 134)

**rural ideal** Concept advanced by the landscape architect Andrew Jackson Downing urging the benefits of rural life, it was especially influential among middle-class Americans making their livings in cities but attracted to the suburbs. (p. 540)

**salutary neglect** British colonial policy during the reigns of George I (r. 1714–1727) and George II (r. 1727–1760). Relaxed supervision of internal colonial affairs by royal bureaucrats contributed significantly to the rise of American self-government. (p. 92)

**scalawags** Southern whites who joined the Republicans during Reconstruction and were ridiculed by ex-Confederates as worthless traitors. They included ex-Whigs and yeomen farmers who had not supported the Confederacy and who believed that an alliance with the Republicans was the best way to attract northern capital and rebuild the South. (p. 457)

**scientific management** A system of organizing work, developed by Frederick W. Taylor in the late nineteenth century, designed to get the maximum output from the individual worker and reduce the cost of production, using methods such as the time-and-motion study to determine how factory work should be organized. The system was never applied in its totality in any industry, but it contributed to the rise of the "efficiency expert" and the field of industrial psychology. (p. 524)

**segregation** The policy of racial separation primarily associated with the southern states, which first began passing segregation laws aimed at African Americans in the 1880s. Also known as Jim Crow laws, these statutes required segregation in every type of public facility. These laws were not overturned until after the civil rights movement of the 1950s and 1960s. (p. 791)

**self-made man** The nineteenth-century ideal that celebrated men who rose to wealth or social prominence from humble origins through self-discipline, hard work, and temperate habits. (pp. 312, 748)

**sentimentalism** European cultural movement that emphasized feelings, emotions, and a physical appreciation of God, nature, and other people. Sentimentalism came to the United States in the early nineteenth century and accounted, in part, for marriages being based on love rather than on financial considerations. (p. 260)

**separate spheres** Term used by historians to describe the nineteenth-century view that men and women had different gender-defined characteristics and that, consequently, the sexes inhabited—and should inhabit—different social worlds, with men in the public sphere of politics and economics and women in the private sphere of home and family. In mid-nineteenth-century America this cultural understanding was sharply defined and hotly contested. (pp. 374, 578)

**sharecropping** The labor system by which freedmen agreed to exchange a portion of their harvested crops with the landowner for use of the land, a house, and tools. A compromise between freedmen and white landowners, this system developed in the cash-strapped South because the freedmen wanted to work their own land but lacked the money to buy it, while the white landowners needed agricultural laborers but did not have money to pay wages. (p. 462)

**Social Darwinism** The application of Charles Darwin's biological theory of evolution by natural selection to the development of society, this late-nineteenth-century principle encouraged the notion that societies progress as a result of competition and the "survival of the fittest." Intervention by the state in this process was counterproductive because it impeded healthy progress. Social Darwinists justified the increasing inequality of late-nineteenth-century, industrial American society as natural. (p. 571)

**Sons of Liberty** The members of the (usually) well-disciplined mobs that, after 1763, protested against the new British measures of taxation and control. Most Sons of Liberty were minor merchants and middling artisans. (p. 139)

**special prosecutor** An attorney, not employed by the government, who is appointed by Congress or the Justice Department to investigate a federal official suspected of misconduct. Archibald Cox was the special prosecutor in the Watergate scandal. The appointment is similar to that of independent counsel, the position held by Kenneth Starr, who investigated the scandals connected to President Clinton's impeachment. (p. 920)

**spoils system** The widespread award of public jobs to political supporters following an electoral victory. Underlying this practice was the view that in a democracy rotation in office was preferable to a permanent class of officeholders. In 1829 Andrew Jackson began this practice on the national level and it became a central, and corrupting, feature of American political life. (pp. 332, 567)

**stagflation** An economic condition that results when inflation and unemployment rise at the same time. This condition does not respond to traditional governmental remedies, such as deficit spending and tax reduction. (p. 925)

**states' rights** An interpretation of the Constitution that exalts the sovereignty of the states and circumscribes the authority of the national government. Expressed first by the Antifederalists and then in the Virginia and Kentucky Resolutions of 1798, the philosophy of states' rights became the basis for Southern resistance to the high tariffs of the 1820s and 1830s, legislation to limit the spread of slavery, and attempts by the national government in the mid-twentieth century to end "Jim Crow" practices. (p. 224)

**subtreasury system** A scheme deriving from the Texas Exchange, a cooperative in the 1880s, through which cotton farmers received cheap loans and marketed their crops. When the Texas Exchange failed in 1891, Populists proposed that the federal government take over these functions on a national basis through a "subtreasury," which would have the added benefit of increasing the stock of money in the country and thus push up prices. (p. 588)

**suffrage** The right to vote. In the early national period suffrage was limited by property restrictions. Gradually state constitutions gave the vote to all white men over the age of twenty-one. Over the course of American history, suffrage has expanded as barriers of race, gender, and age have fallen. In the late nineteenth and early twentieth centuries, women activists on behalf of the vote were known as "suffragists." (pp. 210, 451)

**tariff** A tax on imports, which has two purposes: raising revenue for the government and protecting domestic products from foreign competition. A hot political issue throughout much of American history, in the late nineteenth century the tariff became particularly controversial as protection-minded Republicans and pro-free-trade Democrats made the tariff the centerpiece of their political campaigns. (pp. 207, 569)

**task system** A system of slave labor used primarily in the rice fields of South Carolina. Unlike the gang-labor system in which an overseer supervised workers, the task system allowed slaves to work at their own pace but required them to complete an assigned daily task. Once the task was finished, slaves could cultivate their own small plots. (p. 271)

**temperance movement** A long-running series of reform organizations that have encouraged individuals and governments to limit the consumption of alcoholic beverages. Leading temperance groups include the American Temperance Society of the 1830s, the Washingtonian Association of the 1840s, the Women's Christian Temperance Union of the late nineteenth century, and Alcoholics Anonymous in the mid-twentieth century. (pp. 317, 681)

**Third World** This term came into usage in the post–World War II era to describe developing or ex-colonial nations that were not aligned with either the First World, meaning the Western capitalist countries, or the Second World, referring to the socialist states of Eastern Europe. It is currently used in reference to developing countries in Asia, Africa, Latin America, and the Middle East. (p. 829)

**total war** A form of warfare, characteristic of nineteenth and twentieth century conflicts, that mobilized all of a society's resources—economic, political, cultural—in support of the military effort. Armies grew dramatically in size and now were composed of civilian conscripts rather than professional soldiers. Moreover, the civilians and industries that supported the war effort increasingly became the object of enemy attack; examples include Sherman's march through Georgia in the Civil War and the massive American firebombing of Dresden, Hamburg, and Tokyo during World War II. (p. 423)

**totalitarianism, totalitarian** Centralized regimes that systematically repress dissent and exercise dictatorial control over public and private life, usually through the use of force and propaganda. A twentieth-century phenomenon, it is represented by both the Fascist regime of Germany's Adolph Hitler and the Communist rule of the USSR's Joseph Stalin. (p. 781)

**town meeting** The system of local government in New England. The meeting included all male heads of households and was the main governing body. It elected the selectmen, levied local taxes, and regulated markets, roads, and schools. (p. 59)

**trade slaves** Those unfree West Africans who were sold from one African kingdom to another and not considered members of the society that had enslaved them. For centuries Arab merchants had carried trade slaves to the Mediterranean region; around 1440, Portuguese ship captains joined in this trade by buying slaves from African princes and warlords. (p. 23)

**transcendentalism** A nineteenth-century intellectual movement that postulated the importance of an ideal world of mystical knowledge and harmony beyond the world of the senses. As articulated by Ralph Waldo Emerson and Henry David Thoreau, transcendentalism called for a critical examination of society and emphasized individuality, self-reliance, and nonconformity. (p. 353)

**trusts** A term originally applied to a specific form of business organization enabling participating firms to assign the operation of their properties to a board of trustees, but by the early twentieth century, the term applied more generally to corporate mergers and business combinations that exerted monopoly power over an industry. It was in this latter sense that progressives referred to firms like United States Steel and Standard Oil as trusts. (p. 615)

**urban renewal** Process by which city planners, politicians, and real estate developers leveled urban tenements and replaced them with modern construction projects in the 1950s and 1960s. High-rise housing projects, however, destroyed community bonds and led to an increase in crime. (p. 862)

**vice-admiralty courts** Legal tribunals presided over by a judge and without a jury (as in common law courts). The Sugar Act of 1764 required that offenders be tried in vice-admiralty courts rather than in common law tribunals, thereby provoking protests from merchant-smugglers accustomed to acquittal by sympathetic local juries. (p. 136)

**virtual representation** Claim made by British politicians that the interests of the American colonists were "represented" in Parliament by merchants who traded with the colonies and by absentee landlords (mostly West Indian sugar planters) who held property there. (p. 137)

**voluntarism** The view that citizens should act among themselves to improve their lives, rather than rely on the efforts of the state. Especially favored by Samuel Gompers, voluntarism was a key idea within the labor movement, but one it gradually abandoned in the course of the twentieth century. (p. 610)

**war of attrition** A military strategy of small-scale attacks used, usually by the weaker side, to sap the resources and the morale of the adversary. Examples include the southern resistance of the Patriot forces commanded by General N. Greene during the American War of Independence and the tactics of the Vietcong and North Vietnamese during the Vietnam War. (pp. 182, 887)

**welfare capitalism** A system of labor relations that stresses management's responsibility for employees' well-being. Originating in the 1920s, welfare capitalism offered such benefits as stock plans, health care, and old-age pensions and was designed to maintain a stable workforce and undercut the growth of trade unions. (p. 698)

**welfare state** A nation that provides for the basic needs of its citizens, including such provisions as old-age pensions, unemployment compensation, child-care facilities, education, and other social programs. Unlike the major European countries, such provisions appeared in the United States only with the coming of the New Deal in the 1930s. (pp. 601, 761)

**yellow journalism** Term that refers to newspapers that specialize in sensationalistic reporting. The name came from the ink used in Hearst's *New York Journal* to print the first comic strip to appear in color in 1895 and is generally associated with the inflammatory reporting leading up to the Spanish-American War of 1898. (p. 561)

**yellow-dog contract** An agreement by a worker, as a condition of employment, not to join a union. Employers in the late nineteenth century used this along with the blacklist and violent strikebreaking to fight unionization of their workforce. (p. 528)

**yeoman** In medieval England, a farmer below the level of gentry but above the peasantry. A freeholder, he owned his own land, which released him from economic obligations to a landlord. In America, Thomas Jefferson envisioned a nation based on democracy and a thriving agrarian society, built on the labor and prosperity of the yeomen. (p. 15)

# CREDITS

**CHAPTER 1**

"Friar Bernardino de Sahagún: Aztec Elders Describe the Spanish Conquest." From *The Florentine Codex: General History of New Spain*, translated by Arthur J. O. Anderson and Charles E. Dibble. Copyright © 1975 by the University of Utah Press and the School of American Research. Reprinted courtesy of the University of Utah Press.

**CHAPTER 4**

"Runaway Servants and Slaves." From *Blacks Who Stole Themselves: Advertisements for Runaways in the Pennsylvania Gazette, 1728–1790* by Billy G. Smith and Richard Wojtowicz. Copyright © 1989 by Billy G. Smith. Reprinted by permission of the University of Pennsylvania Press.

**CHAPTER 5**

"Lieutenant Colonel Francis Smith: A British View of Lexington and Concord." From *Proceedings of the Massachusetts Historical Society, 1876*, p. 350ff. Reprinted courtesy of the Massachusetts Historical Society.

**CHAPTER 6**

"Mary Hooks Slocumb: The Meaning of War." From *The Women of the American Revolution* by Elizabeth F. Ellet. © 1969 by Elizabeth F. Ellet. Reprinted by permission.

"Alexander Coventry: The Character of Northern Slavery." From *Memoirs of an Emigrant: The Journal of Alexander Coventry*, M.D. Published by the Albany Institute of History & Art (1978). Reprinted by permission.

**CHAPTER 7**

"Abigail and John Adams: The Status of Women." Excerpts from select letters reprinted from *The Adams Papers: Adams Family Correspondence, Volume I: December 1761–May 1776*, edited by L. H. Butterfield. The Belknap Press of Harvard University Press. Copyright © 1963 by the Massachusetts Historical Society. Reprinted by permission of the publisher.

**CHAPTER 8**

"Alexis de Tocqueville: Law and Lawyers in the United States." From *Democracy in America* by Alexis de Tocqueville, translated by Henry Reeve. Copyright © 1945 and renewed 1973 by Alfred A. Knopf, a division of Random House, Inc. Used by permission of Alfred A. Knopf, a division of Random House, Inc.

**CHAPTER 10**

"John Gough: The Vice of Intemperance." From *Antebellum American Culture: An Interpretive Anthology*, edited by David Brion Davis. Reprinted by permission of the author.

**CHAPTER 12**

"An Illinois 'Jeffersonian' Attacks the Mormons." From *Antebellum America: An Interpretive Anthology*, edited by David Brion Davis. Reprinted by permission of the author.

# INDEX

*A note about the index*: Names of individuals appear in boldface; biographical dates are included for major historical figures. Letters in parentheses following pages refer to: *(f)* figures, including charts and graphs; *(i)* illustrations, including photographs and artifacts; *(m)* maps; and *(t)* tables.

**Abbott, John,** 264
Abenaki (or Abnaki) Indians, 75
*Ableman v. Booth* (1857), 400
abolition, 189–190, 192*(m)*. *See also* emancipation; Emancipation Proclamation
   as central war aim, 428–429
   economic consequences of, 460–464
   government power and, 442
   opposition to, 412, 429
   Radical Republicans and, 428–429, 451
   of slave trade, 210, 267–268, 271, 275, 371, 398
   support for, 417, 432
abolitionism, 367–374
   African resettlement and, 268
   attacks on, 371–372
   evangelical, 368–371, 374
   free blacks and, 272, 274–275, 367
   Fugitive Slave Acts and, 398–400
   and Garrison, 352
   in Kansas, 382, 402–403
   Lincoln and, 407, 412, 428–429
   politics and, 372, 382–383, 390–391, 394–396, 402
   religion and, 268, 284, 368–371
   slavery and, 327*(i)*, 344
   in the South, 382–383
   transcendentalism and, 358, 371, 374
   *Uncle Tom's Cabin* and, 400
   women and, 370, 372, 373*(m)*, 376–378, 456–457
Acadia, 75, 76*(m)*, 179. *See also* Nova Scotia
Acadians, 121

Acoma pueblo, destruction of, 40
Acts of Trade and Navigation. *See* Navigation Acts
**Adams, Abigail,** 188
   on equality of women, 199, 200, 201
**Adams, Charles Francis,** 393, 396, 432
**Adams, Henry,** 428
**Adams, John** (1735–1826), 257, 325
   Abigail Adams and, 188, 200
   appointment of Marshall to Supreme Court (1801), 251
   as Boston lawyer, 136, 142
   on Boston Tea Party, 152
   as diplomat, 183–184, 207
   on elite politics, 92
   foreign policy of, 222
   "midnight appointments" of, 237–238
   peace negotiations and, 183
   political theory of, 114
   as president (1797–1801), 222, 237–238
   republicanism and, 282, 284
   Second Continental Congress and, 167
   on Sons of Liberty, 139, 142
   as vice president, 215
   view of legislature, 197–198
   women's rights and, 200, 260
**Adams, John Quincy** (1767–1848), 393
   American System and, 327–328, 336, 342
   ceding of Florida and, 244–245
   1824 elections and, 318*(m)*, 325–326
   1828 elections and, 328–330
   Indian policy of, 328–329
   as president (1825–1829), 326–330
   slavery and, 327*(i)*
   Treaty of Ghent and, 244
**Adams, Samuel** (1722–1803), 207
   Committees of Correspondence and, 151–152
   Constitution and, 213
   pre-Revolutionary views of, 143–144, 150, 167
Adams-Onís Treaty (1819), 245, 386

Africa. *See also* West Africa
  Arab civilization in, 18
  Atlantic slave trade with, 6–7, 21(*m*), 23,
    78(*m*), 271
  colonization by freed slaves in, 268, 407
  gender relations in, 80
  Guinea company in, 33
  migration from. *See* Middle Passage
  Protestant missions in, 283(*m*)
  slave trade in, 20, 21(*m*), 23
  society of, 20–21, 80
  trade with, 14, 20
African Americans. *See also* abolition;
    abolitionism; free blacks; racism; slavery;
    slaves
  alleged inferiority of, 384–385
  Baptists and, 118, 277–278, 280–281
  citizenship for, 432, 446, 450
  Civil War and, 412, 432–433
  in colonial America, 99, 104, 106–107, 109, 117
  community of, 84–86
  Congressional Delegation (1872) of, 459(*i*)
  culture of slavery and, 84–86, 271–273
  Democratic Party and, 457–458
  *Dred Scott* and, 405–406
  education of, 265, 284, 461(*i*)
  emancipation and, 446–450
  equality of, 272–275, 277–278, 280–281
  Ethiopian Regiment, 167
  Fugitive Slave Acts and, 399–400
  hostility to, 424, 465–467
  John Brown and, 409
  leadership of, 458, 460
  Methodism and, 268, 274, 277–281
  origins of, 271–272
  as percent of population, 172
  prejudice against, 317
  in public life, 349
  Reconstruction and, 444, 470
  Republican Party and, 457–460
  resettlement in Africa of, 268, 407
  revivalism and, 277–281
  Revolutionary War and, 157–158, 167–168,
    172, 180–182, 188–191, 192(*m*)
  rights of, 395. *See also* civil rights
  sex ratio of, 85
  Shakers and, 360
  sharecropping and, 463(*m*)
  social class and, 50–51
  in South Carolina, 333
  stereotypes of, 458
  in Union Army, 433(*i*)
  violence against, 445, 450–451, 452(*i*), 465–467
  voting rights and, 371
  white women as caretakers of, 384–385
African Methodist Episcopal Church (AME),
    268, 274, 460
African School, 274(*i*)
**Agreda, Maria de Jesus de,** 40(*i*)
agricultural societies, 7–9, 14–16, 20–21
agriculture. *See also* corn; cotton; farmers;
    freehold society; grain; sugar; tobacco;
    wheat
  African, 20–21, 83–85
  capitalists in, 106
  Columbian Exchange and, 28
  cotton, 462
  crop-lien system in, 462, 464
  crop rotation in, 235
  in the East, 235
  in England, 33
  in English colonies, 37, 46–50, 48(*i*), 51
  in Europe, 14–16
  evangelicalism and, 114, 116, 283(*m*)
  expansion of, 232–237
  exports of, 104, 110, 123–124, 135, 150, 292,
    308–309
  farm life and, 101–106, 116
  household mode of production and,
    100–101, 104
  irrigation for, 9, 11
  laborers in, 102, 297. *See also* farmers
  medieval methods of, 14–16
  in Middle Atlantic colonies, 104–106
  of Mormons, 364
  Native Americans and, 9–14, 230
  Native American women and, 12, 14, 231
  in New England, 100–104
  outwork and, 106
  of Shakers, 360
  in the South, 308
  tariffs and, 295
  technology for, 105–106, 233, 235, 294,
    307–308
  transportation and, 302–305
  in the West, 270
Aix-la-Chapelle, Treaty of (1748), 95
Alabama
  admission to Union of (1818), 268
  migration to, 233, 269(*m*), 270, 303(*m*)

Reconstruction and, 452, 457, 465
  secession and, 398, 413, 414(m)
  slavery in, 268–270, 276(m), 383
  voting rights in, 259, 259(m)
*Alabama* (Confederate warship), 432
the Alamo, 387, 388(i)
Alaska, 388, 391
Albany, New York, 175, 234
  Dutch in, 43
  Erie Canal and, 303–304, 306(m)
*Albany Argus* (newspaper), 324
Albany Congress (1754), 119, 137
Albany Plan (Plan of Union; 1754), 119, 154
Albany Regency (Albany, New York), 324
**Albemarle, duke of,** 68
Albemarle County, Virginia, rebellion in, 69
Albemarle Sound, 45(i)
alcohol, temperance movement and, 314,
  316–319
Aleut peoples, 7
Alexandria, Egypt, 19
Algonquian Indians, 42–44
  "praying towns" of, 61
Alien and Sedition Acts (1798), 224, 237
Allegheny River, 63
**Allen, James,** 367
**Allen, Richard,** 268, 274
**Allen, Thomas,** 458
Alton, Illinois, 372
American and Foreign Anti-Slavery Society,
  372, 395
American Anti-Slavery Society, 370
American Bible Society (1816), 282
American colonies. *See also* colonization;
  *individual colonies by name*
  agriculture in, 37–39, 46–50, 48(i), 51,
    103–106, 247–249
  Anglicanism in, 108, 108(m), 112,
    117–118, 158
  British reform measures in (1763–1765),
    131–138
  British Restoration and, 69–72
  British troops in, 132–133, 137–138
  colonial assemblies in, 91–92
  constitutional rights of, 136–138, 145–146
  control of trade by, 89(m)
  economic growth in, 123–124
  elite in, 91–92
  Enlightenment in (1740–1765), 112–118, 143
  European spheres of influence in, 120(m)
  evangelicalism in, 117–118
  freehold society in, 103–104, 105(m), 117, 125
  French and Indian War and, 119–122, 155
  governments of, 44, 46–48, 53–56, 58–59
  independence of. *See* Revolutionary War
  land conflicts in, 124–125
  mercantilism and, 33, 70–72, 89(m), 94–96
  Navigation Acts and, 95
  patronage in, 87, 94
  proprietary, 69, 73
  royal, 69
  salutary neglect and, 92–94, 94(i), 96
  seaport society in, 90–91
  self-government in, 91–96, 131
  slave labor in, 76–91
  tenant farmers in, 104–106, 125
  tobacco in, 47–52
  urban growth in, 88–90
  women in, 57–58, 89–90
American Colonization Society, 268, 369
American Education Society (1815), 282
American Home Missionary Society (1826),
  282, 283(m)
American Lyceum, 355
American Party. *See* Know-Nothing Party
American Philosophical Society, 113
American Red Cross, 425
"The American Scholar" (Emerson), 355
*American Slavery as It Is: Testimony of a
  Thousand Witnesses,* 370
American Sunday School Union (1824), 282
American System (Clay), 325, 349, 391, 426
  Jackson and, 329–330, 332–334, 336, 340–342
  John Q. Adams and, 327–328, 336, 342
American Woman Suffrage Association, 457
**Ames, Adelbert,** 467
**Ames, Fisher,** 206
Anabaptists, 30
Anasazi Indians, 11
**Anderson, Jourdon,** 447
**Anderson, Robert,** 415
Andover, Massachusetts, 58, 60(m)
**Andros, Edmund,** 72–73
Anglicanism (Church of England), 31, 47,
  53–54, 56, 72–73, 127
  American, 193
  in American colonies, 69–70, 72, 108,
    108(m), 117–118, 158
  Columbia University and, 116
  as established church, 73, 117

Angola, West Africa, 20

**Anthony, Susan B.** (1820–1906), 379–380, 456–457

Antietam, battle of, 419(*m*), 420, 421(*i*), 423, 429

Antifederalists, 212–215

Antigua, land in, 464

anti-Masonry, 344

Anti-Slavery Conventions of American Women, 370

Anti-Slavery Society, 372

Apache Indians, 7

Apalachee Indians, 12, 38

Appalachian Mountains, 59, 204, 228, 232, 235

    western expansion and, 125, 126(*m*), 133(*m*), 270, 301

    as western frontier, 119, 122, 133(*m*), 154(*m*)

*An Appeal . . . to the Colored Citizens of the World* (Walker), 367–368

**Appleton, Nathan,** 295

Appomattox Court House, Virginia, 440, 442

Arabs, 18–20. *See also* Muslims

    effect on Europe of, 18–19

    Mediterranean commerce and, 18

    scholarship of, 18–19, 19(*i*)

Arawak Indians, 24–25

architecture

    Aztec, 9–10

    Federal style, 220

Aristocratic-Republicanism, 257, 266–277, 281

Aristotle, 355

Arizona, 11, 38

Arkansas

    in Civil War, 430

    migration to, 302, 303(*m*)

    Reconstruction and, 465

    secession and, 414

    slavery in, 386

**Arkwright, Richard,** 295

Army of Northern Virginia, 431

Army of the Potomac, 419–420, 430, 434

**Arnold, Benedict,** 182

art. *See also* Mayas

    Native American, 9, 11

    Renaissance, 20

Articles of Confederation (1777)

    provisions of, 202–205

    revision of, 208–211

artisan republicanism, 345

artisans, 247–249, 345. *See also* mechanics

    among free blacks, 274

    in colonial America, 104, 106, 109, 113, 116

    education for, 264

    European, 20

    in industrial age, 297, 299–301, 319

    Native American, 9, 11–12, 65

    as new Democrats, 329, 336

    on plantations, 266

    as Sons of Liberty, 139–140, 152

    South Atlantic system and, 90

    taxation on, 258

Asante people, 80

**Ashby, Robert,** 118

Asia, 6, 20, 23, 401. *See also particular countries*

assemblies, colonial, 91–92

    restrictions on, 146, 153

    self-government and, 132, 137–138, 146

    struggle with royal government and, 119, 132–133, 137–138, 146

assembly line, 293–294, 294(*i*)

assimilation, cultural

    Franciscans and, 38–40

    Native Americans and, 29, 37–41, 228

**Astor, John Jacob,** 246

astronomy

    Arabic, 19(*i*)

    Mayan, 9

asylum reform

    Dix and, 375

    Reconstruction and, 459

    women's rights and, 375

**Atchison, David R.,** 402

**Atherton, Joshua,** 213

Atlanta, Georgia, 434

    fall of (1864), 438(*m*)

    as railroad hub, 307(*m*)

**Attucks, Crispus,** 150

Augsberg, Peace of (1555), 30

**Austin, Moses,** 386

**Austin, Stephen F.,** 386

*Autobiography* (Franklin), 113, 312

Azores, 20

Aztecs

    culture of, 9–10, 12

    European diseases and, 26–27

    human sacrifice among, 10, 12

    social structure of, 9–10, 25

    Spanish conquest of, 25–28, 28(*i*)

**Babcock, Orville,** 468
**Backus, Isaac,** 116, 194
**Bacon, Nathaniel,** 52–53, 61
Bacon's Rebellion (1676), 52–53, 69, 87
Bad Axe Massacre, 337
Bahamas, 24
**Balboa, Vasco Núñez de,** 25
**Ball, Charles,** 281
**Baltimore, Lord.** *See* **Calvert, Cecilius;**
       **Calvert, George**
Baltimore, Maryland
    British attack on (1812), 242, 243(*m*)
    business elite of, 310
    free blacks in, 274
    secessionists in, 416
    transportation and, 305, 309
    West Indian trade and, 88–89
Bank of England, 346
Bank of North America, 246
Bank of the United States, 238
    First, 246, 426
    Jackson's attack on Second, 334–336
    Second, 251–252, 325, 328, 334–335, 335(*i*),
       347, 349, 426
    Washington and, 217
banks
    American System and, 327–328, 336, 341
    bankers and, 308–310
    charters for, 324, 335
    in Civil War, 426
    Hamilton on, 216–217
    investment in, 343
    national, 347, 349, 391
    National Banking Acts and, 427
    private, 345
    regulation of, 325, 334–336
    savings, 316
Bank War, 325, 328, 334–336, 335(*i*), 347, 349
**Banneker, Benjamin,** 274
Baptists, 127, 189–190
    abolitionism and, 368, 376
    African Americans and, 118, 277–278, 280–281
    Brown University and, 116
    child rearing and, 264
    in colonial America, 102, 108, 108(*m*),
       111, 116
    egalitarianism of, 117–118, 277–278,
       280(*i*), 284
    evangelicalism of, 277–281, 280(*i*),
       283(*m*), 285

    National Convention of, 460
    separation of church and state and, 116
Barbados, 69, 77, 80–82, 464
Barbary States, 238
Barrow Plantation, 463(*m*)
**Barton, Clara,** 425
**Bayard, James,** 225
**Beard, Ithamar A.,** 313
**Beauregard, P.G.T.,** 393, 418, 421
**Beckley, John,** 241
**Beckwith, Abijah,** 395
**Beecher, Catharine,** 375
**Beecher, Henry Ward,** 346
**Beecher, Lyman,** 282, 314–315
**Bell, John,** 405(*m*), 410
Belle, Anne, 425(*i*)
**Bellini, Jacopo,** 20
**Bellows, Henry W.,** 352
Benevolent Empire activities, 314–317
**Benezet, Anthony,** 190
Benin, Africa, 80–82
Bennington, Vermont, 174(*m*), 176
**Benton, Thomas Hart,** 336
Bering Strait, 7
**Berkeley, William,** 52–53
**Bernard, Francis,** 137
**Bernard, Thomas,** 262
Bethel African Methodist Episcopal
       Church, 268
**Bethune, Joanna,** 315
*The Bible against Slavery* (Weld), 370
**Biddle, Nicholas,** 334–335, 335(*i*)
Bill for Establishing Religious Freedom
       (1786), 193
Bill of Rights. *See also* Constitutional
       amendments
    Madison and, 215, 241
    ratification of Constitution and, 213, 215
    of William and Mary, 73
**Bingham, Caleb,** 264
**Bingham, William,** 246
**Birney, James G.,** 372, 391
birth control, declining birth rate and,
       261–262, 285
birth rate. *See also* population
    Colonial era and, 101(*i*)
    declining, 261–262, 285
    of European peasants, 16
    women and, 100–101, 261–262
Black Ball Line, 309

black churches, 268, 274, 277, 281, 460. *See also particular denominations under* African Americans
Black Codes, 445, 459
Black Death, 14
**Black Hawk** (1767–1838), 337–338, 339(*i*)
blacklist, workers' rights and, 345
Black Robes. *See* Jesuits
**Blair, Francis Preston,** 332
**Bland, Richard,** 136
"Bleeding Kansas," 403–404
*The Blithedale Romance* (Hawthorne), 358
Board of Trade, British, 119, 121, 132, 146
Bonus Bill (1817), 251, 328
*The Book of Mormon* (Smith), 363
**Booth, John Wilkes,** 442
**Booth, Nathaniel,** 258
**Boston, Absalom,** 274(*i*)
Boston, Massachusetts
    British troops in, 149, 149(*m*), 153, 155, 158
    news of Glorious Revolution in, 73
    popular power in, 92
    South Atlantic system and, 89(*m*)
    transportation and, 306, 306(*m*), 307(*m*), 309
    West Indian trade and, 88, 89(*m*)
Boston Manufacturing Company, 295–297, 308
Boston Massacre, 150
Boston Tea Party, 140(*i*), 152
**Bowdoin, James,** 207
**Bowie, Jim,** 387
boycotts. *See also* nonimportation
    of 1765, 139, 145, 147(*i*), 148, 156
    of 1768, 145, 148
    effects of, 145, 148
    pre-Revolutionary War, 145–146, 147(*i*), 148, 150, 156
**Boyleston, Nicholas,** 113
**Boyleston, Thomas,** 187
**Braddock, Edward,** 121
**Bradford, William,** 54
**Bradley, Joseph P.,** 470
**Brady, Matthew,** 408(*i*)
**Brant, Joseph** (Thayendanegea; Chief Joseph; Mohawk chief), 172, 173(*i*)
**Braxton, Carter,** 202
Brazil, 77, 80, 82
    African slaves in, 44
    economy of, 464
    trade with, 309

**Breckinridge, John C.,** 405(*m*), 409–410
**Brisbane, Arthur,** 361
*Briscoe v. Bank of Kentucky* (1837), 341
British East India Company, 33, 122, 151–153
British Empire. *See also* England; Great Britain
    in America (1660–1750), 68–98, 132–138
    in Boston, 150, 155, 158
    colonial land grants and, 103
    debts of, 124, 132, 134, 144, 155
    expansion of, 99, 119–122, 133(*m*)
    impressment and, 141
    in India, 121–122, 152
    Industrial Revolution in, 123
    mercantilism and, 94–96
    Navigation Acts and, 135–137
    navy and, 121–122, 132, 141, 155
    politics of, 91–96
    profits of, 121
    reforms in, 131–138, 143, 145
    taxation and, 134–153
    trade in, 135. *See also* trade, Anglo-American
    in West Africa, 121–122
British Guiana, 464
Brook Farm, 357–358, 359(*m*)
**Brooks, Preston,** 382
**Brown, John,** 403
    raid of (1859), 409
**Brown, Joseph,** 424
**Brown, Moses,** 295
**Brown, Susan,** 296–297
**Brownson, Orestes,** 345
Brown University, founding of, 116
**Bruce, Blanche K.,** 458
**Brunelleschi, Filippo,** 20
**Buchanan, James** (1791–1868), 400
    Mormons and, 366
    as president (1857–1861), 403, 405–406, 414–415
    as Secretary of State, 392, 395
    on slave vs. free state conflict, 397, 405–406
Buffalo, New York, 234
    transportation and, 304–305, 306(*m*), 307(*m*)
Bull Run (Manassas Creek), battle of, 418, 420
**Burgoyne, John,** 174(*m*), 175–176, 183
burial mounds, Native American, 11–12
**Burke, Edmund,** 92
**Burnside, Ambrose E.,** 420
**Burr, Aaron,** 218(*i*), 224
    duel with Hamilton, 240

Bussell, Joshua H., 360(*i*)
Bute, Lord, 134
Butler, Andrew P., 382
Butler, Benjamin, 428
Butler, Pierce, 209
Butterfield Overland Mail, 389(*m*)
Byzantine civilization, 19

Cahokia (Mississippian civilization), 11–12
calendar
  Catholic, 17
  Mayan, 9
Calhoun, John C. (1782–1850), 241, 382,
    406, 413
  Bonus Bill and, 251
  expansionism and, 395
  on majority rule, 333
  as presidential candidate, 325
  as secretary of state, 391
  on slave vs. free state conflict, 397
  as vice president, 333, 336
  as vice presidential candidate, 329
  Whig Party and, 342
California, 41
  annexation of, 390, 395, 403
  attempt to buy, 392
  British and, 391
  China trade and, 389
  Compromise of 1850 and, 398, 399(*m*)
  gold rush in (1849–1857), 396, 397(*i*)
  Mexican culture in, 390
  Mexican War and, 392–393
  migration to, 390
  statehood for, 396, 398, 401
  voting rights in, 456
California Trail, 389(*m*)
Californios, 390
Calvert, Benedict, 73
Calvert, Cecilius (Cecil; 2nd Baron Baltimore),
    47, 71(*i*)
Calvert, George (1st Baron Baltimore),
    69, 71(*i*)
Calvert, Leonard, 48
Calvin, John, 30–31
Calvinism, 32, 55, 315
  in Europe, 30–31
  Jonathan Edwards and, 114
  predestination and, 278, 281, 284
  Quakers and, 70
  transcendentalism and, 354

Cambridge, Massachusetts, 158
Camden, South Carolina, 180–182, 185
Camino Real, 389(*m*)
camp followers, 175
Canada, 13, 41. *See also* Montreal; Quebec
  African Americans in, 367
  American invasion of, 167
  British conquest of (1754–1760), 121–122,
    132–133
  Burgoyne's army and, 176
  Civil War and, 432
  French loss of, 179
  immigrants from, 301
  Loyalist emigration to, 187
  settlement of boundaries with,
    243(*m*), 244
  War of 1812 and, 241–242, 243(*m*), 244,
    245(*m*)
canals, 293, 308, 324–325, 327–328
  Erie, 235, 283(*m*), 302–305, 304(*i*), 306(*m*),
    309, 315–316, 316(*i*), 363
  foreign investment in, 303, 305, 346
  labor for, 303, 304(*i*), 316
Canary Islands, 20, 23
Cane Ridge revival, 278, 283(*m*)
Cape of Good Hope, 23
capitalism
  in agriculture, 106
  communalism and, 358, 361
  Fourierism and, 361
  free-market, 246–249, 342, 344
  Mormons and, 363, 366
  Oneida Community and, 362
captives, Indian, 63–65
Caribbean Islands (West Indies)
  Columbus in, 24
  economy of, 464
  expansionist foreign policy and, 401
  French, 95–96, 179–180, 182, 219–220, 240
  governance of, 25
  Molasses Act and, 96
  Navigation Acts and, 95
  Revolutionary War and, 167, 179–180,
    182–184, 187
  slavery in, 68, 76–78, 80, 83, 86, 333, 398,
    401, 415
  South Atlantic system in, 77–80
  sugar and, 106, 122, 133(*m*), 135, 156
  trade with, 69, 88, 89(*m*), 206, 246
  War of Austrian Succession and, 95

Carib Indians, 24
Carolinas, 69, 74, 77. *See also* North Carolina;
    South Carolina
carpetbaggers, 457–458
**Carroll, Charles,** 52, 85
Cartagena, Colombia, 95
**Carter, Robert, III,** 88
**Cartier, Jacques,** 41
cartoons, political, 156(i), 221(i), 335(i), 343(i)
**Cartwright, Peter,** 302
**Cass, Lewis,** 395–397, 400, 405(m)
**Catharine of Aragon,** 31
Catholicism
    in America, 38–39, 41, 43, 47–48, 65, 73
    in California, 390
    in colonial America, 108(m)
    conversions to, 40, 40(i), 41
    Democratic party and, 342
    in Europe, 17–18
    in Maryland, 73
    missions of, 37–40, 65
    mob revolt against, 320
    vs. Protestantism, 29–33, 47–48
    rhetoric against, 387
    of slaves, 86
    Spanish conquest and, 29
Catholics, 108, 110, 277
    Acadians and, 121
    anti-Catholicism and, 153–154, 319–320
    Know-Nothing Party and, 402–403
    prejudice against, 141, 153–154, 154(m),
        319–320
**Caverly, Azariah,** 312(i)
Cayuga Indians, 63
Cemetery Ridge, 431, 431(m)
Central America. *See* Mesoamerica
Chaco Canyon, 11–12
**Champlain, Samuel de,** 41
Chancellorsville, Virginia, 430, 431(m)
**Chandler, Samuel,** 103
**Channing, William Ellery,** 281
charitable activities
    of Benevolent Empire, 314–317, 349
    of women, 262, 315, 349
**Charles I,** king of England (r. 1625–1649), 54,
        56, 138
**Charles II,** king of England (r. 1660–1685), 56,
        68–70, 124
*Charles River Bridge Co. v. Warren Bridge Co.*
    (1837), 341

Charleston, South Carolina, 180, 181(m),
        188, 234(i)
    free blacks in, 274–275
    South Atlantic system and, 89(m)
    transportation and, 306(m)–307(m), 309
    West Indian trade and, 89
Charlestown, Massachusetts, 158, 320
charters, 249, 253
**Chase, Salmon P.,** 398, 409, 426, 428, 454
**Chastellux, marquis de,** 266
**Chatham, earl of.** *See* Pitt, William
Chattanooga, Tennessee, 434, 438(m)
chattel slavery, 50
**Chauncy, Charles,** 116
checks and balances, 212, 454
Cheney Family, 101(i)
Cherokee Indians, 12, 125, 172
    removal of, 337, 339, 340(m)
*Cherokee Nation v. Georgia* (1831), 337
Chesapeake Bay
    class in, 87–88
    colonies of, 38, 47–51
    economy of, 219, 233
    governance of, 69
    peoples of, 46–47, 52
    plantations in, 49(i)
    planters of, 104, 118, 157, 267(i), 269–270,
        269(m)
    Revolutionary War and, 176, 181(m),
        182, 185
    slavery in, 80, 83, 85, 104, 190, 192(m),
        267(i), 269–271, 269(m)
    tobacco in, 47–52
    in War of 1812, 242, 243(m)
*Chesapeake* (ship), 240
**Chesnut, James,** 385
**Chesnut, Mary Boykin,** 385
Chicago, Illinois, 230, 310
    transportation and, 306, 306(m)–307(m),
        309
Chickasaw Indians, 12, 337
**Chigabe** (Chippewa chief), 14
**Child, Lydia Maria,** 282, 457
children
    as indentured servants, 102
    in medieval Europe, 16–17
    rearing of, 260–265, 263(i), 285
    republicanism and, 263–265, 263(i)
    republican motherhood and, 261–265,
        263(i), 374

social reform and, 375
working, 296–297, 296(*i*)
China, 14, 23, 464
trade with, 389
Chinese immigrants, 397(*i*), 456
Chipewyan Indians, 229, 229(*i*)
Chippewa Indians, 14
**Chittendon, Ebenezer,** 100
Choctaw Indians, 337
Christiana, Pennsylvania, 400
*The Christian Evangelist* (periodical), 317
Christianity. *See also* evangelicalism; Protestant
    Reformation; revivalism; *particular*
    *denominations*
    African American, 118, 268, 274, 277–281, 460
    in Europe, 16–18
    French Revolution and, 220
    Inquisition and, 24
    vs. Islam, 18, 20, 29
    vs. Judaism, 29
    Native Americans and, 230–231, 232(*i*)
    in New World, 24, 37–41
    vs. paganism, 17–18
    slave imports and, 83
church and state, separation of, 190, 193–194,
    257
Church of England. *See* Anglicanism
Church of Jesus Christ of Latter-day Saints. *See*
    Mormons
Church of Scotland, 31
Churubusco, battle of (1847), 393
Cíbola (mythical seven golden cities), 38
Cincinnati, Ohio, 236, 367
    slaughterhouses of, 293, 294(*i*)
    transportation and, 306(*m*)–307(*m*), 308
cities. *See also* urbanization
    as commercial hubs, 308–309
    growth of, 89–90
    population growth and, 308–309
    poverty in, 310, 313–314, 319–320
    social divisions within, 310–314
    West Indian trade and, 88
city-states, 14, 19
civic humanism, 19
civil disobedience, 356
civil rights. *See also* natural rights
    Fourteenth Amendment and, 450–451, 453,
        455(*t*)
    Fifteenth Amendment and, 455(*t*), 456
    of freed slaves, 449–450

individual, 73
land and, 464
Reconstruction and, 446
Civil Rights Act (1866), 446, 450, 455(*t*)
Civil Rights Bill (1870), 468
Civil War (1861–1865), 412–441
    African Americans and, 412, 432–433
    Antietam, 419(*m*), 420, 421(*i*), 429
    black soldiers in, 432–433, 433(*i*)
    Bull Run, 418, 420
    casualties of, 420, 440
    civilians in, 423–425, 435
    Constitution and, 207
    cost of, 427, 440
    crisis of Union and, 382–411
    disease in, 423–425
    Eastern campaigns of, 419(*m*)
    Gettysburg, 412, 424, 430–431, 431(*m*)
    martial law in, 424
    military draft in, 423–424
    mobilizing resources in, 426–428
    nurses in, 424–425
    Reconstruction and, 442, 470
    Shiloh, 421
    slavery and, 412, 417, 428–430, 432–433
    taxation in, 427
    as total war, 423–428
    trench warfare in, 434
    turning point of (1863), 428–432
    Union victory in (1864–1865), 432–440
    Virginia campaign (1864–1865), 435(*m*)
    war bonds in, 427
    in the West, 420–423, 422(*m*), 430
    women in, 424–425
**Clark, William,** 240
Clarke family, 104
class. *See* social structure
**Clay, Henry,** 268, 400, 413, 415
    American System of, 325–330, 332–334,
        336, 340–342, 391, 426
    Compromise of 1850 and, 398
    1824 elections and, 318(*m*), 325–326
    1832 elections and, 336
    1840 elections and, 347
    1844 elections and, 391
    freemasonry and, 344
    Missouri Compromise and, 276
    national mercantilism and, 426
    Second Bank and, 250–251, 335–336
    War of 1812 and, 244

*Clermont* (ship), 305
Cleveland, Ohio, transportation and, 306(*m*)–307(*m*), 309
**Clinton, De Witt,** 242, 303
**Clinton, George,** 212
**Clinton, Henry,** 180
closed-shop agreements, 345, 347
**Cobbett, William** (Peter Porcupine), 223(*i*)
Coercive Acts (1774), 153, 155, 157, 171, 174
**Colden, Cadwallader,** 141
Cold Harbor, battle of, 434, 435(*m*)
**Coleridge, Samuel Taylor,** 353
College of New Jersey. *See* Princeton College
College of Rhode Island. *See* Brown University
**Collins, R. M.,** 412
**Collins, Samuel W.,** 299
colonization. *See also* British Empire; Dutch colonization; English colonization; French colonization; Spanish colonization
   of Florida, 122, 132, 133(*m*)
   by freed slaves in Africa, 268, 407
   Portuguese, 18–22, 21(*m*)
   of Quebec, 122, 132, 133(*m*)
   slavery and, 268, 407
**Colt, Samuel,** 294
Columbia, South Carolina, 437
Columbian Exchange, 28
Columbia River, 240
Columbia University, 131
   founding of, 116
**Columbus, Christopher,** 6
   slave trade and, 24
Committees of Correspondence, 151–153
Committees of Safety and Inspection, 156
common law, 102, 136, 142, 253
   inheritance and, 263
   women and, 102
   worker's rights and, 300, 345, 347
*Common Sense* (Paine), 170–171
commonwealth system, 249–250
*Commonwealth vs. Hunt* (1842), 347
communalism. *See* utopian communities
*Comprehensive Orders for New Discoveries* (1573), 38
Compromise of 1850, 398, 399(*m*)
   political realignment and, 405(*m*)
Concord, Massachusetts, 249, 354–355
   British troops in, 158
   Patriot movement in, 156, 158
   Revolutionary War battle (1775), 167, 185

Conestoga Indians, 125
Confederate States of America, 416, 424–425, 432, 453(*m*). *See also* Civil War; secession
   collapse of, 440
   inflation in, 427–428
   proclamation of, 413
Confiscation Acts (1861 and 1862), 428–429
Congo, Africa, 20
Congregationalism, 55, 193–194
   abolitionism and, 369
   in British colonies, 72
   in colonial America, 101, 108(*m*), 114
   "separatists" and, 116
   social reform and, 314
   women in, 284
   women's rights and, 376
Congress, U.S. *See also* House of Representatives, U.S.; Senate, U.S.
   abolitionism and, 371–372, 373(*m*)
   Crisis of 1877 and, 469–470
   1848 elections and, 393
   1864 elections and, 437
   Ku Klux Klan and, 465–466
   Mormons and, 363, 366
   vs. President, 450–452
   Reconstruction and, 443–452
   secession and, 415
   slavery and, 428
   slave vs. free states and, 397–398, 405–406, 408
   Wilmot Proviso and, 395
**Conkling, Roscoe,** 468
Connecticut
   claims to Western lands, 202
   as corporate colony, 72
   land grants in, 103
   Litchfield Law School in, 261
   migration from, 124
   voting rights in, 324
Connecticut River Valley, 56
   religious revival in, 114–116
conquistadors, 25, 27
conscience Whigs, 393, 402
conscription. *See* military draft
Constitution, 207–215, 237
   abolitionism and, 373
   Bill of Rights and, 213, 215
   Civil War and, 207
   contract clause of, 253
   evolution of, 251

Federalism and, 212–215, 224
Garrison and, 369
impeachment and, 454
implementation of, 214–215
on interstate commerce, 252
ratification of, 211, 214(m), 215
Reconstruction and, 445
revision of, 244
secession and, 443
slave vs. free states and, 397–398, 407
Constitutional amendments, 397, 415, 457, 470
First, 224
Fifth, 406
Thirteenth, 437, 445, 455(t)
Fourteenth, 450–451, 453–454, 455(t)
Fifteenth, 455(t), 456
Constitutional Convention (1787), 207–211,
    253, 277
Great Compromise in, 210
New Jersey Plan of, 209
protest against, 211–214
Virginia Plan of, 208–209
Constitutional Crisis (1798–1800), 222–225
constitutional monarchy, 91
constitutional rights, 150, 155
of colonies, 136–138, 145–146
and republicanism, 257
of Southern states, 275–277
Constitutional Union Party, 405(m), 410
constitutions, state, 197–199, 224, 341, 454
consumerism, 124
Continental army, 172–183, 185, 202
Continental Congress, First (1774), 153,
    155–156, 158
Continental Congress, Second (1775), 185
affairs of colonies and, 202, 207
alliance with France, 179–180
Articles of Confederation and, 202–205
Britain and, 167–168, 171–172, 175–176,
    178, 180
delegates to, 208
finances of, 178
independence and, 171–172
new governing institutions and, 197
contrabands, 428, 432
Cooke, Jay, 427, 468
Cooper, Thomas, 328
Coosas Indians, 38
Copernicus, 112
Copley, John Singleton, 201(i)

corn, 8–9, 14. See also grain
production of, 103–104, 270, 302–303,
    303(m)
Cornish, Samuel D., 367
Cornwallis, Charles, Lord, 180, 181(m),
    182–183
Coronado, Francisco Vásquez de,
    38, 39(m)
corruption, political, 324, 460, 468–469
Cortés, Hernán, 25
cotton
Civil War and, 426
as diplomatic weapon, 426
exports of, 219, 292, 308, 426
Panic of 1837 and, 346
production of, 383–386, 462
Reconstruction and, 458
sharecropping and, 462, 464
slavery and, 233, 267(i), 268–270, 269(m),
    383–386
the South and, 268–270, 269(m), 295, 301,
    303(m), 308, 343, 383–386
tariff battle and, 328
technology for, 233, 295–299
textile industry and, 294–298
cotton gin, 219
Country Party (England), 134
court system, 215, 237–238. See also judiciary;
    Supreme Court
trial by jury and, 136, 138–139, 142, 274
vice-admiralty, 136, 142, 146
covenant, 55
Coventry, Alexander, 191(i)
crafts, of Shakers, 360
craftsmen. See artisans
Crawford, William H., 318(m), 325–326
Creek Indians, 12, 74–75, 242, 243(m),
    328–329, 337, 339, 340(m)
Crèvecoeur, St. Jean de, 258
Crittenden Plan, 415
Crockett, Davy, 387
Cromwell, Oliver, 56, 72
crop-lien system, 462, 464
crops. See agriculture
Crusades, 18
Crystal Palace Exhibition, London, 299
Cuba, 74, 122, 391
economy of, 464
expansionism and, 395, 401
Cumberland River, 421

currency
  land banks and, 96
  paper, 177–178, 177(i), 187, 206, 427–428
  state, 341
Currency Acts
  of 1751, 96
  of 1764, 134
Currier and Ives, 459(i)

Dahomey, Africa, 78(m), 79
**Dale, Thomas,** 46
*The Dangers of an Unconverted Ministry*
    (Tennent), 116
**Daniel, Jackson,** 429
**Dartmouth, Lord,** 155
*Dartmouth College v. Woodward* (1819), 253, 341
*Dartmouth* (ship), 152
Daughters of Liberty, 147(i), 148. *See also* Sons
    of Liberty
**Davis, David,** 469
**Davis, Jefferson** (1808–1889), 409
  black soldiers and, 438
  as Confederate president, 413
  1863 elections and, 431
  on Emancipation Proclamation, 429
  expansionism and, 395
  Fort Sumter and, 415
  General Sherman and, 438
  inauguration of (1861), 418
  resources of the South and, 423, 427
  strategy of, 430
**Davis, Robert,** 177
death. *See also* disease
  Civil War, 420, 440
  seasonal patterns of, 16
  slavery and, 78(m), 80–81, 83
debt
  British Empire and, 124, 132, 134, 144, 155
  of colonists, 119, 124, 206
  of farmers, 207
  foreign, 207–208, 211
  imprisonment for, 197, 206–207, 323, 345
  of Mexico, 391
  national, 211, 216, 238, 250
  public, 206–211
  of southern states, 460
  war, 216–217
Declaration of Independence, 171, 184,
    197, 222
  women's rights and, 378, 457

Declaration of Rights (1689), 91
Declaration of Rights and Grievances
    (1774), 155
Declaration of Sentiments
    (1848; Seneca Falls), 378
Declaration of the Causes and Necessities of
    Taking Up Arms, 167
Declaratory Act (1766), 145, 155
**Deere, John,** 307
deism, 113
Delaware, 70, 416
  free blacks in, 274
  secession and, 414, 418
Delaware Indians, 119, 121–122, 125, 229
Delaware Iron Works, 307
Delaware River, 63
democracy
  Civil War and, 413
  in England, 91
  immigrants and, 417
  meaning of, 322
  political evolution of, 323–330
  transcendentalism and, 355
  views of, 196, 322, 357
*Democracy in America* (Tocqueville),
    254(i), 322
Democratic Party. *See also* elections; Peace
    Democrats
  black political leaders and, 458
  Compromise of 1850 and, 398
  Crisis of 1877 and, 469–470
  divisions in, 400, 402
  1848 elections and, 396
  1852 elections and, 401
  1858 elections and, 408–409
  1862 elections and, 430
  1868 elections and, 456
  in 1870s, 467, 469–470
  impeachment and, 454
  Ku Klux Klan and, 465
  labor and, 347
  Mexican War and, 393–394
  Northern, 416, 424
  Oregon and, 391
  origins of, 324, 329
  realignment of, 405(m)
  Reconstruction and, 444, 464–465, 467
  slave vs. free states and, 396–398, 409
  Southern, 409
  Texas and, 387

vs. Whigs, 255, 322, 330(*f*), 342–345, 347–349

Whitman and, 356

Democratic-Republicans, 219, 258–265. *See also* Republican Party

political equality and, 258–259, 286

*Democratic Review* (periodical), 387

**Dennison, William,** 415

depressions, 358, 361. *See also* panics

of 1837–1843, 346

of 1839, 347

of 1857, 301

of 1873, 468–469

Deseret, Mormon state of, 364(*m*), 366

Detroit, Michigan, 122, 230, 242

transportation and, 307(*m*), 308

*The Dial* (journal), 356

**Dias, Bartholomeu,** 23

**Díaz, Bernal,** 29

**Dickinson, John,** 147, 167

*Diedrich Knickerbocker's History of New York* (Irving), 265

**Dinwiddie, Robert,** 119, 121

diplomacy

cotton and, 426

in Revolutionary War, 183–184

disease. *See also* smallpox

cholera, 319

in Civil War, 423–425

dysentery, 16, 23

effect on Native Americans, 26–27, 37–41, 43, 54, 61, 63, 65

environment and, 45–46, 49

epidemic, 80, 83, 112–113, 319

of Europeans in Africa, 23

influenza, 27

malaria, 23

measles, 27, 112

seasonal cycle and, 16

tuberculosis, 11–12

yellow fever, 23

*Dissertation on the English Language* (Webster), 265

District of Columbia (Washington, D.C.), 419(*m*)

abolitionism and, 371, 373

as capital, 272

in Civil War, 430

Compromise of 1850 and, 398

slavery in, 268, 407, 429

War of 1812 and, 242, 243(*m*)

divine right, 73

**Dix, Dorothea** (1802–1887), 375, 425

Doeg Indians, 52

*Domestic Manners of the Americans* (Trollope), 279, 322

domestic manufacture, 106, 148. *See also* household production

Dominican Republic, 24

Dominion of New England, 72–74, 92, 138

**Doniphan, Alfred A.,** 394(*m*)

**Douglas, Stephen A.** (1813–1861), 408(*i*), 416

Compromise of 1850 and, 398

debates with Lincoln, 408

1852 elections and, 400

1860 elections and, 405(*m*), 409–410

expansionism and, 395

on Kansas, 406

Kansas-Nebraska Act and, 401–402

popular sovereignty and, 397–398, 402

on slave vs. free state conflict, 397–398

**Douglass, Frederick** (1818–1895), 370, 428, 432

Free-Soil Party and, 395

Fugitive Slave Acts and, 400

women's rights and, 456–457

dower right, 102

draft riots (Civil War), 424

*Dred Scott* decision (*Dred Scott v. Sandford*; 1857), 252, 405–406, 408

Dry Dock Bank, 346

**Duer, William,** 217

**Dunmore, Lord,** 180

Dutch colonization, 116–117

vs. British, 44, 51, 68, 182

commercial activities and, 33, 122, 152

fur trade and, 43–44, 63, 65

in Hudson River Valley, 104, 124–125

Navigation Acts and, 69

New Amsterdam, 43–44

New Netherlands, 33, 43–44, 68–69, 71, 104, 105(*m*)

in New World, 6, 33

slavery and, 191(*i*)

sugar plantations and, 77

Dutch East India Company, 43

Dutch Reformed Protestants

in colonial America, 104, 116–117

Rutgers University and, 117

Dutch West India Company, 104

Duveyier de Hauranne, Ernest, 417
Dwight, Timothy, 102

Early, Jubal, 435
eastern woodland Indians, 12, 14, 65
East India Company. *See* British East India
    Company
East Indies, 18, 121–122
Eaton, Peggy, 336
economic development, 249–250. *See also*
    agriculture; industrialization;
    manufacturing; ranching, cattle
  in Civil War, 426
  colonial, 100, 104–106, 123–124
  eastern, 227–228
  Jackson and, 341–342
  John Q. Adams and, 327–329
  nonimportation and, 147(i), 148, 150,
    155–156
  Whig program for, 426
economic policy, 186–187, 329, 403
economic sanctions, 418
economy. *See also* capitalism; depressions;
    inflation; market economy; mercantilism;
    panics; trade
  abolition and, 460–464
  agricultural, 77, 219, 232–237, 308, 464
  British imperial, 76–94, 249
  changing (1790–1820), 232–237
  Civil War destruction of, 437, 440
  commonwealth system, 249–250
  of communal utopias, 358, 360, 362
  cotton, 383–387
  Embargo Act of 1807 and, 241
  entrepreneurial enterprise and, 247, 342
  free-market capitalist, 246–249, 342, 344
  inequality and, 105–106
  laissez-faire, 342, 347
  living standards and, 237, 352
  merchant-based, 246–249
  of Mexico, 392
  Middle Atlantic (1720–1765), 104–106
  military power and, 71
  of Mormons, 366
  Northern maritime, 88–91
  plantation, 383–387, 402
  politics and, 91, 391
  Reconstruction and, 458–459
  reform and, 352
  slave, 76–91, 266–277, 267(i), 269(m), 280–281

social structure and, 90–91
South Atlantic system, 76–80
Southern, 219, 308, 458–459, 464
tobacco, 48–52
westward migration and, 235–237
women in, 425
education
  of African Americans, 265, 284, 368,
    461(i)
  elementary, 197, 201–202
  free blacks and, 367
  middle-class culture and, 311
  in New England, 264, 266
  popular, 355
  public, 264–265, 375, 460
  reforms in, 265, 369, 375
  republicanism and, 258, 263–265
  teachers and, 265, 286
  of women, 199–202, 262, 284–286, 375
Edwards, Jonathan, 101, 114, 116
Egypt, 426
elections. *See also* presidential elections
  Crisis of 1877 and, 469–470
  local, 322–323
  Mormons and, 363, 365
  of 1800, 224
  of 1818, 253
  of 1824, 318(m), 325–326
  of 1828, 328–330, 330(f)
  of 1832, 335–336
  of 1836, 344
  of 1840, 347–349, 348(i)
  of 1844, 390–391
  of 1846, 393
  of 1848, 394–396, 405(m)
  of 1852, 400–401, 405(m)
  of 1856, 403–406, 405(m)
  of 1858, 407–408
  of 1860, 405(m), 408(i), 409–410, 412–413
  of 1862, 429–430
  of 1863, 431
  of 1864, 434, 436–437
  of 1866, 450–452
  of 1868, 455–456
  of 1872, 468
  of 1875, 467
  of 1876, 469–470
electoral college, 210, 215, 224, 456, 469
  1824 elections and, 318(m), 325–326
  1828 elections and, 326, 330

1836 elections and, 344
1860 elections and, 409–410
**Elgin, Lord,** 307*(m)*
**Eliot, John,** 61
elite, 91–92. *See also* middle class; nobility;
    social structure
    business, 301, 309–310, 342
    planter-merchant, 77
    Reconstruction and, 444, 458
    Southern, 87–88, 384
    taxation of, 459–460
**Elizabeth I,** queen of England (r. 1558–1603),
    31, 32*(i)*, 44, 70
**Ely, Ezra Stiles,** 282, 284
emancipation, 267–268, 281, 333. *See also*
    abolition; abolitionism
    African Americans and, 446–450
    antiabolitionism and, 372
    in Caribbean, 267, 464
    Civil War and, 428–430, 437
    Democratic Party and, 436
    gradual, 192*(m)*, 368, 418, 464
    Lincoln and, 407
    Missouri crisis and, 275–276
    Reconstruction and, 442, 458
    Revolutionary War and, 188–190, 192*(m)*
    state legislation for, 368
Emancipation Proclamation (1862),
    429–430, 437
    outcome of, 432, 464
Embargo Act (1807), 241
**Emerson, Ralph Waldo** (1803–1882), 265, 322,
    354*(i)*, 362
    at Brook Farm, 358
    on industrial revolution, 293
    literary influence of, 355–357
    on slavery, 371
    transcendentalism and, 353–355
emigration. *See also* immigrants; migration
    of Loyalists, 187–188
eminent domain, 250
empiricism, 112
enclosure acts, 34
*encomenderos* (land owners), 39
*encomiendas* (grants), 27
England. *See also* British empire; Great Britain
    agriculture in, 33
    democracy in, 91, 323
    vs. Dutch, 44, 51, 68, 182
    duties on goods and, 135–136

enclosure acts of, 34
France and, 74
Industrial Revolution and, 123, 292
industry in, 34
mercantilism in, 33
merchants in, 150
migration to America from, 33–34, 37,
    44–47
new world trade monopolies of, 51
Price Revolution in, 33–34
Protestant Reformation and, 29–31
Puritan exodus from, 53–56
religious civil war in, 56, 72–73
vs. Spain, 32–33, 38
Whig Party in, 91–93, 134, 143
English colonization, 120*(m)*
    colonial self-government and, 131–132
    early attempts, 44–59
    fur trade and, 63, 65
    migration of ideas and traditions and,
        33–34, 37, 54–56
    Native Americans and, 6, 59–63
    in New England, 53–61, 60*(m)*, 100–104
    population growth and, 99
    social causes of, 33–34
English language, 85
Enlightenment, 170–171, 193, 204, 219
    in American colonies (1740–1765),
        112–118, 141
    American revolutionary thought
        and, 141
    child rearing and, 264
    religious thought and, 281
    slavery and, 189–190
    transcendentalism and, 353
    witchcraft accusations and, 58
    women's rights and, 376
Enrollment Act (1863), 424
entrepreneurial enterprise, 247, 342
environment, 9, 27, 249
    effects of fur trade on, 65
    health and, 45–46, 49
Episcopal Church, 127, 264, 277–278. *See also*
    Anglicanism
equality
    of African Americans, 272, 274–275,
        277–278, 280–281, 446
    antiabolitionism and, 372
    before the law, 446, 450, 465
    within marriage, 258, 260–261

equality (*cont.*)
  Quakers and, 109, 310
  republicanism and, 257–260, 281, 286
equal opportunity
  Jackson and, 336
  Whig ideal of, 343–344
equal rights, 345, 349
Equal Rights Association, 457
**Equiano, Olaudah** (Gustavus Vassa), 81
Era of Good Feeling, 255
Erie Canal, 235, 283(*m*), 302–305, 304(*i*),
    306(*m*), 309
  Mormons and, 363
  revivalism on, 315–316, 316(*i*)
Erie Indians, 63
Erie Railroad, 306
*Essay Concerning Human Understanding*
    (Locke), 112–113
Ethiopian Regiment, 167
ethnic diversity, 70, 99, 104, 106, 108–111
Europe, 14–20. *See also* migration; Protestant
    Reformation; *particular countries*
  American colonies and, 37–66
  American politics and, 322–323
  artisans in, 20
  immigration from, 99–103, 106, 108
  impact on new world of, 37–40
  maritime expansion and, 18–20
  medieval era in, 14–18
  political innovation and, 20
  Price Revolution in, 33–34
  religion in, 16–18, 29–31
  Renaissance in, 18–20
  rural life in, 14–16
  social values of, 17–18
  transcendentalism and, 353
evangelicalism. *See also* Protestantism;
    revivalism
  abolitionism and, 368–371, 374
  camp meetings and, 278–279, 280(*i*), 283(*m*)
  child rearing and, 264, 285
  Great Awakening and, 112–118, 141, 281–282
  in Middle Atlantic colonies, 117–118
  in New England, 114–116, 278, 283(*m*)
  Oneida Community and, 361–362
  political freedom and, 116–117, 141
  Presbyterian, 324
  republicanism and, 281–282, 284
  Second Great Awakening and, 257, 277–284,
    283(*m*), 315, 319

  slavery and, 315
  social reform and, 315–318, 353
  Whigs and, 342, 344
  women's rights and, 278, 280–281,
    284–286, 457
  women's role and, 100–102, 116, 278,
    280–281, 284–286, 317
**Evans, Oliver,** 294
**Everett, Edward,** 342
**Ewell, Richard B.,** 430
expansionism. *See also* westward expansion
  as foreign policy, 394, 401
  Manifest Destiny and, 383–391
  Ostend Manifesto and, 401
  slavery and, 392–398
exports. *See also* trade
  colonial, 104, 110, 123–124, 135, 155, 292
  cotton, 219, 292, 308, 426
  grain, 103–104, 110, 308
  manufactured goods, 294
  rice, 123–124
  sugar, 135–136
  tobacco, 123–124

factory system. *See also* industrialization;
    manufacturing; mills
  assembly line and, 293, 294(*i*)
  division of labor and, 293–294, 294(*i*)
  mass-production techniques in, 307–308
  technology and, 293–299, 294(*i*)
  women in, 425
**Fairfax, Lord,** 125
Fallen Timbers, battle of, 229(*i*), 230
family, 84–85, 101(*i*). *See also* birth control;
    children; patriarchy; women
  child rearing and, 260–265, 263(*i*), 285
  farm life and, 100–103
  inheritance and, 100, 102–103, 260–262, 310
  marriage and, 102, 108–109, 111, 260–263,
    263(*i*)
  middle class culture and, 311, 312(*i*)
  republican motherhood and, 261–265,
    263(*i*), 285
  slavery and, 270–273
farmers. *See also* agriculture; tenant farmers;
    yeomen farmers
  bankruptcy of, 126, 128
  debt of, 207, 235
  education for, 264
  evangelicalism and, 112, 116

Jackson and, 329, 335–336
land sales for, 302, 303(*m*)
as loyalists, 157
Political power and, 199, 212
Revolutionary War and, 175, 177–178,
    182, 188
tariffs and, 327–329
taxation and, 140, 155
Western migration of, 233
farming. *See* agriculture
**Farragut, David G.,** 423
**Faucit, Walter,** 111
federal government, 19
    abolition and, 442
    centralized system of, 210–211
    civil rights and, 468
    Indian removal and, 336–339, 340(*m*)
    Ku Klux Klan and, 465
    powers of, 329–330, 400, 415, 442, 451
    Second Bank and, 334–336
    slavery and, 407
    small, 341–342
    states and, 252
    voting rights and, 456
*The Federalist,* 212
Federalists, 259–260, 265, 325
    commonwealth idea and, 250–251
    Constitution and, 212–215, 224
    declaration of War of 1812 and, 241–242
    decline of, 253, 255
    financial policy and, 216–219
    the judiciary and, 237–238
    New England, 240, 242, 244
    opening of West and, 227
    pro-British foreign policy of, 241
    vs. Republicans, 218–219, 221–222, 224
**Fell, Margaret,** 70
Female Charitable Society, 262, 316
Female Guardian Society, 375
Female Moral Reform Society, 375
feminism, 457. *See also* women's rights
**Ferdinand,** king of Spain (r. 1474–1516), 24
**Field, David Dudley,** 352
"Fifty-four forty or fight!", 391, 393
Filipinos. *See* Philippines
**Fillmore, Millard** (1800–1874), 398, 403, 405
    as president (1850–1853), 307(*m*)
**Finley, James,** 278
**Finney, Charles Grandison,** 315–317, 316(*i*),
    355, 361, 369, 375

**Finney, Lydia,** 316, 375
firearms industry, 294, 299. *See also* guns
**Fish, Nathaniel,** 59
fishing industry, 88, 135
**Fithian, Philip,** 103
**Fitzhugh, George,** 385
Five Nations, Iroquois, 14, 41, 63. *See also*
    Iroquois Indians
*Fletcher v. Peck* (1810), 253
*Florentine Codex: General History of New Spain*
    (Sahagún), 26
Florida
    British colonization of, 122, 132, 133(*m*)
    Reconstruction and, 453(*m*), 457
    Republican government in, 467, 469
    as sanctuary for escaped slaves, 272
    secession of, 413
    Seminole Indians in, 337, 339, 340(*m*)
    slavery and, 69, 182
    Spain and, 25, 38, 39(*m*), 41, 69, 74, 86,
        184, 245
Force Bill (1833), 334
*Foreign Conspiracy against the Liberties of the
    United States* (Morse), 319
foreign policy, 222, 224
    1852 elections and, 401
    expansionist, 394, 401
    pro-British, 221, 241
**Forrest, Nathan Bedford,** 465
Fort Beauséjour, Nova Scotia, 120(*m*), 121
Fort Bridger, 364(*m*)
Fort Donelson, 421
Fort Duquesne, 120(*m*), 121–122. *See also*
    Pittsburgh, Pennsylvania
Fort Fisher, 433(*i*)
Fort George, 141
Fort Henry, 421
Fort McHenry, 242
Fort Orange, 43
Fort Pitt. *See* Pittsburgh, Pennsylvania
Fort Stanwix, Treaty of (1784), 229
Fort Sumter, 440
    secession and, 414(*m*)
    seizure of, 415–416
Fort Ticonderoga, 176
Fort Wagner, 433
**Forten, James,** 367
"forty-niners," 396, 397(*i*). *See also* gold rush
Forty-ninth parallel, 244–245
**Fourier, Charles** (1777–1837), 361

Fourierism, 361, 366(i)
Fowler, Philemon, 374
Fox, George, 70
Fox, Henry, 346
Fox Indians, 65, 337–338, 339(i)
Frame of Government (1681; Pennsylvania), 70
France. See also French colonization; New
     France; Paris, Treaty of; Versailles,
     Treaty of
   American alliance with, 178–184, 181(m)
   England and, 68, 74, 94–95
   loan from, 178
   migration to New World from, 41–43
   peace talks with, 183–184
   slave trade and, 77–78
   vs. Spain, 38
   sugar islands and, 122, 135
   Texas and, 386
   War of Austrian Succession and, 95
   XYZ Affair, 221(i), 222
Franciscan friars
   cultural assimilation and, 38–41
   exploitation of Native Americans by, 38–40
   missions and churches of, 38–40
Franklin, Benjamin (1706–1790), 111, 125,
     171, 186
   Albany Plan (Plan of Union) and, 119
   Constitution and, 207, 211
   as diplomat, 179, 183, 207
   in England, 137, 143, 147
   Enlightenment and, 113–114, 193
   George III and, 170
   pre-Revolutionary views of, 147–148,
     150–151
   as scientist, 297
   on slavery, 113
   on work ethic, 312, 317
Franklin Institute, 297
Fredericksburg, Virginia, 420, 430
Free African Society, 274
free blacks, 86, 272–275
   abolitionism and, 272, 274–275, 367
   accomplishments of, 272, 274–275
   black churches and, 268, 274, 460
   in Charleston, 274–275
   Dred Scott and, 406
   education of, 461(i)
   Fugitive Slave Acts and, 399–400
   labor of, 304(i), 445, 448(i)
   Patriot cause and, 189

   prejudice against, 268
   Reconstruction and, 443, 445–446, 458
   sharecropping and, 462–464
   as tenant farmers, 272
   terrorism against, 465–467
   voting rights for, 259–260, 272, 371, 456
   women, 462
Freedman's Savings and Trust Company, 469
Freedmen's Bureau, 445–446, 448–450, 458,
     461
freedom of speech, 224
Freedom's Journal, 367
freehold society
   in Middle Atlantic colonies, 105, 105(m),
     117, 125
   in New England, 100–104
   property rights and, 100–104, 105(m),
     124–125
   republicanism and, 156
Freeman, Elizabeth, 189(i)
Freemasonry, Order of, 344
Freeport Doctrine (Douglas), 408
Free Presbyterian Church, 316
Free-Soil Party, 395–396, 398
   "Bleeding Kansas" and, 403
   elections and, 401
   political realignment and, 405(m)
   Republican Party and, 402
Frelinghuysen, Theodore Jacob, 114
Frémont, John C., 392–393, 394(m), 405, 417
French and Indian War, 119–122, 172. See also
     Seven Years' War
French colonization, 6, 12, 14, 99, 119–122,
     120(m), 132–133, 135–136
   British Empire and, 96
   Christianization and, 41, 43, 63, 65
   fur trade and, 41–44
   Iroquois and, 63, 65
   in Louisiana, 13, 41
   in West Indies, 71, 96, 179–180, 182,
     219–220
French Revolution
   division of Americans and, 219–221
   ideological impact of, 220, 223(i)
Fugitive Slave Act
   of 1793, 371
   of 1850, 398
   resistance to, 399–400
Fulani Indians, 22(i)
Fuller, Margaret (1810–1850), 356–357

INDEX I-19

Fulton, Robert, 305
Fundamental Constitutions
    (Carolina; 1669), 69
fur trade, 37–38, 119
    British, 388
    Dutch, 43–44, 63, 65
    environmental effects of, 65
    French, 41–43
    Indian wars and, 41–43, 63–65
    inland peoples and, 63–65

Gadsden, James, 401
Gage, Thomas, 125, 138, 141, 149, 155, 158
gag rule, 372
Gallatin, Albert, 238, 244, 248
Galloway, Joseph, 154
Gama, Vasco da, 23
gang-labor system, 352, 383, 448–449, 461, 464
Garrison, William Lloyd (1805–1879), 352,
    368–370, 369(i)
    Free-Soil Party and, 395
Garsed, Richard, 297
Gaspée (ship), 151
Gassaway, Robert, 166
Gates, Horatio, 174(m), 176, 180
Gazette of the United States, 224
gender roles. See also women
    in Africa, 80
    of free blacks, 449
    Mormons and, 366(i)
    Native American, 12–14, 231–232
    reform and, 352–353
    transcendentalism and, 356
    utopian communalism and, 358, 360–362
    women's rights and, 374, 376
General Union for Promoting the Observance
    of the Christian Sabbath, 315
Geneva, Switzerland, 30–31
Genius of Universal Emancipation
    (newspaper), 369
gentry class, 69, 87–88. See also elite
    defined, 34
George I, king of England (r. 1714–1727),
    92, 94(i)
George II, king of England (r. 1727–1760),
    92, 94(i)
George III, king of England (r. 1760–1820),
    167, 168(i), 170–171, 179, 188, 253
    Declaration of Independence and, 171
    policies of, 132, 138, 143–145, 151–152

rebellion against, 138
repeal of Stamp Act and, 168
Georgia
    antiabolitionism in, 372
    as colony, 94–95, 153
    economy of, 219
    evangelicals in, 118
    freed slaves in, 446
    Ku Klux Klan in, 465
    migrants from, 386
    Native Americans and, 337, 339
    plantations in, 233
    Reconstruction and, 456, 458
    secession and, 398, 413, 414(m)
    sharecropping in, 463(m)
    Sherman's march through, 437
    slavery in, 94, 118, 268, 269(m), 276(m), 383
    war with Spain and, 94–95
Germain, George, 175
Germans
    in colonial America, 104–106
    draft and, 424
    immigration of, 70, 126, 309, 314, 317, 319,
        349, 402, 416–417
    as Loyalists, 157
    in Maryland, 110(i)
    in Pennsylvania, 70, 106–109, 157
    Pietism and, 114
Germantown, Pennsylvania, 70
Germany, 30, 95
Gettysburg, battle of (1863), 412, 424,
    430–431, 431(m), 434
Ghent, Treaty of (1814), 244
Gibbons, Thomas, 252
Gibbons v. Ogden (1824), 252, 305
Gibraltar, 75, 180, 184
Giddings, Joshua, 393
Gilbert, Humphrey, 44
Giles, John, 118
Glorious Revolution (1688), 72–74, 91, 93, 96,
    143
Godey's Lady's Book, 375
Godwyn, Morgan, 68
gold
    Spanish conquests and, 24, 28, 33, 38, 39(m)
    trade in, 20, 21(m)
    Virginia company and, 45
gold rush (California; 1849–1857), 396, 397(i)
Goliad, Texas, 386, 387(m)
Gorges, Ferdinando, 44

**Gough, John** (1817–1886), 318
**Graham, Isabella,** 315
grain. *See also* corn; Price Revolution; rice;
    wheat
    exports of, 103–104, 110, 308
    production of, 105–106
    transportation for, 304–309
Grand Canyon, 38
**Grant, Ulysses S.** (1822–1885), 418
    1868 elections and, 455–456
    Ku Klux Klan Act (1871) and, 465
    Lee's surrender and, 440
    at Petersburg, 436
    as president (1869–1877), 467–468
    Reconstruction and, 454, 460, 469
    Richmond campaign (1864) and, 435(*m*)
    scorched earth campaign of, 435
    Sherman and, 439
    Shiloh and, 421, 423
    as Union Army commander, 433–435
    Vicksburg campaign of, 430
    in the West, 421, 430, 434
Great American Desert. *See* Great Plains
Great Awakening, 112–118, 141, 277, 281–282.
        *See also* evangelicalism; revivalism; Second
        Great Awakening
    Edwards and, 114
    George Whitefield and, 114–116
    political aspects of, 116–117
    religious fervor of, 114–117
Great Britain. *See also* British Empire; England;
        English colonization
    American empire of (1713), 76(*m*)
    boundaries of western lands and, 243(*m*),
        244, 245(*m*)
    Civil War and, 432
    civil war in, 69
    colonial trade of, 68
    Confederacy and, 426, 432
    control of trade by, 89(*m*)
    France and, 74
    Mexico and, 391
    nineteenth-century immigration from,
        318–319
    Oregon and, 388, 393
    slave trade and, 77
    Spain and, 74, 86
    territorial disputes with, 237
    War of Austrian Succession and, 95
    West Indian trade and, 88

Great Lakes, 11, 63, 184, 230, 244, 344
    migration to, 302, 303(*m*)
    transportation to, 304–305, 306(*m*)
Great Plains, 28, 386, 389
Great War for Empire. *See* Seven Years' War
Greece, 19
**Greeley, Horace,** 361, 428, 468
greenbacks, 427. *See also* currency
**Greene, Nathanael,** 182
**Greenleaf, Simon,** 377
Greenville, Treaty of (1795), 229(*i*), 230, 231(*i*)
**Grenville, George,** 134–138, 135(*i*)
**Griffin, James B.,** 423
**Grimké, Angelina,** 370, 372, 376–377
**Grimké, Sarah,** 370, 372, 376–377
**Grimké, Thomas,** 262
Grund, Francis, 292
Guadalupe Hidalgo, Treaty of (1848), 395
Guatemala, 7, 9
guilds, 20
Guinea Company, 33
Gulf of Mexico, 11, 41
Gullah dialect, 84–85, 271
guns, 294
    Remington rifles, 299
    Rifle Clubs, 467
    rifle-muskets, 426, 431
**Guttridge, Molly,** 185(*i*)
Guy Fawkes Day, 141

Haas, Philip, 327(*i*)
habeas corpus, 424
Haiti, 24, 238
    economy of, 464
    slave revolt in, 267, 464
**Haldimand, General,** 152
**Halifax, Lord,** 121
**Hall, Basil,** 322
**Hall, John H.,** 299
**Hall, Prince,** 367
**Haller, Albrecht von,** 37
**Hamilton, Alexander** (1755–1804)
    assumption plan of, 217
    banking system and, 336
    Constitution and, 252
    duel with Aaron Burr, 240
    *The Federalist* and, 212
    fiscal program of, 216–219
    Jefferson and, 217–219, 218(*i*)
    on national bank, 216–217

at Philadelphia Convention, 208
plan for Northern Confederacy and, 240
pro-British foreign policy of, 221
program of national mercantilism, 250
on public credit, 216
as secretary of the treasury, 216–218
Hamilton Manufacturing Company, 313
**Hammond, James,** 266
**Hammond, John Henry,** 384
**Hancock, John,** 136, 142
**Handsome Lake** (Seneca chief), 230
**Harding, Chester,** 251(*i*)
**Harper, Frances,** 457
Harpers Ferry, Virginia, 299, 420, 426
    Brown's raid on (1859), 409
**Harris, Anna,** 270
**Harris, David,** 438
**Harris, Jim,** 428
**Harris, William,** 62–63
**Harrison, William Henry** (1773–1841),
        241–242
    death of, 349
    1836 elections and, 344
    1840 elections and, 347–349, 348(*i*)
    as president (1841), 349
Hartford, Connecticut, 56, 185, 244
    manufacturing in, 294
    transportation and, 308
Harvard College, 144
hat making, 249
Hawaii, 283(*m*)
Hawikuh Indians, 39
**Hawthorne, Nathaniel,** 304, 357–358
**Hayes, Rutherford B.** (1822–1893), as
        president (1877–1881), 469–470
**Heaton, Hannah,** 101–102, 115
**Helper, Hinton,** 414
**Henrietta Maria,** queen of England
        (r. 1625–1649), 47
**Henry, Patrick** (1736–1799), 138–139, 139(*i*),
        150, 157, 167, 208
    church taxes and, 193
    on Hamilton's financial program, 216
    on ratification of Constitution, 213, 221
**Henry,** prince of Portugal (r. 1394–1460), 20
**Henry VIII,** king of England (r. 1509–1547), 31
heresy, 18, 30, 58
**Hernandes, Harriet,** 466
**Higginson, Francis,** 37
**Higginson, Thomas Wentworth,** 432–433

**Hillsborough, Lord,** 148–150
Hispaniola, 24–25, 27
**Hoff, John,** 247
hog production, 270, 293–294, 294(*i*), 302, 305
Hohokam culture, 11
Holland. *See* Dutch colonization
Holland Land Company, 235
**Holloway, Houston H.,** 442
**Holmes, Isaac,** 271
Holy Roman Empire, 30
Homestead Act (1862), 426–427
**Hood, John B.,** 436, 438(*m*)
**Hooker, Joseph** ("Fighting Joe"), 420, 430
**Hooker, Thomas,** 56
**Hoole, Axalla John,** 382, 404
Hopewell Indians, 10–11
Hopi Indians, 11
**Hopkins, Samuel,** 282
horses, 27–28
Horseshoe Bend, battle of (1814), 242, 243(*m*)
household production
    in colonial America, 100, 104, 148
    outwork and, 106, 148, 293, 300
House of Burgesses, Virginia, 46–47, 51–53
House of Commons, England, 34,
        137–138, 144
House of Lords, England, 34
House of Representatives, U.S.
    abolitionism and, 372
    impeachment and, 454
    Know-Nothing Party in, 402
    Republican Party and, 409
    Wilmot Proviso and, 395
**Houston, Sam,** 387
**Howard, Oliver O.,** 446
**Howe, Julia Ward,** 457
**Howe, William,** 172–175
**Hudson, Henry,** 43
Hudson Bay, 75
Hudson River, 41, 63, 172–173, 176, 252
    Erie Canal and, 235
    manors on, 105, 105(*i*), 234
Hudson River Valley
    Dutch in, 104–105, 124–125
    land conflicts in, 124–125, 126(*m*)
    loyalists in, 157
    settlement of, 105(*m*)
Hudson's Bay Company, 388
Huguenots, 31, 41, 108–109
human sacrifice, 10, 12

**Hume, David,** 143
hunter-gatherers, 7
**Huntington, Susan,** 101
Huron Indians, 41–43, 63, 65
**Hus, Jan,** 30
**Hutcheson, Francis,** 143
**Hutchinson, Anne,** 55–56
**Hutchinson, Thomas,** 139, 151–152, 155

Icaria, Texas, 359(m)
Ice Age, 7, 8(m)
Illinois, 230
    Civil War and, 418
    Lincoln and, 407–408
    migration to, 301, 303(m)
    Mormons and, 363, 364(m), 365
    slaves in, 405
    voting rights in, 258, 259(m), 322
Illinois Indians, 65
immigrants, 222. See also Irish immigrants;
        migration
    in British America, 102, 104–105
    Canadian, 301
    Chinese, 397(i), 456
    class distinctions and, 309–310, 319–320
    democracy and, 417
    draft and, 424
    earliest, 7, 8(m)
    English, 31, 33–34, 37–38, 44–59,
        318–319
    European, 99–103, 106, 108
    French Canadian, 301
    German, 70, 126, 309, 314, 317, 319, 349,
        402, 416–417
    Know-Nothing Party and, 402
    nineteenth-century, 318–319
    poverty of, 310, 313–314, 319–320
    Puritan, 53–61
    voting rights and, 456
immigration laws, 222, 224, 237–238
impeachment, 454
imports, 110, 123, 295. See also boycotts;
        exports; nonimportation; trade
impressment, 267. See also military draft
Inca civilization, 27
indentured servants, 34, 109, 134, 168, 175,
        210, 292
    in Chesapeake, 50–53
    children sold as, 102
    vs. slavery, 464

Independence, Missouri, 390
Independent Order of Good Templars, 375
Independent Treasury Act (1840), 347
India, 18, 23, 426
    as British colony, 121, 152
    indentured servants from, 464
    Protestant mission in, 283(m)
Indiana, 230
    migration to, 234, 301, 303(m)
    revivals in, 317
    Shakers in, 284
    voting rights in, 258, 259(m), 322
Indian Ocean, 23
Indian Removal Act (1830), 337, 339(i)
indigo, 124, 269(m)
individualism, 353–358
    meaning of, 353
    Mormons and, 363, 366
    transcendentalism and, 353–355
    utopian communalism and, 357–358, 361
Indonesia, 18, 23
industrialization, 426. See also factory system;
        manufacturing; mills
    artisans and, 297, 299–301, 319
    Civil War and, 434
    market economy and, 317
    Republican Party and, 402
    transcendentalism and, 355, 358
    unemployment and, 301, 309, 319
    urbanization and, 308–309
    working conditions and, 353
Industrial Revolution, 172, 349
    in America, 292–301
    in England, 123, 247, 292
    labor for, 293, 295–298, 296(i)
    political parties and, 324
    social structure and, 292–293, 309–314,
        312(i)
    U.S. Patent Office and, 297
    Whig policy and, 342
inflation, 34
    during American Revolution, 186–187
    in Confederacy, 427–428
    excess of currency and, 177–178, 187
influenza, 27
**Ingersoll, Jared,** 140
inheritance, 102–103, 310
    marriage and, 102, 260–262
    primogeniture and, 263
    women's rights to, 260–261

inland Indians, 63–65

Inquisition, 24

*Institutes of the Christian Religion* (Calvin), 30

Intolerable Acts (1774), 153

Inuit Indians, 7

Iowa, 302, 303(*m*)

Ireland, 155
    famine in, 319

Irish immigrants, 110, 222, 304, 349. *See also*
        Scots-Irish
    cultural conflict and, 319–320
    draft and, 424
    1852 elections and, 402
    nineteenth-century, 301, 303, 304(*i*), 309,
        314, 317, 319–320

Irish Test Act (1704), 110

iron industry, 299, 307, 342
    tariffs on, 295, 328

Iroquois Indians, 7, 19, 119, 121, 229
    adopted captives of, 63, 65
    "covenant chain" of military alliances, 75
    Five Nations of, 14, 41, 63
    French and, 63, 65, 75
    fur trade wars of, 41–44, 63, 65
    Six Nations of, 75, 172, 173(*i*), 176

irrigation, 9, 11, 83

Irving, Washington, 265

Isabella, queen of Spain (r. 1474–1516), 24

Islam, 24, 85
    vs. Christianity, 18, 20

Isthmus of Darien (Panama), 25

Italian Revolution (1848), 356

Italy, 19, 356


Jackson, Andrew (1829–1836)
    abolitionism and, 372
    American System and, 329–330, 332–334,
        336, 340–342
    antimonopoly policies of, 329, 341
    Democratic Party and, 324, 347
    1824 elections and, 318(*m*), 325–326
    1828 elections and, 328–330
    freemasonry and, 344
    inauguration of, 331
    Indian Removal Act of, 337, 340(*m*)
    as military commander, 242, 243(*m*), 244
    Native Americans and, 329, 336–340
    nullification and, 333–334, 343, 415
    as president (1829–1837), 331–342, 332(*i*),
        335(*i*), 343(*i*), 387

Second Bank and, 334–336
    on states' rights, 329, 333–334, 341
    Supreme Court and, 341

Jackson, Patrick Tracy, 295

Jackson, Rebecca Cox, 360

Jackson, Thomas J. ("Stonewall"), 419(*m*), 420

Jacksonian Democrats, 324

Jacobins, 220

Jamaica, 77

James, duke of York, 69

James I, king of England (r. 1603–1625), 44, 54

James II, king of England (r. 1685–1688),
        72–73, 138

James River, 46, 49(*i*), 182

Jamestown, 46, 53

Japan, 24, 401

Jay, John (1745–1829), 323
    *The Federalist* and, 212

Jay's Treaty (1795), 230

Jefferson, Thomas (1743–1826), 86, 157
    agrarian vision of, 218–219
    Bill for Establishing Religious Freedom
        (1786), 193
    Constitution and, 239
    death of, 257
    Declaration of Independence and,
        171–172, 184
    as diplomat, 208
    on education, 264–265
    Embargo act and, 241
    Enlightenment and, 143
    Hamilton and, 217–219, 218(*i*), 224
    on John Q. Adams, 328
    on manufacturing, 219, 297
    on Missouri crisis, 277
    Mormons and, 365
    Northwest Ordinance and, 204
    as president (1801–1809), 237–240
    primacy of statute law and, 252
    republicanism and, 218–219, 282, 284
    Revolution of 1800 and, 237
    slavery and, 190, 219, 367
    states' rights and, 224, 333, 335
    the West and, 239–240

Jenkins' Ear, War of (1740), 95

Jerome, Chauncey, 292

Jesuits, 43, 65

Jews, 24, 108(*m*)

Johnson, Andrew (1808–1875), 442
    campaigning by, 451

**Johnson, Andrew** (*cont.*)
vs. Congress, 450–452
Fourteenth Amendment and, 450–451
impeachment of, 454
as Lincoln's running mate, 436
as president (1865–1869), 444–446
Reconstruction plan of, 444–446, 444(*i*), 450–451, 461
veto of civil rights bill by, 450
veto of Reconstruction Act by, 454
**Johnson, Gabriel,** 92–93
**Johnson, Samuel,** 188
**Johnson, Sir William,** 99, 119
**Johnston, Albert Sidney,** 421
**Johnston, Joseph E.,** 436
**Johnston, Joshua,** 272
**Jones, Nathaniel,** 166
**Joseph, Chief** (Mohawk chief). *See* **Brant, Joseph**
judicial review, 252–253
meaning of, 238
judiciary, 198. *See also* common law; court system; law; Supreme Court
trial by jury and, 136, 138–139, 142, 274
Judiciary Acts (1789, 1801), 215, 237–238
**Julian, George W.,** 451
July Fourth, 257
Lincoln's speech on, 418

Kansas, 38
abolitionism in, 382
admission of, 406
African American regiments in, 432
"Bleeding Kansas," 403–404
popular sovereignty in, 399(*m*)
Kansas-Nebraska Act (1854), 399(*m*), 401–403, 407
**Kant, Immanuel,** 353
**Kearney, Stephen,** 394(*m*)
**Kelley, Abby,** 372
**Kempe, John Tabor,** 187
**Kendall, Amos,** 332
Kendall, Keziah, 377
Kennesaw Mountain, battle of, 436
Kentucky, 233–234
migration from, 302, 303(*m*)
revivals in, 278, 283(*m*)
secession and, 414, 416, 418, 421
Shakers in, 284

slavery in, 268, 276(*m*)
westward migration from, 390
Kickapoo Indians, 65
**King, Charles Bird,** 339(*i*)
King George's War (War of the Austrian Succession; 1740–1748), 95
King Philip's War (Metacom's Rebellion), 61–63, 62(*i*)
King's College. *See* Columbia University
King's Mountain, South Carolina, 182
Know-Nothing (American) Party, 402–403, 405, 405(*m*)
**Knox, Henry,** 207, 215, 228
**Knox, John,** 31
**Knox, William,** 133
Kongo, Africa, 86
Ku Klux Klan, 465–467, 467(*i*)
Ku Klux Klan Act (1871), 455(*t*)
failure to enforce, 465, 467

labor. *See also* indentured servants; labor unions; slavery
of African Americans, 445
capital and, 343–344
division of, 293–294, 294(*i*)
forced, 40, 462
free black, 304(*i*), 445, 448(*i*)
gang, 352, 383, 448, 461, 464
Industrial Revolution and, 293, 295–298, 296(*i*)
manufacturing and, 295, 309
Reconstruction and, 442
slavery and, 402, 417
wage, 343, 361, 448(*i*), 449, 461–462, 464
of women, 449
laborers
education for, 264–265
farm, 102, 297
as journeymen, 299–300
Pietism and, 112
rights of, 300, 345–347
as Sons of Liberty, 141, 152
urbanization and, 310, 313–314, 319, 336
women, 301
labor theory of value, 300–301
labor unions, 299–301
closed-shop agreements and, 345, 347
emergence of, 299–301, 345–347
Panic of 1837 and, 346

strikes and, 300–301
working hours and, 300, 347
**Lafayette, marquis de,** 181(*m*), 182
Lake Champlain, 63
    battle of, 243(*m*), 244
Lake Erie, 242
Lake Texcoco, 9
Lancaster, Pennsylvania, 90, 250
Lancaster Turnpike Company, 250
land
    for freed slaves, 451
    grants of, 103, 119, 124
    ownership of, 446, 449, 461, 464. *See also*
        freehold society; property rights
    policies on, 46, 51–52, 58–59
    public, 461
    taxation of, 384
Land Act, 239
land banks, 96
Land Ordinance (1785), 463(*m*)
**Lane, Dutton,** 118
Lane Theological Seminary (Cincinnati, Ohio),
    369
**Lansing, John,** 209
**Larcom, Lucy,** 296, 298
**Larkin, Thomas Oliver,** 390, 392
**La Salle, Robert de,** 41
Latin America. *See* South America
Latter-day Saints, Church of Jesus Christ of. *See*
    Mormons
**Laud, William,** 54, 56
**Laurens, Henry,** 185
law. *See also* common law; court system;
        immigration laws; judiciary; Supreme
        Court
    equality before, 446, 450, 465
    statute, 252
Lawrence, Kansas, 403
lawyers, 142
*Leaves of Grass* (Whitman), 356
Lecompton constitution (Kansas), 402–403,
    406
**Lee, Mother Ann,** 284
**Lee, Richard Henry,** 171, 188
**Lee, Robert E.,** 419(*m*)
    black soldiers and, 438
    Gettysburg and, 430–431
    Grant and, 434, 435(*m*)
    invasion of North by, 420, 431(*m*)
    Lincoln and, 416

in Mexican War, 393
    surrender of, 435(*m*), 440
Leeward Islands, 77
Legal Tender Act (1862), 427
**Leggett, William,** 345
**Leisler, Jacob,** 73–74
Leisler's revolt (1689), 73–74, 129
**Leo X, Pope** (1513–1521), 29
*Letters from a Farmer in Pennsylvania*
    (Dickenson), 147
*Letters from an American Farmer*
    (Crèvecoeur), 258
Levant Company (Turkey), 33
**Lewis, Meriwether,** 240
Lexington, battle of (1775), 158, 185
**Libby, Owen,** 214(*m*)
*The Liberator* (newspaper), 370, 374
Liberia, Africa, 268
Liberty Party, 372–373, 391, 395
*The Life of George Washington* (Weems), 265
**Lincoln, Abraham** (1809–1865), 408(*i*).
        *See also* Civil War; Emancipation
        Proclamation
    assassination of, 442
    debates with Douglas of, 408
    early life of, 407
    1860 elections and, 405(*m*), 409–410, 412
    1864 presidential campaign of, 436–437, 456
    Grant and, 421, 434
    McClellan and, 419–420
    national mercantilism under, 426
    Reconstruction and, 442, 470
    Republican Party and, 402, 406–410
    slavery and, 409–410, 412
    the South and, 412
    speeches of, 408, 413, 418, 442
    states' rights and, 334
    suspension of habeas corpus by, 424
    Union victory and, 432–440
**Lincoln, Benjamin,** 180
**Lincoln, Mary Todd,** 407
Lisbon, Portugal, 23
Litchfield Law School, 261
literacy, 368, 402, 456, 458
literature
    antislavery, 385, 400
    republican, 265
    transcendental, 355–357
Little Round Top, 430
**Little Turtle** (Miami chief), 230

Livingston, Robert, 239
Livingston family, 104–105, 124
Locke, John, 73, 112–113, 189, 264
    on natural rights, 113, 143, 184
Loco-Foco (Equal Rights) Party, 345
log cabin campaign (1840), 348(i)
London, England, 14
Long, Stephen H., 386
Long Island, New York, 44, 73
    battle of, 173, 185
Longstreet, James, 430
lost colony. See Roanoke
Louisbourg, siege of (1745), 95, 122
Louisiana, 11
    Acadians in, 121
    admission to Union, 245, 268
    African American regiments in, 432
    in Civil War, 430
    Emancipation Proclamation and, 429
    as French colony, 13, 41
    migration to, 233, 302, 303(m)
    Napoleon and, 239
    Reconstruction and, 443, 453(m), 457, 461
    Republican government in, 467, 470
    secession of, 413
    slavery in, 268–271, 269(m), 276(m), 437
    voting rights in, 323
Louisiana Purchase (1803), 227, 239–240,
    245(m)
    slavery and, 276(m), 397, 401
    Texas and, 245, 386
Louisville, Kentucky, 306(m), 307(m), 308
Louis XIV, king of France (r. 1643–1715), 41,
    72, 94
Louis XVI, king of France (r. 1774–1792), 179,
    182, 221(i), 223(i)
    execution of, 220
L'Ouverture, Toussaint, 239
Lovejoy, Elijah P., 372
Low, Thomas, 265
Lowell, Francis Cabot, 295
Lowell, Massachusetts, 296–298, 301, 308, 342
Loyalists, 157
    British strategies and, 172–176, 180–182
    emigration of, 187–188
    vs. Patriots, 166–167, 172, 176
lumber industry, 135
Lundy, Benjamin, 369
Lunt, Dolly Sumner, 439
Luther, Martin, 30, 116

Lutheranism, 277
    in colonial America, 104, 108, 108(m)
Lynn, Massachusetts, 247, 300

MacAllister, Alexander, 99
McClellan, George B., 416, 418–420, 436–437
McCormick, Cyrus, 294, 309
McCormick and Hussey, 308
McCulloch v. Maryland (1819), 252
McDougall, Alexander, 141
McDowell, Irwin, 418
McGready, James, 278
Machiavelli, Niccolò, 20
machinery
    industrialization and, 294–296, 294(i), 296(i)
    interchangeable parts and, 292
    tool making and, 299
Macon, Nathaniel, 275
Madeira Islands, 20, 23
Madison, James (1751–1836), 157–158, 168,
    208–209. See also Virginia Plan
    Bill of Rights and, 215, 241
    Bonus Bill and, 251, 328
    Embargo Act and, 241
    First Bank and, 247
    on Hamilton's financial plan, 216–217
    Marbury case and, 238
    political theory of, 114
    as president (1809–1817), 237–238,
        241–242
    religion and, 193
    as secretary of state, 238, 241
    on slavery, 267
    states' rights and, 333
Magna Charta, 142
Magnum, W. P., 344
Maine, 44, 360(i)
    admission as free state, 275–276, 276(m)
    Massachusetts and, 73
    settlement of, 233
    temperance movement and, 382
    voting rights in, 272
    women's rights in, 378
"Maine law," 382
maize, 8–9. See also corn
Malcolm, John, 140(i)
Manassas Creek (Bull Run), 418, 420
Manhattan Island, 43. See also New York City
Manifest Destiny, 383–391
    origin of term, 387–388

Manifesto and Declaration of the Indians (Bacon), 53

**Mann, Horace,** 375

**Mansfield, Sir James,** 143

manufacturing. *See also* factory system; industrialization; mills
  American System and, 327–328
  business elite and, 301, 310
  education and, 265
  in Midwest, 307–309
  in Northeast, 292–301
  rural, 247–249
  water power and, 294–295, 308

**Marbury, William,** 238

*Marbury v. Madison* (1803), 238, 252

**Marcy, William L.,** 332, 401

**Marion, Francis** (Swamp Fox), 182

market economy, 349
  class divisions and, 292–293, 309–314, 312(*i*), 317
  cycles of, 358
  expansion of, 301–309
  industrialization and, 319

**Marquette, Jacques,** 41

marriage. *See also* women
  arranged, 102, 260–261
  companionate, 260–261
  complex, 362
  divorce and, 261
  domestic abuse and, 261
  dower right and, 102
  equality within, 258, 260–261
  within ethnic group, 109, 111
  inheritance and, 102, 260–262
  interracial, 371, 412–413
  medieval, 16–17
  Mormons and, 366(*i*)
  polygamous, 363, 366, 366(*i*)
  republican, 260–261, 263(*i*)
  slaves and, 271, 449
  utopian communalism and, 358–359, 362
  women's rights and, 374, 378

marriage portion, 102

Married Women's Property Acts (1839–1845), 378

**Marshall, John** (1755–1835), 240, 250–253, 251(*i*), 305. *See also* Supreme Court
  on commerce clause, 341
  death of, 341
  *Fletcher v. Peck* (1810), 253

*McCulloch v. Maryland* (1819), 252–253
*Marbury v. Madison* (1803), 238, 252
  Native American cases and, 339
  three principles of, 251

**Martin, Henry Byam,** 234(*i*)

**Martin, Josiah,** 168

**Martineau, Harriet,** 322

Martinique, 122

**Mary II,** queen of England (r. 1688–1694), 72–74, 91

Maryland. *See also* Baltimore, Maryland
  Catholicism in, 47–48, 73
  Civil War and, 416, 420
  claims to western lands and, 202
  as colony, 47–48, 52, 69, 73, 85
  emancipation in, 429, 437
  freed slaves in, 448
  ratification of Constitution and, 213
  revolts in, 73
  Scots-Irish in, 110
  secession and, 414, 418
  Second Bank and, 252
  slavery in, 80, 83, 85, 270
  South Atlantic system and, 89–90
  voting rights in, 258, 259(*m*), 323
  wheat production in, 124

*Maryland Gazette,* 233, 265

**Mason, George,** 193, 210

Masons. *See* Freemasonry, Order of

Massachusetts
  claims to Western lands, 202
  free blacks in, 272
  Fugitive Slave Acts and, 400
  Know-Nothing Party in, 402
  ratification convention in, 213
  revivals in, 278
  separation of Maine from, 275
  transportation in, 235
  voting rights in, 324
  women in, 199–201, 375, 378

Massachusetts Bay Colony. *See also* Boston, Massachusetts
  assembly of, 91
  Dominion of New England and, 72–74
  General Court of, 54, 132
  government of, 54–55
  House of Representatives in, 136–138, 158
  land grants in, 103
  Native American attacks on, 75
  Navigation Acts and, 71–72

Massachusetts Bay Colony (*cont.*)
  religious intolerance in, 55–56
  revolts in, 73–74
  "taxation without representation" and,
    136–137, 149–150
*Massachusetts Gazette,* 148
*Massachusetts Spy,* 152
Massacre of Saint George Fields, 150
**Massatamohtnock.** *See* **Opechancanough**
**Mather, Cotton,** 58, 112–113
matrilineal societies, 14
Mayas, 9, 12
Mayflower Compact, 54
*Mayor of New York v. Miln* (1837), 341
**Meade, George G.,** 393, 430–431, 431(*m*)
mechanics, 295, 297, 313. *See also* artisans
  unemployment and, 319
Mechanics' Union of Trade Association, 300
medieval period, 14–18
  agriculture in, 14–16
  marriage in, 16–17
  religion in, 17–18
  seasonal cycle in, 15–16
  social order in, 16–17
Mediterranean Sea, 18–21, 21(*m*)
**Melville, Herman,** 357
Memphis, Tennessee, 450
Mennonites, 109
mercantilism, 89(*m*), 94–96. *See also* South
  Atlantic system
  American, 249–250, 426
  British, 33, 94–95
  in British colonies, 70–72
  commonwealth system and, 249–250
  meaning of, 20, 33
  politics of, 94–95, 97–98
merchants, 89(*m*), 106. *See also* shopkeepers
  as business elite, 301, 308–310
  Dutch, 70, 122
  education and, 265
  in England, 150
  Enlightenment and, 112–113
  as loyalists, 147(*i*), 148, 150, 158
  Navigation Acts and, 95
  of New England, 135–136
  revolution and, 139, 141–142, 152, 157
  sharecropping and, 462, 464
  South Atlantic system and, 88–91
  textile industry and, 293
  trade with Britain and, 123–124

Mesoamerica, 7, 8(*m*), 9–12, 27.
  *See also* Aztecs
  trade with, 95
*mestizos,* 29, 390
Metacom's Rebellion (King Philip's War),
  61–63, 62(*i*)
**Metcalf, Seth,** 131
Methodism, 114
  abolitionism and, 368, 376
  African Americans and, 268, 274, 277–281
  child rearing and, 264
  evangelical, 277–281, 283(*m*)
Mexican War (1846–1848), 382, 392–394,
  394(*m*)
  Democratic Party and, 393, 396
  presidential candidates and, 400
  slavery and, 371
  victory in, 393–396
Mexico, 7, 9, 245(*m*)
  California and, 390
  cession of land from, 398
  economy of, 392
  foreign debts of, 391
  independence of, 386
  Mormons in, 363–364, 364(*m*)
  purchase of land from, 401
  Spanish conquests in, 25, 27
  Texas and, 386–387
Mexico City, 9, 393
Miami Indians, 65
**Miantonomi** (Narragansett chief), 37
**Michelangelo,** 20
Michigan, 302, 303(*m*), 361
Micmac Indians, 10
Middle Atlantic colonies (1720–1765)
  economic inequality in, 104–106
  religious diversity in, 99, 104–111,
    108(*m*)
Middlebury Female Seminary, 285
middle class
  Civil War and, 424, 427
  culture of, 311, 312(*i*), 317
  in government, 342, 344
  Lincoln and, 402, 407
  politics and, 323–324, 336
  racism and, 372
  reform and, 353
  Republican Party and, 402
  South Atlantic system and, 90
  taxes and, 427

transcendentalism and, 354(i), 355
women of, 311, 312(i), 375
Middle Passage, 78(m), 81, 82(i), 267(i)
Middlesex County Congress (1774), 158
the Midwest
   democracy in, 323
   Jackson and, 329
   John Q. Adams and, 327
   manufacturing in, 307–309
   migration to, 234, 298, 301–302, 303(m)
   wheat production in, 302–305, 303(m)
migration. See also emigration; immigrants
   to California, 390
   internal, 8(m), 232–235
   to and from Midwest, 234, 298, 301–302,
      303(m)
   Native American, 7
   from New England, 124–125, 233–234, 298,
      301–302, 303(m), 307
   to old Southwest, 267(i), 268, 269(m),
      301–302, 303(m)
   religious conflict and, 31
   social causes of, 16, 33–34
   to and from the South, 232–233, 302,
      303(m)
   trans-Appalachian, 122, 126(m), 133(m),
      262, 283(m), 301–302, 303(m)
   to the West, 323, 383, 386–390, 389(m)
military. See also Army of Northern Virginia;
      Army of the Potomac
   African Americans in, 432–433, 433(i),
      438, 440
military draft (Civil War), 423–424, 433, 438
militia, 185. See also Minutemen
   colonial, 121, 128–129, 132, 158
   mob control and, 320
   service in, 259(m), 324
Militia Act (1862), 424
Mill Dam Act (1795), 250
Miller, Lewis, 267(i)
Millerites, 379(i)
mills. See also factory system
   colonial, 106
   textile, 294–298, 301, 308
   on waterways, 247
Mimbres Valley, 11
Minutemen, 158
missionaries. See also Jesuits
   Catholic, 37–40, 65
   missions of, 38–40

   to Native Americans, 37–41, 43, 65
   Protestant, 282, 283(m)
Mississippi, 233, 467
   admission to Union, 268
   migration to, 302, 303(m)
   Reconstruction and, 456–458, 465
   secession and, 398, 413
   slavery in, 268, 269(m), 270–271,
      276(m), 383
   women's rights in, 378
Mississippian civilization, 13, 27
Mississippi River, 244
   Civil War and, 416, 420–421, 422(m),
      423, 430
   early explorers and, 41, 63
   navigation of, 184, 236
   resettlement of Indians and, 337–340,
      340(m)
   Treaty of Paris and, 184
Mississippi River Valley
   cotton production in, 268–270, 269(m)
   land sales in, 303(m)
   Native Americans in, 6, 9, 11, 13,
      119, 120(m)
Missouri
   Civil War and, 416–417
   emancipation in, 429, 437
   migration to, 301–302, 303(m)
   Mormons in, 364(m), 365
   racism in, 409
   secession and, 414, 418
   slavery in, 383, 386
   statehood for, 275–277, 276(m)
   westward migration from, 390
Missouri Compromise (1821), 275–277,
      276(m), 397, 415
   Dred Scott and, 406
   Kansas-Nebraska Act and, 401
Missouri River, 240, 420
Mittelberger, Gottlieb, 111
mobs. See also draft riots; Sons of Liberty
   antiabolitionist, 371–372
   antiblack, 367
   anti-Catholic, 320
   anti-Mormon, 363
   in Britain, 150
   British troops and, 128–129, 141, 150
   colonial land rights and, 125, 128
   colonial taxation and, 131, 134, 139, 140(i),
      141–142

*Moby-Dick* (Melville), 357
**Moctezuma,** 25–26
Mogollon culture, 11
Mohawk Indians, 44, 62–63, 75
Mohawk River, 63
Mohegan Indians, 62
Molasses Act (1733), 96, 132, 135–136
Mongolia, 18
monopolies, chartered, 341, 345
**Monroe, James** (1758–1831), 268
　Era of Good Feeling and, 255
　Louisiana Purchase and, 239
　as president (1817–1825), 237, 245
Montauk Indians, 37
Monterrey, Mexico, 393
**Montesquieu, Charles-Louis de,** 143, 212
Montreal, capture of (1760), 122
**Moody, Paul,** 295
Moore's Creek Bridge, battle of, 168–169
**Morgan, Daniel,** 182
**Morgan, William,** 344
Mormons, 359(*m*), 362–366, 364(*m*)
　polygamy of, 363–364, 366
　in Utah, 364, 366
　violence against, 363
Mormon Trail, 389(*m*)
**Morris, Gouverneur** (1752–1814), 105(*m*),
　210, 211(*i*), 253
**Morris, Robert,** 178, 186, 202–204, 207–208, 234
**Morris, Samuel,** 117
**Morris, Thomas,** 329, 394
Morristown, New Jersey, 185
**Morse, Samuel F. B.,** 319
**Morton, Oliver,** 451
*Mother's Magazine,* 285
**Mott, Lucretia,** 370, 372, 378
mound building, 11–12
**Murray, Judith Sargent,** 201, 201(*i*)
Muslims, 18, 20–21, 29. *See also* Arabs; Islam
Mutual Benefit Society, 300
*My Life in the South* (Stroyer), 273
mysticism, 354

Nantucket, Massachusetts, 274(*i*)
**Napoleon Bonaparte,** 239
Napoleonic Wars (1802–1815), 240
Narragansett Indians, 37, 55, 61–62
Nashoba, Mississippi, 359(*m*)
Nashville, Tennessee, 444
**Nast, Thomas,** 452(*i*)

Natchez Indians, 6, 12–13
National Banking Acts (1863, 1864), 427
nationalism, 207
National Road, 302, 328, 333
National Trades' Union, 300
National Union Party, 436, 451
National Woman Suffrage Association, 457
Native American Clubs, 319–320
Native Americans, 6–14. *See also individual
　peoples*
　adopted prisoners of, 63, 65
　agriculture of, 9–14, 230–232
　alleged inferiority of, 388
　art of, 9, 11
　assimilation of, 38–41
　in California, 390
　Carolina, 45(*i*)
　changed world of, 59–65
　cultural destruction of, 27–28, 37–43, 65
　cultural diversity of, 63–65
　defense against, 132, 149(*m*)
　of eastern woodlands, 12–14
　encounters with immigrants and, 99,
　　109, 111
　English settlers and, 46–47, 59, 61
　European diseases and, 26–27, 37, 39–41,
　　43, 54, 61, 63, 65
　vs. European military technology, 25
　European wars and, 74–75
　as farmers, 27
　French and Indian War and, 122
　fur trade and, 41–44, 63, 65
　Kansas-Nebraska Act and, 401
　land of, 11, 52, 227–230, 231(*m*)
　languages of, 44
　Marshall Court and, 337, 339
　matrilineal societies of, 14
　in Mesoamerica, 7, 8(*m*), 9–10, 12, 27
　migrations of, 7
　missionaries to, 37–40, 65
　in Mississippi valley, 6, 9, 11, 13
　mixed-blood, 337
　Mormons and, 364(*m*)
　policies toward, 328–329
　political status of, 349
　Pontiac's uprising and, 122, 123(*i*), 132
　population changes of, 52, 63, 65
　Puritan treatment of, 61
　religions of, 9–10, 13
　removal of (1820–1843), 336–339, 340(*m*)

resistance of, 46–47, 52, 61, 228–232
Revolutionary War and, 172, 173(i), 176, 184
in southwest U.S., 11–12
Spanish conquest of, 25–29, 38–40
trade with, 69, 75
tribal politics of, 65
wars of, 52, 61
women's role among, 12–14, 65
nativism, 319–320. See also Know-Nothing Party
    anti-Catholic, 402
Naturalization Act (1798), 222, 238
natural resources. See environment
natural rights, 113, 143, 184, 189–190
Nauvoo, Illinois, 363, 365
Navajo Indians, 7
Navigation Acts (Acts of Trade and Navigation;
    1651–1751), 51, 147, 249
    British Empire and, 135–137
    British mercantilism and, 68, 70–72, 95
    resistance to, 95, 97–98
    South Atlantic system and, 77, 89–90
    vice-admiralty courts and, 136–137
    West Indian trade and, 95, 206
Nebraska, 399(m)
**Neolin,** 122
Netherlands. See Dutch colonization
New Amsterdam, 43–44. See also New York
    City
New England
    agriculture in, 100–104
    black tenant farmers in, 272
    California and, 390
    China trade and, 389
    Currency Act and, 96
    Dominion of, 72–74, 92, 138
    economy of, 88–91
    education in, 264, 266
    elite politics in, 92
    English colonization in, 53–61, 60(m),
        100–104
    evangelicalism in, 114–116, 278, 281–282,
        283(m)
    farm life in, 100–104
    fishing industry in, 185
    freehold society in, 100–104
    governance of, 69, 72
    manufacturing in, 292–301
    merchants of, 135–136
    migration from, 124–125, 233–234, 298,
        301–302, 303(m), 307

population of, 99, 103
    Puritans in, 100, 103–104, 114, 121, 131,
        141, 143, 148, 153. See also Pietism
    republicanism and, 141, 148
    Shakers in, 360
    tenant farmers in, 102
    textile industry in, 247–249, 293–298, 301,
        308, 342
    transcendentalism in, 353–358
    utopian communities in, 362
    War of 1812 and, 242, 243(m), 244
    women's rights in, 377
New England Anti-Slavery Society, 369
New England Emigrant Aid Society, 402
Newfoundland, 44, 75, 76(m), 184
    as British colony, 122, 149(m),
        153, 154(m)
New France, 41. See also Canada
New Hampshire, 103, 233, 253
    constitution of, 184
    migration from, 301, 303(m)
    ratification of Constitution by, 213
    as royal colony, 72
    Shakers in, 284
    South Atlantic system and, 89–90
New Harmony, Indiana, 359(m)
New Jersey, 185, 252
    as colony, 69, 72, 91
    land disputes in, 125
    popular power in, 91–92
    Quaker settlements in, 106, 109
    revivalism in, 114
    in Revolutionary War, 174(m), 177
    settlement of, 104, 106
    voting rights in, 201, 259(m), 260
New Lights, 115–118, 127, 170
New Mexico, 11, 38–41
    annexation of, 395
    attempt to buy, 392
    Compromise of 1850 and, 398, 399(m)
    Mexican War and, 393
New Netherlands, 33, 43–44, 68.
        See also New York
    British occupation of, 69, 71
New Orleans, battle of, 243(m), 244
New Orleans, Louisiana, 41, 239, 243(m),
        244, 423
    business elite of, 274–275
    Emancipation Proclamation and, 429
    free blacks in, 274–275

New Orleans, Louisiana (*cont.*)
    Reconstruction and, 443
    transportation and, 305,
        306(*m*)–307(*m*), 308
Newport, Rhode Island, 55, 88, 89(*m*), 182
newspapers, 143. *See also New York Tribune*
    abolitionist, 369–370, 374
    political cartoons in, 156(*i*), 221(*i*),
        335(*i*), 343(*i*)
    politics and, 324, 329, 335(*i*)
**Newton, Isaac,** 112
New York
    British occupation of, 69, 71, 185
    colonial, 14, 43–44, 69, 71–74
    Dutch in, 43–44, 104, 105(*m*)
    Erie Canal, 302–305, 304(*i*), 306(*m*)
    *Hudson River manors, 104, 105(m)*
    *land disputes in, 124–125*
    land in, 104
    Mormons in, 364(*m*)
    New England immigrants, 302
    politics in, 324
    popular power in, 92
    ratification of Constitution by, 213
    representative assembly in, 74
    revivals in, 283(*m*)
    revolts in, 73–74
    in Revolutionary War, 172–176,
        174(*m*), 185
    utopian communities in, 360–362
    voting rights in, 259(*m*), 260, 324
    West Indian trade and, 88–89
    wheat production in, 124
    women's rights in, 375, 378, 380
New York City
    business elite of, 310
    colonial, 43–44, 73
    corruption in, 469
    draft riots in (1863), 424
    foreign trade and, 309
    Panic of 1837 and, 346
    reform movement in, 317
    during Revolutionary era, 149(*m*),
        182, 185
    slavery in, 90
    slums of, 313
    as transportation hub, 303–306,
        306(*m*)–307(*m*)
    West Indian trade and, 88–89, 89(*m*)
New York Humane Society, 282

*New York Tribune,* 309, 458, 468
    Fourierism and, 361
    Fuller and, 356
**Nicholson,** Lieutenant Governor, 73
*Niles' Weekly Register* (periodical), 292
*Ninety-five Theses* (Luther), 30
Nipmuck Indians, 61
nobility
    in medieval Europe, 16
    Price Revolution and, 34
nonimportation, 147(*i*), 148, 155. *See also*
        boycotts
the North
    communal experiments in, 359(*m*)
    Compromise of 1850 and, 398
    economy of, 88–91, 459
    education in, 375
    Fugitive Slave Acts and, 399–400
    population of, 426
    racism in, 367
    Republican Party and, 402, 410
    slave vs. free states and, 396–398, 401–404
    vs. the South, 383, 413, 449
    *Uncle Tom's Cabin* and, 400
**North, Lord,** 172, 174, 182
    compromises of, 149–150
    naval blockade and, 155
North Anna, battle of, 435(*i*)
North Carolina
    as colony, 44, 69, 75, 91
    freed slaves in, 449
    industrial capacity in, 426
    Ku Klux Klan in, 465
    land disputes in, 126, 128–129
    migration from, 301–302, 303(*m*)
    ratification of Constitution by, 213
    Regulators in, 125–126, 126(*m*), 128–129,
        128(*i*), 180, 233
    revivalism in, 317
    salutary neglect and, 92–93
    secession and, 414, 416
    slave labor in, 270, 276(*m*), 384
    voting rights in, 324
the Northeast. *See also* New England; New York
    Jackson and, 329
    John Q. Adams and, 327–328
    manufacturing in, 292–301
Northern Pacific Railroad, 468
Northwest Ordinance, 203(*m*), 204, 405–406
Northwest Territory, 221

notables, 323–324
*Notes on the State of Virginia* (Jefferson), 219, 239
Nova Scotia (Acadia), 10, 75, 76(m), 179, 184
  as British colony, 121, 149(m), 153, 154(m)
  control of fisheries off, 184
**Noyes, John Humphrey** (1811–1886), 361–362
Nueces River, 392
*nuevo mundo* (new world), 24–25
nullification of tariffs, 333–334, 336, 343, 415
nurses, Civil War, 424–425, 425(i)

Oberlin College, 316(i)
Ochasteguins. *See* Huron Indians
**Ogden, Aaron,** 252
Oglethorpe, Georgia, 311
Ohio, 10, 230, 234
  migration to, 234, 301–302, 303(m)
  Shakers in, 360
  slavery in, 386
  utopian communities in, 361–362
  voting rights in, 259(m), 260, 323–324
  westward migration from, 388
Ohio Company, 119–121, 126(m)
Ohio River, 63, 65, 236, 241, 416, 420–421, 422(m)
Ohio River Valley
  expansion of Quebec and, 153–154
  French and Indian War and, 119–121, 120(m)
Old Lights, 116
Old Republicans, 328
Old Southwest (Alabama, Mississippi, Louisiana), 233
  migration to, 267(i), 268, 269(m), 301–302, 303(m)
Old Whigs, 145. *See also* Whig Party (England)
**Oliver, Andrew,** 139
**Oliver, Robert,** 246
Olmec Indians, 9
Omaha, Nebraska, Mormons in, 364(m)
**Oñate, Juan de,** 40
Oneida Community, 359(m), 361–362
Oneida Indians, 63
Onondaga Indians, 63
"On the Equality of the Sexes" (Murray), 201
**Opechancanough,** 46–47, 61
Order of the Star-Spangled Banner, 402
Ordinance of Nullification, 333–334
Oregon, 389(m), 393, 395
  annexation of, 391

  1844 elections and, 391
  migration to, 388–390
Oregon Trail, 364(m), 389(m), 390
Orphan Asylum Society, 315
Ostend Manifesto (1854), 401
**Ostram, Mary Walker,** 374
**O'Sullivan, John L.,** 387–388
**Otis, James,** 138, 142
Ottawa Indians, 65, 122, 123(i), 229, 229(i)
outwork system, 247–248
  in agriculture, 106
  household production and, 106, 148, 293

pacifism
  abolitionism and, 372
  Garrison and, 352
  in Pennsylvania, 70
  Quakers and, 109, 111, 125, 157
**Paine, Sarah Cobb,** 185
**Paine, Thomas** (1737–1809), 166, 170–171, 173. *See also Common Sense*
  attack on George III, 170
  on word "republic," 184
**Palladio, Andrea,** 20
Panama (Isthmus of Darien), 25
panics. *See also* depressions
  of 1819, 247
  of 1837, 346, 358, 361
  of 1857, 301, 311
  of 1873, 468
pantheism, 355
Paris, France, 14
Paris, Treaty of (1763), 133(m), 154(m), 184, 228, 230
Paris, Treaty of (1783), 231(m)
  western lands and, 227–230, 231(m)
Parliament, English, 34
  taxation and, 132–138
**Paterson, William,** 209
patriarchy, 16–17, 87, 100–103
  vs. republicanism, 260–261
Patriots, 131, 138–140. *See also* Sons of Liberty
  alliance with France and, 179–180
  ideological roots of, 142–143, 151
  vs. Loyalists, 166–167, 172, 176
  Radical Whig, 175, 216
patronage
  in colonies, 87, 94, 132
  John Q. Adams and, 329
  Van Buren and, 324

Paxton Boys, 125, 126(m)
Peace Democrats, 436
**Peale, Charles Willson,** 173(i), 263(i)
**Peale, James,** 263(i)
**Pearce, Charles H.,** 460
peasants, 9, 14–17, 272
peddlers, Yankee, 247, 248(i)
**Pelham, Henry,** 121
**Pendleton, Edmund,** 168
**Penn, John,** 125
**Penn, William,** 70, 91, 124
Pennsylvania, 127
    assembly of, 91
    as colony, 70
    German settlements in, 108–111
    Know-Nothing Party in, 402
    Quakers in, 70, 106–109
    revivalism in, 114, 317
    transportation in, 235
    voting rights in, 258, 259(m)
    West Indian trade and, 90
    wheat production in, 124
*Pennsylvania Gazette,* 114
peonage (forced labor), 462
Peoria Indians, 43
Pequot Indians, 59, 61
perfectionism, 361–362
**Perry, Oliver Hazard,** 242
Persia, 19
Peru, 7, 9, 27, 28(m)
Petersburg, Virginia, 434–436
phalanxes (Fourierist communities), 361
Philadelphia, Pennsylvania, 72
    abolitionist convention in (1830),
        367–368
    agitation against George III in, 170
    antiabolitionism in, 372
    Committee of Resistance in, 170
    Committee on Prices in, 186
    Continental Army in, 176
    free blacks in, 268
    Howe's attack on, 174(m), 176
    Patriot traders in, 188
    during Revolutionary era, 149(m)
    slavery in, 90
    South Atlantic system and, 89–90
    Tom Paine in, 170
    transportation and, 250, 305–306,
        306(m)–307(m)
    unions in, 300
    West Indian trade and, 88–90, 89(m)
    women of, 376
Philadelphia Convention (1787), 266
Philadelphia Female Anti-Slavery Society, 370
**Philip, King** (Metacom; Wamponoag chief),
    61–62, 62(i)
**Philip II,** king of Spain (r. 1556–1598),
    31–33, 38
Philippines, 122
**Phillips, Wendell,** 368, 429
**Pickett, George E.,** 431
Piedmont region, 123
**Pierce, Franklin** (1804–1869), 400–401
    as president (1853–1857), 402
Pietism, 99, 112, 114–115
**Pike, James M.,** 468
Pilgrims, 53–56. *See also* Puritans
**Pinckney, Thomas,** 446
Pinckney's Treaty (1795), 239
Pine Bluff, Arkansas, 449–450
**Pitt, William,** 121–122, 137, 145–146, 155
Pittsburgh, Pennsylvania. *See also* Fort
        Duquesne
    transportation and, 305, 306(m),
        307(m), 308
**Pius IX, Pope,** 319
**Pizarro, Francisco,** 27
plantations, 123–124. *See also* the South
    cotton and, 302, 308, 383–384
    culture of, 124
    impact of sharecropping on, 464(m)
    Kansas-Nebraska Act and, 402
    religion of, 112, 117–118
    river, 49(i)
    slavery and, 80–83, 266–273, 267(i),
        269(m), 280–281
    Southern gentry and, 87
    sugar production and, 77
pluralism. *See also* ethnic diversity
    religious, 99, 104, 108–111, 108(m)
Plymouth colony, 72–73
    legal code in, 54
**Poague, William,** 416
**Pocahontas,** 46
Poland Hill, Maine, 360(i)
political crisis of 1790s, 215–225
political parties. *See also* elections; *particular
        parties*
    fragmentation of, 409–410
    new, 401–402

nineteenth-century changes in, 398–406
and political machine, 324
realignment of (1848–1860), 405(m)
regional vs. national, 405(m)
rise of, 221–222, 323–325
workingmen's, 345
political theory, 113
politics
  abolitionism and, 372, 382–383
  African Americans and, 446
  American, 322–323
  British, 91–96
  corruption in, 324, 460, 468–469. *See also*
    patronage
  elite, 91–92
  imperial, 68–76
  middle class and, 323–324, 336
  newspapers and, 329
  religion and, 324
  rise of popular, 323–330
  sharecropping and, 464
  slavery and, 383, 396–398
  women in, 348–349
Polk, James K. (1795–1849), 396
  expansionism of, 391–392, 394–395, 401
  as president (1845–1849), 392–395
poll taxes, 258, 456
Ponce de León, Juan, 25
Pontiac (Ottawa chief), 123(i)
  rebellion of, 122, 132
Pony Express, 389(m)
*Poor Richard's Almanack* (Franklin), 113
Popé (shaman), 40
popular sovereignty, 252, 339
  original meaning of, 197
  slavery decisions and, 397–398, 399(m),
    400–403, 407–408
population
  in colonial America, 99, 103, 124, 126(m)
  disease and, 26–27
  in England, 33
  environment and, 9
  first census (1790) and, 228
  in Middle Atlantic colonies, 104
  Native American, 9, 26–27, 63, 65
  of North vs. South, 426
  seasonal patterns and, 15–16
  Spanish conquests and, 27–28
  urbanization and, 308–309
Port Bill (1774), 153

Port Hudson, Louisiana, 430
Portugal, 6, 23, 32, 77
  maritime expansion and, 18–22, 21(m)
Postlethwayt, Malachy, 68
Post Office Act (1792), 305
Potomac River, 419
Pottawatomie massacre (1856), 403
poverty
  of immigrants, 310, 313–314, 319–320
  of women, 313, 315
Powhatan, 46
praying towns, 61. *See also* Algonquian Indians
predestination, 55
Preemption Act (1841), 349
Presbyterians, 31, 193
  abolitionism and, 369
  in colonial America, 104, 108, 108(m),
    110–111, 114
  egalitarianism of, 117, 310
  Enlightenment and, 264
  evangelical, 324
  New Lights, 115–118, 127, 170
  Old Lights, 116
  Princeton and, 116
  social reform and, 314–317, 374
  synods of, 277
presidential elections
  Adams, John (1796), 222
  Adams, John Quincy (1824), 318(m),
    325–326
  Buchanan, James (1856), 403–405
  Grant, Ulysses S. (1868), 455–456
  Grant, Ulysses S. (1872), 468
  Harrison, William Henry (1840), 347–349,
    348(i)
  Hayes, Rutherford B. (1876), 469
  Jackson, Andrew (1832), 335–336
  Jefferson, Thomas (1800), 224, 237
  Lincoln, Abraham (1860), 405(m), 408(i),
    409–410
  Lincoln, Abraham (1864), 434, 436–437
  Madison, James (1808), 237
  Madison, James (1812), 237, 242
  Pierce, Franklin (1852), 400–401
  Polk, James K. (1844), 391
  Taylor, Zachary (1848), 396, 405(m)
  Van Buren, Martin (1836), 344
  Washington, George (1788), 215
presidios (forts), 390
Price Revolution, 33–34

primogeniture, 17, 263
*The Prince* (Machiavelli), 20
Princeton, New Jersey, battle of, 173, 174(m)
Princeton College, founding of, 116
*Principia Mathematica* (Newton), 112
printing industry, 113, 142–143, 148
Prison Discipline Society, 314
prisons
    abolition of, 352, 372
    debtors', 197, 206–207, 323, 345
    as reforming institutions, 314–315
    reform of, 372, 375, 459
Privy Council (British), 146, 152
Proclamation for Suppressing Rebellion and
        Sedition, 167
Proclamation Line (1763), 122, 132–133,
        133(m), 154(m), 157
Prohibitory Act (1775), 180
property
    common ownership of, 353, 358–359, 361
    ownership of, 233, 446, 448
    political rights and, 91
    private, 246, 251–253
    protection of, 210, 448, 461
    slaves as, 449
    taxation of, 459
    voting rights and, 92, 322–324, 456, 464
property rights, 197, 199, 251–253
    abolitionism and, 371
    in Confederacy, 428
    conflicts over, 125–129
    corporate, 253
    *Dred Scott* and, 406
    freeholders and, 100–104, 105(m)
    inheritance and, 102, 260
    Mormons and, 366
    Reconstruction and, 461
    slavery and, 383, 418, 429
    of women, 87, 100, 102, 109, 378–380
Prophetstown, Indiana, 241
proprietorships, 69–70, 73–74
**Prosser, Gabriel,** 190, 272
**Prosser, Martin,** 272, 281
prostitution, 375
*The Prostrate State* (Pike), 468
protectionism. *See* tariffs: protective
Protestantism, 73, 85. *See also* evangelicalism;
        *individual denominations*
    anti-Catholicism of, 141, 153, 154(m),
        319–320

French (Huguenots), 31, 41, 108–109
    Know-Nothing Party and, 402
    Manifest Destiny and, 388
    missionary action and, 282, 283(m)
    in New World, 37–38, 41, 47–48
    social reform and, 277, 282, 314
    Whigs and, 342
    women and, 262, 284–286
    work ethic and, 311
Protestant Reformation, 29–31. *See also*
        Calvinism; Luther, Martin
    in England, 31
    in Holland, 31–32
    Roman Catholic Church and, 29–33
Providence, Rhode Island, 55, 88, 295
Pueblo Indians, 11–12, 27, 38–40
    revolt of, 40
Puget Sound, 389
Puritans, 31, 53–61, 103–104, 131
    coercive policies of, 54–56
    vs. English government, 56
    as freeholders, 100
    during French and Indian War, 121
    Great Awakening and, 113–115
    vs. hierarchichal institutions, 56
    Mormons and, 363
    Plymouth colony and, 53–54, 72–73
    republicanism and, 143, 148, 282
    Revolution of, 56, 138, 141
    seizure of Indian lands by, 55, 59
    transcendentalism and, 353
    witchcraft fears of, 57–58
    women and, 55–56, 100–102
putting-out system, 247

Quakers, 102, 104, 106–109, 278
    abolitionism and, 189–190, 368, 370, 376
    Calvinism and, 70
    as merchants, 309
    in Nantucket, 274(i)
    in New Jersey, 106, 109
    pacifism of, 109, 111, 125, 157, 284
    in Pennsylvania, 70, 106–109
    social equality and, 106, 109, 310
    women of, 70
Quartering Acts
    of 1765, 138, 146
    of 1774, 153
Quebec, 6, 41–42, 63, 75
    battle for (1758), 122

capture of (1759), 122
colonization of, 122, 132, 133(m)
Quebec Act (1774), 153, 154(m), 157
Queen Anne's War (War of the Spanish
    Succession; 1702–1713), 74, 76(m)
Queen's College. See Rutgers University
Queen's Own Loyal Virginians, 167
Quetzalcoatl, 25

race. See also particular groups
    reform and, 352
    status and, 29, 51
racism, 80, 268, 272–275, 408
    abolitionism and, 371–372
    Free-Soil Party and, 395
    interracial marriage and, 371, 412–413
    Manifest Destiny and, 388
    middle-class, 371–372
    military service and, 433
    Reconstruction and, 450
    voting rights and, 257, 259–260
Radical movement, southern, 409–410, 413
Radical Republicans, 443, 445, 451–452, 461,
    468–470
railroads, 293, 307(m), 426, 434
    destruction of, 436
    Erie, 306
    expansion of, 305–307, 306(m)–307(m)
    hub for, 307(m)
    investment in, 301, 341, 343
    Northern Pacific, 468
    Reconstruction and, 458–459
    transcontinental, 401, 403
Raleigh, Walter, 44, 45(i)
Ramsay, David, 166, 227
ranching, cattle, 305, 390
Randolph, Edward, 71
Ranke, Leopold von, 196
Rankin, Christopher, 275
Raphael, 20
ratification conventions, 208–211
reconquista, 24
Reconstruction (1865–1877), 442–471
    Presidential, 443–452
    quest for land in, 460–464
    Radical, 452–464, 453(m), 468–470
    Republicans and, 442
    role of black churches in, 460
    undoing of, 464–470
    violence and, 451

Reconstruction Act (1867), 453, 455(t)
Redeemers, 465, 467
redemptioners, 109
Red Jacket (Sagoyewatha; c.1758–1830),
    230, 232(i)
Red Shirts, 467
reform. See also social reform
    British (1763–1765), 131–137, 143, 146
    economic, 353
    educational, 265, 375
    government, 341–342
    moral, 375
    Republican Party and, 403
Reform Bill of 1832 (England), 323
regionalism, 318(m), 405(m)
Regulators, 157
    in North Carolina, 125–126, 126(m),
        128–129, 128(i), 180, 233
religion, 37–41, 53–56. See also evangelicalism;
        Great Awakening; Protestant Reformation;
        revivalism; Second Great Awakening;
        particular denominations
    abolitionism and, 268, 284, 368–371, 374
    African, 85
    African American, 117–118, 268, 274,
        277–281, 460
    anti-Masonry and, 344
    Crusades and, 18
    diversity of, 99, 104, 108–111, 108(m)
    English civil war and, 56, 69, 72–73
    Enlightenment and, 281
    established church and, 257
    in Europe, 17–18, 29–33
    freedom of, 55, 70, 190, 193–194
    intolerance and, 55–56
    justification of slavery and, 384
    vs. laws of nature, 58
    medieval, 17–18
    in Middle Atlantic colonies (1720–1765), 99,
        104, 108–111, 108(m)
    Native American, 9–10, 12–13, 40, 42–43
    on plantations, 112, 117–118
    politics and, 324
    reform and, 352–381
    separation of church and state, 190,
        193–194, 257
    society and, 54–56
    taxation and, 193–194
    wars of, 18, 56
    women's rights and, 374

Renaissance
    American, 265
    impact of, 18–20
    Muslim influences on, 18–19
Reorganized Church of Jesus Christ of Latter-
        day Saints, 364
representative government, 136–141
republic, 171, 184–185
republicanism, 171, 184–194. *See also*
        constitutional rights
    artisan, 345
    charters and, 250
    Civil War and, 413
    condemnation of, 319
    definition of, 322
    education of children and, 263–265
    evangelical Christianity and, 281–282, 284
    ideals of, under wartime pressure,
        184–187
    institutions of, 196–215
    literary culture of, 265
    of Puritans, 143, 148, 282
    religion and, 190, 193–194
    as representative government, 257
    rights of women and, 260–263, 263(i), 281
    social classes and, 258, 310, 342
    the South and, 458
    testing of, 184–187
    Virginia Plan and, 208–209
republican motherhood, 261–262, 263(i),
        285, 374
Republican Party (1850s-on)
    Crisis of 1877 and, 469–470
    Crittenden Plan and, 415
    Democrats and, 329, 436–437
    draft riots and, 424
    1858 elections and, 408–409
    1860 elections and, 409–410
    1862 elections and, 430
    1863 elections and, 431
    free-soil policy of, 426
    Ku Klux Klan and, 465, 467
    Lincoln and, 406–410, 423
    national mercantilism and, 426
    origins of, 402
    Peace Democrats and, 436–437
    realignment of, 405(m)
    Reconstruction and, 442–446, 450–452,
        460–461, 468–470
    slavery and, 409, 412, 415

in the South, 457–460, 469
    women's rights groups and, 457, 459
Republican Party (Jeffersonian), 251
    agricultural expansion and, 237, 239
    commonwealth idea and, 250
    factions of, 255, 325
    vs. Federalists, 219, 221–222, 253, 255
    War of 1812 and, 241
"Resistance to Civil Government" (Thoreau),
        371
Restoration (Great Britain), 69–72
Restraining Act (1767), 146
**Revels, Hiram,** 459(i)
Revenue Acts
    of 1673, 71
    of 1762, 132
    of 1767, 146
**Revere, Paul,** 158
revivalism, 316(i), 349. *See also* evangelicalism;
        Great Awakening; Second Great
        Awakening
    abolitionism and, 370
    in colonial America, 114–118
    in postcolonial America, 257, 260
    Second Great Awakening and, 257, 277–284,
        283(m), 315, 319
    social reform and, 315–318, 316(i)
    women's rights and, 374
Revolutionary War
    armies and strategies in, 174–175
    battles in, 158, 167, 172–182, 174(m),
        181(m), 185
    British strategies in, 172–176, 180–182
    causes of. *See* Revolutionary War (prewar
        events)
    diplomatic triumph in, 183–184
    financial crisis in, 177–178
    in the North, 172–176, 174(m)
    paper money in, 427
    partisan warfare in Carolinas, 180–182
    political legacy of, 199
    publishing and, 143
    response in Britain to, 183
    rights of man and, 112–113, 142–143
    social and financial perils in, 176–178
    in the South, 180–182, 181(m)
    Treaty of Alliance with France (1778), 179
    women in, 185(i)
Revolutionary War (prewar events)
    Boston Massacre, 150

Boston Tea Party, 140(*i*), 152
boycotts, 139, 145, 147(*i*), 148, 150, 153
Committees of Correspondence, 151–153
Daughters of Liberty, 147(*i*), 148
Intolerable Acts (1774), 153
Loyalists, 157
militia, 121–122, 128–129, 158
Quartering Acts, 138, 146, 153
Sons of Liberty, 139–142, 140(*i*), 147(*i*), 152
Stamp Act (1765), 131, 137–147, 150
taxation, 131–138, 155–157
Tea Act (1773), 151–152
**Rhett, Robert Barnwell,** 409, 413
Rhode Island, 55, 203, 208, 211, 213
currency in, 96
revocation of corporate charters, 72
voting rights in, 324
**Rhodes, Elisha Hunt,** 412, 423
rice
African knowledge of, 83
exports of, 123–124
production, 269(*m*), 270–272
slavery and, 83
in South Carolina, 83, 94, 126
Southern production of, 269(*m*), 270–272
Richelieu River (River of the Iroquois), 63
Richmond, Virginia, 419(*m*)
in Civil War, 418, 426, 428, 434, 436, 440
food riots in, 428
free blacks in, 274
manufacturing in, 299, 306(*m*)–307(*m*), 308
Rio Grande River, 11, 392
Roanoke Island, 45(*i*)
Roanoke (lost colony), 44
**Robespierre, Maximilien,** 220
**Robinson, John,** 56
**Rochambeau, Comte de,** 182
Rochester, New York
revivalism in, 316–317
transportation and, 305, 307(*m*)
**Rockingham, Lord,** 145
Rocky Mountains, 11, 240, 245
**Rodgers, John,** 282
**Rogers, Robert,** 123(*i*)
**Rolfe, John,** 46
Roman Catholic Church. *See* Catholicism;
    Catholics
Romanticism, 260, 353
Rome, ancient, 18–19
Roosevelt family, 105(*m*)

**Rowlandson, Mary,** 64
Royal African Company, 78
**Ruffin, Thomas,** 384
rum, 88, 96
rural life
of African Americans, 86
in Europe, 14–16
manufacturing and, 247–249
**Rush, Benjamin,** 163, 170, 185, 262, 264
Rush-Bagot Treaty, 244
Russia, Alaska and, 391
**Russwurm, John,** 367
Rutgers University, founding of, 116

Sacramento Valley, California, 392
**Sahagún, Friar Bernardino de,** 26
St. Augustine, 38–39, 39(*m*)
St. Lawrence River, 41, 122
**St. Leger, Colonel Barry,** 171(*m*), 176
St. Louis, Missouri, 11
transportation and, 306(*m*), 307(*m*),
    308–309
St. Mary's City (first settlement), 47
Salem, Massachusetts, 55
popular power in, 92
witchcraft trials in, 58
**Salisbury, Stephan,** 206
*Salmagundi* (Irving), 265
saloons, 314. *See also* taverns; temperance
salutary neglect, 92, 94(*i*), 96, 132, 136
San Francisco, California
gold rush and, 396
Mexican War and, 382
Sanitary Commission, U.S., 424–425
San Jacinto, battle of (1836), 387
**Santa Anna, Antonio López de,** 386–387,
    393, 394(*m*)
Santa Fe, New Mexico, 39(*m*), 40, 393
Santa Fe Trail, 389(*m*)
Saratoga, battle of (1777), 174(*m*), 175–176,
    179, 183, 185
Sauk Indians, 65, 337–338, 339(*i*)
Savannah, Georgia, 180, 181(*m*), 188, 437
scalawags, 457–458
*The Scarlet Letter* (Hawthorne), 357
**Schneebeli, Heinrich,** 109
**Schuyler, Philip,** 175
Scots-Irish, 104
in colonial America, 99, 110, 117, 119
merchant credit of, 123–124

Scots-Irish (*cont.*)
  in Middle Atlantic colonies, 110–111, 114,
    123–124
  in Pennsylvania colony, 106
**Scott, Winfield,** 339, 393, 394(*m*), 416, 418
  as presidential nominee, 400
Sea Islands, 446, 448
**Sears, Isaac,** 141
secession, 412–441
  Compromise of 1850 and, 398
  Constitution and, 443
  Democratic Party and, 409
  elite southerners and, 444
  insurrection and, 415
  Lincoln and, 410
  process of, 414(*m*)
  Reconstruction and, 445
  Republican Party and, 405
  slave vs. free state conflict and, 397–398
  southern leaders and, 410
  Upper South states and, 414, 414(*m*),
    416, 418
Second Bank of the United States, 251–252
  war against, 334–336, 335(*i*)
Second Great Awakening (1820–1860), 257,
    277–284, 283(*m*), 315, 319, 352. *See also*
    evangelicalism; Great Awakening;
    revivalism
  abolitionism and, 367
  child rearing and, 264
  women's rights and, 374
Second Party System, 342–344, 348(*i*)
  end of, 398–406
self-government. *See also* democracy;
    representative government; republicanism
  colonial assemblies and, 137–138, 146, 150,
    154, 158
**Sellars, John,** 297
**Sellars, Samuel,** 297
Seminole Indians, 12, 272, 337, 339, 340(*m*)
Senate, U.S.
  impeachment and, 454
  Lincoln and, 407
  Wilmot Proviso and, 395
Seneca Falls Declaration (1848), 378
Seneca Indians, 14, 63, 229–230, 232(*i*)
Senegal, Africa, 20
Senegambia, Africa, 23
sentimentalism, 260
separate spheres, 374

separation of powers, 212. *See also* checks and
  balances
**Sequoyah,** 337
Seven Years' War, 121–122. *See also* French and
  Indian War
**Sewall, Samuel,** 57
**Seward, William H.,** 398, 406, 409
sexuality
  Oneida Community and, 361–362
  Shakers and, 359–360
  utopian communities and, 362
  women's rights and, 374–375
**Seymour, Horatio,** 429, 456
Shakers, 284, 358–360, 359(*m*), 366(*i*)
shaman, 40
sharecropping, 462–464
Sharpsburg, Maryland, 420
**Shaw, Lemuel,** 347
Shawnee Indians, 119, 125, 229(*i*), 230,
  232, 241
**Shays, Daniel,** 206–207, 213
Shaysites, 220
Shays's Rebellion, 206–208, 220
**Shelburne, earl of,** 99, 146
**Sheldon, Lucy,** 236(*i*)
**Sheridan, Philip H.,** 435
**Sheridan, Robert,** 272
**Sherman, William Tecumseh** (1820–1891),
    434, 469
  capture of Atlanta, 436–437
  land for liberated slaves and, 446
  march to the sea, 437–438, 438(*m*)
  total war and, 437–438
Shiloh, battle of, 421, 423
shipbuilding industry, 88–90
shoemaking, 293
shopkeepers, 104, 106, 141
Siberia, 7
Sierra Leone, Africa, 188
Singer Sewing Machine Company, 299
Six Nations, Iroquois, 75, 172, 173(*i*), 176. *See
  also* Iroquois Indians
**Slater, Samuel,** 295
"Slave-Power" conspiracy, 395,
    401–403, 407
slave rebellion, 85–86, 267, 272, 281, 409
  abolitionism and, 367–368
  Emancipation Proclamation and, 429
  fear of, 333, 384, 412
  in Haiti, 239

slavery, 76–91, 189(i). *See also* abolition; cotton; Middle Passage; plantations; the South
  abolition of, 188–192, 327(i), 344, 437, 442–443, 464
  among Native Americans, 86, 337
  antislavery movement and. *See* abolitionism
  British Empire and, 68, 96
  in Chesapeake colony, 80, 83, 104, 267(i), 269–271, 269(m)
  Civil War and, 412, 417, 428–430, 432–433
  in colonial America, 50–51, 53, 99, 117–118, 126, 157–158
  colonization and, 268, 407
  communal experiments and, 359(m)
  Constitutional Convention and, 210
  cotton and, 233, 267(i), 268–270, 269(m), 383–384
  culture of, 329
  economics of, 313
  in 1800, 192(m)
  evangelicism and, 315
  expansion of, 204, 267(i), 268–270, 269(m), 302, 303(m), 392–398, 399(m), 402
  family life and, 270–273
  fugitive slave laws and, 267
  justifications for, 384
  legalization of, 53
  Lincoln and, 407–409
  Mexican War and, 395
  in Mexico, 386
  in Middle Atlantic colonies, 104, 106
  military service and, 433
  Mormons and, 366
  Northwest Ordinance and, 204
  politics and, 391, 396–398, 405(m), 409–410
  popular education and, 355
  positions on, 113, 329
  in postcolonial America, 266–277, 267(i), 269(m), 276(m)
  property rights and, 275–276
  protection of, 409, 415
  Quakers and, 109
  reform movement and, 352–353
  republicanism and, 188–190, 192(m)
  Republican Party and, 402
  resettlement to old Southwest and, 267(i), 268, 269(m), 302, 303(m)
  Revolutionary War and, 167–168, 172, 180, 182, 188–191, 192(m)
  secession and, 414(m), 429
  slave vs. free states and, 396–398, 405–406
  in the South, 317, 343
  Union threat to, 427
  in West Indies, 68, 77, 80, 83, 86, 333
  westward expansion and, 390–391, 401–402
  women and, 83, 385
slaves
  African, 24, 50–51, 53
  arming, 438, 440
  auctions of, 234(i)
  British and, 188
  in Civil War, 426–427
  denial of education to, 85, 368
  draft and, 423
  Dutch and, 77
  emancipation of, 188–190, 192(m), 267–268, 275–276, 281, 333, 437, 449, 458
  freed, 376
  fugitive, 210, 398, 428, 430, 432
  Indian peoples and, 86
  labor gang system and, 352, 383, 448, 461, 464
  manumission of, 189–190
  in Middle Atlantic colonies, 104, 106
  Muslim beliefs and, 85
  Native American, 47
  as percentage of population, 172, 228
  as property, 210, 428–429
  relocation of, 267(i), 268, 269(m), 302
  resettlement of freed, 268, 407
  resistance by, 85–86, 384–385
  three-fifths rule for, 210
  westward migration and, 233
slave trade
  abolition of, 210, 267–268, 271, 275, 371, 398
  in Africa, 20, 21(m), 23
  with Africa, 6, 20–23, 21(m), 78(m), 89(m), 271
  South Atlantic system and, 76–80, 76(m), 90
*Slave Trader, Sold to Tennessee,* 267(i)
**Slidell, John,** 392
**Sloat, John,** 393, 394(m)
**Slocumb, Mary Hooks,** 169
smallpox, 26–27, 54, 59, 63, 113
**Smallwood, William,** 175
**Smith, Adam,** 77, 219
**Smith, Joseph** (1805–1844), 363, 364(m), 365
**Smith, Joseph, III,** 364
**Smith, Margaret Bayard,** 331
**Smith, Melancton,** 212

**Smith, Seba** (Major Jack Downing), 335*(i)*
**Smith, William,** 276
smuggling, 96, 134, 136
*Social Chaos on the Carolina Frontier* (Woodmason), 126–127
*The Social Destiny of Man* (Brisbane), 361
socialism, 361
social mobility
    African, 51
    as republican ideal, 258
    Republican Party and, 402
    work ethic and, 311–312, 317
social reform
    asylums and, 375
    children and, 375
    evangelicalism and, 315–318, 353
    of nineteenth century, 314–319
    prisons and, 314–315, 372, 375
    Protestantism and, 277, 282, 314
    religion and, 352–381
    revivalism and, 315–318, 316*(i)*
    women and, 375
    women's rights and, 375, 380
social structure. *See also* elite; gentry class; middle class
    in Africa, 21
    African Americans and, 50–51
    Aztec, 9–10, 25
    of British colonies, 69
    in Chesapeake colonies, 87–88
    Confederacy and, 438
    English, 34
    European medieval, 14–20
    hierarchy in, 16–17
    immigrants and, 309–310, 319–320
    Inca, 27
    Industrial Revolution and, 292–293, 309–314, 312*(i)*
    market economy and, 292–293, 309–314, 312*(i)*, 317
    matrilineal societies and, 12–14
    Native American, 9, 12
    Oneida Community and, 362
    peasants in, 34
    politics and, 322–324
    race and, 29, 51, 372
    Republican Party and, 402
    revolt and, 51–53
    slavery and, 402
    in the South, 257, 266, 320, 384

South Atlantic system and, 88–91
    in Spanish America, 27, 29
    yeomen, 34, 51–52, 58–59
social values, in new world, 53–56
Society for Promoting Christian Knowledge, 284
Society for the Free Instruction of African Females, 284
Society for the Promotion of Industry, 315
Society for the Relief of Poor Widows, 284, 315
Society of Friends. *See* Quakers
Society of Journeymen Tailors, 345
socioeconomic status. *See* social structure
*Sociology for the South; or, the Failure of Free Society* (Fitzhugh), 385
Solemn League and Covenant, 156
Sons of Liberty, 139–142, 140*(i)*, 147*(i)*, 152, 157, 220. *See also* mobs
**Soto, Hernán de,** 12, 38, 39*(m)*
the South. *See also* Civil War; cotton; plantations; slavery
    abolitionism and, 372, 376, 382–383
    agricultural economy of, 308
    American System and, 325
    Civil War destruction of, 437, 440
    class distinctions in, 257, 266, 320, 343–344
    communal experiments in, 359*(m)*
    Compromise of 1850 and, 398
    debt of, 460
    Democratic Party in, 409
    economy of, 458–459, 464
    1860 elections and, 409–410
    elite life in, 384
    Fugitive Slave Acts and, 399–400
    gentry class in, 87–88
    home rule for, 469
    Lower vs. Upper, 414*(m)*, 416, 418
    migration to and from, 232–233, 301–302, 303*(m)*
    vs. the North, 383, 413, 449
    policies of John Q. Adams and, 328
    popular education in, 355
    population of, 426
    race in, 257
    Reconstruction and, 442
    Republican Party and, 405
    sharecropping and, 464
    slavery in, 266–277, 267*(i)*, 317, 329, 343, 417
    slave vs. free states and, 396–398, 401–404

tariffs and, 328–329, 333–334
tenant farmers of, 266
westward expansion and, 390–391
South America, 29. *See also* Mesoamerica
slavery in, 415
trade with, 309
South Atlantic system, 76–80
Navigation Acts and, 95
social structure and, 88–91
urbanization and, 88, 90–91
South Carolina
abolitionism and, 382
African American regiments in, 432
Civil War and, 437
class in, 87–88
as colony, 69–70, 75, 83–85
economy of, 219
evangelicals in, 118
freed slaves in, 446, 448(i)
indigo production in, 124
kinship in, 85
Ku Klux Klan in, 465–466
migration to and from, 233, 301–302,
    303(m)
nullification and, 333–334, 336, 343
ratification of Constitution and, 213
Reconstruction and, 453(m), 457–458, 460
Regulators and, 125–126, 126(m), 128–129
Republican government in, 467, 469–470
revivals in, 278
rice in, 83, 94
secession and, 398, 413, 415
slavery in, 83, 85–86, 118, 266, 269–273,
    269(m), 276, 276(m), 333, 383–384
tariffs and, 333–334
voting rights in, 258, 259(m)
war with Spain and, 95
*The South Carolina Exposition and Protest*
    (Calhoun), 333
Southern Homestead Act (1866), 461
Southern Rights Democrats, 398, 409
**Southgate, Eliza,** 261
Southwest, Old (Alabama, Mississippi,
    Louisiana), migration to, 267(i), 268,
    269(m), 296, 301–302, 303(m)
Spain
Cuba and, 391, 401
vs. England, 32–33, 38, 94–95
vs. France, 38
Islam in, 18

maritime expansion of, 18, 24
Mexican independence from, 386
missions of, 38–40
Napoleon and, 239
peace talks with, 183–184
Portugal and, 32
vs. Protestantism, 31–33
in Revolutionary War, 180, 183–184
territorial disputes with, 237
Texas and, 386
wars with, 86, 94–95
the West and, 245(m), 390
Spanish Armada, 33
Spanish colonization, 24, 38–41, 39(m), 75, 272
Catholicism and, 29, 38–41
conquest of Aztecs and Incas, 9, 25–29,
    28(i), 28(m)
Florida and, 69
gold and, 24, 28, 33, 38
in Mexico, 25–28
in North America, 99, 120(m), 121, 132,
    154(m), 245(m)
in Texas, 245
Spanish Netherlands, 32. *See also* Dutch
    colonization
specie, 334, 346. *See also* currency
Specie Circular (1836), 347
spheres of influence, in American colonies,
    120(m)
spinning, 248
spoils system, 332, 342, 349
Spokane Indians, 6
Spotsylvania Court House, battle of, 434,
    435(i)
squatter sovereignty, 395, 397
Stamp Act (1765), 131, 137–147, 180, 206
repeal of, 145, 168
resistance to, 137–142
Stamp Act Congress (1765), 138, 142
**Stanley, Ann Lee** (Mother Ann), 358–360
**Stanton, Edward M.,** 454
**Stanton, Elizabeth Cady,** 372, 380, 456–457
Seneca Falls and, 378
states
constitutions of, 197–199, 224, 341, 454
formation and Indian cessions, 231(m)
governments of, 249–250, 341–342
secession of, 405
slave vs. free, 382–383, 393–394, 396–398,
    401–406

states (*cont.*)
  voting rights and, 456
  women's rights and, 378
states' rights, 275–277, 341, 343, 349
  Calhoun on, 333
  Confederacy and, 427
  draft and, 424
  Fugitive Slave Acts and, 400
  Indian removal and, 337, 339
  interstate commerce and, 305
  Reconstruction and, 445, 450
  Second Bank and, 334–335, 335(*i*)
  slavery and, 382
steam power
  manufacturing and, 294
  steamboats and, 305, 308–309
**Stephens, Alexander,** 418, 436, 445
**Steuben, Baron von,** 178
**Stevens, Thaddeus,** 428–429, 451
**Stewart, Maria W.,** 376
**Stiles, Ezra,** 129, 196
**Stone, Lucy,** 457
**Stone, Samuel,** 259
Stono Rebellion (1739), 86, 95
**Story, Joseph,** 251, 330
**Stowe, Harriet Beecher,** 376, 385, 400
strikes, 300–301
**Stroyer, Jacob,** 272
**Stuyvesant, Peter,** 44
suffrage. *See* voting rights
sugar, 461
  duties on, 135–137
  Molasses Act and, 96
  plantations and, 77, 80
  planter-merchant elite and, 77
  related industries and, 78–79
  slavery and, 68, 76–80, 76(*m*), 83, 86
  in the South, 268, 269(*m*)
  West Indies trade and, 88, 89(*m*), 106,
    135–136
Sugar Act (1764), 135–138, 145, 180
*A Summary View of the Rights of British
    America* (Jefferson), 171
**Sumner, Charles,** 382, 385, 428, 451, 457, 468
Supreme Court, 210, 215, 224, 237–238,
    250–253, 454
  Civil Rights Bill (1870) and, 468
  *Dred Scott* and, 405–408
  Fugitive Slave Acts and, 400
  *Gibbons v. Ogden,* 252, 305

interstate trade and, 305
  Marshall and, 250–253
  Native American cases and, 337, 339
  Roger Taney and, 341
  slavery and, 407–408
Susquehanna Company, 124
Susquehannock Indians, 52, 63
**Sutter, John A.,** 396
Swamp Fox. *See* Marion, Francis
Sweden, 44

Taino Indians, 24
**Talleyrand, Charles,** 222
**Tallmadge, James,** 275
**Taney, Roger B.,** 332, 341
  *Dred Scott* and, 406
  Fugitive Slave Acts and, 400
  Second Bank and, 336
**Tappan, Arthur,** 317, 370–371
**Tappan, Lewis,** 317, 370, 372
Tariff of Abominations, 328–329, 333
tariffs, 207, 213, 217
  of 1816, 328, 334
  of 1828, 328, 333
  in Civil War, 426–427
  Jackson and, 329, 333–334, 336
  during John Q. Adams's administration,
    327–328
  Know-Nothing Party and, 403
  for manufacturing, 295, 297
  nullification of, 333–334, 336
  protective, 336, 342, 347, 349
  for road and canal building, 325, 327
  textile industry and, 310
taverns, 140
taxation. *See also* Shays's Rebellion
  Articles of Confederation and, 202
  in Civil War, 427
  in colonial America, 131–138, 155–157
  colonial assemblies and, 91
  Confederacy and, 202, 206, 427
  Constitution and, 206
  excise levies and, 134, 217, 238, 310
  exemption for churches, 193
  hidden currency, 187
  increases in, 73
  Jefferson and, 238
  land, 384
  in New England colonies, 71, 73
  occupation tax, 258

political rights and, 91
poll tax, 258
power of, 252
of property, 459–460
rebellion and, 69
Reconstruction and, 459–460
religion and, 193–194
Revolutionary War and, 175, 178, 183
self-government and, 257
Shays's Rebellion and, 206
smuggling and, 134, 136, 152
Southern gentry and, 87
of stocks and bonds, 345
of wealthy, 345
without representation, 136–139, 377
women's rights and, 377
**Taylor, Zachary** (1784–1850), 392
1848 elections and, 396, 405(*m*)
Mexican War and, 393, 394(*m*)
as president (1849–1850), 396
slave vs. free states and, 396
Tea Act (1773), 151–152, 180
technology. *See also* machinery
abolitionism and, 370
in agriculture, 105–106, 294, 307–308
cotton production and, 233, 295–299
in factories, 293–299, 294(*i*)
Republican values and, 219
textile industry and, 219
tidal, 83
**Tecumseh** (Shawnee chief), 241–242
**Teedyuscung,** 75
temperance movement, 316–319, 344, 349, 382
abolitionism and, 369
free blacks and, 367
in Maine, 382
reform and, 353
societies of, 314, 317
women's rights and, 375, 379
tenant farmers, 232–235
in England, 149–150
in Hudson River Valley, 105(*m*), 124–125, 157
in Middle Atlantic colonies, 104–105
in New England, 102, 272
in Pennsylvania, 106
in Virginia, 117–118, 266
**Tennent, Gilbert,** 114, 116, 170
**Tennent, William,** 114
Tennessee, 233, 242, 414, 416, 430
emancipation in, 429, 437

industrial capacity in, 426
Ku Klux Klan in, 465
public education in, 460
Reconstruction and, 445, 453
revivals in, 278, 317
secession and, 414, 414(*m*)
westward migration from, 390
Tennessee River, 236, 421, 422(*m*)
Tenochtitlán, 9–10, 25, 27–28
Ten Percent Plan, 443
**Tenskwatawa** (Lalawethika), 241
Tenure of Office Act (1867), 454, 455(*t*)
Teotihuacán culture, 9, 14
terrorism
against blacks, 465–467
in Civil War, 435
**Terry, Eli,** 292
Texas
admission to Union of, 382
American settlement in, 386–387, 387(*m*),
389(*m*)
annexation of, 391–392
in Civil War, 430
Compromise of 1850 and, 398
independence of, 386–387
rebellion in, 386–387
Reconstruction and, 456, 465
secession of, 413
slavery in, 386–387, 398
Spanish, 245
textile industry
British competition and, 294–297
growth of, 308
innovations in, 294–299
Navigation Acts and, 95
in New England, 342
tariffs and, 310, 328
technological innovation and, 219
trade in, 78, 247–248
women in, 293, 296–298, 296(*i*), 301,
309, 315
Thames, battle of the, 242
**Thayendanegea** (Mohawk chief). *See* **Brant,
Joseph**
**Thoreau, Henry David** (1817–1862), 355–357,
371, 409
*Thoughts on Female Education* (Rush),
262
*Thoughts on Government* (John Adams),
198, 212

Tidewater region, 117, 123
Tikal, 9
**Tilden, Samuel J.,** 469
timber industry. *See* lumber industry
Timucua Indians, 12
Tippecanoe, battle of, 241, 347
tobacco, 73, 77–80, 83
    colonial production of, 157
    decline of, 268
    duties on, 134
    economy based on, 48–52
    exports of, 124
    Southern gentry and, 87
    Southern production of, 268, 269(*m*), 270
    trade in, 89(*m*)
    transportation for, 306(*m*)
Tobago, 184
**Tocqueville, Alexis de,** 254(*i*), 322, 353
Toleration Act (1649), 48
Tory Association, 158
town meetings, 58–59
**Townshend, Charles,** 96, 145–146
Townshend Act (1767), 145–148, 147(*i*),
    151–152
trade, 19. *See also* exports; imports; South
    Atlantic system; *particular commodities*
    Anglo-American, 119, 123–124, 135–136,
        145, 148, 150, 155
    British empire and, 121
    with California, 390
    of Confederacy, 426–427
    with Confederacy, 415
    control of, 89(*m*)
    duties on, 110, 135–137
    free, 322
    of manufactured goods, 309–310
    New York City and, 309
    slave, 71, 76–83, 82(*i*), 233, 234(*i*)
    West Indian, 88, 106, 135–137, 155
trade routes, 20, 21(*m*), 24
Trail of Tears, 339
transcendentalism, 353–355, 362
    abolitionism and, 371, 374
    industrialization and, 358
transportation system. *See also* canals; railroads
    bottleneck in, 235–237
    financing of roads and canals, 293, 302,
        324–325, 327–328, 333, 341, 344
    revolution in, 293, 302–308, 304(*i*), 306(*m*)
    water, 235–236

*Treatise on Domestic Economy* (Beecher), 375
Tredegar Iron Works, 299, 426
Trenton, battle of, 173, 174(*m*), 184(*m*)
trial by jury, 136, 138–139, 142, 274
**Trollope, Frances,** 279, 322
**Troup, George M.,** 329
**Trumbull, Lyman,** 445–446, 450
**Truth, Sojourner,** 379(*i*), 457
**Tryon, William,** 128–129
**Tubman, Harriet,** 370–371
Turkey, 19(*i*), 33
**Turner, Henry M.,** 449
**Turner, Nat,** 368
**Turner, Randolph,** 382
turnpikes, 293, 302
Tuscarora Indians, 7, 75
*Two Treatises on Government* (Locke), 73, 113
**Tyler, John** (1790–1862), 347
    1844 elections and, 391
    as president (1841–1845), 349

*Uncle Tom's Cabin* (Stowe), 376, 385, 400
underground railroad, 370–371
Underwood Company, 311
unemployment, 301, 309, 313, 316, 319, 346
Union. *See* Civil War
Union Army, 433–435
    African Americans in, 433(*i*)
    black veterans of, 448, 458
Unionists, 416
unions. *See* labor unions
Unitarianism, 353–354
Universalists, 278, 283(*m*), 324
urbanization. *See also* cities
    in American colonies, 88–90
    individualism and, 355
    industrialization and, 308–309
    labor and, 310, 313–314, 319, 336
    South Atlantic system and, 88, 90–91
Utah
    Compromise of 1850 and, 398, 399(*m*)
    Mormons in, 364, 364(*m*), 366, 366(*i*)
Utica, New York, 372, 374
utopian communities, 357–366
    Brook Farm, 357–358, 359(*m*)
    Fourierist, 361
    Mormon, 359(*m*), 362–366, 364(*m*)
    Oneida, 359(*m*), 361–362
    Shaker, 284, 358–360, 359(*m*), 361
Utrecht, Treaty of (1713), 75, 76(*m*)

Valley Forge, Pennsylvania, 178
**Van Buren, Martin** (1782–1862), 387
  1836 elections and, 344
  1840 elections and, 347–348
  1844 elections and, 391
  1848 elections and, 396, 405(*m*)
  1852 elections and, 401
  Independent Treasury Act of 1840 and, 347
  Jackson and, 328–329
  party government and, 323–325
  party politics and, 322–325
  patronage and, 324
  as president (1837–1841), 339, 347
  as vice presidential candidate, 336
  Wilmot Proviso and, 395
**Vance, Zebulon,** 424
**Vann, James,** 337
**Van Rensselaer, Kiliaen,** 43
Van Rensselaer family, 124
**Vassa, Gustavus** (Olaudah Equiano), 81
Venezuela, 309
Venice, Italy, 19
**Vergennes, Comte de,** 179
Vermont
  land grants in, 103
  migration from, 301, 303(*m*)
  settlement of, 233
  voting rights in, 258, 259(*m*), 272
Versailles, Treaty of (1783), 184
**Vesey, Denmark,** 272
**Vespucci, Amerigo,** 24–25
Vicksburg, Mississippi, 430–432, 434
**Vinci, Leonardo da,** 20
Virginia
  vs. Chesapeake peoples, 46–47, 52
  claims to Western lands, 202, 233
  as colony, 44–52
  elite politics in, 92
  Emancipation Proclamation and, 429
  end of Civil War and, 440
  evangelicals in, 117–118
  House of Burgesses of, 51–53, 87, 138, 148, 151, 157
  industrial capacity in, 426
  land disputes in, 125
  migration from, 302, 303(*m*)
  presidency and, 237
  ratification of Constitution and, 213
  Reconstruction and, 453(*m*), 456
  river plantations in, 49(*i*)

  Scots-Irish in, 110
  secession and, 414, 414(*m*), 416
  slavery in, 50–51, 80–81, 83, 86, 157–158, 281, 368
  tenant farmers of, 117–118, 266
  voting rights in, 324
  wheat production in, 124
Virginia Company, 44–46
Virginia Plan, 208–209
Virginia planters. *See also* plantations
  culture of, 113, 117–118
  revolution and, 157
Virgin of Guadalupe, 29
voting patterns, changes in, 330(*f*)
voting rights. *See also* Constitutional amendments: Fifteenth
  African American, 446, 451, 453–454, 457, 464, 467
  for free blacks, 272, 371
  intimidation and, 466–467
  Know-Nothing Party and, 402
  movement for, 379, 457
  property qualifications for, 92, 197, 199
  republicanism and, 258–260, 259(*m*), 285–286
  Southern gentry and, 87
  universal, 322, 349
  white male, 258–259, 259(*m*), 322–324, 341
  for women, 379, 456–457

Wade-Davis Bill (1864), 443
**Wadsworth, Benjamin,** 100
wages
  abolitionism and, 371
  labor for, 361, 448(*i*), 449, 461–462, 464
  slavery and, 402
  of women, 375, 380
*Walden, or Life in the Woods* (Thoreau), 355–356
Walden Pond, 355
**Walker, David** (1785–1830), 367–368
**Walker, John,** 275
**Waller, John,** 118
**Walpole, Sir Robert,** 92–95, 94(*i*)
Waltham plan, 296
Wampanoag Indians, 54, 61. *See also* Metacom's Rebellion
Wappinger Indians, 124–125
War of 1812, 237, 347
  causes of, 242

War of 1812 (*cont.*)
  Congressional vote on declaration of, 242
  emancipation and, 268
  Indian peoples and, 337
  Jackson and, 325
  terms of, 268
  Washington, D.C. and, 242, 243(*m*)
War of the Austrian Succession (King George's
      War; 1740–1748), 95
War of the Spanish Succession (Queen Anne's
      War; 1702–1713), 74
**Warren, Joseph,** 143
**Warren, Mercy Otis,** 260
**Washington, George** (1732–1799), 157
  in battle of Long Island, 173
  cabinet of, 215
  church taxes and, 193
  on closing of Boston Harbor, 153
  as commander of Continental army, 167,
      175–176, 183
  creation of national bank and, 217
  as delegate to Constitutional Convention, 208
  on expansion of West, 227
  Federalists and, 222
  freemasonry and, 344
  in French and Indian War, 121
  John Jay and, 220
  nationalist faction and, 207
  on national system of taxation, 202
  Native American resistance and, 230
  as president (1789–1797), 215
  Proclamation of Neutrality, 219
  return to plantation, 196
  soldiers' pensions and, 179
  southern strategy of, 182
  at Valley Forge, 178
  Whiskey Rebellion and, 220
  Zachary Taylor and, 396
*Washington Globe,* 332
Washington, D.C. *See* District of Columbia
water power
  manufacturing and, 294–295, 297–298,
      308
  mills and, 247
**Wayne, "Mad Anthony,"** 230
wealth. *See also* economy
  of business elite, 301, 309–310
  inheritance and, 310
  per capita income and, 293, 308
*The Wealth of Nations* (Smith), 77, 219

**Webster, Daniel,** 242, 253, 342, 413
  Compromise of 1850 and, 398
  1836 elections and, 344
  1840 elections and, 347, 349
  on Jackson, 330
  Second Bank and, 335
  Whig Party and, 347, 349
**Webster, Noah,** 265
**Weed, Thurlow,** 344
**Weems, Parson Mason,** 265
**Weld, Theodore,** 369, 372
*The Well-Ordered Family* (Wadsworth), 100
**Wentworth, Governor,** 158
**Wesley, John,** 114
the West, 184, 202–205. *See also* westward
      expansion
  American sovereignty and, 241
  American System and, 325
  cession to U.S. of, 244–245
  Civil War in, 420–423, 430
  claims to, 202–204, 203(*m*)
  communal experiments in, 359(*m*)
  Free-Soil Party and, 395
  Jackson as first president from, 330
  migration to, 323, 383, 387–390, 389(*m*)
  opening up of, 202–204, 227–237
  removal of Indians to, 337–340, 340(*m*)
  Second Bank and, 336
  settlement of, 227, 232–237
  slavery in, 398
West Africa, 84. *See also* Africa
  as British colony, 121
  culture of, 20–22
  Dutch trade in, 43
  Mediterranean trade and, 21, 21(*m*)
  slave trade in, 21(*m*), 23
Western Confederacy (Shawnees, Miamis, and
      Potawatomis), 229(*i*), 230, 241
West India Company, 33, 43
West Indies. *See* Caribbean Islands
West Virginia
  creation of, 416
  secession and, 414(*m*), 418
westward expansion, 126(*m*), 132, 153–154,
      157, 227–237, 240, 253. *See also*
      migration
  Louisiana Purchase and, 276(*m*)
  Manifest Destiny and, 383–391
  migration and, 119, 122, 232–237, 301–302,
      303(*m*), 323, 383, 387–390, 389(*m*)

Missouri Compromise and,
275–277, 276(m)
Native Americans and, 99, 119–121, 125
postcolonial, 262
of slavery to old Southwest, 233, 267(i), 268,
269(m), 302, 303(m)
slave vs. free states and, 396–398,
401–402, 406
Treaty of Paris and, 133(m), 154(m)
Wethersfield, Connecticut, 56, 60(m)
**Wetmore, Ephraim,** 206
whaling industry, 274(i)
wheat
colonial production of, 103, 110(i), 124
exports of, 124, 135, 292
Midwest production of, 302–305, 303(m)
from North in Civil War, 432
prices of, 219
western, 235
**Wheeler, Adam,** 206
Whig Party, 426
Compromise of 1850 and, 398
creation of, 342
decline of, 400–401
vs. Democratic Party, 255, 322, 330(f),
344–345, 349
economic program of, 403
1844 elections and, 391
evangelical moralism and, 342, 344
first national convention of, 347
ideology of, 342–344
Lincoln in, 407
Mexican War and, 393, 395
Radical, 134, 141, 143, 150, 175, 216
realignment of, 405(m)
salutary neglect and, 92
slave vs. free states and, 396, 398, 402
support in the South, 343–344
Whig Party (England), 91–93, 134, 143, 145, 198
Whiskey Rebellion (1794), 220, 238
Whiskey Ring, 468
**White, Hugh L.,** 344
**White, John,** 45(i)
**Whitefield, George,** 114–116, 115(i),
117, 278, 284
white supremacy, 408, 413, 445, 450, 465–467.
*See also* Ku Klux Klan; racism
**Whitman, Walt** (1819–1892), 356–357, 396
**Whitney, Eli,** 233, 299
Wilderness, battle of the, 434, 435(i)

**Wilkes, John,** 134, 150
**Wilkinson, Eliza,** 199
**Wilkinson, James,** 240
**Wilkinson, Jemima,** 284
Willamette Valley, Oregon, 388
**Willard, Emma,** 285
**William III,** king of England, 91
**Williams, Roger,** 55–56
**Wilmot, David,** 394
Wilmot Proviso, 394–396, 407, 429
Windsor, Connecticut, 56
**Winthrop, James,** 212
**Winthrop, John,** 54, 59
Wisconsin, 11, 41
Fugitive Slave Acts and, 400
slaves in, 405
utopian communities in, 361
**Wise, John,** 113
witchcraft executions, 58
**Wolfe, James,** 122, 132
**Wollstonecraft, Mary,** 262
Wolof Indians, 23
*Woman in the Nineteenth Century* (Fuller), 356
women. *See also* children; gender roles; marriage
abolitionism and, 370–372, 373(m),
376–378, 379(i), 457
African American, 462
Baptists and, 118, 280–281
birthrates and, 100–101, 261–262
charitable institutions and, 315, 349
in Civil War, 424–425, 425(i)
in colonies, 58
divorce and, 261
as domestic servants, 319
dower right and, 102
education of, 199–202, 262, 284–286
emancipation and, 449
equality of, 199–202, 372
evangelicalism and, 101–102
on farms, 100–101, 109, 110(i), 148
feminism and, 457
Fourierism and, 361
free black, 462
Free-Soil Party and, 395
Garrison and, 369(i)
gentry, 87–88
household production and, 185–186
Ku Klux Klan and, 466
labor of, 449
in medieval Europe, 16–17

women (*cont.*)
  middle class, 311, 312*(i)*
  moral reform and, 375
  Native American, 12–14, 64–65, 231–232
  in the North, 375
  Oneida Community and, 361–362
  political status of, 199–202, 348–349
  poverty and, 313, 315
  Puritan, 55–56, 100–101
  Quaker, 70
  Radical Reconstruction program and,
    456–457, 459
  republican motherhood and, 261–262,
    263*(i)*, 285
  in Revolutionary War, 185, 185*(i)*
  role of, 101*(i)*, 273–274, 278, 280–281,
    284–286, 317
  slavery and, 83, 173, 385
  social reform and, 375
  in South Atlantic system, 90
  as teachers, 286
  in textile industry, 293, 296–298, 296*(i)*, 301,
    309, 315
  transcendentalism and, 356
  utopian communalism and, 361–362
  westward migration and, 390
women's rights, 366*(i)*
  Abigail Adams on, 199, 200*(i)*, 201
  Douglass on, 456–457
  evangelicalism and, 116, 278, 280–281,
    284–286
  Garrison and, 352
  German settlers and, 109
  inheritances and, 260–261
  John Adams on, 260
  in labor force, 301
  movement for, 374–380
  to property, 100, 102, 109

  social reform and, 375
  voting, 260, 262, 456–457
**Wood, Jethro,** 308
**Woolman, John,** 189
Worcester, Massachusetts, 379
*Worcester v. Georgia* (1832), 339
work ethic, 311–312, 317
Working Men's Party, 300
World Anti-Slavery Convention (London;
    1840), 378
World War I (1914–1918), 434
World War II (1939–1945), 420
Wyandot Indians, 229
Wyoming Valley, Pennsylvania, 124, 126*(m)*

Yale College, 283*(m)*
Yamasee people, 69
**Yancey, William Lowndes,** 409
**Yates, Robert,** 209
Yellowstone region, 11
yeomen farmers, 34, 52–53, 235, 384, 414
  draft and, 423
  Free-Soil Party and, 395
  Lincoln and, 407, 409
  migration to America, 34
  Reconstruction and, 444
  secession and, 414*(m)*, 416
  slavery and, 393, 395
  social structure of, 58–59, 260
  Southern, 87, 343, 458
  taxes and, 427
  westward expansion and, 386
Yorktown, battle of (1781), 181*(m)*, 182
**Young, Brigham,** 364, 364*(m)*, 366
Yucatán peninsula, 9, 11

**Zoffany, Johann,** 168
Zuni Indians, 11

CANADA

MINNESOTA
Duluth
Fargo
WISCONSIN
St. Paul
Minneapolis
Sioux Falls
Madison
Milwaukee

Lake Superior

MICHIGAN

Lake Michigan

Lake Huron

Lansing
Detroit
Lansing

IOWA
Des
Moines
Omaha
Lincoln

ILLINOIS
Springfield

Chicago
Gary
Toledo

INDIANA
Indianapolis

OHIO
Columbus
Cincinnati

Wheeling
Cleveland

MAINE
Augusta

Burlington
Montpelier    N.H.    Portland
VT.    Concord
Manchester    Boston
Albany    MASS.    Providence
Hartford    RHODE
ISLAND
CONNECTICUT

Lake Ontario
NEW YORK
Buffalo

Lake Erie

Allegheny R.

PENNSYLVANIA
Harrisburg
Pittsburgh

Newark
New York
Trenton
NEW JERSEY
Philadelphia

Baltimore
MD.
Washington, D.C.    Dover    DELAWARE
Annapolis

Topeka
Kansas
City
Jefferson
City
Wichita
MISSOURI

St. Louis
Louisville
Frankfort

KENTUCKY

Missouri R.

Mississippi R.

Illinois R.

Wabash R.

Ohio R.

WEST
VIRGINIA
Charleston

Cumberland R.

VIRGINIA
Richmond
Norfolk

Roanoke R.

APPALACHIAN MOUNTAINS

Knoxville
Nashville
TENNESSEE

NORTH
CAROLINA
Raleigh
Charlotte

Cape Fear R.

ATLANTIC
OCEAN

Tulsa
Oklahoma
City
Little
Rock

ARKANSAS

Memphis

Arkansas R.

Tennessee R.

Birmingham

Atlanta

SOUTH
CAROLINA
Columbia

Charleston

Savannah

Santee R.

Chattahoochee R.

Fort Worth
Dallas

LOUISIANA

MISSISSIPPI
Jackson

ALABAMA
Montgomery

GEORGIA

Tallahassee

Jacksonville

Alabama R.

Altamaha R.

Austin
Houston

Baton Rouge
New Orleans
Mobile

Trinity R.
Sabine R.
Red R.

FLORIDA

Tampa

Miami

Gulf of Mexico

BAHAMAS

67°W    66°W
ATLANTIC OCEAN
San Juan
PUERTO RICO
18°N    Ponce
Caribbean
Sea    0   25   50 miles
0   25   50 kilometers

CUBA

### Elevation

| Feet | Meters |
|------|--------|
| 9,843 | 3,000 |
| 6,562 | 2,000 |
| 3,281 | 1,000 |
| 1,640 | 500 |
| 656 | 200 |
| 0 | 0 |
| Below sea level | Below sea level |

0    200    400 miles
0    200    400 kilometers

Wisconsin R.

St. Lawrence R.

Hudson R.

Potomac R.

Ohio R.

Mississippi R.

95°W    90°W    85°W    80°W

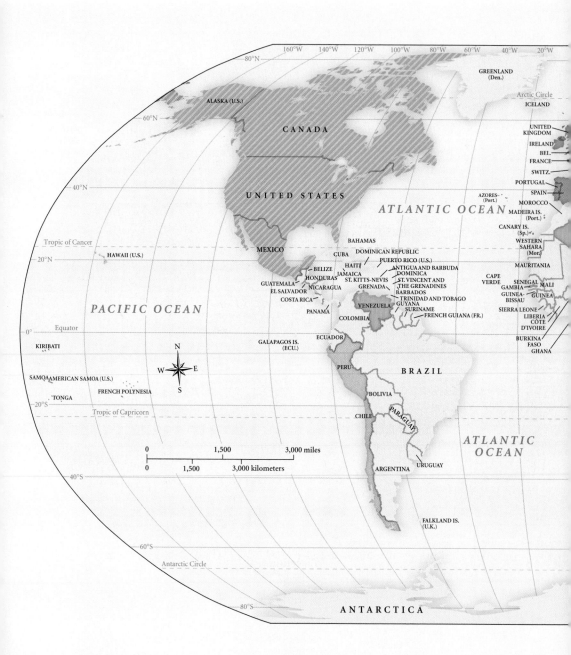

Political divisions as of May 2004

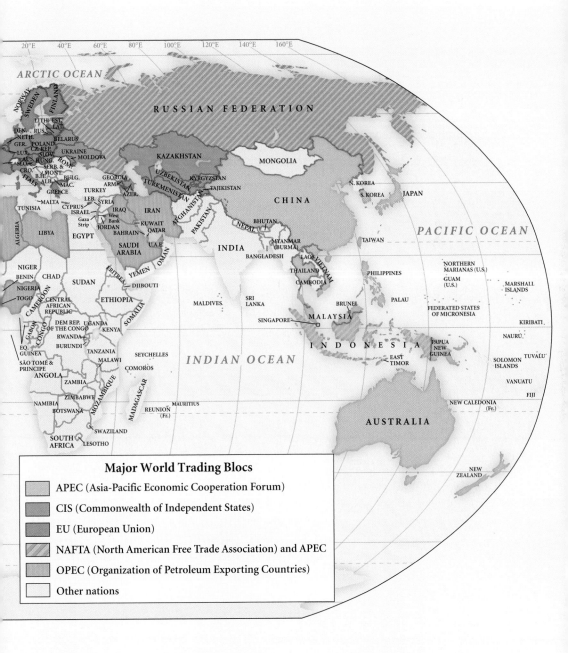

20°E  40°E  60°E  80°E  100°E  120°E  140°E  160°E

*ARCTIC OCEAN*

RUSSIAN FEDERATION

NORWAY
SWEDEN
FINLAND
LITH. EST.
DEN. RUS. LAT.
NETH.
GER. POLAND
LUX. CZ.REP.
AUS. SLOV. BELARUS
SLO. HUNG. UKRAINE
CRO. SERB.& MOLDOVA
ITALY B.H. MONT.
MAC. BULG.
GREECE GEORGIA
MALTA TURKEY ARM.
TUNISIA CYPRUS LEB. AZER.
ISRAEL SYRIA
Gaza West IRAQ
Strip Bank KUWAIT
JORDAN QATAR
BAHRAIN
EGYPT SAUDI U.A.E.
ARABIA

KAZAKHSTAN
MONGOLIA
UZBEKISTAN KYRGYZSTAN
TURKMENISTAN TAJIKISTAN
N. KOREA
CHINA S. KOREA JAPAN

IRAN
AFGHANISTAN
PAKISTAN
NEPAL BHUTAN
TAIWAN

ALGERIA
LIBYA

NIGER
BENIN CHAD
NIGERIA SUDAN
TOGO
CAMEROON CENTRAL
AFRICAN
REPUBLIC
EQ. GABON CONGO
GUINEA DEM REP. UGANDA
OF THE CONGO KENYA
RWANDA
BURUNDI
SÃO TOMÉ & TANZANIA
PRINCIPE MALAWI
ANGOLA
ZAMBIA
ZIMBABWE
NAMIBIA
BOTSWANA
SWAZILAND
SOUTH LESOTHO
AFRICA

ERITREA
YEMEN OMAN
DJIBOUTI
ETHIOPIA
SOMALIA
SEYCHELLES
COMOROS
MADAGASCAR
REUNION
(Fr.)

INDIA
BANGLADESH
MYANMAR
(BURMA)
LAOS VIETNAM
THAILAND
CAMBODIA

MALDIVES
SRI
LANKA

SINGAPORE
MALAYSIA

*PACIFIC OCEAN*

PHILIPPINES

NORTHERN
MARIANAS (U.S.)
GUAM
(U.S.)

BRUNEI PALAU
FEDERATED STATES
OF MICRONESIA

MARSHALL
ISLANDS

KIRIBATI

NAURU

*INDIAN OCEAN*

I N D O N E S I A

PAPUA
NEW
GUINEA
EAST
TIMOR

SOLOMON
ISLANDS
TUVALU

VANUATU

NEW CALEDONIA
(Fr.)

FIJI

MAURITIUS

AUSTRALIA

NEW
ZEALAND

## Major World Trading Blocs

APEC (Asia-Pacific Economic Cooperation Forum)

CIS (Commonwealth of Independent States)

EU (European Union)

NAFTA (North American Free Trade Association) and APEC

OPEC (Organization of Petroleum Exporting Countries)

Other nations

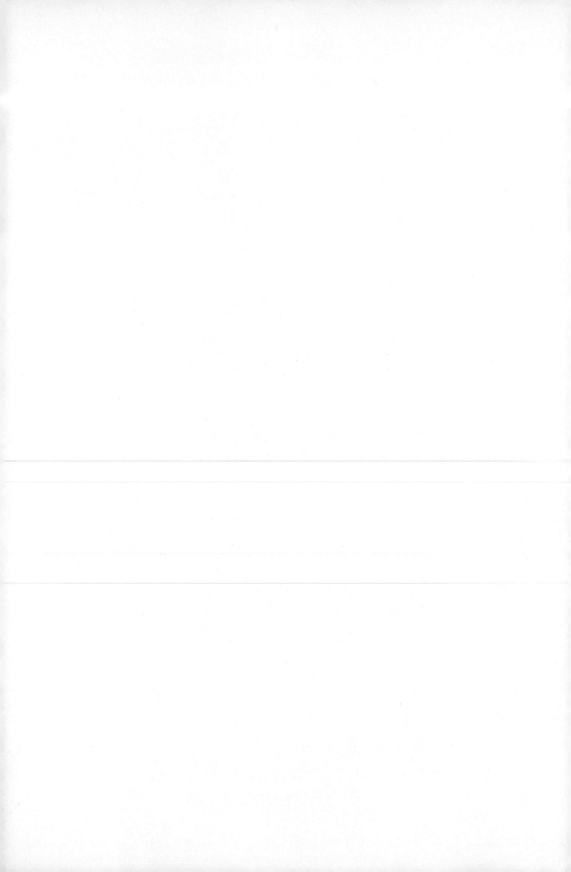

# Understanding History through Maps

Working with maps deepens your understanding of the basic issues of geography and how they relate to historical studies. Understanding these five themes — location, place, region, movement, and interaction — will enrich your readings of maps and the historical situation they depict.

## Location

"When?" and "where?" are the first questions asked by historians and cartographers. Every event happens somewhere and at some point in time, and maps are the best devices to show a particular location at a particular time.

## Place

Human activity creates places. Locations exist on their own without the presence of people, but they become places when people use the spots in some way. As human enterprise thickens and generation after generation use a place, it accumulates artifacts, develops layers of remains, and generates a variety of associations held in a society's history and memory.

## Region

A region highlights common elements, tying certain places together as a group distinguishable from other places. Perceiving regional ties helps the reader of historical maps because they suggest the forces binding individual interests together and encouraging people to act in common.

## Movement

All historical change involves movement. People move in their daily activities, in seasonal patterns, and in migration to new places of residence. To understand a map fully, the reader must always envision it as one part of a sequence, not unlike a "still" excerpted from a motion picture.

## Interaction

The interaction between people and the environment goes both ways. On the one hand, people change their environment to suit their needs. Human ingenuity has found ways to put almost all places to some use. On the other hand, climate and topography present constraints on how people use the land and force people to change their behavior and culture as they adapt to their natural surroundings.